CAMBRIDGE LIBRARY

Books of enduring scholar

The Naval Chronicle

The *Naval Chronicle*, published in 40 volumes between 1799 and 1818, is a key source for British maritime and military history, and is also sought after by those researching family histories. Six instalments per year were produced (and often reprinted with corrections) by Bunney and Gold, later Joyce Gold, in London, and bound up into two volumes per year. Printed economically, on paper of varying weights and often with very small type, the extant copies have been heavily used over the course of two centuries, present significant conservation challenges, and are difficult to find outside major libraries. This reissue is the first complete printed reproduction of what was the most influential maritime publication of its day. The subjects covered range widely, including accounts of battles, notices of promotions, marriages and deaths, lists of ships and their tonnages, reports of courts martial, shipwrecks, privateers and prizes, biographies and poetry, notes on the latest technology, and letters. Each volume also contains engravings and charts relating to naval engagements and important harbours from Jamaica to Timor, Newfoundland to Canton, and Penzance to Port Jackson.

Volume 28

Volume 28 (1812) concentrates on the Anglo-American War of 1812. It discusses events surrounding the war, and reprints state papers detailing America's grievances with Britain and the British declaration of war itself. It also describes the proposed construction of a breakwater in Plymouth Sound and its estimated costs, and includes a chart and description of the Cape of Good Hope.

Cambridge University Press has long been a pioneer in the reissuing of out-of-print titles from its own backlist, producing digital reprints of books that are still sought after by scholars and students but could not be reprinted economically using traditional technology. The Cambridge Library Collection extends this activity to a wider range of books which are still of importance to researchers and professionals, either for the source material they contain, or as landmarks in the history of their academic discipline.

Drawing from the world-renowned collections in the Cambridge University Library, and guided by the advice of experts in each subject area, Cambridge University Press is using state-of-the-art scanning machines in its own Printing House to capture the content of each book selected for inclusion. The files are processed to give a consistently clear, crisp image, and the books finished to the high quality standard for which the Press is recognised around the world. The latest print-on-demand technology ensures that the books will remain available indefinitely, and that orders for single or multiple copies can quickly be supplied.

The Cambridge Library Collection will bring back to life books of enduring scholarly value (including out-of-copyright works originally issued by other publishers) across a wide range of disciplines in the humanities and social sciences and in science and technology.

The Naval Chronicle

Containing a General and Biographical
History of the Royal Navy of the United
Kingdom with a Variety of Original Papers on
Nautical Subjects

VOLUME 28: JULY-DECEMBER 1812

EDITED BY JAMES STANIER CLARKE
AND JOHN MCARTHUR

CAMBRIDGE UNIVERSITY PRESS

Cambridge, New York, Melbourne, Madrid, Cape Town, Singapore,
São Paolo, Delhi, Dubai, Tokyo

Published in the United States of America by Cambridge University Press, New York

www.cambridge.org
Information on this title: www.cambridge.org/9781108018678

© in this compilation Cambridge University Press 2010

This edition first published 1812
This digitally printed version 2010

ISBN 978-1-108-01867-8 Paperback

This book reproduces the text of the original edition. The content and language reflect
the beliefs, practices and terminology of their time, and have not been updated.

Cambridge University Press wishes to make clear that the book, unless originally published
by Cambridge, is not being republished by, in association or collaboration with, or
with the endorsement or approval of, the original publisher or its successors in title.

NAVAL CHRONICLE.

VOL. XXVIII.

Bacon Jun.r del.

Erected at the public expence, to the Memory of
Capt.n George Duff,
who was killed the 26th of Oct.r 1805;
commanding the Mars,
in the Battle of Trafalgar:
in the 42d Year of his Age, and the 29th of his Service.

THE

Naval Chronicle,

FOR 1812:

CONTAINING A

GENERAL AND BIOGRAPHICAL HISTORY

OF

THE ROYAL NAVY

OF THE

United Kingdom;

WITH A VARIETY OF ORIGINAL PAPERS ON
NAUTICAL SUBJECTS.

UNDER THE GUIDANCE OF SEVERAL
LITERARY AND PROFESSIONAL MEN.

VOL. XXVIII.

(FROM JULY TO DECEMBER.)

Tu regere imperio popvlos Britanne memento
Hae tibi ervnt artes————————

" These are imperial arts, and worthy thee."

LONDON:

PRINTED AND PUBLISHED BY AND FOR *JOYCE GOLD*, 103, SHOE-LANE;

And sold by Messrs. Longman, Hurst, Rees, Orme & Brown, Messrs. Wilkie & Robinson, Messrs. Sherwood, Neeley, and Jones, and Mr. Walker, *Paternoster-row;* White and Co. *Fleet-street;* Mr. Asperne, and Messrs. Richardsons, *Cornhill;* Messrs. Black, Parry, and Co. *Leadenhall-street;* Messrs. Crosby and Co. *Stationers'-hall-court;* Messrs. Scatchard and Letterman, and Mr. Law, *Avemaria-lane;* Mr. Lindsell, *Wimpole-street;* Mr. Andrews, *Charing-cross;* Mr. Booth, *Duke-street, Portland-place;* Messrs. Mottley and Co. *Portsmouth;* Mr. Woodward, *Portsea;* Messrs. Congdon, Hoxland, and Platt, *Dock;* Messrs. Haydon—Rees, and Curtis—Smith—Rogers—and Nettleton, *Plymouth;* Mr. Godwin, *Bath;* Messrs. Norton and Son, *Bristol;* Mr. Robinson, *Liverpool;* Mr. Wilson, *Hull;* Messrs. Manners and Miller, Mr. Creech, and Mr. Constable, *Edinburgh;* Mr. Turnbull and Mr. Lumsden, *Glasgow;* and the principal Booksellers in the different Seaport Towns throughout the United Kingdom.

TO

THE RIGHT HONORABLE

ALEXANDER ARTHUR HOOD,

VISCOUNT AND BARON BRIDPORT, OF CRICKET-ST. THOMAS,
IN THE COUNTY OF SOMERSET,

KNIGHT OF THE MOST HONORABLE AND MILITARY ORDER
OF THE BATH,

ADMIRAL OF THE RED SQUADRON, VICE-ADMIRAL OF
ENGLAND, AND GENERAL OF MARINES:

THIS TWENTY-EIGHTH VOLUME OF THE

Naval Chronicle

IS RESPECTFULLY DEDICATED,

BY THE PROPRIETOR,

Joyce Gold

PLATES IN VOLUME XXVIII.

From Original Designs.

PLATE | Page

FRONTISPIECE.—Representation of the Monument erected in St. Paul's Cathedral, to the Memory of the late GEORGE DUFF, R.N. Engraved by HALL,

CCCLXVII. Portrait of the late Captain JOHN STEWART, R. N. Engraved by PAGE, from a Drawing in the possession of WILLIAM ADAM, Esq. 1

CCCLXVIII. View of PUERTO-SANTO, near MADEIRA. Engraved by BAILY, from a Drawing by POCOCK. 53

CCCLXIX. View of BRIMSTONE HILL, ISLAND OF ST. CHRISTOPHER. Engraved by BAILY, from a Drawing by G. T. 116

CCCLXX. Chart of SALDANHA BAY, Cape of Good Hope. 148

CCCLXXI. Portrait of GEORGE LEGGE, Lord Dartmouth, Admiral of the Fleet in the Reign of James the Second. Engraved by Page, from a Painting by SHIPSTER. 177

CCCLXXII. Plymouth Sound, with the projected Breakwater. Reduced by ROWE, from the Chart ordered by the House of Commons to be printed, 1812. 233

CCCLXXIII. Portrait of Captain HENRY WHITBY, R.N. Engraved by PAGE. 265

CCCLXXIV. View of FORT ST. ANGELO, on the Cotonea Side, in the Island of Malta. Engraved by BAILY, from a Drawing by BENNET. 308

CCCLXXV. Portrait of Captain SALUSBURY PRYCE HUMPHREYS, R.N. Engraved by PAGE, from an original Miniature. .. 353

CCCLXXVI. View of a MOSK in PANWELL RIVER, DEKHAN CHINA. Engraved by BAILY from a Drawing by W. WESTALL, A.R.A. 400

CCCLXXVII. View of APE'S HILL, on the Barbary coast. Engraved by BAILY, from a Drawing by BENNET. 477

CCCLXXVIII. Chart. The Cape of Good Hope. 497

CCCLXXIX. Frontispiece to the Volume.

PREFACE

TO THE TWENTY-EIGHTH VOLUME.

IN Prefaces, the pomposity of literature, and the literary cant of humility, are alike obnoxious to censure. If the writer of a Preface be deficient in respect for himself, it is impossible for him to be entitled to that of his readers; and, if he enjoy not the grateful consciousness, that his exertions deserve, though they may not command success, he ought not to stand forward as a candidate for public favour. Unlike those imprudent authors, to whom the quaint Spanish proverb applies—"Aviendo pregonado vino, venden vinagre" (having cried up their wine, they sell us vinegar)—the conductors of the NAVAL CHRONICLE would not, by injudicious boasting, bespeak attention, and expose imagination to disappointment; but, aware of what is reciprocally due, between themselves and the public, they only wish to attune the minds of their readers into a proper harmony of ideas, so that their tone may respond to the emotions which they are anxious to excite;—that the want of such a publication as the present may be felt, as a desire not elsewhere to be gratified.

As the Editors of the NAVAL CHRONICLE have only two opportunities, in each year, personally to address its readers, they avail themselves of the present, to solicit co-operation, on their parts, both in point of contribution, and in that of extending the publicity of the work. On the latter point, the Editors take leave to observe, that, as the NAVAL CHRONICLE is only occasionally advertised in the daily prints, and is left to maintain its ground, and to make its way by its own intrinsic merits and utility, there is reason to believe, that, from the necessary dispersion of so fluctuating a body as the navy, its very existence, even at the end of fourteen years, is unknown to many naval men. It is, therefore, respectfully requested, that every officer, of whose library it may form a part, will bear this in mind; and, as an equitable and liberal return for the amusement, or instruction, which he may have derived from it, that he will grant it his patronage—at least so far as the making of it known to his messmates, or other professional associates, by mentioning it in such terms as he may think it deserves, or, more particularly, by allowing it to be seen by the junior members of the body.

It may here not be deemed improper to remark, that the NAVAL CHRONICLE, from its commencement, in the year 1799, contains a general and biographical history of the Royal Navy, with a variety of original papers on nautical subjects; that it is specially devoted to the interests of the British Navy, of the Royal Marines, &c.; that it also pays due attention to those valuable branches of the nautical profession, the Honourable East India Company's Marine, and the mercantile shipping interest; that the monthly lists of promotions, appointments, births, marriages, and deaths, at home and abroad, which are diligently and faithfully recorded in the Chronicle, are found particularly interesting to, and worthy of the attention of naval families in general; that the NAVAL CHRONICLE forms, in itself, a comprehensive nautical library, not only for mariners, but for every one interested in maritime affairs; and that, consequently, merchants, and gentlemen in their employ, cannot take out a venture more likely to sell to advantage, particularly in the East and West Indies, the Continent of America, &c.

The Editors take leave to add, that, although the Volumes of the NAVAL CHRONICLE are numbered, from 1. to XXVIII. that circumstance does not entail the absolute necessity of commencing a Subscriber, from the beginning; for each Volume (any of which may be had separate), instead of being a mere fragment of a voluminous work, constitutes a whole in itself, and forms a complete naval history of the time to which it refers. Another advantage is, that, from the reprint which the respective volumes and numbers of the work, from time to time undergoes, particular parts, lost at sea, or otherwise, may at any time be replaced.

The expediency and importance of rendering the NAVAL CHRONICLE the common centre for all nautical information, has been repeatedly urged. Nothing can so certainly promote, or effectuate this object, as the exertions of individuals. Professional contributions are, at all times, peculiarly acceptable; and, as most officers, in the course of service, meet with occurrences deserving of record, conceive ideas which are entitled to publicity, and form plans which ought to be promulgated, the surprise is, not that the NAVAL CHRONICLE has made so conspicuous a figure in this light, as it has of late done, but, that its pages have not been crowded with communications. Particular pleasure will always be felt, in diffusing, through the medium of those pages, the opinions and suggestions of well-informed men, upon subjects relating to, or connected with, their profession; and, howsoever bold may be the truths, which such persons may sometimes find it necessary to advance, their communications, when expressed in terms of due respect to constituted authorities, will never be rejected.

Among the Correspondents, whose miscellaneous contributions enhance the value of the present Volume, the thanks of the Editors are particularly due to MULCIBER, for Captain Tillard's narrative, relating to a sub-marine volcano, near the island of St. Michael; to Mr. Bampfield, surgeon of H. M. S. Warrior, for his account of the mode adopted by him for preserving the health of mariners on long voyages; to C. Y. for his remarks on the situation of Masters in the Royal Navy; and to A FRIEND TO NAVAL MERIT, and to OCEANUS, for their various favours. Many others are also entitled to acknowledgment; but a deficiency of space precludes the pleasure of enumerating them.

Naval Biography, so interesting to the profession in particular, and to the public at large, has uniformly experienced a cordial attention from the Editors of the NAVAL CHRONICLE. Those who are desirous of assisting them in this branch of the work, will find their labours materially facilitated, by attending to the *Biographical Interrogatories* of PLUTARCH, inserted at page 114.

Two of the memoirs in the present Volume, it is presumed, have been particularly well-timed. At the commencement of a contest so important in its nature, as that which has unfortunately taken place between Great Britain and America, any documents that were calculated to elucidate the cause of quarrel could not be otherwise than acceptable. The memoir of Captain Whitby, who commanded the Leander, at the time when an American seaman was alleged to have been killed by a shot from that ship; and the memoir of Captain Humphreys, who commanded the Leopard, when Admiral Berkeley's orders for her searching the U. S. S. Chesapeake, were executed, will, in this light, be found of material moment.—Much interesting and original information, relating to Captain Stewart's services in the Levant Seas, &c. will be found in the life of that lamented officer. The memoir of Admiral Lord Dartmouth, an ancestor of the present Admiral Legge; and that of Sir John Balchen, will be read with satisfaction by those who love to dwell upon the recollections of past times. Mr. Horsburgh, to whose labours in hydrography the British nation is eminently indebted, is the subject of the last biographical sketch in the volume.

On the subject of Hydrography, the Editors again solicit all persons, whether in the Royal Navy, in the service of the East India Company, or in the mercantile marine, who may possess information respecting the situation of any rock, shoal, or danger, yet unpublished, to transmit the same to the Hydrographer of the NAVAL CHRONICLE, and to state the authority on which their information is grounded.—Captains Byng and Flinders, and J. S. S. are particularly entitled to the acknowledgments and thanks of the Editors, for their attentions in the course of the present volume.

The NAVAL CHRONICLE is the only publication which has taken due notice of that great national work, the Breakwater at Plymouth. In addition to an engraved plan, copied from that which was published by order of the House of Commons, it contains various documents, letters, &c. elucidatory of the nature and extent of the undertaking.

The State Papers, in the present Volume, are more than usually numerous and important. The value, and general utility of such documents are self-evident.

Of the original miscellaneous articles in the succeeding sheets, the Editors have room only to direct the attention of the reader to Lieutenant O'Brien's Narrative, which, in its progress, will record some of the most extraordinary adventures and escapes, that ever fell under the cognizance of the public.

The Editors of the NAVAL CHRONICLE have now only to repeat their exhortation, that every friend of the work—and they are not conscious that it possesses, or ought to possess, a single enemy—will unite in their endeavours to promote its circulation; on the double ground of affording benefit to the nautical world, and of presenting a just reward for the pains and perseverance of its Proprietor.

⁎ As a medium of advertisement for scientific literature, for the sale of naval articles, and for the circulation of maritime information, by Navy Agents, Ship Owners, Ship Brokers, Dealers in articles of naval outfit, and publishers of nautical works, the wrappers of the NAVAL CHRONICLE are found peculiarly advantageous.

---

†‡† Authors or publishers of Naval Works are invited to transmit them to the NAVAL CHRONICLE Office, for the purpose of being reviewed; and a continuation of contributions from our kind Correspondents, is requested, which will always meet with early attention.—For the accommodation of Correspondents, &c. at the west end of the town, a letter-box is open at Mr. Andrews's, Naval print-seller, Charing-Cross.

CAPTN. JOHN STEWART RN.

MEMOIR OF THE PUBLIC SERVICES

OF THE LATE

CAPTAIN JOHN STEWART, R.N.

COMMANDER OF H.M.S. SEAHORSE.

" Peace to each manly Soul that sleepeth!
Rest to each faithful ye that weepeth!
Long may the fair and brave
Sigh o'er the Hero's grave."
(Anacreon Moore.)

THE friends of this distinguished officer and excellent man, have, in justice to his professional merit, determined, that a memoir of his public services should thus be given to his country : Lest it should be said of him, as Johnson once asserted of a most distinguished character, " His contemporaries, however they reverenced his genius, left his life unwritten ; and nothing, therefore, can be known, beyond what casual mention and uncertain tradition have supplied."

Mr. John Stewart, the second son of William Stewart, Esq. of Castle Stewart,* in the shire of Galloway in Scotland, was born on the 21st of December, 1774. His mother was the sixth daughter of Lord Fortrose ; to whose eldest son the title of Earl of Seaforth was restored, which had been forfeited in the year 1715.

Mr. Stewart was educated in Scotland until the year 1788 : when, shewing an inclination for the sea service, he was sent to the Naval Academy, at New Cross, Deptford, where his attention to the scientific objects of his profession was conspicuous. During the ensuing year (1789), he embarked as a midshipman on board the Rose frigate,† Captain Waller, on the 9th of May, 1789;

---

* This family was very ancient and respectable, and was an early branch from the Earls of Galloway. Captain Stewart had two paternal uncles, who died in the service of their country and were generals. He had also a brother in the engineers, and one in the artillery, who lost their lives, at an early period, in the West Indies.

† A brother officer, and intimate friend, observes in a letter—" I think he has told me, that he was on the books, and had been on board (though never regularly at sea before), with his relation, the late Commodore Keith Stewart:" but the dates do not appear to confirm this idea.

but availed himself of an opportunity of returning to his academy, which had been removed to Eltham, while the Rose was in port.

After two voyages to Newfoundland and America in that frigate, he left her on the 16th of April, 1790, and was entered on board the Discovery, Captain Vancouver, on the 16th of January, 1791. During her tedious and perilous voyage, Mr. Stewart's talents for nautical astronomy were soon observed by Mr. Whidbey,* the skilful master of that ship; who then commenced an intimate friendship with our young seaman, which ended only with his death. Mr. Stewart often took the lead in every branch of service on which the ship was sent, as appears from many pages in Vancouver's Voyage, the principal part of which was executed under circumstances extremely hazardous, since the examination of the N. W. coast of America, could only be performed in small open boats, that were often absent from the ship at the distance of 30, and even 40 leagues; during which, the boats were constantly harassed and often attacked, by Indians of a most savage and ferocious character. In these dangerous expeditions, Mr. Stewart always accompanied Captain Vancouver, to assist him in surveying; and the extraordinary escape which they both one day had from being murdered, and probably devoured by a very large tribe of the natives, has been preserved by some friends of Captain Stewart, in the following interesting memoranda of his own conversations relative to that event :—

........" We generally landed at some sequestered spot to cook our dinner; and upon one occasion, we were certainly in the most imminent danger of being murdered. Our boat was in the mouth of the river, now called Mackenzie's river—(and, by the bye, on comparing my journal with Sir A. Mackenzie's narrative, I find we left the coast on the very day he came in sight of the ocean.) We had been employed in taking soundings; and the other boat which had been in company during the morning, had separated to survey a small bay, at a little distance. A point of land lay between us, and we thought it might take them a considerable time to rejoin. We, therefore, determined to land, and dine at a spot which seemed sheltered and free from any savages. However, on nearing it, a few were discovered; but, from them, Vancouver thought there was nothing to fear. We accordingly neared the shore, and landed, when

---

* Master Attendant at Woolwich, now conducting that great national work, the Breakwater, at Plymouth; one of the ablest and most upright characters in the navy. See preceding Vol. p. 485.

other savages were observed to make their appearance from behind a small eminence, that had hitherto concealed them; and on their approach, we perceived that many of them had put on their war dress, and were armed with spears, bows, and war clubs. By this time our boat had got into shoal water, and was close to the beach, within reach of their arrows. Vancouver began to talk of retreating, yet did not like to shew any symptom of fear: he ordered the arm chest to be opened, and that every man should arm himself. The moment the savages saw this, they rushed towards the boat, and plunging into the sea, got under our oars, so that they could not be used; others laid hold of the boat, and endeavoured to haul it on shore. Vancouver in vain endeavoured to hold a parley with them, and to explain that no harm was intended; they every minute became more insolent and audacious, and I saw clearly that they intended mischief. We looked round at that instant, for our companions in the other boat, but they could not be seen.

" The savages had now put themselves into threatening attitudes. My station was in the stern sheets, where providentially lay a pair of large horse pistols. I took one of them, and a midshipman, who stood by me, took the other. We had scarcely done this, when two tall, strong, horrid looking savages, rushed into the water, within a few feet of us, dressed in their war dress of buffalo hide; each armed with a long spear, and their faces painted with all sorts of colours. The savage who was opposed to me, threw himself back a little, elevated his spear, and seemed in the very act of hurling it through my body: when suddenly his eye caught mine, and he observed that the muzzle of my pistol was directed to his breast. He instantly was horror struck, and remained fixed in his terrific attitude. Aware of the efficacy of fire arms, he dreaded instant death, if he made his intended throw at me. I had sat down in the stern sheets to avoid their arrows: but my pistol was rested on the gunwale of our boat, and my eyes were sternly rivetted on his. I acknowledge I was frightened, but I thought not of death. I thought of nothing, but the horrid savage before me, and whether it were possible, that my pistol might fail in going off, or the ball in penetrating the buffalo hide which he had on. I resolved to sell my life as dear as I could; and in this state of awful suspense we remained a considerable time, utterly regardless of any thing that passed around us.

" At this critical instant, and when Vancouver had been knocked down by a war club, and several of our boat's crew had been wounded severely* with their spears, our shipmates in the other boat hove in sight! They immediately saw what was going on, and fired upon the savages. The Indians then retired in consternation; and, with the assistance of our companions, we pushed into deep water and rowed off.

During this voyage, Mr. Stewart became intimately acquainted with a distinguished young officer, whom he much regarded, and

---

* One man was speared through the thigh by the savages, with such force, as to be pinioned to the side of the boat.

whose keen feelings he always sedulously loved to abate,—the much injured and ever to-be lamented Lord Camelford. The pages of our CHRONICLE must use the language of truth, however at variance with popular and received opinions. We sincerely trust that the future naval historian will do justice to the memory and liberal zeal of this unfortunate seaman ; and, like the Monk in Sterne, will gather the nettle which should never have been suffered to grow on the tomb of one, who was beloved and is now regretted, by many leading characters in the British navy.

Mr. Stewart served as midshipman and master's mate on board the Discovery, until the 3d of November, 1795. Captain Vancouver, on his arrival at St. Helens, strongly recommended his young companion to Mr. Stewart's relation, Lord Keith, then Sir G. K. Elphinstone; who patronised him in a conspicuous manner, and placed him in situations where his great abilities might appear.

On the 3d of November, 1795, Mr. Stewart passed his examination as lieutenant, with great credit, and was appointed second in the Arab, on the 6th of that month. After a voyage to New York, and whilst cruising off the French coast, the Arab struck on a rock in hazy weather, and in less than twenty minutes became a mere wreck. Perceiving there was no hope of saving the ship, Lieutenant Stewart had thrown himself into the sea, but without the precaution of taking off his shirt ; which had nearly proved fatal to him, from its gathering round his shoulders and arms, and thus nearly preventing his swimming. Providentially he reached a spar, which he had thrown overboard, and swam with it to clear the eddy that was occasioned by the sinking of the ship : when hearing voices that proceeded from the jolly boat full of people, he called out for assistance. His voice was recognized by a seaman of the name of Johnson, who called out, " that is Lieutenant Stewart, let us stop and take him in at all events." He then put back to the floating wreck of the Arab, and saved four persons more. Captain Seymour's voice was once thought to have been heard in the water, amidst the fog, but they could not find him. He was lost with the surgeon and 23 of the crew. The survivors, many of whom were picked up by fishermen, on reaching the French coast were infamously treated, and even marched naked into the country, to Quimper, where they received much kindness and assistance from a Miss Coppinger, who had been a Nun.

The surviving officers, who were nine in number, being without money, and no rations being allowed whilst on parole, were compelled to go to prison with their men. They were afterwards marched to Brest, and Morlaix, and exchanged. A French captain, named Bergeret, gave them money; and the relations also of those for whom they were exchanged were very kind. Lieutenant Stewart arrived at Plymouth in July, 1796; and, after paying a visit to his family in Scotland, on the 5th of the ensuing September, he was appointed to the Revolutionnaire frigate, and joined her at Falmouth.

In 1797, Lieutenant Stewart joined Lord Keith on board the Queen Charlotte, having left the Revolutionnaire on the 20th of July, in that year. When his Lordship's flag was struck, Lieutenant Stewart served in the Formidable; and afterwards successively with the noble Admiral, on board the Tonnant, Foudroyant, Barfleur, and Queen Charlotte.

He joined the Foudroyant on the 19th of November, 1798, at Plymouth, and had previously continued in the Channel fleet. Lord Keith's flag was on board, going out second in command in the Mediterranean. The Foudroyant joined Earl St. Vincent at Gibraltar in December; who, being severely indisposed, gave charge of our fleet off Cadiz to Lord Keith, with his flag on board the Barfleur: and in that ship Lieutenant Stewart remained employed on the blockade of the Spanish fleet,* until the beginning of the month of May, 1799: when the French fleet, under Admiral Bruix, consisting of 24 sail of the line, and nine smaller vessels, being overawed by the imposing attitude which the British fleet had assumed, consisting only of 15 sail of the line, one frigate, and one sloop, abandoned the project of attempting to enter the port of Cadiz; and, passing through the Straits in the night, made the best of their way towards Toulon. Lord Keith having ascertained that fact, returned with his squadron to Gibraltar to receive the instructions of the commander-in-chief.

During all the preceding service, as well as in the subsequent

---

* Consisting of twenty-two ships of the line, and a correspondent number of smaller vessels, ready to put to sea at a minute's notice.

pursuit of the French fleet by Earl St. Vincent, and of the combined fleets by Lord Keith, Mr. Stewart continued to do the duty of that Admiral's flag lieutenant ; and by his prompt conception of all public applications, his immediate attention to the object of them, his respectful but manly demeanour to his superiors, his kind and liberal behaviour to his brother officers, and the habitual urbanity of his manners to all ; he conciliated the respect, and secured the esteem of all ranks and degrees, confirming the favourable impression which his valuable talents and amiable disposition had originally made upon his patron's mind.

On Lord Keith's return to England, Lieutenant Stewart remained attached to the Channel fleet, for about three months : but returned with that Admiral to the Mediterranean, on his receiving orders to repair thither as successor to the Earl of St. Vincent; when his flag was again hoisted on board the Queen Charlotte, which sailed about the middle of November, 1799, from Spithead. Having been foiled in his design of entering the port of Lisbon by the weather, Lord Keith successively visited Gibraltar, Minorca, Leghorn, Palermo, and the canal of Malta, for the purpose of distributing and stationing his ships ; and of holding communications with his Majesty's military officers, and those of his allies, as also with the King's ministers at Florence, Naples, and Palermo, and with the Sicilian Court. Lieutenant Stewart being in the habitual confidence of his Admiral, was thus afforded frequent opportunities of access on public business, to foreign ministers, military officers, and other persons of distinction ; for intercourse with whom he had laboured to qualify himself, by the acquisition of the Italian language.

On the 7th of March, 1800, Lord Keith returned to Leghorn, to co-operate with the Austrian army against the French, under the command of Massena, who at that time occupied the city and territory of Genoa. While the necessary arrangements for the service were going on, the Queen Charlotte † was unhappily destroyed by fire, on the 17th of March. Lieutenant Stewart had gone on shore on the preceding evening ; but, on the first alarm in the morning, he hastened to the Mole, and cutting a tartan loose, compelled the crew to put off to give immediate assistance :

---

† For a detailed account, refer to Vol. III. p. 299.

in which gallant and dangerous enterprise, he was assisted by an old schoolfellow whom he chanced to meet on the Mole.

When the Tartan reached the Queen Charlotte, then in a perfect blaze, she was stationed by Lieutenant Stewart as near as safety would permit, under the care of his friend; whilst he himself went in a little boat, to save people who were hanging by ropes from the bowsprit, and sprit-sail-yard, &c. Another small boat on the same service, was swamped by the numbers that dropped into her, when two men who had volunteered their assistance, were drowned.

Captain A. Duff, who was then third lieutenant of the Queen Charlotte, has favoured us with the following testimony to these humane exertions of his brother officer, who was second lieutenant:—" To the active and intrepid conduct of that lamented ornament of the British navy, the major part of those who escaped, owe their preservation. Stewart had been early in the morning informed of the dreadful situation of our noble ship. The burning of Troy could not have been a more tremendous or awful sight to Æneas. The ship was one blaze from stem to stern, with her guns going off in all directions, from the flames. Lieutenant Stewart's heroic conduct was followed by two other boats, and, to the honour of some American vessels, who were at Leghorn, one was directly manned by three of their men; but too incautiously going alongside of the Queen Charlotte, she fell a sacrifice to the impetuosity of the unfortunate crew, who, urged by the flames, flocked in numbers for deliverance. She sank alongside, with all on board.

" Lieutenant Stewart's ardour in the cause of humanity was only equalled by his judgment in affording us relief, when he had reached the Queen Charlotte; which lay at the distance of twelve miles from the shore. He judiciously dropped his Tartan under the bows, where almost all the remaining crew had taken refuge. Little more than an hour had elapsed, after this assistance had been given, before the ship blew up. All that had been left unburnt, immediately sunk down by the stern; but when the ponderous contents of the hold had been washed away by the waves, she, for an instant, recovered her buoyant property; and was suddenly seen to emerge almost her whole length from the deep ; and then immediately turning over, she floated on the surface, with her burnished copper glistening in the Sun. Amidst the various wonders of the deep, which are beheld by those who go down to the sea in ships, this certainly formed a most sublime and awful event. I had been roused from sleep by the going off of the guns, and had escaped from the surrounding flames by jumping from the poop, in order to swim to the launch that was astern, at that time full of men. I providentially reached the launch, just as they were in the act of casting off the tow rope ; and after some entreaties and consultation, I was taken in, and had the happiness of being afterwards conducive to the preservation of several lives. I also witnessed, whilst in the launch, the exertions of the boats under the bows of the ship, directed by Lieutenant Stewart. We had only one oar and the rudder in the launch, and were consequently at the mercy of the wind and sea."

Captain Stewart had the gratification to find, amongst the number who had been preserved by himself, his most intimate friend, the Honourable Lieutenant (now Captain) Dundas, of the Euryalus, and also Mr. Francis Loch, midshipman, who was under his particular care.

The Admiral, in a state bordering on distraction, had continued, after Lieutenant Stewart's going off in the Tartan, to use every possible effort and persuasion with the Italians belonging to the country boats in the Mole, to put to sea: but which, notwithstanding the active interference of the government of the town, and of the president of the chamber of commerce, had only an effect on a few, and on fewer still with any beneficial effect. Could the activity, energy, and humanity, that would have actuated the seamen of a British port on such an occasion, have been transferred to the drones in the Mole of Leghorn, many more valuable lives would have been saved.—The Admiral most highly appreciated Lieutenant Stewart's services on that disastrous day, as also those of Mr. Greenway, master's mate, who went off in a merchant ship's boat : as well as those of Mr. T. Parkinson, Mr. Isaac Crabb, and Mr. James Cutline, masters of transports ; and of Mr. Lewis, master of the English ship Alexander, of Mr. William Robinson, master of the American ship Castor and Pollux, with the crews of their respective vessels.

After this melancholy event, Lieutenant Stewart was left employed by Lord Keith on shore at Leghorn; whilst the Admiral proceeded, on the 3d of April, 1800, to the blockade of Genoa, then besieged by the Austrians. Lieutenant Stewart intercepted whatever supplies were attempted to be sent thither. Corn for that purpose having actually been embarked on board Italian vessels, which were thus immediately stopped by him, who was the only Englishman in the place. A message was in consequence sent to Lieutenant Stewart by the Austrian general, to let the vessels sail, as they had his passports, and were destined for a town occupied by the Austrian forces; but the former resolutely refused without orders from his Admiral, well knowing they were intended as a supply for the French army. The Austrian, who had received a bribe, preferred silence to any farther appeal, and the enemy were thus reduced to the utmost distress.

On the 29th of April, 1800, Lieutenant Stewart was appointed by Lord Keith to the command of the Mondovi sloop, of 14 guns, and continued co-operating with the squadron in the blockade, and seconding the operations of the Austrian army on the coast until the 16th of May, when he was sent to Leghorn, to arrange the conveyance of some Austrian troops to the Genoese territory. Lieutenant Stewart was at the same time confidentially instructed, to apply his attention to an object esteemed by the Admiral of the utmost importance to the ultimate success of the campaign—*The total suppression of the clandestine exportation of grain, from the ports of Tuscany.* For this important purpose, he was finally stationed at Leghorn. Where, by his judicious and temperate representations, and the prompt and decided interposition of an honest mind, he was enabled, and particularly in one case of great extent, to palsy the speculations and designs of individuals; who had been led to sacrifice both principle and duty, to the enormous profit, which was at that time to be derived from the conveyance of supplies to the nearly famished and distressed enemy in the port of Genoa. Captain Stewart fully justified the confidence that had been thus reposed in him by the commander-in-chief.

Many of the desperate and sanguinary conflicts that almost daily took place on that coast, between the Austrian and French armies, being within view of the British squadron, had been distinctly witnessed by Captain Stewart, before he was detached on other duty. But there was one event of considerable importance, that he did not witness, and which it is our duty as faithful Naval Chroniclers to notice—" The surrender of the important City of Geroa to the British Squadron."—The Austrians never fired a gun,against that place, and its reduction was wholly caused by famine, which the vigilance and severity of our sea blockade had occasioned. This achievement in our naval annals would not have failed to have shone forth as it deserved, had not the disastrous result of the battle of Marengo, and the Convention of Alexandria, between Baron de Melas and Buonaparte, overwhelmed Europe with astonishment and dismay.—The great object of our Biographical Memoirs is, to preserve and elucidate Naval Facts, and Dates, for the future historian, and we have, therefore, thus paid the tribute that was here due, to the friend and Admiral of the distinguished subject of our present attention.

On the 25th of June, 1800, soon after the termination of the Genoese campaign, Captain Stewart was detached by Lord Keith, to cruise under the orders of the senior officer employed off Lisbon and Oporto: where, with the exception of some occasional absence at Minorca, and whilst off Cadiz, he continued employed until the commencement of the Egyptian expedition. A great debarkation had been contemplated at Cadiz, in the beginning of October, but was subsequently abandoned in consequence of the yellow fever which prevailed.

Captain Stewart sailed in the Mondovi on the Egyptian expedition with Lord Keith, to Marmorice, on the coast of Anatolia, December 31, 1800. That great armament consisted of about 100 ships of war, the greater part of which were ships of two decks, and frigates, with an equal number of large transports, having from 25, to 30,000 men on board. Its arrival at the appointed rendezvous, excited the astonishment and admiration of the inhabitants of the Asiatic shores, and gave a new and magnificent appearance to the extensive surface of the hitherto solitary, but beautiful and romantic Bay of Marmorice.

(1801.) Amongst the numerous difficulties, with which this extensive and important expedition had to contend; but which it

is not the object of this biographical memoir to explain—was that
of bringing forward the small armed vessels, which the Turkish
Government had engaged to provide for co-operating with the
armament. And, however limited and unavailing any assistance
of that nature proved, in the issue, to be, it certainly appeared
incumbent upon the commander-in-chief, to exert all his influence
for procuring it to the greatest practicable extent. The harbour
of Rhodes, opposite to Marmorice, and distant from it about 40
miles, was the port in which these vessels were intended to be
equipped. The presence, therefore, of an officer of activity,
temper, discretion, and judgment, and one whom the Admiral
could admit confidentially into his views, was required. Captain
Stewart was accordingly selected for this service, and, on the 2d
of January, 1801, he was sent to Rhodes, under special instructions from Lord Keith, to take the chief charge of naval affairs at
that Island; to consult, in the Admiral's name, with Hassan Bey,
the Governor; to expedite the refitting of such of his Majesty's
gun-boats as were there; to hasten them to Marmorice, as well as
some Turkish gun-boats that had been built at Constantinople;
to encourage the Governor to fit out other dismantled gun-boats
that were lying at Rhodes, and to prevail upon him to admit into
each of them an intelligent British seaman, who could understand
the established signals. Captain Stewart was also directed, to
despatch to Marmorice, as soon as they were ready, all such
transport vessels as might be hired for the quarter-master-general's,
and commissary-general's departments by a master of the navy,
who had been appointed to engage them, and to superintend the
embarkation of their horses, mules, oxen, wood, water, and
other stores.—Captain Stewart was also to apply to the Governor,
for suitable buildings for the reception and accommodation of the
sick on board our fleet at Marmorice.—In the able discharge of
these intricate and multifarious duties, this officer remained at
Rhodes until the armament was ready to sail for the coast of
Egypt; and he maintained throughout, not only a continued confidential intercourse with Lord Keith, but what was much more
difficult, he, at the same time, secured by his temperate and conciliating conduct, the favour of the despotic and uninformed
Chief, with whom he had to act, for the successful attainment of
the objects of his mission.

On the 22d of February, 1801, the armament proceeded to its destination; and, on the 8th of March, the debarkation of our brave soldiers, under the ever-to-be-lamented Sir Ralph Abercrombie, took place. The Mondovi, Captain Stewart, had been selected for the meeting of our General and Admiral; around which the flotilla and armed boats were to assemble.* Both General Abercrombie, and Lord Keith, afterwards removed to the Tartarus bomb vessel, that was anchored still closer to the shore. The particulars of the glorious descent that was made, are too well known to need repetition. Captain Stewart was on shore on the 13th of March, with our army, when the second engagement with the French took place; and having slept in the British camp on the night of the 20th, he witnessed, during the ensuing day, that desperate but unsuccessful attack of the enemy upon the position of our troops, when the death of the renowned Abercrombie may be said to have sealed the termination of the Egyptian campaign: although it could not be brought to a final close by his gallant successor, Lord Hutchinson, owing to a combination of various circumstances, for several months afterwards.

On two different occasions, after the 21st of March, the Admiral had detached the Mondovi to the port of Alexandria, from Aboukir Bay, with some prisoners, whom the French General Menou was well inclined to receive: but the vigilance and jealousy of the enemy, prohibited all intercourse whatever.

On the 10th of April, 1801, Captain Stewart was promoted, by the Admiral, to the command of the Africaine frigate, of 38 guns; but, in consequence of Admiralty arrangements, he was afterwards removed by Lord Keith to the Haerlem, a troop-ship, of 64 guns. In this ship, he conveyed the Honourable General Fox, the successor of Sir Ralph Abercrombie, as commander of his Majesty's land forces in the Mediterranean, from Minorca to Malta, where he arrived on the 25th of August.—Captain Stewart had been previously known to that respectable and valuable officer, and continued in the most friendly intercourse with him until his return from the Straits.—On the 6th of August, 1801, Captain Stewart was confirmed in his post rank, by a commission from the Admiralty; and, on the 17th of October, took the command of H. M. S. the Europe, to which he had been nomi-

---

* See the end of this memoir.

nated, on her arrival at Malta.—This ship continued in the Mediterranean until the 15th of June, 1802; when Captain Stewart received the commander-in-chief's orders to proceed with her to England; and was charged to give his particular attention to H. M. S. the Genereux, then proceeding from Gibraltar to England, in a very infirm and defective state. Both ships arrived safely in England, and the Europa was paid off on the 4th of August, 1802.

* * * * * *

(1803.) On the re-commencement of hostilities, in May, 1803, Lord Keith was appointed commander-in-chief of all his Majesty's ships employed in the North Sea, and in the English Channel, as far to the westward as Selsea-Bill. The nature of this extensive and complicated command, required that the Admiral should be established on shore, at some convenient station, for maintaining his correspondence with the Admiralty Board, and with the flag officers and commanding officers respectively employed under his command, in the Downs, at Dungeness, at Sheerness, Yarmouth, and Leith, and upon the different stations within the limits of his flag; as well as for the purpose of regulating the distribution and stations of the block-ships, which it had been judged necessary to employ for the defence of the entrance to the River Thames. The number of the ships of the line appointed for the station, did not admit, agreeably to the then existing practice of the navy, of the appointment of a first captain to the fleet. Much assistance, however, of that kind, was required. The Admiral naturally turned his attention to those who had served him long and well; and the Board of Admiralty shewed a disposition to attend to all he desired in this respect. Captain John Clarke Searle (now chairman of the Victualling Board), an officer of distinguished merit, who had been chosen by Lord Keith as the captain of his flag-ship during the Egyptian campaign, and with whom Captain Stewart had long lived in cordial friendship, which continued until the time of his death, was, accordingly, on his Lordship's application, again appointed to the command of the flag-ship. Captain Stewart immediately received an appointment to H. M. S. the Ceres, then in commission on the establishment of an hospital ship, under the command of a lieutenant, in order that Lord Keith might avail himself of his services on any part of his extensive command, and for that purpose the Lords of the Admiralty granted him a general leave of absence from his ship. The following general order that was issued, by the Admiral, to the fleet, on Captain Stewart's appointment, will explain the nature of this duty :—

" *Vlieter, at the Nore,* 22d *May*, 1803.

" It being my intention that Captain John Stewart, of H.M.S. the Ceres, is to attend to the detailed duties of the fleet under my orders, the respective captains and commanders are hereby required and directed to comply with all such general and particular memoranda as are issued by him, on my authority, in the same manner as if they proceeded immediately from myself.

" KEITH."

" *To the respective Captains and Commanders of his Majesty's Ships and Vessels on the North Sea Station.*"

From the date of this appointment, until the commencement of the winter of 1805, Captain Stewart continued with his Admiral; sometimes embarked, but generally resident upon the Isle of Thanet, which had been fixed on as the most convenient station for superintending our stationary ships, and maintaining a correspondence throughout all points of Lord Keith's command. Captain Stewart visited, in execution of the orders of the commander-in-chief, occasionally, the anchorages of the fleet, and the signal stations, and kept up a daily intercourse with the flag-ship in the Downs; thus uniformly conducting all the branches of his varied duty, with the same zeal, diligence, and discretion he had formerly displayed. In the early part of this command, he accompanied Lord Keith, attended by his much valued friend, and fellow circumnavigator, Mr. Whidbey, of Woolwich dock-yard, to establish signal stations on the coasts of Essex, and Kent. In the month of November, 1803, and again in June, 1804, he was sent by the Admiral, most strictly to reconnoitre and report upon the state of the enemy's preparations for invasion, at Dunkirk and Ostend; but more especially at the latter port. He was accompanied by the best pilots for the enemy's coast, and was particularly instructed to ascertain, as satisfactorily as possible, if any fair prospect existed for bombarding and destroying the enemy's gun-boats and small craft, that had been assembled in these ports for the boasted threatened invasion of our coast. The result was, that no bombardment was attempted; there being every reason to apprehend, after the closest inspection, and most deliberate consultation with the pilots (who were perfectly acquainted, not only with the soundings, but with the locality of the place), that the enemy had the power, and on the shortest notice, of withdrawing all their small craft completely out of the reach of our bomb-vessels and guns: and that any such attack must have been attended with a positive and extensive expence, together with the probable loss of vessels, and the sacrifice of valuable lives, without the prospect of any commensurate advantages.

On many occasions, during the continuance of Captain Stewart on this service, he was employed by the Admiral, in communications with the military officers, commanding in the district, relative to the embarkation of troops, and other points of service: and he obtained the favourable opinion of all, which he never failed to secure. In his numerous communications with the flag-officers, who served under Lord Keith's command, during that period, he was equally fortunate. And it is believed, that, in the exercise of a duty, which very frequently required intercourse, and interference, on the part of the Admiral, with captains of rank superior to his own, no instance occurred of Captain Stewart's having afforded any cause for dissatisfaction or complaint.

From his private letters, during the above-mentioned period, we have selected three. The first is dated June 28, 1804, addressed, like the rest, to Captain Stewart's intimate friend, James Loch, Esq.

" Dear Loch: * * * * * The minister will find it difficult to persuade *Bonny* to destroy his boats: independently of every thing else, it is to be considered, that most of them, or at least a large proportion, are private property, certainly just now in requisition, but which, during a peace, would be returned to their owners; who, by means of the canals, carry on with those boats most of the commerce of Flanders, and of the fisheries on the coasts, and on the North Sea Banks.—They, at home, may talk a great deal about the force in the Downs; but it is not very different from what it was, except in having attached to it a parcel of merchantmen, with guns of a small calibre, and which have each a naval captain in them, but as yet no men.....We want more ships off Havre, which may contain a greater force than we know of. You need not be much afraid of the invasion: he cannot get his Boulognese across, unless he could bring a fleet up to cover them; which is certainly possible to happen, but not probable —So the people may still come to Ramsgate.

"The scheme of making Cherburg a great port, which was carried on at a vast expence, and with immense labour during the long peace, certainly failed; as the cones were washed away, and I conclude the French have not done very much to it this war. What has been inserted in their papers, alludes to shelter for small vessels, and not for a fleet of men of war, which was their original intention.—But I am speaking from supposition, having never seen the place, and therefore can give you no idea whether they intended to excavate and have an artificial back water, or whether there is a natural one.

Respecting an *Establishment on the Sandwich Islands*, I never heard that there was an intention of forming one. There, certainly, are abundance of proper situations, particularly on *Owhyhee*, *Mowea*, and *Woahu*, or *Atooi*. But for what purpose would you settle them, unless as a place for refreshment, which is now unnecessary, as the fur trade is almost, if not quite, over, and most probably will never again be much in our power, since the Russians, from killing their own sea otters, can afford to undersell us very much. Some traders, sent out by Curtis and others, formed a kind of establishment at *Woahoo*, made syrup from sugar canes (of which there are abundance), and salted pork, &c. for their vessels employed in the fur trade; but they soon quarrelled with the natives, who put some of them to death, and the rest fled, and so that ended; since which, I know nothing of the country. From its climate, it would produce every thing in our West Indies—but then where would be the market.

"I cannot say whether the Sandwich Islanders resemble the New Zealanders more than the Otaheiteans, because I never saw a New Zealander. Those of *Otaheitee* and the *Sandwich Islands*, always appeared to me to be one nation. I lived much amongst them. The Sandwich Islanders are more muscular, darker, and neither so handsome nor so tall as the Otaheitean; yet seemed to me to be evidently the same race, and I should account for their apparent difference, in a great measure, from their own lives, which in time may have had an effect in altering the appearance of an whole race: The Sandwich Islander earns his bread by the sweat of his brow, and cultivates the earth. The Otaheitean finds bread hanging on his trees, and does little else but sleep and play under their shade, and of course becomes more effeminate. This difference in their lives, is pointed out by the nature of their respective countries, which lying in the same climate, are very different in their formation. The *Sandwich Islands*, in general, rise gradually from the sea, to the height of mountains; and then form three regions, *the cultivated, the woody,* and *the snowy*; though in most of them are only two, *the cultivated,* and *the woody*. There are scarcely any low lands; of course little bread fruit, and few cocoa nuts. They chiefly cultivate and live on the sweet potatoe and taro, which latter is their chief article of food; besides these, they have a great deal of sugar canes and plantains, of which their fences are formed. The island of Otaheitee is a steep mountain, surrounded by a slip of low land, on which the Indians dwell; and which is covered with cocoa nut and bread fruit trees, with a great many plantains; upon these fruits the natives live, and never give themselves the trouble to cultivate any thing. Now and then,

Indeed, you see a few yams or sweet potatoes; but the only thing they take the least trouble to rear, is the cloth plant.

"I never was at the *Navigators Islands*, and never saw a New Hollander; but am persuaded he is totally a different being from a South Sea Islander. I do not think there is the slightest resemblance to the Chinese, in either the Sandwich Islander or Otaheitean : if I recollect, the latter has a full shining black eye, and not the pig's eye of China. The South Sea Islander, I should conjecture, comes nearer to the Malays, than to any other nation; but I do not much remember the Malays, of whom I saw only a few at the Cape. The women of Otaheitee have a light brown complexion, a pretty round face, not so thin as the East Indians, a clear black eye, with no red in the white—neither a Roman nor a Grecian nose, nor the least approach to a Negro one : in fact they are, what you would call, pretty but not beautiful. It is, however, ten years since I have been amongst those people ; so unless my memory is good, my replies may be incorrect.

From the same to the same, dated H. M. S. Monarch, off Dungeness, September 30, 1804.

"Dear Loch : Here we are, on our way to Boulogne, where all the squadron are now assembled ; what we are going for, I am unable to say. Yesterday 30 sail of praams, schooners, and brigs, put into Calais, on their way from Dunkirk to Boulogne. They are a part of those which lately left Ostend, and if they continue where they are, we shall put a few shells in amongst them. Buonaparte can have only two reasons for thus concent'ring his force—either to frighten us the more, and to keep up our suspense, or else, he hopes to be able to get his fleet up Channel, to clear the way for his flotilla's crossing—we must be very unlucky indeed, if this takes place : however, it is a speculation."

On the 3d of October, Captain Stewart returned to the Downs, after the attack which had been then made on the enemy ; and on the next day sent the following to his friend, Mr. Loch, at Richmond Park :—" We returned last night from Boulogne, after exercising our destructive qualities, as you will see in the newspapers.............If these kind of explosion vessels had been got into the harbour, they would have done infinite mischief ; as it was, from the extended situation of the enemy, I fancy we did not destroy many, if any ; but must have killed a good number, by the immense quantity of stones, and stuff, thrown on their decks.—We had not a man wounded, from

the nature of the invention; for after it is once set a going, its effect is certain. You may set it to any time, and if an enemy board the vessel, he cannot stop its effect, for in attempting to do that, he must inevitably make it explode. Lord Melville made his appearance in the night, in a frigate, and saw the whole. To be sure, nothing could be grander as a sight—the whole enemy's coast a line of fire, with every now and then a great explosion. On our part not a single shot fired. All was still. I know Lord Melville was much disappointed, as he and others expected great things from it. They wanted to persuade people to get the things into the harbour; but no man in the fleet could be got fool-hardy enough to attempt it.................
We shall be pestered with this burning story for some time; the *Moniteur* will be grand upon the occasion, they of course will say, they suffered nothing. We saw a few bowsprits and jib-booms gone in the morning, and much confusion."—Captain Stewart's opinion was always against the plan of attack that had been thus adopted—he saw its fallacy from the first, with the experienced eye of a seaman: he had been close to the Queen Charlotte when she blew up, and declared that the vessel he was in had received no harm; that the Amphion frigate blew up in Hamoaze alongside the sheer-hulk, yet although she was completely blown away from the hulk, tearing away the lashings and throwing two of her guns on the hulk's deck, still the latter received no damage.

Captain Stewart after this was afflicted with ill health, and was at length compelled by it to abandon his situation with Lord Keith; not being any longer able to support the sharp easterly winds and winter duty. He had served under the Admiral as Adjutant-general, with the title of Assistant-captain to the Fleet, but with only the pay of a frigate, and no prize-money.

(1805.) After residing for some time with his relation, W. Adam, Esq. at Richmond Park, and with his friend, H. Davis, Esq. at Clifton, he returned to London; having received great relief in his asthmatic complaints, from the advice of Dr. Bree, who then resided at Birmingham. The correspondence that was afterwards kept up between him and Dr. Bree, was productive of a sincere and permanent friendship.

On his recovery, Captain Stewart received a commission to command the Seahorse frigate, off Cadiz, which he joined in March, or April, 1806 ; and, after serving in the blockade of that port and at Gibraltar, he brought her home to Sheerness to refit; which being completely done, he was ordered again to the Mediterranean.—On leaving the Downs, in a thick fog and tremendous gale of wind, the Seahorse struck on the Varne shoal; and was only saved by the prompt and judicious exertions of her captain, who brought her into the Downs without the rudder and false keel. She was ordered into dock at Plymouth, and sailed again for the Mediterranean. On her arrival at Malta, Captain Stewart was selected by Lord Collingwood, to serve in the Archipelago ; his Lordship, with the British squadron, and that of Russia, were lying off the Island of Imbros, outside of the Dardanelles : Sir Arthur Paget being on board with Lord Collingwood, endeavouring to negotiate with the Turks. On the conclusion of peace between France and Russia, the Russian squadron came down the Mediterranean, and soon afterwards Lord Collingwood set sail ; leaving Captain Stewart * to maintain our footing in the Archipelago, and to preserve the Greek Islands, whence we had drawn our supplies and from which a great deal of trade was carrying on to Malta, from the ravages of their Turkish Agas, who had left them on our approach.

The following letter from Captain Stewart to Rear-admiral Martin, is dated Miconi, September 30, 1807 :—

" Sir : I have just heard that Mr. Vertot, the Russian Consul at this place, has chosen to find fault with my conduct, in having, as he says,

---

* " You will probably," (says a Correspondent to whom we are much indebted) " be able to make out from Captain Stewart's papers what authority Lord Collingwood had given him, with respect to keeping open the intercourse with the Porte. That the steps taken for that purpose had the ultimate and entire approbation of Lord Collingwood, I have every reason to believe : but Captain Stewart told me, at the time, that his Lordship had thrown the responsibility of the communications off his own shoulders, by disavowing his having given Captain Stewart authority to go so far as he did; which more particularly related to a proposal made by him, and received by the Turkish Government, for the preservation of their fleet, in the event of an invasion then apprehended from France on the side of Dalmatia."

threatened to punish Russian subjects, in a paper I circulated amongst the Islands, with a hope of bringing them into some kind of order.

" In the first place there is no such threat, as the Ionian Islands are now French, and every one of the privateers were from thence; and in the next place, if it had been so, the necessity was obvious, as those Consuls have no power to punish these fellows (as we have seen from the first), and they have oftener encouraged than prevented their excesses. Until the Ionian privateers were driven away, it was impossible to establish or protect private property; as their crews lived at free quarters on the defenceless inhabitants. At the island of Naxia alone, they had taken away 300 oxen, and other stock in proportion. At Santorin, they had robbed and plundered many houses, particularly one called the Tower, in which their wealthiest people had put their valuables; and besides all this, they had extorted a large sum of money from them. Paros has also suffered excessively, and Sino considerably; in short, every one of the islands groaned under their lash. One might almost, after hearing this, say, any measure whatever could not be too strong against such villains, particularly as the Consuls had no power to remedy the evil, but oftener were concerned in the privateers.

" I send you a copy of my orders, to which I have only to add, that Lord Collingwood verbally desired me to use strong measures, if necessary: from these orders, and his intentions, I drew out the paper; and, from the nature of the people it is addressed to, made it somewhat prolix and pompous, but in no way to hurt RUSSIAN DELICACY. On the contrary, I cautiously worded the whole, *to save the Russian Admiral's honour*; who, by the bye, ought to have relieved the islands from the oppression he had laid on them by turning loose these banditti. It was necessary to make these people believe we were sincere in intending to relieve them, and to punish aggressors; as otherwise the primates would not act. The good effect of the measure is already seen and felt in all of the islands. I have been twice there, and am pretty certain there are few, if any, of the privateers, or their men, now remaining. At every island we have been at, large parties of them had just set off on hearing of our approach, or fled immediately on our arrival. I have made the primates of the different islands establish guards for their own defence, and I have no doubt things will now go on quietly; as the people seem thankful and obedient. In the islands where difference of religion had split them into parties, I have extorted a written acknowledgment from the heads of the religious, to act together for the peace of the island. In short, I can assure you, that in the whole of the service I have acted as appeared to me for the best, and meaning to offend none but the guilty. I send you a copy of Lord Collingwood's letter to the Consul at Santorin, relative to the tribute: a subject, which, as it was not in my orders, I have not touched upon, but merely sent a copy to each island, leaving them to act as they judged fit: saying, I concluded his Lordship's intentions relative to all the islands to be the same. I hope after this explanation, that should M. Vertot make any complaint of my conduct, you will do me the justice to approve of what I have done, and of the motives which have guided me.

"I have the honour to be, &c.

(Signed) "JOHN STEWART."

But the principal detail of Captain Stewart's services in the Archipelago, is given by himself, in a long letter to Mr. Loch, dated Seahorse, off Candia, November 7, 1807 : and is particularly interesting, as containing a faithful portraiture of Stewart's sanguine and chivalric disposition, ever ready to succour the oppressed, and to chastise the oppressor. It is worthy of forming an episode, even in the beautiful ROMAUNT OF CHILDE HAROLDE.

" I left Gibraltar July 14th, after putting my prizes in a fair train, and arrived at Malta after a fine weather passage of fourteen days. There I found orders to proceed to Messina for news, and then join Lord Collingwood at Tenedos, whom I found under the rocky Imbros of Homer. A position which he had taken, as from it he could fetch the Turkish fleet with the N.E. winds, which at that season are periodical. This he could not have done from Tenedos, which is to leeward, and towards which a continued strong current sets from the Dardanelles : this intention of his Lordship was in consequence of the Turkish fleet being outside of the Dardanelles, when he first arrived at Tenedos ; but the moment they heard of our fleet's arrival, they moved above the first Castles ; and, by the time he had worked to windward, were quite secure. They remained outside, not caring much for the Russians; who have had two actions with them, and only took one line-of-battle ship, besides driving two, I believe frigates, ashore. I leave you to judge of Siniavin's manœuvres and conduct, when you are informed, that the Russians were some days between the Turks and the Dardanelles, that the Turks never put into any other port, and did actually land a body of men on Tenedos, who retook and held it for some time : what would we give for such an opportunity ! The consequence of these Russian manœuvres is, that as they have a particular talent for burning and destroying, the town and island of Tenedos, which was one of the most productive of the small islands, are now, except the vines and fig-trees, a total desert. I went all over it—there was an abundance of game, but not a human being to be seen. I found a profusion of the finest grapes and figs, and plenty of corn for our stock. All of which every ship in the fleet used to gather in any quantity they pleased.—The town had been burnt to the ground, and was still a mass of smoking ruins. Its small harbour was totally ruined, and nearly filled up, and there was not a house but what had been perfectly gutted. All this I beheld on my return to Lord Collingwood, after visiting the Cyclades, where I had already seen most of the unfortunate inhabitants of Tenedos begging their bread.

But to begin with the islands.—Imbros,* where I found the fleet, appeared to me rocky and miserable. My stay was too short to visit the interior ; but those who did informed me, its northern side was very fertile, and, that after crossing the hills from the south, you descend into a well cultivated and inhabited side by some beautiful vallies covered with wood. Here are no Turks. The Greeks pay a regular tribute, and govern themselves by their own laws, of which I shall speak hereafter.—As Lord Collingwood thought it probable the fleet might be obliged to winter in this sea, he sent me to examine the ports in the Cyclades, and to report as to their capacity, means of refreshment, water, &c. He also directed me to go to any islands which had shipping, and where commerce might be introduced; and to offer them facility for carrying on a trade with Malta. This order has procured me one of the pleasantest cruises I ever was employed on ; and, with my second trip to the Cyclades, afforded me an opportunity of exploring them which few have enjoyed.

" You ought first to know, that from their never having Turks over them, and only paying tribute, both the Russians and ourselves considered them as neutral : they, from their ultimate intention of holding them, and a wish to conciliate the Greeks in general; we, both from the latter desire, and also the advantages they offer as places of security and refreshment to our ships—with the cruelty it would be to attack a set of defenceless though restless devils.

" I left Lord Collingwood, August the 21st (1807) and the next day, after a run of about 60 leagues, anchored in Port Trio, on the S. side of the island of Paros. This port had been represented as a very fine one, and as being constantly used by the Turkish fleet : It is, however, only a good summer port, well sheltered from the strong N. winds of that season. Here the Turks have made an excellent watering place, and had conveyed down, by an aqueduct, a large run of very fine water. The Russians ruined it in the former war, though fortunately they could not spoil the water. Whilst the ship continued at this port, I visited the great marble quarries in Paros. I found many that had been dug into like caves, and in which lights must have been used. On the side of one was a rough carved procession of men and women, with a Greek inscription ; probably executed by some one of the many sculptors, who used to work here, as a memorial. Paros is a fine island, but is very thinly inhabited, and even those are a miserable set. Its town is now called Parecchia. No remains of antiquity are seen, except that the walls of a castle in ruins, which was built by the Genoese, are, in great measure, formed of immense slabs of white sculptured marble, and the fragments of columns which are placed

---

* *Imbros*, or *Imbrus*, noted for its great number of hares, whence its name, which is supposed to be of Phœnician original. Imbros was antiently governed for some time by its own laws, but afterwards became subject to the power of Persia, Athens, Macedonia, and the Kings of Pergamus, and at length to the Romans.

on their sides, with their ends outwards. From Port Trio I went in my boat to visit the Grotto of Antiparos, and provided myself well with false and port fires, ropes, flambeaus, &c. It was well worth seeing; we found there a rope ladder left by Captain Donnelly, of the Narcissus, by means of which, and our ropes, we descended a very considerable way under ground, until we came to a large hall, which we lighted up most brilliantly. The petrifactions, as usual, were seen in great numbers, hanging in curious shapes from the roof. We also observed many sprouting up like shrubs from the ground, formed no doubt from drops of water, which, as they fell, petrified upwards. *Antiparos* has only one small village, and but few inhabitants. I left the rope, as a legacy to future travellers, in charge of the primate or chief of the village, who also has the ladder in store.

" From Port Trio we went to *Milo*, a fruitful island, in which is a most excellent harbour. It would every way suit a fleet to winter in, as to security, but there is hardly any good water, and the island is unhealthy. About 80 years ago a plague destroyed 9000 people, and it has never since recovered its consequence. The modern town of Milo is nearly in ruins, and has not more than about 800 people in it. The village of *Castro*, where all the pilots in the Archipelago live, is most romantically situated on a very high rock on your left as you enter the harbour, and looks like an eagle's nest. Here are about 900 people; and these two numbers constitute the present population: in the town every body looks unhealthy, at the village every face displays the picture of health. The antient town of *Melos* stood in a valley, on the side of a hill on your left, as you go into the harbour; you may still trace the walls, some parts of which remain, and you also see broken pieces of columns and cornices on the top of a hill, on which appears to have been a temple. There are likewise many sepulchres; from one that had six stone recesses for bodies, I took two small jars; the first, a black ground with red figures, the other a white ground with red figures; and I also got a thing which seems to have been used for holding ink. The town came down to the sea side, and along the cliffs are many recesses neatly cut out, generally into two chambers, which most probably were inhabited. *Milo* is a volcanic island: towards the head of the harbour, close in with the edge of the sea, there is a warm spring, I should think hot enough to boil an egg; and inland, a little way from that spring, are some warm sulphureous ones, too strong for me to go down. On the very summit of a tolerably high hill, about a mile inland from the S.E. side of the harbour, is a very fine natural steam bath. I remained in it for a few minutes, and found it not the least sulphureous, but remarkably pleasant. The inhabitants appear formerly to have made use of this bath, as the way up to it is arched, and there are the remains of several chambers, which, no oubt, were used by the bathers. At this island, I found it necessary to rectify the disorders in the government; for, in consequence of the war, and a supposition that the Turks were never to have power over them again, which they were promised by the Russians, an intriguing priest had, by hiring some of our broken regiment of Froberg, who had mutinied at Malta, created himself governor for the time being; and was actually levying the revenue of the island, having displaced the old primates. I landed a party of marines, called a meeting of the people, sent for the Greek bishop of Siphno,* and secured the priest. The old primates were reinstated, to the great joy of the inhabitants, and the bishop of Siphno took upon himself to punish the priest. You will admire the punishment—he fined him about 30*l*. and had him bastinadoed in his own presence ; since which, the island has been particularly quiet.

" From *Milo* I went to *Miconi*, a barren unproductive island, but until the war it had a good deal of commerce, the inhabitants being either merchants or sailors. The town is populous, and the people look well and healthy. Here we admired considerable beauty in several of the women, and found them very affable. Italian is the language in general use. Nothing curious was to be seen at this island : but *Delos* was only about two miles distant, and I passed a day in wandering over it, amongst heaps of indistinct ruins. Madam Diana could not have had much room to hunt, for her Mount Cynthus is a hill but of moderate size, and the whole island not above two and an half miles long, and very narrow. The Temple is now quite demolished : you can, however, make out where it stood, and there are still a great number of pieces of large broken columns, &c. lying about it. I am told that numerous columns were standing until the last Russian war; many of them were removed by the Russians, and I was shewn a number of columns, which had been taken from thence, in a Greek church at *Naxia*. Besides the scite of the Temple, you can make out the ruins of the Mole for sheltering their vessels, a place which they say was the *Naumachia ;* but in truth it appeared to me too small, and I should have thought that it had been a large reservoir for preserving water, after the periodical rains, for the use of the city—but I am no judge of antiquities. Round it, there is first a vacant flat place, as if it had been a walk, and then the base of a large wall or building. You also see very distinct remains of a Theatre and its chambers, and an arch which seems to stand, on what one would naturally suppose to have been the way from the Temple to Mount Cynthus. There are many other ruins, and much rubbish, which I cannot call by any other particular, being ignorant of the ancient situations of places ; but the town and buildings seem to have covered nearly half the island, and to have reached quite across it in the middle part.

" From *Miconi* I went to *Tino*, which is by far the pleasantest of the islands, though probably one may except *Naxia*. This island is naturally barren ; but the industry of its inhabitants exceeds any thing I ever saw, except at Malta. *Tino* contains nearly 20,000 souls, two-thirds of whom are of the Greek religion, the remainder Catholics ; and never was religious animosity stronger than it is here. The inhabitants are a healthy looking race, and the women very beautiful and lively. They are accustomed to the company of Europeans, as most of the women servants

---

* A town of the island of *Nansio*.

and nurses at Smyrna and Constantinople go from this island, and, after gaining some money, settle quietly at home. In going through the villages, you are almost sure to meet with some one, who has been employed by or in the service of the English; they always ask you in and entertain you with their best fare. When we were there, the Greek party, who also considered themselves as being the Russian, were carrying it with a high hand over the others, who are supposed to be inclined towards the French, and certainly have been supported by their ambassador at the Porte. The Greeks, from being the strongest party, and I will also say the boldest men, were committing many excesses against the other, and many complaints came to me, praying for redress. I promised to lay their case before the Admiral; for, beside their own quarrels, the Russian privateers were living at free quarters upon them. This, indeed, was the case throughout all the *Cyclades*.

" I must, in the next place, recount my Adventures here: and if I entered on them with all the chivalric zeal of Don Quixote, I had nearly been as roughly treated, or even worse, than that celebrated Knight Errant—my motives, I assure you, were equally disinterested. Having heard that a remarkably pretty damsel in the Catholic side of the village, had been carried off, ravished, and forced to marry a Greek of the same place, I determined to enquire into the truth, and to afford her instant redress. But, like Don Quixote, instead of going with a sufficient force to support me, I sat off merely attended by young Hatton as my Squire, with an interpreter, and not even a case of pistols. Upon reaching the village, the girl's father and her friends, advised me not to go into the Greek part of it, as the Greeks were all half intoxicated, and had determined not to give her up. Her father also shewed me his arm, which had been cut by one of them, on his trying, some days before, to rescue his daughter.—I admit that my resolve was not prudent, but the spirit of chivalry was up; and I determined to see and to speak with the damsel, and if her story were true, to relieve her—So on we went.

" At the entrance of the Greek part of the village, we met with five or six ruffian looking fellows, of whom I demanded—which of them spoke Italian? I replied to the one who answered, that he did—" That I had heard of some people carrying off a girl, that I was determined to know if it were true, and was come to satisfy myself from her own mouth, before I would determine how to act."—At first he declared, that she was not in the village: but on my again insisting to see her, and declaring, that I would enter every house until I was satisfied whether she were there or not, he promised, after consulting with those who stood around for a few minutes, that if I would walk into her husband's house, she should appear before me. Here I saw the crown of ribbons and flowers, which had been placed on the girl's head during the marriage ceremony. They declared, she had been married with her own consent; and I now began to think that it really had been the case, and that only her parents had been against it. However, in about ten minutes she came in, followed by nearly 18 or 20 men and women. She was really remarkably beautiful, and about 16,

Her tears flowed incessantly; and perceiving she was lame (as appeared afterwards from an attempt to escape), I requested her to sit down, and as she could not speak Italian, I was obliged to resort to my interpreter. We endeavoured to get her story from her own mouth, but she was too much alarmed to deliver it; and being of opinion that she was awed by the presence of the Greeks, I ordered every soul of them to leave the room, which they did not do over willingly. She now told us her whole Story.

" She had been carried off by a party of men, when going to the well for water: an exact parallel to which occurs in the most sacred and antient records that remain. She was confined for some time in a house, had sprained her ancle in jumping out from the window, had been seized a second time, and forced to marry, entirely contrary to her inclination, after the forms of the Greek Church. Still, however, she intended to run away again, as soon as she had recovered from her sprain, and enjoyed an opportunity. I offered to carry her immediately to her parents, and she took hold of my arm; but upon opening the door, the instant she was assailed by the savage looks of her husband (and he was in truth an ill looking dog), and also heard the threats of her mother-in-law,—she drew back and said, *she did not want to go*.—I again cleared the house, and asked, what all this meant? She said, the truth was, " That if I carried her to her parents they could not defend her, and the Greeks had already done them mischief enough, and she was sure would either kill them or carry her off again, as there was no law in the land. She cried, and said she should be glad to go any where from those wretches."—I again opened the door, as if to lead her off; when the crowd exclaimed, *It shall fall on her family!* She trembled, hesitated, and wept. *I am miserable, indeed,* she exclaimed, *but I must remain where I am, and I will endeavour to escape hereafter.* The people now declared, " That I was worse than a Turk, and wanted to take her away by force; for it was clear she wished not to go:" So I felt the uproar was too powerful, and was obliged to retreat; threatening them, however, with my vengeance at my next visit, and declaring, That the whole village should answer for it, if she were not released.—I thus left my adventure unfinished: but that I may not have to revert to this painful subject again, I will at once inform you in what manner it ended. On our return to this island, the moment the fair Captive heard that the Seahorse had anchored, she escaped, and took refuge in a large Roman Catholic village; sending me a message, *That she hoped I would still protect her.* So I sat off again, and we met like old friends. She now told me more fully her whole history, and that they had treated her better after I went; that all she had said was true, and that she earnestly hoped I would cause her to be protected. I naturally took a lively interest in her feelings; and before I left the island, I extorted a written obligation from the Primates to protect her. It is her intention to go to Smyrna, and to procure a servant's place when she can get there, and a fine handy girl she is.—*Tino* is called the Island of the Winds, and well was it named; for while we lay under its lee, it blew a continued gale of wind, the N. and N.E. winds came over the mountain in furious gusts;

but on shore, these winds are delightful, and keep the air cool and salubrious. They prevail throughout the Archipelago during the end of the summer and autumn, and were called by the ancients, the *Etesian* winds. They were so conscious of their utility, that they used to offer sacrifices for them. We next went to *Ipsera*, a small barren island near *Scio*, inhabited by a set of sailors; who, in time of peace, employ about 50 sail of shipping, that now were laid up. They, as well as the people of *Miconi*, &c. declined entering into Commerce at present, solely from fear of the Russian privateers, who respect neither nation, property, nor passport.— I rejoined Lord Collingwood September 11, and found that our Negotiation was just where I had left it; but that Siniavin and his fleet were gone, upon hearing of the peace with France.—Here endeth the first Lesson.

" *November* 15.

" I have been very busy chasing vessels of all descriptions, of course too much engaged to think of writing—it is only to day that we are quite idle and nearly becalmed. After staying about a week with the fleet at *Imbros*, Lord Collingwood moved us all over to *Tenedos*, as it was near the time when we might expect S. winds, and that place afforded better shelter than the other. Sir Arthur Paget went at the same time in the *Thetis*, with a flag of truce, to get a final answer from the Turks, and returned the fourth day, when war seemed perfectly certain. Lord Collingwood determined to sail with half the fleet, and sent the Hind frigate to Alexandria, relative to the evacuation; he also ordered me to proceed again through all the *Cyclades*, to put all their governments into the hands of the old Primates, to punish offenders, and to drive from amongst them all the vessels that had been privateering under the Russian flag; but who being Ionian Islanders, now lived on the defenceless inhabitants, and in short were pirates. I sailed on this service, September 17, and continued going from island to island, until the middle of October, by which time I had nearly put them all in order, and had effectually performed the last part of my instructions: for as soon as I made known by a circular paper, the service I was come upon, it spread like wild-fire—the islanders finding it to be their interest to frighten the banditti, and though I only remained three days at *Miconi*, where I published the paper, I found that the Ionians had every where got on board their vessels, and had set off as fast as they could, after having committed the greatest devastation in several islands. It was really shameful that Siniavin should leave all these wretches to prey on the world. He sneaked off so suddenly, and so shabbily, that he never sent a single vessel of war round, to order the privateers away. His reason for this, I afterwards found out. On the Russians declaring war against the Turks, the former addressed a proclamation to the Greeks, calling upon them to arm against their natural enemies, and promising not to leave the business unfinished, as had been done before; for that now Russia would establish the Greek Empire on the ruins of the Ottoman Government. This proclamation had the effect of arming one or two islands on the shore of the Morea, particularly *Hydra* and *Speria*; the consequence of which has been, that the Turks having repossessed those islands, a large proportion of the inhabitants were obliged to emigrate, and mostly, I believe, to the Ionian Islands.

" In making this second round of the *Cyclades*, though I went to many islands, I shall only notice *Naxia*, *Santorin*, and *Argentiera*. The first, is the largest and, apparently, the most fruitful of the *Cyclades*, but has no port. The town stands opposite to the roadsted of St. Mary's in *Pagos*, and is situated on the N.W. side of the island; it is not large, but for that country contains several good houses. Excepting at *Santorin*, the Catholics are by far the most respectable inhabitants; they have an archbishop here, as well as at *Tino*, but the number of Catholics bears no proportion to the number in *Tino*, though they far exceed them in respectability. In *Naxia* are reckoned about 25,000 inhabitants, chiefly Greeks. This island was the seat of the Dukes of the Archipelago. There is a family who call themselves lineal descendants from the Duke of Naxos. With respect to antiquities, the gate of the Temple of Bacchus is to be seen. It is arched, and consists of three immense slabs of white marble, two of which are vertical, with a cross piece; and from its massiveness the destroyers of all nations have been obliged to let it remain. Many seriously assert, that when the Russians were carrying off some of the columns, as they could not move this, they fired several shot at it.

" The Temple stood on a small island close to the town of Naxia, and from the boundaries which are distinctly seen, it must have been large. You may also trace the remains of the aqueduct which conveyed water to it from the main. The Fountain of Ariadne is still shewn, and like in that of Arethusa at Syracuse, you constantly behold the Nymphs washing. There is a large grotto in the Mountain of Jupiter, but by no means equal to that at Antiparos; and about 20 miles to the N.E. of the town, at a place called Appollona, you are shewn a rough formed colossal statue of about 30 feet, lying down, which they tell you is Apollo's: but though the whole is very unfinished, you plainly discern that the gentleman was intended to have a huge beard, which would be more like *Nep*, or *Jupiter*.

" *Santorin* is an island totally different in appearance from any of the rest, and is altogether one of the most extraordinary looking places I ever beheld. It is an immense heap of lava and pumice stone. You sail into an excessive large bason, protected by islands, and would naturally expect good anchorage: but when your pilot comes off, he tells you—That except a small place off the S. end of the southernmost of the islands, there is no anchorage for you; as the only place beside that, in the whole bay, where you can find bottom, is a spot between the town and the islands, on which is four fathom rugged, bad ground; and which, from its becoming gradually shoaler, they believe to be an island rising gradually from the sea, as some of the others have done about 100 years ago. As this place off the S. end of the island, was not large, and only good anchorage with N. winds, the pilot carried us out of the bay, and anchored the ship under the S. end of the island of *Santorin* itself, in an open roadsted. In going out of the bay, we beheld on all sides a most remarkable sight: On the right a cluster of volcanic islands, the two innermost absolute heaps of lava and cinders —not a green blade to be seen ; and a spot is pointed out upon one, where the volcano is yet smoking just at the water's side, which there has a turbid yellowish appearance. Between these two inner islands, lies a narrow channel, in which were some merchant vessels waiting for their cargoes; during winter they are lashed to both islands, and hang between them. On your left, all round the bay, a steep, high, rugged, black cliff presents itself; about the middle of which, and on its very verge over your head, the town is seen, ranging along for above a mile, with its ancient castle reared on a nearly unconnected rock on the N. side. A zigzag stair, or road, is cut from the town in only one place, as a way down to load their vessels. I remained at this island six days, with our Consul, a very respectable Catholic merchant. The whole country is a vineyard. The Greeks had committed considerable depredations on the Catholics, and the Ionians who had escaped had levied a good deal of money on the latter. I had much trouble in putting them to rights ; however, I left them apparently well satisfied, at least as much so as you can ever hope to make Greeks and Catholics. *Santorin* produces nothing but wine; and their sweet wine is out of comparison the richest in the Greek Sea ; their common white wine is also, in my opinion, remarkably good, which is sold at only 9d. a gallon. The soil is a continued mass of pounded pumice stone, and as the ground slopes gradually from the top of the cliff over the bay, to the sea on the opposite shore, you have an absolute precipice on one side of the island, and a very gentle descent on the other. There are here many Catholic merchants, by far the most respectable people we had seen in those seas. The two Nunneries at *Santorin*, were the only ones I visited : the Roman Catholic contained many beautiful young women ; that belonging to the Greeks looked miserable, and all the nuns were old and haggard : but the Greek religion, with all its superstition, prevents women from becoming nuns until after thirty.

" From *Santorin* I went to *Argentiera*, which I only notice to say, I was entirely disappointed in what I saw. The French, who had formerly resorted hither in times of peace, under their Consul, had so much extolled *Argentiera* and its women, in their books of travels, that we expected to have enjoyed something a little like society : whatever might have been formerly its merits, it either had them not, or else was certainly beheld by us with very different eyes.—Having now done with these Islands, I shall only add, that the government of them is placed by the Turks in the hands of the Greeks, who elect the chief magistrates, called Primates, from amongst themselves. These Primates collect the tribute which arises from a moderate capitation tax, and a tenth is levied on the produce. I have subjoined an account of the *Population and Tribute of the Cyclades*, which the person who gave it me declared to be correct. The Primates also carry on the civil government, and can fine, but not punish capitally for any offence : a murderer or robber must be sent to the Capitain Pacha, under whose jurisdiction the islands remain ; and I was told, that if the offender should be rich, he can generally if not always buy himself off. This leads to the

Greeks frequently taking vengeance themselves, and they in general carry arms, so that the Primates may be said to possess but little power. Sometimes a person rents the tribute of the Pacha; he is then I believe called a *Waivode*, and of course makes all he can. My opinion of the Greeks is, that they are a faithless, sordid, cruel set. I never, if possible, would trust to, or deal with any one of them. Their meanness may indeed be attributed to their fear of the Turks; but I cannot give the latter the credit of causing those other bad qualities, which I hold them to possess.

POPULATION AND TRIBUTE OF THE CYCLADES.

	Inhabitants.	Tribute (*in Piastres, nearly* 1s. 6d.)
Naxos	15,000	40,000
Paros	7,000	12,000
Tino	20,000	40.000
Miconi	7,000	10,000
Sira	4,000	7,500
Zea	5,000	20,000
Thermia	4,000	10,000
Argentiera	700	3,000
Milo	2,000	7,000
Policandro	2,000	2,500
Sikino	2,000	2,500
Santorin	13,000	52,000
Nanfia	1,500	1,500
Astampalia	2,000	2,500
Nio	3,000	5,000
Anti Paros	200	1,000
Andros	15,000	45,000
Siphno	3,000	6,000
Siphanto	7,000	15,000
Amorgo	3,000	7,000
		289,500

" These islands, generally speaking, with the exception of *Tino* and *Santorin*, might produce sufficient abundance to feed a much greater population than they now contain; but at present they can barely support their own inhabitants, and export but little. *Santorin* has a considerable commerce with its wine, but imports every thing else; it produces also a little corn and cotton. *Naxia* is fruitful, and exports some corn and oil. *Sira* produces only wine, which it exports, and in return gets corn, oil, &c. *Milo* is very fruitful, but is considered unhealthy, and has not inhabitants to cultivate its surface. *Miconi* is obliged to import every thing. *Andros*, I believe, produces enough for itself, and of the other islands I know but little. *Tino* does not produce enough for its population, they import corn and oil, and make excellent silk stockings very strong, some raw silk is also exported.

" After leaving the Islands, I took up my station from the Morea to Candia, and cruised on it until Sir A. Paget came past in the Thetis; he left the Dardanelles October 19.. I found the Turks would not make peace, and it was fairly owned in private, that the French would not let them. So now we have a certain war, and Turkish prizes are worth looking after." -------------

Captain Stewart after this went to Milo, with a person who conveyed a letter from Sir A. Paget to the Pacha. He then continued to cruise, but did not meet with any vessels until November 10, when he chased a ship into *Retimo*. During the ensuing night, they took a Turkish vessel, laden with grain, biscuit, hung beef, maccaroni, &c. bound from *Eno*, the port for Adrianople, to *Canea*; and the next morning at day-light, when it was nearly calm, they saw four more, which had left *Canea* during the night; they were laden with soap, chesnuts, oranges, raisins, &c. Captain Stewart afterwards took a Xebeque, of six guns, and other vessels, and remained on that station until the 1st of December, when he went to Malta.

" We continued," adds he, in his letter to Mr. Loch, to cruise about Cerigo and Cape Matapan, until the first. I was in hopes, as we knew the French had sent two frigates and a corvette to Corfu, that one of them might be coming on with troops to possess Cerigo, which is one of the seven islands, but we heard nothing of them. I took a bombard and large boat near Cape Matapan; the former was laden with sour wine, so I released her—the latter with dried figs, so we eased her of three tons of them, and let the Johnies have as many as they pleased.—Cape Matapan and the ridge of land from it, to the head of the Gulf of Coron, are inhabited by a tribe of independent Greeks, called MANIOTS, who never have allowed the Turks to enter their country. It consists of a heap of mountains towards the Morea, and on the E. side; but there seems some tolerably good land, and plenty of olive trees on the W. side, towards the sea shore. The shores are steep and safe. I sailed a great way along it, nearer than a mile, and saw numbers of the inhabitants who were out gazing at the ship; they were the most savage looking animals I ever saw, very dark coloured and ill clad. The country appeared to be covered with villages, and to be well peopled. They have towns on the tops of the hills, and in every village are a number of turrets, as I supposed, to retire to in case of any Turks landing, which I am told they have sometimes done. I do not know what race these MANIOTS are of, nor when they first made themselves independent. The Turks found their country too strong on the land side, and whenever they came from seaward, the natives took refuge in the mountains: so, I believe, both parties found it would be for their mutual interest, if the MANIOTS paid a trifling acknowledgment, and the Turks promised not to molest their country. They were long the terror of

the Archipelago, living by piracy and pillaging both ships and islands, until about three years ago, our Narcissus frigate found 50 of them at Delos, whom they seized and sent to Constantinople, where they were all executed: since which, they have kept at home. The adjacent parts of the country, such as about Cape Angelo, were very subject to their visits; so much so, that all the towns are moved up to the summit and sides of the hills, instead of being near the shore, as they generally are, in the other parts. Adieu. Yours ever sincerely,
" JOHN STEWART."

(1808.) At the beginning of the ensuing year, 1808, we find Captain Stewart's active mind zealously intent on the commercial resources of these Islands, according to the orders he had received from the commander-in-chief; as appears from a long and interesting letter on that subject, which he addressed to Sir W. Ball, at Malta, February 8 :—

" The Island of *Ipsera*," said he, " has made a most pressing application for leave to carry pitch, tar, rosin, grain, &c. to Malta, if allowed to seek for those articles..........I mention *Ipsera*; but at *Tino*, *Zea*, and *Miconi*, are also English agents, who are only speculating on the probability of the trade from the Islands to the Continent, being thrown open entirely. I hate the whole of it, and wish it were off my hands. I have, however, written my sentiments to Lord Collingwood. We can get all the country produce from thence, but let us do it in our honest manner, and at once give the vessels their passports to go to any specified place for the cargo. I beg of you not to be deceived by the representations of interested persons; who, from being fixed at the islands, may for this express reason wish that to be the course of trade. For, believe me, there is not a Greek, who could not, if he chose, tell you in an instant, at what continental port he could get his cargo; and every Greek has access to any continental port he chooses. By way of example: I met a Scopolo ship the other day, with a passport from you, to go to any port and seek a cargo of provisions for Malta: he had been at two or three, *and it did appear had carried different things from each;* but he would have told you, *if he had not been a Greek*, that *Scopolo* is close to the mouth of the Gulph of Volo, where grain, provisions, &c. are probably cheaper than in any part of the Turkish Empire, and where he could load his ship for Malta, as soon as he dropped his anchor. I beg to assure you, that particularly with respect to grain, there can be no doubt of the quantity you can get; as the immense supply formerly exported on this side of the Euxine Sea to Europe, has now no market but Malta............There is another subject, to which I am anxious to call your attention, and that is—*Privateers coming into these parts in the event of war being continued:* I seriously think it would be attended with much mischief. King's ships, however severe they may be upon the enemy, are guided by a sense of honour; and the private property of individuals is always respected. Here, in this country, we allow small boats, with grain, to pass to the islands, as the inhabitants cannot (on some of them) live without it, and we religiously pay for what we get at these islands. I cannot give your Malta privateers credit for so much honesty, and indeed the facility of forcing things from the Greeks, would be too strong a temptation."----------

On his arrival at Malta from a four months' cruise, he thus wrote to his friend Mr. Loch, April 11, 1808 :—

" I am going back to Commodore it in the Archipelago. I am tired of it: indeed these last three months we have had most terrible weather. I took three prizes, and destroyed, God knows how many ; but it seems labour in vain: we have a new way with the Turks. Our officers are ordered in every way to destroy and annoy their trade, but the Admiralty Courts are not directed to condemn : so they put the naval officers in the light of pirates, and will not publicly avow their hostility. All the cargoes brought in here are rotting unsold. The Turks are frightened to death ; and indeed nothing can save them, but a jealousy between France and Russia. When asked by Sebastiani, why such preparation had been made? they said, ' It was to defend themselves against their real and presumable enemies.' They would gladly make peace with us, if they dared."

(1808.) Before we endeavour to furnish fresh information respecting Captain Stewart's distinguished night action with the Turkish frigates,* during this year, it is necessary to subjoin the following short historical retrospect of what had passed ; with which we have been favoured by a naval friend :—

" A Band of EPIROTS, who had been taken into the pay and service of Russia, being on the conclusion of the peace of Tilsit disbanded, and left at the mercy of their former masters ; had taken possession of two islands in the mouth of the Gulf of Salonica, from whence with large boats they laid the coast, as far as the Dardanelles, under contribution, and made prize of all vessels going to Constantinople. The tribute from these countries being principally paid in corn, was thus intercepted, and the Turks having no force outside of the Dardanelles, sufficient to crush this nest of pirates, made application to Captain Stewart, to know whether he would interfere with any squadron sent for that purpose? To which he replied—*That he should repel by force any ships attempting to come out.* The Turks were not, however, ignorant of the force in the Archipelago ; and being anxious to suppress the pirates, sent a squadron of two frigates, two sloops of war, two mortar vessels, and some xebecs, for this purpose : which having anchored off the island of Silo Dromo, made a landing, and surrounded the town of the pirates, situated on a peak. On the approach of the Turkish squadron, the pirates despatched a fast-sailing boat, with one of their chiefs, to the island of *Zea*, where the Seahorse then lay by

---

* For the official account, see Vol. XX. p. 330.

herself, to apprize Captain Stewart of the Turks being out.—Without calculating the enemy's force, Captain S. immediately weighed, and proceeded in search of the enemy, and on the second day, in working up towards the island, fell in with the two frigates, whom he engaged on the night of the 5th of July, within hearing of the other Turkish squadron; which it was well known was but a very few miles off: success, however, always favours enterprise, and the Turks, about the time the action closed in the morning, weighed anchor and made sail for the Dardanelles."

The following is Captain Stewart's own private narrative of this splendid event, as sent to a most intimate friend:—

" In working to the N. amongst the islands, I found the consternation of the Greeks general : from each place I received accounts of the Turkish ships being out, and most of the accounts exaggerated. As I knew that whatever the Turkish force was, it would be certainly much superior to my ship, I devised in my head most of the cases likely to arise ; and determined, if the disparity of force was not excessive, to attack them, and if they were under sail, to do so in the night. I felt my situation critical. I was alone ; and could not get assistance for some time. If I were driven out of the Archipelago, the whole of the islands would be instantly over run by the Turks, and our character and influence suffer in consequence. On the contrary, if I could strike a blow on the first of the Turks coming out, it would give them an earnest of what the English could do : it might possibly prevent the rest from coming out, and would certainly exalt our character with the Greeks, especially if it saved their islands from pillage. Add to this, that I was ambitious and longed for glory; and a pretty good judgment may then be formed of my feelings, between the 1st and 5th of July, when I first got sight of two Turkish men of war, between the islands of Scohilo and Killidroni. It was a fine morning when we saw them; we were standing towards Sciatho. I could not think how they came there, as I had only that day been positively assured the Turkish ships were still in *Sciatho*; I feared it might be the line-of-battle ships coming to reinforce the others, and was distressed at the thought of it. They passed to windward of the island, and we worked up with light winds towards it. In the afternoon there suddenly came on a strong north wind : I continued snug under the island, knowing they would come to leeward of it before night, if they could not get to *Sciatho*, which the wind did not seem to admit of.

" I was walking the deck with much anxiety; when, at half-past six, a large frigate,* with 15 ports on a side, was observed coming through the

---

* The BADERE ZAFFER, *Captain Scanderli Kichuc Alli*, a very fine frigate of the largest dimensions, which was taken : she carried 52 long brass guns, 24-pounders, on the main-deck, except two, which were 42-pounders, and twelve-pounders on the quarter-deck and forecastle. The other ship was the ATIO FEZAN, 24 18-pounders, and two mortars, *Captain Daragardi Alli*, complement 230 men.

passage between *Schohilo* and *Killidroni*. Then followed a smaller ship, with 13 ports on a side, and then a galley. This seemed within my compass. I knew my crew to be brave active men, well practised at manœuvering : they made all sail with undeseribable alacrity; we stood towards the Turks, with our yards all braced up, as if for sailing on a wind. I suddenly hauled the wind, when I found we could weather them, and purposely kept from engaging them until dark; when I judged we should have a greater advantage in manœuvering.

" We began engaging at half-past nine. We first attacked the large ship, and had disabled her before the smaller one came up, and tried to run us on board. We were prepared for her, with every gun double shotted; and in ten minutes totally dismasted her, and set her on fire. She blew up forward; and we left her, to go and attack the large one again. After much fatigue, and great exertion, we had knocked every thing away by half-past twelve; after that, it was downright slaughter, as he would neither say he struck, or fire only musketry when we hailed. I ought to have said, the galley, after putting most of her men into the frigates, made off. As I was anxious to carry in one of our opponents, I did not like to sink the large one, so laid by her till day-light, when we fired two broadsides into him, and he struck; but I found the captain was held. On board the Turk, was the most frightful scene I ever saw : there were 70 dead on the decks, and really almost every creature wounded. She had in all about 170 killed, and 200 wounded, (she had 543 men in all), of the latter, many died before we left *Miconi*, where I got her with much difficulty. The Turks worked and pumped on being promised their liberty; though the savage of a captain tried to blow her up, after I had allowed him to return on parole to her. We had five killed, and 10 wounded, in this extraordinary action. We refitted ourselves and the prize in three days, and I gave all the Turks their liberty, making the Greeks send them to Constantinople, and Smyrna, in ships; giving them provisions from the Seahorse. Before we sailed from *Miconi* for Malta, I wrote to the Captain Pacha, telling him that he must have foreseen what would happen, after all that had passed, and Lord Colllingwood's answer, if he sent out ships. I recommended his not sending any more, as it would only irritate the two nations against each other, who I was sure both wanted peace.

" We had a good passage to Malta, where I refitted; and I was just going to sail for the Archipelago, when I heard that Mr. Adair was come to Palermo, on his way to Turkey, and doubted, after hearing of the action, how to proceed. I volunteered to Sir A. Ball to go over to him, which I did, and he soon determined to go up in the Seahorse.

" We arrived at Tenedos the 18th September, and entered the Dardanelles the 11th November; where just as the negociation began, another revolution broke out at Constantinople, which delayed the business considerably. However, peace was signed 5th January, 1809, and I sailed up to Constantinople the 28th January. I stayed some time with Mr. Adair, who was very kind to me.. I was honoured with marked civility by the

Turks; which, as I had almost the whole conduct of the war against them, I attributed to my having personally well treated all their countrymen whom I had taken. From Constantinople I went to Smyrna, to see that our factory was re-established; and finding all right, I returned to Malta."

Captain Stewart* received a medal from the King, and the following liberal commendation from his commander-in-chief:—

........" Notwithstanding the high opinion I have ever entertained of the excellent discipline and order which are established in the Seahorse, and the firmness and enterprise which are manifest in every service on which she is engaged; yet I cannot sufficiently express my admiration of the result of this action against a force so much superior: and which can only be attributed to the eminent skill with which it was conducted. The exertions of Lieutenant Downie,† the other officers, and ship's company, deserve every regard. I have transmitted your letter to the Lords Commissioners of the Admiralty, who will doubtless pay all due attention to their merit; and I will take an early opportunity of doing what is in my power for Mr. Lester and Hully, the gunner's mate. I beg you to accept my sincere congratulations on your success, and am, &c. &c. &c.

" COLLINGWOOD."

Lord Mulgrave, in his letter from the Admiralty, dated January 4, 1809, after expressing great satisfaction at transmitting the naval medal which accompanied it, as a mark of his Majesty's gracious approbation of the skill and gallantry that had been displayed by Captain Stewart on the 5th of July, 1808, added—

" The best testimony that I can bear of the sense which I entertain of the distinguished service of that day, will be found in the enclosed list of promotions, which the Admiralty Board has made in the several ranks on board the Seahorse. I have the honour to be, with the highest esteem, &c. &c. " MULGRAVE."

Lieutenant George Downie, to the rank of Commander.
Mr. William Lester, to be Lieutenant of the Seahorse.
Mr. Thomas Hully, to be Gunner.

A memorandum is made at the Admiralty, for the promotion of the Purser, Boatswain, and Carpenter of the Seahorse, to better Ships.

Lord Collingwood, in a second letter, dated December 25, 1808, thus expressed, as commander-in-chief, the approbation of the Admiralty:—

---

* From the length to which this memoir has been already extended, we must reserve some of these honourable testimonies for another opportunity.
† Now Captain Downie.

".......... " I am commanded by their Lordships to express to you, the high sense they entertain of your meritorious conduct in that encounter. The ability with which it was conducted, and the success which ensued, have given their Lordships a satisfactory proof, That the skill, bravery, and discipline, of British seamen and marines, when guided by officers of enterprise and talent, are irresistible.—It is their Lordships' directions, That you make known to the officers and ship's company of the Seahorse, their approbation of their zealous and gallant conduct: A conduct so in unison with the high character which British seamen have on all occasions maintained in their country's service"

(1809.) At the beginning of the ensuing year, Sir Alexander Ball wrote to Captain Stewart, to congratulate him on Mr. Adair's successful negociation with the Porte—" He has spoken, my dear Stewart, of your services in the most flattering terms."—It was impossible for a man of Mr. Adair's liberal and grateful mind to act otherwise; since both his faculties and his feelings were congenial with those of Captain Stewart. In answer to a letter which Mr. Adair had written to the commander-in-chief, Lord Collingwood replied—" I shall at all times have great pleasure, in paying every possible regard to your request and suggestions. No officer is in higher estimation, in my mind, than Captain Stewart; because I have experienced his ability and judgment, wherever he was employed, and know that he is suited to the most important services." ...... But in addition to this and other generous testimony of Mr. Adair to the great reputation of this now lamented naval officer, who was afterwards cut off in the very bloom of his distinguished faculties and professional talents; we are enabled to subjoin the following eloquent eulogium, which Mr. Adair has been pleased to transmit to the writer of this biographical memoir.—

" SIR, " *Queen Street, May Fair, April 3d,* 1812.

" Understanding from Mr. Meyer,* that you are about to publish a biographical memoir of the late Captain Stewart, of the Seahorse, and that you have expressed a desire, that I should contribute such materials as may be in my possession, towards a more faithful delineation of his character: it strikes me, that I can fulfil your wishes in no manner so effectually, as by stating under what circumstances I came to know him; and

---

* A rising character in the diplomatique line, now employed in the mission to Malta.

what opportunities I had, during a service in which we were, to a certain degree, mutually engaged, of discerning those qualities; which won for him, so generally, the affection and confidence of all men. And I adopt this mode the rather, because the benefits which, during my negociation at the Dardanelles, I derived from his conduct while he had the command upon that station—(very different from those achievements which so eminently distinguish his professional life in the same year): had their origin in a class of virtues, which adorned him no less than his valour: but which, from being of a milder cast, could only be discovered by the habits of continued intercourse in which we lived, and through the unrestrained association of private friendship with public duty.

" But it will be necessary for me first, briefly to advert, as far as I can do with propriety, to some points in the history of that event, which brought us together, namely the war between Great Britain and Turkey in 1806.

" That war was produced by the adherence on our part to our engagements with Russia. Turkey, influenced by France, had in many instances infringed the treaty of triple alliance, entered into by Great Britain, Russia, and herself, to protect her against the French power during the war of the Revolution. These infractions happened during the summer and autumn of 1806, and were of a nature to provoke, and almost to invite, acts of hostility on the part of Russia. In the mean time, Buonaparte, after destroying the Prussian monarchy at Jena, had established himself on the Vistula, and was preparing to penetrate into the heart of the Russian empire. The English government, aware of the temptations which a Turkish war had at all times presented to Russia, in the easy conquest of Moldavia and Walachia, and anxious to avert the mischief which they saw must inevitably result to the common cause, if any part of the Russian force were diverted from the Vistula to the Danube; exerted their utmost endeavours, both at St. Petersburg and Constantinople, to bring about an accommodation. Their representations at St. Petersburg were successful; and they soon obtained from that Court, not only the unequivocal renunciation of all views of conquest and aggrandizement on the side of Turkey, but the manifestation of a strong desire to restore peace on any reasonable conditions. On the other hand, acting in the spirit of good faith towards Russia, and guided by a public policy, which was rendered indispensable by the then circumstances of Europe; they instructed Mr. Arbuthnot, their Ambassador at Constantinople, to insist firmly on the re-establishment of the treaty of triple alliance; and they sent a squadron to the Dardanelles, with orders to co-operate with him, and to support his negociations.

" In giving effect to this policy, they were well seconded by Mr. Arbuthnot; for although, during this time, the French influence at the Porte was at its height, so prudently did he conduct himself, and such was the real deference of Turkey towards Great Britain, that he had actually obtained the consent of the Divan to restore the treaty in its principal points; when the entry of the Russian troops into Moldavia, in consequence of the first orders from St. Petersburg, destroyed in one moment the whole effect of his exertions. This false step of the Russian Cabinet, enabled General

Sebastiani to compleat the rupture, and us a necessary consequence, to ruin irrecoverably the influence of Great Britain at the Porte.

" Every thing, indeed, conspired just then to favour the views of France. In consequence of our interference at the Court of St. Petersburg, and the dispositions produced by it, despatches of a pacific nature were prepared by the Russian government, and forwarded to their Ambassador, Count Kalinsky, both by the usual road, and by the Black Sea. The first set of these despatches was intercepted on the frontiers; and the corvette containing the duplicates, was detained at the entrance of the Bosphorus, on the ground of her being a ship of war. Count Kalinsky, it is true, had by this time quitted Constantinople; but Mr. Arbuthnot remained there, availing himself of every opportunity to promote a reconciliation. Had he gotten possession of these papers, there is scarcely a doubt that, in consequence of his preceding arrangements, peace would then have been restored; but they never were delivered to him, and their contents consequently remained unexecuted.

" Sebastiani availed himself of these advantages with so much industry, that the British Ambassador in a short time became a sort of prisoner in his palace; and was even deprived of the means of communicating either with his government, or with the dependencies of his embassy.

" In this situation, Mr. Arbuthnot took the resolution of embarking on board the Endymion, then at anchor in the port of Constantinople, and of joining the fleet under Admiral Duckworth. With this fleet he shortly afterwards passed the Dardanelles; intending to proceed strait up to the walls of the Seraglio, and to propose his terms of accommodation, under the auspices of the British flag. The circumstances which prevented the full execution of this intention, are not matter for inquiry in this place. Suffice it to say, that the squadron came to an anchor at the Prince's islands, that a negociation was begun with the Turkish government, that it failed, and that war ensued.

" When the news of this event arrived in England,* the ministers sent out an embassy, under Sir Arthur Paget, escorted by a squadron under Lord Collingwood, to endeavour to restore peace, in concert with a Russian Plenipotentiary,† who at about the same time had been despatched on a similar mission to Admiral Siniavin's fleet in the Archipelago. But before Sir Arthur could reach the Dardanelles, the Emperor of Russia had made his terms with France, and renounced the alliance of Great Britain. To bring about this important change, Buonaparte had adopted a course directly opposite to that pursued by Great Britain, in respect to the Turkish war. He knew the value attached by the Russian nobility to the possession of Moldavia and Walachia; and he knew likewise what with him was the main consideration of all, that by establishing Russia in those provinces, he was laying the foundation for interminable strife between that power and Austria. Inviting, therefore, the Emperor Alexander to a

---

* The administration was changed by this time.

† W. Pozze di Borgo, a Corsican Chief of an high principle and character.

personal interview with him at Tilsit, in July, 1807, he there gave that monarch the promise, that under certain circumstances, France would not oppose his making the Danube the boundary of his empire. This he did to gain Russia; while on the other hand, to maintain his ground with the Turks, and to keep them still at variance with Great Britain, he proposed, on condition of their continuing so at variance, to mediate a peace for them, on the principle of preserving the integrity of their empire; and in order the more completely to dupe them, and to make them believe that he was exerting his utmost power to favour their interests, he caused two articles to be introduced into the Treaty of Tilsit, the one for an armistice on the Danube, which he assumed the credit with them of having extorted from Russia, and the other, providing that the troops on both sides * should evacuate the provinces during the negociation.

" The effects of this policy were decisive in both quarters: on the part of Russia, the pacific views with which we had inspired her towards Turkey were instantly reversed, and Moldavia and Walachia were considered as finally secured to her empire. On the part of Turkey, the promised mediation on the principles announced to her, coupled with the articles for an armistice, and for evacuating the provinces, kept the Divan firm to the French interests. By the time, therefore, that the Russian and the English plenipotentiaries reached the Dardanelles, they found; the first, that his commission was annulled, and the second, that no favourable issue could be hoped for from that with which he was charged. Under these circumstances, after an unsuccessful effort for peace, Sir Arthur Paget returned to England towards the end of the year 1807.

" I have entered thus far into the history of our war with Turkey, to shew, that, unless in the mode of conducting hostilities some fresh cause of animosity should arise, it was of a nature to admit of an easy termination, whenever the French influence at the Porte could be counteracted. It will be seen, therefore, how materially the preservation of those favourable dispositions which the Turks still professed towards Great Britain could depend upon the conduct of the officer appointed to the command on that station.

" No military operations being intended in those seas, Lord Collingwood returned with his squadron to the Mediterranean, leaving Captain Stewart as senior officer in the Archipelago, with the usual orders to act against the ships of war and trade of an enemy. And here I come to the point from whence the country has to reckon those obligations towards this invaluable officer, to which I am about to bear my testimony.

" Our acquaintance began shortly after his appointment to this station. I was introduced to him by the late Sir Alexander Ball;—a man, whose use of power, in a post very far from an easy one, although contracted to a few wretched acres of rock and sand, exhibited an ability, a judgment, a moderation, and a spirit of true legislative wisdom, from which no

---

* There were none but Russian troops at this time in the provinces, except the Turkish garrisons.

Governors, however exalted their rank, or however extensive their
authority, may be ashamed to receive a lesson in administering the sacred
trust of a people's happiness. Returning from my mission at Vienna, in
the spring of 1808, I landed at Malta ; where, soon afterwards, Captain
Stewart arrived in the Seahorse, with some important information respecting the state of affairs in Turkey. This intelligence was immediately forwarded to Lord Collingwood, and likewise to Mr. Canning, then secretary
of state for foreign affairs ; who lost no time in making out a commission
for me to renew the negociations. After transacting some business in
England, I returned to the Mediterranean, and reached Palermo on the
third of August. During this impotant interval, the conduct of Captain
Stewart had been most judicious. Steadily adhering to the conciliatory
system with which he had set out, his disinterestedness was never shaken,
even by the temptation of advantages fairly within his reach, but he regarded
his instructions to capture and distress the Ottoman trade, rather as the
means of bringing a mistaken enemy to his senses, than as a source of
emolument to himself. On the other hand, and in conformity with the same
spirit, which is ever best allied to firmness, while he suffered the inhabitants of the Archipelago to carry on their traffic from island to island unmolested, he strictly enforced two conditions on the Turks, as the price of his
forbearance ; the one, that they should collect no revenue in the Greek
Islands, the other, that no Turkish ship of war should appear in those
seas. It is not, therefore, to be wondered at, that the Greeks regarded
him rather as their protector than their enemy, and that, as such, they
should venerate him to this hour. With every disposition, however,
to give a marked character of mildness to the hostility which two nations,
so long friendly, were now compelled to exercise against each other, he
found it impossible, on one occasion, to avoid inflicting upon the Turkish
marine, one of those severe lessons, which every naval state, in hostility
with us, has been doomed to experience in its turn. It happened, that
under a pretence of destroying pirates, the Captain Pacha thought fit, this
year, to send a squadron of frigates into the Ægean Sea ; in contravention
of the understood compact already mentioned. Information of this having
reached Captain Stewart, he proceeded immediately in search of them, and
coming up with two of the frigates and a galley off the island of Scopolo,
he remonstrated with the Turkish commodore upon his proceedings. On
being made acquainted, by that officer, with the purpose for which he had
been sent out, Captain Stewart readily offered to take that service upon
himself, provided he would return to port ; but he told him, at the same
time, that if he remained there, he must attack him. The Turk, scarcely
thinking his adversary in earnest, and relying upon his immense superiority ;
his own ship mounting 52 guns, and his consort 34, while the Seahorse had
but 38 in all ; preferred the risk of an engagement : and after seeing his
comrade driven out of the action, so completely beaten and crippled as to
render it doubtful whether she could gain a port, he was himself compelled
to surrender, at the end of a conflict of four hours, in which (to use Captain Stewart's words in his official letter) ' *he was rendered a motionless
wreck.*' with the loss of 350 of his men.

"This event, the glorious details of which are in every one's knowledge, happened a very few days before my arrival at Palermo. When I learned it, I confess that, on a first view, I could not but consider it as extremely embarrassing. It was impossible to judge, either what change so desperate an encounter might not produce on the pacific dispositions of the Turks; or whether the encounter itself, might not rather have been occasioned by a previous alteration in those views; and this embarrassment, coming in addition to what I had also just learned of a fresh revolution at Constantinople, in which the Sultan, to whom I was accredited, had been deposed, and most of the ministers supposed to be friendly to us, had been put to death, caused me to hesitate for a moment as to the course most proper to be pursued.

"From any apprehensions, however, as to the bad effects likely to result, from Captain Stewart's vigorous proceeding with the Turkish frigates, I was relieved, on my first interview with him. Indeed I soon found that, in one sense, it was likely to assist rather than impede my negociation. As, besides the benefit of the example, it enabled me to ascertain the true character of the revolution which had just happened, and which at first sight appeared fatal to my mission.

"Having embarked on board the Seahorse on the 3d of December, we proceeded to the Dardanelles, and anchored off Tenedos on the 26th. We remained there until the arrival of a Turkish plenipotentiary to open the conferences with me; and then removed to Barbieri bay, an anchorage between the first and second line of castles which defend the Straits. During our stay at Tenedos I thought it advisable, although the negociation had not yet commenced, that the Turkish trade, which at this time was carrying on with considerable activity, should be suffered to pass unmolested to the capital. Captain Stewart acceded without hesitation to my wishes, and by this additional act of disinterestedness, helped to keep alive, and to confirm the prevailing good humour of the Divan; a service the most essential, as it afterwards turned out, for on the very day preceding my first conference with the Turkish plenipotentiary, another insurrection broke out at Constantinople, and was followed by the death of the deposed Sultan, the slaughter of ten or fifteen thousand Turks, and the burning of a third part of the city.

"In this, as in the whole of his preceding conduct, I conceive myself greatly indebted to Captain Stewart, for the success of the negociation entrusted to me. There are other points of his public services at this period, on which I might descant, were I not restrained by obvious considerations. Between the commencement of the negociation and its close, which was not until the 5th of January, 1809, and during the time which we afterwards passed together at Constantinople, where he remained until the end of March, nothing occurred to assist me further in tracing out the distinct lines of his character, except in its amiable and social parts: yet even here I could observe the tendency, as I felt the full power, of such a character to create firm and lasting friendships. Such, it is true, are rarely the growth of our riper years. In that period of life they have to win their way through the inveteracy of habit, they find the ground pre-occupied by former affections, and are checked in their beginnings by the very virtues which are to secure their durability; yet there is something in the daily contemplation of a sound and steady mind, directed by an honest heart, and working with us in a course of common action for the public service, that carries us forcibly over all these obstacles, and sanctions the sentiments of our nature even by the calculations of our prudence. This, Sir, was my title, I hope it is a just one, to be ranked among the friends of Captain Stewart. I acquired it, not only through his constant kindness towards myself and the gentlemen of my embassy, but by having hourly before my eyes, for nearly seven months without intermission, his behaviour to his officers, to the young men whom he was educating to tread the paths of glory after him, and to his sailors, whose every nerve, fibre, and faculty, he could command to the very gates of death. If this imperfect sketch can help you in any way towards the drawing a more perfect likeness of this excellent man, you have my free consent to make whatever use of it you may think proper.

" I am, Sir,
" Your very obedient humble servant,
" ROBERT ADAIR."

* * * * * *

(1809.) Before Captain Stewart left Constantinople, he sent the following account of the Turkish Navy to Lord Collingwood, dated March 24th :—

" MY LORD,

" I am at last able to leave this place, where I have been detained much longer than I wished ; but at the express desire of Mr. Adair, who required my assistance in two or three things which he had to settle with the Turkish Government : particularly to assist at a conference that was held relative to a proposed co-operation in case of their being at war with Russia.

" On the 23d instant, I attended Mr. Adair to the Porte, where we met the Reis Effendi, a person of the Ulema, called the Plenipotentiary of the conferences, and Wakil Effendi : The principal subject was the co-operation of a British squadron in the Black Sea, to attack, or at least threaten, Sebastopolis and the Crimea ; and thus draw a large detachment of the Russian troops from the Danube. The Turks held themselves equal to meet the Russian fleet in the Black Sea ; but said, that a British force would both give confidence to their fleet, and inspire fear in the enemy. They asked for four sail of the line, two frigates, and four bombs, the latter in case Sebastopolis should be attackable from the sea. I learnt from Mr. Adair, that he had had communication with your Lordship on the subject of the Black Sea, where the impossibility of protecting the retreat of a British squadron had been discussed: I, therefore, asked the Turkish ministers, if the British government sent the ships they required, would they take the necessary steps for destroying the cannon on the north side of the Bosphorus, in case of the rapid advance of the

Russians? Their answer was, " that though they had no idea of such an advance, still there could be no doubt they would do so ;" and they added, *but if the Russians were to get there, our Empire in Europe is gone ;* and surely England, on whose account we are now going to war, would not grudge the injury which a few of of her ships might sustain." Mr. Adair told them of the crippled state of your Lordship's fleet, and the probability that you could not spare any ships : they said, the assurance of his application to the government for them, was sufficient, as they counted every. thing on our friendship. I added, That unless the squadron went into the Black Sea, before the N.E. winds set in, it could not get up there this year. They seemed to think, that the very idea of being attacked in the Black Sea by our squadron, would make a strong impression on the Russians. I afterwards told them all I knew about the Archipelago; recommended their attention to the fortresses of *Suda, Napoli,* and *Romania,* &c. &c. and, above all, pressed their immediately securing, or turning away from the Islands, all the Russians, and French partizans. They begged me to give them all the information I could in writing ; which I did the next day. They asked a good deal about Buonaparte's Berlin Decree, and our Orders in Council ; a copy of all which I left with Mr. Adair for them. By all I can learn, my Lord, the Russians have eight sail of the line, four frigates, and a number of small vessels fit for sea, two or three of which are three-deckers ; they are at Sebastopolis ; which port I have not been able to get a good account of, as no merchant ships go there : I enclose an account extracted from a book, containing descriptions of the different places in the Black Sea : An Austrian captain told me, it is strongly fortified on both sides of the entrance. The Turks have fifteen sail of the line, ten of which (viz. three 3-deckers, and seven 2-deckers) are nearly ready for sea. One 74 is just launched, and the other four refitting ; they have five frigates nearly ready for sea, and two refitting: they have besides in Constantinople, seven corvettes, two bombs, and two brigs ; three sail of the line are building at Militine, Bondroum, and Rhodes. I went up the Bosphorus in a boat as far as the Buyulidari : till you come to that place there are no batteries to signify, but from thence to the Black Sea, are a great many, and seemingly in better order than the batteries in the Dardanelles passage.

The Caimacan Ali Pacha has been made Captain Pacha, and will take upon himself the office the moment the Grand Vizier arrives : he is a man of great bravery, but no sailor. Siad Alli was made Pacha by the Janizary party after the late revolution, and the Sultan always determined to remove him, as soon as his own authority should be consolidated. Siad Alli is banished to Broresa : he persuaded Sir A. Paget, that he was a great friend of the English ; on the contrary, he seems to have been totally inimical to them, and to be connected with the French : he undoubtedly protracted the negociation, by suggesting and urging the claim for restitution of ships. A claim Mr. Adair always suspected came from French advice, and which I have no doubt did.

" I have the honour to be, &c.

(Signed) " JOHN STEWART."

As he expresses himself in a letter to his friend, Mr. Loch—His attendance at the public audience at Constantinople, was certainly a curious termination to his previous services and warfare in the Archipelago. On leaving THE PORTE, Lord Collingwood had intended to place him as chief of the squadron in the Adriatic, and actually sent him orders to that effect; but the war between Austria and France prevented it. On joining the commander-in-chief, Captain Stewart had his choice of situation, and volunteered a confidential service, of which he obtained the command, " To annoy the enemy's shores, procure intelligence, and communicate with Sir John Stuart in regard to his Continental Expedition." This service was executed with boldness, and great success. A reference to our twenty-second Volume (1809, page 255) will give the Gazette notice of two official letters from Captain Stewart to Lord Collingwood, reporting the destruction of the enemy's forts on the small Islands of *Gianuti* and *Pianosa*, on the coast of Italy:* on which service distinguished gallantry had been shewn, by the officers and men who were employed under the directions of Lieutenants Bennett and Pearse, of the Seahorse and Halcyon. To which we are now enabled to add the following answer from the commander-in-chief:—

" SIR, " *Ville de Paris, at Sea, Nov.* 5, 1809.

" Having transmitted to the Secretary of the Admiralty, your letter of the 10th of May, informing me of the capture of the Islands of *Pianosa* and *Gianuti*, I have the satisfaction to inform you, That their Lordships are pleased to express their high approbation of your conduct on that occa-

---

* The following anecdote, so illustrative of the character and prevailing superstitions of seamen, also marks the address with which Captain Stewart could humour the prejudices and anxious minds of his men, and yet preserve the necessary discipline and authority which must ever prevail in a King's ship. In one of these cruises off the Italian coast, he had passed some days without seeing a ship; when it came to his ears, that the men ascribed this to their captain's having taken a black cat on board from the last port they had touched at. He immediately called the men aft, and asked them if it really were so; they without hesitation confirmed the report. *Overboard with the black cat !* " That," exclaimed an old seaman, " is worse still, she must be landed." *Then lower away the jolly boat,* said the captain. Which having been done, the cat was safely landed with much formality on an island in sight. And as a coincidence of circumstances brought it about, that same night, they took the best prize which they had captured in the Mediterranean.

sion, and of the officers, seamen, and marines, who were employed on it; and which you will please to communicate to them."

There is also a letter from Lord Collingwood to Captain Stewart, on the nature of his services in Italy: with his Lordship's opinion that the English army should be landed in Tuscany; which may be reserved for another opportunity.

From the period of Lord Collingwood's death in March, 1810, until January, 1811, Captain Stewart was constantly employed on various important services in the Mediterranean, more especially at Sicily and Malta. He was decidedly adverse from the party and principles of the Queen;* one of whose messengers was stopped by him, but not before he had found time to destroy his despatches. Captain Stewart afterwards brought home Lord Amherst and his suite, from Palermo. The Seahorse being worn out, as well as her commander, was paid off at Woolwich in June, 1811. The severe internal complaints under which Captain Stewart had long laboured, did not at first seriously attract either his own notice, or those of his relations and friends; and an apparent improvement, which took place in his general appearance, tended to encourage the most delusive hopes: He soon, however, began to grow rapidly worse; and towards the middle of October, 1811, fatal symptoms announced a premature death. He expired on the 26th of that month, at the house of his intimate and disconsolate friend, Mr. Hawthorn. A general wish being signified, that the body might be opened, leave was granted; when it was ascertained, that this indefatigable and zealous servant of his King and Country, had died from a continual exertion of mind and body, too great for his strength and constitution to support; which the anxious and laudable spirit of his ardent mind had fatally prolonged.

Captain Stewart's remains were attended to an honourable grave, in the great National Sepulchre of his Country, WESTMINSTER ABBEY, by the following distinguished mourners:—The Marquis of Downshire, Lord Holland, Lord W. Fitzroy, the Hon. Mr. Fullarton, Mr. Elphinstone, Mr. Adair, the Hon. Mr. Law, Mr. Hart Davis, Mr. Adam, Mr. Hawthorn, Commissioner Brown,

---

* A very valuable and favourable statement of Sicilian politics, and from one who could be depended on, appeared in The Morning Post, October 12, 1811, signed by *A Man of Plain Notions*.

Mr. Whidbey, and many others. The Duke of Bedford and Lord Keith, were only prevented from attending, by being out of town. A small neat marble tablet is preparing by Westmacott, with an inscription from the pen of Mr. Adair, to preserve the memory of an officer who was so generally beloved and respected, and to consecrate his faithful services to the emulation of posterity.

The quickness with which he comprehended the bearings of the most intricate and difficult service, denoted superior talents; the firmness and courtesy with which he executed the orders that were intrusted to him, marked a great and a humane mind. The glowing ardour of his martial genius, and the natural enthusiasm which it displayed, frequently resembled the daring and romantic character of his renowned countryman, WALLACE; and *The Scotts that ha' with* STEWART *bled*, will long venerate the memory of their Chief. Like WALLACE, Captain Stewart always provided against every emergency; and like him, had determined, to use his own words—*Never to be taken alive.* And what shall we say more; since time and space would both fail if we attempted more fully to delineate the character of a man, whom nature had originally formed, and the Spartan School of the British Navy had disciplined, both to know how to obey, and how to command. We shall therefore conclude, with the following extract of a letter from one of his officers :—*Captain Stewart's character as a Captain of a ship, may be considered as a perfect model of propriety: firm and even strict in discipline; yet with a degree of kindness and consideration for those under his command, that extended throughout his crew, from the first to the lowest of his ship's company.*

⁎⁎ *The following Order is referred to at preceding page* 12.
(COPY.)
" MEM.   " *Foudroyant, Aboukir Bay, March 8th,* 1801.
 " It is the Admiral's directions, that any six flat boats, having slides, and fitted for carronades, are immediately manned, and armed with a carronade, and to proceed to the Mondovi, and there follow the orders of Captain Stewart; they are to take three days' provisions with them, and water.
" By command of the Admiral,
(Signed)   " WM. YOUNG."

HERALDIC PARTICULARS.

Captain Stewart's arms as *Cadet* of the GALLOWAY Family, were the same as those borne by that Earl.

NAVAL ANECDOTES, COMMERCIAL HINTS, RECOLLECTIONS, &c.

NANTES IN GURGITE VASTO.

MEANS TO PREVENT DROWNING.

MEN are drowned by raising their arms above water, the unbuoyed weight of which depresses the head. Other animals have neither notion nor ability to act similarly, and therefore swim naturally. When a man falls into deep water, he will rise to the surface by stoppage, and will continue there if he do not elevate his hands. If he move his hands under the water, in any manner he pleases, his head will rise so high as to allow him free liberty to breathe; and if he move his legs, as in the action of walking (or rather of walking up stairs), his shoulders will rise above the water; so that he may use less exertion with his hands, or apply them to other purposes. These plain directions are recommended to the recollection of those who have not learnt to swim in their youth, as they may be found highly advantageous in preserving life.

COMMERCIAL LICENSES.

THE following account of the number of Commercial Licenses, granted during the last ten years, distinguishing the years, has been published by order of the House of Commons:—1802, 68; 1803, 836; 1804, 1141; 1805, 791; 1806, 1620; 1807, 2606; 1808, 4910; 1809, 15,226; 1810, 18,356; 1811, 7602.

LEGITIMATE RUSE DE GUERRE.

IT has long been a well known fact, that Napoleon draws off the efficient troops of each subjected nation, and sends them to carry on the work of slavery in *other countries*, whilst he is pillaging *their's*. This he is the more easily enabled to effect, by stopping all letters, or other information, on the way to the armies, so that those who may still possess some patriotic spirit, are kept ignorant of his enormities. At present there are many Dutch soldiers in Spain; and it would surely be sound policy in our ministry to cause thousands of placards, descriptive of the present state of Holland, to be printed in Dutch, and disseminated in Spain. The expense would be trifling; nay, much less than has often been incurred in one night in the House of Commons, by some would-be politician moving for the printing of papers which nobody would read, nor perhaps understand if they did!

IMPROVEMENT IN FIRE-ARMS.

MR. T. NOON, of Burton-upon-Trent, has obtained a patent for improvements in fire-arms, &c.—His invention consists in a different construction of the pan, hammer, and plate. The parts chambered out of the hammer, and pan, next the barrel, or breech, at the touch-hole, are made to receive a swell, or bulge, left on the barrel or breech, opposite to the chamber; and the barrel, or breech, is hollowed out round the swell or bulge. At the bottom of the chamber is a hole, through the plate, under the pan. When the lock and barrel are put together, the water that may insinuate itself between them, will run down the projection to the hollow in the barrel, or breech, and from thence escape through the hole, without touching the powder in the pan, provided the chamber and this projection be made to fit close.

AMERICA *versus* FRANCE.

THE *Repertory Advertiser*, one of the American Federalist Papers, a short time since presented the following allegations, in opposition to one of the democratic prints, distinguished by its support of the French cause :—

" 1st. Above forty millions of American property have been seized in France, and countries acting under the Imperial Decrees, which have not been restored.

" 2d. A great number of American captains, mates, and sailors, have been treated in France with a brutality not justifiable, and not practised towards prisoners of war. They have been marched across the country at the point of the bayonet, half starved, and imprisoned.

" 3dly. Great numbers of American seamen have been kept on bread and water, with a scant allowance even of them, and treated with the utmost rigour, to compel them to enter on board of French privateers ; to which many have consented, to avoid a miserable, lingering death. Yet the Paper alluded to heads a column with the following assertion, printed in a conspicuous type :—" England the only Aggressor."

" The feelings of every American, not devoted heart and soul to the tyrant who has inflicted wrongs and insults on our country, such as never nation endured before, will afford a sufficient comment on such a daring, unblushing falsehood. Who now will presume to say we have not traitors in our own bosoms ?—Traitors, too, who have the hardihood to glory in displaying their corruption."

THE MISSING INDIA SHIPS.

WE have now been so long without any account of the seven missing East India ships, that all hope of the escape of any person belonging to them from the fury of the elements must be given up. It is, however, very extraordinary, that no part of the wreck has been found. Some gratification would arise from the discovery of any thing that conjecture could connect with, or approximate to their fate ; but nothing of that description has yet appeared, except the following account of a large wreck, supposed to be the remains of a ship of 1,000 or 1,200 tons burthen, which was seen from the Isle of Bourbon in the end of December, 1811, taken from *The Bourbon Gazette* of the 5th of January following :—

" *To the Editor of the Bourbon Gazette.*

" SIR—Mr. Delestrac, sen. being at his house, at Brulé, the day before yesterday (December 31), observed out at sea (as did also his steward, cook, and the greater part of his negroes), a body, which corresponded in size with a vessel of 1000 or 1,200 tons burthen, driving along before the wind and current. Both he and his slaves are positive that it could be nothing else but a ship, with the bottom upwards. Sometimes it was entirely enveloped in the waves, and then again the hull showed itself, apparently from 140 to 150 feet in length. It was followed by a quantity of wreck, which he took to be the masts broken, no doubt, but still probably attached and dragged along by the shrouds and chain-wales.

" This object was first descried about half-past ten in the morning, by Mr. Delestrac's steward, who immediately reported the circumstance to his master. It was at that time opposite to the Berter, and about a league and a half distant from the land. As it approached, it was driven by the force of the wind (and perhaps of the current also) close to the beach, and it passed within about 200 fathoms of one of the ships in the roads, which was moored farther off than the others from the shore. At length, about five in the evening, it passed Cape Bernard, and could no longer be seen.

" This occurrence excited so much anxiety in Mr. Delestrac's mind, that he would immediately have sent information of what he had seen to St. Denis, but the object was so near to the land, and to the ships in the roads, that he never doubted but that many persons must have observed it, and he thought it useless, therefore, to disturb his negroes. To day, however, he has learnt, with much surprise, on his arrival at St. Denis, that nothing was known here of the matter: and he regrets, therefore, exceedingly, having omitted to give the information in time, so that some person might have been sent to examine the object, which he, and his negroes likewise, are well convinced is a wreck. It was in sight for the space of six or seven hours, without intermission; and, considering the direction in which the winds and waves were carrying it, there is reason to think that it might even yet be found, if boats were sent to explore the coast.

" I have thought it my duty, Mr. Editor, to apprize you of these circumstances, which, though doubtless calculated to disquiet the public mind, may, be of use to excite further inquiries.

" I have the honour to be,
' *St. Denys, Jan.* 2, 1811. " BRUNIQUEL."

CATCHING HAKE.

THE following account of a new method of catching hake, is copied from an Irish paper :—

" During the summer season, a quantity of the fish called hake, resort to the Court M'Sherry bay, and amongst other modes of taking them made use of by the neighbouring peasantry, is a net called a trammel. The net is about 25 feet deep, its mesh five inches, and its length indefinite; heavy leaded at the bottom, thickly corked at the top, and when set stands erect in the sea, about three fathoms from the ground. The shoals of fish, as they pass in the night, strike against it and are taken. The use and benefit of this new-discovered net over the common mode of line-fishing, is manifest, as the net, attended to by one boat's crew for the night, will take from one to five hundred fish without any trouble; whereas the boat at the line fishing may not take twenty fish, and very often not the fourth part, although the fish are extremely plenty, and must be taken if the trammel is set."

NAVAL CONJUGAL CORRESPONDENCE.

The following is given in a Cornwall paper, as a correct copy of a letter received some time since by a woman in Truro, from her husband, a seaman on board the Edgar, then lying at Plymouth:—

" MY DEAR GRACE, " *H. M. S. Edgar, at Plymouth Dock.*
" This coms with my kind love, hopine it will find you as it leves me. I hope if the child is a boy, you will cale it after my nam for my sak, and as i dozen intind never to see you agen, you may be married as son as you wil, for I shall be married as son as I can.—So no mor at presant from your afectinate husband. " J. M."
" To Mrs. G———, *in the Work-House.*"

THE CHATHAM, SHIP OF WAR.

The following *jeu d'esprit,* addressed to the Editor of the *Morning Chronicle,* appeared some time ago in that paper:—

" SIR,

" When I first read in your paper, that the Walcheren ship, just launched, was to be called the CHATHAM, in honour of the Earl of that name, I took it for a sly attempt at irony by some roguish Correspondent; but finding the same thing gravely announced in *The Courier,* and *The Morning Post,* I could no longer refrain from examining into the matter with my own eyes; and sure enough, the first thing I saw at the dock, was this very ship, with the Earl's effigy at the bowsprit.

" The master carver has been fortunate in the choice of his log of wood, which is indeed an exact resemblance of the original: the stockings are ungartered, and hang down negligently, and the night cap is still on. The various attributes, though but the common place emblems of war and commerce, are not badly executed: his feet are resting on a cannon presenting its breech, and his head and arm recline gracefully on a keg of hollands.

" There is also an image of Fame, exceedingly large, but at the same time made subordinate to the main figure, by the concealment of her face under his robe; and by holding her trumpet behind her, in a position which appears to me awkward, if not indecorous.

" The circumstance of time is pointed out, by introducing contemporary characters; and the stout little legs of Mr. Perceval are well contrasted with the thinner ones of Mr. Wilberforce. The Twin Secretaries also, Canning and Castlereagh, are seen scratching at each other with one hand, and clinging to the Earl's blue ribband with the other.

" On the stern is a representation of the great Hospital at Flushing; and, over it, is a very distant prospect of Antwerp."

JACK JUNK'S JOURNAL.

HOVE out of Portsmouth on board the Britannia fly—a swift sailor—an outside birth—rather drowsy the first watch or two—like to have slipped off the stern—cast anchor at the George—took a fresh quid and a supply of grog—comforted the upper works—spoke several homeward-bound frigates on the road, and after a tolerable smooth voyage, entered the port of London at ten minutes past five, post meridian, steered to Nan's lodgings, and unshipped my cargo—Nan admired the shiners, so did landlord —gave them a handful a piece—emptied a bowl of the right sort with landlord, to the health of Lord Nelson—All three set sail for the play,— got a birth in a cabin on the larboard side—wanted to smoke a pipe, but the boatswain would not let me—Nan, I believe, called the play Pollzaro, with Harlkin Hamlet—but d—n me if I knew stem from stern—remember to rig out Nan like the fine folks in the cabin right a-head—saw Tom Junk aloft in the corner of the upper deck—hailed him—the signal returned— some of the lubbers in the cockpit began to laugh—tipp'd 'em a little forecastle lingo 'till they sheered off—emptied the grog bottle—fell fast asleep —dreamt of the battle off Camperdown—My landlord told me the play was over—glad of it—crowded sail for a hackney coach—got on board—squally weather—rather inclined to be sea-sick—arrived at Nan's lodgings—gave the pilot a two pound note, and told him not to mind change—supped with Nan, and swung in the same hammock—looked over my rhino in the morning—great deal of it to be sure—But I hope, with the help of a few friends, to spend every shilling of it in a little time, to the honour and glory of Old England.

THE ROYAL OAK.

" The monarch Oak, the patriarch of the trees,
Shoots rising up, and spreads by slow degrees:
Three centuries he grows, and three he stays
Supreme in state; and in three more decays."—DRYDEN.

THE injuries and mutilations which a considerable portion of the Oak-trees throughout England (in Scotland and Ireland the custom is not general), is, by a sort of prescription, doomed annually to suffer, about the spring season, are irreparable and incalculable. It is a notorious fact, that the stock of this species of timber, which is so essential to our security, our prosperity, and to our very existence as an independent nation, has greatly diminished of late years, and is confessedly inadequate to the supply of our dock-yards,—a circumstance which obliges us to resort to, and become dependent upon, foreign countries, to supply the deficiency of our home growth. Noblemen and gentlemen of landed property, who have a due regard for their own interest, and the paramount interest of their country

would do well to consider this fact, and to use their utmost endeavours, not only to promote the culture of the Oak upon their demesnes and wastes, but also to manifest as much anxiety and diligence for the preservation of their woods and plantations from Royal Oak-day depredators, as they universally do for the protection of their trout-streams and fishponds, their game, and other territorial rights and privileges, against poachers and plunderers of every denomination. We would also recommend it to the more respectable classes of the community, to contribute their assistance for the extinction of a custom, which, though originating in laudable motives, would now be more " honour'd in the breach than in the observance," by discouraging, as much as possible, the exposure on the sides of their houses, sign-posts, market-places, &c. of the mutilated members of " the monarch of the woods." But the mischief is not confined to the unseasonable and unskilful lopping of trees ; the most promising plants are taken indiscriminately, with boughs and underwood, and exhibited with impunity in almost every town and village in England, under an erroneous notion of *loyalty*, which, it ought to be recollected, can never be at variance with genuine patriotism. It would be desirable if the Legislature could, consistently with that right which land-owners possess, in common with other subjects, in the disposition and appropriation of their property, pass a law, compelling them to plant Oaks in a given proportion to other timber on their estates, on wastes, in hedge-rows, along the margins of commons and public highways ; and if it could at the same time devise some effectual means for protecting them from injury and spoliation, till they arrive at maturity, the produce of our own soil might, in less than a century, be commensurate with the consumption, and render us independent of other countries; but as such a measure would be considered too arbitrary for adoption under a free government, it becomes more emphatically the duty of every loyal subject, of every lover of his country, to cherish, protect, and venerate the Oak, on which the security, prosperity, and independence of the British empire, mainly depend.

> " Let India boast her plants, nor envy we,
> The weeping amber, and the balmy tree ;
> While by our Oaks the precious loads are borne,
> And realms commanded which those Oaks adorn."

PLATE CCCLXVIII.

PUERTO SANTO, or Porto Santo, near Madeira,* is understood to have been the first of the Madeira, or Mattera Islands, discovered by the Portuguese. The Portuguese fleet fell in with it, by accident, in a

---

* In our XIXth Volume, page 108, will be found an *Account of the Present State of the Island of Madeira;* in our XXth Volume, page 386, a View of the East End of the Island of Madeira ; and, in our XXIId Volume, page 213, a View of the Government House, at Funchal, the capital of Madeira.

storm, and gave it the name of Puerto Santo, on account of the safety which it afforded them. It was then uninhabited; but it was soon peopled by its discoverers, in whose possession it has ever since remained.

The Island of Puerto Santo, which does not exceed five leagues in circumference, has a good harbour, and a bay, in which ships may ride securely against all winds, except the S.W. It is in this bay, that ships going to, or returning from India, stop to refit and refresh. The island produces wheat, and other corn, in abundance; also cows, wild boars, and incredible numbers of rabbits; but its most valuable productions for export, are honey, wax, and fish.

CORRESPONDENCE.

MR. EDITOR, *Dover, 15 July*, 1812.

I ANSWER an invitation contained in the preface to your last volume, (that Mulciber* should renew his labors on the interesting, though dreadful phenomena, of earthquakes), by presenting the substance of Captain S. Tillard's narrative, concerning a sub-marine volcano near the island of Saint Michael; which was communicated by Sir Joseph Banks to the Royal Society, on 6th February, 1812 :—

" On Sunday, 12th June, 1811, approaching the island of St. Michael, in H. M. S. Sabrina, we observed occasionally, rising in the horizon two or three columns of smoke, such as would have been occasioned by an action between two ships, to which cause we universally attributed it. This opinion was, however, in a short time changed by the smoke increasing and ascending in much larger bodies than could possibly have been produced by such an event, and having heard, prior to our sailing from Lisbon, that in the preceding January or February a volcano had burst out within the sea near St. Michael, we finally concluded this smoke proceeded from that cause; and on our anchoring the next morning in the road of Ponta-del-Gada, we found this conjecture correct as to the cause, but not as to the time; the eruption of January having subsided, and the present one having burst forth only two days prior to our approach, about three miles distant from the former.†

" Desirous of examining as minutely as possible a contention so extraordinary between two such elements, I set off from the city of Ponta-del-Gada on the morning of the 14th June, in company with Mr. Read, our Consul-general of the Azores. After riding about twenty miles across the N.W. end of the island, we came to the edge of a cliff, from whence the

---

* N. C. XXVII. 315.

† For the account of another prior volcano witnessed among these islands, see N. C. XXI. 105.

volcano burst suddenly upon our view with awful and terrific grandeur. It was only a short mile from the base of the cliff, which was nearly perpendicular, and formed the margin of the sea, being, as nearly as I could judge, from three to four hundred feet high.

" Imagine an immense body of smoke rising from the sea, the surface of which was marked by the silvery rippling occasioned by the light and steady breezes incidental to those climates in summer. In a quiescent state the smoke had the appearance of a circular cloud, revolving on the water like an horizontal wheel, in various and irregular involutions, expanding itself gradually on the lee side, when suddenly a column of black cinders, ashes, and stones, would shoot up in form of a spire, at an angle of from 10° to 20° from the perpendicular, the angle of inclination being universally to windward: this was rapidly succeeded by a second, third, and fourth, each acquiring greater velocity, and overtopping the other, till they had attained an altitude as much above the level of our eye as the sea was below it.

" As the impetus with which the columns were severally propelled diminished, and their ascending motion had nearly ceased, the smoke and falling ashes broke into various fanciful figures, resembling pines, festoons, plumes of feathers, or weeping willow branches. During these bursts, vivid flashes of lightning issued from the densest part; and the cloud of smoke ascending to an altitude much above the highest point to which the ashes were projected, rolled off in large masses of fleecy clouds, gradually expanding before the wind, in a direction nearly horizontal, and attracting those phenomena, denominated water-spouts, which added to the general beauty of the scene.

" That part of the sea was upwards of 30 fathoms deep, and at the time of our view the volcano was only four days old. Soon after our arrival, a peasant said he could discern a peak above the water: we looked, but could not at first discover it; however, in less than half an hour, it became plainly visible to us all, and before we quitted the place, which was about three hours after our arrival, a *crater* was completely formed, not less than 20 feet high on the side where the greater quantity of ashes fell, it's apparent diameter being between four and five hundred feet. The great eruptions were generally attended with a noise like the intermixed firing of cannon and musketry, as also with shocks of earthquakes: while we were sitting within five or six yards from the edge of the cliff, partaking of a slight repast, one of the most magnificent bursts which we had yet witnessed took place, accompanied by a very severe shock. The instantaneous and involuntary movement of each was to spring upon his feet, which was scarcely done, with hardly time to admit of an exclamation, before a large portion of the face of the cliff, about fifty yards on our left, fell with a violent crash. So soon as our first consternation had a little subsided, we removed ten or a dozen yards farther from the edge, and finished our meal.

" On the succeeding day I weighed anchor, and proceeded with the ship towards the volcano, with intention of a night-view; but in this expectation we were disappointed, by the wind freshening, the weather becoming thick and hazy, and also by the more quiescent state of the volcano itself. It seldom emitted lightning, but occasionally as much flame as may be seen to issue from the chimney of a glass-house or foundry. On passing directly under the main cloud of smoke, about three or four miles distant from the volcano, the decks of the ship were covered with fine black ashes, which fell intermixed with small rain. Late on the evening of the next day (16th June), I left St. Michael to complete my cruise.

" On opening sight of the volcano, clear of the N.W. part of the island, after dark, we witnessed one or two eruptions, which appeared one continued blaze of lightning; but the distance, upwards of twenty miles, prevented our viewing it with effect.

" On 4th July, returning towards St. Michael, I was obliged, by the state of the wind, to pass very near the volcano, which by that time had formed an islet about eighty yards above the sea, or nearly the height of Matlock-High-Tor. The circumstance of its being then tranquil induced me to land and explore it more narrowly.

" I left the ship in a boat : as we approached we perceived the new land smoking in many parts, and on our reaching the shore, found the surf very high. Rowing round to the lee side, I jumped on shore with some little difficulty, aided by an oar as a pole, and was followed by some officers, who accompanied me on this excursion. We found a narrow beach of black ashes, from which the side of the volcanic hill rose in general too steep to admit of our ascending; and where we could have clambered up, the mass was too hot to allow our mounting more than a few yards. The declivity under water was equally steep, there being seven fathoms water scarce the boat's length from the shore, and at thrice that distance off, 25 fathoms. From walking round it in about twelve minutes, I should judge it less than a mile in circumference; but the most extraordinary part was, the *crater*, the mouth of which, on the side facing St. Michael, was nearly level with the sea. It formed a basin full of boiling water, emptying itself into the sea by a stream about six yards over, and by which I should suppose it was replenished at high-tide. This stream, close to the edge of the sea, was so hot as only to admit the finger to be dipped in suddenly, and taken out immediately. It appeared evident, by the conformation of this part, that the sea had, during the eruptions, broken into the *crater* at two places : the east side of the streamlet being bounded by a precipice, with a cliff between twenty and thirty feet high, forming a peninsula of about fifty or sixty feet long, which was connected with the islet by an isthmus of somewhat less length; the *crater* rising from the point of junction in the form of an amphitheatre. This cliff, at two or three miles distance, had the appearance of a work of art, resembling a small fort or battery. The top of this we determined, if possible, to attain; but the difficulty was considerable; the side of the isthmus formed of cinders or lava being so steep, that the only mode by which we could effectuate our ascent, was, by fixing the end of an oar at the base, with the assistance of which we forced ourselves upwards and backwards. Having reached the summit, we found it as narrow and steep on both sides as the ridge of a house, so that it not being practicable to walk, we were obliged to throw our legs astride, and moving forward by our hands we at length reached that portion where it gradually widened and formed a flat surface, about fifty feet across.

" Judging this to be the most conspicuous situation, we here planted the Union-flag,* and left a bottle sealed up, containing a brief record of the origin of this island, of our having landed upon it, and naming it ' Sabrina.'

" Within the *crater* we found the complete skeleton of a guard-fish, the bones of which being calcined, fell to pieces upon attempting to lift them; and according to the testimony of the inhabitants on the adjacent coasts, great numbers of fish must have been destroyed during the early time of the eruption, as large quantities, probably suffocated or poisoned, were occasionally drifted into the bays or inlets of St. Michael. The new island, like other volcanic productions, is composed principally of porous substances, generally burnt to a state of cinder, blended occasionally with masses of stone, which I should suppose to be a mixture of iron and lime-stone."

In transcribing the foregoing memoranda, I have scarcely at all departed from the order, and seldom from the words, of the intelligent narrator, except where brevity became requisite, in order to compress the narrative within that compass which would admit of its being given in the NAVAL CHRONICLE at one spell. I could have wished the account had entered into some farther details as to the state of the atmosphere, direction of the winds, and hydrographical site of the volcano, and had also been brought down to a later period, for the purpose of enabling us to judge of its probable permanent effects upon the navigation of those waters: inasmuch as a paper on this subject in the last volume contains intelligence collected from respectable authority, that the island had subsided into a shoal.† If these lines should meet the eye of Captain Tillard, or of Mr. Consul Read, they may perhaps be induced to favour the readers of the NAVAL CHRONICLE with the desired information down to the present day.

MVLCIBER.

MR. EDITOR,

PHILANTHROPISTS have long contemplated with sincere pleasure, the reputation the immortal Cook acquired, by his successful attention to the preservation of the health and lives of his ships' crews, in every variety of climate, and diversity of temperature. The glory of his great discoveries, and the inimitable perseverance displayed in his circumnavigations, are illumined, in the Temple of Fame, by the splendid rays of

* N. C. XXVII. 224. † N. C. XXVII. 226.

lustre, emanating from the virtues of humanity, benevolence, and humility.

It is the lot of human nature to be born to misery, from endless sources. The sailor, when in health, fearlessly launches into the terrors of the ocean, encounters all its dangers with fortitude, and endures all the privations, incidental to his mode of life, with resignation ; but, in the hour of sickness, there is not, perhaps, a situation more depressing and comfortless, or which more requires the consolatory offices of humanity, and the cheering kindness of sympathy ; should, however, this sickness be scurvy, then, indeed, from the nature of his sea diet, which would increase his complaints, is he in famine in the midst of plenty ! and the salted meats are a poison, which slowly corrupts his blood, and destroys the vital energy ; while the digestive functions become so weakened, as to render them incapable of assimilating sufficient nourishment to support life, from the peas and unfermented flour, which constitute the other principal ingredients of his diet. To prevent scurvy in long voyages, should, therefore, always engage the chief attention of every wise commander, and is a subject worthy of the consideration of the government of a commercial nation : to check its fatal ravages, when it does prevail, will demand the exercise of disinterested sentiment, and the generous sacrifice of all the live stock and vegetables of the captain and officers, to the dispensations of invoking humanity ; for experience has decidedly proved, that there is no certain preventive of, or cure for, scurvy, but a combined diet of fresh animal and vegetable food.

The advantage of recording great and good actions, principally consists, in exciting emulation, and in transmitting to posterity, examples worthy of imitation : it is for this reason, that I send for insertion, in the annals of the British Navy, the successful result of the judicious arrangements, and benevolent exertions, of Captain Byng, of H. M. S. Belliqueux, to preserve the health of his ship's company of 491 men, during a voyage from China to England. The voyage was performed in six months, and every man was landed in England alive and in health !—Such a fact deserves the attention of those who annually perform a similar voyage, as the simple means of preservation are within the power of every commander, and equal success will ensure him the gratitude and esteem of those he commands, and the honourable admiration of the benevolent.

H. M. S. Belliqueux had been in the East Indies five years, and previous to leaving India for China, in June, 1810, exchanged about fifty of her healthy men, for a similar number of seamen from other ships, whose constitutions had been much impaired, by a residence of ten years and upwards, in the Oriental tropics:* besides which, there were ordered on board, thirty-two men invalided from various diseases.

---

* A little before this period, the Admiralty, with a just attention to the situation of those seamen, who had been detained long in India, had directed the commander-in-chief, to send home all such as had served ten years in the country.

The Belliqueux arrived in China, in September, 1810, and remained there until February, 1811. Chuenpee roads, lat. 22° 44' N. long. 113° E. near the Boca Tigris, is the anchorage selected by the captains of his Majesty's ships, and tolerated with jealousy by the Chinese government;* here, during part of the month of November, and the months of December, January, and February, a degree of cold prevailed, to which we had been utter strangers in India, and which was suddenly introduced by the north-east monsoon, blowing from the bleak and snow-clad mountains of Manchou Tartary. The thermometer in the shade during this period, ranged from 40° to 62° of Fahrenheit in the day-time; the nights were colder, and in February, ice ½ an inch thick was twice observed on the rivulets, in the rice fields: the sun, on clear days, had considerable power in raising the temperature of the atmosphere.

The ship's company obtained more nutritive and finer beef, than they were accustomed to meet with in India; the improved state of horticulture in China afforded ample supplies of fine vegetables and fruit, which, with the advantages of climate, improved the general appearance and health of the ship's company. It might, therefore, be an arrangement of good policy, to send ships occasionally from India, to winter in China.

The useful experience acquired, by a residence in India, of the most prevailing diseases on long voyages, had taught us, that the scurvy, contrary to received opinion,† is sooner induced in a tropical, than in a cold climate, and is not only most destructive itself, but impedes the cure of all other diseases, or aggravates them; while we had ascertained, that the oriental diseases would commonly yield to experienced medical treatment, if a proper diet could be obtained. Preparations were, therefore, made to check this Boa Upas of sailors, in the East.

Arrangements had been made, to allot a retained proportion of the vegetable money, drawn by the purser, to purchase a sea stock, to which was added a donation of 150 dollars from Captain B. With these sums were purchased, with the captain's sanction, twelve dozen fine capons, two thousand pounds ‡ of potatoes, two hundred pounds of carrots, seven hundred and ninety-eight pounds of pumkins, five hundred pounds of dry onions, two catties of rusk; and about two thousand pounds of onions and nopal leaves were pickled on board, with good vinegar, and plenty of nutmeg, mace, cinnamon, ginger, and pepper, the native spices of India,

---

* A plausible reason of distress and damage, is generally assigned to the visiting Mandarins, by the supple and submissive interpreter, which induces them to permit the ship to remain in good anchorage at Chuenpee, instead of the allotted anchorage, Macao Roads.

† Boerhaave and Culler describe scurvy as peculiar to the north of Europe, and cold latitudes—Inventitur apud Britannos, Batavos, Suecos, Danos, Norvegos, Germanos, &c.; attingit adeoque Boreales populos & frigidiori sub climate viventes. Aphor: 1150. In Regione frigida post victum salitum, &c. Nosologia Cullenii.

‡ Every thing in China is purchased by weight.

under the direction of Mr. W Griffiths, assistant surgeon. Besides which, the captain, with his usual attention to every circumstance, that tended to exemption from disease, and the recovery of the sick, directed six bullocks to be carried to sea, to be killed at different periods of the voyage, for distribution among the sick and scorbutics, and supplied occasionally a quarter of mutton from his own stock. The carrots were packed in dry sand, in the way directed to be preserved by the College of Physicians,* but they fermented, and became putrid in a fortnight. The pomkins should be turned daily, or the juice they contain will gravitate to the most depending part, and occasion putrefaction. With this supply, the Belliqueux weighed from Macao Roads, on the 14th of February, 1811, with the East India Company's ships, Winchelsea, Elphinstone, Wexford, Woodford, Cuffnells, Alfred, and Arniston, under convoy, and we were wild with delight, to direct our course for our native country, which a long absence had more than endeared to us.—

"Such is the Patriot's boast, where'er we roam;
His first, best country, ever is at home."——GOLDSMITH.

A run of four days, with a fine breeze, brought us on the coast of Cochin China, and transferred us from a cold to a torrid climate, which made it agreeable to exchange the English woollens for the light calicoes of India, and the nankeens of China. The convoy glided rapidly through the China seas, and on the 2d of March we entered the Straits of Banca, where we anchored off the Nanka Islands to wood and water, a service in which several men were sun-burnt. The islands are uninhabited, but being covered with trees, afford abundant supplies of fire-wood; the water was obtained from two wells on the west and south sides of the large island; the polite Captain Welsted, of the Alfred, discovered a large rivulet of good water on the north end of the island, which will make an excellent watering place during the S. E. monsoon, and when the N.W. wind does not blow too strong. The watering places are accurately laid out in a masterly chart of the Nanka Islands, drawn from survey, by Mr. William Mackellar, master of the Belliqueux, copies of which were transmitted to the Admiralty, and the Court of Directors.

On the 6th, we weighed, and were detained a little by the Cuffnells grounding on the Sumatra side of the five fathom channel, in passing through the south extremity of the Straits of Banca. On the 7th of March we entered the Straits of Sunda, where we met with adverse currents, and light baffling winds, which prevented us from clearing the Straits of Sunda and Prince Edward's Island, before the 16th. The current from the westward, setting into the Straits against us, on the first day, ran at the rate of five knots an hour. The detention was, however, productive of improvement in the science of navigation. The zeal of Captain B. to promote the interests of the East India Company, and the cultivation of science, again called upon the talents and industry of Mr. Mackellar, who, with his usual

---

* Pharmac. Londinensis, page 58.

ability, took a masterly survey, and drew an accurate chart of the Straits of Sunda, copies of which were transmitted to the Court of Directors, and the Lords of the Admiralty. It is lamented, that for this, and other charts, it does not fall within the comprehensive liberality of that Court, to offer him some adequate recompence. The Admiralty honoured him with a letter of thanks and approbation. After clearing the Straits of Sunda, we crossed the South Pacific Ocean, and had a fine passage until we reached " the stormy spirit of the Cape,"* on the 26th of April. The ship, here, encountered successive gales of wind from the westward, on the Bank of Aguillas, so severe, that she had nearly foundered, and all were indebted to the westerly current setting round the Cape of Good Hope, for doubling it in safety, after having sustained seventeen days great fatigue, and three days imminent danger, during which it was expected, that the Belliqueux would finally share the hapless fate of those ships, that had been swallowed up on their passage home in 1809.—

"—Ocean! thou dreadful and tumultuous home
Of dangers, at eternal war with Man!
Death's Capital! where most he domineers,
With all his chosen terrors frowning round."——Young.

On the 25th of May we hailed the Island of St. Helena, as our deliverer, and were glad to terminate our dangers, by anchoring in safety.

During the voyage, 133 men had been placed on the sick list, whose cases happily yielded to medical treatment, to which proper efficacy had been given, by a light and proper diet of fresh food: the number of scorbutics on our arrival amounted to sixty, and several had been cured during the voyage.

The arrangements to prevent the access, and counteract the progress of scurvy, were these: Every man who was sick, or had a small wound or ulceration, or who had evinced a predisposition to scurvy on former voyages, or who became scorbutic in the course of the present one, was supplied with one pound of potatoes on four days in the week, except when beef or mutton was served, and an unlimited allowance of pickles, on the other three days, with his salted meats. The pomkins, with lime-juice, orange peel, and spices, made good mock apple pies. When a bullock was killed, or when a donation of a quarter of mutton was presented from the captain, all were supplied with soup and meat, with abundance of vegetables. The capons, with onions, pompkin, and rusk, made excellent soup, and a light diet for the worst cases of disease, and it was found, that a fine capon, thus cooked, was sufficient to dine from four to eight, and sometimes ten, as the appetite becomes much impaired in all Oriental diseases.

The captain's wines, and other luxuries of his store-room, were at the service of those who wished or required them, and he sometimes condescended to see the ingredients he furnished for soup, put in the kettle himself.

* Pleasures of Hope.

It is well known, that the supply of animal food at St. Helena, is not only very dear, but very limited, and only granted by an order of the Governor in Council. Here was an occasion, that displayed the lively interest Captain B. felt for the health and welfare of the seamen under his command: when the heart dictates, the sentiments are full of energy, and the language is eloquent and persuasive: by his earnest representations to the Governor, and the address he employed in conciliating and gaining his attention, he obtained more bullocks and sheep than had ever been allowed to one ship, while a recent and liberal regulation of the Commissioners for victualling the Navy, furnished ample supplies of vegetables, which, on this island, are good, abundant, and dear. A beautiful waterfall descends from a high precipice, at the extremity of James's Valley, and forms a fine clear rivulet, which, in its meandering course through the valley, exhibits on its surface the green leaf of the water-cress, growing in luxurious abundance. Hither the convalescents and some scorbutics were daily sent to eat this wholesome vegetable, and to perform the task of gathering two or three bags of cresses for the use of the ship's company; they were found in greatest plenty near the water-fall. As St. Helena is the established entrepôt between Europe and the East, it would appear good policy, to form arrangements, for supplying the island, and ships touching at it, with more live stock, as the communication with the Cape of Good Hope offers facilities for obtaining ample supplies, as well as other refreshments useful to seamen, after long voyages: Cape bullocks are large, and the sheep good.

The strength of the people was much recruited, and the scorbutic dispositions corrected, by the salutary refreshments we procured at the island; from which we departed on the 9th of June, with the addition to our former convoy, of H. M. ships Chiffonnée and Menelaus, and the E. I. Company's ships Grenville, Exeter, St. Vincent, Windham, and Charlton. Captain B. directed as large a proportion of vegetables as was deemed necessary, to be reserved out of the liberal allowance of. Government, for a sea stock, and presented a donation of 100 dollars, for the purchase of poultry, sheep, and other articles useful to the sick. Nearly the same quantity of vegetables and pickles was preserved as in China, but the enormous price of ten shillings for a large fowl, greatly limited the stock of poultry, a circumstance which was compensated, by the captain ordering some of the sheep bought for the ship's company, to be exclusively appropriated, during the voyage, to the use of the sick, and those who should become scorbutic. The same enlarged views, and creditable foresight, for the preservation of health, and the continued disposition to supply as much fresh diet as possible, induced Captain B. to despatch the Menelaus and some South Sea whalers, who took convoy, to turn turtle at the Island of Ascension, where they are very large, and sometimes numerous, and where flocks of wild goats are seen to play on the precipices. The turtle were not numerous at this period, and those received were only sufficient to furnish the ship's company with two days fresh soup, although one of them weighed near 400 pounds. The course was shaped from

Ascension to the northward and westward, until we had passed to the north of the Western Isles, when we steered direct for the English Channel, and felt the inexpressible happiness of anchoring in the Downs, on the 8th of August, 1811. Ninety-one cases of disease had been placed on the sick-list, during the voyage from St. Helena to England, and some few scorbutics, but not one of the Belliqueux had been lost from disease, during the whole voyage from China; and on the 30th of August, the ship was paid off at Chatham, and every man dismissed on leave of absence to his friends, exulting to serve in that glorious æra of the British Navy, when such exalted characters as Blane, Trotter, and very many enlightened commissioned and medical officers of the navy, had united sound philosophy, with liberality of sentiment and benevolence, in devising the means of preserving the health and lives of the Bulwarks of Britain, and of establishing it as a maxim, that the efficiency of a ship or fleet depends more on the effective strength and health of the men, than their elegant equipment, and that a strong and vigorous ship's company are, in the terse language of the French, its best equipage. It is pleasing to reflect, that every evil in life, is calculated to elicit some fine feeling of the heart, and to actuate man to deeds of benevolence; thus, the numerous ills of life call into action the virtues of charity and humanity, implanted in the breast of man to relieve them.—Though

" The love of praise is planted to protect
And propagate the glories of the mind,"

it will be needless in me to eulogize the captain of the Belliqueux; his actions and their result are his greatest praise, as the gratification of his own feelings must ever be his highest recompence: but, perhaps, of all gratifications, that, arising from beneficent actions to our fellow creatures, is the most grateful to our nature; and, hence it is, that virtue is its own reward.

R. W. BAMPFIELD,
Late Surgeon of H. M. S. Belliqueux.

H. M. S. Warrior, off Flushing,
June 19th, 1812.

MR. EDITOR,

I SEND you an epitaph, composed several years ago, for a most brave and excellent officer, which you will oblige me by inserting. It was intended to be placed upon a monument, in contemplation to be erected at Lisbon, at that time in the possession of the enemy, and was consequently worded in such a manner as not to afford any reasonable objection to the measure. Whether or not it was done, I have never heard. If this trifling record *did justice to the character it endeavours to commemorate*, it would, indeed, be a very perfect performance. As it stands, however, the only merit, perhaps, *is the attempting it.*

YPSILON.

Sacred to the Memory
of
CONWAY SHIPLEY, Esq.
Late Captain of His Britannic Majesty's Ship, La Nymphe,
Who was killed in an attempt
To cut an Enemy's Vessel out of the Tagus,
On the 23d day of April, 1808.

Circumstances,
Which human wisdom could not foresee,
Nor any exertion of courage obviate,
Rendered the attack unsuccessful:
And closed the short, though distinguished career,
Of the gallant Leader of it.
But, whilst his name will long live
In the records of private friendship,
And the remembrance of his Country,
The Brave and Good of every Nation,
Will venerate his Tomb,
And contemplate with respect
The last Mansion of a HERO.

MR. EDITOR, *Nevis, 4th May,* 1812.

I LOSE no time in communicating to you an account, though imperfect, of the extraordinary phænomenon which took place in this quarter, between the hours of three and four, on the morning of the 1st of May, and is, I greatly apprehend, the result of another convulsion on the Spanish main, still more dreadful and more extensive in its devastation than that of Maunday-Thursday, which overwhelmed the magnificent city of the Caraccas, with its numerous and wealthy population.*

---

* A letter, dated Caraccas, March 29, says—" The dreadful catastrophe that took place in this city on Thursday last, my pen is not able to describe; you will, without doubt, receive the dreadful details from other quarters. My only motive for writing is, to allay your apprehensions relative to my person, and I hope you will receive this letter as soon as the shocking account reaches England. On the day above mentioned, at about seven minutes past four in the afternoon, we experienced one of the most dreadful earthquakes you can imagine. In less than three minutes one quarter of the town was laid in ruins, and the remaining three-fourths of the houses rendered totally uninhabitable.—The number of lives lost is not yet ascertained, but the most moderate accounts estimate it at 5000 souls. Similar accounts have reached us from La Guayra, and various other quarters : what is the extent of the evil in the interior we do not yet know. I fear the calamity has been general throughout the continent."

Another letter, from Captain Cuthbert, of the ship Highlander, dated La Guayra, April 1, gives the following particulars:—Since my arrival here, one of

Upon the morning of Friday last (the 1st of May), a number of explosions were heard by the greater part of the inhabitants of this island, resembling the report of artillery, by which they were roused from their sleep, and not a little alarmed - by those who reside on the northern side of the island, this cannonading was for a considerable time' supposed to proceed from an unfortunate ship in distress, and some actually set out for the beach, in the hope of being able to afford relief, while those who lived on the opposite side of the island entertained a similar idea, and one gentleman, who resides close to Saddle-hill, actually sent to the look-out post to ascertain whether the firing was not in the direction of Redondo and Montserrat; indeed, one of the most striking features of these explosions, was their report appearing in the immediate vicinity of each observer, in whatever part of the island, or at whichsoever side of the mountain he chanced to be. At Charlestown the houses shook as though cannon had been fired in the streets, and the master of the King David, at present in the road, declares his ship shook with the violence of the concussion, insomuch that he conceived the firing to proceed from the fort opposite to the berth in which he was moored — At Mr. Tobin's, about two miles east of the town, and situated near the base of the mountain, the same reports were distinctly heard with equal violence; the loudest explosion taking place exactly at half-past three in the morning. During the whole of Friday, the sea was uncommonly agitated, and a most terrific surf came rolling in from the S.W. in the channel which separates the north-western extremity of this island from St. Christopher's, and is known by the name of the Narrows; the agitation of the water was such as to deter one of those small vessels called *drugers* (which carry sugars from the distant estates near the coast to the ships in the road), from attempting to pass; and all

---

the greatest calamities has occurred at this place that ever happened in any country. On the 26th ult. whilst on board, I heard a most dreadful report of an earthquake; it lasted, as nearly as my recollection will serve, about two minutes. I soon learnt that the town of La Guayra was laid in ruins, and that numbers of the inhabitants were killed and buried in them. The City of Caraccas, I understand, has experienced a still worse fate, and has been totally abandoned by the unfortunate inhabitants. The rocks and mountains were rent asunder; and it is impossible for pen to describe the devastation occasioned by this horrible explosion.—The cargo which I was to have taken on board has shared the fate of nearly all the goods in the city, and has been swallowed up in the general ruin. When the shock was first felt on board, every person was impressed with the feeling that the ship was beating to pieces on the rocks. On my going on shore, the most awful and afflicting scene presented itself; hundreds of the suffering inhabitants were seen mixed with heaps of ruins, and many of them still alive with their heads out, imploring assistance from their fellow citizens, who, instead of affording them aid, were throwing themselves prostrate before images, beating their breasts, and imploring for themselves the protection of their saints. When the alarm had in some degree subsided, the bodies of the dead were sought for; but I have not been able to ascertain the extent of the loss which this hapless city has sustained."

communication with the sister island was prevented for the day. Whether this extraordinary agitation of the water was immediately attendant upon the explosions or not, I cannot say.

The inhabitants of St. Christopher's, were equally alarmed with those of Nevis by these noises; and a brig (the Nautilus, of London), which anchored in the road of Charlestown about noon on Friday, reported having heard the same noises between Guadaloupe and Montserrat; the mate of this vessel declares he distinctly counted 15 separate shots, which he imagined to proceed from an engagement between two ships. Some persons in Charlestown and its vicinity, had the curiosity to count the reports they heard, the number of which, according to some, exceeded 50, with distinct pauses between each. The master of the ship Resolution, of London, which reached this island upon the evening of the 2d instant, states, that being in the fleet bound hither from Europe, last from Barbados, he heard the same firing with that which alarmed us, upon the same morning, apparently to leeward of the island of St. Lucia; in consequence of which, the commodore made sail in the direction of the noise, conceiving it to proceed from a privateer attempting to cut off some of the sternmost ships of his convoy.

From the amazing extent of space through which it thus appears these unaccountable noises were heard, it is evident that the cause which produced them must be of the greatest magnitude; and that we may reasonably look forward with daily expectation to the arrival of news respecting some fresh and extensive calamity affecting the American continent, about the period at which the cannonading was heard, allowing for the slow transmission of sound, especially in a direction contrary to the ordinary current of the wind. Of this event it is most probable that we shall here receive the first intelligence through England; however, as a ship is just sailing for Europe, and this account, imperfect as it is, may probably be the first intimation which you can receive, I have resolved upon no account to miss the opportunity of communicating it.

Since I concluded the preceding, I have seen Captain Hart, of the ship Resolution, of London, which sailed with the fleet from Barbados, I think, upon Wednesday, the 29th of April, and about 2 A.M. on the memorable morning of the following Friday (1st May), being abreast of the island of Martinico, those on board heard a number of explosions, to the amount of at least 100, resembling those which were heard in this island and St. Christopher's, and even as far north as St. Bartholomew's. Captain Hart says, he distinctly heard the report of great guns, with vollies of musketry in the intervals, and the impression of its being an engagement was so strong, that the commodore of the fleet gave chase in the direction of the supposed firing for some time, conceiving that it proceeded from an attempt on the part of a privateer, to cut off some of the sternmost ships of the convoy. The sea at the time was remarkably smooth, and the weather singularly serene, the moon shining in silvery splendour.

By a vessel which made her escape from the island of St. Vincent, upon the eventful morning of the 1st inst. and passed by here yesterday on her way to St. Christopher's, some intelligence has been received of the cause of these terrific noises—as yet, however, the reports which are afloat are no less various than contradictory; there is no doubt, however, that a most fatal and formidable convulsion has taken place in the island of St. Vincent, though I should hope, less fatal in its effects than rumour at present makes it. By one account, we are informed that Kingston, the capital of the island, with the whole of its population, has been swallowed up; but the account which I conceive to be the more probable, is, that the eruption took place in the Caraib district, which occupies the northern extremity of the island, and in which place, about the year 1718, a volcano broke out, and continued burning for some time, as may be seen by a reference to an "Account of the Island of Nevis," written in a series of letters by the Rev. Wm. Smith. I am the more inclined to this latter opinion, from the report of the master of a small vessel, lately arrived here, who states, that passing between the islands of St. Lucia and St. Vincent, on the morning of the 1st of May, he not only heard the noises, I have so often mentioned in this and my preceding letter, but had his decks covered with a shower of hot ashes and cinders.

The following is Mr. Smith's account of the eruption of 1718, which in many of its concomitant symptoms bears a close resemblance to the present:—

"In the year 1718 (or thereabout) one Mr. Boyd, a merchant, going from St. Christopher's in a sloop towards Barbados, and being out of sight of all land, on a sudden, in the forenoon (if I mistake not) the sky grew so dark, and such a horrible noise (far surpassing the loudest thunder) was the same moment heard, insomuch that they all believed the final dissolution of Nature's frame to be just then commencing; there falling likewise instantaneously so thick a shower of ashes, that the sloop's deck was covered two or three inches deep with them. They in fright enough turned back homewards: and Mr. Boyd shewed me some of the ashes, which exactly resembled Holman's Ink Powder. It was soon after found out that a large mountain in the island of St. Vincent (that in my time was wholly inhabited by Negroes who escaped out of a Guinea ship that was cast away unfortunately there many years ago) abounding in veins of sulphur and brimstone, blew up at once, viz. woods, rocks, &c. all together, which must be allowed to cause a most dreadful explosion. As I was always curious in things of a rare nature, I took notice that very day (as I was riding in Gingerland Parish) that I heard six or seven dull bounces of noise, resembling those of cannon, at a great distance, pretty quickly following each other, at the exact time of this explosion: as the sky was quite clear in the eye of the wind, and as none of my acquaintance there took the same notice of the thing, I durst not venture to insist much upon hearing those dull bounces, till I had seen Mr. Boyd. I suppose the weather to be somewhat thick and hazy, which might be the true reason why Mr. Boyd and the sloop's crew did not see land; for they must certainly be nearer to St. Vincent than they reckoned themselves to be. A circumstantial narrative of this uncommon affair was shortly after transmitted home to England.

and printed. (*Natural History of the Island of Nevis, and the rest of the English Leeward Caribbee Islands in America, with many other observations on Nature and Art; particularly an Introduction to the Art of Decyphering. In eleven letters from the Rev. Mr. Smith, sometime Rector of St. John (Figtree) at Nevis, and now Rector of St. Mary, in Bedford; to the Rev. Mr. Mason, B.D. Woodwardian Professor, and Fellow of Trinity College, in Cambridge.*; Cambridge, 1745, p. 60.

The reports which were heard upon the present occasion in this island, were vastly louder than those observed by the Rev. Doctor, and awakened most of the inhabitants from their sleep. The ships in Charlestown-road were shaken as though the fort had fired. It is, however, somewhat remarkable, that the reports heard by the fleet off Martinique, though so much nearer the scene of the melancholy catastrophe, did not exceed in loudness, as Captain Hart declares, those heard in this and the neighbouring islands, where they were universally supposed to proceed from some ship or ships at no great distance from the shore.

This morning, between the hours of four and five, after a heavy fall of rain, a smart shock of an earthquake was felt throughout this island; it has not, however, been attended with any other mischief, than that of increasing the apprehensions which the late formidable events in our vicinity, and almost at our very doors, have excited. I know not whether, like the last shock upon the 11th of April last, this earthquake has been felt at St. Kitt's. A smart shock has, I am informed, been recently experienced at St. Thomas's—and about a year since; a remarkable fissure began to make its appearance in St. Bartholomew's, extending quite across the island from north to south - it created much alarm when first discovered, but habit has long since conquered the fears of the inhabitants —About the same time, during a dreadful storm of wind, rain, thunder and lightning; in which the ship Rachael, of Bristol, was lost at Charleston n, a remarkable subsidence of a considerable portion (at least two acres) of Saddle-hill, in this island, took place, and was for some time erroneously ascribed to a volcanic cause: the fact appears to me, from an attentive examination on the spot, to be simply this, that owing to some accidental cause, certain springs situated at the base of the declivity became choaked, whereby an accumulation of their waters took place within the ground, which partly from this cause, and partly likewise from the torrents of rain which fell at the time, had its cohesive powers so weakened as to be unable to support the superincumbent mass any longer, which of course giving way, gradually subsided till it came to a firmer basis.

I do not find that the Solfaterra, or the hot baths in this island, have been in the least affected by the recent convulsions. I hardly expect that we shall escape without our share in the calamities which befall our neighbours.*

OXONIENSIS.

---

* On this interesting topic much instructive information may be acquired from reference to pages 219, 315, of last volume. The following narrative of a recent

STATE PAPERS.

DECLARATIONS OF THE MEMBERS OF HER MAJESTY'S COUNCIL, RESPECTING THE STATE OF H. M.'s HEALTH.

WE, the underwritten, members of the council appointed to assist Her M. in the execution of the trusts committed to Her M. by virtue of the statute passed in the 51st year of H. M.'s reign, intituled, "An act to provide for the administration of the royal authority, and for the care of H. M.'s royal person, during the continuance of H. M.'s illness, and for the resumption of the exercise of the royal authority by H. M. ;"—Having duly met together, on this fourth day of April, 1812, at the Queen's Lodge near to Windsor Castle, and having called before us, and examined upon oath the physicians and other persons attendant upon H. M. and having ascertained the state of H. M.'s health by all such ways and means, as appeared to us to be necessary for that purpose,—Do hereby declare and certify, That the state of H. M.'s health, at the time of this our meeting, is not such as to enable him to resume the personal exercise of His Royal Authority.

That H. M.'s bodily health is as good as at any of the periods of our former reports.

That H. M.'s mental health is as much disordered as it has been during any part of H. M.'s indisposition.

That all the physicians in attendance concur in thinking, that H. M.'s final and complete recovery is extremely improbable, and they do not expect it; but they also concur in stating, that they do not entirely despair of it.

<table>
<tr><td>C. CANTUAR',</td><td>AYLESFORD,</td></tr>
<tr><td>E. EBOR',</td><td>ELDON,</td></tr>
<tr><td>MONTROSE,</td><td>ELLENBOROUGH.</td></tr>
<tr><td>WINCHILSEA,</td><td>W. GRANT.</td></tr>
</table>

A true copy,
CHETWYND.

---

catastrophe in this island seems also to throw light upon volcanic theory: in fact, the spontaneous ignition of a coal pit is the epitome of a volcano. "On the afternoon of 25th May, one of the most terrible accidents on record in the history of the collieries, took place at Felling, near Gateshead, in the mine belonging to Mr. Brandling, which was the admiration of the district for the excellence of its air and arrangements. Nearly the whole of the workmen were below, the 2d set having gone down before the 1st had come up, when a double blast of hydrogen gas took place, and set the mine on fire, forcing up such a volume of smoke as darkened the air to a considerable distance, and scattered an immense quantity of small coal from the upcast shaft. In this calamity, 93 men and boys perished, 86 of whom are still in the mine, which continues unapproachable. The few men who were saved happened to be working in a distant part of the colliery, to which the fury of the explosion did not reach."—*(Hull Packet, 2 June, 1812.)*

We, &c. [4th July, 1812] do hereby declare and certify, That the state of H. M.'s health, at the time of this our meeting, is not such, as to enable H. M. to resume the personal exercise of his royal functions.

That H. M.'s bodily health is as good as it was at the period of our last report.

That H. M.'s mental health is as much disordered as during any period of H. M.'s indisposition.

That the hope of H. M.'s ultimate and complete recovery is diminished since the period of our last report; but that such recovery is not absolutely despaired of.

(Signed as above.)

HYDROGRAPHY.

SUMATRA.

SIR, *H.M.S. Belliqueux, Croee Bay,* 21 *July,* 1810.

THERE is in this road-sted* a rock, which makes it dangerous for ships approaching the anchorage. It's bearings are as follow: — A remarkable tree close by the entrance of the river, N. 43° E. Resident's house, S. 40° E. Outer point of Selallo rock, S. 9° E. Outer south point of the bay, S. 25° W. I, therefore, recommend your laying a buoy on it, for

---

* It would be desirable to obtain an explanation of the real meaning of the term "road-*sted*," which is rather a favorite expression with naval officers, who seem in their correspondence to shew antipathy to the word road, inasmuch as they are accustomed never to use it but in the plural: this when applied to such places as Toulon, where there is an inner and outer road, may be correct; but cannot be so with reference to Yarmouth, Leith, &c. where there is only one sole undivided anchorage. A well known station affords frequent instance of this corrupt phraseology; namely, the *rade des Basques,* or " road of the Basques," which proper name English mariners almost always translate " Basque roads, instead of Basques'-road, that would surely unite equal brevity to more accuracy. It is impossible to drop this subject without repeating our humble protest against officers of liberal education becoming accomplices to these inroads on our language, either by indiscriminately borrowing the idiom of the vulgar, or sometimes, which is worse, by the affected adoption of *slang.* Local appellations should be held sacred, as far as circumstances allow, and the idiom of science be kept as pure as possible: perhaps a marine dictionary, edited on this principle, with a due regard to etymology, would be a great step towards rendering the nautical dialect in its particular line almost that grand *desideratum,* an universal language; the English are more addicted to *neology,* in its vicious practice, than almost any other travellers: it is only in relation to the " learned" languages that we are fastidious: there, a false concord or false quantity meets with no mercy; but with respect to cotemporary tongues, every piratical license is tolerated, as well by the great as the little vulgar.—(S.).

the safety of ships that may wish to stop here. I beg leave farther to inform you, that I have laid down a temporary buoy about ½ mile from shore, in 3 fathoms; where I would suggest your putting one of a larger size to continue.

James Brown, Esq. Resident, &c.

G. BYNG, Captain.

(Copy) by order of the Marine-Board, Fort William,
    5 December, 1810.

R. SCOTT, Secretary.

Croe, in latitude 5° 15' S. about 7 miles S.E. by E. from Poolo-Pisang, and situated at the bottom of the bay, is an English settlement, on the bank of a small river, navigable by boats at high water, close to the northward of Sillaloo rock. All round the bay, from abreast of Pisang to Croë, soundings of 35 fathoms are gotten about ¼ mile from shore, and they extend farther out from the latter place. Sillaloo rock, when seen at distance, appears like an island: foul ground projects from it about 2 cables' length into 10 fathoms; from thence sandy bottom to 54 fathoms, about ¼ mile off shore. The anchorage is safe in the S. E. monsoon, being well sheltered by Carran-pingan, the point that forms the south side of the bay, off which there are no soundings at ¼ mile from the breakers, and 40 fathoms close-to.—(*Horsburgh*),
S.

ATLANTIC OCEAN.

SHIPS approaching to Madeira generally see a high island, with several peaked hills on it, about 12 or 14 leagues north-eastward from the east end of Madeira: this island is called Puerto-Sancto,* otherwise Porto-Santo; and its geographical site is, according to Horsburgh, in latitude 33° 5' N. longitude 16° 24' W. The " Requisite-Tables," 1802, place it in 33° 5' 35" N. 16° 14' 51" W. The *Connaissance des Tems*, 1808, gives the same latitude as Horsburgh, but makes the longitude 18° 37' 30" W. from Paris, which, reduced to the meridian of Greenwich, is 16° 17' 15". Porto-Santo has a bay on the S.W. side, where there is anchorage, and where water and refreshments are procurable. This road has a rock at it's west end like that of Funchal. Although not so high as Madeira, Porto-Santo may be seen 12 or 14 leagues from a ship's deck; and is easily distinguished from Madeira or the Desertas, by its peaks and inequalities of outline. Rocks even with the water's edge are said to lie N. by W. 28 leagues from Porto-Santo, extending from latitude 34° 30' to 34° 35', or 5 leagues from S. to N. and about 3 leagues E. and W. The southernmost rock of this reef is said to bear N. 5° E. from the east end of Madeira, distant 40 leagues. Horsburgh, who is incredulity personified concerning oceanic dangers, treats the existence of these rocks as imaginary. That hydrographer, however, admits there is a reef in the vicinity of Porto-Santo on which a Dutch ship was lost. This bank was examined by Lieutenant

---

* See Plate CCCLXVIII. page 53 of this Volume.

J. Bowen, in the Falcon, on 10th January, 1802. When the easternmost rock off the N.E. point of the island bore by compass S.E. the N.E. point. S.S.E. ¼ E. the northernmost rock S. ½ W and the W. point S.S.W. ¾ W. The Falcon had 22, 23, and 25 fathoms rocky bottom : the ship's boat at the same time about ¾ mile S. ½ W. from the ship, had 30 fathoms rocky bottom : from whence rowing westward the depth gradually decreased to 16 fathoms, then more suddenly to 12, 8, and 4½, at which last depth the rock was plainly discerned from the boat. When on it in 4¼ fathoms, the N.E. point of Porto-Santo bore by compass S.S.E. the northernmost rock S. by W. and the W. point of the island S.S W. making its true bearing N. 18° W. from the nearest part, distant about 2 leagues. It's extent E. and W. is about one mile, terminating westward in a rocky point, upon which the least water appeared to be 4½ fathoms. When the bearings were taken in the boat, the compass was so agitated by her motion, that they may not be quite correct : but it seems certain that the boat was on the shoalest part, as, from the then state of the weather, the sea must have broken on any spot of it with less water than has been noted. Encrease of wind prevented farther observations. S,

FRANCE,

THE following supplement to the last hydrographic article in the preceding Volume,* is extracted from Horsburgh's " Directions for sailing to and from the East Indies," &c. (1809).

" The only places in the bay which seem to afford good shelter for large ships in westerly gales, are, probably, Belle-isle, in latitude 47° 18′ N. longitude 3° 5′ W. and Basque road, near Rochefort. Belle-isle is high, and may be seen at a great distance : the N.W. end is surrounded by rocks, and directly in the line from it to the isle Grouais, nearly mid-way, is the bank Bervidaux. The north end of Belle-isle is in 47° 23′ and the south end in 47° 15′ N. If a ship, with the wind at N.W. or W.N.W. keeps between these latitudes in running for the island, when she approaches it, should steer along the south side, at 2 miles distance, to point du-Canon, the S.E. extremity, she ought, when abreast of this point, to haul up for point Locmaria, which is the easternmost point of the island, distant about a league from the former; and anchor under it in 8, 10, or 15 fathoms, where she will be sheltered from a north-westerly wind. Should it veer southward, she may run to the northward of the point, and anchor on the north-east side of the island. The isle Hédic, about 7 miles eastward from the east end of Belle-isle, has many rocks around it. To the S.E. is a cluster called the Cardinals; the largest is distant from Hedic about 1 mile, and is always above water. Should a ship be driven to the eastward of Belle-isle, she may pass southward of the Cardinals at a mile distant ; then haul up northward, and anchor on the east side of them and of isle Hedic, in 9, or 10 fathoms, sand and mud." S.

---

* N. C. XXVII. 475

NAVAL HISTORY OF THE PRESENT YEAR, 1812.
(June—July.)
RETROSPECTIVE AND MISCELLANEOUS.

THE American Senate has passed a resolution for declaring war against Britain; and circumstances have transpired which strongly indicate, that that resolution has been sanctioned by the President of the United States.—On the 25th of July, as we learn from the " *Hampshire Telegraph,*" the Mackarel schooner arrived at Portsmouth, from Halifax, with despatches from Admiral Sawyer, relating, that, on the 24th of June, the Belvidera frigate, commanded by Captain Richard Byron (one of the ships under his command), was cruising off Sandy Hook, but not in sight of land, when she fell in with an American squadron, consisting of the President, United States, Congress, and Essex frigates, and Hornet sloop of war, which ships, as soon as they were within point blank shot, *without previous communication with the Belvidera,* immediately commenced firing upon her.—The Belvidera, of course, made sail from so very superior a force, and the Americans pursued her, maintaining a running fight with her, as long as she was within reach of shot; in the course of which she had two men killed, and Captain Byron was hurt in the thigh, by a gun falling upon him. The Belvidera made her way to Halifax, to acquaint Admiral Sawyer of the transaction, and repair her damages. On her arrival there Admiral Sawyer sent Captain Thompson, in the Colibri sloop of war, *with a flag of truce,* to New York, to request an explanation of the matter ; despatched the Rattler to Bermuda, and the different cruising stations, to order all his squadron to assemble at Halifax ; and sent Captain Hargrave in the Mackarel to England, with despatches for Government.—Captain Byron is said to have captured three American vessels, on his way to port, but Admiral Sawyer released them.

Our Government has expressed an opinion, that the attack made upon the Belvidera had neither resulted from any new orders of the American Government, nor was any proof that war had been decided on. The American frigates, it was thought, had acted in conformity to a previous order of the Government of the United States, not to permit vessels of war belonging to foreign powers to cruise within their waters.

Buonaparte has crossed the Niemen, and, according to the latest accounts, was proceeding on his route towards St. Petersburg, the Russian army retreating before him.

The Regency of Tripoli has declared war against Spain.

It has transpired, from the French papers, and the truth of the statement has been acknowledged in Parliament, that when the intercourse took place between the British and French Governments, in the month of April last, a proposition for peace was made, on the basis that the reigning dynasty should be acknowledged Sovereign of Spain (the integrality of the Spanish dominions to be guaranteed in his family, which is termed " the

Nav. Chron. Vol. XXVIII.   L

present, or actual dynasty:") that Naples should remain in the hands of Murat, and Sicily in that of its legitimate Sovereign; and that each power should retain the portion, of which the other could not deprive it by war. To this proposition Lord Castlereagh replied, that ministers had no objection to treat of a peace; but, with respect to the proposed basis, he wished to be informed, whether, by the "actual dynasty" were really meant Joseph and his kin; as, if so, the obligations of good faith did not permit the Prince Regent to attend to the proposition. Buonaparte offered no explanation, and thus the correspondence terminated.

Letters on Service,
Copied, verbatim, from the LONDON GAZETTE.

ADMIRALTY-OFFICE, JUNE 30, 1812.

REAR-ADMIRAL SIR EDWARD BULLER has transmitted to John Wilson Croker, Esq. a letter from Captain Hopkins, of H. M. sloop the Helicon, giving an account of his having, on the 25th instant, captured, off the Isle of Bas, La Zulma, a French lugger privateer, carrying nineteen men, with small arms, out two days from Abervrach without making any capture.

JULY 4.

Admiral Lord Keith has transmitted to John Wilson Croker, Esq. a letter from Captain Sir Home Popham, dated on board H.M.S. Venerable, off Lequitio, the 21st of last month, giving an account of an attack made upon the French troops in possession of that place by the Spanish Guerillas, aided by Sir Home, and the officers and men of H. M. ships under his orders.

The enemy had possession of a hill fort commanding the town, calculated to resist any body of infantry; and also two hundred men posted in a fortified convent within the town, the walls of which were impervious to any thing less than an eighteen pounder.

The convent might have been destroyed by the ships; but, as the town would have materially suffered, and as the guns of the Venerable made no visible impression on the fort, it was determined to erect a battery on a hill opposite to the latter, which the enemy considered as quite inaccessible to cannon, and in that confidence rested his security.

A gun was accordingly landed in the forenoon of the 20th (chiefly by the exertions of Lieutenant Groves, of the Venerable), notwithstanding the sea was breaking with such violence against the rocks at the foot of the hill, that it was doubtful whether a boat could get near enough for that purpose. It was then hove up a short distance by a moveable capstan; but this was found so tedious that men and bullocks were sent for to draw it; and it was, at length, dragged to the summit of the hill by thirty-six pair of bullocks, four hundred guerillas, and one hundred seamen, headed by the Hon. Captain Bouverie. It was immediately mounted, and fired its first shot at four in the afternoon.

The gun was so admirably served, that at sunset, a practicable breach was made in the wall of the fort, and the guerillas volunteered to storm it. The first party was repulsed, but the second gained possession without any considerable loss; several of the enemy escaped on the opposite side, and got into the convent.

In the course of the evening the sea abated a little, and a landing upon the island of St. Nicholas was effected, though with some difficulty, by Lieutenant O'Reilly, of the Surveillante; marines were also landed from that ship, the Medusa, and Rhin, with a carronade from each ship; and Captain Malcolm took the command of the island during the night, whilst Captain Sir George Collier was in the Venerable's battery on the hill.

At dawn of the 21st, a 24-pounder was brought to the east side of the town, within two hundred yards of the convent, and another was in the act of being landed upon St.Nicholas, to bombard it, when the French Commandant Gillort, Chef de Battalion, beat a parley, and surrendered with the remainder of his party, consisting of 290 men of the 119th regiment.

The enemy's loss had not been ascertained, but it was supposed to be considerable, as the guerillas, who were better posted and fired with more celerity, had 56 men killed or wounded. Not a man was hurt in H. M. squadron, either by the surf or the enemy.

There were two 18 pounders mounted on the fort, and three small guns in the barracks; the latter, with the muskets, were given to the guerillas, who were also supplied with every description of military stores of which they stood in need. The guns in the fort were rendered useless, the fort destroyed, and the convent blown up.

Sir Home Popham commends, in high terms, the conduct of all the officers and men employed on this occasion; and expresses his sense of the assistance rendered by Sir Howard Douglas and General Carrol, who had embarked in the Venerable, and volunteered their services wherever they could be employed.

Vice-admiral Sir Edward Pellew has transmitted to John Wilson Croker, Esq. two letters, addressed to him by Captains Campbell and Thomas, of H. M. ships Leviathan and Undaunted; the former giving an account of an attack made on the 29th of April last, by the boats of the Leviathan, under the directions of Lieutenant Dobbs, on a French privateer and several merchant vessels at Agay; four of the latter were brought out, and the privateer, a brig of 14 guns and 80 men, was taken possession of; but, having been hauled on shore she could not be got off, and being set on fire, it was afterwards extinguished by the enemy: the vessel was carried without any loss on our part, but during the endeavours made to bring her off, two men were killed and four wounded by the enemy's fire from the shore.

The latter reporting an attack made on the same day on a French convoy near the mouth of the Rhone, by the boats of the Undaunted, Volontaire, and Blossom, under the directions of Lieutenant Eagar, of the first ship; of twenty-six vessels composing the convoy, seven were brought out, twelve burnt, and two left stranded on the beach: a national schooner of four 18-pounders and 74 men was amongst the vessels burnt. This service was performed without any loss, the boats being ably protected by Captain Stewart in the Blossom sloop.

Copy of a Letter from Captain Usher, of H. M. S. Hyacinth, addressed to Commodore Penrose, at Gibraltar, and transmitted by the latter to John Wilson Croker, Esq.

SIR,   *H. M. S. Hyacinth, off Almunecar, May* 27, 1812.

I had the honour to inform you, in my letter of the 20th instant, that the Termagant had destroyed the castle at Nersa, and that the guerillas came down from the mountains and entered the town; I have now to acquaint you that I went on shore with Captain Hamilton, and waited upon the guerilla leader, who informed me that the French had retreated to Almunecar, seven miles to the eastward, and that they had 300 men there; and considering himself strong enough to attack them, he proposed marching upon it without loss of time. As I was desirous to render the guerillas every assistance in my power, I promised him to anchor the ships in a position to place the enemy between our fire, which gave him great satisfaction, and his men great confidence. I accordingly bore up at four o'clock the following evening (20th instant) with H. M. ships as per margin,* and anchored at point blank range before the castle, which we silenced in less than an hour. As the guerillas were to have arrived at seven o'clock, and there was no appearance of them at eight, Captain Hamilton volunteered to return to Nersa in his gig, to learn if any thing had occurred to prevent their moving forward ; and, at four in the morning he returned, and informed me that a reinforcement which they expected had not arrived, and that they waited for them before they could advance. At seven o'clock the enemy again opened his fire, having, during the night, mounted a howitzer in a breach made in the covered way to the castle; but by ten o'clock he was again silenced, and driven, with great loss, into the town, where they fortified themselves in the church and houses. Desirous of sparing the unfortunate inhabitants, whom the French had thus cruelly exposed, I ceased firing ; and having destroyed a privateer which lay at anchor under the castle, I, at two o'clock, weighed and ran down to Nersa, for the purpose of concerting plans with the guerillas. On my arrival I had the satisfaction to meet a division of Ballesteros's guerillas, commanded by Colonel Febrien, an officer of the truest patriotism, who, partaking of all the zeal of his general, immediately put himself and troops at my disposal. The roads through the mountains being very tedious, and as no time was to be lost, I resolved to take the infantry, consisting of about 200, on board ; and I ordered the cavalry to move forward through the mountains immediately, and take a position in the rear of the enemy, whilst the infantry, with all the small arm men and marines, were to land on his flanks. I am sorry that the delay of a calm gave the enemy time to learn our combined movement, as he instantly fled with great precipitation, and joining a corps of 200 at Motril, within four miles of Almunecar, he retreated upon Grenada.

As soon as I arrived at my anchorage, I sent Lieutenant Spilsbury and a guerilla officer to hoist the respective flags on the castle; and immediately began to demolish the works, which are exceedingly strong, as it is built on a peninsula or high rock, scarped all round the sea-face, and a wall thirty feet high. At the land side the rock is excavated nearly thirty feet deep and sixty wide, with a narrow drawbridge, which is the only entrance into the castle. I intend to fill up as much of the ditch as possible, by springing mines under each bastion. I found in the castle two brass 24-pounders, six iron 18-pounders, a 6-pounder, and howitzer, which were spiked by the enemy. He has left a number of deserters, principally Germans and Flemings, who inform me that they were the whole of the foreigners in this battalion of the 32d regiment; they likewise inform me that they have long looked for an opportunity to desert, as they were dragged from their families, and forced into the French service : one of them has been eight years from his country. The enemy's loss was very severe, but cannot be ascertained, as the wounded were carried off in waggons.

I feel greatly indebted to Captain Hamilton for the able assistance he rendered me, and the judicious position he anchored his ship in ; likewise

---

* Termagant, Basilisk.

to Lieutenant French, of the Basilisk, who opened and supported a warm and well-directed fire upon the enemy, while the ships were heaving in their springs to bring their broadsides to bear.

I am happy to inform you that we have had no loss, except the Termagant one man wounded, and the Basilisk one slightly. The privateer was one of Barbastro's small vessels, armed with two guns and thirty or forty men. I cannot conclude without informing you that the officers and men wounded so recently at Malaga came to their quarters. Lieutenant Spilsbury, whose wound is still open, and Mr. Bell, the boatswain, who lost his arm, did not spare themselves.

I have the honour to be, &c.

To Commodore Penrose, Gibraltar. THOS. USHER.

JULY 7.

Copy of a Letter from Lieutenant Simmonds, commanding H. M. Gun-Vessel Attack, addressed to Rear-admiral Foley, and transmitted to John Wilson Croker, Esq.

H. M. Gun Brig *Attack,* Dover Roads,
SIR, July 5, 1812.

It is with much satisfaction I have the honour to inform you, that in executing your orders, to cruize in H. M. brig under my command, for the protection of trade and the annoyance of the enemy, at six P.M. yesterday evening, Calais Cliff bearing S. by E. four miles, I observed a transport galliot, a sloop, and a privateer, coming out of Calais Harbour, and endeavouring to run along shore: perceiving this to be their intention, and knowing that the shewing a disposition to make an immediate attack would cause them all to put back, or run their vessels on shore, I made sail to windward, in the hope of decoying them so far from their own shore as to be able to cut them off. Judging this to be the proper opportunity for such an attempt, I immediately made all sail in shore, and at half past eight, manned and sent the gig away, with six men, under the direction of Mr. Couney, the second master, still keeping H.M. brig towards the enemy. At twelve, there being light airs, and within half gun-shot of the enemy's shore, the second master discovered the galliot in tow of the privateer.

Mr. Couney, undaunted by such an unequal force, and under the galling fire of their musketry, immediately boarded the transport, while on the other side she was boarded by the privateer's men; but on the second master's having killed one of their men in boarding, they thought it prudent to desist and sheer off, leaving the boat's crew in possession of their prize. She proves to be the transport galliot No. 637, of 256 tons burden, manned with sixteen men, and armed with muskets; the privateer was armed with a 6-pounder, swivels, cohorns, and musketry, and a complement of thirty men, commanded by Lieutenant de Vaisseau Gröthe.

It is with great pleasure I have to state, that it has pleased God to spare the lives of the little crew of H. M. brig engaged in this contest, who have escaped, to a man unhurt.

The gallantry displayed by Mr. Couney and the men employed with him, merits any approbation that can be bestowed on them, for, independent of the fire of the enemy's musketry, the vessel was exposed to the batteries, which kept up a fire of round and grape upon them. From H. M. brig being becalmed from the time the boat shoved off, I was unable to close with them; my anxiety was great for the fate of the people, but, from my knowledge of Mr. Couney's conduct since he has been with me, I had great confidence in him.

I cannot conclude without mentioning the steady conduct of my officers

and men throughout the whole of the affair; and had we been so fortunate as to have had a breeze, we, no doubt, should have captured the whole.
I have the honour to be, &c.
R. W. SIMMONDS, Lieut. and Com.

Rear-admiral Foley, Commander-in-Chief,
&c. &c. &c. Downs.

JULY 11.

Copy of a Letter from Admiral Young to John Wilson Croker, Esq. dated on board H. M. S. Impregnable, off West Capel, the 5th instant.

SIR,
I have great pleasure in transmitting for their lordships' information, a letter from Captain Lennock, of H. M. sloop Raven, giving an account of his having attacked fourteen of the enemy's brigs, and driven three of them on shore.
I have no doubt of their lordships being pleased with Captain Lennock's quickness in deciding on, and his skill and spirit in executing this attack; the merit of which is greatly enhanced, and the gratification attending the success of it heightened, by its being obtained in the enemy's port; under the guns of his forts, and in the face of his fleet.
I have the honour to be, &c.
W. YOUNG.

SIR,   *H. M. S. Raven, off the Scheldt, July 4, 1812.*
I have the pleasure to inform you, that when hauling over the Droograan yesterday afternoon, I perceived several of the enemy's flotilla that had been exercising considerably to leeward in the Weiling, and was induced to stand on to ascertain if there was a possibility of cutting any of the detachment off, which consisted of fourteen brigs; on proceeding into the Weiling, about a quarter past six P. M. found we could fetch some of them, but, from the haziness of the weather, was unable to make it known to you by signal, and as standing back to do so would lose the opportunity of disturbing their manœuvres, we plied up with them as far as Wulpen, firing occasionally in passing. The wind blowing strong on shore our superior sailing and working enabled us to overtake seven, four of which were obliged to anchor close to the surf under their batteries; the other three were driven on shore, and, at half-past seven, were still lying on the beach with the sea beating over them. I trust you will deem all has been performed on this occasion that was practicable, in face of an enemy's fleet, in an intricate passage, and on a lee shore; only one shot struck us, near the stern port. From Lieutenant Berriff I had every assistance to be expected from an old officer, and the officers and ship's company behaved with that steadiness which, I trust, would prove successful in a more serious contest. On reconnoitring this morning, the three brigs were on the beach, and probably bilged.
I have the honour to be, &c.
Commodore Owen.   G. G. LENNOCK, Commander.

JULY 14.

Admiral Lord Keith has transmitted to John Wilson Croker, Esq. a letter from Captain Sir Home Popham, of H. M. S. the Venerable, dated near the bar of Bilboa [Bilbao],* the 25th of last month, giving an account of his proceedings subsequent to the surrender of the French troops at Lequitio, as stated in the Gazette of the 4th instant.

---

* Vide N. C. XXVI. 478.

In the afternoon of the 20th the enemy had collected about 1100 men in the neighbourhood of the above place, but on hearing from the peasantry that 2000 men had been landed from the English squadron, they retired; and intercepted letters were transmitted to Sir Home Popham, by which the Commandant of Gernicò was instructed to prepare rations for a French General and 2600 of the Imperial Guards.

On the 23d, in the afternoon, the squadron being on its way to co-operate in an attack intended to be made by a Spanish general upon Bilboa and the wind being unfavourable for getting round Machichaco, a part of the squadron fetched the anchorage of Bermeo, and parties were prepared to land by six in the evening. The enemy were found to have retired, leaving a small magazine of provisions in a fortified convent, which was taken possession of, and distributed to the poor, and the ships in want of water were completed. The battery on the hill of Bermeo, consisting of five 18 pounders, was destroyed, and the guns rendered useless, and all the fortified places of which the enemy had had possession, were blown up.

On the 24th the Venerable arrived off Plencia, where parties from the Rhin and Medusa were destroying the works; and some of H. M. vessels were immediately despatched to commence the operations of dismantling the batteries, and destroying the guns on each side of the inlet below the bar of the Bilboa river.

In the afternoon of the same day, Sir Home Popham landed at Algorta, with the captains of the squadron, General Carrol, and Sir Howard Douglas, and a detachment of the royal marine force, under his orders; but, as the country was particularly close, and calculated for a surprise, they re-embarked before night. The castle of Galea was destroyed by Captain Bloye; it consisted of eight 18 and 24-pounders; the guard-house and gun-carriages were burnt, and the trunnions knocked off the guns. The batteries of Algorta and Begona were destroyed by Lieutenants Groves and O'Reilly, the former mounting five 18 pounders, and the latter four. On the opposite side of the inlet the batteries of El Campillo las Quersas and Xebiles, mounting eleven guns, 18 and 24-pounders, were destroyed by Lieutenants Coleman and Arbuthnot.

On the 25th, at dawn, parties of the enemy were seen advancing, and, at five, entered the destroyed batteries of Algorta, but soon retired from thence on the squadron's making a disposition to stand up the inlet. They afterwards formed on the plain, and were found to consist of 2000 men at Algorta, while 400 were sent to Puerta Galetta. Three of H. M. sloops closed with the fort at the latter place, silenced it, and drove the enemy from it. Sir Home expresses his belief that the enemy's corps was the one for which rations had been ordered at Guernico, and which was, therefore, completely diverted from its original destination.

Sir Home Popham concludes by commending the zeal and exertions of the officers under his orders on these several occasions, in all which the squadron has not had a single man hurt.

JULY 18, 1812.

Copy of a Letter from Vice-admiral Sir James Saumarez, Bart. and K.B. to John Wilson Croker, Esq. dated on board H. M. S. Victory, Wingo Sound, July 8, 1812.

SIR,

I have the highest satisfaction in transmitting to you, to be laid before the Lords Commissioners of the Admiralty, the enclosed letter which I have this day received from Captain Stewart, of his Majesty's ship Dictator, detailing the particulars of a most gallant exploit performed by him and the two sloops and the gun-brig named in the margin,* upon the Danish frigate Nayaden, three large sloops of war, and numerous gun-boats, within the rocks of Mardoe, on the coast of Norway, supported by batteries on the shore; in which the enemy's frigate has been totally destroyed, and the sloops of war completely disabled, besides several of the gun-boats sunk.

It is impossible for me to express in an adequate manner, the undaunted spirit displayed by Captain Stewart, and all the officers and men under his orders, in this arduous enterprise, which I am assured will be duly appreciated by their Lordships.

Captain Stewart speaks in the strongest terms of the gallantry and zeal of Captain Robilliard, of the Podargus, and Captain Weir, of the Calypso, and Lieutenant Thomas England, commanding the Flamer gun-brig; also of Lieutenant William Buchanan, first of the Dictator.

Herewith is also transmitted, the list of the enemy's force, with the returns of the killed and wounded on board his Majesty's ships.

I have the honour to be, &c.

JAMES SAUMAREZ.

SIR, *H. M. S. Dictator, in the Sleeve, July* 7, 1812.

I have the honour to inform you, that yesterday evening being off Mardoe with the brigs named in the margin, the mast heads of the enemy's squadron were seen over the rocks; and Captain Robilliard, of the Podargus, in the most handsome manner volunteered to lead the squadron in to attack them, he having a man on board acquainted with the place; and as neither the masters or the pilots of either of the ships conceived themselves equal to the charge, I did not hesitate to accept his kind offer, well knowing that the British flag would meet with nothing but honour in such hands.

In the entrance of the passage the Podargus unfortunately took the ground; by which circumstance I was deprived of the valuable and gallant services of her commander during the remainder of the day, and was, in consequence, obliged to leave the Flamer to her assistance; but in Captain Weir, of the Calypso, I found every thing that could be wished for, which, in a great measure, made up for the loss which I had sustained in the Podargus and Flamer. By this time, half past seven P. M., we had arrived within one mile of the enemy, who were running inside the rocks under a press of sail; the Calypso which had also grounded for a short time, was now leading us through the passage, and both she and ourselves engaged with the squadron and numerous gun-boats. However, at half-past nine, I had the satisfaction, after sailing twelve miles through a passage, in some places scarcely wide enough to admit of our studding sail booms being out, of running the Dictator's bow upon the land with her broadside towards the enemy (within hail) as per margin,† who were anchored with springs on their cables, close together, and supported by gun-boats, in the small creek of Lyngoe, the Calypso most nobly following us up.

In half an hour the frigate was literally battered to atoms, and the flames bursting forth from her hatchways; the brigs had also struck, and most of the gun-boats were completely beaten, and some sunk. The action had scarcely ceased, and the ship afloat, than we found ourselves

---

* Pordargus, Calypso, Flamer, gun-brig.
† Nayaden, Laaland, Samsoe, Kiel.

again attacked by the gun boats which had retreated on seeing the fate of their squadron, and were again collecting from all quarters ; but Captain Weir of the Calypso, having taken a most advantageous position, engaged them with the greatest gallantry and effect ; indeed I am at a loss how to express my approbation of the prompt exertion of this gallant and meritorious officer.

The Podargus and Flamer in the meantime were warmly engaged with numerous batteries and gun-boats, both brigs being aground ; but by the uncommon exertion and extreme gallantry of Captain Robilliard, and the officers and crews of the brigs, they at last got afloat very much cut up : on this occasion Lieutenant England particularly distinguished himself.

At three A. M. having got the Dictator, Calypso, and prize brigs in the fair way, we attempted to get out through the passages, when we were assailed by a division of gun-boats from behind the rocks, so situated that not a gun could be brought to bear on them from either vessel ; in this situation both prize brigs grounded, and notwithstanding every exertion on the part of Lieutenant James Wilkie of this ship, in the Laaland, who had extinguished a fire on board her which was burning with great fury, and Lieutenant Hooper, of the Calypso, in the Kiel, we had to abandon them complete wrecks, humanity forbidding our setting them on fire, owing to the number of wounded men they had on board.

I cannot conclude this letter without mentioning in terms of praise Mr. William Buchanan, the first Lieutenant of this ship, a most gallant and excellent officer.

From the nature of the attack, I have been obliged to lengthen my report, probably more than the service performed justifies, but in that case, I trust you will only attribute it to my anxiety to endeavour to do justice to a set of officers and men who, I am sure, have done their duty to admiration. The conduct of every individual on board his Majesty's ship I have the honour to command, has been highly meritorious, and I cannot omit to add the names of Lieutenants Duell, Dutton, and Edwards, Captain Triscot, Lieutenant James Baker, and Lieutenanr F. M'Namara, of the royal marines, Mr. R. West, the master, and Mr. John Luckomlee, the Purser. The skilful attention of Mr. Hay the Surgeon, to our own men as well as our enemies, has been beyond all praise and he speaks in the highest terms of Mr. Sanderson, his assistant. Captains Robilliard and Weir, mention the conduct of all their officers and men to have been such as characterize Britons on such occasions, and I am sure I can with great justice add my tribute of applause.

Enclosed I have the honour to transmit a list of the killed &c. although I cannot help deploring the loss of so many brave men, it is much less than could be reasonably expected. The Danes acknowledge to have lost about three hundred killed and wounded ; I rather suspect five.

Our ships have suffered extremely in their hulls, masts, and rigging.

I have the honour to be, &c.

J. P. STEWART, Captain.

To Sir Jas. Saumarez, Bart. and
K. B. Vice-admiral and Com-
mander-in-chief, &c.

Statement of the Enemy's Force.

Nayaden, of 38 guns, mounting 50, long 24-pounders on the maindeck, and 320 men.
Laaland, of 20 guns, long 18-pounders, and 125 men.
Samsoe, of 18 guns, long 18-pounders, and 125 men.
Kiel, of 18 guns, long 18-pounders, and 125 men.
Twenty-five gun-boats, carrying each two long 18 or 24-pounders, and from 50 to 60 men.

Return of Killed, Wounded, and Missing, on board His Majesty's Ships Dictator, Podargus, Calypso, and Flamer.

Dictator—5 killed; 16 severely, 8 slightly wounded.
Podargus—4 severely, 5 slightly wounded.
Calypso—3 killed; 1 severely wounded; 2 missing.
Flamer—1 killed; 1 severely wounded.
Total—9 killed; 26 severely, 13 slightly wounded; 2 missing.

J. P. STEWART, Captain.

List of Killed and Wounded on board H. M. S. Dictator, 7th July 1812.

Killed.—Thomas Barnes, seaman; Christopher Lewis, ditto; John Sullivan, ditto; Abraham Ladd, marine; William Rolf, boy.

Wounded.—John Merick, seaman, dangerously; John Lloyd, private marine, severely; William Rogers, ditto, ditto; John Goodhew, seaman, ditto; Jos. Bull, ditto, ditto; Samuel Davis, ditto, ditto; John Dixon, ditto, ditto; Francis Emanuel, ditto, ditto; James Kendal, ditto, ditto; James Chandler, ditto, ditto; Richard Sanders, ditto, ditto; James Black (1), ditto, ditto; Moys Hulon, ditto, ditto; William Lamb, ditto, ditto; John Manuel, boy, ditto; William Quick, ditto, ditto; Mr. Hooper, midshipman, slightly; Thomas Broderick, private marine, ditto; John Nesbit, ditto, ditto; Thomas Farmer, captain's clerk, ditto; John Ball, seaman, ditto; Jeremiah Wanlien, ditto, ditto; William Richards, ditto, ditto; John Flynn, ditto, ditto.

J. P. STEWART, Captain.
ANDREW HAY, Surgeon.

List of Wounded on board H.M. Sloop Podargus, in Action the 7th July 1812.

Wounded.—John Ladan, able seaman, severely; William Clary, ordinary seaman, ditto; John Cook, ditto, ditto; William Lane, supernumerary, belonging to H.M.S. Dictator, ditto; Mr. Garratt, purser, slightly; Mr. Robilliard, volunteer, 1st class, ditto; James Boyle, able seaman, ditto; John Rock, ordinary seaman, ditto; William Marlow, private marine, ditto.

WM. ROBILLIARD, Commander.
J. DADD, Surgeon.

List of Killed and Wounded on board H. M. Sloop Calypso, on the 7th of July 1812.

Killed.—John Ward, marine; James Blake, ditto.
Wounded.—William Todman, ordinary seaman, dangerously (since dead); Nept Mussared, able seaman, severely.

H. WEIR, Commander.

List of Killed and Wounded on board H. M. Brig Flamer, on the 7th July 1812.

Killed.—Donald M'Neal, ordinary seaman.
Wounded.—Mr. James Powell, midshipman, slightly.
　　　　　　　THOS. ENGLAND, Lieutenant and Commander.

Copy of a Letter from Captain Weir, of H. M. Sloop Calypso, to John Wilson Croker, Esq. dated off Yarmouth, the 14th Instant.

SIR,

I beg you will be pleased to inform my Lords Commissioners of the Admiralty, that on my passage through the Sleeve yesterday, I spoke the Nimble cutter, which had been despatched to reconnoitre the enemy's position in Norway; the commander of which informed me, that besides the frigate, one sloop was totally destroyed, and the rest disabled; which account corresponds with my own observation during and subsequent to the action.

I enclose a report of the Danish force prior and since the battle, from which I trust their Lordships will be satisfied they can effect nothing of importance this summer.

　　　　　　　　I have the honour to be, &c.
　　　　　　　　HENRY WEIR, Commander.

Danish Force, 6th and 7th July 1812.

Nayaden, of 48 guns, 24-pounders, and 335 men; burnt.
Logan, of 20 guns, 24 and 18-pounders, and 120 men; burnt.
Laaland, of 20 guns and 120 men; taken, much burnt, but afterwards abandoned, as it grounded.
Kiel, of 18 guns, 18-pounders, and 120 men; ditto, ditto.
Samsoe, of 18 guns, 18-pounders, and 120 men; struck.
Alaart, of 16 guns, 18-pounders, and 100 men; laying at Christiansand.
Seagull, of 16 guns, 18-pounders, and 100 men; laying at Christiansand.
Langeland, of 18 guns, 18-pounders, and 120 men; ditto.
Alren, of 18 guns, 18-pounders, and 120 men; ditto.
Gun-boats out of number.

　　　　　　　　　　HENRY WEIR.

Copy of a Letter from Captain Ross, of H. M. Sloop, Briseis, addressed to Rear-admiral Martin, and transmitted by Vice-admiral Sir James Saumarez to John Wilson Croker, Esq.

SIR,　　　*H. M. Sloop Briseis, off Pillau, June* 29, 1812.

I have the honour to inform you, that, in pursuance of your orders, I stood in yesterday to communicate with the merchant vessel Urania, in Pillau Roads, when I perceived her to be in possession of the French troops, and that it was intended to destroy her on our approach; I tacked and stood off, judging it the most likely way to save the ship (which was employed by Messrs. Sully and Son on the part of Government) from destruction, and the remainder of her cargo from falling into the hands of the enemy, to surprise her in the night. Lieutenant Thomas Jones (2d), first of the Briseis, Mr. Palmer, midshipman, and eighteen men, were sent in the pinnace on that service at midnight; when within pistol-shot, they were hailed and fired upon by the enemy, who had six guns and four swivels on board the Urania, which was surrounded by craft and boats; but every obstacle was overcome by the gallantry of

Lieutenant Jones and his crew, who gave three cheers, boarded over the craft, and drove the enemy off deck into their boats on the opposite side, leaving behind part of their arms; the cable was then cut, and she was brought out, together with a French scout that was employed unloading her.

On our side I have to regret the loss of one seaman (John Cooper) killed; Joseph Cook, serjeant of royal marines, badly; Mr. Palmer, midshipman, and one seaman (Robert Starkins), slightly wounded; but the enemy must have suffered far more severely, from being exposed, in their turn, to the fire from the Urania after they had abandoned her.

I am, &c.
JOHN ROSS, Commander.

To Rear-admiral T. B. Martin.

Promotions and Appointments.

WHITEHALL, JUNE 26, 1812.

His Royal Highness the Prince Regent has been graciously pleased, in the name and on the behalf of his Majesty, to give and grant unto George Wickens Willes, Esq. a commander in the royal navy, his Majesty's royal licence and permission, that he may accept and wear the insignia of a Knight of the Third Class of the Royal Sicilian Order of St. Ferdinand and of Merit, which his Sicilian Majesty had been pleased to confer upon the said Captain George Wickens Willes, in testimony of his royal approbation of the great courage and intrepidity displayed by him as first lieutenant of his Majesty's ship Spartan, in the action fought by that frigate, against a squadron of the enemy in the bay of Naples, on the 3d day of May 1810:

And also to command, that the said royal concession and declaration be registered, together with the relative documents, in his Majesty's College of Arms.

Admirals and Captains appointed.

Vice-admiral Sir William Sidney Smith, to be second in command in the Mediterranean.

Captain C. T. Smith is appointed flag-captain to Vice-admiral Sir Sidney Smith.

Captains.—Michael Head, to the Curlew; Hon. ——— Paget, to the Superb; J. Hewitt, to the Gladiator; J. Graham, to the Laurestinus; George Wyndham (posted), to the Bristol; William Kent, to the Union; B. S. Bluett, to the Childers; George Augustus Hire, to the Bittern; Hon. William Gordon, to the Java; ——— Foley, to the Zenobia.

Lieutenants, &c. appointed.

H. W. Hoare, to the Minden; John Dawson, to the Castilian; Randall Vans, to the Princess Carolina; George Bignall and Thomas Gardiner, to the Dover; Thomas Dickinson and J. Thompson, to the Andromache; N. Kortwright, to the Experiment; James M. Shipton and David Ogilvie, to the Curlew; Robert A. Wadham, to the Royal William; John A. Moore, to the Cordelia; William Green, to command the Resolute G.B.; ——— Oake, to command the Abundance S.S.; J. Petit, to command the Sprightly cutter; J. Carter, to the impress service at the Isle of Wight; T. Evans (1), to the Mullet schooner; M. Raynham, to the Laurestinus; C. H. Bowen, to the Cornwall;

NAVAL HISTORY OF THE PRESENT YEAR, 1812.   85

J. Cririe, to the Narcissus; G. Glasscock, to the Clarence ; John Reeve, to the Prometheus ; J. Chrystie, to the Vengeur.
J. Smith (7), of the Dictator; ———— Keenah, of the Resolute; ———— Read, flag-lieutenant to Admiral Hope; and J. W. Gabriel; to the rank of commanders.

Messrs. R. Otway, C. Simon (Sparrowhawk), A. Henry, D. Ramsay (Victory), and John Fraser (Armide), to the rank of lieutenants.

Pursers.—T. Beatty, to the Queen Charlotte; ————- Williamson, to the Scipion ; William Peake, to the Blenheim ; W. Coe, to the Terrible; J. H. Simmons, to the Robust; —— Richards, to the Conquistadore; J. J. Ault, to the Atlas; John Goldsmith, to the Skiold ; J. Ross, to the Nymphe ; T. Reed, to the Nymphen ; T. Crisp, to the Temeraire; J. M. Perkins, to the Carriere ; J. Bryan, to the Madagascar ; J. Baker, to the Laurel ; T. Stone, to the Emerald; J Thompson, to the Wolf; H. Bamber, to the Fairy; W. W. Humphry, to the Andromeda; J. Overy, to the Aurora; E. Scott, to the Java.

Mr. Bruff, master of the Royal William, is appointed to superintend the Breakwater at Plymouth.

Richard Haig, Esq. to be secretary to Rear-admiral Langharne, at Malta, *vice* Rev. D. Evans, who returns from ill health ; J. Wilkinson, Esq. to be secretary to Admiral Martin.

Masters appointed.

John Jones, to the Phipps; William Petre, to the Orestes; George Tilferd, to the Snake; J. E. Harfield, to the Fox; J. Oake, to the Abundance store ship ; John Lewis, to the Hamadryad; J. Grant, to the Cornwall ; J. E. Rivers, to the Echo; K. M'Kenzie, to the Jasper; A. Burns, to the Ulysses; J. Hepburn, to the Impetueux ; J. T. Crout, to the Minden; W. Yeams, to the Acasta; T. Wiley, to the Crane; G. Stuart, to the Alonzo; R. Cubitt, to the Briton; A. M'Lean, to the San Juan ; Thomas Alltoft, to the York ; D. Murphy, to the Clarence; G. Scott, to the Narcissus; L. Fitzmaurice, to the Semiramis ; T. Kirkby, to the Valiant ; J. Selby, to the Tremendous ; N. Squires, to the Bellona ; James Wilshire, to the Cherokee ; Thomas Spence, to the Curlew ; Richard Haines, to the Stork ; William M'Cullock, to the Dover; John Tucker, to the Nassau; R. Worth, to the Ardent; J. Huntington, to the Salvador del Mundo ; T. Ruckhert, to the Namur; E. Strode, superintending master at Sheerness; Lewis John, to the Royal William ; P. Dall, to the Racoon ; Thomas Stapledon, to the Clarence ; S. Blyth, to the San Domingo; M. Robertson, superintending master at Portsmouth ; P. Inskip, to the Jalouse; D. Murphey, to the Minden ; C. Leach, to the Sabrina ; G. Turner, to the Egmont.

A List of Midshipmen who have passed for Lieutenants in June and July.

JUNE.

Sheerness.—R. Rust, William Hewett, G. P. Eyre, D. Rice, William Flynn, E. Hanswell, F. Coppin, E. Kennedy, T. Fowler, G. Inglis.

Portsmouth.—C. Batton, J. T. Appleby, W. Johnston, J. Faulkner, J. Godfrey, J. Foneraux, J. Dunn, R. Gibbes.

Plymouth.—R. Freeman, C. G. Randolph, A. Darley, C. W. Payne, A. T. Cope, G. H. Bowlby, A. H. Kellett, E. Dennis.

JULY.

Sheerness.—N. C. Whitmore, T. Carew, R. Hea, J. Jackson, G. Bunster, W. West, R. Bowen.
Portsmouth.—J. H. Rothery, R. Uniacke, T. D. Barron, J. Wood, W. Rolfe, J. Roche.
Plymouth.—John Fraser, R. Easto.

Surgeons, &c. appointed.

William Corsan, to be surgeon of the Shark; John Todd, to the Prometheus; R. H. Rogan, to the Minstrel; J. P. L. Michod, to the Crane; James Scott (2), to the Sybille; William Cupples, to the York; Thomas Alexander, to the Fox; James Caie, to the Ceres; William Shoveller, to the Cornwall; John Speer, to the Indian; A. Bennett, to the Arve Princen; J. J. Inger, to the Prometheus, *vice* John Todd, dismissed the service; Joseph M'Leod, to the Myrtle; James Clark, to the Colibri; G. S. Rutherford, to the Cherokee; H. Baillie, to the Clarence; J. Angus, to the Doterelle; James Campbell, to the Narcissus; Thomas Jones (2), to the Indefatigable; John M'Keen, to the Beaver; W. C. Brown, to the Dover; William Petrie, to the Alfred; William Jamison, to the Sampson P.S.; Edward Williams, to the Minden; William Aiton, to the Sabrina; Charles Stormouth, to the Union; William Graham, to the Curlew; Alexander Ross, to the Volontaire; G. H. Weatherhead, to the Prometheus: Ant. Patrickson, to the Helicon; John Williams, to the Circe; R. C. Swann, to the Fortunée; John Power, to the Buzzard; John Griffiths, to the Laurestinus; William Dartler, to the Thisbe; Primrose Lyon, to the Tweed; William Petrie, to the Childers; G. Cuming, to the Tyrian; J. Brydone, to the Asia; Patrick Walsh, to the Bittern; Robert Evans, to the Boyne; Thomas Heron, to the Brunswick P.S.; James Black, to the Raven; Alexander M'Pherson, to the Helicon; Donald Cameron, to the Sprightly cutter.

Assistant-Surgeons, &c. appointed.

John Temple, Peter Reid, Charles Stodart, George Wilson, John Beckett, to proceed as supernumerary assistant-surgeons to the Baltic; James Rae, to the Narcissus; Robert Macdowall, to be an hospital-mate at Antigua; Thomas Barnes, to the Mullet; John Curtis, to the Arrow; D. P. Williams, to the Minden; William Black (2), to be an hospital mate at Plymouth; Samuel Cumings, to the Locust G.B.; John Paterson, to the Pompée; A. M'Robert, to the Alfred; Alexander Gordon, to be hospital-mate at Norman Cross; John Cameron, to the Tribune; James Carruthers, to the Swift S.S.; George Webster, Alexander Linton, Archibald Campbell, to proceed to the Mediterranean as supernumeraries; M. Power, to the Impetueux; M. Burnside, to the Furious G.B.; Andrew Henderson, to the York; W. T. Hawke, to be hospital-mate at Plymouth; William Price, to the Clarence; Walter Gray, to be an hospital-mate at Plymouth; John Campbell, to the Cornwall; Thomas Thomas, to the Growler; Edward Keilly, to the Strenuous G.B.; Charles Sherratt, to the Barbados; Evan Bowen, to the Gloire; James Campbell, to the Clarence; William Black (1), to the Theseus; John Corsan, Thomas O'Gara, to Jamaica, as supernumerary surgeons; H. Compton, to be an hospital-mate at Haslar; D. Campbell, to the Clarence; C. B. Maguire, to the Martin; James Hill, to the Crocodile;

Charles Norman, to the Martial ; A. Kift, to the Urgent ; John Gilchrist, to the Dover ; William Plampin, to the Latona ; John Campbell, to the Sussex H.S.; Thomas Wallington, to the Emma convict ship ; J. Pollock, to the Porpoise ; John Hewitson, to the Royal Sovereign ; N. Roche, to the Impetueux ; James Burrell, to the Cornwall ; John Henderson, to the Elizabeth ; J. Nicol, to the Dictator ; Andrew Tymon, to the Gladiator ; Thomas Allison, Daniel Schaw, Alexander Watson, John Anderson, Thomas Rosser, Edward Joyce, Robert Wood, David Findlay, Alexander Heastie, William Price, to proceed to the East Indies as supernumeraries in the Minden ; William Burnie, to the Elizabeth ; Evan Bowen, to the Stately ; David Kissock, to the Vengeur ; William Price, to be an hospital mate at Plymouth ; Francis Cole, to be ditto at Haslar ; Thomas Robertson, to the St. Domingo ; George Glasson, to the Royal William ; Alexander Thompson, to the Andromache.

BIRTHS.

At Southampton, the lady of Captain Volant Vashon Ballard, R.N. of a daughter.

At Belmont Castle, the lady of Captain Prevost, R.N. of a daughter.

At Fareham, the lady of Captain Wainwright, R.N. of a son.

The lady of Lieutenant Bailey, R.N. of a daughter.

The lady of Captain Sir Peter Parker, Bart. of H.M.S. Menelaus, of a son.

June 24, at Hythe, the lady of Joseph Williamson, Esq. of H.M.S. Royal William, prematurely, of a still-born son.

MARRIAGES.

Lately, at Teignmouth, Devon, James Harding, Esq. of Upper Gower-street, Bedford-square, to Miss Pym, sister of Captain Pym, R.N. of H.M.S. Niemen.

At the Cove of Cork, Captain Young, R.N. to Mary, daughter of the late Sir Edwin Jeynes, of Gloucester.

Mr. Shoveller, of Portsea, surgeon of H.M.S. Conqueror, to Miss Marshall, of Hardway, near Gosport.

Mr. Jessop, purser R.N. to Miss Mary Pridham, daughter of Mr. John Pridham, merchant, of Plymouth.

The Hon. Captain Waldegrave, R.N. brother of Earl Waldegrave, to Miss Whitbread, daughter of Samuel Whitbread, Esq. M.P.

June 20, at Lisbon, the Earl of Euston, eldest son of the Duke of Grafton, to Mary, youngest daughter of the Hon. Admiral G. C. Berkeley, and niece to the Duke of Richmond.

June 28, at All Saints Church, Ryde, Lieutenant Wining, R.N. to Miss Crane.

OBITUARY.

Lately, at Java, Mr. Hamilton, assistant-surgeon of H.M.S. President.

At Jamaica, Captain Perkins, R.N.

At Mahon, Lieutenant Harrington, of H.M.S. Ocean.

At Plymouth, G. Gifferena, Esq. aged 78. He was many years secretary to the late Admiral Lord Graves, of Thancks, in the county of Cornwall.

At Portsea, aged 79, Mr. Crane, late first-master-attendant at Portsmouth. This gentleman went into the navy in the year 1755.

At Saltwood, the Rev. Brook John Bridges, brother to Lieutenant Sir Brook W. Bridges, Bart. R.N. and rector of Saltwood cum Hythe, Kent.

At Fowey, of a decline, Mrs. M'Cleverty, wife of Mr. H. M'Cleverty, master of the Hibernia.

Mr. W. Pollard, late of the Marine Library, Brighton.

At Belle-Vue Terrace, Southsea, the infant son of Captain John Price, R.N.

Lieutenant R. Heacock, commander of the St. Antonio prison ship, Portsmouth.

At the advanced age of 82, the Rev. Richard Keats, rector of Bideford and King's Nympton, in the county of Devon, and father of Vice-admiral Sir R. G. Keats, K.B.

In April, on board the Mackerel schooner, on her way to New York, Lieutenant Parker, the commander of the schooner: he was killed by the falling of a man upon him from the mast head.

April 29, Mr. George Atkinson, midshipman on board H.M.S. Leviathan, son of Mr. Atkinson, brandy-merchant, of Bath. He fell by a grape-shot, whilst in the act of cutting the cable of a privateer of 14 guns, which he had boarded in an affair near Villa Franca.

June 2, at Paris, Admiral De Winter. This officer commanded the Dutch fleet in the battle of Camperdown, October 11, 1797; and it is said, that, after a most gallant defence, he was the only man left on the quarter-deck of his ship, who was not either killed or wounded. He struck his flag to Admiral Duncan, and was brought prisoner to London.*—Admiral De Winter, who always bore the character of a brave and honourable man, was greatly esteemed. He commanded in the Texel during the last winter.†

July 4, at Brockhurst Cottage, near Gosport, John Dredge, Esq. 40 years in the navy, and purser of his Majesty's ship Le Pegase.

July 7, at Stonehouse, Captain Jardine, R.M.

July 10, at Dundalk, in Ireland, in the 23d year of his age, the Hon. James Bligh Jocelyn, second son of the Earl of Roden, and a lieutenant in the R.N.

July 21, Mr. Henry Methuen Bailward, late of the Pomone frigate.

---

* The details of this memorable engagement will be found in our Memoir of Admiral Lord Duncan, N. C. iv. 107.

† *Vide* his Report to the Minister of the Marine and Colonies, relating to the loss of H.M.S. Manilla, N. C. xxvii. 417.

BIOGRAPHICAL MEMOIR

OF THE LATE

SIR JOHN BALCHEN, KNT.

ADMIRAL OF THE WHITE SQUADRON, AND GOVERNOR
OF GREENWICH HOSPITAL.

" Such were the laurels which your fathers won;
Such Glory's dictates in their dauntless breast."

SIR JOHN BALCHEN, whose name stands high upon the list of our naval worthies, was born on the 2d of February, 1669. With his particular services, prior to his attainment of post rank, we are unacquainted; but he is known to have made a very early choice of a naval life; and, by every writer, who has noticed his professional progress, it is agreed, that he passed regularly, and with the highest credit, through every subordinate gradation.

If the monumental record of his services, in Westminster Abbey, be correct, Mr. Balchen entered the navy about the year 1686. He was appointed captain of the Virgin, or Virginia Prize, a frigate of 32 guns, on the 25th of July, 1697; but it was not until ten years after that period, that he is known to have been employed in any affair of note.—In 1707, he commanded the Chester, of 50 guns; and, in the month of September, in that year, he was ordered, with the Ruby, of the same force, to convoy the fleet to Lisbon. The protection of this fleet was of the utmost consequence; as, independently of its intrinsic value, the whole of the provisions, and stores, and upwards of a thousand horses, for the service of the ensuing campaign, in Spain, were on board. It was consequently thought proper to strengthen the convoy, by the addition of two ships of 80 guns each, and one of 76. The convoying squadron then stood as follows :—

Ships.	Guns.	Commanders.
Cumberland	80	Commodore Richard Edwards.
Devonshire	80	Captain John Watkins.
Royal Oak	76	———— ————.Wilde.
Chester	50	———— John Balchen.
Ruby	50	———— ———— ————.

With the Cumberland, Devonshire, and Royal Oak, it was intended that Commodore Edwards * should see the fleet fifty leagues to the S.W. of Scilly, where, it was presumed, they would be completely out of danger of the Dunkirk squadron.

The fleet sailed on the 9th of October; and, as the French were not, at that time, believed to have any force of consequence at Brest, not the least apprehension as to its safety was entertained. A want of due information, however, on that point, proved fatal. By the treasonable conduct of individuals, the enemy were, from time to time, accurately apprized of the equipment, force, and destination of this squadron; and, on the 10th of October, the very day after it sailed, it was encountered, off the Lizard, by the combined squadrons of le Comte de Forbin, and M. du Guai Trouin. With a force so decidedly superior—consisting of at least twelve ships of the line—it was scarcely possible to contend, with any hope of success. The commodore, however, took every measure which prudence could suggest, and gallantry impel; and, in his meritorious efforts, he received from

---

* This officer was appointed second lieutenant of the Plymouth, on the 3d of September, 1688; on the 10th of March, 1690, he was made post in the Greenwich; in 1693, he was captain of the Kent, of 70 guns, in the Channel fleet; in 1695, he commanded the Chichester, of 80 guns, one of the ships belonging to the small squadron which was sent under the command of Lord Berkeley and Sir Cloudesley Shovel, to attack the smaller French ports; in 1696, he removed into the Severn, of 50 guns; and, after the accession of Queen Anne, he was appointed to the Berwick, of 70 guns, one of Sir George Rooke's fleet, in the expedition against Cadiz. On that occasion, Captain Edwards acted as one of the seconds to Rear-admiral Graydon; and, in the subsequent attack on Vigo, he was stationed as one of the seconds to Sir Stafford Fairborne, who commanded the third division. In 1703, he went to the Mediterranean, under Sir C. Shovel, and was stationed to lead the van of the British squadron, on the starboard tack. Returning to England, in the following autumn, he quitted the command of the Berwick; and nothing farther is known of him, till the year 1707, when he was appointed commodore of the squadron that was to convoy the Lisbon fleet. He was released from captivity in the following year, tried by a court martial for the loss of his ship, and most honourably acquitted. He is not known to have gone to sea again; but, in 1711, he was appointed Commissioner of the Navy, at Plymouth. He held that office till 1714, when he retired on a pension of 250*l.* a year. He died on the 2d of March, 1723.

his colleagues all the support which the most determined bravery could afford. Having formed his line, Commodore Edwards made a signal to the merchant ships, to make all the sail they could, and then dropped in between them and the enemy. A desperate action commenced. About noon, M. du Guai Trouin himself, supported by his two seconds, attacked the commodore's ship (the Cumberland), which, after an obstinate and bloody conflict, was compelled to strike. The conduct of Captain Watkins, in the Devonshire, was not less conspicuous. He defended himself for nearly three hours, against seven of the enemy's ships, and, for four hours more, against five. The approach of night then seemed to hold forth some chance of success; but, suddenly, the Devonshire took fire, blew up, and, with the exception of two men, consigned the whole of her crew to eternity!* Captain Balchen's ship, the Chester, after a defence which rendered her worthy of her companions, became the prize of le Comte de Forbin himself; who, notwithstanding the overwhelming superiority of his force precluded every claim to glory, was wonderfully elated with his success, which, with their accustomed adroitness, the French took ample care to magnify.† The Ruby (the name of whose captain we are unacquainted with) was also overpowered by numbers, and compelled to submit; but the Royal Oak, Captain Wilde, after a vigorous resistance, got safe into Kinsale harbour.‡ During the engagement, the merchantmen crowded sail, and, subsequently, arrived in safety at Lisbon.

---

* This brave officer was made post in the Seaford, on the 14th of August, 1696. In 1706, he commanded the St. George, of 90 guns, Sir John Jennings's flag-ship, in the Mediterranean; and he distinguished himself at the storming of Alicant, being the third officer who entered the town. In the autumn of the same year, he removed, with Sir John Jennings, into the Devonshire, and went to the West Indies. He returned from the West Indies, in April, 1707; and, in October, as appears above, / he sailed with the squadron to convoy the Lisbon fleet. The merchants, whose ships escaped the fate of their protectors, attributed their safety, in a great measure, to the noble defence made by this unfortunate commander.

† Campbell, however, candidly observes, that " all the French relations do us the justice to own, that our captains behaved extremely well, and that their victory cost them very dear."

‡ Captain Wilde's escape was the subject of much censure and party

Captain Balchen was exchanged in the autumn of the following year (1708); and, on the 27th of October, he was tried by a

contention. That he fought bravely, cannot be denied; but that he broke the line, and pushed through the French squadron, to save himself, before the commodore, or any of his companions, had surrendered, is fully apparent. The facts of the case seem to be circumstantially related in the following extract of a letter, from on board the Royal Oak, dated Kinsale, October 12, 1807:—

" On the 10th instant, off the Deadman, Commodore Edwards, in the Cumberland, with the Devonshire, Chester, Ruby, and Royal Oak, discovered fourteen French ships, five between sixty and seventy guns, five of fifty, and four of forty guns. The commodore made a signal for a line abreast standing under top-sails, the enemy bearing down upon us at twelve at noon; the commodore of the French, after having passed the Chester, and received her broadside without returning so much as a musket, made directly to the commodore. As soon as they were abreast, they both began to fire, as did several others of the enemy's ships, and engaged the Chester and Ruby; at the same time a ship of seventy guns came along our starboard quarter, endeavouring to board us. We began to fire; but finding the enemy would not come alongside, gave our ship a yaw to the starboard, upon which his bowsprit carried away our ensign staff and lanthorn. As he passed under our stern he fired a broadside into us; but, as he shot along our larboard quarter, we returned it with double and round. In firing along our larboard, we saw, he had a design to board us upon the bow, another ship of 60 guns coming up to sustain him. We clapt our helm hard a-starboard, and came so near, that our bowsprit took his quarter, and carried it away with our head, which brought him to. As he came up along by our starboard side, we gave him again our broadside, with double and round. He immediately took fire, but it was extinguished in five minutes; and after the smoke was over, we saw him on the careen. In less than an hour's time, we saw our commodore's fore-mast, mizen-mast, and bowsprit, shot away, and a cluster of five or six ships on board each other, without firing on either side. *Hereupon our captain, after a consultation with his officers, thought fit to endeavour at saving the ship. The Devonshire at the same time bore down upon us, and was soon after followed by seven sail of the enemy; upon which we made all the sail we could.* The Devonshire made sail with her larboard tacks, and we quartering with our starboard tacks, all the seven sail made after the Devonshire, by reason, as is supposed, of the convoy a-head. As long as we could see their hulls, the Devonshire maintained the fight. We had in this engagement, twelve men killed, twenty-seven dangerously wounded, and the ship very much damaged."

Captain Wilde, as well as Commodore Edwards and Captain Balchen, was tried by a court martial; but, while they were honourably acquitted, he was dismissed from the service. The treatment which he subsequently

court martial, for the loss of his ship, and most honourably acquitted.

He is not mentioned again, till the year 1717, when he commanded the Orford, of 70 guns. At that time, the Swedes very much annoyed our trade in the Baltic; and Sir George Byng was consequently sent thither, with a fleet of twenty-one ships of the line, besides frigates. Captain Balchen went with this fleet, which remained in the Baltic the whole of the summer, in a state of comparative inactivity, and then returned.

In the following year, he accompanied Sir George Byng to the Mediterranean; where, on his arrival, he became captain to Viceadmiral Cornwall, who hoisted his flag on board the Shrewsbury, as second in command of the fleet.*—Campbell, and other naval

---

experienced, however, seems to indicate, that even the Sovereign thought him rather unfortunate than criminal—that his misconduct originated in an error of judgment, and not in a defect of personal bravery. He was afterwards restored to the service, and allowed to rank from the 7th of October, 1707, three days before the action took place; and, in the year 1724, he obtained his original seniority, and, consequently, became a Rear-admiral.

This officer (Baron Wilde, or Wylde), according to Hardy, took post rank in the Winchelsea, on the 24th of December, 1694. In 1695, he commanded the Northumberland, of 70 guns, one of the ships employed, under Sir Cloudesley Shovel, in the blockade of Dunkirk, and in the bombardment of Calais. In 1703, he was tried by a court martial, at Portsmouth, and honourably acquitted; but the charges against him are not upon record. In 1704, he commanded the Firm, of 70 guns, in which he greatly distinguished himself in the battle of Malaga. In the spring of 1707, he was employed, in the Royal Oak, as senior officer, or commodore, of a squadron which was appointed to convoy the trade to Portugal and the West Indies. Unfortunately, he fell in with the Dunkirk squadron, commanded by le Comte de Forbin, who attacked him, and, after a very obstinate contest, captured two of the English ships of war (the Grafton and the Hampton Court) out of three, and several of the merchant vessels. Forbin's squadron consisted of ten sail of the line, a frigate, and four large privateers. Captain Wilde drew five of the stoutest merchantmen into the line, and fought bravely for two hours and a half. He compelled two of the French men of war to sheer off, greatly disabled, and at length got safe into Dungeness.—The damages which the Royal Oak had sustained in this action were scarcely repaired, when Captain Wilde was employed on a similar service, as appears above, under Commodore Edwards.—After attaining the rank of Rear-admiral, he died on the 25th of September, 1733.

* The Spaniards having sent a powerful fleet and army to attack the

historians, down to Schomberg, place the Shrewsbury in the van division of Sir George Byng's fleet, when it engaged that of the Spanish Admiral Castaneta, off Cape Passaro, in Sicily, on the 11th of August, 1718; but Charnock is of opinion, "from many concurrent circumstances," (not one of which, however, does he specify) that, for some service or other, the Shrewsbury had previously been detached. In the present case, the point, perhaps, is not of much importance; but it is worth noticing, that Sir George Byng, in his account of the engagement, makes no mention of Admiral Cornwall, or of his flag-ship, the Shrewsbury.

After Captain Balchen's return from the Mediterranean, he was appointed to a 70-gun ship, the command of which he retained till he became a flag-officer, and was consequently always employed in those annual and harmless expeditions, which took place during the remainder of the reign of George the Ist.—In the spring of 1720, he sailed with Sir John Norris into the Baltic, with the view of protecting the Swedish coasts against the Russians. In 1721, the Russians still continuing hostile to the Swedes, Captain Balchen again proceeded to the Baltic with Sir John Norris; and, being one of the oldest captains in the fleet, he was stationed to lead on the larboard tack. In 1726, it was resolved to send a strong fleet into the Baltic, to overawe the Czarina; and, the command having been given to Sir Charles Wager, Captain Balchen accompanied him thither, as one of his seconds: in 1727, he filled the same post to Sir John Norris, on the same station. In the former year, the Russians were incompetent to resent the appearance of the British fleet; and, in the latter, the death of the Czarina prevented any hostilities from taking place.

On his return from the Baltic, in 1727, Captain Balchen proceeded to Gibraltar, under the command of Sir George Walton, who was sent thither with a reinforcement to Sir Charles Wager. He remained there, without meeting with any interesting occurrence; excepting that he was appointed temporary commodore of

---

possessions of the King of Naples, on the island of Sicily, the British Government, which had determined to protect the House of Austria in its rights, and to maintain the neutrality of Italy, sent Sir George Byng, with a powerful fleet, to the Mediterranean, for that purpose.

a small squadron, which was ordered to cruise between Cape St. Mary and Cadiz, till the month of January, 1728, when he returned to England with Sir George Walton.

On the 19th of July following, Captain Balchen was promoted to the rank of Rear-admiral of the Blue Squadron; having, at that time, been forty-two years in the service, thirty-one of which he had passed as a private captain. On the 4th of March, 1729, he was advanced to be Rear-admiral of the White; but he did not hoist his flag till the summer of the year 1731, when he went out second in command of the fleet which was sent, under Sir Charles Wager, to Cadiz and the Mediterranean. The objects of this expedition were, to take possession of Leghorn; to place Don Carlos on the throne of Naples; and to see other points of inferior consequence carried into effect, according to the treaty of Vienna.

Charnock states, that Rear-admiral Balchen first hoisted his flag in the Dreadnought, at Spithead; but that, soon after the arrival of Sir Charles Wager from the Downs, with part of the fleet, he shifted it into the Princess Amelia, in which he continued during the remainder of the expedition. On this occasion, Schomberg's list of Sir Charles Wager's fleet, which places the Rear-admiral's flag in the Norfolk, of 80 guns, Captain Roberts, seems preferably entitled to credit.

The fleet arrived at Cadiz on the 6th of August, and was joined by a Spanish squadron under the command of the Marquis de Mari. Sir Charles Wager then went to Madrid; and, with Mr. Keene, the British envoy there, concerted such measures as were necessary to be pursued on the occasion; after which he returned to Cadiz, and resumed the command of the combined fleet. He put to sea on the 6th of October, and, on the 15th, arrived at Leghorn: where, after some conferences holden with the Grand Duke of Tuscany's minister, the Spanish troops were permitted to land.—The objects of the expedition having been effected, the fleet left the Mediterranean, and arrived at Spithead on the 10th of December.

On the 16th of February, 1733, the subject of this memoir was promoted to the rank of Vice-admiral of the White; and, in 1734, he was appointed commander-in-chief of a small squadron, which was collected at Plymouth, with the view of being sent as a reinforcement to Sir John Norris, on the Lisbon station, should not the dispute between Portugal and Spain be amicably adjusted. The storm, however, blew over, and the Vice-admiral's services were, for a time, dispensed with.—On the 2d of March, 1736, he was advanced to the Red Squadron; but he was not employed till 1739; when, Spain continuing obstinate in the refusal of the terms which were offered her by Great Britain, it became necessary to prepare for war. Many ships were, consequently, put into commission; war was declared on the 23d of October; and Vice-admiral Balchen was amongst the first officers who were selected for important commands. He was sent to the Mediterranean, with six sail of the line, to reinforce Admiral Haddock,* and to take the chief command. " The first intended enterprise of their united force was, to intercept the Assogue ships, which were daily expected at Cadiz from Vera Cruz, laden with the usual tribute of treasure, the annual produce of that part of the Western World dependant on Spain. This fleet was actually on its passage, and steering a course which would have inevitably thrown them into the hands of the English, but, unfortunately, Admiral Pizarro, who commanded the convoy, having, by mere accident, received information of the situation of affairs in Europe, he stretched to the northward, and instead of making the Madeiras, and steering for Cadiz by that which was the usual route, he stood away to the northward of the Bahamas, and returned to Europe in the track used by the ships bound from the West Indies for the British Channel. He actually made the Lizard; and from thence standing over to Ushant, by creeping close under the shore he eluded the vigilance of the British cruisers, both off the coast of Spain and in the Bay of Biscay, and arrived in perfect safety at the port of St. Andero." †

The Vice-admiral's services being no longer necessary in the Mediterranean, he returned to England, and, during the latter end of the year 1740, he had the command of a squadron in the Channel.

---

* N. C. XXVII. 97.

† Charnock's *Biographia Navalis*, Vol. III. page 158.

On the 9th of August, 1743, he was made Admiral of the White Squadron; and, early in 1744, as a just reward for his long and faithful services, he was appointed (as the successor of Sir John Jennings, who died on the 23d of December, 1743) to be Governor of Greenwich Hospital. Soon afterwards, his Majesty was also pleased to confer upon him the honour of knighthood.

The year 1744 is, on many accounts, memorable in the annals of the British navy. In the month of January, a French fleet, consisting of twenty-three sail of men of war, which had been equipped at Brest, entered the Channel, with the view of sailing to Dunkirk, where it was to be joined by a fleet of transports, with Charles Edward, son to the Pretender, and an army of 20,000 men on board, for the purpose of invading England, and supporting the Pretender's claims. Aware of this armament, the British Government appointed Sir John Norris, with a superior force, to cruise in the Downs, and the intentions of the enemy were, in consequence, frustrated. On the 20th of March, France issued a formal declaration of war against England; and, on the 31st of the same month, the compliment was returned on the part of the British. His Majesty also wrote a letter to the States General, to request the aid of a naval force, as stipulated by treaty; and, of twenty sail, for the equipment of which directions were immediately given, fifteen actually arrived, in a short time. Various other circumstances, which it is here unnecessary to enumerate, contributed to render this a very critical period. Amongst others, however, Sir Charles Hardy, who had convoyed the trade, and a number of store-ships, to Lisbon, with eleven sail of the line, was blocked up in the Tagus, by a greatly superior French force, under the command of M. le Comte de Rochambault.* Sir John Balchen, it might have been expected, would be allowed to pass the remainder of his life in peaceful and honourable retirement; more particularly as he had reached an advanced age, and as he laboured under many infirmities, the natural result of his long and active services. Such, however, were the necessities of his country, and such was the spirit of this

---

* N. C. XIX. 94.

brave and gallant officer, that he did not hesitate to accept the command of a fleet, which it was found necessary expeditiously to equip, for the purpose of releasing Sir Charles Hardy.

Early in July, a fleet of fourteen British ships of the line had assembled at Spithead; and Sir John Balchen hoisted his flag, as commander-in-chief, on board the Victory, of 110 guns, the largest and finest ship in the navy. " She was manned," says Charnock, " with a chosen crew of 1100 men; and had, besides, upwards of fifty young gentlemen on board, some of them belonging to families of the first distinction, who entered as volunteers, ambitious to serve, and learn the first rudiments of naval tactics under so worthy and able a commander. On the 15th a squadron of seven Dutch ships of the line, and two frigates, came up to Spithead, under the command of four admirals; and Sir John having a special commission for that purpose, assumed the command of the whole."

The combined force was then as follows:—

British Division.

Ships.	Guns.	Commanders.
Victory	110	{ Sir J. Balchen, Knt. Admiral of the White. { Captain S. Faulknor.
Hampton Court	70	——— S. Mostyn.
Augusta	60	——— Hon. J. Hamilton.
Captain	70	——— T. Griffin.
Princess Amelia	80	——— Edward Spragge.
St. George	90	{ Vice-admiral Wm. Martin. { Captain R. Martin.
Suffolk	70	——— T. Grenville.
Falkland	50	——— Edward Pratten.
Exeter	60	——— T. Broderick.
Duke	90	{ Vice-admiral James Stewart. { Captain T. Trevor.
Sunderland	60	——— J. Brett.
Monmouth	70	——— H. Harrison.
Prince Frederick	70	——— H. Norris.
Princess Mary	60	——— T. Smith.
Etna } Fire-ships. Scipio }	8 8	——— David Brodie.
Fly sloop	14	——— Hon. A. Steuart.

Dutch Division:

Haerlem	76	Admiral Baccarest.
Dordrecht	54	Vice-admiral Hooft.

Ships.	Guns.	Commanders.
Damiata	54	Captain Schryver.
Leeuwenhorst	54	Rear-admiral Reynst.
Edam	54	Captain Fransel.
Assendelft	54	—— Boudaan.
Delft	54	—— Wallestyn.
———— } Frigates.	—	—— ———.

This formidable fleet left Spithead on the 7th of August, and proceeded for Portugal, with upwards of 200 sail of merchant ships under its convoy; but, impeded by contrary winds, and encumbered by the extensiveness of its charge, it did not arrive off the rock of Lisbon till the 9th of September. Count Rochambault, apprized of the approach of this superior force, had prudently retreated to Cadiz. Sir John Balchen was immediately joined by Sir Charles Hardy, with his squadron, and the store-ships which were with him; and the fleet then proceeded to Gibraltar, the reinforcement, and supply of which, with provisions and military stores, had been the first object of Sir Charles Hardy's voyage.

After Gibraltar had been succoured, and placed in a proper posture of defence, Sir John Balchen returned to cruise off the coast of Portugal for some days, in the hope that, with the view of getting back to Brest, Rochambault might have taken an opportunity of slipping out. In this expectation he was disappointed; and, finding that Rochambault cautiously confined his fleet within the harbour of Cadiz, he quitted the coast of Gallicia on the 28th of September, and, on the 30th, entered the Bay of Biscay on his return to England. On the 3d of October, the whole fleet was dispersed in a violent storm, and many of the ships were, with the greatest difficulty, prevented from foundering. Excepting the Victory, however, all of them, though in a very shattered state, arrived at Spithead by the 10th of October. That noble ship separated from her companions on the 4th, and was never heard of afterwards! It is supposed that she struck upon a ridge of rocks, off the Caskets; as, from the testimony of the men who attended the lights, and of the inhabitants of the island of Alderney, many signals of distress were heard on the nights of the 4th and 5th of October, but the weather was too tempestuous for boats to venture out. Thus, instantaneously, as it were, perished the finest ship of the finest navy in the world, with her veteran commander, and nearly twelve hundred of his brave associates!

"———— Poor souls, they perished!
Had I been any god of power, I would
Have sunk the sea within the earth, or e'er
It should the good ship so have swallowed, and
The freighting souls within her."

For a time, this sudden and unforeseen calamity overwhelmed the nation with sorrow. A naval event, so poignantly distressing, had not occurred since the loss of Sir Cloudesley Shovel, on the rocks of Scilly, in the year 1707.

His Majesty, to compensate the mourning widow, as far as a pecuniary grant might be considered a compensation, for a loss so severe—or rather as a reward for the long and faithful services of the deceased—settled a pension of 500*l. per annum* on Lady Balchen. That Lady, in commemoration of the virtues, public actions, and premature death of her husband, caused a small, but elegant monument to be erected in Westminster Abbey, bearing the following inscription :—

" Sir John Balchen, Knight, Admiral of the White Squadron of his Majesty's Fleet, who, in the year 1744, being sent out commander-in-chief of the combined Fleets of England and Holland, to cruise on the enemy, was, on his return home, in his Majesty's ship the Victory, lost in the Channel by a violent storm ; from which sad circumstance of his death we may learn, that neither the greatest skill, judgment, or experience, joined to the most unshaken resolution, can resist the fury of the winds and waves: and we are taught from the passages of his life, which were filled with great and gallant actions, but accompanied with adverse gales of fortune, that the brave, the worthy, and the good man, meets not always his reward in this world. Fifty-eight years of faithful and painful service he had passed, when, being just retired to the government of Greenwich Hospital to wear out the remainder of his days, he was once more, and for the last time, called out by his King and Country, whose interest he ever prefered to his own ; and his unwearied zeal for their service ended only with his life, which weighty misfortune to his afflicted family became heightened by many aggravating circumstances attending it. Yet, amidst their grief, they had the mournful consolation to find his gracious and Royal Master mixing his concern with the general lamentations of the public for the calamitous fate of so zealous, so valiant, and so able a commander; and, as a lasting memorial of sincere love and affection borne by his widow to a most affectionate and worthy husband, this honorary monument was erected by her.

" He was born February 2d, 1669. Married Susannah, the daughter of Colonel Apreece, of Washingly, in the county of Huntingdon. Died October the 7th [4th] 1744, leaving one son and one daughter; the former of whom, George Balchen, survived him but a short time, for, being sent to the West Indies, in 1745, commander of his Majesty's ship the Pembroke, he died, at Barbados, in December the same year, aged twenty-eight, having walked in the steps, and imitated the virtues and bravery of his good, but unfortunate father."

Captain Balchen, whose name is recorded on his father's monument, is understood to have been brought up in the profession, under the immediate eye of Sir John. On the 12th of September, 1740, he was made captain, in the Greyhound; and, in 1742, he commanded the Folkestone, of 44 guns, on the Mediterranean station, and, under Commodore Barnet, bore a distinguished share in the encounter with the Chevalier de Caylus. After he returned to England, he was promoted to the Pembroke, and ordered to the West Indies, where he died in the prime of life, universally regretted, on the 18th of December, 1745.

NAVAL ANECDOTES, COMMERCIAL HINTS, RECOLLECTIONS, &c.

NANTES IN GURGITE VASTO.

MERIT AND GRATITUDE.

AFTER the Prince Regent's levee, on Friday, 29 May, the following address was presented to Captain (now Sir Christopher) Cole, R.N. by Mr. Barker, of Portsmouth, in the name of H. M. S. Caroline's crew, accompanied by the donation of a sword :—

" Sir ! I am requested by James Macdowal, and others, on behalf of the crew of H.M.'s frigate Caroline, to present you with this sword, as a testimony of the high esteem and respect they entertain for you as their late commander, in return for the marked attention you, at all times, paid to them ; for the gallant manner in which you took them into action, and for the honourable manner you brought them out; for the unceasing zeal you invariably have manifested for your country's cause, and for the comforts they enjoyed whilst they served under your command,—they humbly trust you will accept the same, as a pledge of gratitude and token of veneration for you, which time can never efface from their memory. I remain, Sir, in behalf of the crew, your most obedient and humble servant,

"*Portsmouth, May* 28, 1812.   " JOHN BARKER."
" Captain C. Cole, *late of H. M.'s Frigate*
Caroline."

A present and an address of this kind, from private men to their *late* commander, is a new thing, and must be regarded as a compliment of the highest and most valuable description. Captain Cole having ceased to command these brave fellows, it is obvious that no feelings can exist, but those of the respect, admiration, and gratitude which they profess; and, by the same circumstance, this proceeding is exempted from those exceptions which, in the view of strict discipline, some persons might otherwise be disposed to make, to any such demonstrations from military persons, toward those to whom they are subordinate.

SHIPS, COLONIES, AND COMMERCE.

A GENTLEMAN, recently arrived from Paris, states, that Buonaparte's grand plan, on which he depended for a supply of sugar, has been totally abandoned. It was found that the extract from the beet-root did not answer the purpose, on several accounts. The grape produced a saccharine substance, nearest in resemblance to sugar produced from the cane; but there was this disadvantage attending the manufacture of sugar from grapes, that when the juice was kept to a certain season of the year, a fermentation took place, which spoiled the whole process. Indigo has also failed, but cotton has succeeded, and is stated to be equal in quality to the best article of the kind from Berbice. Several cargoes which had been produced in Italy had arrived in France from Naples, and was a circumstance of great congratulation.

ICHTHYOLOGY.

A SUN-FISH, of the enormous weight of 342*lbs.* 7*oz.* was taken off Plymouth a short time ago. This remarkable fish, which appears to be almost peculiar to the Devon and Cornish coasts, is termed by Pennant, the oblong diodon. In form it resembles the bream, or any other deep seafish, *cut off in the middle.* One of these remarkable fish, which weighed 500*lbs.* was taken about the beginning of the present century, near Plymouth, but they are mostly found near Mount's Bay, in Cornwall.

IMPROVEMENT IN THE KEEPING OF WATER, IN SHIPS.

A SLOOP arrived lately at Portsmouth, with 52 cast-iron water-tanks which are to be fitted into H. M. S. Minden. They hold two tuns each; and the object is, to find a substitute for the present mode of keeping and preserving water on board ship, and in a more compact form.

A SAILOR'S JOKE.

WHEN the Pigmy cutter some time last war had just come to an anchor off Venice, she was visited by one of the state gondolas or barges from the town, the awnings and other equipments of which were made (as they all in general are) of black velvet, richly ornamented with tassels, &c. The boatswain's mate, who attended the side upon the occasion, came below immediately afterwards, and addressed one of his companions with " D— my eyes, Jack, what d'ye think's just come alongside—a hearse by G—d!"

IRISH PRISONERS IN FRANCE.

PIERCE KIRWAN, of Dungarvan, and Marcus M'Causland, of Belfast, have recently returned to the places of their nativity, having effected their escape from the *dépôt* of British prisoners at Auxonne. The details of the plans they adopted to secure their deliverance, of the manner in which they travelled, and of the treatment they experienced, are not in our possession—but some idea may be formed of the toils and perils which the love of liberty and of home induced them to encounter, from the bare mention of the countries through which they traversed. Having accomplished their escape from custody, they passed through Switzerland, Bavaria, Austria, Hungary, and part of Turkey—in one of the ports of the last of these countries, they embarked for Malta, and were thence conveyed in safety to the British Empire. At the time of their departure from the *dépôt*, on the 19th of January, 1811, they left behind them the following prisoners, belonging to the City of Waterford :—Allen Crawford, Thomas Walsh, John Power, Thomas Hogan, James Waters, John Cluine, Alexander Ross, Thomas Street, James Neill, and Mr. Crawford's mate.

One of these prisoners, a young gentleman who has long witnessed and deeply deplored the sufferings of his unhappy countrymen, has written several impressive letters in their behalf to his brother in Waterford, in which he details their privations and distress in most pathetic terms. In one of these letters, he says :—

" The persons who are prisoners in this *dépôt*, (Auxonne) belonging to Waterford and its vicinity, are in a situation miserable beyond the power of language to describe. They are but few in number, and even a small sum would be of essential and infinite service. It is true, that some money has been remitted for their relief, but the person, to whose care the distribution was entrusted, gave it without discrimination, and thus, unhappily, rendered it of little avail. The English prisoners are in a state of much greater comfort, for they are supported by liberal subscriptions, raised in the various districts to which they belong."

In another letter, the same benevolent youth speaks in the following terms, and subjoins a list which must be peculiarly interesting :—" I must remind you again, of the miserable condition of the poor fellows in this *dépôt* (Auxonne), belonging to Waterford and its vicinity. I give you their names, and assure you, that some of them, whose friends at home are unable to send assistance, are in a state the most lamentable and afflicting. I have represented to some of them, who are in extreme distress, that I would write to you on the subject, in the full expectation, that the merchants, and other charitable inhabitants of Waterford and its vicinity, would, on a representation of circumstances, collect something for their support, and they rest in the most sanguine confidence, that their hapless lot will not be forgotten."—The names are as follows :—Thomas Walsh, Allen Crawford, Daniel Croneen, James Prendergast, John Ryan, Thomas Hogan, James Sly, Richard Phelan, Joseph Phelan, Martin Power, Daniel Mahony, James Phelan, Francis Fitzgerald, John Power, John Buckley, Thomas Street, John Phelan, James Neil, William Tobyn, Nicholas Conden, Daniel Merrigan, Joseph Hearn, James Carew, Peter Mealey.

The above-mentioned prisoners were subsequently removed from Auxonne to Longwy.—The following Irish prisoners were, not long since, at the places specified :—

At Arras.—Richard Phelan, James Phelan, James Bryan, James Prendergast, Darby Bryan, Laurence Delahunty, Edward Hobin, James Carey.

At Bitche.—Laurence Callahan, Patrick Murphy.

At Cambray.—Edmond Manigan; Chapel-lane, James Bryan, do. J. Keough, George's-street, William Morgan, do. Andrew Lannen, George's Square, J. Spleen, Patrick-street, Andrew Madden, Patrick Square, Edward Morgan.

PARTICULARS OF THE ACTION BETWEEN H. M. S. BELVIDERA, AND AN AMERICAN SQUADRON, OFF SANDY-HOOK.*

Extract of a Letter from an Officer on board H. M. S. Belvidera, dated Halifax, June 27.

" You will perceive by reports, which doubtless have reached England, that our little vessel can do something for her country. The event has been fortunate, and a source of joy and happiness to us. On the 23d, at daylight, five sail were seen in chase of a merchantman, all standing before the wind. We chased, and discovered them to be men of war. The tables were soon turned, by our being chased: at twelve o'clock, the headmost ship, the President, was within gun-shot and an half; the United States within two gun-shots; and the Essex about three gun-shots. At half-past twelve the President topped his sprit-sail-yard to windward. We then expected a shot, but all remained quiet ;—piped to dinner ;—the President at some distance till three o'clock, when she began to draw on us, having got the wind first; the whole of us being before the wind : at about ten minutes before four, she then being three cables length from us, she gave us a shot right through the rudder-coat, which damaged the rudder; two more shots were fired, the second of which killed one man, and wounded several others. This shot being of a bad quality, it split into about fifty pieces. One of the men, who died twenty-four hours after his wounds, had his arms amputated high up, and would have lived had not two of his ribs been fractured and driven into his lungs ; notwithstanding which, after his wounds were dressed, he wanted to go on deck to have another shot at the cowards (so he termed them). The rest of the

* *Vide* page 73.

wounded have merely flesh wounds, except one, who has a large splinter in the knee, but will not lose the limb. Our captain, officers, and men, were cool and determined. The fine fellows asked the captain if they should give it them?

" Poor Captain Byron has received a violent contusion in the upper and inside part of the thigh, which, by the surgeon's account, will turn to an abscess, and will be well in about a fortnight. The President's commander is a coward; he might have been alongside of us had he chosen it. He gave us seven or eight broadsides, independent of his bow guns; we tickled him with four, and only four stern chasers, which were well applied to his bows. They were thrown into confusion, and I doubt not that many of the Yankeys have left off messing. Our stern is cut much with their grape, but that did not kill any men. Six shots struck our counter, one went through our main-top-mast, and another through our cross-jack-yard, from their trying to disable us in our rigging, and we to hull them. The annexed is a statement of our weight of metal, as compared with that of our American antagonists :—Belvidera, twenty-six 18-pounders, two 9-pounders, fourteen 32-pounders, 42 guns; President frigate, mounting 64 guns, 42 and 24-pounders; Constitution, 54 guns; United States, 51 guns; Essex, not certain; Argus, 20 guns."

BOTH SIDES OF A SAILOR'S LIFE.

" How melancholy is the life of a sailor! (exclaims Mr. Semple, at the commencement of his *Sketch of the present State of Caracas.*) From the first hour of embarkation, his habits and modes of life become essentially different from those of his brethren on shore. His habitation is not fixed, and seems without foundation; now leaning to this side, now to that; acted upon by every wave and by every breath of wind. Even his food is unnatural, engenders diseases, and can be relished only through long habit. Often for months he does not behold the cheerful face of woman, nor green fields, nor cottages. So sad are the watery desarts which he traverses, that a solitary and sterile land becomes to him an object of interest. At night he slumbers in a narrow hammock, from which, in the midst of dreams of home, he is often roused by the sound of danger. Rushing upon deck, he finds the vessel driving before the blast, or laid down upon her side by a sudden gale. The rest of the night is spent amidst cold and wet, and darkness, and storms. Even the morning light is hardly welcome, since it serves only to discover a turbulent and boundless ocean, in which he may possibly, ere long, be overwhelmed, and no sad memorial of him remain to tell his fate."

This is the gloomy side of the picture, not overcharged, however, but pourtrayed with the colour of truth. The opposite side of the picture is equally natural.

" Yet to some, how pleasant is the life of a sailor! For ever roving about, he enjoys, without care, that variety which the epicurean so sedulously, and often so vainly, seeks, as alone capable of giving a zest to the pleasures of existence. The fruits, the productions, the manners of distant climates, become to him as familiar as those of his own country. He sees nature under every aspect; and the widely varying races of mankind, the Chinese and the Negro, the Indian and the Malay, are brothers with whom he has often conversed. It is the duty and pride of a sailor to struggle with the tempest, which inures his mind and body to fatigue and danger. But storms do not always vex the surface of the deep, nor do clouds always darken the face of Heaven. Favourable breezes at intervals bear him smoothly along. He sees the Sun rise in all his glory from the eastern waves, and disappear in the evening as in a sea of fire. He contemplates with pleasure the tropical clouds, the rich and splendid colours which bid defiance to the art of the painter, and awaken to admiration even the rudest mind. He alone with his level horizon can contemplate in all its magnificence the star-light canopy of Heaven, or the Moon reflected on every side from a thousand broken waves. Who would not undergo a few hardships and privations, to arrive at the enjoyment of objects so sublime? How pleasant is the life of a sailor!"

EXTRAORDINARY IMPULSE.

The following narrative, communicated by our Correspondent, ROBUR, deserves preservation, as it records an instance of what may be termed (if not a supernatural interference) a very extraordinary prepossession, in a person who lived early in the 18th century:—

One Richard Hutton, master of the Michael of London, burthen 330 tons, bound for Lisbon, and designing to take in St. Ubes salt, for Gottenburgh, sailed out of the Downs on the 4th day of the month, and on the 6th, about two in the morning, in a violent storm, struck upon the Casketts, near Alderney, and was immediately staved to pieces. The master and six men were drowned, and nine saved; the mast falling on the rock, some, who were on the shrouds, fell with it, and some swung themselves on by parts of the rigging. They did not save any bread, or other provision, but lived 14 days on the ship's dog, which they ate raw, and on limpets and weeds which grow on the rocks. They once had sight of the Express advice boat, but were not perceived by her. About the 18th or 19th of the month, one Taskard's son, who had been apprentice to a master of a ship at Lymmington, dreamed that he was taking up several men about the Casketts. He related his dream to his father, who took no notice of it; but on the 20th the old man set sail in his bark for Guernsey, bound to Southampton. When he came in view of the Casketts, the boy said there were men on them: his father chid him, and contradicted him; but the boy insisting on it, the old man took his glass, by which he saw a man on the top of the rock, waving his cap; upon which he steered for the rock, and came to anchor on the leeward of it, there being a great sea. He took the men all into his little boat, carried them on board the bark, and the next day brought them safe to Hampton. The feet of all the men, except one, were very much swelled and sore; viz. Stephen Hutchins, second mate, who was a stout man, and heartened his companions all the time they were on the rock.

CORRESPONDENCE.

MR. EDITOR,

I OBSERVED in the NAVAL CHRONICLE for May last, a letter from " A FRIEND TO NAVAL MERIT, proposing measures for giving employment to those officers of the navy that are on half-pay ; many of whom are kept so, contrarily to their inclinations, in consequence of the present system of distributing the different classes of officers. The writer not having specified the best means for lieutenants being kept in actual service, I am induced to suggest the following plan, together with the plain reason, why such a plan is necessary, and the judicious effect it would produce if carried into execution. The duty that lieutenants in sloops of war have to perform will be rendered less severe, and consequently be executed with more satisfaction to their own feelings, and to those of their captains, and will also give employment to officers who are now soliciting it in vain.

That two lieutenants are incompetent to perform strictly the various duties imposed on that class of officers serving in sloops of war, all those who are acquainted with the naval service of this country will doubtless acknowledge. It is certain that at present the duties are performed, but in a manner quite different from what they should be; this also, they who have sailed in any of his Majesty's sloops, or have any knowledge of the service, I dare say will allow to be true : therefore, for the better performance of such duties, and for the relief of those officers who are attached to ships now bearing only two lieutenants, let there be an additional one appointed; the duty would then become lighter, be executed in a manner creditable to the service, and with more real pleasure than I imagine it is at present ; for every experienced officer in the navy, if he judges impartially, will not hesitate in saying—that the life of a junior lieutenant serving in a sloop of war, is a life of slavery, when compared with that of his brother officers employed in any other class of ships. It appears by the present list of the royal navy, that there are 229 vessels in commission, bearing only two lieutenants each ; therefore, the Lords Commissioners of the Admiralty have it in their power, by appointing an additional lieutenant to every ship as above stated, not only to rescue from obscurity a great number of deserving officers, who are dragging out a miserable life on shore (occasioned by their not obtaining appointments, being unfit for any other employment, and obliged to *exist* on the scanty means produced by the mere pittance allowed them for past services), but perhaps save many a deserving young man from gaol, and from disgrace.

It would also be rendering essential service to the navy, by their Lordships' adding a fourth lieutenant to each frigate in commission (109), as the master generally acts in that capacity, and it is well known that the duties which that particular class of officers is made to perform (in a great degree from the whims of the captains), are completely altered from those specified in the naval printed instructions.

The master not only navigates the ship, and is subject to be called upon to attend the deck, at any period of the day or night, but is obliged to keep a regular watch in harbour, and at sea; to follow dock-yard duty, row guard, answer signals, and in fact to execute in his turn, any, and every one of the different points of service which a lieutenant performs. Much is wanted to be done! and if I am not too presumptuous in saying so, their Lordships cannot shew their attention to the navy more, than by inquiring into, and relieving such oppressive measures as are positively carried on in the service. Although the masters of the navy have borne the pressure of double duty so long, it does not follow that they in consequence should always be made to labour under the weight of such unfair, and improper treatment. It may be said, there are three lieutenants to each frigate, and as the watches are divided into that number, that there is no occasion for the master to keep watch—to which I reply, that as the first lieutenant is the officer nominated to regulate the internal discipline of the ship, to work her, &c. when all hands are called, and to see that all orders issued by the captain are properly, and punctually obeyed, he is therefore, for these cogent reasons, exempt from keeping watch, and that part of his duty unperformed by himself, is imposed on the master, whenever there is not a mate or midshipman sufficiently experienced to be entrusted with the charge of the deck. Every man who is acquainted with the naval service, and is at all considerate, will certainly allow, that if a master attends properly to the navigating of the ship, the stowing and keeping her holds in a proper state, the regulating of the warrant officer's stores, and seeing the rigging kept in order, he will have quite enough to occupy his attention. That he should attend particularly to the first point of service, is strictly necessary, for the preservation of the ship, and all on board her; that the second also should be attended to, is highly proper, that the ship might be kept in trim, and the provisions and spirits preserved; that there might not be a wasteful expenditure of stores, it is equally proper that he should give his attention to the third; and, to the fourth, for the credit of the ship and his own professional character. It is consequently expedient for the good of his Majesty's service, that masters should not be allowed to keep watch; neither is it proper that they should be made to do the duty of lieutenants.

July 28th, 1812. OCEANUS.

MR. EDITOR,

THE enclosed effusion, which came into my hands a few days ago, is, I understand, the composition of Captain Belchier, of the navy, and was, I believe, written in the early part of the present war: I know not who it is addressed to, but it breathes so noble a spirit, and is so prophetic of what has since been achieved by British arms, that I have taken the liberty of requesting you to insert it in your valuable publication.

July 4th, 1812. A CONSTANT READER.

The British Lion is awake, and has drowsily placed himself upon his haunches; at this eventful period, he should be standing collected in his strength, his mane erect, his eyes flashing indignant fire, and his tremendous roar resounding throughout the universe. There should be a spirit, a resentment in the country, to be allayed only by the total subjugation and ruin of our enemy, obstinately inveterate in our turn, for the insults and injuries we have received; a stream of fire, expressive of the most fixed contempt and national hereditary hatred, should flame from every mouth; the anger of Britain must be stern and vindictive, her proud and menacing attitude such, that France herself shall tremble, for the weak and uncemented foundations of her empire.

This spirit exists in the country, but exists a smothered flame, half suffocated in its own ashes. It is the duty, and I am conscious it is in the power, of ministers to draw it forth, a flame of patriot fire. We must hear no more of those disgraceful fears of the enemy's landing on our coasts, but of one warm and generous wish, that they may escape the vigilance of our fleets, and on British ground receive the punishment of their temerity. Enough has been done for naval honour: the rostral column of our triumphs stands a magnificent monument of glory to our country, and of emulation to our youth; its capital crowned with a wreath of unfading laurels, woven by the noble hands of a St. Vincent, a Nelson, a Duncan, and a Howe; and, should the gallic standard ever be unfurled in this country, I shall behold its sister pillar rise majestically by its side. Its pedestal has been formed for ages by those architects of honour, the heroes of Cressy, Poictiers, and Agincourt; its shaft we have seen proudly rising by the labours of Marlborough and of Wolf, and strongly cemented by the blood of Abercromby.

May the kindred laurels of those heroes entwine, adorn, and mutually support each other: it is under their shade only, that an oppressed and insulted world can find repose.

To the Right Hon. Lord Viscount Melville, First Lord of the Admiralty, &c.

MY LORD,

I LATELY ventured to call your attention to the situation of the officers of his Majesty's navy, and truly, however inadequately depicted the claims that invaluable but neglected class of men have upon the generosity, or more properly, *upon the justice*, of their country. Independent of the exalted station you hold in the government, by which the grand security of the nation is committed to your care, there is an hereditary popularity attached to your name and title, which, while it commands the respect and regard of every rank in the service, also naturally leads them to form ardent hopes, and to entertain great, and I fervently trust, well grounded expectations.—I shall now, my Lord, trespass again, upon a subject intimately connected with the former, and equally worthy your serious consideration. I allude, my Lord, to the condition of the widows and orphans of those officers, who have fallen in the battles, or have dedicated their lives and faculties to the welfare of the state. The provision, my Lord, *if it deserves that name*, which is made for these unfortunate persons, is so paltry, so wretched, and so contemptible, that I can scarcely conceive any degree of human misery, *I had almost said of human degradation*, greater than that which is inflicted upon those who are under the necessity of receiving it. It is, my Lord, a disgraceful fact, that the widow of an Admiral, who may, perhaps, have served for half a century, is not, by the present regulation, entitled to a larger, *and very probably to a smaller*, annual stipend, than that which you confer upon your housekeeper, and, that the allowance to the widows of inferior officers *sinks still lower in the scale*, to a parallel even with the wages of your chambermaid, or your scullion,—the lowest and least valued menials of your establishment!— When you reflect upon this, and when you consider, my Lord, that the people so circumstanced, have moved in high, or at least in reputable circles—that the recollection of *what has been*, clings closer round the heart in every reverse of fortune—and, that there is no method open to them of increasing their income, whilst the changed and sordid spirit of the present generation *deems poverty a disgrace!* you surely must admit, that they merit from their country a better and more exalted fate. It cannot, my Lord, be denied, that there are a few instances, *the more conspicuous from the smallness of their number*, of competent pensions being given to the widows and orphans of particularly distinguished characters; but these trifling exceptions, *only confirm the necessity of a general extension*. It is not, *it cannot be*, the good fortune of every officer, however able or enterprising, to enrol his name in the annals of glory. Yet, his exertions may have been eminently useful, and his constitution impaired or destroyed, by a series of active, *though silent services*, more harassing to the mind, and sometimes not less beneficial to the nation, than those brilliant exploits, which ensure immortality.—Besides, the provision ought not to be considered as a matter of favour, *but as a right*, devolving to the wife, upon the death of the husband, and it should be so ample, as to prevent the necessity of addition, except under very peculiar circumstances, and when the spontaneous bounty of the Sovereign should direct it. It should likewise, my Lord, be sufficiently large, to alleviate, as far as competence can alleviate, the anguish of the severest of all human privations—to soothe the cares of declining age—and to enable the relict so to educate and provide for her children, that her last moments may not be agonized with the idea, of leaving those for whom alone she cherished existence, *to the scanty and cautious charity of mankind*, or, what is yet worse, *the chilling and repulsive benevolence of relations*. In reflecting upon the slightness of the allowance under consideration, it is impossible to avoid drawing a comparison between the compensations awarded *to warlike and to civil services*— to those of the hero and the clerk—the man, who devotes his best days, exposes his life, and exhausts his energies, to maintain the dignity, enhance the fame, and enlarge or secure the conquests of his country; and, *he* who dozes in torpid inaction over his office desk, rejects applications with contemptuous insolence, and makes them with despicable meanness—whose mind never soars beyond the dull monotony of his employment, and whose genius can barely comprehend a newspaper paragraph. Yet, my Lord, such animals as these, after a few years of *scribeship*, retire with pensions *superior to the half-pay of the weather-beaten veteran*, and, with remainders to their wives and children, unclogged by the paltry and vexatious limitations, which attach to the miserable provision allowed to the widows of the bulwarks of the state. So prevalent is this partiality to civil situations, that it is even extended to the navy, when any of its officers are appointed to them, notwithstanding such appointment is solely attributable to their naval rank. The relict of a Commissioner has about fourfold that of an Admiral! I am far from conceiving, that the pension of the former should be less; on the contrary, I would wish to see it increased. But, I cannot but think, that a due regard should be had to relative rank, and, that the widow of the Admiral should not suffer, in consequence of her husband having preferred the more difficult and dangerous, if not the more useful, service.

Having touched upon the incompetence of these pensions, I shall now shortly advert to the manner in which they are enjoyed.—They are held, my Lord, it is almost needless to mention, only while the lady continues unmarried, and not at all, should she be in possession of a certain income; in other words, my Lord, they are lost, should she gratify an honourable ambition, indulge an innocent inclination, or by accident or inheritance, become mistress of a bare subsistence. This last, carries with it such evident marks of injustice, that it is quite unnecessary to comment upon them. And, allowing, my Lord, that the pension to the widow *should cease*, upon her losing that character, why should her offspring become the victims of it? The original intention in granting the provision, had certainly in view the children of the deceased. Why then, my Lord, should a young and helpless family, be subservient, for the common aliments of life, to the caprice of a step-father, no way interested in their happiness or welfare? It is making them suffer for conduct, over which they could have no controul; for, whether that conduct be laudable or condemnable, whether it raises the parent to affluence, or consigns her to misery, *it equally removes the only certain barrier between them and want*. If I might presume an opinion, I would recommend in such cases, that the pension should descend, for a certain period, to the children; and, that a regular provision for orphans, subject to some positive regulation, should be made by the Government. The expense would be but little; and, when, my Lord, the magnitude of the object is properly appreciated, when it is considered how many, now pining in indigence, would be gifted with comfort—how many countenances, overcast with sadness, be lighted up with satisfaction—how many deserving officers, whose domestic felicity is embittered by the idea of posterity unprovided for, would then meet their last summons with content and resignation; surely, my Lord, when all these things are duly weighed, there could not, I humbly hope, be one dissentient voice, to the benevolent measure I am solicitous to advocate. *Distress has a sacred title*, and in this case, it is increased by every circumstance which can give it additional importance. The very names of widow and orphan interest our feelings, even when unacquainted with the persons, or their affairs. Should the latter be a female, the claim upon humanity is perhaps the strongest, which the varied and ever-varying features of misfortune can exhibit. Imagine, my Lord, the daughter of an aged warrior left in this situation, in the bloom of youth, glowing with every grace, replete with every charm, and adorned with every virtue; nursed with the tenderest affection, educated with the fondest care, and possessed of every accomplishment, which can fascinate the heart, engage the inclinations, and awaken the sensibilities!—What, my Lord, is to be the fate of such a being, thus left unprotected? How is she to repel the allurements of the vitiated, or resist the pressure of calamity? The shameful, I should rather say the infamous custom, of these times, seems to have closed every avenue to female exertion; *and a set of wretches, of neither sex,* are now employed in all the effeminate offices, which, however galling they would naturally be to such a character as I have delineated, would afford a shelter from ignominy, and a palliative to misfortune. That such instances as the above do sometimes occur, I am warranted in asserting, as *more than one* has fallen under my observation!—That they should occur, seems a national disgrace. Their removal may be accomplished, or assisted by your influence. Let then, my Lord, the navy indulge the expectation, that, under your generous care, all their wounds may be healed. The blessings of the father and the husband, the widow and the orphan, will be your recompense. To a benevolent heart, this is the highest of all human gratifications—It can never appeal in vain to that of your Lordship.

JUSTICIUS.

MR. EDITOR,

I THINK the following liberal testimony of Lieutenant T. Gill, addressed to the Commissioners of the Transport Board, in favour of Mr. A. Gordon, is well worthy of insertion in your CHRONICLE.

TIM. WEATHERSIDE.

(COPY.)

These are to certify the Honourable the Commissioners of the Transport Board, that, having been invalided from his Majesty's ship Sultan, and not being able to procure a passage home from Gibraltar in a man of war, Commodore Penrose ordered me one in the Economy transport, Alexander Gordon, master; that said transport parted from the convoy, during a long and heavy gale of wind, after every exertion 'had been used to prevent doing so. That said transport was attacked on the morning of the 8th of January, 1811, by a French privateer schooner, of the largest dimensions, mounting twelve guns, and full of men, which, after a very close action of thirty minutes, she beat off. That said transport was not only defended in a most gallant and determined manner by the master and his little crew, but Mr. Alexander Gordon shewed, in his arrangements for receiving the enemy, such coolness and presence of mind, that I have never seen surpassed by any officer I have ever known in the British navy. That said transport was dodged by three other privateers, but Mr. Gordon prepared to receive them in such a resolute way, that they did not think proper to attack him; and I have also to state, that said transport having lost her rudder a little to the westward of Scilly, was three days beating about in the Channel in a gale of wind, and I firmly believe that said transport would have been lost, but for Mr. Gordon's exertions and seaman-like conduct.

Given under my hand at Tillingham Grange, Signal Station, this 17th day of July, 1812.

THOMAS GILL, (2d) Lieutenant in his Majesty's Navy.

MR. EDITOR,

AS it is some time since I have seen the NAVAL CHRONICLE, I know not whether you have published the Narrative of John Anderson, one of the survivors of the unfortunate crew of the St. George. This was sent to Admiral Reynolds's family; and, if you have not received it, it is much at your service. A. F. Y.

" On the 22d of December, 1811, lying off Salls, the wind at W.S.W. made signal for a pilot, who came on board. The wind chopped round to the N. by E stood off to sea, and shaped a course for England.

" Sunday 23d, the wind N. by W. we continued our course. Monday evening the wind came round to the W.N.W. blowing a strong gale, with a heavy sea; at nine lost sight of the Defence; at nine 30 the Cressy passed us to leeward, and stood to the southward. About 11 the wind changed to N.N.W.; at 12 the Admiral made the signal to wear and stand to the westward; in vain we tried to hoist the jib, but it was blown away before half up; after it was gone, hands were sent up to loose the foretop-sail; it was no sooner gone from their arms, before it was blown away. All our head sails being gone, we got the hammock cloaths in the forerigging, which, however, had no effect. Then got a nine-inch hawser, and bent it to the spare anchor, the stock and one fluke being gone.

" Then taking the opportunity of a lull, let go the anchor and put the helm down, trying to club-haul her, and get her round on the other tack, but the hawser catching the heel of the rudder, carried it away. All we had to trust to then was our anchors. We immediately sent two watches below to arrange the cables, and kept one watch on deck to strike lower yards and top-masts; finding we had only 12 fathom, let go the S. bower, and by the time the best bower was gone, she struck. This was between five and six of the morning of the 24th; orders were then given to cut away the masts, and sent hands down to the pump; but finding she gained so much water, all hands were obliged to fly to the poop, where they continued from the 24th, till we left the ship on the 25th, when the whole that remained were either dead, or dying very fast. We looked in vain for boats coming to our assistance ; the sea ran so high it was impossible for boats to live: two yards being all we had left, we contrived to make a raft of them alongside ; we then got on it, some lashed and some not, those who were not were swept off by the first sea.

" The Admiral remained in his cabin till the 24th ; when the sea came in he was obliged to be hoisted through the skylight on the poop, where he and the captain (Guion) lay close to each other ; at half-past three on the 25th he died, the captain lying alongside of him.

" Those who were lashed, myself and three others, got on shore, but so weak as not to be able to get off the raft without assistance. Seven men got on shore afterwards, on planks or pieces of the wreck, as the ship broke up. On coming to our senses we could only muster eleven hands.

(Signed)   " JOHN ANDERSON."

MR. EDITOR,   Dover, 1 July, 1812:

BIOGRAPHY occupies deservedly so considerable a proportion of the Naval Chronicle, that I conceive any suggestion tending to the advancement of that branch of the work, can hardly fail of being favourably received. Contemplating the difficulty of collecting genuine information on this subject, sufficient for the constant demand created by the successive publication of a biographical memoir every month, coupled with the occasional call for revision and correction of those which have already appeared, I have been induced to devise some expedient for facilitating research, and abridging the task of your correspondents ; most of whom, doubtless, belong to that description of persons whose avocations leave them as little leisure, as their habits may give them little inclination, for epistolary employment; and upon whom any appearance even of literary labor must operate as a discouragement. The result of my meditations has been the formation of a biographical catechism ; which, if the respondent will take the trouble of answering in due detail, becomes at once a skeleton of each individual, by no means difficult to animate. My aim has been to combine compendious brevity with that extent of inquiry capable of embracing the most material circumstances attending naval life. In conformity to this idea, I have drawn up a string of twenty-five interrogatories, which I recommend to your adoption, for circulation, in a standing numerical order, to serve as a guide for the transmission and uniform arrangement of replies, which may be made in a detached form.

PLUTARCH.

BIOGRAPHICAL INTERROGATORIES

CONCERNING

[*Officer's Name, &c.*   ]

1. Date of this officer's birth or baptism ?—2. Place of nativity or family settlement?—3. Parents' names, and immediate affinities?—4. Genealogical and heraldic particulars?—5. Brothers or sisters ?—6. Place and

mode of education?—7. Period and circumstances of entry into the navy?—8. First and other ships he ever sailed in?—9. Earliest and principal professional patrons?—10. How did he serve his time?—11. Date, &c. of first commission as lieutenant?—12. The same as commander?—13. The same as captain, from which he was allowed to take post rank?—14. The same as flag-officer?—15. Marriage and issue?—16. Particular exploits or memorable services?—17. Wounds, casualties, shipwrecks, or remarkable escapes?—18. Honors or rewards?—19. Death and burial?—20. Can reference be made to official, literary, or civil records of his public life?— 21. Was he author of any published work or approved invention?—22. His most intimate ship-mates or associates?—23. Any portrait extant?— 24. Juvenile or miscellaneous anecdotes illustrative of individual character?—25. Addenda and recollections?

MR. EDITOR, *Hereford, July* 11*th,* 1812.

CONCEIVING a plan of the intended Breakwater that is to be made for the improvement of Plymouth Sound, would tend to illustrate your valuable work, and shew more clearly to your readers (than mere description) who are unacquainted with the place, the manner in which the improvement is to be made, I beg leave to offer the distances (as accurately ascertained by one of the oldest and best pilots for the above-mentioned place) of the different points, shoals, &c. adjacent, and which may be taken as an assistant in forming the plan, should my suggestion meet your idea.—I have not a plan of the Sound, otherwise I would have reduced it so as to suit your publication. A constant Reader,
W. Y. E.

	Feet.
From the Garrison Flag-staff to Maker Tower	12,750
Do. to Penlie Beacon or Tower	19,650
Do. to Rame-Head	26,875
Do. to the Eddystone	72,950
Do. to Peak of Mew Stone	21,150
Do. to Flag-staff, Staddon Bay	8,585
Do. to the Tower on Mount Batton	2,580
Do. to Old Sugar House	2,270
Do. to the New House	2,955
Do. to Tor House	11,620
Do. to Block House, Stoke	9,575
Do. to Dock-yard Chapel	10,490
Do. to the Obelisk at Passage	9,800
Do. to Block-House, Devil's Point	6,960
Do. to Drake's Isle	4,690

From low water, part of Mount Batton shoal extends 650 feet to the westward; from thence it is 550 feet to the east end of the Mallard; from the east to the west end of the Mallard is 520 feet; from the west end of the Mallard to the east end of Winter Rock, is 700 feet; from the east end of Winter Rock to the west end of ditto, is 620 feet; from the west end of Winter Rock to the Asia buoy, is 1,050 feet; from the Asia buoy to the Island is 1,500 feet; from Melampus shoal to Melampus buoy, is 410 feet; and to the Island is 1,700 feet; from the west end of the Shovel to the Panther, is 2,150 feet; from the Panther to the Knap, is 2000 feet; from Block House, on Devil's Point, to Mount Edgecumbe, is 1,200 feet.

PLATE CCCLXIX.

THE island of St. Christopher, distant about fourteen leagues from Antigua, was first discovered by Columbus, from whom its present name is derived, in the year 1493. By the natives, it was called Liamuiga, or the Fertile Island. Its climate is hot, but, from the height of the country, less so than might be expected. The air is pure, and salubrious; and the soil, though light and sandy, is very fruitful, and well watered by several rivulets, which run down both sides of the mountains. The island is about fifteen miles in length, and, generally, four in breadth, but, towards the eastern extremity, not more than three; and, between that part and the rest of the island, is a strip of land three miles in length, which does not measure half a mile across. In the interior are many rugged precipices, and barren mountains; the most lofty of which is Mount Misery, evidently an extinct volcano, rising 3,711 feet perpendicularly from the sea. About 17,000 acres of land are appropriated to the growth of the sugar-cane, and 4000 to pasturage. The average annual produce of sugar is 16,000 hogsheads, of 16 cwt. each. Cotton is cultivated, but not to a great extent. The usual fruits, &c. of the West India Islands, are found here in abundance.

No settlement was made in the island of St. Christopher, till the year 1623, when an association was formed in England for that purpose, under the conduct of a Mr. Warner. Soon after the English settlement had been effected, a party of French arrived in the island, under M. Desnambuc. Warner's company had lived on friendly terms with the natives, who supplied them liberally with provisions; but, having seized on their lands, the consciousness of deserving retaliation made the united colonists apprehensive of an attack; and, falling on the Caraibs by night, they murdered upwards of a hundred of the stoutest, and drove the rest from the island, excepting such of the women as were young and handsome, whom they reserved for concubines and slaves.—In 1627, the island was formally divided, agreeably to a treaty of partition, between the English and French. The Spaniards, contemplating the flourishing state of St. Christopher's with jealousy, sent a formidable expedition against the island; the result of which was, that the French abandoned their allies, and fled to Antigua and Montserrat, and the English were obliged to submit to evacuate their possessions, under pain of death. Very few of them, however

Brimstone Hill, Island of St. Christopher

left the island, and, the French returning, the injury which had been sustained by the plantations was speedily repaired.—In the first Dutch war, in the reign of Charles the IId. the King of France declaring for the United States, his subjects in the island of St. Christopher attacked the English planters, and drove them out of their possessions. They were, however, restored by the treaty of Breda. In 1689, the year after the English revolution, the French inhabitants espoused the cause of the self-exiled monarch, and, a second time, attacked and expelled their English neighbours, laying waste their plantations, and committing the most dreadful excesses. After the French had continued sole masters of the island for about eight months, the English returned in great force, under General Codrington, compelled the French inhabitants to surrender, and actually transported 1800 of them to Martinique and Hispaniola. By the treaty of Ryswick, in 1697, reparation was stipulated to be made to the French; but, as war again broke out between the two nations, in 1702, the French planters derived but little advantage from the clause which had been agreed to in their favour. In 1705, a French armament committed such ravages on the possessions of the English, in the island of St. Christopher, that the British Parliament found it necessary to distribute the sum of 103,000*l.* amongst the sufferers, to enable them to re-settle their plantations. At the peace of Utrecht, however, the island was wholly ceded to the English, and the French possessions were publicly sold, for the benefit of the British Government.

The island of St. Christopher is divided into nine parishes, and contains four towns and hamlets: *viz.* Basseterre, the present capital, as it was formerly that of the French, containing about 800 houses Sandy Point, which always belonged to the English; Old Road; and Deep Bay. Of these, the two first are ports of entry, established by law. The fortifications are, Brimstone Hill (*vide* plate) and Charles Fort, both near Sandy Point; three batteries at Basseterre; one at Fig-tree Bay; another at Palmeto Point; and some smaller ones of no great importance. Most of the houses are built of cedar, and the lands hedged with orange and lemon trees. The white inhabitants, in number about 4000, are celebrated for the urbanity of their manners; and their habitations, which are clean and commodious, are delightfully adorned with fountains and groves.

The island has no harbour; but, on the contrary, the surf is continually beating on the sandy shore, at the few places that are fit for landing at; which not only prevents the building of any quay or wharf, but renders the landing or shipping of goods always inconvenient, and frequently dangerous. For the shipment of heavy goods, a small boat, called a moses, of a peculiar construction, is used. This boat leaves the ship with some active and expert rowers, who, when they see what is called a lull, which is an abatement of the violence of the surge, push to land, and lay the sides of the moses on the strand: a hogshead is then rolled into it, and conveyed to the ship. In this inconvenient and hazardous manner the sugars are conveyed on board by single hogsheads. Such goods as will bear the water are generally floated both to and from the ship.

Brimstone Hill was the scene of much active exertion, in the year 1782. Early in January, the Count de Grasse, with a squadron of thirty-three ships of the line, landed 8000 men on the island of St. Christopher, under the command of the Marquis de Bouille. General Fraser, with his little garrison of 600 men, retired, in consequence, to Brimstone Hill. The enemy prosecuted the siege, with unabating vigour, till the 13th of February, when a practicable breach was made in the works. The General and Governor having given up all hopes of succour, in order to spare the farther effusion of blood, which must have been the consequence of an assault, and the garrison not then numbering more than 500 effective men, they embraced the offer of a capitulation, and surrendered. The whole island consequently fell into the hands of the French; but, by the peace of 1782, it was restored to Great Britain, in whose possession it has ever since remained.*

NAVAL AND HYDRAULIC ARCHITECTURE.

THE BREAKWATER IN PLYMOUTH SOUND.

(Continued from Vol. XXVII. page 487.)

MY LORDS, *London, September 24, 1806.*

IN consequence of your directions, I have considered what appears to me the best manner of proceeding with the various preparations for carrying into execution the great Mole, or Breakwater, proposed to be constructed in Plymouth Sound. I beg leave to state the following, as what occurs for that purpose:

The first and most material step is to procure a sufficient quantity of rock, which may be quarried, for the Breakwater. The greatest part of the margins of Plymouth Sound, Cawsand Bay, and Catwater, may be said to be rock; but, except what is at the upper end of the Sound between Plymouth Dock, and what is in Catwater, the rest is all rock, apparently much intersected with fissures. To raise stones thereof of large magnitude from such places, proper for this purpose, will, I doubt, be attended with great expense, as well as much delay. It is, however, possible, that after quarries are opened in several of these places, the rock may turn out to be more suitable to the purpose, than what, on a cursory inspection, they appear capable of affording.

The rock at the head of the Sound, which lies between Plymouth and Dock, is mostly limestone; and a considerable part of it appears very suitable to the purpose in question, as well as most of the rock in Catwater. The sides of Plymouth Sound and Cawsand Bay are very much exposed,

---

† For a detailed account of the capture of the island of St. Christopher, in 1782, *vide* memoir of Admiral Lord Hood, N.C. II. 14 to 18.

according as the winds blow; Cawsand Bay, and all towards Mount
Edgecombe, to south, south-easterly, and easterly winds; Bouvisand Bay,
Staden-Point within the Withy-Hedge, and all the head of the Sound, to
south, south-westerly, and westerly winds: And as these are the prevailing winds in this country, the seas that break on these shores are such as
to prevent the possibility (if the winds are at all considerable) of vessels
taking in cargoes of stone from places so exposed.

The interior part of Catwater, where the principal quarries are, is sheltered from all winds; and though the distance from the work to be performed is greater than many of the other places, and although the going
into and coming out of it is more difficult, yet the advantage of being able
to load at all times, and lie in security when loaded, is so great, that it is
peculiarly eligible for such a work as this. I have, therefore, to advise,
that the rock around the Sound and Bay should be tried, and such places
as will produce proper stone be purchased, that advantage may be taken of
them when the winds and weather will permit. But I am persuaded that
Catwater will ultimately be found the best, and indeed the principal place
from which the great supply of stones must be procured, and therefore
that the great purchases should be made there: the rock is also known to
be suitable to the purpose; a sufficiency should therefore be procured there
for the principal part of the work.

The quantity of limestone rock in Catwater is very great: I have given
a person directions to survey it, but this will require time. After I have
got his report, I shall state the particulars to your Lordships. I know it
will be urged by the proprietors of the rock in Catwater, of what immense
advantage it is to the country, as a manure; and I fully believe the truth
and extent of this assertion. But I would propose, that all the rock or
stone which is not fit for the purpose of the Breakwater, be sold to the
country for lime, at a price something under what they now pay. It is as
good for their purpose as the large stones, and as it will come cheaper,
they will be considerable gainers. By this, the public will also be gainers,
by selling what is not fit for their purpose. But I will suppose, that in
time all this rock should be exhausted; still there is enough between Plymouth and Dock for the purposes of the country, for many centuries to
come: and when the Breakwater is completed, this situation will be so
sheltered, as to enable small vessels to frequent it with great ease.

Supposing a sufficient quantity of rock to be purchased in the Catwater
and in the other situations I have mentioned, it appears to me that this
rock should be parcelled out in lots or pieces, and that these pieces should
be given to different people, and who, supplied with a certain number of
convicts, should be paid a certain price per ton for the quantity of stones
they quarry and deliver on board of vessels, such as shall afterwards be
mentioned. I am not sufficiently acquainted with the manner in which the
convicts are supported by the public; but if they are hired to those contractors at a certain rate per day, and supplied with provisions, &c. at the
public expense, those contractors will make such bargains afterwards with
the convicts as they can agree on, and no doubt will make them perform

their due quantity of work. All the small stones, not fit for the work, should remain the property of the public, and be by them sold to the country, as I have mentioned.

The vessels which appear to be most proper for the work, are those from 40 to 100 tons. If they were made with wells in them, to discharge the stones by a valve or door in their bottoms, perhaps this would be the easiest mode; but if this kind of plan was to be adopted, vessels must be built on purpose, which probably would occasion a heavy expense to the public. Under these circumstances, I am inclined to think, vessels with a crane fixed in their decks, to take out the stones and throw them into the water, will be found, under all circumstances, the most economical; and a false floor might be placed in their holds, to keep the stones higher, and thus render them easier unloaded.

If this latter kind of vessel is used, they might be furnished by contracts in small numbers. The vessel, being the property of the contractor, would be better taken care of, and he might agree to carry stones by the ton, from the place where they are taken on board, to that where they are to be deposited, and also unload them; and if all the vessels were to be correctly gauged, the quantity of stone each took would be easily ascertained, and this might serve both for the quarrying and carriage. I am persuaded contractors to any necessary extent might be found for this purpose, and provision should be made at starting for sixty or seventy vessels.

The line of Mole, or Breakwater, should be correctly buoyed out by proper buoys and chains, and landmarks should be established to see that they keep their places. A sufficient number of moorings should likewise be laid down, for the purpose of making them fast during the time they are unloading their cargoes. These buoys, perhaps, had better be placed in a double row, one at each side of the proposed Mole, and the moorings between them; this would shew the extent of the work, and the vessels would be more easily directed to the place where they are to unload. This is a most essential part of the work, and must be done with great care and attention; for if the stones were to be scattered about the Sound, much injury would be done, and the expense of taking them up again would be very great. The mooring chains and buoys should be prepared without delay, that they may be ready to lay down in the spring.

A person of skill in maritime affairs, of ingenuity, intrepidity, and capable of superintending and directing the whole of these operations, should be appointed; he should be a man of integrity, and have those resources within himself, which would enable him to act with discretion, when any difficulties arise in the management of them employed under him. He should have proper clerks and assistants, to see that all the accounts are kept correctly; that the quantity and dimensions of stone delivered, are according to the specification; that the vessels work in their proper places, that the buoys and moorings remain where placed, and that the work is carried on in a regular and scientific manner: he should also have power to discharge any of his clerks or assistants who do not act properly, and appoint others in their place.

All the accounts of the work performed should be regularly specified by the said superintendent each month; and these accounts, so certified, should be put in a proper train for payment, by bills drawn on the Treasurer of the Navy, or such other Treasurer as the Lords of the Admiralty shall be pleased to appoint. And each contractor should give proper security for the performance of his contract. The work should be begun on the Shovel, and extended each way; and a monthly report should be made of its progress and effects. Soundings should likewise be taken monthly, to ascertain whether the water becomes shallower in any one place, and in general what effect it produces in quieting the water in the Sound; and whether the effects of the storms are increased in any situation, so that the works may be extended more to one side or the other, as may be found advisable. The manner the waves are reflected from any part of the work should likewise be observed, and how they affect the shipping entering or going out of the Sound: that such variations may be made during the progress of the work, as shall, on the whole, appear most beneficial. It is likewise of considerable importance, to observe what effect the sea may produce on the stones so deposited, in moving them from their places, that no larger stone be used than what is necessary; for, the smaller the stones that can with propriety be used, the cheaper the work becomes. But this ought to be carried no farther than necessary, for in a work of this importance, no risk should be run that can be avoided. I have stated above what appears to me the most eligible mode of proceeding, but many improvements will appear during the execution of the work, that cannot at present be foreseen; this, however, will be reported from time to time to your Lordships, and measures may be taken accordingly.

The Lords of the Admiralty.   JOHN RENNIE.

GENTLEMEN,   *Admiralty-Office*, 2d *August*, 1810.

I am commanded by my Lords Commissioners of the Admiralty, to send you herewith a sketch of Plymouth Sound, whereon is delineated the plan of a proposed Dyke or Breakwater to be formed for shelter to ships at that anchorage; which you are immediately to forward, through the Commissioner, to Mr. Jackson, the master-attendant, with directions to take the same into his mature consideration, and, taking for granted the practicability of the works, and the same to be completed, he is to answer the following questions; viz.

1st. How many ships of the line could be moored in security within the said Dyke, or Breakwater?

2d. Is there any danger to be apprehended, in consequence of the moderate depth of the water, of ships striking on their own anchors, or those of the ships lying near them, in the event of driving, or in the act of unmooring in the usual way, at low water, &c. &c.?

3d. Would ships be able to get out of the Sound and proceed to sea, with the wind from S.E. to south, with as much, or nearly as much facility, as from Torbay, with the wind between those points?

Navy Board. J. W. CROKER.

[*Follows a Letter from the Navy Board to J. W. Croker, Esq. dated 10th October, 1810, with Mr. Jackson's Reply. Signed* T. J. HARTWELL, WM. RULE, E. BOUVERIE.]

HONOURABLE SIRS, *Plymouth Yard*, 15*th August*, 1810.

In consequence of your letter of the 3d inst. to Commissioner Fanshawe, desiring his directions to me to take into my mature consideration the plan of the Dyke or Breakwater proposed to be formed in Plymouth Sound, for the security of his Majesty's ships resorting to that anchorage, and (taking for granted the practicability of the works, and the same being *completed*) to answer the questions therein stated respecting the same; I beg leave (in the absence of the commissioner) to acquaint you, that I have maturely considered the same accordingly, and the following are the answers which I humbly beg to submit as the result thereof; *viz.*

Question 1st. How many ships of the line could be moored in security within the said Dyke or Breakwater?

Answer. Thirty-six ships of the line may be moored in security in Plymouth Sound, within the said Dyke or Breakwater.

Question 2d. Is there any danger to be apprehended, in consequence of the moderate depth of the water, of ships striking on their own anchors, or those of the ships lying near them, in the event of driving, or in the act of unmooring in the usual way at low water, &c. &c.?

Answer. I would beg to observe, that in the sketch of the Sound transmitted by the Honourable Board for my inspection, the depth of water stated is calculated at the very *lowest runs*, such as very seldom happen, and only two instances of which have occurred within the last six years. I consider that there is from a foot to 18 inches more water than shewn by the said sketch, in the general run of spring tides at low water; but notwithstanding this small addition, I must still allow the depth to be but moderate for ships of large draught. But when I consider the great advantage a Breakwater would render to the safety of line-of-battle ships riding or moored in the Sound, as the water would be smooth, and thereby a ship would not increase her draught by pitching; and the well-known good quality of the bottom, occasioning the anchors to hold even at a short stay-peak, though but a few hours down; and that at all times when the anchor is laid fair, one arm is found to have been buried in the mud; I am of opinion, that even if a weather anchor should prove foul, and a ship in a gale should bring the same home, she would not drift so fast, with a whole cable out, but that a third anchor might be dropped, to prevent her going over her own lee anchor, or the anchor of any ship that might be near her. A ship in the act of unmooring in the usual way, might, at all times, with the assistance of one of her hawsers, jib, or fore-top-mast stay-sail, drop or veer on one side of the anchor she is going to take up, or that of any other ship she might be near, even was she circumstanced so as to unmoor at the very *lowest run*. And, moreover, by ships being properly moored with a cable on each anchor, under the shelter of the Breakwater, in smooth water, and the yards and top-masts being duly attended to, and struck in heavy gales, the anchor would never start. Under all these favourable circumstances, I am of opinion, there is not any danger to be apprehended of ships striking on their own anchors, or those of ships lying near them, in the event of driving, or in the act of unmooring in the usual way at low water, &c. &c.

Question 3d. Would ships be able to get out of the Sound and proceed to sea, with the wind from south-east to south, with as much, or nearly as much facility, as from Torbay, with the wind between those points?

Answer. I beg to observe, that the west end of the proposed pier, and outer part or south-east extremity of the Adder Rocks, lying off Penlee Point, bear by compass east-north-east, and west-south-west; therefore, a ship passing the west Pier-Head, at a cable's length, and making her way good south-west, and by west, would be carried a cable and a half without the said rocks; but should it blow fresh at south-south-east, by taking every advantage (while in smooth water under the lee of the Breakwater) by having a suitable well set sail in the ship, and choosing a proper distance to pass the Pier-Head, it is evident that a ship of war would go clear out to sea. The wind at south-east would be two points more favourable; and with the wind at south the ship would, after passing the west Pier-Head, fetch under the lee of Penlee Point, and the next tack, tack short of the Tinker, and, on the larboard tack, if not blowing very fresh, would go round the Ramhead. Therefore, under the foregoing circumstances, I am fully of opinion that ships of war would be able to get out of the Sound, and proceed to sea, with the wind from south-east to south, with even more facility than from Torbay, with the wind between those points.

In the event of a Dyke or Breakwater being formed, I would submit, that a transporting buoy be placed on the north-west side of Duke Rock, or the foul ground lying off Statten Heights, and one just within the Shovel Shoal; also two buoys, one on the *south-west*, and the other on the *north-east* end of the Scot's ground: the two transporting buoys, for enabling ships to get under weigh from, and would very frequently be found useful to moor or unmoor by; the two latter buoys, to shew the danger of the shoal, which I conceive would be necessary, for the guidance of large ships in turning into or out of the Sound. At present our pilots have charge of line-of-battle ships when passing through the Sound to or from Hamoaze; but I would recommend that a proper well qualified person, with full authority, should be appointed to see the ships properly placed and moored, in case of the Breakwater in question being erected.

J. JACKSON.

SIR,   *Chatham Dock-yard,* 15*th October,* 1810.

I have received your letter of the 11th instant (enclosing a copy of Mr. Jackson's remarks relative to the plan of the Dyke or Breakwater, proposed to be formed in Plymouth Sound), wherein you desire I would consider and report to you, for the information of the Right Honourable the Lords Commissioners of the Admiralty, my opinion on the said remarks. I beg leave to acquaint you, that having attentively considered the answers of Mr. Jackson to the several questions put to him, I have no hesitation in saying, that I perfectly agree with him in opinion upon all that he has said on the occasion. I have only further to observe, that during the ten years I was master-attendant at Plymouth dock-yard, I never heard of any ship getting on her anchors in the Sound, or on any other ships' anchors. The anchoring ground in the Sound is superior to most roadsteads. I am likewise of opinion, that Plymouth Sound has certainly the advantage of Torbay, for ships to proceed to sea with the wind from S.E. to south. In Plymouth Sound, the tide of ebb runs strong, occasioned by the great quantity of backwater which comes down from the different rivers and out of Catwater. In Torbay, there is no backwater, and not much tide. A ship, by turning about four miles to windward from her anchorage in the Sound, may shape her course for the Lizard; whereas at Torbay a ship must turn fourteen or sixteen miles directly to windward, before she can weather Start Point, which in the winter season, and night approaching, is very unpleasant. Under similar circumstances, when a ship gets out of the Sound, she has the benefit of the Eddystone Light.

John Barrow, Esq.   SAMUEL HEMMANS.

[*Follows a Letter from the Navy Board, to J. W. Croker, Esq. dated* 26*th October,* 1810; *enclosing further Remarks from Mr. Jackson. Signed* WM. RULE, S. GAMBIER, H. LEGGE.]

HONOURABLE SIRS,   *Plymouth Yard,* 23*d October,* 1810.

In obedience to your directions of the 15th instant, to insert in circular spaces, in the sketch of Plymouth Sound which accompanied the same, the space that each of the thirty-six ships of the line would occupy, when moored at their own anchors within the proposed Dyke or Breakwater, and to mark the general outline of the anchoring ground; also to point out the places proposed for buoys to be laid on; and to return the sketch when done with;—I beg leave to acquaint you, that, in compliance therewith, I have marked the spaces where the said number of ships are prepared to be placed, the same being calculated for a first rate, (Caledonia.)

I propose to moor each ship S.S.E. and N.N.W. with the best bower to the northward, and have left sufficient room for a ship to veer and take up her anchor, without the risk of veering over the weather anchor of the ship astern or to leeward of her, by allowing a space of 210 fathoms between the centres of each ship on the line of mooring, calculating that when a line-of-battle ship is moored at what is termed a cable each way, she has not more than 85 fathoms from her hawsehole to the anchor. Even in a small class 74 gun-ship, allowing the splice to be abreast the jeer capstan, the biting, tailing, and clinch, take fifteen fathoms; which will leave a space of 40 fathoms between the lee anchor in taking up, when unmooring, and the weather anchor of the ship astern or to leeward, which will be about eight fathoms from the ship's stern port, when the ship unmooring has veered sufficiently to take up her lee anchor. I have placed the ships so far asunder, in order that they may unmoor at any time of tide, without danger of coming near the anchor of the ship astern, as well as for getting under sail; and which plan has consequently placed the outer ships further to the N. N. W. than would have been otherwise necessary, but which I consider as the best, as there can be no danger, when short for casting, of nearing the next ship's anchor. I beg to observe, that I consider the three fathoms inserted in the sketch S.W. by S. of Donstone or Blackball Point, as a mistake in copying, and should have been five fathoms; neither myself nor any of the pilots having ever found less than five fathoms. I further beg to remark, that the ground to the northward of the northernmost ship is excellent holding ground.

Hon. Navy Board. J. JACKSON.

[To be continued.]

SHIP OWNERS' RESOLUTIONS RESPECTING EAST INDIA SHIP BUILDING.

AT a general meeting of the committee of ship owners for the port of London, held this 9th of April, 1812, John W. Buckle, Esq. in the chair,

Resolved unanimously, that, although this committee, in common with the rest of his Majesty's subjects, contemplate the great advantages which are likely to ensue from a free intercourse with the countries to the eastward of the Cape of Good Hope; yet they look with the utmost alarm to the dangerous and destructive consequences which will arise to the maritime interests of Great Britain, by the great influx of East India built ships, which must be the natural result of such intercourse, unless restricted by legislative regulation, and that trade confined to British built ships.

Resolved unanimously, that the opening of the trade to the eastward of the Cape of Good Hope, in British built ships only, will prove highly beneficial to the maritime interests of this country.

Resolved unanimously, that the consequences of continuing to admit ships built in India, which are navigated by natives of that country, to a participation in this trade, will prove ruinous, not only to the various classes of the people interested and employed in the building, repairing, and equipment of British built ships; thus sacrificing "great national interests and establishments, to support one of dubious utility, and of unquestionable danger in the East Indies, where the most confident politician cannot be secure, that at no distant period it will not be made a powerful engine of annoyance to the mother country, which so imprudently admitted its establishment, and since has raised it to its present dangerous state."

Resolved unanimously, that it will be an act of great injustice to the owners of British built ships, and to the persons engaged in the building and equipment of them, who contribute so largely to the revenue of the mother country, to allow India built ships the privileges of the former, as the owners and builders of the latter are exempt from such contributions, and the articles used by them in ship building, are not liable to any duties whatever, whilst those used in the building and equipment of British built ships are subject to a very heavy taxation.

Resolved unanimously, that the employment of India built shipping in the general trade of the empire, will annihilate the principal market for British timber, discourage its cultivation, and render the supply of it for his Majesty's navy more precarious than at any former period.

Resolved unanimously, " that the building, equipment, and employment of such ships will reverse the natural order of the India trade; estrange the affections of the parties engaged in it from the mother country; make India the commencement and termination of their voyages, and lay the foundation of a system which will render more equivocal and precarious the continuance of British influence and British power in that quarter of the globe."

Resolved unanimously, that a petition be presented to both Houses of Parliament, that in future, East India built ships may be prohibited by statute from being admitted to registry, and to the privileges of British built ships.

COMPARISON OF THE CAPACITIES AND PRINCIPAL DIMENSIONS OF HIS MAJESTY'S SHIPS HIBERNIA AND CALEDONIA, OF 120 GUNS EACH.

THE Caledonia, of 120 guns, is supposed to be the most perfect ship ever built in England, as she is found to possess every good quality desirable in a ship of war.

The following comparative statement of the capacities and principal dimensions of that ship, and the Hibernia, of the same force, was made with the greatest care by the officers in the surveyor's department at the Navy Office: it may be depended on as authentic, and considered as a valuable document for ship-builders, as well as for sea-officers,

	Hibernia.		Caledonia.	
	Feet.	In.	Feet.	In.
Length	201	02	205	0
Breadth	53	0	53	6
Depth of hold *	22	4	23	2
Hanging of the gun-deck	2	3¼	1	8
Depth of keels { Main	1	8¼	1	8½
{ False	1	1	1	0
Height from the upper side of the main keel to the lower cill of the midship port	26	11½	27	9¼
Mean draft of water when launched, excluding the effect of ballast on board, or the difference of the false keels †	17	2	17	0
Draft of water when completed to five months { Aft	25	9	26	0
{ Fore	25	7	24	10
Broke from the sheer when { launched	0	3	0	2⅝
{ loaded	0	7	0	5
Lower cill of midship port above water when complete	4	8	5	6

	Tons.		Tons.	
Displacement of water by the inch, at the height of 14 feet 5 inches from the upper side of the keel	20	$\frac{16}{35}$	20	$\frac{6}{35}$
Displacement, &c. at 22 feet 3¼ inches, &c. as above	23	$\frac{14}{35}$	23	$\frac{10}{35}$
Total displacement *per* plan at a height of 22 feet 3¼ inches from the upper side of the main keel	4647		4557	
Quantity immersed at the extremes, by ships' breaking from their sheer‡	54		39	

---

* The Caledonia, by having 7 ¼ inches less hanging to her gun-deck, has the advantage of carrying her midship port so much higher above flotation, with but little loss of stability ; as the guns and decks are, *in toto*, raised but half that quantity; probably still less hanging on a straighter deck would be better, especially for all three-deckers.

† The Hibernia had 50 tons iron ballast on board when launched, with an inch more false keel than the Caledonia, which last ship had only 40 tons of iron ballast ; the Hibernia's actual mean draft at launching was 17 feet 5 ¼ inches ; the Caledonia's actual mean draft at launching was 17 feet two inches.

‡ A third of the quantity due to an immersion of the ship the same number of inches the ship has broke from her sheer, when complete, is allowed for the displacement of water by the extremities : thus, by immersing the Hibernia 7 inches, she would displace 163 tons, a third of which quantity is added for the quantity immersed by her extremes.

	Hibernia.	Caledonia.
	Feet. In.	Feet. In.
Entire displacement, or weight of the ship and all its contents, when completed to five months	4701	4596
Quantity displaced after launching, until completed to five months *	2140	2140
Weight of the hull when launched †	2561	2456

FOUNDATION OF THE PLYMOUTH BREAKWATER.

ONE of the Plymouth Papers, under the date of August 12, 1812, has furnished us with the following account of the ceremony of laying the foundation stone of the Breakwater:—

" This being the anniversary of the birth-day of his Royal Highness the Prince Regent, was ushered in with ringing of bells in all the churches, and the hoisting the Royal Standard and Union Flags on board the Salvador del Mundo, Admiral Sir R. Calder, and the Government-house, the Dockyard, Ordnance-wharf, Royal Hospital, and the Guildhall. At noon the guns of the citadel, and all the batteries, fired a royal salute, which was re-echoed by three excellent vollies from all the regiments of artillery and infantry. Five thousand men were drawn up in front of the Government-house. At half-past twelve a grand procession took place, from Hamoaze, of the barges of Admiral Sir R. Calder, and Rear-admiral Buller, with their respective flags flying in the bow and stern sheets, from the flag-ship in Hamoaze, attended, according to seniority, by all the captains' barges of the fleet, their crews dressed in white, with black velvet-caps, their pendants also flying in the stern-sheets. They proceeded through the Narrow of Devil's Point, the Sound, to the Panther Rock Shoal, where, in due form, the foundation-stone of the new Breakwater was dropped, by Admiral Sir R. Calder, Bart. amidst the loudest acclamations. This was the grandest nautical spectacle ever witnessed in the Port of Plymouth; and the Sound was literally covered with pleasure yachts and boats of all descriptions. The ceremony being performed, all the men of war, per signal, being dressed, let fly, as through enchantment, their various colours,

---

* This is very near the truth; the displacement by the respective plans correspond very accurately with the computation of the quantities received.

† The method adopted for fastening the Caledonia's beams to her sides is in effect above 80 tons less in weight to her top side than the mode used for the same purpose in the Hibernia; and the timbering the top side is about six tons less weight in the Caledonia: these circumstances, with the ten inches more depth in hold, enable the Caledonia to carry her midship port 5 feet 6 inches, and is found sufficiently stiff under her canvas.

which, reflected on by the sun's beams, had a very pleasing effect; the ships saluting, in succession, with 21 guns, and cheering. Mount Edgcombe, Mount Wise, Staddon Heights, the two Hoes, Devil's Point, the Island and Citadel, were literally covered with thousands of spectators, assembled to witness the commencement of this grand national undertaking. The barges and boats rowed back after the ceremony, in the same order, to the flag-ship, and then dismissed. The foundation-stone is about seven tons, and has an inscription engraven on it as follows:—

G. P. R.
August, 1812.
S. R. C.
Dept.

" Grand dinners and balls were given here, at Dock, and at all the Mess-Rooms, in honour of the day, which finished with the greatest harmony and conviviality."

HYDROGRAPHY.

BRITAIN.

THE Lords Commissioners of the Admiralty having given directions for a vessel fitted as a floating light to be moored off the point of Bembridge, at the east end of the Isle of Wight, as a guide to shipping bound in or out of St. Helen's road by night or by day; notice was, on 20th July, given by the corporation of the Trinity-house at London, that the said floating light will be completed and moored at the station above-mentioned, by the 29th day of September next, from and after which time, lights will be exhibited thereon every night, and continued constantly, from sun-set to sun-rise, for the benefit of H. M.'s ships, and of navigation in general. And masters and pilots are to observe, that two distinct lights will be shewn from this vessel, in two lanthorns, suspended from two separate masts, at forty-three feet distance asunder, and hung at different heights; the one lanthorn at twenty-five feet, the other at eighteen feet height above the vessel's deck; by which this floating light will be readily distinguishable from the Owers floating light, and other lights in that vicinity.

Due notice will be given of the marks and bearings, as soon as the vessel is placed, and the lights exhibited.

AFRICA.
SALDANHA.

SALDANHA * is about 16 leagues N.N.W. of Table bay. This is an excellent harbour, where any number of ships may lie sheltered from all

* See Plate CCCLXX.

winds: the entrance is between two islands called Jutten and Malgasen. A little farther in is Marcus island; which may be passed on either side. On the larboard side is a bay called Hoetjes, in which the anchorage is good for ships of any size, with deep water close to a natural mole of granite on the west side. Ships may lie in safety at all seasons; but in winter the anchorage of Hoetjes is preferable, for the purpose of getting more easily to sea with the prevailing winds, than from the southern parts of the bay: from whence in the summer months the S. easterly winds will carry them out with equal facility. Ships in want of repairs, particularly careening, are sent hither from the Cape of Good Hope: and if a ship in distress should fall to leeward of Table bay when strong southerly winds prevail, she had better make for this place: where refreshments are procured in abundance from the neigbouring inhabitants, and usually at more moderate prices than at the Cape. The greatest disadvantage here is the scarcity of fresh water; no spring in the vicinity affording a sufficient supply for a small squadron in the dry season: but during the winter months, the quality as well as quantity of this article is much improved by the rains. Horsburgh places the entrance of Saldanha bay in latitude 33° 7′ S. Neither that author, nor the Requisite Tables, nor the *Connoissance des temps*, give its longitude: it must, therefore, be ascertained by approximation to that of Cape town, the mean at present adopted for which is 18° 28′ 30″ E. even that remarkable position not having been yet definitively determined. The magnetic variation on this coast was 25° 40′ W. in February, 1800. The tide seldom rises more than 5 feet perpendicular hereabouts. Between Saldanha and Table bay regular soundings afford a safe guide in approaching the land. S.

ORIENTAL SEAS.

SUMATRA.

CAPTAIN BYNG, R.N. of H.M.S. Warrior, having observed the notice of the Belliqueux shoal, discovered at Croee, in Sumatra, recorded at page 70 of this Volume; that officer has, in a manner equally demonstrative of his professional zeal, and politeness of character, contributed to the Hydrography of the NAVAL CHRONICLE the following copy of a letter addressed by him when commanding the Belliqueux, to Rear-admiral Drury, then commander-in-chief upon the East Indian station, containing farther particulars of that anchorage:—

" SIR,   " *H. M. S. Belliqueux, at Sea, 25th July*, 1810.

" Having remained at anchor several days in the Road of Croee, on the west coast of Sumatra, I think it a duty to communicate the information I have acquired respecting it, and to point out the practical benefit his Majesty's ships may derive from touching there, for refreshments, and other purposes.

" I also do myself the honour to send you a survey, taken under my own inspection, by Mr. M'Kellar, master of H.M.S. Belliqueux, by which you will perceive, we have discovered a very dangerous shoal, not laid down either in the charts given me by the Admiralty, in a survey of Captain Watson, in 1762, or any other chart that I have on board. It is ¼ of a mile from the anchorage of Croee, and about ½ a mile from the shore, which, from the boldness of the shore laid down in the charts, with the land wind off, might induce captains working in to stand so close as to endanger their ships.

" I am satisfied that I must, in working to my anchorage, have been very close to it.

" At low water the shoal had on it 2¼ fathoms in its deepest part.

" The anchorage is excellent in 18 feet water, on a soft clayey bottom, at rather more than half a mile from the shore; the water is smooth, and the anchorage secure from the south-east monsoon. Water can be obtained from a small river, at the distance of fifty yards from the beach; the casks should be filled at half ebb and flood, as the water is brackish at the time of high water. A considerable surf sometimes breaks on the beach; but it is never so heavy as to prevent the casks from being rafted off; about forty tons may be easily towed off by the ships' boats in a day, and, by proper arrangement, two or three ships may water with ease at the same time. Wood is abundant, and is cut by the natives at the rate of 5 dollars for a thousand billets.

" The fresh beef supplied by Mr. Brown, the British resident, is infinitely superior to any I have received in India, and will not exceed 6d per pound. The cattle are of Mr. Brown's own breeding, during his nine years residence at Croee, and are a private property, which he wishes to dispose of, as he is on the eve of departure for Europe. About fifty head of cattle remain, and when they are diposed of and killed, it will depend on the next resident's disposition, to continue the same laudable plan, of breeding a fine race of bullocks. Buffaloes, however, can be procured much cheaper than at Bencoolen, where the price is extortionate, and where the charges for water are exorbitant; indeed, Croee is superior to Bencoolen, for every species of supplies and refreshments for a ship's company. To the southward and eastward of the roads there are abundance of fine turtle, which the seamen may be employed in turning. I, however, preferred buying them from the natives, at the rate of four for a dollar; goats, ducks, and fowls, can be purchased at reasonable prices.

" We obtained tolerable supplies of those fruits and vegetables, which are common in India, particularly limes, pomkins, and yams.

" At the distance of seven miles from our anchorage, is the island of Poulo Pesang, where the resident grazes his cattle, and from whence it was necessary to transport them. By sending our boats away at four o'clock in the morning, they always returned before eight at night. I am assured, that the anchorage of Poulo Pesang is safe in the N.W. monsoon, but time did not admit of my fully investigating and ascertaining it. I cannot conclude my statement to you of this place, without expressing, in the strongest terms, the obligation I feel to Mr. Brown, for his great zeal and attention to get supplies for the ship, as well as for his private attention to myself and all the officers, and to the seamen on shore filling water. The resident possesses almost sovereign authority in this part of the country, which is rather thinly inhabited, and has promised to encourage the rearing of poultry, and the culture of vegetables, by the natives, who (he justly thinks) will be disposed to feel an interest in meeting his wishes, when they find a ready sale for their commodities, by his Majesty's ships touching there occasionally. I left a temporary buoy on the shoal, but the resident, on my pointing out the necessity of it, promised to lay a larger one down.

"I have the honour to be, &c. &c.

"*Rear-admiral Drury, &c.*" "GEORGE BYNG."

STATE PAPERS.

MESSAGE OF THE PRESIDENT OF THE UNITED STATES TO CONGRESS.

I COMMUNICATE to Congress certain documents, being a continuation of those heretofore laid before them, on the subject of our affairs with Great Britain.

Without going beyond the renewal in 1803, of the war in which Great Britain is engaged, and omitting unrepaired wrongs of inferior magnitude, the conduct of her government presents a series of acts hostile to the United States as an independent and neutral nation.

British cruisers have been in the continued practice of violating the American flag on the great highway of nations, and of seizing and carrying off persons sailing under it, not in the exercise of a belligerent right, founded on the law of nations against an enemy, but of a municipal prerogative over British subjects. British jurisdiction is thus extended to neutral vessels, in a situation where no laws can operate but the law of nations, and the laws of the country to which the vessels belong; and a self-redress is assumed, which, if British subjects were wrongfully detained and alone concerned, is that substitution of force for a resort to the responsible Sovereign, which falls within the definition of war. Could the seizure of British subjects, in such cases, be regarded as within the exercise of a belligerent right, the acknowledged laws of war, which forbid an article of captured property to be adjudged without a regular investigation before a competent tribunal, would imperiously demand the fairest trial, where the sacred rights of persons were at issue. In place of such trial, these rights are subjected to the will of every petty commander.

The practice, hence, is so far from affecting British subjects alone, that under the pretext of searching for these, thousands of American citizens, under the safeguard of public laws, and of their national flag, have been torn from their country, and from every thing dear to them,—have been dragged on board ships of war of a foreign nation, and exposed, under the severities of their discipline, to be exiled to the most distant and deadly climes, to risk their lives in the battles of their oppressors, and to be the melancholy instruments of taking away those of their own brethren.

Against this crying enormity, which Great Britain would be so prompt to avenge if committed against herself, the United States have in vain exhausted remonstrances and expostulations: and that no proof might be wanting of their conciliatory dispositions, and no pretext left for continuance of the practice, the British Government was formally assured of the readiness of the United States to enter into arrangements, such as could not be rejected, if the recovery of the British subjects were the real and the sole object. The communication passed without effect.

British cruisers have been in the practice also of violating the rights and the peace of our coasts. They hover over and harass our entering and departing commerce. To the most insulting pretensions they have added lawless proceedings in our very harbours, and have wantonly spilt American blood within the sanctuary of our territorial jurisdiction. The principles and rules enforced by that nation, when a neutral nation, against armed vessels of belligerents hovering near her coasts, and disturbing her commerce, are well known. When called on, nevertheless, by the United States, to punish the greater offences committed by her own vessels, her Government has bestowed on their commanders additional marks of honour and confidence.

Under pretended blockades, without the presence of an adequate force, and sometimes without the practicability of applying one, our commerce has been plundered in every sea; the great staples of our country have been cut off from their legitimate markets; and a destructive blow aimed at our agricultural and maritime interests. In aggravation of these predatory measures, they have been considered as in force from the dates of their notification; a retrospective effect being thus added, as has been done in other important cases, to the unlawfulness of the course pursued: and to render the outrage more signal, these mock blockades have been reiterated and enforced in the face of official communications from the British Government, declaring, as the true definition of a legal blockade, " that particular ports must be actually invested, and previous warning given to vessels bound to them not to enter."

Not content with these occasional expedients for laying waste our neutral trade, the Cabinet of Great Britain resorted, at length, to the sweeping system of blockades, under the names of Orders in Council, which has been moulded and managed as might best suit its political views, its commercial jealousies, or the avidity of British cruisers.

To our remonstrances against the complicated and transcendent injustice of this innovation, the first reply was, that the Orders were reluctantly adopted by Great Britain, as a necessary retaliation on decrees of her enemy, proclaiming a general blockade of the British Isles, at a time when the naval force of the enemy dared not to issue from his own ports. She was reminded, without effect, that her own prior blockades, unsupported by an adequate naval force actually applied and continued, were a bar to this plea; that executed edicts against millions of our property could not be retaliation on edicts confessedly impossible to be executed; that retaliation, to be just, should fall on the party setting the guilty example, not on an innocent party, which was not even chargeable with an acquiescence in it.

When deprived of this flimsy veil for a prohibition of our trade with Great Britain, her Cabinet, instead of a corresponding repeal, or a practical discontinuance of its Orders, formally avowed a determination to persist in them against the United States, until the markets of her enemy should be laid open to British products; thus asserting an obligation on a neutral power to require one belligerent to encourage, by its internal regulations, the trade of another belligerent; contradicting her own practice towards all nations in peace as well as in war; and betraying the insincerity of those professions which inculcated a belief, that, having resorted to her Orders with regret, she was anxious to find an occasion for putting an end to them.

Abandoning still more all respect for the neutral rights of the United States, and for its own consistency, the British Government now demands as pre-requisites to a repeal of its Orders, as they relate to the United States, that a formality should be observed in the repeal of the French Decrees, no wise necessary to their termination, nor exemplified by British usage; and that the French repeal, besides including that portion of the Decrees which operates within a territorial jurisdiction, as well as that which operates on the high seas against the commerce of the United States, should not be a single special repeal in relation to the United States, but should be extended to whatever other neutral nations unconnected with them may be affected by those Decrees.

And as an additional insult, they are called on for a formal disavowal of conditions and pretensions advanced by the French Government, for which the United States are so far from having been themselves responsible, that, in official explanations which have been published to the world, and in a correspondence of the American Minister at London, with the British Minister for Foreign Affairs, such a responsibility was explicitly and emphatically disclaimed.

It has become, indeed, sufficiently certain, that the commerce of the United States is to be sacrificed, not as interfering with the belligerent rights of Great Britain—not as supplying the wants of their enemies, which she herself supplies—but as interfering with the monopoly which she covets for her own commerce and navigation. She carries on a war against the lawful commerce of a friend, that she may the better carry on a commerce with an enemy—a commerce polluted by the forgeries and perjuries which are for the most part the only passports by which it can succeed.

Anxious to make every experiment short of the last resort of injured nations, the United States have withheld from Great Britain, under successive modifications, the benefits of a free intercourse with their market, the loss of which could not but outweigh the profits accruing from her restrictions of our commerce with other nations. And to entitle those experiments to the more favourable consideration, they were so framed as to enable her to place her adversary under the exclusive operation of them. To these appeals her Government has been equally inflexible, as if willing to make sacrifices of every sort, rather than yield to the claims of justice, or renounce the errors of a false pride. Nay, so far were the attempts carried to overcome the attachment of the British Cabinet to its unjust edicts, that it received every encouragement, within the competency of the executive branch of our Government to expect, that a repeal of them would be followed by a war between the United States and France, unless the French edicts should also be repealed. Even this communication, although silencing for ever the plea of a disposition in the United States to acquiesce in those edicts, originally the sole plea for them, received no attention.

If no other proof existed of a pre-determination of the British Government against a repeal of its Orders, it might be found in the correspondence of the Minister Plenipotentiary of the United States at London, and the British Secretary for Foreign Affairs in 1810, on the question whether the blockade of May, 1806, was considered in force or as not in force. It had been ascertained that the French Government, which urged this blockade as the ground of its Decree, was willing, in the event of its removal, to repeal that Decree; which being followed by alternate repeals of the other offensive edicts, might abolish the whole system on both sides. This inviting opportunity for accomplishing an object so important to the United States, and professed so often to be the desire of both the belligerents, was made known to the British Government. As that Government admits that an actual application of an adequate force is necessary to the existence of a legal blockade, and it was notorious that if such a force had ever been applied, its long discontinuance had annulled the blockade in question, there could be no sufficient objection on the part of Great Britain to a formal revocation of it; and no imaginable objection to a declaration of the fact that the blockade did not exist. The declaration would have been consistent with her avowed principles of blockade, and would have enabled the United States to demand from France the pledged repeal of her Decrees; either with success—in which case the way would have been opened for a general repeal of the Belligerent Edicts—or without success, in which case the United States would have been justified in turning their measures exclusively against France. The British Government would, however, neither rescind the blockade, nor declare its non-existence, nor permit its non-existence to be inferred and affirmed by the American Plenipotentiary. On the contrary, by representing the blockade to be comprehended in the Orders in Council, the United States were compelled so to regard it in their subsequent proceedings.

There was a period, when a favourable change in the policy of the British Cabinet was justly considered as established. The Minister Plenipotentiary of his Britannic Majesty here, proposed an adjustment of the differences more immediately endangering the harmony of the two countries. The proposition was accepted with a promptitude and cordiality, corresponding with the invariable professions of this Government. A foundation appeared to be laid for a sincere and lasting reconciliation. The prospect, however, quickly vanished. The whole proceeding was disavowed by the British Government, without any explanation which could, at that time, repress the belief, that the disavowal proceeded from a spirit of hostility to the commercial rights and prosperity of the United States: and it has since come into proof, that, at the very moment when the public Minister was holding the language of friendship, and inspired confidence in the sincerity of the negociation with which he was charged, a secret agent of his Government was employed in intrigues, having for their object a subversion of our Government, and a dismemberment of our happy union.

In reviewing the conduct of Great Britain towards the United States, our attention is necessarily drawn to the warfare just renewed by the savages on one of our extensive frontiers; a warfare which is known to spare neither age nor sex, and to be distinguished by features particularly shocking to humanity. It is difficult to account for the activity and combinations which have for some time been developing themselves among the tribes in constant intercourse with British traders and garrisons, without connecting their hostility with that influence; and without recollecting the authenticated examples of such interpositions heretofore furnished by the officers and agents of that Government.

Such is the spectacle of injuries and indignities which have been heaped on our country; and such the crisis which its unexampled forbearance and conciliatory efforts have not been able to avert. It might at least have been expected, that an enlightened nation, if less urged by moral obligations, or invited by friendly dispositions on the part of the United States, would have found in its true interests alone a sufficient motive to respect their rights and their tranquility on the high seas; that an enlarged policy would have favoured the free and general circulation of commerce, in which the British nation is, at all times, interested, and which in times of war is the best alleviation of its calamities to herself, as well as the other belligerents; and more especially that the British Cabinet would not, for the sake of a precarious and surreptitious intercourse with hostile markets, have persevered in a course of measures which necessarily put at hazard the invaluable market of a great and growing country, disposed to cultivate the mutual advantages of an active commerce.

Other councils have prevailed. Our moderation and conciliation have had no other effect, than to encourage perseverance, and to enlarge pretensions. We behold our seafaring citizens still the daily victims of lawless violence, committed on the great and common highway of nations, even within the sight of the country which owes them protection. We behold our vessels freighted with the products of our soil and industry, or returning with the honest proceeds of them, wrested from their lawful destinations, confiscated by prize courts, no longer the organs of public law, but the instruments of arbitrary edicts, and their unfortunate crews dispersed and lost, or forced or inveigled in British ports into British fleets; whilst arguments are employed in support of these aggressions, which have no foundation but in a principle equally supporting a claim to regulate our external commerce in all cases whatsoever.

We behold, in fine, on the side of Great Britain, a state of war against the United States; and, on the side of the United States, a state of peace towards Great Britain.

Whether the United States shall continue passive under these progressive usurpations, and these accumulating wrongs, or, opposing force to force in defence of their natural rights, shall commit a just cause into the hands of the Almighty Disposer of events, avoiding all connections which might entangle it in the contests or views of other powers, and preserving a constant readiness to concur in an honourable re-establishment of peace and friendship, is a solemn question, which the constitution wisely confines to the legislative department of the Government. In recommending it to their early deliberations, I am happy in the assurance, that the decision will be worthy the enlightened and patriotic councils of a virtuous, a free, and a powerful nation.

Having presented this view of the relations of the United States with Great Britain, and of the solemn alternative growing out of them, I proceed to remark, that the communications last made to Congress on the subject of our relations with France, will have shewn, that since the revocation of her Decrees, as they violated the neutral rights of the United States, her Government has authorized illegal captures by its privateers and public ships; and that other outrages have been practised on our vessels and our citizens. It will have been seen, also, that no indemnity had been provided, or satisfactorily pledged, for the extensive spoliations committed under the violent and retrospective Order of the French Government against the property of our citizens, seized within the jurisdiction of France.

I abstain at this time from recommending to the consideration of Congress definitive measures with respect to that nation, in the expectation, that the result of the unclosed discussions between our Minister Plenipotentiary at Paris, and the French Government, will speedily enable Congress to decide with greater advantage, on the course due to the rights, the interests, the honour of our country.

Washington, June 1, 1812. JAMES MADISON.

AN ACT,
Declaring War between the United Kingdom of Great Britain and Ireland, and the Dependencies thereof, and the United States of America, and their Territories.

Be it enacted, by the Senate and House of Representatives of the United States of America, in Congress assembled, that War be, and the same is hereby declared to exist, between the United Kingdom of Great Britain and Ireland, and the dependencies thereof, and the United States of America and their territories; and that the President of the United States be, and is hereby authorized, to use the whole land and naval forces of the United States, to carry the same into effect; and to issue to private armed vessels of the United States, commissions or letters of marque and general reprisals, in such form as he shall think proper, and under the seal of the United States, against the vessels, goods, and effects of the Government of the said United Kingdom of Great Britain and Ireland, and the subjects thereof.

June 18, 1812.—(*Approved.*) JAMES MADISON.

NOVA SCOTIA.

THE following Proclamation has been issued by his Excellency Lieutenant-General Sir John Coape Sherbrooke, Lieutenant-governor, and commander-in-chief of Nova Scotia and its Dependencies :—

" Whereas the Government of the United States of America, by an Act of Congress on the 18th day of June last, has declared war against the United Kingdom of Great Britain and Ireland, and it is expedient that this Act should be made as public as possible, in the province under my government, I have, therefore, thought fit, by and with the advice and consent of his Majesty's Council, to issue this Proclamation, in order to make known the said Declaration, that his Majesty's subjects, having this notice, may govern themselves accordingly.

" J. C. SHERBROOKE."

ORDER FOR A GENERAL EMBARGO ON AMERICAN SHIPPING.

(From the London Gazette, August 1, 1812.)

AT the Court at Carlton-House, the 31st of July, 1812, Present, his Royal Highness the Prince Regent in Council.

It is this day ordered, by his Royal Highness the Prince Regent, in the name and on the behalf of his Majesty, and by and with the advice of his Majesty's Privy Council, that no ships or vessels belonging to any of his Majesty's subjects be permitted to enter and clear out for any of the ports within the territories of the United States of America, until further order: and his Royal Highness is further pleased, in the name and on the behalf of his Majesty, and by and with the advice aforesaid, to order, that a general embargo or stop be made of all ships and vessels whatsoever, belonging to the citizens of the United States of America, now within, or which shall hereafter come into any of the ports, harbours, or roads, within any part of his Majesty's dominions, together with all persons and effects on board all such ships and vessels; and that the commanders of his Majesty's ships of war and privateers do detain and bring into port all ships and vessels belonging to the citizens of the United States of America, or bearing the flag of the said United States, except such as may be furrished with British licenses, which vessels are allowed to proceed according to the tenor of the said licenses; but that the utmost care be taken for the preservation of all and every part of the cargoes on board any of the said ships or vessels, so that no damage or embezzlement whatever be sustained; and the commanders of his Majesty's ships of war and privateers are hereby instructed to detain and bring into port every such ship and vessel accordingly, except such as are above excepted : and the Right Honourable the Lords Commissioners of his Majesty's Treasury, the Lords Commissioners of the Admiralty, and Lord Warden of the Cinque Ports, are to give the necessary directions herein as to them may respectively appertain. CHETWYND.

ADMIRALTY ORDER FOR THE REVOCATION OF LICENSES.

(From the London Gazette, August 1, 1812.)

By the Commissioners for executing the Office of Lord High Admiral of the United Kingdom of Great Britain and Ireland, &c.

WHEREAS by an Act, passed in the forty-third year of the reign of his present Majesty, for the better protection of the trade of the United Kingdom during the present hostilities with France, a power is vested in us to grant license to vessels to sail without convoy, and we have, in pursuance of the said Act, granted sundry licenses accordingly ; and whereas we see fit to revoke certain of these licenses, as hereinafter specified, we do hereby revoke and declare null and void, and of no effect, all licenses granted by us to any ship or vessel to sail without convoy to any port or place of North America, Newfoundland, the West Indies, or the Gulf of Mexico, which ship or vessel shall not have cleared out before this revocation shall be known to the collector or other officer of the customs of the port at which such ship or vessel shall be.

Given under our hands, and the seal of the Office of Admiralty, the 31st of July, 1812.

(Signed) MELVILLE.
WM. DOMETT.
GEO. J. HOPE.

To all whom it may concern.

By command of their Lordships,

J. W. CROKER,

PEACE BETWEEN GREAT BRITAIN, RUSSIA, AND SWEDEN.

(From the London Gazette Extraordinary, July 31, 1812.)

Foreign Office, Downing-street, July 31, 1812.

VISCOUNT CASTLEREAGH has this day received, by Lieutenant Dobree, of H.M.S. Victory, despatches from E. Thornton, Esq. his Majesty's Plenipotentiary in Sweden, transmitting a Treaty of Peace and Friendship between his Majesty and the Emperor of all the Russias; and a Treaty of Peace and Friendship between his Majesty and the King of Sweden, signed at Orebro, by Mr. Thornton, and the respective Plenipotentiaries of the two Powers, on the 18th instant.

DECREE REGULATING THE OPENING OF THE SWEDISH PORTS.

ARTICLE 1. From the 15th of August all the ports of Sweden shall be opened to vessels of every flag and nation, but every foreign vessel is only allowed to import such goods as are either produced or manufactured in that very country or its colonies.

2. All goods imported by foreign vessels to pay 40 per cent. more duty than such as arrive in Swedish ones; every vessel acting against the above order, and imports such goods as are not derived from her home country, shall be confiscated, together with its cargo.

3 Swedish vessels are allowed to import all goods from every place of the world. The exports are equal for Swedish as for foreign vessels.

REVOCATION OF THE ORDER FOR REPRISALS AGAINST RUSSIA.

(From the London Gazette of August 11, 1812.)

AT the Court at Carlton-House, the 5th of August, 1812,

PRESENT,

His Royal Highness the PRINCE REGENT in Council.

WHEREAS, by his Majesty's Order in Council, bearing date the eighteenth day of December, one thousand eight hundred and seven, his Majesty was pleased to order and command, " That general reprisals be granted against the ships, goods, and subjects of the Emperor of All the Russias ."

And whereas it is expedient that the said Order should be revoked, his Royal Highness the Prince Regent, in the name and on the behalf of his Majesty, is pleased, by and with the advice of his Majesty's Privy Council, to revoke and annul the said Order, and the same is hereby revoked and henceforth annulled.

And the Right Honourable the Lords Commissioners of his Majesty's Treasury, his Majesty's Principal Secretaries of State, the Lords Commissioners of the Admiralty, and the Judge of the High Court of Admiralty, and the Judges of the Courts of Vice-Admiralty, are to give the necessary directions herein as to them may respectively appertain.

CHETWYND.

THE SPEECH OF THE LORDS COMMISSIONERS TO BOTH HOUSES OF PARLIAMENT, ON THURSDAY, JULY 30, 1812.

My Lords, and Gentlemen,

IN terminating the present Session of Parliament, his Royal Highness the Prince Regent has commanded us to express to you the deep concern and sorrow which he feels at the continuance of his Majesty's lamented indisposition.

His Royal Highness regrets the interruptions which have occurred in the progress of public business, during this long and laborious session, in consequence of an event which his Royal Highness must ever deplore. The zeal and unwearied assiduity with which you have persevered in the discharge of the arduous duties imposed upon you by the situation of the country, and the state of public affairs, demands his Royal Highness's warmest acknowledgments.

The assistance which you have enabled his Royal Highness to continue to the brave and loyal nations on the Peninsula, is calculated to produce the most beneficial effects.

His Royal Highness most warmly participates in those sentiments of approbation which you have bestowed on the consummate skill and intrepidity displayed in the operations which led to the capture of the important fortresses of Ciudad Rodrigo and Badajoz, during the present campaign; and his Royal Highness confidently trusts, that the tried valour of the Allied forces, under the distinguished command of General the Earl of Wellington, combined with the unabated spirit and steady perseverance of the Spanish and Portuguese nations, will finally bring the contest in that quarter to an issue, by which the independence of the Peninsula will be effectually secured.

The renewal of the war in the north of Europe furnishes an additional proof of the little security which can be derived from any submission to the usurpations and tyranny of the French Government. His Royal Highness is persuaded, that you will be sensible of the great importance of the struggle in which the Emperor of Russia has been compelled to engage; and that you will approve of his Royal Highness affording to those powers who may be united in this contest every degree of co-operation and assistance, consistent with his other engagements, and with the interests of his Majesty's dominions.

His Royal Highness has commanded us to assure you, that he views, with most sincere regret, the hostile measures which have been recently adopted by the Government of the United States of America towards this country. His Royal Highness is nevertheless willing to hope, that the accustomed relations of peace and amity between the two countries may yet be restored; but if his expectations in this respect should be disappointed by the conduct of the Government of the United States, or by their perseverance in any unwarrantable pretensions, he will most fully rely on the support of every class of his Majesty's subjects, in a contest in which the honour of his Majesty's crown, and the best interests of his dominions must be involved.

Gentlemen of the House of Commons,

We have it in command from his Royal Highness to thank you for the liberal provision which you have made for the services of the present year: His Royal Highness deeply regrets the burthens which you have found it necessary to impose upon his Majesty's people, but he applauds the wisdom which has induced you so largely to provide for the exigencies of the public service, as affording the best prospect of bringing the contest in which the country is engaged to a successful and honourable conclusion.

My Lords, and Gentlemen,

His Royal Highness has observed, with the utmost concern, the spirit of insubordination and outrage which has appeared in some parts of the country, and which has been manifested by acts, not only destructive of the property and personal safety of many of his Majesty's loyal subjects in those districts, but disgraceful to the British character. His Royal Highness feels it incumbent upon him to acknowledge your diligence in the investigation of the causes which have led to these outrages, and he has commanded us to thank you for the wise and salutary measures which you have adopted on this occasion. It will be a principal object of his Royal Highness's attention, to make an effectual and prudent use of the powers vested in him for the protection of his Majesty's people; and he confidently trusts that, on your return into your respective counties, he may rely on your exertions for the preservation of the public peace, and for bringing the disturbers of it to justice. His Royal Highness most earnestly recommends to you the importance of inculcating, by every means in your power, a spirit of obedience to those laws, and of attachment to that constitution, which provide equally for the happiness and welfare of all classes of his Majesty's subjects, and on which have hitherto depended the glory and prosperity of this kingdom.

Then a Commission for proroguing the Parliament was read, After which the Lord Chancellor said,

My Lords and Gentlemen,

By virtue of the Commission under the Great Seal, to us and other Lords directed, and now read, we do, in obedience to the commands of his Royal Highness the Prince Regent, in the name and on behalf of his Majesty, prorogue this Parliament to Friday the second day of October next, to be then here holden; and this Parliament is accordingly prorogued to Friday the second day of October next.

NAVAL LITERATURE.

Twelve Letters, addressed to the Right Honourable Spencer Perceval. Wherein a View is taken of the present Magnitude of the British Navy, the Royal Establishments for its Equipment and Reception, compared with those at different periods of its Strength, and with the Demands the Country now has for its Services, and which must continue with her Power: also of the Policy of the Measures about to be adopted for the supplying of the evident Defects in the present Anchorages and Royal Dock Yards. From JAMES MANDERSON, *Esq. Captain in the Royal Navy; Author of a " Letter addressed to the Prime Minister, and First Lord of the Admiralty, on the Extension of the Naval Establishments of the Country;" and of an " Examination into the true Cause of the Stream running through the Gulf of Florida."* 8vo. pp. 150.

THE object of these letters is explained in the title-page of the pamphlet; and we perfectly agree with Captain Manderson, where, in his introduction, he observes, that

" There is certainly much information necessary in the present day, when choosing a situation for a great naval arsenal. One that might be proper two hundred years ago, or when Holland was the most powerful adversary which England had to contend with by sea, when she had little to do with the Atlantic Ocean, might be extremely improper in the present day. This is so evident, that the greatest wonder is, how a doubt can exist in any mind upon the subject, who is possessed of any information.

" To run from the great ocean westward, near a hundred and twenty leagues east, a hundred of these through a strait blown over by westerly winds three-fourths of the year, to a remote situation, where the country experiences extreme inconvenience, from having so many naval establishments there already, discovers that the subject is not yet properly digested.

" To form expensive breakwaters to procure a mere anchorage in a dangerous situation, the fatal consequence of which no man can pretend to foresee, and this to the rejection of a safe harbour better situated for national services, when the country is aghast from being uncertain of what will become of her navy in peace, that right arm of her power, the shield of her shores, and the protection of her wealth, proves that some strange misconception stands in the way; and, therefore, that impartial deliberation is still necessary before the hand shall be rashly put forth."

These letters have fallen under our cognizance at a time particularly favourable, to enable the readers of the NAVAL CHRONICLE, by the analysis and extracts which we shall offer, to form a due estimate of their merits; especially with reference to the Breakwater, in Plymouth Sound. To the insertion of official documents, relating to that great national undertaking, a considerable portion of our preceding volume was devoted; and as, in addition to the remainder of those documents, yet to appear, we possess a variety of private communications, the subject can scarcely fail of receiving adequate elucidation. The remarks of practical men are entitled to pre-eminent notice; and, on that ground, Captain Manderson's letters will, we conceive, be found deserving of serious consideration.

The Plymouth Breakwater, however, is not the first object of his animadversions. These letters, which, their author informs us, " were at one time intended to make their appearance anonymously, through one of the daily papers," appear to have been projected about the time, when a grand naval establishment, at Northfleet, was in contemplation. The abandonment of the plan, which certainly had many very able and scientific supporters, has not rendered obsolete Captain Manderson's reasoning upon the subject. He decidedly prefers Falmouth to Northfleet. In a former Volume (XXV. 286) we presented, from our Correspondent, TIM WEATHERSIDE, a tolerably fair exposition of the views and motives in which the Northfleet project originated. Captain Manderson's opinions, in favour of Falmouth, with the reasonings on which those opinions are founded, shall be here inserted.

" Lay before you, Sir," says he, addressing himself to the deceased Minister, " a map of the world; trace the connection of the Atlantic with the Indian Ocean, and the British possessions there; then let your eye come back to the Cape of Good Hope, thence to Cape Horn, and pass along the various regions of South America; stand and ponder the probable destinies of the nations inhabiting that extensive country westward to the great Pacific, and their more than probable unrestrained intercourse hereafter with Great Britain, by means of her ascendancy on the seas. When this is fully contemplated, pass on to the Caribbee and Antilles islands, behold the British power there established by her arms; then scan the coast of North America, with whom Britain must one day contend, and teach the lesson she has taught mightier nations; cross the ocean to the Straight of Gibraltar, enter the Mediterranean sea, and consider the various nations inhabiting its shores, the important interests and connections Great Britain has to defend there, against the power and influence of France; then come back to Cape Trafalgar (proud name for England!) pass along the coast of Spain and Portugal; visit minutely that of France, and her naval ports and arsenals; stand on the Island of Ushant; look to the north-west; then step over to the Lizard, there take post, and with the eye of political wisdom, view again the different regions you have passed over; then consider the extreme urgency of a speedy communication with the ocean westward; turn suddenly eastward with your eyes full open; where is the Thames? Cast your eye near three hundred nautical miles, along that straight of the ocean called the English Channel, there you will see the South Foreland, and near it the Downs, that dangerous roadstead; eight leagues northward, beyond these shoals, sand banks, and flats, you will perceive the mouth of the Thames.—Ponder attentively the *distance* and *navigation* between your *station*, and that *river;* turn, over in your mind the general state of the winds in the English Channel, their frequent fluctuations from south-west to north-west, and back again; then seriously ask yourself, in any exigency of service, how is a squadron of ships of war to get from the Thames into the Atlantic, during the prevalence of such winds, which often continue for months together, and more often for several weeks?

"Ask yourself in the common calls of the service, how long ships and squadrons may be in getting from the Thames as far westward as your station, to its great impediment and delay? and how disastrous it might prove, in cases of urgency, without the English Channel, to depend upon any portion of the navy so far eastward? and what excuse could be made for it, when there cannot be the smallest plea of necessity, arising from the want of a western harbour?

"This is so plain a circumstance, that it requires no seamanship, or the art of a navigator, clearly to comprehend the difficulties that stand in the way of ships of war clearing the Channel from the mouth of the Thames, in all urgent demands of the service, which cannot be limited to any time or season, when easterly winds are sooner or later to be expected, for at least some days.

"The mercantile fleets that leave that river every year for the western ocean, are no proof of the eligibility of the situation for a great naval station, designed to give facilities and preponderance to the naval power of Britain; their history would prove quite the contrary. Their being delayed by natural causes is only individual loss; but a great part of the navy being so detained, might not only prove a national loss, but be also attended with circumstances highly disastrous, and casting a gloom over pages of the history of the country? What weight has a mere convenience of land and water, against the preponderating considerations in the opposite scale? If it were the only place that the coast of England offered for such a purpose, that would silence all objections: but turn your eyes a few miles northward from where you stand; behold that secure harbour; that, Sir, is the harbour of Falmouth. Mark well its situation, as connected with the Atlantic Ocean, and, therefore, with all the regions you have passed over. It invites you to its entrance, to examine minutely the truth of contradictory reports you have no doubt heard, and to an impartial consideration of its advantages, compared with Northfleet or any other place."

Captain Manderson thus concludes his first letter. In his second, after admitting certain advantages to be derived from the establishment of a naval arsenal at Northfleet, he proceeds to inquire how the case stands, as it respects the active operations of the navy.

"Two squadrons are immediately wanted for service in the Bay of Biscay, the Mediterranean, the West Indies, the coast of America, or any where else connected with the Atlantic Ocean; one is to be furnished from Falmouth, and the other from Northfleet. They are ready on the same day, the wind is at north-west ; that from Falmouth sails free into the ocean, that from Northfleet can get no farther than the Downs. The wind keeps in that quarter for a day or two, then veers to the south-west, and so continues for weeks, veering between south and north-west. One squadron is in the Mediterranean, the West Indies, or at the Cape of Good Hope, according as it may have been ordered ; but the other is not to the westward of Spithead. This is by no means an improbable case, but one that would frequently occur, as you may convince yourself, by consulting a correct register of the wind for any year past; whoever endeavours to persuade you to the contrary, keeps out of sight the main point at issue, and the most important advantages the country would derive from its adoption as a naval station. Before this, the winding of the Thames at Northfleet and its western shore sink into indifference.

" Should it be answered, it is not intended that Northfleet should furnish squadrons for urgent services connected with the Atlantic, but with the German Ocean; this would bring me to what I proposed to notice farther, its vicinity to four out of the six royal dock-yards which the country possesses; those of Deptford and Woolwich are in the Thames; those of Chatham and Sheerness in the Medway; and the communication of all with the North Sea may be considered as at the same point.

" If these four naval establishments be not sufficient to furnish ships and vessels for the service of the North Sea and Baltic, what establishments are to furnish them for the numerous and various services of all the regions southward and westward ? It may be answered, Portsmouth and Plymouth are on a larger scale than any of those eastward, and therefore could furnish as many ships as the other four. But experience has proved, that where one ship or vessel, generally speaking, has been required eastward of the South Foreland, at least two have been wanted southward and westward of the Land's End."

Having established the truth of the latter assertion, he examines, on what grounds Portsmouth has been denominated a western port.

" Look, Sir, at its situation on a chart, and give me leave to ask, whether it be nearer to the Atlantic than the German Ocean ? You will perceive it is twice the distance from the former that it is from the latter; being 31 leagues from the South Foreland, and 63 from the Land's End of England. It can have no claim then, from situation, to the appellation, a *western port*: what has it from the general state of the winds? Here it is as far from proving any claim, as three-fourths of the year they generally blow from the western quarters. How then comes it to be called a *western port* ? No reason can be assigned, but because it is to the westward of the four royal dock-yards in the Thames and Medway. But to call it a western port, when speaking of the eastern and western coasts of England, or of the German and Atlantic Oceans, is to adopt the error of common acceptation, which ought to be carefully avoided in all matters of national concern. How would it sound in your ears to call Plymouth an eastern port ? Yet Plymouth is but eight leagues farther from the North

Sea than Portsmouth is from the Atlantic; and when the prevalence of westerly winds in the Channel is taken into consideration, it has a much stronger claim to furnish ships and vessels of war for services eastward, than Portsmouth can have for services westward. It is as near to Boulogne as to the Start; yet some men have called Portsmouth a *western port !* It is nearer to the Scheldt than to the Land's End of England; what right then has it to be called a *western port ?* It is as near to the Scheldt as Northfleet to the Texel; yet it is *supposed* to be a *western port.*

" Men may talk as they please, as best suits their partialities and prejudices; but here is the plain matter of fact before you, which no one can disprove or controvert: what call then has the country for another eastern naval arsenal? None—Positively none.

" Place yourself on the Isle of Groin, opposite Sheerness; if Northfleet were adopted, five royal dock-yards out of the seven the country would possess, one of them exceeding in magnitude all the others, are crammed into the space between the south banks of the Medway and Thames, whose point of confluence is the Nore.—Where is the Atlantic Ocean ? Is not the question enough to make a British Minister start with alarm, when, from the station you have taken, you view such a mass of naval establishments near you, thrust into a space that has no communication but with the North Sea, and this through many leagues of sand banks, shoals, and flats."

Opposing the arguments in favour of a new eastern establishment, and contending for the necessity of a western one, Captain Manderson thus closes his fifth letter :—

" It has been shewn, that out of the six royal dock-yards, four belong to the North Sea, being situated in the Thames and Medway: that the fifth at Portsmouth, though called by some a western establishment, has no just claim to the appellation, being only half the distance from the North Sea on the east, that it is from the ocean on the west: and that from the prevalence of westerly winds in the Channel of England, it has at least three times the opportunities of sending ships any where into the sea eastward, that it can find of sending them westward half the distance to the ocean ; no particular instances of the prevalence of easterly winds can affect the general position : and, lastly, that the only remaining naval establishment at Plymouth is very little nearer to the Atlantic, than Portsmouth is to the German Ocean; but from the general state of the winds, before noticed, it finds the task three times as difficult to get ships and vessels from its anchorage, into the ocean westward, that Portsmouth finds to get them into the sea eastward. These, Sir, are no specious theories, dogmatic opinions, or groundless assertions ; they are undeniable facts. Let those who wish to keep them out of sight disguise them as they may to the eyes of those whom they wish to believe otherwise, ought not their language to be understood by every one who wishes to see the essential interests of his country attended to before all other representations? Ought it not to be particularly intelligible to the government ?"

[To be continued.]

PLATE CCCLXX.

SALDANHA BAY, on the S. coast of Africa, is to the N. westerly from the Cape of Good Hope,* (see Hydrography, page 129 of this volume). The entrance, which goes in due E. and then runs down to the S.E. parallel to the coast, so as to form a peninsula. Nearly S. from the northern point of the entrance is a rocky island, with foul ground between it and the main, but round the S. side ships may run due E. into the bay for the point of the peninsula, giving it a small berth on the starboard, between the two islands which lie before the inner entrance. There is good anchorage within the N.E. island, and within the point of the peninsula, is from 5 to 7 fathoms, more or less, according to the distance from the shore. Within the peninsula to the S.E. are several shoals, between which are channels of sufficient depth for most ships; but they are unnecessary, as there is sufficient shelter within the island and point of the bay already mentioned. The water is much deeper between the islands, and without them to the southward of the rocky island first noticed.—[MALHAM'S *Gazetteer*.]

Naval Poetry.

ADELMORN AND ANGELINE.

THE tapers bright in Lord Mowbray's tow'r,
    Shone many a mile away;
But there was no light in his daughter's bow'r,
    Save the misty Moon's pale ray.

The maiden's sigh, the maiden's groan,
    Echoed the loud and stormy wave;
She wept to quit her native home,
    Alas! she thought not of a grave.

She heard not in the owlet's cry
    An omen sad of dire mischance,
She mark'd not in the northern sky
    The fatal meteor shoot askance;

---

* For particulars relating to the Cape of Good Hope, *vide* N. C. III. 361; V. 417 (View); XI. 14; XII. 380 (View); XIV. 194; XV. 248, 250, 261.

SALDANHA BAY.

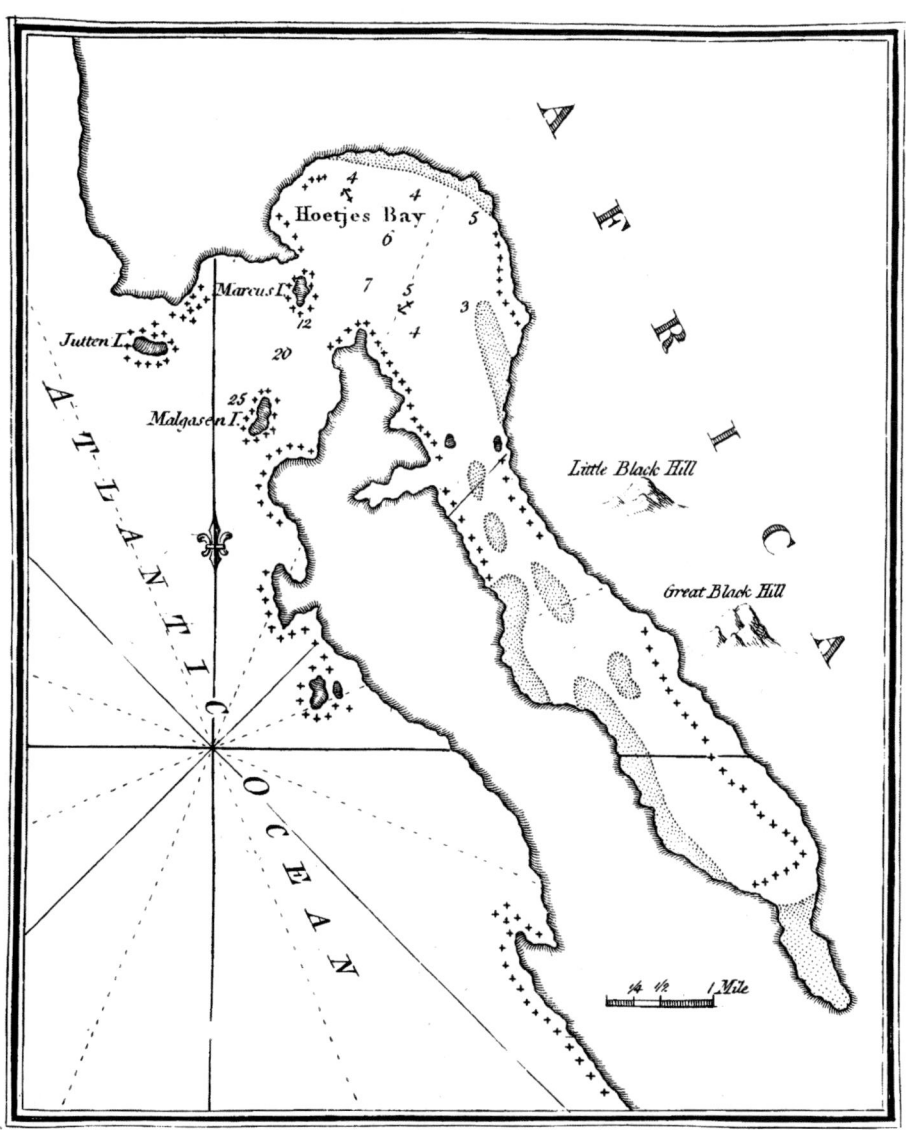

Published August 31, 1812, by Joyce Gold, Naval Chronicle Office, 103, Shoe Lane, London.

But plain she heard the boatman's song,
    And plain she heard the dashing oar,
And saw the vessel glide along,
    'Mid beating winds and billows' roar.

And plain she saw the stately form,
    That tower'd o'er the gallant crew;
Right well she guess'd 'twas Adelmorn,
    His silver casque, his plume, she knew.

She saw him from the vessel's side,
    Leap through the waves' surrounding foam—
The maiden's heart within her died—
    " Oh God! I cannot quit my home."

She paused, for accents known and dear,
    Soft as the gentle breath of e'en,
Came in sweet cadence to her ear—
    " Why weeps the lovely Angeline?

" The howling wind and stormy wave,
    May well that timid breast alarm;
But Adelmorn would die to save,
    His worship'd Angeline from harm:

" Cheer thee, our bark is trim and gay,
    And fearless are my sailors all;
The first faint peep of morning's ray,
    Shall find thee in my Castle Hall."

" I weep not at the rising storm,
    I care not for the angry wind,
But bitter, bitter, do I mourn,
    The friends, the home, I leave behind.

" I hear my honour'd father's rage,
    I see my angel mother's woe;
A sickening chill, a dread presage,
    Informs me that I must not go."

But ah! as winter's snows dissolve,
    Before the Sun's meridian beam,
So perish'd every high resolve
    Of fair ill-fated Angeline.

Yet often did she turn around,
 To view each well-lov'd scene she fled;
Oft press her cold lips to the ground,
 She never was again to tread!

And as the boat forsook the shore,
 Above the tempest's hollow moan,
Above the billow's lengthened roar
 Was heard her agonizing groan.

Ah! never to her father's tower,
 Shall she, the vent'rous maid, return,
Or joyful view, at morning hour,
 The promised halls of Adelmorn.

Long may his mother mount the cliff,
 To view with anxious eyes the main,
And think each distant sail the skiff,
 She never shall behold again.

In Mowbray's hall the childless pair
 May hopeless set from morn to e'en,
And wipe, with trembling hand, the tear
 That constant falls for Angeline.

Oft from their Castle's rocky steep,
 In moonlight hour, are seen to glide,
Dim airy forms upon the deep,
 Slow flitting o'er the silver tide;

And oft, at midnight, sounds are heard,
 That stay the listening sailor's oar;
Not the shrill scream of ocean bird,
 Nor yet the distant billow's roar:

The mermaid's wild and mournful song,
 As o'er the grave of Angeline,
She sweeps her scaly length along,
 And waves her locks of dewy green.

MARY.

Marine Law.

REPORT OF THE FRENCH MINISTER OF THE MARINE, TO HIS MAJESTY THE EMPEROR, RELATIVE TO THE PROCEEDINGS OF LA RENOMMEE, LA NEREIDE, AND LA CLORINDE.*

SIRE,

" I AM about to fulfil the painful task of laying before your Majesty, an account of the occurrences which have taken place with respect to the division of frigates under the orders of Captain Roquebert, on the 20th of last month, as they have been represented by the several reports which have been received.

" The division, consisting of la Renommée, commanded by Captain Roquebert, la Nereide, Captain Lemaresquier, and la Clorinde, Captain St. Cricq, being on the 19th of May in the latitude of Tamatava, in the island of Madagascar, Captain Roquebert sent two armed boats into the bay of that place, to take some vessels which had anchored there.

" The expedition, which took place in the night, did not experience any obstacles, and the person who commanded the boats exceeding his orders, surprised the fort, and took 100 prisoners.

" On the 20th, at day-break, the boats had not yet reached their ships, when a division came in sight of three of the enemy's frigates, and a large sloop of war, several leagues to windward.

" Captain Roquebert determined to attack this division, but instead of acting on such a determination, he remained the greater part of the day lying-to, while the enemy was endeavouring to come up, with a press of sail; in the mean time, one of the boats, which had been taking possession of Tamatava, came on board.

" At three quarters of an hour after three o'clock, the two divisions were within cannon-shot, on opposite tacks, and the firing commenced. They soon, by a manœuvre of the enemy, came on the same tack, but were at so great a distance, that the carronades did no execution.

" Captain Lemaresquier, of the Nereide, which was the sternmost ship of the squadron, came up, intending to engage the sternmost of the enemy.

" This manœuvre not being seconded either by la Renommée, or la Clorinde, these two vessels consequently remained at a distance from la Nereide.

" It now fell a dead calm, and an English frigate and a sloop of war were towed up by their boats, in order to succour the frigate which had been engaged by Captain Lemaresquier, who now had two frigates and the brig on his hands.

" During this time, la Renommée and la Clorinde were kept stationary by the calm, but kept up a fire from a distance on the third English frigate.

---

* For Captain Saint Cricq's report of the proceedings of la Clorinde, and Captain C. M. Schomberg's Gazette letter, vide N. C. XXVI. 388 and 481.

" The action of la Nereide alone with the three English ships, appears to have lasted from four o'clock till five, when she was relieved for a few minutes by the other two frigates.

[It is proper to remark here, that through the whole course of the business, the different reports with respect to the manœuvres and the time vary.]

" The calm returning, from six o'clock till seven the Nereide was at a considerable distance from the other frigates, and had still to sustain a contest with the whole of the enemy's division which had rallied against her.

" At a quarter after seven la Renommée and la Clorinde, favoured by a slight breeze, came up to the assistance of la Nereide; and on their approach, they having suffered but little, the enemy sheered off and neared the land, where our people lost sight of them in the darkness of the night.

Captain Lemaresquier was killed, and was replaced by Lieutenant Ponee, who fought the Nereide in the most gallant manner.

" This officer was congratulated through a speaking trumpet by the commander of the division, whom he informed that the frigate was not in a state to continue her manœuvres, but that she had still her guns and a brave crew in a perfectly fighting condition.

" Captain Roquebert now spoke the Nereide, desiring her to make the land, that he would take care to protect her, and ordered her to repair during the night, that she might be able to fight again the next day.

" At the same time he ordered la Clorinde to follow Renommée at a slight distance.

" After this communication between the three frigates, la Renommée and la Clorinde beat to windward, without being able to discover the enemy, and got a distance from the Nereide, though she did her utmost to keep up with them.

" In a tack of the two frigates, a man of la Clorinde fell overboard, and Captain St. Cricq endeavoured to save him; the manœuvre necessary for the purpose, however short its duration, threw la Clorinde to a considerable distance behind la Renommée.

" It was scarcely begun, when the interchange of shots between la Renommée and the English division, which now hove in sight, was heard. La Clorinde abandoned the drowning man, to take part in the engagement, but she, as well as la Nereide, was no longer perceived by la Renommée, which vessel, though she was at a distance from la Clorinde, made no attempt to bring her up before she began to fire, and thus found herself engaged single-handed with the enemy's division.

Captain Roquebert was killed, and a short time afterwards his lieutenant was wounded; this officer, however, did not quit the deck for more than a few minutes, and then returned to his post.

" At half after ten o'clock, la Renommée, surrounded by the four vessels with which she was engaged, was obliged to strike, after an engagement of an hour's duration, according to the report of the commander of that frigate; of three quarters of an hour, according to that of the captain of la Nereide; and of twenty minutes, according to that of Captain St. Cricq.

" This officer, however, had not reached the enemy till the firing ceased. He declares, that he did not observe that la Renommee and la Nereide were unable to fight any longer; and that he attributed the discontinuance of the firing on both sides to an apprehension of mistakes, arising from the darkness of the night.

" He made repeated signals to the frigates, but without success; they did not answer him, and he was soon satisfied that he was in the midst of the enemy, at the distance only of pistol-shot, between two of their vessels, and without succours.

" One of the frigates fired two shots at him, which he did not return, because he was endeavouring to discover where the other vessels were lying.

" Having been for some time thus employed, without success, he was obliged to crowd sail, in order to coast the land, which he supposed the two frigates to have made.

" This required manœuvres which he could only have recourse to when he got some respite from the enemy, two of whose frigates kept up a close fire on him from their bows.

" However, as he carried more sail than the enemy's frigates, he shot a-head, and had got out of sight of them by four o'clock in the morning.

" The further occurrences which took place with respect to la Clorinde have no connection with this affair.

" As to la Nereide, which had received orders to lie along shore, she was not in a state to move, and that, when morning appeared, no vessel whatsoever was in sight.

" The commander of la Nereide states, in his report, that, at half-after nine o'clock he perceived a tolerably brisk cannonade, which was the engagement of la Renommée; but he adds, that he did not consider it a very serious affair, because he conceived that he saw, by the light of the flashes, la Clorinde to windward, at a little distance, and that she did not attempt to take any part in the action.

" La Nereide being thus isolated at day-break in such a state as could not be repaired at sea, the commander determined to make the port of Tamatava, in order to provide for her repairs, which required considerable labour, and he was thus engaged, when, on the 25th of May, two frigates and a brig summoned him to surrender. La Nereide was not in a situation to resist; nevertheless, Lieutenant Ponée, availing himself of such means of resistance, as it appeared possible for him to have recourse to, obtained terms of capitulation, according to which he delivered to the enemy the fort and the frigate, upon conditions that his crew should be sent to France, where they are hourly expected.

" As I have already stated, the recital of these particulars varies in the three different reports which have reached me, but such is the total which they appear to furnish.

" We must bestow every proper tribute to the memory of Captains Roquebert and Lemaresquier, both of whom fell bravely fighting, and their loss is the more vexatious, because the unfortunate termination of the action may be attributed to faults which it would have been easy to avoid.

" It was at six o'clock in the morning, that the enemy's division was perceived six leagues to windward. It was superior in force to the French division by a vessel of twenty 32-pound carronades.

" Captain Roquebert was at perfect liberty either to give battle or to decline it. He is not to be blamed for the determination he formed to fight, and even to engage in a decisive action, for which, according to the report of Captain St. Cricq, he made the signal. But when this resolution was taken, how had it happened that, in place of bearing down upon the enemy together, and in order, he spent eight or nine hours in tacking, so that the action did not commence till four o'clock in the afternoon, whereby he exposed himself to all the variations of the wind, which, at the time, was in his favour, and to all the chances of a nocturnal engagement, from which he had no advantage to gain?

" How came it that he did not profit by this delay of nine hours, to concert with the captains upon his plan of attack, and the manœuvres which it would be necessary to make? When resolved upon a decisive action, why had he not engaged the enemy at such a distance, as would not only render his musketry useless, but be without the range of his carronades?

" Why had he not, when at the commencement of the battle he saw the Nereide more to leeward than himself, bring the Clorinde and Renommée up, in order to close equally with the enemy? and, above all, why had he not hurried this movement of closing with the enemy, when he saw the Nereide obeying his signal to the very letter, and every moment nearing still more, with a view to engage yard-arm and yard-arm the compact line of the enemy? Why, when the enemy had recourse to his sweeps to rally three ships against the Nereide, had not Captain Roquebert practised the same manœuvre to cover her, in place of remaining with the Clorinde, to engage at a great distance a single enemy's frigate?

" When towards evening the Renommée and Clorinde had disengaged the Nereide, which they perceived in a condition rendering her incapable of manœuvering, why had not orders been given to the Clorinde to take her in tow, the sure means of preserving her, and which would have prevented the fatal separation that took place a few hours afterwards?

" In short, why had not the Renommée, when she could no longer perceive the Clorinde in her wake, manœuvred with a view to rejoin that vessel, and why had she exposed herself singly to the fire of the whole English squadron, without foreseeing what must be the result of these partial actions, in which, whilst each vessel contended separately, they must all be captured one after another?

" There hangs over this last resolution, by which Captain Roquebert threw himself singly into the midst of the enemy's division, a veil which cannot be removed until the arrival of the officer who succeeded him in the

MARINE LAW. 155

command of the Renommée, for this officer concludes in these words the report which he has addressed to me:—' It is impossible for me to explain to you how Captain Roquebert came singly into the midst of the enemy before the ships of his division were rallied. It is a misfortune of which I can give only a verbal account.'

" These questions, which I have put to myself, are independent of those which the council of war will have to decide upon; 'and I disguise them the less, because it is of importance to call the attention of the officers of your marine to such faults as may have been committed, in order that they may, by reflection, prepare themselves so as to avoid similar, or any other faults, upon every occasion.

" It is of importance that they should be penetrated with this idea, that an honourable death is by no means a justification of fault, and that your Majesty is too firmly convinced of their courage to consider it as a merit in them; but that what you require of them is, a prudent foresight before battle, a sound judgment in the orders to be given, and a wise combination in the manœuvres and the attack.

" The Renommée had 93 men killed and wounded in this action; the Nereide 77, of whom 25 were killed; and the Clorinde but one man killed, and six wounded.

" Lieutenants Duplanty, of the Renommée, and Ponée, of the Nereide, whatever prepossessions may be entertained in favour of their defence, should, according to the regulations of the service, be tried by a council of war for the surrender of the frigates, to the command of which they had succeeded.

" The circumstances also of the Clorinde having taken a share in the action, from which she alone has escaped after the loss of the two other frigates, and particularly of the commandant of the division, require, in like manner, that the conduct of Captain St. Cricq should be submitted to the judgment of a council of war. A provision has been made for this case by the Ordinance of Marine of the 25th of March, 1763, article 54; inasmuch as the simple fact of the return of the Clorinde proves that she had quitted her commandant, and the council of war alone can decide, whether or not there has been any guilt in having so come away from her commodore."

To the copy of the above Report, published in the *Moniteur*, was affixed the following Order, from Buonaparte:—

" The Minister of Marine shall put the laws of the Empire in force. The Commandant of the Clorinde shall be brought before a Council of War, for having taken so small a share in the action—for having abandoned his Commodore—for having preferred his life to his honour—and for not having fulfilled his mission and executed the orders he received, to proceed to Batavia, and carry thither his cargo and the troops he had on board.

(Signed)   " NAPOLEON.
" The Minister Secretary of State,
(Signed)   " Count DARU."
" *Palace of St. Cloud, Nov.* 23, 1811."

The consequence of this Order was, a COUNCIL OF WAR; or, *French Naval Court Martial*; the proceedings of which are thus related in the *Moniteur*:

" *Paris, March* 20.—A Council of War was held on the 13th instant, on Captain St. Cricq, late commander of the frigate Clorinde, on charges: 1st, for not doing all in his power in the action of May 20, 1811, in which the frigate Renommée was captured: 2dly, for having separated himself from his commander almost at the instant of the action, when he should have kept very near, and have made no movement which could have carried him to a distance: 3dly, for not having, although the Clorinde was in a sufficient condition, made any attack on the enemy a little while after the separation from the Renommee, and almost at the moment when the enemy ceased his fire on that ship; the result of which attack might have been the abandonment by the enemy of his pursuit of the Renommée, if she were not too much reduced, or, on the other hand, if the enemy had been rendered unable to take possession of her: and, 4thly, for having voluntarily failed in his mission to the Isle of Java, which was prescribed to him by his instructions, dated December 22, 1810, should he be unable to enter the Isle of France.

The Council sat, by adjournments, till the 18th inst. and examined a number of witnesses; one of whom, Gerot Fabritius, a native of Enkhuysen, Lieutenant in the Clorinde, not being familiar with the French language, was, at his own request, examined in the English tongue.

" On the evening of the 18th inst. the Council decreed, by a majority of six voices to two, as follows:—

" In the name of the emperor and king.

" Napoleon by the grace of God, &c. to all present and to come, greeting.

" On 13 March, 1812, the council of war, formed by H. M.'s decree of 7 February, convoked at Paris by Vice-admiral Count Rosilly, the members of the court being Vice-admirals, Rosilly, Gantheaume, Missiessy; Rear-admirals, Dordelin, Cosmao, Hamelin; Captain Lemarant; Vice-admiral Emeriau, imperial procurator and reporter [judge-advocate]; Sanson, naval commissary and *greffier* [clerk], proceeded to try St. Cricq, *capitaine-de-vaisseau*, late commanding the frigate Clorinde; Ponée, *capitaine-de-fregate*, late commanding the frigate Nereide; and Defredot-Duplanty, *lieutenant-de-vaisseau*, late commanding the frigate Renommée. And the trial was continued by adjournments until the 18th, when the council finally declared, unanimously, François Ponée not guilty in respect to the surrender of Nereide: he is discharged, honourably acquitted; and it is ordered that his sword shall be restored to him by the president. The council unanimously declare Defredot-Duplanty not guilty in surrendering Renommée on the night of the 20-21st August, 1811. The charge is dismissed, and his sword will be restored by president.

" The council have determined (by a majority of six voices against two) that Jacques St. Cricq is guilty of disobedience to orders, but not so in the presence of the enemy, and they sentence him to be cashiered and declared unworthy of the service, as far as relates to not taking any part in the second engagement, when Renommée struck, and of having abandoned that frigate, through false manœuvre, irresolution, and want of judgment; and that, in conformity with the article of the law (which was read by the president), " *Every Commander of a ship of war, guilty of disobeying the orders or signals of his Commander, shall be deprived of his command; and if his disobedience occasions a separation, either of his own or another vessel of the squadron, he shall be cashiered, and be unworthy to serve; if this takes place in the presence of the enemy, he shall be condemned to death;* " the Council condemned the accused, Jacques St. Cricq, to three years imprisonment, in such place as the government shall appoint. They farther condemned him to be degraded from the Legion of Honor, and to pay all the costs of the process, in conformity to the law of 18 *germinal*, VII.; and ordered 200 copies of the judgment to be publicly affixed."

Immediately after reading the above sentence, the president made the condemned prisoner stand before him, and declared, in the name of the Legion of Honor, that he ceased from thenceforth to be a member of that corporation. It appears, that of the two dissentient voices, one was for capital punishment, and the other applied to the offence the 38th article of the law of 22 August, 1790.

NAVAL HISTORY OF THE PRESENT YEAR, 1812.
(July—August.)
RETROSPECTIVE and MISCELLANEOUS.

IN consequence of the hostile conduct of the American Government, towards Great Britain, Mr. Foster, our Envoy, left New York on the 14th of July, in the Atalanta sloop of war, and arrived at Portsmouth on the 19th of August. Mr. Baker, Secretary to the Envoy, remained at Washington, to act as occasion might require.

A large portion of the daily press in England has been engaged in promulgating errors with regard to America; by which the public has been induced more or less to approve of the measures which have now produced so serious a calamity as a new war. We have been persuaded to believe that our hostile system was useful, and that the American government had not the power, if it had the spirit, to resent provocation. The state of affairs between the two countries now stands thus: There have existed disputes on our celebrated Orders in Council; on the impressment of American seamen; and on certain points relating to Florida. Of these the first only has been settled by the revocation which took place on 23d June,[*] and that step

---

[*] N. C. XXVII. 28, 215, 466, 468, 471. XXVIII. p. 49, 73, 132, 137, 138, 139.

was too late in its adoption to prevent war, which was in fact declared on 18th June by America, who had been preparing many months. In consequence of which, an Order in Council was issued on 31st July, for an embargo on American vessels in our ports, and also for detaining them at sea. The next question now appears to be, whether, when that government hears of our repeal, they will revoke their declaration. On this momentous point the same sort of infatuation appears still to prevail in some degree. The writers who are instrumental thereto seem to forget, that two important points of difference, out of three, still remain at issue: that the declaration of war in America is a legislative act, and that to do away its effect another act must pass: that it is the people, and not merely the government of the United States, who have declared war; and that the people must be consulted before that declaration can be annulled. In short we are, contrary to all political prediction, at war with America; and before we can have peace again we must have a treaty. This is a question in which hundreds of thousands are interested, and relative to which we have felt it our duty to lend our aid towards dispelling deception, by stating the case distinctly and fairly.

Respecting the justness, policy, or probable success of the war, there is, in America, much difference of opinion. Various resolutions, and counter-resolutions, have been passed upon the subject. In an address for a public meeting, in the state of New York, are the words: " Disguise it as they may, one fact is too palpable for denial: the Rulers of our Government are compelling a free people to connect their destinies with those of the French Empire, and to unite in war with the Tyrant of Europe, for the destruction of England."—It may also be mentioned, that, while the House of Representatives of the State of Massachusetts have addressed their constituents in disapprobation of the war with England, the Senate of the same State have issued a counter-declaration in favour of the war.

The latest intelligence we have from America is by the Bloodhound gun-brig, which sailed from Annapolis, on the 24th of July, with Mr. Schaw the messenger, on board, who is returned to England, after delivering despatches to Mr. Baker, the British Secretary of Legation at Washington. At the departure of the Bloodhound, no intimation had been received at the seat of Government in America, of the revocation of the Orders in Council, or of any intention to that effect on the part of the British Government. We have still, therefore, to learn what effect may have been produced in America, by the arrival of the Gleaner, or any other vessel that took out accounts of the repeal of the Orders in Council. In the mean time, the Americans were making preparations for war according to their means, particularly in fitting out a number of privateers, by which they hoped to annoy the trade of this country. It was said to be a favourite scheme of the American Government to seduce British seamen who may happen to be made prisoners, to enter the American navy. For this purpose it had agents employed at the different ports where captured vessels were likely to arrive; and it is said, that upwards of 30 of the Bloodhound's crew had been induced to desert.

Great expectations were formed in America of Commodore Rodgers falling in with the Jamaica fleet, and capturing the greater part of it. H. M. S. Thetis, however, and the whole of the convoy, from Jamaica, arrived in the Downs on the 24th of August. On the 6th, Commodore Rodgers's squadron hove in sight of the convoy, upon which the Æolus, the Shannon, and the Belvidera frigates, which were escorting it across the Atlantic, parted company, in chase of the enemy.

On the 14th of August, Admiral Sir J. B. Warren sailed from Portsmouth, in the San Domingo, 80, Captain Gill, for the coast of America.— The Poictiers, 74, Sir John Poo Beresford; Sophie, Captain Lockyer; Magnet, Captain Maurice; and Mackarel schooner, sailed with him. The Tenedos, Captain Hyde Parker; and the Niemen (frigates), Captain Pym, were to follow as soon as possible.—Sir John, we understand, is gone out with powers to negociate, as well as to act offensively with the ships under his orders; but proposals of conciliation are, in the first instance, to be made. He goes direct to Halifax, and from thence to New York with his squadron.—He was spoken with by the Marlborough packet, from Lisbon, on the 19th of August, in lat. 46° 50′ N. long. 8° 25′ W.

On the 22d of July, Lord Wellington obtained a signal victory over Marmont, in the neighbourhood of Salamanca. Marmont himself was severely wounded, and is since dead; in killed, wounded, and prisoners, the enemy lost from 16 to 18,000 men; and King Joseph, who had left Madrid, with a corps of 15,000 men, for the purpose of reinforcing Marmont, very narrowly effected his escape, by flight. For his services on this occasion, Lord Wellington has been raised to the dignity of a Marquis of the United Kingdom.—Sir Home Popham, for his exertions on the North coast of Spain, has been honoured with Lord Wellington's particular approbation.

There has been much severe fighting, but no general action, between the French and the Russians. At the date of the latest accounts (August 4th) the French had gone into quarters of refreshment, in consequence, as it was said, of the great heat of the weather. The army was then at Witepsk, in the direction of Moscow.—The English Admiral, Martin, remains at Riga, and, by his judicious disposition of the gun boats, &c. has contributed greatly to the defence of that City.

The birth-day of his Royal Highness the Prince Regent was distinguished by a Naval Promotion which then took place. (*Vide* Promotions and Appointments, in a subsequent page.)

A few days before H. M. S. Niemen, Captain Pym, left her station off Rochfort, four of her boats were manned and sent in to attack a convoy, which were lying in an assailable position. The vessels, however, moved unperceived in the course of the night, excepting one *chasse marée*, which a boat, commanded by Mr. Downey (son of Mr. Downey, surgeon, R.N.) took possession of; but, unfortunately, the tide soon turned with very great strength, and a brig came out of the Loire, and re-captured her, with Mr. Downey, and 15 men.—The other boats returned safe to the Niemen.

Letters on Service,

Copied, verbatim, from the LONDON GAZETTE.

ADMIRALTY-OFFICE, JULY 21, 1812.

Copy of a Letter from Vice-admiral Sir Edward Pellew, Bart. to John Wilson Croker, Esq. dated on board the Caledonia, off Toulon, June 10, 1812.

SIR,

I HAVE the honour to enclose, for the information of the Lords Commissioners of the Admiralty, the copy of a letter and its enclosures, which I have received from Captain Rowley, of H. M. S. America, stating the particulars of a spirited attack upon the enemy's batteries at Languillia, and the capture of a convoy that had taken shelter under them.

I have the honour to be, &c.

EDW. PELLEW.

SIR, *H. M. S.* America, *off Languillia, May* 10, 1812.

I have the honour to inform you, that having yesterday, in company with the Leviathan and Eclair, fallen in with a convoy of eighteen sail of the enemy deeply laden, which took shelter under the town and batteries of Languillia, and Captain Campbell concurring in opinion with me as to the practicability of bringing them out or destroying them by getting possession of the batteries, the marines of both ships, under the direction of Captain Rea, of the America, were landed this morning at daybreak to effect it.

A party under Captain Owen, royal marines, of the Leviathan, was detached to carry a battery of five twenty-four and eighteen-pounders to the eastward, which he performed in a very spirited and judicious manner, the French officer who commanded falling in the attack; the main body in the mean time rapidly advancing through a severe fire of grape, carried the battery adjoining the town of Languillia (consisting of four twenty-four and eighteen-pounders and a mortar), though protected by a strong body of the enemy posted in a wood, and in several contiguous buildings, upon the latter of which the guns were immediately turned with much effect. The enemy were now driven from the houses lining the beach, by the fire of the Eclair, and the boats then proceeded to bring out the vessels that were secured by various contrivances to the houses and beach, their sails and rudders being mostly removed on shore: sixteen were towed off (as per enclosed list) which being accomplished, the marines were re-embarked in the most perfect order, under cover of the fire of the Eclair, and without molestation from the enemy, though a strong party was advancing from the town of Alassia to reinforce them.

I regret to state that our success has been clouded, and our loss on this occasion much extended, by an unfortunate accident which occurred in landing the party; the America's yawl being sunk by a chance shot from the only gun that could bear on the boats, and before assistance could be afforded, I lament to say, ten marines and one of the crew were drowned.

I have great satisfaction in the favourable report I feel it my duty to make of the officers, seamen, and marines, employed on this occasion; the gallant and able conduct of Captain Rea, who commanded the marines, was very conspicuous, and he reports in the most favourable manner of Captain Owen, and Lieutenants Neame, Cock, Cardon, and Hill, and of the orderly good conduct of the whole detachment. To Captain Bellamy I was much indebted for the handsome manner in which the Eclair was swept in, and the fire she kept up to cover and protect the troops and boats during their operations. The ships being prevented by the light and baffling winds from getting close enough to act. The services of the boats in landing and embarking the troops, and (being all armed with guns or carronades) assisting with their fire, and the expedition with which the enemy's vessels were brought out does much credit to Lieutenant Richardson, first of this ship, who had the direction of them, as also to Lieutenants Molesworth and Moodie, of the America, and Dobbs and Hambly, of the Leviathan, who were employed in them. I cannot conclude without requesting permission to recommend to your notice Mr. John Harvey, master's mate of this ship, who has particularly distinguished himself both on the present and other late occasions of boat service. I have the honour to be, &c.

Vice-admiral Sir Edward Pellew, Bart.   JOSIAS ROWLEY.
Commander-in-chief, &c.

List of Merchant Vessels captured and destroyed by his Majesty's Ships America, Leviathan, and Éclair, at Languillia, on the 10th day of May, 1812.

Settee, No. 9755, of 80 tons, laden with leather and sundries; captured and brought out.
Settee, No. 3084, of 50 tons, laden with wine; captured and brought out.
Settee, No. 7093, of 120 tons, laden with salt; captured and brought out.
Settee, No. 5097, of 70 tons, laden with leather and sundries; captured and brought out.
Settee, la Volante, of 160 tons, laden with salt; captured and brought out.
Settee, la Conception, of 80 tons, laden with salt; captured and brought out.
Settee, l'Assomption, of 40 tons, laden with wine; captured and brought out
Settee, l'Assension, of 60 tons, laden with wine; captured and brought out.
Settee, Notre Dame du Carmel de Penes, of 90 tons, laden with salt; captured and brought out.
Settee, No. 7249, of 70 tons, laden with leather and sundries; captured and brought out.
Settee, No. 2294, of 30 tons, laden with wine; captured and brought out.
Settee, No. 1116, of 25 tons, laden with wine; captured and brought out.
Settee, name unknown, of 40 tons, laden with brandy; captured and brought out.
Settee, name unknown, of 60 tons, laden with wine; captured and brought out.
Settee, name unknown, of 25 tons, laden with salt; captured and brought out.
Settee, name unknown, of 35 tons, laden with salt; captured and brought out.
Settee, name unknown, of 4 guns, and 90 tons, laden with salt; burnt in the harbour by the boats.
Settee, name unknown, of 60 tons, laden with salt; damaged by the shot and could not be got afloat.

                                          JOSIAS ROWLEY.

A List of Seamen and Marines belonging to his Majesty's Ship America, killed and wounded in an Action with the Enemy at Languillia, 10th May, 1812.

Killed.—John Hoan Davey, serjeant of marines; John Paine, private marine.

162   NAVAL HISTORY OF THE PRESENT YEAR, 1812.

Drowned.—James Fox, private marine; George Plum, ditto; Nicholas Segona, ditto; Edward Moriarty, ditto; Casper Bomb, ditto: Hendrick Bawker, ditto; Thomas Wilson, ditto; William Paole, ditto; John Hake, ditto Hewit Snell, ditto: James Ealey, able seaman.

Wounded.—Thomas Jones, able seaman, slightly; George Wheeler, private marine, ditto; William Lavercombe, ditto, severely; Jacob Banks, ditto, badly; Dennis Ford, ditto, dangerously (since dead); Charles Mills, ditto, badly; Robert Shipley, ditto, ditto; Conrad Elders, ditto, ditto; John M'Nabb, corporal of Marines, severely; Richard Brean, private marine, slightly; William Bromwell, ditto, severely; Edward Carr, ditto, slightly; Thomas Ashley, ditto, ditto.

Total killed—1 serjeant of marines, 1 private marine.
Total drowned—10 private marines, 1 seaman.
Total wounded—1 corporal of marines, 11 private marines (1 since dead), 1 seaman.

JOS. ROWLEY, Captain.
E. Y. BLOMLEY, Surgeon.

A List of Seamen and Marines of H. M. S. Leviathan, killed and wounded in Action with the enemy at Languillia, May 10, 1812.

Killed.—Corporal Rex; John Mills, seaman.

Wounded.—Thomas Williams, seaman; Michael Dunn, private marine dangerously; Robert Shorn, ditto, ditto; Isaac May, ditto, severely; Thomas Smallwood, ditto, ditto; Thomas Moore, seaman, ditto; Corporal Harrison, severely; Henry Collins, private marine, ditto.

PATRICK CAMPBELL, Captain.
R. GRIFFITH, Surgeon.

Copies of Two Letters from Captain Napier, of H. M.S. Thames, addressed to Rear-admiral Fremantle, and transmitted to John Wilson Croker, Esq. by Vice-admiral Sir Edward Pellew, Bart.

SIR,   *H.M.S. Thames, April* 16, 1812.

I enclose you a letter from Captain Nicholas, of the Pilot, by which you will observe he has taken ten vessels without loss; he speaks highly of Lieutenant Campbell, and Mr. Langlands, acting master, an excellent and brave officer.   I have the honour to be, &c.

CHARLES NAPIER.

Thomas Francis Fremantle, Esq. Rear-admiral of the Blue, &c.

SIR,   *H. M. Sloop Pilot, off Cape Palinuro, April* 16, 1812.

Having observed nine coasting vessels of the enemy hauled up on the beach near the town of Policastro, I thought it practicable to take them off by anchoring the Pilot close to the shore, which was immediately done, and her fire opened to drive away the armed force that was collected for their protection, and nearly at the same moment a party of seamen and the marines were landed, under the direction of Lieutenant Alexander Campbell, assisted by Mr. Langlands, the acting master, and through their gallantry and exertions above eighty of the civic militia were obliged to retire, and were kept in check by the marines and small arm men, whilst the vessels were launched, which was fully accomplished in about four hours, notwithstanding they were hauled very high up, and had been much stove by their crews. They proved to be laden with oil, and were from Pezzo bound to Naples.

I have great pleasure in reporting, that no person belonging to the Pilot was hurt in this affair, and which, from the enemy's having kept up almost a constant fire of musketry from behind trees and hedges, is to be attributed to the able conduct of Mr. Langlands, who had the charge of the people in advance at small arms, and I trust you will make it known to the rear-admiral, as he is a young man of great merit, and has repeatedly been recommended for his conspicuous bravery.

I have the honour to be, &c.
J. TOUP NICHOLAS, Commander:
Captain Napier, H. M. S. Thames.

SIR, *H.M.S. Thames, Sapri, May* 14, 1812.

I this day, in company with the Pilot, attacked the port of Sapri, defended by a strong battery and tower, mounting two thirty-two pounders, with an officer and thirty-eight men, which surrendered at discretion, after being battered for two hours within pistol-shot; but in consequence of their gallant defence, I allowed him to march out with the honours of war, but not to serve against us in this expedition. We found twenty-eight large vessels on the beach, loaded with oil, some of them nearly a quarter of a mile in the country, all of which were launched, and the battery in ruins before sun-set.

I owe much to the support I received from Captain Nicholas, who flanked the battery in a most judicious manner, and afterwards commanded the launching, assisted by my first lieutenant, Alexander Campbell, an officer of six years' standing, as well as Mr. Langlands, acting master of the Pilot, who, by his able disposition of the marines who were under his command (there being no officer of that corps on board), kept upwards of two hundred armed peasantry in check, and had only one man wounded.

The firing of both ships' companies was superior to any thing I ever saw, and their conduct on shore was no less praise-worthy. Neither ship lost men on board: our bowsprit wounded in three places, is the only material injury we have suffered. *I have, &c.*

Thomas Francis Fremantle, Esq. Rear-   CHAS. NAPIER.
admiral of the Blue, &c.

A letter has been received from Vice-admiral Sir Edward Pellew, to John Wilson Croker, Esq. dated off Toulon, the 23d of June, stating, that a small twenty-gun ship having escaped into Ciotat, where a new store-ship was fitting for sea, an attack was intended to be made upon the place on the 1st ultimo, with a detachment of the marines of his Majesty's squadron. The marines had reached the point intended at day-break; but the wind having fallen, and the ships appointed to cover the debarkation not being able in consequence to enter the bay, without whom it was not intended the marines should land, the latter were recalled without going ashore.

His Majesty's ship Kent was unfortunately struck by a chance shot from one of the batteries, by which accident Lieutenant Walton and one seaman were killed, and three or four wounded; the only casualty on the occasion.

Vice-admiral Sir Edward Pellew has transmitted to John Wilson Croker, Esq. a letter from Captain Hope, of H. M. S. Salsette, giving an account of his having, on the 21st of April last, captured, and afterwards destroyed, la Comete, a French privateer, of 2 eighteen-pounders, and 45 men: and also two letters from Lieutenant Charles Phillips, acting in the command of the Onyx sloop, and Lieutenant James J. Osborne, commanding the

Fearless gun-vessel, to the Honourable Rear-admiral Legge, the former giving an account of the burning of a brig on the beach of Conil, under the protection of a battery and musketry, by the boats of the Onyx and Desperate, under Lieutenant Biddulph, of the former; and the latter, stating the capture of a French privateer of one gun and eight men, with small arms, by the Fearless.

Copy of a Letter from Vice-admiral Thornborough, Commander-in-chief of his Majesty's Ships and Vessels on the Coast of Ireland, to John Wilson Croker, Esq. dated at Cork, the 15th Instant.

SIR,

I have to acquaint you, for the information of the Lords Commissioners of the Admiralty, H. M. S. Sybille captured, on the 10th instant, in latitude 49° 6' north, and longitude 8° 22' west, the French cutter privateer l'Aigle (formerly the Chesterfield Guernsey packet), commanded by Alexander Black, mounting fourteen guns, eight of which were thrown overboard in the chase, and having sixty-one men on board; the said privateer arrived this morning.

Captain Upton states the l'Aigle was only three days from Bennodet, near Quimper, and had captured, on the morning of the 10th, the brig Alicia, from Bristol bound to Gibraltar. I am, &c.

E. THORNBOROUGH, Vice-admiral.

Vice-admiral Sir Edward Pellew has transmitted to John Wilson Croker, Esq. a letter from Captain Moresby, of his Majesty's sloop Wizard, giving an account of his having, on the 3d of April, captured in the Archipelago, the Corcira, a xebeck privateer, of eight guns, and 60 men, belonging to Corfu; and also a letter from Captain Down, of his Majesty's sloop Redwing, stating his having, on the 8th of May, taken, off Cape St. Vieto, a small Neapolitan privateer, of one gun.

JULY 25.

Vice-admiral Murray has, in his letter to John Wilson Croker, Esq. of the 21st instant, reported the arrival at Yarmouth of the Eole French lugger privateer, of 14 guns (only five mounted), captured on the 16th, near Heligoland, by the boats of his Majesty's sloops Osprey, Britomart, and Leveret.

JULY 28.

Admiral Lord Keith has transmitted to John Wilson Croker, Esq. despatches from Captain Sir Home Popham, of H. M. S. Venerable, giving an account of his further proceedings subsequent to those reported in his former letters, and inserted in the Gazette of the 14th instant.

On the 2d, the squadron under his orders being off Guetaria, an attack was intended to be made upon that place, and two companies of royal marines were landed under Major Williams, accompanied by General Carrol, for the purpose of reconnoitering; but some parties of the enemy being discovered crossing the hills, and the Guerillas, whose co-operation had been expected, being engaged with the enemy in a different quarter, the plan of attack was relinquished, and the marines re-embarked, but without loss.

The Guerillas had been employed in an action with a detachment of the enemy conducting eighty prisoners from Asturias. One hundred and thirty of the enemy are stated to have been killed, and fifty taken, who had been left wounded on the field of battle, and the Spanish prisoners were liberated.

On the 6th, Sir Home Popham arrived off Castro, where a 24-pounder and a company of marines had been landed by Sir George Collier, from the Surveillante, to assist Colonel Longa in an attack on the place. Information was, however, received of the approach of two thousand five hundred French troops, whose arrival obliged Longa to retire, and the parties landed from the squadron were again re-embarked without loss. In the evening the enemy were seen marching into the town.

On the 7th the enemy were driven from the town by the fire of the squadron, and took post on the hills, and preparations were made for a landing and attack on the castle on the following morning, which accordingly took place on the 8th, when the commandant of the castle surrendered, with one hundred and fifty men, the remainder of the enemy's force having marched towards Larido. Twenty-six guns of different sizes were found in the town and castle of Castro; those in the former were withdrawn, and the latter was put into a state of defence, and garrisoned by the marines and Spanish artillerymen of the Iris, Captain Christian.

On the 10th the squadron proceeded off Puerta Galletta, to co-operate in an attack upon it with the Spanish troops under Longa; and, on the 11th much firing was kept up against the batteries; but the enemy being found to be stronger than the Spaniards had expected, the attack was abandoned. During the morning, Captain Bloye of the Lyra, landed with a party of marines, and knocked off the trunnions of the guns in the Bagona battery, and destroyed one mounted on a height.

On the 12th the Venerable anchored off Castro, which had been feebly attacked by the enemy the evening before; one of the imperial guards was wounded and brought in a prisoner.

On the 15th, the enemy's moveable column having been drawn by a feint to Santona, from whence it could not reach Guetaria in less than four days, another attack was intended to be made upon the latter place, in concert with the Guerillas under Don Gaspar, and with the promised aid of one of the battalions under General Mina.

Early in the morning of the 18th, one 24-pounder under Lieutenant Groves, and a howitzer under Lieutenant Lawrence, of the marine artillery, were landed from the Venerable, and mounted on a hill to the westward of Guetaria, under the directions of Captain Malcolm, of the Rhin, while the Hon. Captain Bouverie landed with two guns (one short 24-pounder and one 12-pounder carronade) from the Medusa; and, after many difficulties in drawing them up, mounted them on the top of a hill to the eastward. The Venerable's guns began firing at noon, and continued till sunset, when those of the enemy on that side were silenced; and the Medusa's were put in readiness to open on the following morning. During the night, however, intelligence was received of the approach of a body of French troops, which afterwards proved to be a division of between two and three thousand men, that had just arrived at St. Sebastian's from France, and was immediately sent forward by forced marches to Guetaria.

The uncertainty with respect to the enemy's force, and the disposition of the Guerillas to oppose their advance, prevented the re-embarkation of the guns and men landed from the squadron, until the retreat of the Spaniards, after some skirmishing with the superior numbers of the French, in which the latter are stated to have suffered severely. Captain Bouverie then destroyed the two guns from the Medusa, and re-embarked with all his men, and every thing belonging to the guns; Captain Malcolm was detained longer, by a message brought to him by one of Don Gaspar's aid-de-camps, stating that the enemy had been beaten back, and urging him to remain in his battery; finding, however, that the enemy was advancing fast, he gave orders to re-embark, and brought off his party, with the exception of three midshipmen and twenty-nine men, who were taken prisoners, but fortunately without having one man killed or wounded.

Sir Home Popham had sent to propose an exchange of the men taken on this occasion for some of the French prisoners on board the squadron, and was in hopes of succeeding in this proposal.

The Spaniards lost a captain of artillery, and had a serjeant and ten men badly wounded. Those in want of surgical aid were received on board the Venerable.

The detachment expected from General Mina's army arrived the morning after the action, and joined Don Gaspar, having marched eighteen Spanish leagues in two days.

JULY 28.

Copy of a Letter from Lieutenant Thomas Warrand, commanding H. M. Schooner Sealark, addressed to Admiral Sir Robert Calder, Bart. and transmitted by the latter to John Wilson Croker, Esq.

SIR, H. M. Schooner Sealark, July 23, 1812.

I have the honour to inform you, that on the 21st instant, when cruizing off the Start, in the execution of your orders, at eight A.M. a signal was made from the signal station, of an enemy being in the S. E. quarter; after running for three hours in that direction, I discovered a large lugger under English colours, chacing and firing at two large merchant ships steering up Channel, which I believe were West Indiamen. On the lugger discovering the Sealark to be a cruizer, she altered her course to starboard, and made all possible sail; but finding the schooner gaining on her, she shortened sail, hoisted English colours, and cleared for action, and wore repeatedly, to endeavour to get to windward of the schooner; but, fearing she might escape if she had so done, I was determined to lay her on board, which I accomplished between her fore and main-chains, when an action commenced, which lasted one hour and thirty minutes; during which time a most severe fire was kept up with great guns and musketry, the enemy using hand grenades, &c. when, perceiving that she had taken fire, I then directed Mr. James Beavor, the acting master, to board her, which he did in the most spirited manner, and carried her. She proves to be the Ville de Caen, Captain Cocket, of sixteen guns and seventy-five men, belonging to St. Maloe's; had sailed from the Isle of Bas the day before, had taken nothing, and is the same vessel which had beaten off the Sandwich lugger some time since. I am sorry, Sir, to acquaint you, that our loss has been very severe, having had seven men killed (amongst whom was my clerk), and myself and twenty-one men wounded, several of them dangerously. The enemy's loss, as nearly as I can collect, has been fifteen killed, who, with the captain, were found on deck when taken possession of; and sixteen wounded, most of them severely. I beg particularly to recommend to your notice the steady, brave, and good conduct of Mr. Beavor, the acting master, with the pilot, and every other petty officer, seaman, and marine engaged in this arduous and unequal contest. I enclose a return of the killed and wounded.

I have the honour to be, &c.

THOMAS WARRAND, Lieut. and Com.

Admiral Sir Robert Calder, &c. &c. &c.

A List of Men killed and wounded in the Action with the French Lugger Privateer La Ville de Caen, of Sixteen Guns, Captain Cocket, off Portland, 21st July, 1812.

Killed.

Mr. John Purnel, clerk; Joseph Cattano, able seaman; Thomas Morgan, marine; Isaac Gould, able seaman; Joseph Hill, ditto; Alexander Brodie, ditto; John Barglehole, boatswain's mate.

Wounded.

Lieutenant Warrand, commander; William Birket, quarter-master; Daniel Brade, able seaman; John Harris, ditto; John Robinson, ditto; John M'Minis, ditto; Thomas Dunsford, ditto; John Heath, marine; Richard Griffiths, able seaman; John Phifer, ordinary seaman; Thomas Ashley, ditto; George Sales, ditto; William Evans, able seaman; John Millwright, ditto; William Robson, ditto; Gracious Gain, marine; James Cumings, gunner's mate; James Jackson, able seaman; Thomas Bradbury, ditto; Henry Johnston, ditto; John Wakeham, corporal; Mr. Alexander Gunn, midshipman.

T. WARRAND, Lieut. and Com.
F. BLESSMAN, Assist. Surg.

AUGUST 8.

Vice-admiral Sir Edward Pellew has transmitted to John Wilson Croker, Esq. a letter from the Hon. Captain Waldegrave, of H. M. S. Volontaire, giving an account of the capture of the Colombe French felucca, carrying one long gun and eight swivels, with forty-five men, on the 23d of June, off Cape Croisette, by the boats of the Volontaire, under the directions of Lieutenant Shaw. One midshipman and two seamen were wounded in the boats; and, on the side of the enemy, three were killed and seven wounded.

The felucca was commanded by an Enseigne de Vaisseau, and sent out expressly to attack the Volontaire's boats, which were waiting to intercept the coasting trade from Marseilles.

AUGUST 11.

Copy of a Letter from Captain Campbell, of H. M. S. the Leviathan, addressed to Captain Rowley, of the America, and transmitted by Vice-admiral Sir Edward Pellew to John Wilson Croker, Esq.

H M. S. Leviathan, off Cape del Mello,
SIR,   June 27, 1812.

A convoy of eighteen sail of square and latine rigged vessels having assembled at Languillia and Allassio; the Curaçoa having joined, which, with the Imperieuse and Eclair you had formerly placed under my orders, made our force, I conceived, sufficient to attack both places, either to destroy or bring the vessels out.

This morning, about an hour before day-break, the marines were landed between the towns, under the command of Captain Owen (royal marines), of this ship, covered by Eclair. They had hardly formed on the beach before they were attacked by treble their number. Prisoners report they had upwards of five hundred men in the two towns, a company having come to each in the evening, independent of one in each as its garrison; the 52d regiment of the line, consisting of thirteen hundred men, having been detached from Genoa a few days before, to the different towns along the coast: but nothing could withstand our brave fellows; they dashed at them with the bayonet, and drove them from their batteries (one of five guns, the other of four and a mortar), into the towns, killing a great many (upwards of twenty being counted, besides two officers) and taking fourteen prisoners, all Frenchmen. After spiking the guns and destroying the carriages, they were embarked; but, though the ships were anchored within less than musket shot of the towns, and Eclair on her sweeps, going where she could be of most effect, the launches, and other boats with carronades, keeping up a heavy fire, we could not effectually drive them from the houses to enable our boats to take the vessels off, who were made fast in all manner of ways, with sails unbent, rudders unshipt, &c. without risk of great loss, we therefore destroyed them with our guns.

I want words sufficiently to express my admiration of the conduct and gallantry of Captain Owen, and the officers, non-commissioned officers, and privates of royal marines, as also of the officers and seamen employed in the boats. I feel much indebted to Lieutenant Dobbs, first of this ship, for his judicious arrangement in disembarking, embarking, and covering the marines, as they advanced to the different batteries.

It is most painful to me to add, we have suffered severely; an account of which I send enclosed.

I have the honour to be, &c.
PATRICK CAMPBELL.

A List of killed and wounded in Storming the Batteries, &c. at Languillia and Allassio, on the 27th of June, 1812.

Leviathan—1 seaman, 1 marine, killed; 2 seamen, 9 marines, severely wounded; 1 midshipman, 5 marines, slightly wounded.

Curaçoa—3 marines, killed; 1 marine, severely; 2 marines, slightly wounded.

Imperieuse—1 seaman, 3 marines, killed; Lieutenant William Walpole, 1 seaman, 5 marines, severely wounded; 4 marines, slightly wounded.

PAT. CAMPBELL.

Admiral Young has transmitted to John Wilson Croker, Esq. a letter from Lieutenant William Henry Dixon, of H. M. sloop the Britomart, to Captain Hunt, her commander (of which the following is a copy) giving an account of the capture of L'Eole French privateer; the arrival of which at Yarmouth was announced in the Gazette of the 25th of last month.

H. M. Sloop Britomart, Heligoland Harbour,
SIR, *17th July,* 1812.

As senior officer, I have the honour to acquaint you, for the information of Captain Clinch, of H. M. sloop Osprey, as well as that of the commander in chief, that I proceeded yesterday agreeably to your order, with our cutter manned and armed, in company with the boats of the Osprey and Leveret, in chace of an enemy's lugger, eight or nine leagues N. W. of this island. At half past one, being about five or six leagues, observed the lugger at anchor; but immediately on seeing us she weighed and made sail. I then cheered the boats, and sallied on till half past three, and being the leading boat, opened my fire on her, about musket-shot distance, which was returned from the lugger, when she hoisted French colours and wounded one of my men. The Osprey's boat then closing with me, I thought the enemy of too great a force to attempt boarding without the assistance of the Leveret's boat, which was at that time about half a mile distant. On her coming abreast of us, and being in the enemy's wake, our situations were such as to enable me to take the larboard, the Leveret's the starboard quarter, and the Osprey's boat the stern; we then cheered, and prepared for boarding. The Osprey's boat and ours grappled his stern, and from their well-directed fire and spirited defence, it was nearly ten minutes before we could make good our boarding. On our getting on board we still met with a well-contested resistance for the space of ten minutes, when they struck their colours and called for quarter. We then ceased the attack, but they still continued to fire pistols up the hatchways, which wounded one or two of our people, till we perfectly silenced them, took possession, and hoisted the English ensign. She proved to be L'Eole French lugger privateer, of fourteen guns, but only six mounted, commanded by Captain

Dubost, with a complement of thirty one officers and men,· belonging to Dunkirk, out one day from Schiermonnikoog on a cruize, but had made no captures.

I beg leave to state to you the support I received from Lieutenant Malone, and boat's crew of the Osprey, who behaved in a most determined and gallant manner in boarding; likewise that of Lieutenant Romney, of the Leveret; but, unfortunately, his oars getting foul of my boat, obliged him to drop astern, and prevented his sharing in this glorious and unequal contest.

Any further encomiums from me of their gallant conduct, would be needless; suffice it to say, they behaved with the coolness and intrepidity of British seamen.

I beg leave also to enclose herewith a return of the killed and wounded in the attack, and have the honour to be, &c.

W. H. DIXON, Senior Lieut.

*To William Buckly Hunt, Esq. Commander
of H. M. Sloop Britomart.*

*List of killed and wounded in the Attack of the French Lugger Privateer
L'Eole, on the 16th July, 1812.*

Osprey's Boat—William Cox, quarter-master, killed; Abraham Barker, ship's corporal; William Hunt, quarter-master's-mate, dangerously wounded; Samuel Adams, ship's coxswain, ditto; Joseph Antony, sailmaker's crew, ditto; John Colwood, able seaman, ditto; Duncan Crawford, captain of forecastle, severely wounded; John Vintner, captain of foretop, ditto.

Britomart's Boat—Peter Brewer, ordinary seaman, killed; Ralph Crump, able seaman, severely wounded; Lieut. W. H. Dixon, slightly wounded; John Smith, able seaman, ditto; Luke M'Carty, landman, ditto; William Comp, private marine, ditto.

Leveret's Boat—None killed or wounded.

AUGUST, 15.

Extract of a Letter from Vice-Admiral Sir James Saumarez, Bart. K. B. &c. to John Wilson Croker, Esq. dated on board His Majesty's Ship Victory, in Hawke Road, 5th August 1812.

Herewith I have the honour to enclose, for the information of the Lords Commissioners of the Admiralty, a letter I have received from Rear-Admiral Martin, dated Riga, the 25th ult. transmitting the accompanying official paper, giving an account of a spirited attack by Prince Bagration on a large body of the enemy's cavalry, which were completely routed, and one thousand men made prisoners.

Extract of a Letter from Rear-Admiral Martin to Vice-Admiral Sir James Saumarez, dated at Riga, the 25th July, 1812.

This instant, on my return from our advanced post, where Captain Stewart is stationed with a division of gun-boats, I have the satisfaction to learn that a Messenger arrived during my absence, with intelligence of the Prince Bragation having attacked Davoust's cavalry in a most spirited manner, the result of which is made public at this place by the inclosed official paper.

(Translation.)

Intelligence of the Operations of the Army, which has been received here this day, dated at Polotzk, the 7th (19th) July.

In the first engagement of consequence which has taken place, victory has declared itself in favour of our native country and of humanity. Prince Bagration, who was employed in the execution of the movements entrusted to him, in order to effect a junction with the first army, fell in, on his march with his avant-garde, with the whole of the enemy's cavalry. The Russian troops, who had long been eager for battle, fell in upon them, and after the most resolute resistance of the enemy, which rendered this battle the more conspicuous, nine regiments of the enemy were completely cut down, above 1000 men, and upwards of 50 Staff and upper Officers, made prisoners. The difficulties which the enemy had endeavoured to lay in the way of the operations of the second army are now removed. Nothing now stands in the way to prevent these two armies, with their united strength, from preparing for the swarm of their enemies the fate with which every desolating conqueror has ended, so far as the history of nations has taught us. This praiseworthy battle we can consider as the pledge for further brilliant deeds. While victory will conduct our feelings in a new battle, the victims of our opponent will diminish their confidence in the fortune of war, as well as their power and inclination for making resistance.

Riga, 13*th* (25*th*) *July*, 1812.

Extract of another Letter from Vice-Admiral Sir James Saumarez, Bart. and K. B. &c. to John Wilson Croker, Esq. dated on board the Victory, in Hawke Road, 7*th August*, 1812.

Herewith I transmit a Letter I have this morning received by express from Hano, from Rear-Admiral Martin, dated Riga, the 27th ultimo, informing me of the junction of General Barclay de Tolli, Commander in Chief of the Russian army, with the corps of Prince Bagration.

Extract of a Letter from Rear-Admiral Martin to Vice-Admiral Sir James Saumarez, dated at Riga, the 27*th July*, 1812.

General Barclay de Tolli, the Commander in Chief of the Russian army, has announced his junction, by forced marches, with the corps of Prince Bagration at Witepsk, where the Messenger who is just arrived left him on the 24th instant.

The Emperor Alexander had himself reached Smolenski, probably to stimulate by his presence the natives of that loyal province to exertions suited to the danger with which they are threatened.

The Emperor's activity and earnestness in the prosecution of the war, affords an admirable example to his subjects who in Old Russia are devoted to his cause.

The Nobles of Moscow have offered to raise one hundred thousand men at their own expence, besides a voluntary contribution of two millions of silver rubles, to be at the Emperor's disposal.

We learn by the same Messenger, that the Peace with Turkey is ratified.

Copy of another Letter from Vice-Admiral Sir James Saumarez, Bart. and K. B. &c. to John Wilson Croker, Esq. dated on board the Victory, in Hawke Road, 8*th August* 1812.

SIR,

Herewith I enclose a copy of intelligence of the operations of the Russian army, published at Riga, which I received yesterday evening from Rear-Admiral Morris, to whom it had been transmitted by Rear-Admiral Martin, in a merchant vessel, which you will please to lay before their Lordships.

I am, &c.   J. SAUMAREZ.

(Translation.)

Intelligence this day received of the Operations of the Army.

The objects of the battle, which the advance of Prince Bagration's army victoriously sustained with the enemy, is accomplished. The first west army has effected a junction with that of Prince Bagration, and now both hasten mutually to the attack of the enemy.

At the same time, the agreeable intelligence of the final conclusion of peace with the Ottoman Porte, is received. With united force the Russian armies now stand opposite the enemy, whose operations have hitherto been confined to preventing their junction, but which objects they have been unable to accomplish.

Their brethren in arms on the Danube, now turn from their conciliated opponents towards them, to take part in their deeds, from the result of which, Russia has to expect immortal glory, and oppressed Europe, the dawn of freedom.

(Signed) ESSEN, Lieut. Gen.
and General Governor of Riga.

Riga, 15 (27) *July* 1812.

Admiral Lord Keith has transmitted to John Wilson Croker, Esq. letters from Captain Sir Home Popham, of His Majesty's ship Venerable, dated the 30th ult. and 1st and 4th instant; the two former giving an account of an attack made upon the town of Santander and the Castle of Ano, at the mouth of its harbour, by a detachment of the Royal Marines, embarked on board the squadron under the orders of Sir Home, in conjunction with the Spanish Guerrillas under General Porlier. The castle was taken possession of by the Marines, but the garrison of Santander having received reinforcements, which made it much stronger than had been expected, General Porlier was unable to advance upon the place, and the Marines which had pushed on to co-operate in the attack, were obliged to fall back upon the castle, with some loss. Captains Lake, of the Magnificent, and Sir George Collier, of the Surveillante, who commanded the detachment, were wounded, as also Captain Noble, of the Marines, who was taken prisoner.

The last letter from Sir Home Popham states, that on the 3d instant the French evacuated the town of Santander; of which a detachment of Marines from the frigates lying in the harbour immediately took possession. Twenty guns, of different sizes, were found in it, with a quantity of ammunition.

Vice-Admiral Murray has transmitted to John Wilson Croker, Esq. a letter from Captain Willis, of His Majesty's sloop the Leveret, giving an account of his having, on the 4th instant, captured the French lugger privateer Le Brave, of four guns and twenty-two men, out four days from Groningen.

AUGUST 18.

Copy of a Letter from the Right Hon. Lord Keith, K.B. Admiral of the Red, &c. to John Wilson Croker, Esq; dated on board His Majesty's ship San Josef, off Ushant, the 15th instant.

SIR,

The Goldfinch has this moment joined me from Basque Roads with a dispatch which Sir Home Popham delivered to Captain Waller at St. Andero, on the 9th instant.

I lose no time in transmitting a copy thereof, and congratulate their Lordships upon the highly satisfactory intelligence that it contains.

It is gratifying to observe that the operations of the squadron upon the north coast of Spain have been serviceable to the army; and that the arrangements made by Sir Home for seconding his Lordship's further intentions appear to be judicious.

I have, &c.   KEITH, Admiral.

Venerable, Harbour of Santander, August 2d, 1812.

I have the honour to enclose, for your Lordship's information, a copy of a letter which I have just received from Sir Howard Douglas.

I feel a great degree of satisfaction that the Earl of Wellington should have so handsomely marked his approbation of the services of the squadron which your Lordship has placed under my orders, and I am not a little happy at having anticipated the wishes of his Lordship.

HOME POPHAM.

Admiral Lord Keith, K.B, &c. &c. &c.

Medina del Campo, Sunday, August, 2d, 1812.

The army is advancing; head-quarters at Cuellar. The enemy still retiring, having abandoned Valladolid with 4000 sick and wounded, and stores, ammunition, &c. We are now a part of the allied army.

I had an opportunity, in a long conference with Lord Wellington, of giving a detailed account of your operations; and am happy to inform you, that his Lordship is fully satisfied of the use they have been of to his movements. An intercepted letter from Caffarelli proves this, by stating, in answer to an order he had received to join Marmont, that a British armament being on the coast, he could not detach a single man; indeed some troops which he had already sent, were recalled on the appearance of our squadron.   HOWARD DOUGLAS.

Promotions and Appointments.

CARLTON-HOUSE, JUNE 1, 1812.

His Royal Highness the Prince Regent has been pleased, in the name and on the behalf of his Majesty, to approve of the nomination of the Rev. James Stanier Clarke, F.R.S. Chaplain to the Household, and Librarian to his Royal Highness, to be Historiographer to his Majesty, in the room of the late Rev. L. Dutens.

ADMIRALTY-OFFICE, AUGUST 12, 1812.

This day, in pursuance of the pleasure of his Royal Highness the Prince Regent, in the name and on the behalf of his Majesty, the following Flag-officers of his Majesty's Fleet were promoted, viz.

Admirals of the White.—Robert Man, Esq. John Henry, Esq. to be Admirals of the Red.

Admirals of the Blue.—Sir Charles Henry Knowles, Bart. Hon. Thomas Pakenham, Robert Deans, Esq. James Hawkins Whitshed, Esq. to be Admirals of the White.

Vice-admirals of the Red.—Edward Tyrrel Smith, Esq. Sir Thomas Graves, K.B. Thomas Macnamara Russell, Esq. Sir Henry Trollope, Knt. Sir Henry Edwyn Stanhope, Bart. to be Admirals of the Blue.

Vice-admirals of the White.—Sir Isaac Coffin Greenly, Bart. John Aylmer, Esq. Samuel Osborn, Esq. Richard Boger, Esq. John Child Purvis, Esq. Theophilus Jones, Esq. to be Vice-admirals of the Red.

Vice-admirals of the Blue.—John M'Dougall, Esq. James Alms, Esq. Eliab Harvey, Esq. Sir Edmund Nagle, Knt. John Wells, Esq. Richard Grindall, Esq. George Martin, Esq. Sir Richard John Strachan, Bart. and K.B. Sir William Sidney Smith, Knt. Thomas Sotheby, Esq. to be Vice-admirals of the White.

Rear-admirals of the Red.—Robert Devereux Fancourt, Esq. Sir Edward Buller, Bart. Hon. Robert Stopford, Mark Robinson, Esq. Thomas Revell Shivers, Esq. Francis Pickmore, Esq. John Stephens Hall, Esq. John Dilkes, Esq. William Lechmere, Esq. Thomas Foley, Esq. to be Vice-admirals of the Blue.

Rear-admirals of the White.—Rowley Bulteel, Esq. William Luke, Esq. Isaac George Manley, Esq. John Osborn, Esq. Edmund Crawley, Esq. Charles Boyles, Esq. Sir Thomas Williams, Knt. Thomas Hamilton, Esq. Sir Thomas Boulden Thompson, Bart. John Laugharne, Esq. William Hargood, Esq. George Gregory, Esq. John Ferrier, Esq. Richard Incledon Bury, Esq. Robert Moorsom, Esq. to be Rear-admirals of the Red.

Rear-admirals of the Blue.—William Bligh, Esq. Lawrence William Halsted, Esq. Edward Oliver Osborn, Esq. Sir Harry Neale, Bart. Sir Joseph Sydney Yorke, Knt. Hon. Arthur Kaye Legge, Francis Fayerman, Esq. Right Hon. George Earl of Galloway, Thomas Francis Fremantle, Esq. Sir Francis Laforey, Bart. Philip Charles Durham, Esq. Israel Pellew, Esq. Alexander Fraser, Esq. Benjamin Hallowell, Esq. George Johnstone Hope, Esq. Right Hon. Lord Amelius Beauclerc, William Taylor, Esq. James Nicoll Morris, Esq. George Burdon, Esq. William Brown, Esq. Thomas Byam Martin, Esq. to be Rear-admirals of the White.

And the undermentioned Captains were also appointed Flag-officers of his Majesty's Fleet, viz.

William Johnstone Hope, Esq. Right Hon. Lord Henry Paulet, Charles William Paterson, Esq. George Cockburn, Esq. Thomas Surridge, Esq. Samuel Hood Linzee, Esq. James Carpenter, Esq. Robert Barton, Esq. Graham Moore, Esq. Matthew Henry Scott, Esq. Joseph Hanwell, Esq. Henry William Bayntun, Esq. Hon. Francis Farington Gardner, Sir Richard King, Bart. Edward Griffith, Esq. Edward James Foote, Esq. Richard Lee, Esq. William Pierrepont, Esq. Peter Halkett, Esq. William Bedford, Esq. to be Rear-admirals of the Blue.

Admirals and Captains appointed.

Admiral Sir John Borlase Warren, Bart. K.B. is appointed commander-in-chief of H.M.'s squadron on the Halifax and West India stations, and down the whole Coast of America.

Rear-admiral Cockburn to succeed the Hon. Admiral Legge in the command at Cadiz. The Marlborough is to be fitted for his flag-ship.

Captains.—Sir Home Popham, John Harvey, and William Hotham, to the Royal Yachts; David Milne, to the Dublin; J. Broughton, to the Cornwall; E. R. Baker, to the Warspite; Charles Ross, to the Marlborough; Sir John Gore, to the Revenge; Sir Thomas Hardy, to the Ramillies; H. Lambert, to the Java; G. Harris, to the

Belle Poule; C. D. Pater, to the William and Mary yacht; A. W. Schomberg, to the York; G. Hayes, to the Magnificent; R. Barrie, to the Grampus; A. Shippard, to the Asia; T. B. Cochrane, to the Magicienne; A. Brine, to the Sheldrake; H. J. Lyford, to the Erebus; C. M'Donald, to the Scylla; J. Harper, to the Saracen; T. Flynn, to the Cephalus; ———— Squire, to the Onyx; T. Warrand, to the Sea Lark (the establishment of which, in acknowledgment of Captain W.'s late gallantry, has been increased); ———— Pechell, to the San Domingo; C. Gill, to the Cleopatra; James Brisbane, to the Vengeur; ———— Hanwell, to the Dictator; N. Mitchell, to the Nimrod; ———— Hornby, to the Stag; John Bedford, to the Childers; Edward Grey, to the Fairy; S. Leslie, to the Baracouta; E. S. Clay, to the Raisonable; A. King, to the Rainbow; E. S. Dickson, to the Swiftsure; G. R. Sartorius, to the Boxer; ———— Owen (brother of Commodore Owen), to the rank of post captain, in the Cornelia; A. W. J. Clifford, of the Cephalus; ———— Pringle, of the Sparrowhawk; E. R. Sibly, of the Swallow; H. Weir, of the Calypso; to the rank of post captains.

The following twenty Commanders were also promoted to the rank of Post-captain on the Prince Regent's birth-day:—E. Ellicott, to the Hebe; A. Milner, to the Gorgon; J. Barker, to the Morriston; P. Rye, to the Providence; J. Veitch, to the Alonzo; A. Mott, to the Prince William; J. Gifford, to the Sheldrake; T. Clinch, to the Osprey; G. L. Geyt, to the Stork; B. S. Bluett, to the Childers; H. G. Morris, to the Jalouse; S. Chambers, to the Arachne; W. Autridge, to the Erebus; E. A. Down, to the Redwing; T. Whinyates, to the Frolic; W. Hellard, to the Snake; J. Thompson, to the Brune; A. Atchison, to the Scylla; G. Moubray, to the Moselle; A. Cunningham, to the Bermuda.

Captain John Hearding, quay-master at Milford Haven, to be the East India Company's agent at Milford.

Lieutenants, &c. appointed.

Matthew Hewson, M. Cowan, Robert Andoe, and Henry Wise, to the Clarence; Nathaniel Ball, George N. Jackson, Henry Frederick Sewell, and C. Bennet, to the Cornwall; David M'Crery, to the Mutine; Thomas Jager, to the Laurestinus; James Robertson (1), to the Rifleman; Thomas Shepherd, to the Bittern; George Bassan, to the Dannemark; Thomas Patton, to the Egeria; Francis Fead, to the Queen; James G. Gordon, to the Egmont; Thomas W. Kent, to the Childers; Hugh B. White, to the Pompée; Daniel W. Randall, to the Christian VII.; Charles Adams, to the Theseus; James Lambert, to the Parthian; James Campbell (2), to the Elephant; William Stone (1), to the Royal William; George Hall, to the Adamant; Flowers Beckett, to the Bittern; George Jackson and J. Scott, to the Indefatigable; A. Wray, to the Minden; ———— Moore, to the Cordelia; H. E. Stanhope, to the Norge; G. Pechell, to the San Domingo; H. R. Rokeley, to the Impetueux; John Sissons, to the Childers; James Hewett, to the Crocodile; W. P. Croke, to the San Domingo; J. L. Meik, to the Barfleur; Rob. Watts, to the Fox; Fred. Houghton, to the Magnet; John Wilkinson, to the Trinculo; Thomas Hughes, to the Mackarel; T. M. Blaney, to the Circe; G. A. Westphall, James Caunes, G. C. Urniston, W. Roberts, W. D. Bigland, to the Marlborough; W. Cobb, to the Poictiers; D. W. Randall, to the Christian; H. D. Chadds, W. A. Herringham, and G. Buchannan, to the Java; J. Davis, to the Fox; G. Pidlaw, to the Grampus; J. Pakenham, to the Magicienne;

W. F. Spence, to the Justitia ; R. Roper, to the Saracen ; H. Squire, to the St. Antonio ; J. Hellard, to the Gladiator ; H. F. Pogson, to the Bold ; ——— Reid, to the Arrogant ; J. Smith, (7) (made commander) to the Stromboli ; ——— Norton (made commander) to the Wilhelmina ; Henry T. Browne Collier, D. Roberts, ——— Keenan, J. Stoddart, T. Warrand, E. Hall, J. C. G. Roberts, H. Jenkinson, and T. Eyre, to the rank of commander ; Messrs. R. Edwards, H. Paddon, Low, Williams, W. Woodley, ——— Keeling, T. Denston, and M. Derewzey, to the rank of lieutenant.

Pursers.—G. W. Harrison, to the Minden ; Simeon Bishop, to the Childers ; T. Watson, to the Paulina ; ——— Lane, to the Genereux ; James Henderson, to the St. Domingo ; ——— Tackle, to the Canada ; ——— Williams, to the Rodney ; ——— Godwin, to the Salsette.

Secretaries.—Richard Speare, Esq. to Vice-Admiral Sir W. S. Smith ; George R. Hulbert, Esq. to Admiral Sir J. B. Warren.

Masters.—T. Hodgson, to the St. Domingo ; John Lamb, to the Poictiers ; G. Garson, to the Magnificent ; W. F. Baker, to the Stag ; J. Russell, to the Brunswick ; R. Lesby, to the Success ; M. Grose, to the Diomede ; P. Dall, to the Dublin ; P. Willins, to the Nimrod ; W. B. Stevenson, to the Racoon ; T. M. Copplestone, to the Childers ; R. Ashford, to the Pylades ; G. Pearth, to the Grampus ; G. Thoms, to the Marlborough ; B. Robinson, to the Java ; T. Gransden, to the Bellepoule ; J. Gritton, to the Laurestinus ; J. Norie, to the Colossus ; J. H. Sparke, to the Dryad ; T. Miller, to the Desirée.

A List of Midshipmen who have passed for Lieutenants in August :—

Sheerness.—P. Wright, J. A. Moore, P. Stokes, P. Barnes, W. Barker, T. Beasley, W. Nash, E. Keane, S. Link, J. Jane, E. Ackland, and E. Montagu.

Portsmouth.—E. H. Jacob, A. Ross, H. Fortescue, W. Boyce, and R. Charlesson.

Surgeons, &c. appointed.

Mr. James Guthrie, to the Asia ; John May, to the Dublin ; John Lind, to the battalion of marines now forming at Portsmouth ; Stephen Lawson to the Dradlin ; John Gooch, to the Sheerwater ; John Workman, to the Stately ; William Duncan, confirmed in the Magnet ; William Williamson, to the Tremendous ; James Glen, to the Grampus ; William Greene, to the Stag ; W. H. Trotman, to the Nimrod ; James Ayres, to the Dwarf ; Andrew Mannin, to the Sheldrake ; Richard Harris, to the Hibernia ; William Farr, to the Goldfinch ; John Naughton, to the Victorious ; William Edmonds, to the Sampson, P.S. ; and David James (1) to the Crown Prince.

Assistant-Surgeons, &c. appointed.

W. Robert Dick, to the Attack, G. B. ; Geo. Johnston, to the Raisonable ; G. T. Millett, to the Caton, P.H.S ; John M'Gowan, to the Pegase, P.H.S ; James Stitt, to the Curlew, ; James Wills, to the Argonaut, H.S. ; James M'Conkey, to the Dublin ; Jos. Seed, to the marine battalion ; Charles Roberts, to the Horatio ; Thomas Dunn, to the Bramble schooner ; George Currie, to be hospital mate at the prison dépôt at Dartmoor.

BIRTHS.

At Cork, the lady of Captain Upton, of H.M.S. Sybille, of a daughter.
At Bath, the lady of Captain Nesbitt, R.N. of a son.
July 17, at Doncaster, the lady of the Hon. Captain F. F. Gardner, of a son.
July 30, the wife of Lieutenant W. H. Douglas, R.N. of a daughter.
August 2, in Wimpole street, the lady of Captain Henry Lambert, R.N. of a son.
August 3, the lady of Captain Wise, R.N. of a son.
August 10, at Norwich, the lady of Captain Burt, R.N. of a daughter.

MARRIAGES.

Lately, the Hon. Basil Cochrane, (brother of the Earl of Dundonald, and of Admiral Sir Alexander Cochrane) to Mrs. Lawry, widow of the Rev. S. Lawry.
At Mary-le-bone Church, Charles Williams, Esq. to Miss Metcalfe, daughter of the late Captain Metcalf, R.N.
July 22, by special license, at St. George's Church, the Right Hon. Lord Walpole, one of the Lords of the Admiralty, to Mary Elizabeth, eldest daughter of the late Mr. Falkner, clerk of the privy council.
July 28, at St. Mary-le-bone church, Major William Markham Coombe, R.M. to Miss Barclay, eldest daughter of Lieutenant-general Barclay, resident commandant of the royal marines in London.
July 29, at Plymouth, P. Laffer, Esq. Adjutant of the Royal Marines, to Miss Rogers, daughter of the late Capt. James Rogers, R.N.
July 30, at Weymouth, Lieut. Lipson, R.N. to Eliz. eldest daughter of Wm. Took, Esq. of Weymouth.
(Same day) Wm. Nesbitt, Esq. Commanding the Huddart East Indiaman, to Miss Samuel.
July 31, at Portsmouth, Lieut. Henry Davies, R.N. to Miss Mayton, of Faversham.
Aug. 13, (and not before) at Southill, Bedfordshire, the Hon. Wm. Waldegrave, (brother to Earl Waldegrave, and to Admiral Lord Radstock) to Eliz. eldest daughter of S. Whitbread, Esq.
Aug. 21, at St. Ann's Church, Soho, James Baillie, Esq. late Secretary to the Hon. Admiral Berkeley, to Lady Burton, widow of Sir John Burton, of Soho Square.

OBITUARY.

In November last, at Trichnopoly, in the East Indies, John Byng, Esq. Judge and Magistrate of that District, third son of the Hon. John Byng, and brother to Capt. Byng, of H.M.S. Warrior, aged 33 years.
Lately, at Bombay, Lieut. Colonel Hardyman, of His Majesty's Ceylon regiment, eldest son of Captain Hardyman, of Portsmouth, and brother of Capt. Hardyman, R.N.
At Mahon, Mr. Young, Purser of H.M.S. Rodney.
Mrs. Stewart, wife of Capt. Wm. Stewart, of H.M.S. St. Albans, and daughter of Major Clubly, of Portsmouth.

GEORGE LEGGE   LORD DARTMOUTH

Admiral of the Fleet.

BIOGRAPHICAL MEMOIR

OF

GEORGE LEGGE, LORD DARTMOUTH,

ADMIRAL OF THE FLEET,

IN THE REIGN OF JAMES THE SECOND.

" To the time's warfare, simple or refin'd,
The time itself adapts the warrior's mind,"

LORD DARTMOUTH lived in times of severe political trial. His character has consequently been censured, when it ought to have been praised. Regarded as the agent of a despot, by some, by others he has been condemned for betraying the cause of his Sovereign. The task of the biographer, as well as of the historian is, to place truth in its clearest light; and, in the performance of that task, we trust it will be made to appear, that the subject of this memoir was neither disloyal to his King, nor a recreant to his country.

George Legge, who, for his various public services, was raised to the peerage, by the title of Baron Dartmouth, was born in the year 1647. He descended from a very ancient and honourable family in Venice; where, according to the Sieur Amelot, the original stock continued to flourish, in the highest rank of nobility. A branch of this family migrated to England, some time prior to the reign of Edward the IId. and, as appears by SPEED's *Map of Kent*, was long settled at Legge's Place (to which it, of course, gave the name) near Tunbridge. The Legge family has also been settled in Herefordshire, for some centuries. The first of its descendants, whom we find particularly noticed, was Thomas Legge, who served the office of Sheriff of London, in the eighteenth, and Lord Mayor in the twentieth, and twenty-eighth years of Edward the IIId. He was also twice chosen representative in Parliament for the City, first, in 1349, and again in 1352. From him descended Simon Legge, whose grandson, William, settled in Ireland. His only son, Edward, was appointed Vice President of Munster, by Charles Blount, Earl of Devonshire, who was at that time Lord Lieutenant. William, the eldest son of Edward, quitted Ireland, under the patronage of Sir Henry Danvers, Earl of Danby, who undertook, and faithfully fulfilled, the superintendence of his education. This gentleman, who was the father of Lord Dartmouth, passed an active, perilous, and glorious life. He first distinguished himself, as a volunteer, in the Low Countries, under Prince Maurice, of Orange; after which, on his return to England, he had the honour of being presented to Charles the 1st, by his patron, the Earl of Danby. The introduction was fortunate. His Majesty, soon conceiving a strong attachment to him, made him groom of his bedchamber, and, afterwards, Lieutenant-general of the Ordnance. Subsequently to the commencement of the civil war, he was made Governor, first of Chester, and then of Oxford. Firmly attached, by principle—perhaps also by personal feeling—to the cause of royalty, he was amongst the most strenuous supporters of Charles the IId. when he marched into England with the Scots. His life nearly fell a sacrifice to his loyalty. The known favour in which he had ever been with Charles the 1st, and the intrepid zeal which he had shewn in the service of his son and successor, rendered him peculiarly obnoxious to the Parliament. He was taken prisoner soon after the unfortunate battle of Worcester; and, in consequence of the hatred which he had incurred, his murder, under the mockery of a trial, for having been in arms against the Parliament, was fully resolved on. The ingenuity of his lady, however, rescued him from the infliction of their vengeance, by contriving and effecting his escape from Coventry Gaol, in woman's apparel. He immediately joined his exiled sovereign. Charles the IId has frequently, and, perhaps, with justice, been charged with ingratitude. In the present instance, however, he did not forget his friend, when the days of prosperity returned. After the Restoration, he re-appointed Colonel Legge to the offices which had been so honourably filled by him, in the preceding reign, and, at the same time, made him superintendant and treasurer of the Ordnance.

During the civil war, Colonel Legge married Elizabeth, the eldest daughter of Sir William Washington, of Packington, in Leicestershire, by Anne Villers, daughter to Sir George Villers, of Brookesby, and sister to the first Duke of Buckingham of that family. The first offspring of this marriage was George, afterwards Lord Dartmouth, whose services we now proceed to record.

At an early period of life, he was destined for the naval profession; and, in his eighteenth year (1665) his father placed him under the care of that very brave and celebrated commander, Sir Edward Spragge.* A more illustrious tutor, it has been justly observed, could not, perhaps, have been found, nor a pupil more likely to do justice to his instructions. A circumstance which rendered this arrangement the more eligible was, the relationship which subsisted between the parties, the mother of Sir Edward Spragge being the second sister of Colonel Legge.

Having distinguished himself, as a lieutenant, during the greater part of the first Dutch war, he was, towards the close of the year 1667, " without deriving the smallest advantage from his connexions, and the loyal attachment of his parent," promoted to the rank of captain. Hardy represents him to have taken post rank in the Fairfax, but makes it a query, whether he were not captain of the Pembroke, in 1667, and in 1671, of the Fairfax. Charnock states his first command to have been " of a new ship, called the Pembroke, a promotion unenvied, notwithstanding his youth, because all persons were convinced it was deservedly made."

In consequence of the peace, Captain Legge had not, for some time, any farther opportunity of increasing his professional reputation. His time, however, was not passed in idleness, for he applied himself assiduously to the study of the mathematics, especially to such branches of that extensive science, as bore any relation to the military art. His exertions were crowned with success. Having attained great skill, as an engineer, he was employed by Charles the IId in that character. In the year 1669, he succeeded his father, in the command of an independent company of foot; † and, in 1670 (December 7) he was appointed Lieutenant-general of the Ordnance.

---

* The name of Sir Edward Spragge has long been upon our list; and it is probable that a memoir of his services will appear in the course of a few months.

† Captain Legge's father, who attained the age of 83, died at his house in the Minories, on the 13th of October, 1670; he was buried in a vault, in the Chapel of the Trinity, near that place.

Early in the year 1671, Captain Legge was appointed to the Fairfax, of 50 guns; one of the ships belonging to the squadron which was fitted out, and ordered to cruise in the Channel, under Sir Robert Holmes, to intercept the Dutch Smyrna fleet. The English, it would appear, not forgetting the insult which had been offered to them, about four years before, by the Dutch sailing up the Medway, were anxious for an opportunity of vengeance. The Smyrna squadron was descried, by the advanced frigates, on the 13th of March. Sir Robert Holmes immediately gave chase, and, on his approach within gun-shot, fired at the Dutch ships of war, to make them pay the usual compliment to the flag. The Dutch commander, refusing to comply, returned the fire: an obstinate action ensued, and a running fight was maintained for three days; at the expiration of which, one of the Dutch men of war, and five of the richest of the merchant ships, were taken. The remainder effected their escape into the different ports of Holland.*—The States General were so much enraged at this act of hostility, that, without hesitation, they issued a declaration of war against England.

In the above-mentioned action, Captain Legge is understood to have distinguished himself in a very particular manner; and, in the battle of Solebay, which took place in the succeeding year, his behaviour was, if possible, more exemplary.—France, having joined England in the war against the Dutch, sent over a fleet of thirty-six men of war, to Portsmouth. The combined naval force of Great Britain and France, consisting of 101 sail, carrying 6,018 guns, and 32,530 men, then sailed for the Downs in three divisions; the Duke of York (afterwards James the IId.) commanding the red, the Earl of Sandwich the blue, and le Comte d'Estrées, Vice-admiral of France, the rear, bearing a white flag. From the Downs, this force sailed to Solebay; where, on the morning of the 28th of May, 1672, it was surprised by the appearance of the Dutch fleet, which, at that time, amounted to 91 men of war, 54 fire-ships, and 23 yachts. It was conjectured,

---

* The English squadron consisted of three ships of 70, two of 50, one of 40, and two of 20 guns: the Dutch, of eight ships, mounting, respectively, 50, 48, 46, 44, 38, 34, 32, and 30 guns; with 50 sail of merchant vessels, mounting from 10 to 30 guns each.

that had De Ruyter, the Dutch Admiral, instead of calling a council of war, made an immediate attack, he would have destroyed the combined fleets, which were lying in great disorder. Many of the ships were obliged to cut their cables, with the utmost precipitation, to enable them to get into the line. " The fight began," says the author of the Life of De Ruyter, " betwixt the Earl of Sandwich and Van Ghent; it was terrible and bloody, especially between the blue squadron and Van Ghent, who in the beginning of the battle was shot to death. The brave Earl of Sandwich, who was determined to pawn his life for his honour, overpowered with a number of men and fire-ships, and a hardy Dutch captain, Adrian Brackell, having laid him aboard athwart the hawse, yet still continued the fight with such unshaken courage, that he sunk two or three of the fire-ships that had grappled with him, and forced the Dutch captain to call for quarter; but, at last, his ship being unhappily fired by a third fire-ship, was burnt, and he himself, with many persons of quality, bravely, but unfortunately, perished, to the grief of the King, his master, and unspeakable regret of his country, having left to posterity an immortal proof, that valour, crowned with honour, does not shrink, but swells by its own reward."—For a considerable time, the stress of the action lay upon the St. Michael, the flag-ship of the Duke of York; and it is probable that, had it not been for the very spirited assistance which was afforded to his Royal Highness, by his seconds, of whom Captain Legge was one, his ship would have been destroyed, or taken.—The Duke's squadron, having been deserted by the French, had suffered considerably from the close and powerful attacks of De Ruyter and Bankart; but Sir Joseph Jordaine, who had succeeded the Earl of Sandwich, in the command of the blue squadron, having totally routed Van Ghent, came down to the assistance of the Duke, who had shifted his flag into the Loyal London. The battle then became more equal, and continued, with great bravery, on both sides, till night, when the scattered ships of Van Ghent's division, having rallied, came boldly up to the support of their Admirals, and saved them from destruction. The wretched and disabled state of the Dutch ships obliged them to retreat; and the English, which had equally suffered, were not in a condition to pursue them.

In this action, the Dutch had one ship sunk, one burnt, and one taken: their loss in men was unknown, as, from its great extent, the publication of it was forbidden by the States. The English lost the Royal James (the Earl of Sandwich's flag-ship), and four other smaller ships. Sir Fretchville Hollis, Rear-admiral in the Cambridge; Captain Digby, of the Henry; Captain Piercy, of the St. George; Captain Waterworth, of the Anne; Sir John Fox, of the Prince; and Captain Harman, of the Triumph, were killed; and about 2000 men were also killed and wounded. The French, notwithstanding the little share which they had in the action, lost two ships of war; and one of their flag-officers (Rear-admiral de la Rabinierre), and many men, were killed.

On the death of Captain Turner, in the month of July following, Captain Legge was removed into the York; and, in the spring of 1673, he was appointed to the Royal Catherine, of 84 guns, in which he again signalized himself in a very remarkable manner.—On the 19th of May, it was determined, in a council of war, that, if the Dutch fleet could not be provoked to quit their own coast, they should be attacked upon it. In pursuance of this resolution, the English and French fleets, consisting of 84 men of war, and a number of fire-ships, put to sea, under the command of Prince Rupert, Sir Edward Spragge, and le Comte d'Estrees. On their arrival on the coast of Holland, De Ruyter was discovered with a fleet of 70 men of war, in apparent security, and formed in good order behind the sands of Schonevelt. Prince Rupert, however, notwithstanding their secure position, determined to attack them; and, as a *ruse de guerre*, which completely answered his purpose, on the morning of the 28th, he detached a squadron of 35 frigates, and 13 fire-ships, to stand close in with the sands. De Ruyter, as soon as he discovered the frigates, got under sail, stood out, formed in line of battle, and pursued the decoy squadron, which led him down to the main fleet. Towards noon, the Dutch ships began to fire at the English frigates, and a general action soon commenced, which was maintained with great bravery till night, when De Ruyter again retired behind the sands. "Had it not been for fear of the shoals," says Prince Rupert, in his letter to the Earl of Arlington, "we had driven them into their harbours, and the King would have had a better account of them. But I hope his Majesty will be satisfied, that, considering the place we engaged in, and the sands, there was as much done as could be expected. We lost, in this affair, the Captains, Fowls, Finch, Tempest, Worden : Colonel Hamilton had his legs shot off; and two ships were disabled. Schram, the Dutch Vice-admiral, Vlugh, their Rear-admiral, and six captains, perished, and they lost one ship. Undoubtedly, had the French followed up our operations, our triumph had then been complete." The French, it appears, as in the battle of Solebay, shrunk from the contest ; notwithstanding which, they lost two men of war, and five fire-ships.

The ship which the Dutch lost, in this engagement, was the Jupiter. She surrendered to Captain Legge's ship, the Royal Catherine; but Lediard states, that she was surprised, and retaken, while the English were rummaging her. Captain Legge's good conduct, however, was so apparent, that Prince Rupert, in his letter already quoted, mentions him the first amongst those particularly eminent and meritorious commanders, whom he honoured with the highest commendations. " The officers and men," says he, " generally behaved themselves very well in my squadron, more especially Captain Legge, &c." According to Campbell, Captain Legge distinguished himself in a much more signal manner than might be inferred from Prince Rupert's letter; for he states, that, having been boarded by the Dutch, while his ship, the Royal Catherine, was in the greatest danger of sinking, he drove the enemy back, with considerable loss; and having, in some degree, stopped his leaks, brought the ship safe into harbour.

On the 4th of June, De Ruyter, having refitted and increased his fleet, stood out to sea, and with much apparent boldness bore down to attack the combined squadrons, under Prince Rupert. However, the impetuosity and irregularity with which the Dutch made their attack, soon threw them into confusion, and they retreated to the south-east. The action did not commence till the afternoon; and, though the firing was continued briskly till dark, the whole affair could only be regarded as a skirmish. The French, as in former instances, held back.

Whether Captain Legge were engaged in the action of the 4th of

June, is uncertain ; but, in the third engagement, which occurred on the 11th of August following, and which terminated the second Dutch war, he was very actively concerned. The respective fleets were nearly equal in force. Some time was unavoidably lost by the English, during which the Dutch Admiral gained the wind, and bore down upon the confederates. D'Estrees disregarded the signals of Prince Rupert; and Bankart, freed from all apprehensions respecting the French, joined his squadron to De Ruyter's, and fell upon, and surrounded the Prince, whose destruction consequently appeared almost inevitable. At this time, Captain Legge, with the view of extricating the commander-in-chief, made a diversion, with two fire-ships. This gallant effort was completely successful; and had the French then bore down, as they ought to have done, the entire Dutch fleet must have been ruined.* Even as it was, the Dutch ships were much disabled; and they lost two vice-admirals, three captains, and about a thousand men killed. The English lost the brave Admiral Sir Edward Spragge,† (Captain Legge's naval father) two captains, and a great number of men. After the battle, in which victory was claimed by each party, the English fleet returned to the Thames, and the French to Brest.

At the conclusion of the war,‡ Captain Legge was appointed Governor of Portsmouth, of which he had been, a short time

---

* The conduct of le Comte d'Estrées, the French admiral, upon this occasion, appears to have been the result of pre-determined treachery, rather than of cowardice. Rear-admiral de Martel, who seemed to be the only French commander that had any real design to fight, having been left, not only by the body of the French fleet, but even by the captains of his own division, was attacked by five Dutch ships at once. He fought them for two hours, and with such courage and success, that, having disabled one, the rest were glad to sheer off, and he rejoined the white squadron; where, expostulating with the captains of his own division for deserting him so basely, they told him plainly, *They had orders from the admiral not to observe his motions.* On his return to France, the brave de Martel was sent to the Bastille!

† His ship, the Prince, was so much disabled, that he shifted his flag to the St. George, which was soon also rendered incapable of continuing in the line. Sir Edward was then going to the Royal Charles, when a shot struck the boat, which instantly sunk, and the admiral and crew perished.

‡ Peace was signed, between England and Holland, on the 9th of February, 1674.

before, made lieutenant-governor. At the same time, he was appointed master of the horse, and gentleman of the bed chamber to the Duke of York, with whom he ever appears to have been a great favourite.

On the 15th of June following (1671) he had the honour of entertaining, in his capacity of governor, the King, the Duke of York, and a number of the first nobility in the suite of his Majesty, on a visit which he made to Portsmouth.

Continuing to rise, if possible, in the situation and favour of his Sovereign, he was appointed colonel of a regiment of foot, in the year 1677: on the 28th of January, 1681, he was made master-general of the Ordnance; and on the 3d of March, in the same year, he was sworn a member of the Privy Council.—In the course of the year 1681, or 1682, he also received a special commission to review all the forts and garrisons throughout England; on which occasion he was constituted and appointed commander-in-chief.

On the 2d of December, 1682, Captain Legge was created a peer, by the title of Baron Dartmouth, of Dartmouth, in the county of Devon; and, in the preamble of his patent, the services of his father and of himself were very honourably stated.

By virtue of the marriage between Charles the IId and the Infanta of Portugal, in the year 1661, the city of Tangier,* on the coast of Barbary, had become the property of England. Charles, however, finding the expense of defending this possession far to exceed its value, resolved to rid himself of the incumbrance. In consequence of this determination, Lord Dartmouth was, on the 2d of August, 1683, appointed admiral, and commander-in-chief of a fleet, destined for the demolition of the town, castle, and mole, at Tangier. " The management of this affair," says Campbell, " required great secrecy, and much conduct, in the commander-in-chief, and this probably determined the King to make use of Lord Dartmouth." His Lordship was at the same time made governor of Tangier, and general-in-chief of his Majesty's forces in Africa; that by having the supreme command in

---

* A View of Tangier, accompanied by an historical and descriptive account, and sailing directions, will be found in the IXth Volume of the NAVAL CHRONICLE, page 21. *Vide* also page 198 of the same Volume.

every department vested in himself, those difficulties, which sometimes arise from the disagreement of officers employed to conduct different branches of the same expedition, might be avoided.

Lord Dartmouth hoisted his flag in the Grafton, and proceeded on the execution of this service; some idea of the arduous nature of which may be formed, from the statement, that the mole ran six hundred yards into the sea, and that the stones of which it was composed were so firmly cemented together, that the destruction of the work occupied six months. Nor was this all: the ferocious and determined hostility of the Moors, in their endeavours to preserve the town, and in their reiterated assaults upon the garrison, presented obstacles of a most formidable and serious description. Lord Dartmouth, however, surmounted every impediment, completely achieved the object of the expedition, and returned to England with the greatest possible *eclat*. So delighted does the King appear to have been, so eminently gratified by Lord Dartmouth's success, that, though seldom distinguished by acts of munificence to his servants, he, on this occasion, presented him with 10,000*l*. in money—a large sum in those days—and, amongst several honourable privileges and charters, made him a grant of a fair to be holden twice a year, and a market twice a week, upon Blackheath.

It was not the fortune of Lord Dartmouth to bask much longer in the sun-shine of royal favour. The death of Charles the IId took place soon after his lordship's return from Tangier; and the abrupt termination of the short and troubled reign of his successor, involved him in the misfortunes of the family to which he had ever been a most loyal adherent. On the accession of James the IId he was confirmed in those employments which he had enjoyed in the preceding reign, and was invested with the additional office of Constable of the Tower. " Esteemed as highly by the people," says Charnock, " as he was by the Sovereign, the character he had universally and deservedly established, as a person of the highest rectitude and honour, he ever continued to maintain, in its utmost splendor; so that those unpopular and unconstitutional measures which James, soon after this time, attempted to introduce, are by no means to be attributed to either the counsel, the advice, or the support they received from Lord

Dartmouth. He appears to have considered King James in a two-fold light, first as his sovereign, and next as his friend. As his prince he revered him, he obeyed him, and he served him faithfully: as his friend he loved him. Too wise not to observe, and too honest not to disapprove the conduct of the monarch, which hourly accelerated his own ruin, he failed not to offer such advice as appeared most likely to avert the storm then gathering. But in making this last effort in his power for the service of a prince he dearly loved, he tempered the remonstrance of a friend with the modest submission of a subject. Having thus acquitted his conscience, nothing remained for him but to execute the commands of his sovereign, whom, while he kept possession of the throne, it certainly would have been treason to have disobeyed, at least in the line of his profession."

Amongst the most staunch adherents, and principal favourites of King James, was Sir Roger Strickland; an officer, whose reputation and life seem to have been equally devoted to his Sovereign. Raised to the dignity of Rear-admiral of England, in the autumn of 1687, he was, in the summer following, appointed to the chief command of his Majesty's fleet. Attached to his Prince, as well by his religious principles, as by those of gratitude and loyalty, he imprudently attempted to introduce the exercise of the Catholic religion in the navy. This circumstance excited so violent a clamour, that it was found necessary to remove him from the chief command; a measure the more imperative, as the alarm of invasion, from Holland, had become extremely serious. On the 24th of September (1688) Lord Dartmouth was, in consequence, appointed to supersede Sir Roger Strickland.* On the 21st of October following, the Prince of Orange sailed from Helvoetsluys, with a fleet of 500 sail, formed into three divisions: the centre, commanded by himself, bearing the flag of England, with the motto—" *I will maintain the Protestant Religion,* and

---

* " Strickland having been removed from the command of the fleet, because he was unpopular, Lord Dartmouth, the idol of the seamen, was placed at its head."—*Dalrymple.*—It is said, that the sailors, little relishing the attempt which was made upon their religion, by Sir Roger, were, with some difficulty, restrained by their officers from throwing the reverend fathers, whom he had invited on board the fleet, into the sea!

the liberties of England;", the van, commanded by Admiral Herbert (afterwards Earl of Torrington); and the rear, by the Dutch Admiral Evertzen.

At this time, the English navy amounted to 173 sail; notwithstanding which, remarkable as it must appear, Lord Dartmouth could muster only seventeen sail of the line (chiefly third and fourth rates) three frigates, thirteen fire-ships, and three yachts, to oppose the landing of the Prince of Orange. With this comparatively insignificant force, he, however, sought the fleet of his antagonist, and made every effort, but without success, to engage him.—The Prince, by steering a southerly course, eluded the squadron of Lord Dartmouth, and landed at Torbay, without opposition, on the 5th of November. On the 12th of the succeeding month, James the IId abdicated the throne.

True to his Prince, while that Prince possessed the legitimate rights of royalty, Lord Dartmouth was absolved from allegiance by his abdication; and, as a member of the state, it became his primary duty to submit to the new Sovereign. Actuated by the spirit of genuine patriotism, from the dictates of which he had never swerved, he is understood to have given all the assistance in his power to moderate the distracted state of the nation, and to have paid all due obedience to the preserver of his country's liberty.

It was scarcely to be expected, that the personal friend of an expatriated monarch, should be employed by his successor. Delicacy, it is presumed, would have induced him to decline the honour, had it been proffered. It might, however, have been hoped, that he would be allowed to pass the remainder of an honourable life, in that calm retirement, which, under such circumstances, must be rather grateful than oppressive to a well regulated mind. Unfortunately, that boon was denied; and, as the number is small, even in the refined and elevated sphere of courts, of those who are gifted with magnanimity, the mere circumstance of his attachment to James, rendered him obnoxious to the suspicion of treason. He was consequently arrested, and sent to the Tower; where grief, or indignation, at the treatment which he so undeservedly experienced, is supposed to have accelerated his end. His Lordship died, a state prisoner, on the 21st of October, 1691, in the 44th year of his age.

A stronger proof of the exalted estimation in which Lord Dartmouth's character was holden by King James, need not be offered, than the exclamation of that unfortunate Prince, when he heard of his death:—" Then *faithful* Will Legge's *honest* son George is dead! I have few such servants now!"

King William, also, was fully convinced of his innocence, and had actually determined on his release, which the hand of death prevented. The truth of this assertion is sufficiently apparent from the following memorandum, copied, *verbatim*, from the original, in the hand-writing of his lordship's grandson, William, the second Earl of Dartmouth:—

" After Lord Dartmouth was dead, Lord Lucas, who was constable of the Tower, made some difficulty of letting him be removed; but application being made to the King, he was pleased to order, that the same respect that would have been due to him, if he had died possessed of all the employments he had formerly enjoyed in that place should be paid him; which was done accordingly; and the Tower guns were fired when he was carried out to his funeral: and the King told his son, that if he had lived two days longer he would have been released."

It cannot be doubted, that the honourable and noble mind of William duly estimated and admired the character of the deceased Lord.

HERALDRY.

Thomas Legge, supposed to have been the son of John, third brother of William, father of the first Lord Dartmouth, was made lieutenant of the Mary, on the 24th of May 1688; on the 1st of June, in the same year, he was removed into the Deptford; on the 3d of September, into the Resolution; and, on the 26th of November, he was promoted, by Lord Dartmouth, to be captain of the Dartmouth fire-ship. After the revolution, he again served as lieutenant, on board of different ships; particularly as first of the Rupert, in 1693. In 1696, he was made captain of the Stromboli; from which, soon afterwards, he was removed into the Discovery brigantine, one of the light vessels employed that year, to cover the attack of the French ports. After the accession of Queen Anne, he very conspicuously distinguished himself, under the command of Rear-admiral Dilkes, in an attack upon some French ships in Cancalle Bay. His gallantry on that occasion was rewarded by a gold medal, which was struck purposely to perpetuate the event. He was next appointed to the Antelope, and sent to Gibraltar, under the command of Sir George Rooke.

In that ship he was present at the battle of Malaga. A charge of misconduct, in having been guilty of a breach of orders (on what occasion is unknown) was shortly afterwards preferred against him; in consequence of which, he was tried by a court martial, of which Sir John Leake was president, in the month of January, 1705, and dismissed from the service. The time of his death is not recorded.

William Legge married Elizabeth, eldest daughter of Sir William Washington, of Packington, in Leicestershire, by whom he had George, the subject of the preceding memoir; William, page, and groom of the bedchamber to Charles the IId, and governor of Kinsale; Edward, died an infant; Mary, married Sir H. Gooderick, Bart.; and Susannah, married Thomas Bilson, of Maple Durham, Esq.

George, created Baron Dartmouth, of Dartmouth, in the county of Devon, by patent, on the 2d of December, 1682, married Barbara, daughter and co-heiress of Sir Henry Archbold, of Abbots Bromley, Staffordshire; by whom (who died Jan. 23, 1718) he had issue William Villiers, born October 14, 1672; married, July, 1700, Anne, daughter of Heneage Finch, Earl of Aylesford; created Viscount Lewisham, and Earl of Dartmouth; died Dec. 15, 1750. By his lady, (who died Nov. 30, 1751) he had issue, six sons and two daughters; of whom George, the eldest, who married Elizabeth, sole daughter and heiress of Sir Arthur Kaye, Bart. of Yorkshire, died in the life-time of his father, leaving issue. Edward, the fifth son of William, the first earl, was born in the year 1710, and died, a commodore in the royal navy, in the West Indies, in 1747.[*]—William,

---

[*] On the 21st of May, 1726, the Hon. Edward Legge entered as a volunteer on board the Royal Oak, of 70 guns, one of the ships which were ordered, at the conclusion of that year, for the defence of Gibraltar, then threatened by the Spaniards. On the 5th of March, 1734, he was made lieutenant, in the Deptford; and, on the 26th of July, 1738, he was promoted to be captain of the Lively frigate. At the close of 1739, he was removed into the Pearl, and afterwards into the Severn, of 50 guns, which, in 1740, was ordered out to the South Seas, under Admiral Anson. (*Vide* N.C. VIII. 267, *et seq.*) Nothing remarkable occurred, till after the departure of the squadron from Port St. Julian, in the month of February following. The severe distress which was subsequently encountered by the Severn, in particular, is thus recorded by Captain Legge himself, in a letter dated Rio Janeiro, July 4, 1741:—

" The squadron left St. Julian's the 27th of February, and on the 7th of March passed the Straits of La Maire with great success and fair weather; but the next day met with fresh gales, which from that time increased to such very hard gales from N.N.W. to W.N.W. with such prodigious seas, as exceeded any thing they had ever seen before; it tore their shrouds and sails, and sprung their yards and masts. On the 10th of April, they were

the second earl, born June 20, 1731, succeeded his grandfather, Dec. 15, 1750; married, Jan. 11, 1755, Frances Catharine, sole daughter and heir to the late Sir Charles Gounter Nicholl, K.B. by whom he had issue, George, who succeeded him, born October 3, 1755; William, died October 19, 1784; Charles Gounter, died October 11, 1785; Heneage, died Sept. 2, 1782; Henry, born Jan. 23, 1765; Arthur Kaye, born Oct. 25, 1766, a rear-admiral in the Royal Navy; Edward, born Dec. 11, 1767; Augustus George, born April 21, 1773, married Dec. 15, 1795, Honora

in the latitude of 55° 55' and longitude 91° 54'. That night they lost sight of the commodore and all the squadron, except the Pearl. On the 13th, in the morning, they saw the land at day-break from the W.N.W. to the S.E. very high, and not above five leagues distant; upon sight of which, they endeavoured to wear, which they were more than an hour before they could perform, and then stood to westward as much as the wind would permit them; but the wind coming to N.W. and by W. and W.N.W. and blowing almost a continual storm for forty days together, with exceeding great seas, they beat most of the time under reefed courses. On the 1st of June, they spoke with a Portuguese vessel bound to Bahia, who told them Cape Frio bore W.S.W. 30 leagues; and, on the 30th of June, by the great mercy of God, they arrived safe in this port, where they were received with exceeding great friendship and humanity, after having lost a great number of men by fatigue and sickness, amongst which last were the captain, lieutenant, and ensign of the invalids."

As soon as it was practicable, Captain Legge returned to Europe.—At the end of 1744, he commanded the Strafford, of 50 guns, one of the ships ordered for the West Indies, under Vice-admiral Davers. He sailed from Portsmouth on the 18th of November; and, in the following night, he parted from the squadron, in a violent gale of wind. The wind and weather continued so adverse, that, with the Enterprise, Merlin, and about twenty merchant ships, he was thirty-three days on his passage to Madeira, where he found his admiral, who had got in only three days before him.— After his arrival in the West Indies, he was very successfully employed in cruising. He returned to England with a convoy, in November, or December, 1745; and, in January, 1746, he was appointed to the Windsor, a new ship, of 60 guns. He was, subsequently, one of the members of the court martial, convened for the trial of the Admirals Lestock and Matthews. In 1747, he went out, commodore of a small squadron, to the Leeward Islands; and, on the 19th of September, in the same year, he died at Barbadoes; having, though absent, been just before elected representative in Parliament for the town of Portsmouth.

* This officer, made a post captain, Feb. 6, 1793, was promoted to a flag, July 31, 1810; and, in the late promotion, on the Prince Regent's birth-day (*vide* page 173) he was advanced from the Blue to the White squadron.

Bagot, daughter of the Rev. Walter Bagot; Charlotte, born Oct. 5, 1774, married, Sept. 24, 1795, Charles Duncombe, Esq of Yorkshire.—William, the second earl, dying July 15, 1801, was succeeded by his eldest son, George, who was called up by writ of summons to the House of Peers, June 16, 1801, as Baron of Dartmouth, during the life of his father. He married, Sept. 24, 1782, Frances, sister to the Earl of Aylesford, by whom he had issue, Frances Catherine, born 1783, died 1789; William, born Nov. 29, 1784; George, born 1786, died 1789; Louisa, born 1787; Heneage, born 1788; Charlotte, born 1789; Henrietta, born 1790; Barbara Maria, born 1791; Catherine Charlotte, born 1793, died the same year; Georgiana Caroline, born 1795; Mary, born 1796; Anne, born 1797; Charles, born 1799; and Arthur Charles, born 1800.—His Lordship who was lord chamberlain to his Majesty, K.G. &c. died Nov. 2, 1811; and his remains were deposited in the family vault, in the chapel of the Holy Trinity, in the Minories, where the descendants of the house of Legge have been interred ever since the time of Colonel Legge, father of the first Lord Dartmouth. His Lordship was succeeded by his eldest son, William Viscount Lewisham, major of the Staffordshire Militia.

ARMS.—*Azure*, a stag's head, caboshed, *argent*.

CREST.—Out of a ducal coronet, *or*, a plume of six feathers, *argent* and *azure*.

SUPPORTERS.—On the dexter side a lion, *argent*, powdered with fleurs-de-lis, *sable*, his head adorned with a plume of feathers as the crest issuant from a ducal coronet, *or*.—On the sinister side a stag, *argent*, unguled, *or*, and powdered with mullets, *gules*.

MOTTO.—*Gaudet Tentamine Virtus.*

NAVAL ANECDOTES,
COMMERCIAL HINTS, RECOLLECTIONS, &c.

NANTES IN GURGITE VASTO.

JAVA PRIZE-MONEY, &c.

THE coffee found in the store-houses at Java is estimated at 40,000 tons. The quantities of rice, sugar, pepper, and other spices, are also very large. Subalterns' shares of prize-money had sold as high as 400*l.* each; and a captains' was estimated to be worth 750*l.* The beautiful country mansion of former Dutch governors at Burtenzorg, including a large and profitable estate, has been purchased by Mr. Raffles, for a lack of rupees.

NOCTURNAL TELEGRAPH.

A NOCTURNAL Telegraph was lately exhibited in front of the yard adjoining Lord Glenbervie's house, Whitehall:—On each side of the shutters were two large globular lights, nearly nine inches in circumference—red and blue, to be alternately changed in colour, according to the signals wanted, and the state of the atmosphere. The lights, which are in the form of a cone, may be viewed at a great distance.

STATE OF NEW SOUTH WALES.

LETTERS from New South Wales, of the 20th of May, state, that great improvements have taken place in that colony since the accession of Colonel Macquarrie to the government. The town of Sydney is laid out in regular streets, and divided into districts, with headboroughs, sub-constables, watchmen, &c. Mr. D'Arcy Wentworth has been appointed to the head of the police. Five townships have been laid out on the Hawkesbury and George Rivers, to be called Windsor, Richmond, Wilberforce, Pitt, and Castlereagh. The roads from Sydney to Paramatta and Hawkesbury, which were scarcely passable, have been repaired, bridges thrown over the streams, and turnpikes established. No fears of a scarcity of provisions were to be apprehended, vast quantities of cattle being reared, and the storehouses filled with grain.—Butchers' meat was from 1s. to 1s. 3d. per lb. and the supply equal to the consumption, without assistance from the mother country. Wool was to be their first staple commerce. Settlers of good character were furnished with live stock, from the government stores, in consideration of paying the value, in money or grain, in 18 months. The population of Sydney is estimated at 10,000, of which 8,000 have been sent from England as convicts. Governor Macquarrie was indefatigable in reforming public morals, and in checking drunkenness, concubinage, and other vices.

INTREPIDITY OF JOHN CLARKE, A SEAMAN.

LATELY a seaman, belonging to the Partridge, fell overboard, when Mr. Budgen, second lieutenant, instantly jumped after him, with a rope in his hand: but, having his clothes on, his exertions were soon cramped, and there was great danger that both of them would be drowned.—John Clarke, a seaman, however, was walking on the forecastle with his wife, and the moment it came under his notice, overboard he leaped, brought them to the side of the ship, and they were taken in.

A few weeks before, Clarke was on the fore-rigging of the Partidge, at Spithead, when he saw a man floating past, who had fallen out of a dockyard boat: he leaped out of the rigging into the sea, swam after, and saved him!

REMARKABLE SERIES OF ACCIDENTS.

THE following extraordinary succession of calamities lately occurred on board the United States frigate Constitution:—Two midshipmen, of the names of Morgan and Rogers, went on shore, and fought a duel, in which Rogers was killed, and Morgan wounded. The next day, while the procession of boats was moving, to attend the funeral of the young man, who had thus fallen a miserable victim to the impious laws of honour, a sailor fell from the mast-head of the frigate, and was killed. In a quarter of an hour, another fell from the same place, and was so hurt that he died the next day. While they were lowering the wounded man into the cockpit, another fell backward into it, and badly fractured his leg. Two days after, as the frigate was sailing rapidly up the Delaware bay, a midshipman fell overboard and was drowned: while they were lowering the boats to go to his relief, three men were plunged into the water, from which they were saved with difficulty by the surrounding boats.

ACTION BETWEEN H. M. S. SWALLOW, AND TWO FRENCH SHIPS.

THE subjoined letter, dated H. M. S. Swallow, off Frejus, June 16, 1812, there is reason to believe was written by Mr. Ryan, the purser of the Swallow:—

" This afternoon we have had a very severe engagement with two enemy's vessels, nearly double our own force; it was preconcerted by them for several days, and they stood pledged to the inhabitants to take us into Frejus, that evening, or both go down alongside of us. We engaged, guns nearly touching, and after an action the most sanguinary (in which they four times attempted to board, being full of troops), they made all sail, and took refuge under the batteries of the town. We have been desperately cut up, and I am sorry to add, lost several brave fellows. It is now ten o'clock—the bell done tolling, after burying the dead, and I have just left the deck, after performing the last and melancholy rites due to Christians. This task was the more-painful, as in reading the funeral service over the dead, it also fell to my lot to perform that office for the clerk, who was killed in the act of speaking to me; a person whom I was exceedingly partial to, and one of the finest young men I ever knew. The captain did me the honour to place the marines and boarders under my direction: my hat was twice knocked off by a double-headed shot; I was twice knocked down—but, thank God, have all my legs and arms hanging about me; nor did I suffer any injury, but a contusion of little consequence in my side. These are circumstances I would not acquaint you with, but as all my messmates are writing to their friends, I do not see why I should not do the same, particularly as you will see the business in the papers."

The following account of this dreadfully sanguinary action, is copied from the letter of a young seaman, belonging to the Swallow, named Dennis Graydon, of Cork. Its date is June 20:—

" We have just come from fighting one of the most bloody actions that ever was fought in these seas; but, thanks to the Lord, I have escaped, and I shall always be thankful to him for it. We had a great many killed and wounded, and followed the French, who run away into the harbour, Mr. Ryan, the son of Mr. Brown, who is the purser, had his hat shot off, and one time fell covered all over with blood; when his servant, an old marine, took him in his arms, and was carrying him below, he got to himself on the ladder, and said, ' Where are you taking me?' the servant said, with tears in his eyes, 'Down below.' 'Well, then,' says he, 'take me back again, for I am only stunned, and this here blood is not mine.' I was near to him when he was knocked down, as he was cheering the men at the after guns, and going to fire one. The French fought very well for some time—they had five times as many men as we, and the slaughter must be dreadful. We have not a mast, nor rope, nor sail in the ship but what is cut to pieces; and we expect we shall have to go to England, where all our officers will be promoted. They wanted to board us four times, but we beat them off every time : one time, when we were engaged with the largest on one side, the other came round our bow—the captain saw her— she was full of men, with large blue caps, who were in the rigging, and every where to board. The captain desired Mr. Waller, one of the officers, to get five guns ready at that side, but while he was doing it, his leg was shot off; then Mr. Ryan came to us (myself was at those guns), and, says he, ' My boys, load with double canister, and don't fire a gun until I tell you.' We had then 64lbs. of small shot in every gun ; they thought we did not see them in the smoke—the men were mad to fire at them, but the purser said, he ' would not fire a gun until he rubbed the muzzles of the guns against her sides.' With that, as they were close alongside, he ordered us to put a bag of musket-balls at the mouth of every gun—these bags had 32lbs each, and we had then 96lbs. of shot in every gun. After we fired there was not a man to be seen, but we heard the most dreadful cries, and a great many of them fell overboard, and they never came near to us after. Mr. Brown and his daughter will be glad to hear Mr. Ryan is well ; every man, fore and aft, says he is a brave fellow, and more would be the pity if any thing ailed him."

The extraordinary nature of the action seems to form a sufficient apology for the insertion of the subjoined additional particulars, contained in a letter, dated Port Mahon, July 1 :—

" The Swallow has just anchored here, after a most obstinate and sanguinary engagement : her masts, sails, and rigging, are desperately cut up. The action, on the part of the enemy, had been in agitation for several days. The largest of the French vessels was called the Reynard, and the commander of her was formerly commandant of the Proserpine frigate, at Toulon, with 80 chosen men ; and he stood pledged to the minister of marine to bring the Swallow into Frejus, or to forfeit his existence : nor did he at the time, bargain for the auxiliary assistance of a sixteen gun schooner, which he also brought into the action with him. The America arrived last night : she boarded a fishing-boat, who informed her the brig had every gun dismounted but one, by the shot from the Swallow ; her starboard side almost completely stove in, and 150 men killed and wounded in her and the schooner, the greater part of whom fell in the several attempts they made to board. the Swallow. The little town of Frejus was a scene of mourning, from the number of people belonging to that place who served as volunteers in the enemy's brig and schooner. There were several troops embarked the morning preceeding the action, who all received a promise of being enrolled in the Legion of Honour, after the capture of the Swallow: they were ranged along the gangways, bowsprit, and rigging, coming out. The Swallow passed between the brig and schooner, within 30 yards of the former, and ten of the latter, opening a fire of 64 pounds of canister, and 32 pounds of musketballs, from every gun on both sides. The enemy's brig had a long 9-pounder in her bridle-port, one on each side her forecastle, and nine 32lb. carronades on each side; and the schooner eight long 9-pounders on each side. Thus were they more than double the force of the Swallow; had every advantage, as the water was smooth; and were beaten and followed in under their batteries by fair artillery, the Swallow's superiority in tactics being lost, as there was neither wind nor sea. The Swallow's loss has been severe; but from the nature of the action it could not be expected to be otherwise."

MELANCHOLY AND INTERESTING NARRATIVE.

The affecting little story here related, is from one of the officers of the Swallow:—

In the gallant and sanguinary action (described above) there was a seaman named Phelan, who had his wife on board: she was stationed (as is usual when women are on board in time of battle) to assist the surgeon in the care of the wounded. From the close manner in which the Swallow engaged the enemy, yard-arm and yard-arm, the wounded, as may be expected, were brought below very fast: amongst the rest, a messmate of her husband's (consequently her own), who had received a musket-ball through the side. Her exertions were used to console the poor fellow, who was in great agonies, and nearly breathing his last: when, by some chance, she heard her husband was wounded, on deck: her anxiety and already overpowered feelings could not one moment be restrained; she rushed instantly on deck, and received the wounded tar in her arms; he faintly raised his head to kiss her—she burst into a flood of tears, and told him to take courage, " all would yet be well," but scarcely pronounced the last syllable, when an ill-directed shot took her head off. The poor tar, who was closely wrapt in her arms, opened his eyes once more—then shut them for ever. What renders the circumstance the more affecting was, the poor creature had been only three weeks delivered of a fine boy, who was thus in a moment deprived of a father and a mother. As soon as the action subsided, " and nature began again to take its course, the feelings of the tars, who wanted no unnecessary incitement to stimulate them, were all interested for poor Tommy (for so he was called); many said, and all feared, he must die; they all agreed he should have a hundred fathers, but what could be the substitute of a nurse and a mother? however, the mind of humanity soon discovered there was a Maltese goat on board, belonging to the officers, which gave an abundance of milk; and as there was no better expedient, she was resorted to, for the purpose of suckling the child, who, singular to say, is thriving and getting one of the finest little fellows in the world; and so tractable is his nurse, that even now she lies down when poor little Tommy is brought to be suckled by her. Phelan and his wife were sewed up in one hammock, and, it is needless to say, buried in one grave.

ATTEMPTED ASSASSINATION OF CAPTAIN LINZEE.

On the 3d of June, Andrew Abchurch, ordinary seaman on board H.M.S. Union, then on her passage from Plymouth to the Mediterranean, sent word to Captain Linzee, through the first lieutenant, that he wished to speak to him. Captain L. went upon the quarter-deck with Lieutenant James, to hear what he had to say, when Abchurch, in a low tone of voice, said " there was a mutiny in the ship." On Captain L. asking Lieutenant James what the man said, Abchurch replied, " There is a mutiny in the ship—take that—I am the man ; ' and at the same instant plunged a knife into Captain Linzee's breast. The blow was evidently aimed at the heart; but either from Captain L.'s suddenly turning, or from the confusion of the assassin, the knife penetrated obliquely between the sixth and seventh ribs three inches deep, struck the breast bone, and then turned to the right side, instead of the left. The man was instantly secured; and on the arrival of the ship at Lisbon (into which port, for the preservation of Captain Linzee's life, it was necessary to go), was tried by a court martial, and executed. He was repeatedly urged, in the most solemn manner, by the chaplain of the Union (the Rev. Charles Burne), to declare what his motives were for attempting so atrocious a deed, and he unequivocally declared he never had received any sort of treatment from Captain Linzee which could justify it; but that a sudden thought came into his mind that he must commit murder, and he then determined to do so on the captain, to which he thought he must have been instigated by the devil. He exculpated his shipmates, not one of whom, he said, had the slightest knowledge of his intention ; that he alone contrived and perpetrated the act: he entreated Captain Linzee would forgive him, then he should die in peace.

The necessity of being kept in a tranquil state, compelled Captain Linzee to resign his command ; and he, in consequence, returned to England, in the Sabrina, Captain A. M'Kenzie.—It is highly honourable to the crew of the Union, as it must be consolatory to Captain Linzee, that they wrote the following letter to him, immediately the crime became known amongst them :—

" HONOURED SIR,
" On board H.M.S. Union, at Sea,
June 4th, 1812.

" We, the Petty Officers and Seamen under your command, humbly beg leave to inform you, lest you should entertain the smallest doubt on your mind of there being any of us implicated in the horrid event which occurred last night, that we do most solemnly declare our innocence, and utter abhorrence of so foul and unpardonable a transaction : and it is our most sincere hope, that it may please God shortly to enable you to resume your former command,—having, during the short period which we had the honour of serving under you, experienced both from you and all the officers under your command, the best of treatment; and we do therefore pray for a continuance of your clemency over us ; and should your honour doubt the character of the Temeraires',* they intreat you will apply to their former commanders, who will certify their general characters. We have the honour of subscribing our names to this assertion of our innocence.

(Signed by eight of the Boatswain's Mates, nine Quarter-Masters, twelve Captains of the Forecastle, Tops, and Afterguard, and four of the Gunner's Mates,—in behalf of the Ship's Company.)

PYROTECHNY.

CAPTAIN T. DUNDAS, R.N. has invented a new description of inflammable ball, applicable for besieging a town, and peculiar for its small weight, by which means it may be thrown to a great distance, and takes fire on a very curious plan. It spreads a flame in three distinct opening which is so strong, that the fire extends a full yard in length from the ball itself; and is so powerful, that any thing under, over, or near, cannot escape its effects.

DISCOVERY OF A WRECK.

Extract from the Journal of the Ship Fairy, from Bahia to Liverpool, dated Friday, 19th June, 1812.

" AT six P.M. saw a wreck to the eastward of us; bore down for it and boarded it; found two men (one of them the captain) still alive; they informed us, that they made 191 days since they left Boston, bound to Santa Cruz; the brig (called the Polly) had upset on the third day, but being laden with lumber, and some provisions, would not sink; as soon as they had cut away the masts, she righted; they had existed during the rest of the time partly on the beef and pork they could fish up from the cargo, and afterwards on fish they caught; they had even been obliged to eat some part of one of their shipmates who had died. and had cut up the rest of his body, and put it into pickle, to serve in case of necessity; the two we found were all that remained of a crew of nine. The main-deck was covered with water; they had raised a temporary place in the forecastle to keep them dry and cook their provisions; they produced fire by rubbing violently together two pieces of shingle; when it did not rain they procured fresh water by distillation from salt water, by fixing a piece of board in the top of a pan, and caulking it air tight: underneath (in the middle of the board) they cut a hole, of sufficient size to receive the mouth of a tea kettle, which they inverted in it, and caulked likewise, after filling the pan with salt water; they boiled, and by keeping the spout of the tea-kettle open (the only vent) cool, the steam dissolved, and trickled down into a vessel to receive it; by this means they could make about eight quarts a day. The captain's name was Wm. Leslie Cazuneau."

---

* When this ship was paid off at Plymouth, her crew were turned over to the Union: they highly distinguished themselves in the battle of Trafalgar.

TARRING AND FEATHERING.

THE following ridiculous statement is copied from a New York Paper, of the date of June 27, 1812:—

" A circumstance which occurred on board the frigate Essex yesterday morning having excited considerable anxiety in town, we have taken the pains to ascertain the facts, at the Navy-yard, and detain the press to give them to the public.

" John Irvin, the man who was tarred and feathered, has been known by his own account before and since he belonged to the navy, as a native of Salem, Massachusetts, in which town he says he served his apprenticeship with Mr. Lane, a sail-maker. He entered on board the Essex, at Boston, about ten months since, signed the articles, and took the oath of allegiance. Having behaved well in the service, he was made sail-maker of the ship. On Sunday last, Captain Porter called his crew together, communicated to them the declaration of war against England, and requested that any man amongst them who wished to leave the service, would hand in his name and receive his discharge; to which he received in answer three hearty cheers from every man of the crew.

" Yesterday morning, in consequence of three or four men having straggled from their work, and returned, Captain Porter called all hands again, and addressed them on the subject of the war, repeating his wish, that any man who was unwilling to continue in the service, would give in his name, and receive his discharge; to which the crew, as before, replied with three unanimous cheers. Shortly after, he ordered up the men in their respective gangs, and tendered them the oath of allegiance, which was cheerfully taken by every man on board excepting Irvin, who refused, and declared himself an Englishman. Upon this, the petty officers and crew of the ship, to whom Captain Porter has uniformly submitted the award of punishing offences committed on board his ship, requested permission to inflict severe corporal punishment on the offender; which the captain with his characteristic humanity, refused, and suffered them to dismiss him with a coat of old-fashioned Yankee manufacture, with appropriate labels, in which he appeared in the streets; where he excited so much curiosity, that the police interfered, and took charge of him to prevent a riot."

PROJECTED TRANSFORMATION OF THE THAMES.

A GIGANTIC plan has been announced for converting the River Thames, from Blackwall to the Gallions, and from Deptford to Vauxhall, into docks, for the building, reception, refitting, and repairing of the royal navy, as well as every description of merchant vessels; and for forming bridges, mills, &c. besides other works of great public utility, calculated, according to the projectors, to save the public twenty millions annually. The projectors require to be enabled to convert the bed of the river, from Blackwall to the Gallions, into a grand naval dépôt and arsenal, as well for building and fitting out, as for dismantling and laying up, in perfect security, a large portion of the British navy; and they propose to cut a canal from Long Reach (where ships have deep water at all times) to Woolwich Warren. They propose also to convert the bed of the river between Deptford and Vauxhall, into a dock or basin, for the reception of ships of every description, and to excavate a new channel from Deptford to Vauxhall, for the current of the Thames (which is intended to be of sufficient depth and breadth to allow the passage of vessels of all decriptions). And further, to cut a tide river immediately above the dam at Blackwall, to a point immediately below that at the Gallions.

PRAISEWORTHY CONDUCT OF MR. LOVE.

A LETTER from H.M.S. Boyne, dated off Ushant, July 5, 1812, states as follows:—

" I have much pleasure in mentioning a very noble act performed by Mr. Love, midshipman, of this ship, son of Captain Love, of H.M.S. Tisiphone. When we were close to the enemy's coast, Mr. Sully, a young midshipman, who was playing about the entering-port, fell overboard, and was sinking; when Mr. Love inquired the cause of alarm, and seeing his young shipmate in such imminent danger, he instantly plunged overboard, and rescued him from death. Sir Harry Neale, as an encouragement to enterprise and humanity, immediately promoted Mr. Love to the rank of lieutenant, and appointed him to the Tigre."

ANECDOTES OF CAPTAIN JEREMIAH COGHLAN, R.N.

(Communicated by OCEANUS)

WHILST in the command of his Majesty's sloop Renard, Captain Coghlan fell in with the Lily, a French privateer ship (formerly an English sloop of war, captured by the enemy, on the Halifax station), off St. Domingo, and brought her to action, During the height of the engagement, the French captain, by way, as he supposed, of intimidating our tars, hailed them to " Strike!" Captain Coghlan, who heard it, instantly took his trumpet, and replied, " Aye! I'll strike, and d——d hard too, my lad, directly." The next broadside fired from the Renard, sunk the Lily, with the greater part of her crew.

Whilst commanding the same vessel off St. Domingo, Captain Coghlan had the good fortune to fall in with the French brig of war, Prudent; and, though larger, and carrying more men and guns than the Renard, she struck without firing a shot. On the French captain's coming on board, and observing the comparative smallness of the English vessel, to that which he had but just given up his command of, he with the greatest coolness, requested permission to return to his ship, that he might try his skill in fight; which, of course, Captain Coghlan laughed at. He then, with equal gravity, solicited a certificate, stating, that he had not acted cowardly.—Captain Coghlan replied—" No, I cannot do that; but I will give you one, that shall specify you have acted *prudently.*

IMPROVEMENT IN MECHANIC POWER.

MR. T. SHELDRAKE has made an important discovery in mechanics.

which we are assured, will prove highly beneficial, by improving the effect of machines into which it can be introduced.

By the new application of a principle which it is believed was well known to the ancient mechanics, though so completely lost to the modern, that some have been willing to deny its existence, he is enabled to produce either simple or compound machinery, which shall have either more power, more velocity, or both united, as the subject may require, comprised in less space, and set in motion with less moving power, whether of animals, wind, water, or steam, than the machinery in common use.

The simplicity of the parts, and numerous combinations of which they are susceptible, render it probable that these principles may be applied to many of the engines that are now in use: the inventor has applied it to the following:—

1st. A *Capstan*, for naval, and other purposes, which is allowed by many officers of the navy, and captains in the merchants' service, who have seen it, to have none of the inconveniencies of the capstans that are now made; to have greater power, and, therefore, to perform its work with fewer hands; and in less time than any other capstan.

2dly. A *Windlass*, that possesses all the powers of the best windlasses at present in use; with powers peculiar to itself, which render it equal to the capstan in *effect*, without occupying more room than the common windlass.

3dly. A simple but powerful *movement*, applicable to work the chain or common pump on shipboard, and in other situations, so as to deliver more water in less time and with less moving power, than can be done in the usual way.

4thly. A portable *Crane*, of similar dimensions, but much greater powers, than that in general use. Of the superiority of this invention in compound machinery the following example may be produced:—

A gentleman has a chaff-cutter, with which one horse works two cutters: the horse turns a cog-wheel of 121 teeth: this gives motion to a smaller wheel of 20 teeth; the axis of this wheel turns a larger, over which a band passes into the loft above, and gives motion to the axis which turns the flies that keep the cutters in motion. The opinions of scientifical and practical men differ as to the diminution of power occasioned by friction in machines, but, without entering into that question, it may be sufficient to observe, that there is in this machine the friction of three axes upon their centres, and of 141 teeth upon each other. But in Mr. S.'s design, there are but two wheels besides their flies, consequently there are but *two* axes; the two wheels contain but 29 teeth; of course, whatever may be the absolute effect of friction in abating the power of machinery in general, the effect of friction in Mr. S.'s machine, is, when compared to the effect of friction in the former, as two to three: and twenty-three to one hundred and forty-one.

A boy when set to work this machine, will do as much work as a horse will do with the former. Mr. Sheldrake has printed and privately circulated a demonstration of his theory, which those scientific men who have seen it acknowledge to be just; he has procured patents for his discovery, in England, Scotland, and Ireland, and is preparing to make it public.

SPONTANEOUS IGNITION.*

Letter, dated the 2d of August, 1810, by the Committee appointed to investigate the Causes of the Loss by Fire, of the Honourable Company's Ship Earl Camden.

(Published by order of the Board of Trade.)

" We entered upon this inquiry, with an anxious zeal, to trace the cause of so melancholy an event, impelled not only by a sense of duty, in prosecution of your instructions, but by every consideration of feeling and humanity, to discover, if possible, the source of a calamity, the most dreadful, to which a maritime life is exposed.

" It is, therefore, with great concern, that we close our proceedings, without having been able to arrive at a conclusion, unmixed with doubt, as to the origin of this sudden and destructive conflagration.

" But although no positive proof could be obtained of the cause of this melancholy event, there are, nevertheless, circumstances that have developed themselves in the course of our inquiry, to which, if we apply the information acquired from respectable authority, in treating on voluntary combustion, we cannot help attaching all the force of the strongest presumptive evidence, that they were the existing causes of the loss of this valuable ship.

" From the evidence before us, it appears, that the fire broke out on the larboard side of the gun-room; that linseed oil (that is, paint oil) and spirits of turpentine, were kept in the gun-room, after that part of the ship had been stowed with cotton; that these combustible articles were deposited on the transom and cills of the gun-room ports; that the gunner and his mate were in the habit of repairing to them, to replenish their paint buckets, while they were engaged in the task of painting the ship; that the light, to guide them, proceeded from a glass bull's eye in each gun-room port; and that the gunner always went and returned *on the larboard side,* on which the fire originated.

" From these facts we are irresistibly led to the following inferences:—
First, that oil has accidentally been spilled in replenishing the paint buckets, and that with the inclination of the ship, it has run forward among the cotton.—Secondly, that in conveying the replenished paint buckets along the larboard side of the gun-room, paint has been accidentally spilled on the bales.—Lastly, that the oil absorbed by the gunny of the bales, produced the spontaneous ignition; and that, upon the communication of the current of air, from the gun-room scuttle, and the scuttles cut in the deck, it burst forth into irresistible conflagration.

" Having satisfied our minds, as to the cause of the loss of the Camden,

---

* N. C. XXIII. 448. XXIV. 104, 366.

we are naturally induced, in this part of our report, to suggest such measures of prevention as appear to us necessary to avert from the Honourable Company's shipping, the recurrence of so dreadful an evil.

" We, therefore, proceed to recommend, that it be a standing regulation, that, before a bale of cotton shall be shipped, oil, oil paints, and spirits of turpentine, shall be removed from the orlop deck, to a proper place of security on the poop, and that the commander shall, in writing, report to the superintendant of marine, such removal.

" That no fire shall be allowed, for any purpose, in any boat conveying cotton.

" That no light shall, on any pretence, be allowed to go into the hold, or on the orlop, during the stowage of cotton.

" That no natives of India shall be allowed to go into the hold, or on the orlop, during the receipt of a cotton cargo.

" That no work shall be allowed in the hold, or on the orlop, after six o'clock.

" That within a quarter of an hour of the conclusion of the day's work, all the officers in the ship shall be in the hold, and shall see the seamen up before them, and personally attend the laying on of the hatches and scuttles, the keys of which shall be invariably kept by the commanding officer.

" An instance occurred of ignition from the friction of the iron screw, on the Samson's port, after screwing a bale near the main hatchway, in the Camden's hold, but from the open situation in which this happened, the precautions taken immediately and the circumspection used for some time subsequently, no further effects, we are confident, were produced, than the momentary sparks deposed to. This accident should, however, induce particular caution and attention in the use of the screws in future.

" The Board of Trade not having heard of any instance, of a ship laden with cotton, at this port, sustaining accident from fire, would be glad to receive any information as to the precautions used here for guarding ships laden with cotton against such accident.

" R. C. PLOWDEN,
" Fort William, Oct. 19, 1810.   " Acting Secretary."

The following caution, on the subject of spontaneous ignition, has been circulated in England:—

It is not generally known, that flocks mixed with currier's oil will take fire, and more especially at this season (autumn) of the year. It has been ascertained, that the unfortunate fire at Logmore Mills, near Strond, was occasioned by a quantity of this waste being left on the floor.

DEATH OF AN IRISH SAILOR.

ABOUT an hour before the cessation of the sanguinary contest between H.M.S. Victorious, and the Rivoli,* James Daly, an Irishman, a common

---

* N, C. XXVII. 502, 506.

seaman, was struck at his quarters on the main deck of the Victorious, with a shot, which carried away the entire of the left thigh, so high up that a portion of the hip was attached to it, and shattered the right to pieces. On his way to the cockpit, he observed that one of the guns close to the hatchway was run out, and that the men were nearly in the act of firing; he immediately desired the seamen, who were carrying him down, to stop which they did, when he begged of the men to let him fire it, " and hoped they would allow him to have one shot more at the Frenchmen before he died; after doing which," he added, " he would die content." His request was granted, when he very contentedly permitted himself to be carried down, exclaiming on the ladder, " Fight on, my boys, fight on for your King and Country, until you die." On his arrival in the cockpit, he said to the surgeon, " Sir, I know you will do all you can for me, but I also know, there is nothing in your power." In less than half an hour after, his gallant soul left this for another world.

CORRESPONDENCE.

MR. EDITOR,

SOME time ago, I recollect reading, in the NAVAL CHRONICLE, one or two very curious accounts of a mermaid, which had been seen on some part of the coast of Scotland.* The existence of such an extraordinary animal has been, and no doubt is still considered by many people as fabulous. Indeed, I have been myself one of those who held the mermaid as the mere offspring of the imagination, and preserved in the catalogue of substantial beings by credulity. But I am now convinced of my error; and if you think it will interest or amuse any of your readers, by giving publicity to the following account relating to this animal, I beg you will do so. It may, moreover, call the attention of some able naturalist to the subject; and perhaps he may favour the public, through the same channel, with his opinion, as to the probable economy of this wonderful being.

The day of yesterday being very fine, I joined a party of ladies and gentlemen in a sailing excursion. When we had got about a mile to the S.E. of Exmouth Bar, our attention was suddenly arrested by a very singular noise, by no means unpleasant to the ear, but of which it is impossible to give a correct idea by mere description. It was not, however, unaptly compared by one of our ladies to the wild melodies of the Æolian harp, combined with a noise similar to that made by a stream of water falling gently on the leaves of a tree. The sound, however, had not all the variety, nor the soft cadence of the Æolian notes, but appeared like four or five different notes, each tone repeated several times on the same key. In the mean time, we observed something, about one hundred yards from us, to windward. We all imagined it to be some human being, though at the same time we were at a loss to account for this, at such a distance

---

* *Vide* N. C. XXII. 276; and XXIII. 186.—ED.

from the shore, and no other boat near. We hailed, but received no reply, and we made towards this creature as soon as possible; when, to the great astonishment of us all, it eluded our pursuit by plunging under water. In a few minutes it rose again, nearly in the same place, and by that time we had got sufficiently near for one of the boatmen to throw into the water a piece of boiled fish which he had in his locker.—This seemed to alarm the animal, though it soon recovered from its fears, for we presently observed it to lay hold of the fish, which it ate with apparent relish. Several other pieces were thrown out, by which the creature was induced to keep at a short distance from our boat, and afforded us the opportunity of observing it with attention, and found, to our astonishment, that it was no other than a mermaid. As the sea was calm, and in a great degree transparent, every part of the animal's body became in turn visible. The head, from the crown to the chin, forms rather a long oval, and the face seems to resemble that of the seal, though, at the same time, it is far more agreeable, possessing a peculiar softness, which renders the whole set of features very interesting. The upper and back part of the head appeared to be furnished with something like hair, and the fore part of the body with something like down, between a very light fawn and very pale pink colour, which at a distance had the appearance of flesh, and may have given rise to the idea, that the body of the mermaid is, externally, like that of the human being. This creature has two arms, each of which terminates into a hand with four fingers, connected to each other by means of a very thin elastic membrane. The animal used its arms with great agility, and its motions in general were very graceful. From the waist it gradually tapered so as to form a tail, which had the appearance of being covered with strong broad polished scales, which occasionally reflected the rays of the sun in a very beautiful manner; and from the back and upper part of the neck, down to the loins, the body also appeared covered with short round broad feathers, of the colour of down on the fore part of the body. The whole length of the animal, from the crown of the head to the extremity of the tail, was supposed to be about five feet, or five feet and a half.

In about ten minutes, from the time we approached, the animal gave two or three plunges in quick succession, as if it were at play. After this, it gave a sudden spring, appearing to swim away from us very rapidly, and in a few seconds we lost sight of this wonder-creating animal.

Crowds of boats are this day on the water, in the hope of witnessing such a novel sight, and a medical gentleman of Exeter has offered a reward of 20*l.* to whoever may succeed in catching the animal, and will bring it to him for dissection.—In consequence of this, all the fishermen are very busy in making preparations to endeavour to entangle in their nets this fair nymph of the ocean.

I am, Sir, your most obedient servant,

Exmouth, August 13, 1812.   J. TOUPIN.

P.S. It was reported here a few days ago, that a large strange fish had been seen in the neighbourhood of Torbay, and is supposed to have been this animal.

*** It deserves to be mentioned, that, about the time corresponding with the date of the above letter, the subjoined statement appeared in one of the French Papers:—

"On the 31st of July, an extraordinary animal was seen by five fishermen, in the creek of Port Melin (Morbihan). Its shape resembled that of a man. It had arms, and the bust was completely human, but the lower part terminated in a fish's tail. Its head was bald, with the exception of the fore part, on which was a bunch of black hair, and another bunch was perceptible upon the chin. The seafaring people, who have sent us these particulars, had time to observe the monster at their leisure; it was within half a musket-shot of the shore, between two boats, but they were afraid of it, and did not go any nearer."

MR. EDITOR,

IT is curious to observe in past history, the progress of dominion keeping an exact pace with the improvement of military discipline. The Greeks first overran the world with the invention of their phalanx; the Romans destroyed the Greek phalanx with a new discipline of what they called their Tortoise legion, in which the shields of the soldiers formed as it were a shell to unite and cover a battalion which penetrated the Greek phalanx, and conquered the world. The French have established a system of terror, to force their soldiers on to the most desperate assault, by embodying their army in columns, and empowering every officer, commissioned and non-commissioned, to shoot any person they suspect of cowardice, while the rear ranks are ordered to fire upon the front, if they recoil, and to complete this system of terror, the artillery in the rear threatens to fire upon the whole, if the division should not be triumphant, or moving forward to the assault.

This cowardly tactic was discovered in the experience of the Revolution, and its success has given the whole Continent of Europe to France, in less time than the Greeks or Romans took for the conquest of a single town or province.

This French tactic of artificial prowess is opposed by the moral tactic of sympathy and fortitude in the British nation, which has hitherto triumphed; but the French, aware of the superiority of British bayonets, seem determined never more to deploy their columns into lines to meet the British, so that the cavalry and bayonet of the British will be of no effect against their deep columns, and it will become indispensably necessary to charge in future with the artillery, muzzle to muzzle, by land, as we constantly do by sea, and success is indubitable.

Let us try the theory by experience:—Admiral Villeneuve, at the battle of Trafalgar, when he saw the British fleet advancing without firing a shot, in a hail or shower of French balls or bullets, not opening its fire till close to the muzzle of the French guns, he exclaimed, on his own quarter-deck, "Such cool English fortitude is invincible, and victory must be theirs."

Captain Williams, in a British frigate, in the Irish Channel, took a French frigate with a single broadside, muzzle to muzzle, when the French fled from their quarters before they had returned half the broadside. When the French captain came on board, he told Captain Williams that his crew consisted of 300 grenadiers, that had been in all the battles of the Continent, and though the officers had killed a great number with the discipline of terror, in shooting and stabbing the runaways, they could not force them back to their quarters; and when the officers asked the cause of such dastardly conduct in brave and tried men, they declared they could not stand such close firing with 24 pounders, which British fortitude used like pocket pistols.

If Britons by sea can use this consummate discipline of fortitude, in close fighting with artillery, why cannot British soldiers do the same, and secure victory on both elements by the same infallible means of superior discipline, progressing from the Greek phalanx to the artillery-cap'd columns of British fortitude, in close combat with grape-shot and bayonets.

If Lord Wellington had charged the French army at Talavera with artillery, muzzle to muzzle (not in long-shot cannonade), instead of cavalry and infantry with bayonets, he would certainly have broken their columns in a few minutes, and taken the whole of their artillery, baggage, and great part of the army, prisoners.

It was a cowardly manœuvre of 50,000 French to throw themselves into column to protect them from the bayonets of 20,000 British, and amounted to an avowal, that they were afraid of British fortitude in discipline; and it is impossible to doubt that a single British column, with ten 6-pounders, charging their ranks with grape-shot, would have thrown them into disorder, confusion, and flight. The French army will never more appear in line, but always in column, proved by the late battle of Colonel Craufurd, where 11,000 threw themselves into column against four thousand British, whose bayonets could not penetrate their deep centre, though two 6 pounders, with grape, when the bayonet failed, would have done the business of victory in two rounds; for if they cannot stand one round in a ship's battery, where they are protected from the bayonet, they could not stand half a round when they would be exposed to the bayonet at the same instant.

There seems no other means to triumph over the factitious terror of France, than the natural terror of British fortitude in the charge of artillery; and if, in the indispensable trial of the experiment, our infantry officers should be deficient in zeal and fortitude to conduct it, the commanders of corps must be empowered by law to put in force the discipline of terror by word of command only, upon any occasion that they may judge it necessary, without making it a permanent system, as in France, to disgrace and cowardize a nation.

MUZZLE TO MUZZLE.

MR. EDITOR, *Newmarket,* 26 *May.*

IT has been stated in some of the London papers, that the Galician army, and the people of that province, had not exerted themselves in the way in which they ought to have done.

Allow me, who am well acquainted with them, to inform you, that both the army and the people have performed wonders. They themselves have *bravely* defended their province, without the pecuniary aid of any part of Spain, of South America, or this country (except arms and ammunition, with a little money, at the commencement of the war, the first of which I carried to them in my frigate, the Alcmene).

The French entered that province in pursuit of our army, amounting to 50,000 in all. You know the English embarked and left these poor fellows surrounded by their enemies, who had full possession of their province six months, when the brave and manly Galicians drove every one of them out of it (without the aid of England), except a few sailors from the Lively frigate. Yes, Sir, it was done by the bravery of the Spaniards, in their gallant and well-fought battle at Puente de San-Peyo, near Vigo. Such was the confusion of the French in their retreat, that they had not time to destroy the men of war at Ferrol, which amounted to near twenty sail, eight or ten of the line. And to the credit of the inhabitants of that town, I must not omit to mention, that when the French ordered a contribution on the town, they received for answer, that if they attempted to enforce it, the workmen employed in the dock-yard alone would prevent it; and to them it should be the signal to attack, with such tools as they had in their possession. Hundreds and hundreds of Frenchmen fell in this town by the Spanish *cuchillo,* or knife. Indeed, in all the towns near it, it became a byeword with those who spoke of Ferrol, *Senor, en Ferrol, maten los Franceses, como chinches.* " Sir, in Ferrol they kill the Frenchmen as they would bugs."

The largest army now belonging to Spain is that of Galicia; it is 26,000 strong, commanded by an excellent officer, General Abadia. This account I received from General Walker, who was with him, and reviewed his army in September last, at Astorga, when Marmont advanced against it; at that time General Abadia had just taken the command of it. One-third of this army was without either shoes or stockings, marching over *furze-heaths ;* none of the army had received any rations for three days, neither did they know when they might expect any: all they had to subsist on was a few potatoes, which they themselves dug up out of the cottagers' gardens.

Under all these privations, to the immortal honour of the Galician army, they were perfectly *obedient, quiet,* and *patient ;* so said General Walker, who added, that the character of the Spanish soldier, after what he had seen, was, in his mind, greatly exalted: he also observed, that a colonel of cavalry was reported to General Abadia not to have obeyed some orders; the general calmly replied, " Very well, Sir;" but when he arrived at the head of the colonel's regiment, he stopped and addressed him as follows:—
" Sir, dismount your horse, go your way home, and recollect that you are

no longer a soldier; and that I neither can or will command such men as you, who know not how to obey." The colonel attempted to apologize; the general replied, " I have no further use for your service; but I have for that of your horse, which you will leave here."

This army has been entirely supported by the inhabitants of Galicia, and kept on the frontiers to defend their province : had every other province in Spain acted in the same way, Spain would have been in a very different situation from what it now is. However, their resources are so confined, it will not permit them to leave their province, and take advantage of Lord Wellington's movement. But if this *country would assist them with money*, or proper equipments, I'll answer for their doing every thing that can be expected of them. Besides this army in that province, in September last they had 40,000 men with arms in their hands, ready and willing to come forward at a day's notice, if the Government could pay and subsist them; but, alas! Sir, they have not the power. And these fine fellows leave their homes, their wives and children, without *bounty*, without *fee or reward*, most cheerfully; all they ask is clothes and food; a very little of the latter, and that of a very inferior kind, will suffice them; even a few Callavanzo-beans, an onion, and the water from the brook ; with this alone they will perform longer marches than any other troops in Europe, though well fed. Since I left Galicia, in September last, I have been informed that arms have been given to 50,000 more men in that province ; and besides this, there was a corps of mountain scouts, consisting of about two or three thousand well armed useful men.

I have already stated, that the French army entered 50,000 strong; they remained in it six months, and then left it with only 24,000. Who killed the rest? Or what became of them ?—The English at the battle of Corunna might have killed about 3,000, the rest certainly died by the hands of Spaniards.

It is not the comparatively few men we can send from England that can ever drive the French out of Spain (although it assists very much actually, and by example to the Spaniards), it is the Spaniards who must be the principal actors, and who are ready and willing, if they were furnished with the means. I should imagine this is what the Marquis Wellesley wisely alluded to; was this mode adopted immediately, now that the French armies are in the North, there would not be a Frenchman in Spain this day twelvemonth. You would not then find it necessary to expend twenty milllions annually in the Peninsula, as you are now doing. We ought to recollect the old proverb—" An opportunity once lost cannot be regained."—This applies well to the case in point of Spain, and the situation of the French army in the North.

No one, Sir, can admire the valour that has been displayed by the British troops in the Peninsula more than myself; but I can bring proof of equal valour having been displayed by Spaniards, particularly in the defence of their towns—witness Saragosa, which received 17,000 of the enemy's bomb-shells; Gerona, where even the ladies assisted ; and Tarragona.

I have been a great deal with the Spaniards, and know their generous hearts well. I was the first Englishman in Spain when the Revolution broke out at Madrid. I was there, assisting in their councils three days, when we were, in fact, at war with them. I was residing with them a great part of last summer, and four months the year before, besides being on the station with my frigate, four years since, when I brought over the two Deputies from Galicia; and, as I understand the language pretty well, I think I am able to form a correct judgment.—Therefore, I hope, in justice to our worthy Allies (who, God knows! have suffered every kind of privation possible in their just cause), you will insert this in your valuable Publication, or any part that you think most useful.

W. H. BROWN TREMLETT.

MR. EDITOR,   *September 4th*, 1812.

SEEING in your CHRONICLE for the last month, an account of the loss of the St. George, by one of the Survivors, I send you an account also of that of the Defence, word for word as it was written, by Joseph Page, seaman. The narrative of the St. George has been put into a better dress, than what it was originally written in; but in this I have preferred the rough seaman-like language of the original narrator, as probably will many of your readers.   I am, &c.

NAUTICUS.

" On Monday, the 23d of December, 1811, at 12 P.M. bent the storm-stay-sails, and hauled up the fore-top-sail; it was then blowing a strong gale from W.S.W. The St. George and Cressy in company to leeward.— At 1 took in the fore-top-sail, and lay-to under close reefed main-top-sail. At 3 A.M. slipt the main-top-sail; wind W.N.W. Unbent the main-top-sail, and sent it down on deck; got a fore-top-sail ready for bending, but having no other main-top-sail on board, our captain (Atkins) would not allow it to be bent, for fear of losing it; it was put under the poop awning in readiness, when the weather should moderate. We next hove-to under storm-stay-sails, at 9. 30.; the Cressy wore and stood under our stern to the southward. Our captain ordered to see all clear for wearing; at the same time asking Mr. Baker if the St. George had wore; and was answered, No.—He then said he would stand on with her, or would not wear till she did. We saw no more of the Cressy. At 12 A.M. the watch and idlers turned up to wear ship. At half-past twelve the captain told Mr. Baker he would not wear till the St. George did, but would stay by her. Saw the St. George burning a blue light to leeward. 2. 30. (24th) split the main-stay-sail; hauled down the fore-stay-sail, and lay-to under the storm mizen-stay-sail; blowing a hard gale from the N.W. At 4. 30. the first lieutenant ordered me (captain of the fore-top) to send four men into the top, and went up myself. Just as I got up to the top, the ship struck very easy, and looking to leeward I saw the breakers. I mentioned to Ralph Teazie (one of the men saved), that the ship had struck;

just then falling into a trough of the sea, she struck very heavy, fore and aft. The fore-stay-sail was about half hoisted; the sea making a fair breach over her, washed the men to leeward, rendering them unable to hoist it up. Just as the first lieutenant ordered the masts to be cut away, the main-mast, mizen-mast, and fore-top-sail-yard went over the side; about five minutes after, the foremast went. The sea breaking her, the dismal shrieks of the people, the guns breaking adrift, and crushing the men to death, rendered the whole a dreadful scene. I saw the carpenter's wife, with a little girl in her hand, endeavouring to get on the quarter-deck, when a tremendous sea broke in, which washed her, with many of the people, down the hatchway. The captain was then on the poop, holding on by the howitzer, standing before the mizen-mast. The boats were laying on the lee gangway, all dashed to pieces except the pinnace, with about 20 men in her, and she was immediately washed overboard, and lay bottom upwards.—I now jumped overboard, and got on the mizen-top, and the ship parted by the chesstree and gangway—by the heave of the sea, and rolling of the ship, the sheet anchor was driven athwart the forecastle, and killed several men. The sea was now making a fair breach between the forecastle and quarter-deck; the booms were washed away, with nearly a hundred men holding on by them. I, with several others, were washed off the top—I now made the best of my way from one part of the wreck to another, till I got on the booms, on which were at this time about 40 men. When the sea coming again, made a clear sweep, except three or four.— I got on the raft again, and spoke to John Brown, and told him I thought we were drawing near the land—he told me, yes, he believed we were. There were then again about twenty men on the raft; but on reaching the shore, six only remained. Two Danes, who were on the beach, came to our assistance—my foot was at this time jammed in among the small spars. John Brown, and Ralph Teazie, finding I was not able to get off the raft, were coming to assist me; but the Danes told them, as well as we could understand, to sit down, for they (the Danes) were stronger than us, and they would try to get me off the raft; one Dane made three attempts before he could get to me; the third time he was washed over head and ears; but got hold of my foot, wrenched it out, and took me on shore. He then took me to a little shed, to wait for the carts, most of us being unable to walk; in the course of ten minutes a great number of carts, and gentlemen on horseback, came down to the beach. They put us in two different carts, and drove us to Sheltoz, a small village, on the road. The man who drove us spoke to a woman on the road, and asked if she had any liquor, She took a bottle from her pocket, and made each of us take a drink, *which I believe was the principle of the safety of our lives.* We soon arrived at a house in the village, where we stript, had dry clothes given us, and were put to bed; it was then about eleven o'clock, as near as I can guess; the Danes were very near to us. When I came to myself, I found Thomas Mullins in bed with me; he came on shore some time after me on a piece of the wreck. Just as we reached the shore, the poop and forecastle were turned clean over, and not a man to be seen, but a few on pieces of the wreck. About 5 o'clock, a gentleman who spoke English, came to the bedside where me and Mullins was, and told us there was an officer brought up to the house, and asked us if we were able to get up and see if we knew him. We told him, yes, and, with the assistance of the people, went to the barn, and found it to be our captain. On Sunday, the 29th, he was put into a coffin, and buried in Sheltoz Church-yard. David M'Robb, and John M'Cormic were buried alongside of him. We remained there till the 15th of January, when our captain was taken up and carried to Rizkum, where we fell in with the survivors of the St. George; they were at that time burying the boatswain of Anholt. We then buried our captain, with the honours of war. The St. Georges told us they were going to be sent home.

Names of the Survivors.

Joseph Page, writer of this narrative; John Brown; Ralph Teazie; John Platt; David M'Cormic, came on shore alive, but died going up in the cart; Thomas Mullins.

To the Right Hon. Lord Viscount Melville, First Lord of the Admiralty, &c.

MY LORD,

THE recent alteration in the naval uniform has given, I believe, satisfaction to all classes in the service; but, however gratified the feelings of the officers may be, in having their shoulders decorated with gold, I flatter myself they would be still more so, were their pockets to be ornamented with the substitute, which, through compulsion, has been adopted as the circulating medium, in the United Kingdom, for that valuable article.

I am aware, that the honour of altering the uniform was acquired previously to your Lordship's coming into office, and, consequently, that the merit, if any, attaches to your predecessor. The name your Lordship bears by inheritance ranks deservedly high in the navy, amongst both officers and men, for the facility which has, through your noble parent, been granted them in receiving their pay, and in obtaining a certain proportion thereof for the support of their families. These are not the only acts he performed for their good; but, as the subject of pay is the purport of the present letter, your Lordship will pardon their mention.

It is a notorious fact, that there are few mechanics who have not a greater weekly allowance, than some hundreds of lieutenants (ranking with captains in the army) derive for their half pay, without being compelled to support the characters of gentlemen. The mechanic also possesses *superior advantages* to the officer—he is paid regularly *every week*; by which he is enabled to purchase all the necessaries of life more reasonably. When he receives his stipend, there is no deduction—no, not even the *Income Tax!* and he is certain of receiving the full amount of what he has earned by his labour. I will now, my Lord, point out, (not that I can suppose your Lordship is unacquainted with it) the inferiority of the defenders of their country to the individuals just mentioned. The pay of the officer takes place only *twice in the year*; and although he but too well knows the periods when it is *due*, yet to his sorrow he is in total ignorance of the time of *payment*. How, my Lord, is an individual to support himself, and perhaps a large family, during a period of nearly eight months? The methods of bare existence might be discovered, were it practicable for your Lordship to take a peep into many of the offices belonging to navy agents, where officers may be seen praying advance upon their pay, for which favour they have to pay a certain rate of interest. When the time of payment arrives, there are other stoppages placed on their slender allowance, to which they are compelled quietly to submit.

Thus, it is plain that the mechanic enjoys superior advantages to the officer, all of which are so glaring as to render it superfluous to take up more of your Lordship's time, in adducing proofs. That your Lordship will take the case of the half-pay officers of the navy into consideration, when the multifarious pursuits of your high situation will admit, is my ardent wish; and, that the opportunity now possessed by your Lordship, of your name being firmly fixed in the breasts of some hundreds of grateful individuals may not be lost. The name of " MELVILLE " ranks already high in the navy, and it is now in your Lordship's power to place it on the highest summit, for the admiration of posterity.

I have the honour to be, &c. &c.

Portsmouth, 10*th September*, 1812.   TOM STARBOARD.

NAVAL AND HYDRAULIC ARCHITECTURE.

THE BREAKWATER IN PLYMOUTH SOUND.

(Continued from page 125.)

SIR,   *Harwich, October* 15*th*, 1810.

I HAVE the honour to acknowledge the receipt of your letter of the 11th instant at this place, with a copy of the report on the proposed Breakwater in Plymouth Sound, by Mr. Jackson, master-attendant of Plymouth Yard: and being desired to give my opinion on the said report, I beg you will inform my Lords Commissioners of the Admiralty, that I very much approve of the report in general. Observing that the shoal water in the Sound, as spoken of in the report, will not occupy more than one half of the Sound, where ships of the line can lay; when the proposed Breakwater is completed, the other half of the Sound will have 6 or 7 fathoms at low water spring tides : consequently, the danger that may be apprehended, of ships being liable to receive damage by grounding on their anchors at very low tides, must be very considerably diminished, as ships can never ground on their anchors in that part of the Sound first spoken of. And, indeed, if ships are suffered to ground on their anchors in that part of the anchorage where the water is the shoalest, it must be done for want of care; and I do not recollect ever hearing of any accident of the kind happening with the Sound in its present state. With respect to the number of ships of the line the Sound can contain when the Breakwater is finished, I think Mr. Jackson's report gives under the number; as I do conceive that the water will be so smooth that ships may lay very near each other.

J. W. Croker, Esq. J. WHIDBEY.

SIR, *Plymouth Yard, 31 October,* 1810.

In pursuance of their Lordships' directions, to take into my consideration the report of Mr. Jackson, of the 15th of August last, respecting the plan of the Dyke or Breakwater proposed to be formed in Plymouth, and to report my opinion thereon; I beg leave to acquaint you, for their Lordships' information, that I have considered the same accordingly, and entirely concur with Mr. Jackson, in his replies to the several questions and remarks on the subject. I would beg leave, however, to remark, that though there is ample room for 36 of the line to be moored in security within the proposed Dyke or Breakwater, I had entertained an idea that greater facility might still be afforded for the ships to unmoor and get under way, by confining the number of ships to thirty, which would also allow a space for the possibility of their not being brought to anchor in the exact situations that might be pointed out by the superintendent of the anchorage.

John Wilson Croker, Esq. W. BROWN.

SIR, *London, April* 15, 1811.

Agreeably to the request of the Lords Commissioners of the Admiralty, I have taken into consideration the steps proper to be taken for the purpose of commencing the works of the Breakwater intended to be built in Plymouth Sound; and beg leave to recommend to their Lordships' consideration the following, as the most likely in my opinion to forward that measure with advantage and economy:—The first step which appears to me necessary is, to appoint a proper person to superintend and manage the execution of the whole of the works, and in whose assiduity, skill, and integrity, the utmost reliance can be placed. This person will require several assistants; some to act in the capacity of surveyors and superintendents of the stone quarries; others in the direction of the vessels to be employed in the conveyance and deposition of the stone; and others to keep the accounts, and to check the returns of the quantity of work performed. The principal superintendent, with his assistants, should proceed as early as convenient to Plymouth, for the purpose of surveying and marking out the most suitable places to supply the requisite quantity of stone, and where the piers should be built for the loading of the vessels that are to convey the stone to and deposit it in the Breakwater. The quantity of stone round the margins of Plymouth Sound, and fit for the purposes of the Breakwater, are immense, as will appear by the report I made to their Lordships, dated 29th October, 1806. When the places to supply the stone, and for the other purposes of the Breakwater, are marked out, it will then be for their Lordships to give the necessary directions to procure a sufficiency to complete the whole work, and to afford the other conveniences required. While the foregoing operations are in hand, two mooring chains, of the length of about 1,200 yards each, having their links about two inches diameter, should be procured, as well as four anchors to keep them in their places: one of these chains to be laid beyond the extremity of the outer base, and another beyond the extremity of the inner base or straight part of the Breakwater. And besides these, about fifty smaller chains will be wanted of various lengths, from seven to ten fathoms each, with buoys, to be attached to the large chains, for the vessels to make fast to, while they are depositing their cargoes in the line of the Breakwater. It is probable these chains may be obtained from among the unserviceable mooring chains in the dock-yard; and I should apprehend craft can be spared, with the necessary assistance, to lay them down in the direction of the intended Breakwater. But a stationary vessel, with several boats, will be wanted for the use of the works. The building of the piers at which the vessels are to be loaded, should be put in hand as soon as the ground is procured; and the quarries to supply the stone should also be opened. These, I apprehend, can all be got done by contract, as well as the necessary number of cranes (not less than twenty) for loading the vessels. Vessels also, I would hope, might be procured, to convey such of the stone as are of a moderate size, by contract. But I fear it would be difficult, if not impracticable, to procure such vessels on the coast as will be wanted for conveying the large blocks of stone that must be used in the casing of the outside slope of the Breakwater, as these vessels will require to be made of a particular construction, with machinery adapted to the moving of large masses of stone: I would, therefore, submit to their Lordships' consideration, whether it would not be advisable to direct ten or twelve of such vessels to be built; they will not be wanted until the ensuing spring; and if contractors for this kind of work can be got, these vessels might either be sold to them, or let on proper conditions, and their being ready will greatly accelerate the work. I cannot venture to encourage their Lordships to expect that much, if any, of the actual work of the Breakwater itself will be performed in the course of the present year, as the preparations will necessarily require much time; which I fear will consume the most, if not the whole of the present season. I have annexed an estimate.

J. W. Croker, Esq. JOHN RENNIE.

Estimate of the probable Amount of Money *that will be required for the* Works *at* Plymouth Sound, *in the course of the present Year.*

Mooring chains, anchors, small chains, buoys, and laying them
  down .... £ 5,500
A stationary vessel, with boats 2,600
Purchase of land for quarries, and other purposes, uncertain;
  but say 20,000

Opening quarries, building piers, erecting cranes, and other
conveniences 10,000
Ten vessels for the conveyance of large stone, with their requisite
machinery; say for this year 15,000
Probable deposition of stone, and various miscellaneous articles.. 6,900

£,60,000

ORDER OF THE PRINCE REGENT IN COUNCIL.

At the Court at Whitehall, the 22d day of June, 1811.

PRESENT,

HIS ROYAL HIGHNESS THE PRINCE REGENT

IN COUNCIL.

Whereas there was this day read at the Board, a Report from a Committee of the Lords of his Majesty's Most Honourable Privy Council, dated the 11th of this instant; in the words following :—*viz.*

" Your Royal Highness having been pleased, by your Order in Council of the 9th of last month, in the name and on the behalf of his Majesty, to refer unto this Committee a Memorial from the Right Honourable the Lords Commissioners of the Admiralty, dated the 9th of April last; setting forth, That the said Lords Commissioners, having in the early part of the year 1806, had under their consideration the exposed state of Plymouth Sound, and being deeply impressed with the importance of Plymouth, on account of the natural advantages it possesses as a naval station, directed Mr. Rennie and Mr. Whidbey, whose abilities eminently qualified them for this service, to examine and survey Cawsand Bay, the Sound, Catwater, and Hamoaze; and particularly to state their opinion on the practicability of rendering the Sound a secure anchorage for ships of war; and that those gentlemen, having by their Report of the 21st of April, 1806, submitted to the Admiralty a full statement of all the advantages and disadvantages to which the harbours and roadsteads in the neighbourhood of Plymouth are liable, together with their decided opinion, that if a Pier or Breakwater were constructed in Plymouth Sound, having its eastern end about sixty fathoms east of St. Carlo's Rocks, and its western end about three hundred fathoms west of the Shovel, forming in the whole a length of eight hundred and fifty fathoms, it would, with another pier to be constructed from Andurn Point towards the before-men ioned Breakwater, of about four hundred fathoms in length, having an inclined kant forming an angle of about 120°, completely shelter Plymouth Sound from all storms, without there being any danger of its lessening the depth of water. or any doubt of the practicability of executing the work, thereby enabling a considerable fleet of line-of-battle ships to ride within the Sound in perfect safety in all winds, and in any weather, and with ample room to work out; That the said Lords Commissioners having lately taken the before-mentione subject into their most serious consideration, and having also consulted several of the most intelligent naval officers of his Majesty's dock-yards thereon, by whose reports the opinion stated by Messrs. Rennie and Whidbey, of the practicability of the construction of a Breakwater, in the situation proposed, and of the security it would afford to his Majesty's ships, has been fully corroborated; the said Lords Commissioners have been led, from these reports, and from all information they have been enabled to obtain, as well as from every consideration they can give to the subject, to form the most decided opinion, that it would be highly expedient for the good of his Majesty's naval service, that the said Breakwater should be undertaken without delay, on the plan proposed by Messrs. Rennie and Whidbey, the estimated expense of which amounts to one million one hundred and seventy-one thousand pounds: and therefore, the said Lords Commissioners are induced most humbly to propose to your Royal Highness, that your Royal Highness would be graciously pleased, by your Order in Council, in the name and on the behalf of his Majesty, to authorize them to give such directions for commencing this important work, according to the before-mentioned plan proposed by Messrs. Rennie and Whidbey, as shall appear to the said Lords Commissioners to be most expedient for the benefit of his Majesty's service, and to prepare a supplementary estimate to be laid before Parliament, of such part of the above-mentioned sum as may be found necessary to expend thereon in the course of the present year; the Lords of the Committee, in obedience to your Royal Highness's said order of reference, have taken the said memorial of the Lords Commissioners of the Admiralty into consideration, and do agree humbly to report as their opinion to your Royal Highness, that it may be advisable for your Royal Highness, in the name and on the behalf of his Majesty, to authorize the said Lords Commissioners to give such directions for commencing the important work in question, according to the plan proposed by Messrs. Rennie and Whidbey, as shall appear to the said Lords Commissioners to be most expedient for the benefit of his Majesty's service, and to prepare a supplementary estimate to be laid before Parliament, of such part of the above-mentioned sum, as may be found necessary to expend thereon in the course of the present year."

His Royal Highness the Prince Regent, having taken the said report into consideration, was pleased, in the name and on the behalf of his Majesty, and by and with the advice of his Majesty's Privy Council, to approve thereof: and his Royal Highness, in the name and on the behalf aforesaid, doth hereby accordingly authorize the Lords Commissioners of the Admiralty to give such directions for commencing the construction of a Pier or Breakwater in Plymouth Sound, according to the plan proposed by the said Messrs. Rennie and Whidbey, as shall appear to the said Lords Commissioners to be most expedient for the benefit of his Majesty's service; and do prepare a supplementary estimate, to be laid before Parliament, of such part of the sum of one million one hundred and seventy-one thousand pounds, as may be found necessary to expend thereon in the course of the present year.

W. FAWKENER.

Admiralty-Office, February 1812.

Minute or Paper, from Mr. Bentham to the Navy Board, on the subject of the Breakwater in Plymouth Sound.

Having thought it my duty to consider in what way I should have planned a Pier and Breakwater in Plymouth Sound, supposing this work to be expedient, and that the planning of it had been entrusted to me; and having already contrived two different modes in which that work might be executed, free from the most prominent objections which may be made to the mode (as far as I can, if it be the plan I have seen) proposed by Messrs. Rennie and Whidbey; in either of which two modes of mine, this work might be executed at less than half the expense which that of Messrs. Rennie and Whidbey is estimated at; it seems incumbent on me to acquaint the Board of these circumstances, since they may probably consider it expedient to apprize the Lords Commissioners of the Admiralty, that by a different mode of execution from that ordered, a saving might be made in the work in question of several hundred thousand pounds.

(Copy.   S. BENTHAM,
R. A. NELSON.   24 Sept. 1811.

The Board having looked upon the estimate with which I had been furnished by the Deputy Comptroller, relative to the Pier and Breakwater in Plymouth Sound, and alluded to in my minute of the 24th ultimo, as not sufficiently authentic to serve as the grounds of any statements to the Lords Commissioners of the Admiralty, of the comparative advantage, in point of economy, which might be derived from the substitution of either of the plans mentioned in my said minute, to the plan ordered to be executed, as proposed by Messrs. Rennie and Whidbey, it seems nevertheless incumbent on me to call the attention of the Board to the subject of that work again, for the purpose of bringing to view some of the more important comparative advantages of my plans for that work, in regard to efficiency.

In my above-mentioned minute I spoke of my plans for that work as being either of them free from the most prominent of the objections that may be made to the plan of Messrs. Rennie and Whidbey. The objections I had in view were as follows:—

1st.—That such a work as planned by Messrs. Rennie and Whidbey, as appears by the plan given into the Board by Mr. Whidbey, and from the preparations which the Lords Commissioners of the Admiralty have ordered to be made, even supposing sufficient precautions to have been taken to prevent any injury to the harbour during the execution of it, and that the work were completed in its greatest perfection, would, nevertheless, by opposing throughout its extent a complete interruption to the existing water-way, occasion such extensive eddies in the wake of the work, and such an increased action on the bottom and sides of the parts left open, as could not fail of forming shoals more or less injurious, according to the nature of the soil, and other local circumstances.

2dly.—That the erecting one artificial rock of so great extent in the middle of the entrance of the harbour, and the projecting another from one side of it, and that over a space the greatest part of which seems by the soundings in the plan to be at present navigable for large ships, even at low water, and of course still more so at other times, must be considered as contracting the entrance in a very material amount; insomuch that when it is considered likewise that the Sound, instead of being all of it open for a fleet to run through to the more sheltered parts, would then be contracted into two entrance channels, in which the velocity of the tide would be much increased, and that the remaining part would be entirely eddy, it cannot but appear doubtful at least, whether such a change of circumstances may not occasion an increase of risks to a fleet coming in for shelter, perhaps in the night, which, considering how very few examples there are of the loss of ships in Plymouth Sound, might outweigh the advantages of there being smoother water to lie in, when they should have passed these obstacles.

In the forming of my plans, on the contrary, attention has been paid to the obviating these objections, more or less, completely. By one of my plans, a double row of cylindrical masses of stone-work, built in my new mode, are designed to be deposited in the direction most suitable to a Breakwater (which probably would be different from that fixed on by Messrs. Rennie and Whidbey) in such manner as to leave an interval between each two masses above, equal to their diameter, and that the masses of one row should be placed opposite the intervals in the other, so that while these two rows together form a complete obstacle to direct the course of the waves, the tide or current would be allowed to pass freely between them throughout the whole extent of the Breakwater, as also boats, or even small vessels, in moderate weather.

According to another variety of this mode, a single row of masses more in the form of the piers of a bridge, might be deposited at a greater distance from one another, and other masses of stone might be deposited upon them, so as to form a kind of bridge, but differing from ordinary bridges, inasmuch as that instead of the arch between the piers rising above water, the bottom of the parts intermediate between the piers would be kept sufficiently under low water to afford a complete obstacle to the waves to the required depth, but leaving, nevertheless, very ample space underneath for the constant passage of the tide or current. The upper part of such a Breakwater would be sloped on the side towards the sea, so as to afford an inclined plane for the waves to expend themselves upon in mounting: the interior side of the masses, according to either of these modes, would be perpendicular, and by being hollow, might be converted to various useful purposes, whereby a compensation might be obtained for a considerable part of the expense.

But considering that a diminution of the water-way, even in the above-mentioned lesser degree, would, in some instances at least, be objectionable, and what is of still more importance, that the building of piers or works of masonry of any kind at the entrance of a port, is in fact the forming of artificial rocks, against which ships are as likely to be carried to their destruction as against natural rocks; I thought it expedient to contrive other means of producing the desired effect, which should be free from this objection; in consequence of which, the mode of forming a Breakwater which I should propose in preference, as well to those of masonry built according to my mode as to any other, is as follows:—

To make floating Breakwaters in separate parts, or floats of wood in preference, because that material is sufficiently buoyant without the need for depending on any cavities, which might be liable to be filled with water; to make these floats of a triangular, or rather prismatic form, and to hold them in their places by means of iron chains.

Breakwaters, such as these, would not only leave the whole of the water-way uninterrupted below them, but would also allow a great part of the tide to pass through them; they might, therefore, be extended all across the entrance, so as to afford their protection to the whole of the Sound within it, leaving only in certain parts sufficient intervals between the rows of floats, as well as the contiguous floats, to allow of ships shaping their course between them; more especially since in the event of a ship striking against, or even running over one of these Breakwaters, it would not be likely that such an accident would occasion any material injury to the ship, any more than to the Breakwater.

A farther advantage of these Breakwaters, which must be considered of no small importance, is, that no mischief whatever can be conceived likely to arise to any harbour from the employment of them; they may be tried in different parts of the harbour till experience shall have pointed out the most advantageous situation for them, or they might be entirely taken away, and be employed elsewhere, whenever circumstances might render it desirable. I have also to observe, that this proposal of mine is not founded on theory alone, since I have seen Breakwaters constructed on the same principle, though not in the same manner, in a foreign port, where their good effect was fully exemplified; and indeed I have on one occasion caused one on a small scale to be employed with good effect at Sheerness.

With this view of the subject before me, and referring to that part of the Regulations under which I act, which enjoins that I should " give my advice and assistance in all matters relating to my peculiar profession," that is, of " Civil Architect and Engineer," and to that other part of the same Regulations, which says, " it is of course incumbent on me," in regard to works of every kind, " to suggest such improvements as may occur to me for the benefit of his Majesty's service;" and since the Lords Commissioners of the Admiralty, even at the time of sending back my former minute, have not forbidden my interference in this work, and as they speak of it as a great national work, I cannot but urge the Board to make their Lordships acquainted with my ideas on this subject.

In regard to the opinion which the Board seem to entertain of their being debarred from submitting to their Lordships any thing farther relative to this national work, until they receive farther orders on the subject, I cannot but request the Board to consider, that some of the preliminary measures already ordered are very costly; that in the case of the use of floating Breakwaters being adopted, no stone will be necessary, nor consequently any vessels to carry it, nor any machinery to deposit it.

(Copy.)   S. BENTHAM.
R. A. NELSON.   4 Oct. 1811.

Estimated EXPENSE of a BREAKWATER, 7,000 feet in length, by distinct masses of Masonry; also, of a FLOATING BREAKWATER of the same length, formed by Floats of Wood.

If of STONE, according to the first mode :

A circular mass of Stone 50 feet diameter, 50 feet high, the bottom and sides of an average thickness of 6 feet, of which 2 feet in thickness on the outside, set in Roman Cement and Sand, a strong Coping set in Cement only, and the rest in good under-water Mortar 1,568
Levelling and preparing the bottom of one mass 100
Transporting and depositing one mass 100

                                                   £.1,768
140 No. of Masses, as above 247,520
Contingencies on do. at 15 per cent. 37,128

                           Grand Total .... £.284,648

If of Stone, according to the second mode :—Although a Breakwater of this construction would require less Masonry, yet as the execution would require a little more care and accuracy, the expense may be considered as the same with the former mode.

For a floating Breakwater of WOOD :

One Float, 30 feet in breadth and depth, 60 feet in length,
   paid over with Oil of Tar, and other cheap Oil 0
Four Mooring Chains and Fastenings 430
Laying down the Moorings of one Float 100

                                                   £.1,500
117 Floats, as above 175,500
Preparations and other Contingencies on do. at 15 per cent..... 26,325

                           Grand Total .... £.201,825

                                                                                S. B.

(Copy.)
R. A. NELSON.

                                    (To be continued.)

STATE PAPERS.

AMERICA AND ALGIERS.

THE following is a copy of a Circular sent to all American Consuls in the Mediterranean:

" *On board the American Ship Allegany, at Sea,*
" SIR, *July 25, 1812.*

" I have the honour to inform you, that on the 17th instant the ship Allegany, Ebenezer Eveleth, master, arrived at Algiers from the United States of America, with a cargo of naval and military stores for the Regency, in fulfilment of treaty stipulations; and that on the 20th inst. when they had begun to discharge the cargo, I received a message from the Dey, informing me that he would not receive the same, saying, that the articles were not such in quality or quantity as he expected, and that the ship should leave the Regency immediately, with myself and all other Americans then in Algiers. Every proper measure was taken to prevent the execution of this order, and to restore the former good understanding, but without effect, and I left Algiers this morning in the Allegany, with my family, and all other Americans then in Algiers.

" This act bears such evident marks of hostility, on the part of the Dey of Algiers, towards the United States, that I embrace the first moment to communicate the same, to all Consuls of the United States in the Mediterranean that it may be made known without delay to the commanders of all American vessels in this sea, and others concerned, that they may be on their guard, and secure themselves and their vessels, as effectually as possible, against the danger of capture.

" I therefore request, that you will give this notice to all commanders of American vessels, and other citizens of the United States in your district, and forward the same to all ports and places in this sea, with which you may have an opportunity of communicating, and where it is likely any American vessels may be found.

" On the 13th instant a squadron of cruisers sailed from Algiers to the eastward, consisting of 5 frigates, 3 corvettes, 2 brigs, one zebec, one schooner, one row galley, and 6 gun-boats; and there is reason to apprehend, that they had orders to capture American vessels.

" I shall proceed to Gibraltar, where I shall probably remain, until I can communicate this intelligence to all parts of this sea, or learn something of the conduct of the Algerines towards our vessels.

" I have the honour to be,
" Very respectfully, Sir,
" Your most obedient Servant,
(Signed) " TOBIAS LEAR."

" *To the Consuls of the United States of*
America in the Mediterranean."

MALTA TRADE.

(*From the London Gazette, July* 25, 1812.)

AT the Court at Carlton-house, the 17th of July, 1812, present, his Royal Highness the Prince Regent in Council.

Whereas, in virtue of powers vested in his Majesty by an Act passed in the 41st year of his reign, cap. 103, which Act was, by two other Acts, viz. 43d Geo. III. cap. 12, and 44th Geo. III. cap. 4, further continued until six months after the ratification of a definitive Treaty of Peace, his Majesty was pleased, by his Order in Council, bearing date the 7th day of January, 1807, to make certain regulations for the trade and commerce to and from the isle of Malta :—

And whereas it is expedient that further regulations for the said trade and commerce should now be made ;

His Royal Highness the Prince Regent is pleased, in the name and on the behalf of his Majesty, and by and with the advice of his Majesty's Privy Council, to revoke the said Order in Council of the 7th day of January, 1807, so far as relates to the trade and commerce carried on between the ports of the United Kingdom and the said isle of Malta, and its dependencies:

Provided, nevertheless, that the revocation of the said Order in Council of the 7th day of January, 1807, shall not be taken to revive any former Order of Council relating to the trade and commerce of Malta, which had been revoked by the said Order.

And his Royal Highness the Prince Regent is further pleased, in the name and on the behalf of his Majesty, and by and with the advice of his Majesty's Privy Council, to order, and it is hereby ordered, that from and after the 1st day of August next, no goods or commodities whatsoever shall be exported from any port of the United Kingdom to the said isle of Malta, or its dependencies, in any other than British ships or vessels, owned, navigated, and registered according to law, or in vessels condemned as lawful prize in the isle of Malta, and registered as the law directs, and navigated by one-fourth of British or Maltese subjects ; or natives of the said isle or its dependencies ; and in like manner that, from and after the 1st day of October next, no goods or commodities whatsoever shall be exported from the said isle of Malta, or its dependencies, to any port of the United Kingdom, in any other than British ships or vessels, owned, navigated, and registered according to law, or in ships or vessels condemned as lawful prize in the isle of Malta, and registered as the law directs, and navigated by one-fourth of British or Maltese subjects, or natives of the said isle or its dependencies, or in any ship or vessel belonging to any person or persons whatsoever, and of whatsoever description, and however navigated, to which his Majesty may be graciously pleased to grant his royal license or authority for that purpose.

And the Right Hon. the Lords Commissioners of his Majesty's Treasury, his Majesty's principal Secretaries of State, the Lords Commissioners of the Admiralty, and the Judge of the High Court of Admiralty, and the Judges of the Courts of Vice-admiralty, are to take the necessary measures herein as to them shall respectively appertain.

CHETWYND.

AN ACT,

To prohibit American Vessels from proceeding to or trading with the Enemies of the United States, and for other Purposes.

BE it enacted, by the Senate and House of Representatives of the United States of America, in Congress assembled, That no ship or vessel, owned in whole, or in part, by a citizen or citizens of the United States, shall be permitted to clear out or depart from any port or place within the limits of the United States, or territories thereof, to any foreign port or place, till the owner or owners, agent, factor, freighter, master, or commander, shall have given bond, with sufficient security, in the amount of such ship or vessel, and cargo, not to proceed to or trade with the enemies of the United States. And if any ship or vessel owned as aforesaid, shall depart from any port or place within the limits of the United States or territories thereof, for any foreign port or place, without giving bond with security aforesaid, such ship or vessel, and cargo, shall be forfeited to the use of the United States; and the owner or owners, freighter, factor or agent, master or commander, shall severally forfeit and pay a sum equal to the value of such ship or vessel, and cargo, and the said master or commander, if privy thereto, and being thereof convicted, shall be liable to a fine not exceeding one thousand dollars, and imprisoned for a term not exceeding twelve months, in the discretion of the Court.

Sect. 2. And be it further enacted, That if any citizen or citizens of the United States, or person inhabiting the same, shall transport or attempt to transport, over land or otherwise, in any waggon, cart, sleigh, boat, or otherwise, naval or military stores, arms, or the munitions of war, or any article of provision, from any place in the United States, to any place in Upper or Lower Canada, Nova Scotia, or New Brunswick, the waggon, cart, sleigh, boat, or the thing by which the said naval or military stores, arms, or munitions of war, or articles of provisions, are transported, or attempted to be transported, together with such naval or military stores, arms, or munitions of war or provisions, shall be forfeited to the use of the United States, and the person or persons aiding or privy to the same shall severally forfeit and pay to the use of the United States, a sum equal in value to the waggon, cart, sleigh, boat, or thing, by which the said naval or military stores, arms, or munitions of war, or articles of provision, are transported, or are attempted to be transported; and shall, moreover, be considered as guilty of a misdemeanour, and be liable to be fined in a sum not exceeding 500 dollars, and be imprisoned for a term not exceeding six months, in the discretion of the Court: provided that nothing herein contained shall extend to any transportation for the use or on account of the United States, or the supply of its troops or armed force.

Sect. 3. And be it further enacted, That the collectors of the several ports of the United States be, and the same are hereby authorised to seize and stop naval and military stores, arms, or the munitions of war, or any articles of provision, and ship or vessel, waggon, cart, sleigh boat, or thing by which any article prohibited as aforesaid is shipped or transported, or attempted to be shipped or transported, contrary to this act.

Sect. 4. And be it farther enacted, that no ship or vessel belonging to any citizen or citizens, subject or subjects of any state or kingdom in amity with the United States, except such as at the passage of this act shall belong to the citizen or citizens, subject or subjects, of such state or kingdom, or which shall hereafter be built in the limits of a state, or kingdom, in amity with the United States, or purchased by a citizen or citizens, subject or subjects of a state or kingdom in amity with the United States aforesaid, from a citizen or citizens of the United States, shall be admitted into any port or place of the United States, unless forced by a stress of weather, or for necessary repairs; and any ship or vessel, belonging to a citizen or citizens, subject or subjects of any state or kingdom in amity with the United States as aforesaid, except such ships and vessels as are above excepted, which shall, from and after the first day of November next, enter or attempt to enter, any port or place aforesaid, the same, with her cargo, shall be forfeited to the use of the United States.

Sect. 5. And be it farther enacted, That any British packet or vessel with despatches destined for the United States, and which shall have departed from any port or place in the United Kingdom of Great Britain and Ireland, or its dependencies, on or before the 1st day of September next, shall not be liable to be captured or condemned, but the same shall be permitted to enter and depart from any port or place in the United States: provided, that nothing herein contained shall be construed to affect any cartel, or vessel with flag of truce.

Sect. 6. And be it farther enacted, That the President of the United States be, and he is hereby authorised to give, at any time within six months after the passage of this act, passports for the safe transportation of any ship or other property belonging to British subjects, and which is now within the limits of the United States.

Sect. 7. And be it farther enacted, That every person, being a citizen of the United States, or residing therein, who shall receive, accept, or obtain a license from the Government of Great Britain, or any officer thereof, for leave to carry any merchandize, or send any vessel into any port or place within the dominions of Great Britain, or to trade with any such port or place, shall, on conviction for every such offence, forfeit a sum equal to twice the value of such ship, merchandize, or articles of trade, and shall moreover be deemed guilty of a misdemeanour, and be liable to be imprisoned not exceeding twelve month, and to be fined not exceeding one thousand dollars.
H. CLAY,
Speaker of the House of Representatives.
WM. CRAWFORD,
President of the Senate, pro tempore.

June 6, 1812.   Approved,   JAMES MADISON.

INSTRUCTIONS FOR THE PRIVATEER ARMED VESSELS OF THE UNITED STATES.

1. The tenour of your commission, under the Act of Congress, entitled an Act concerning Letters of Marque, Prizes, and Prize Goods, a copy of which is hereto annexed, will be constantly in your view. The high seas referred to in your commission, you will understand generally to extend to low water mark, but with the exception of the space, neither one league nor three miles from the shore of countries at peace both with Great Britain and with the United States; you may, nevertheless, execute your commission, rather than detain the shore of a nation at war with Great Britain, and even on the waters within the jurisdiction of such nation, if permitted so to do.

2. You are to pay the strictest regard to the rights of neutral powers, and usages of civilized nations; and in all your proceedings towards neutral vessels, you are to give them as little molestation or interruption, as will consist with the right of ascertaining their neutral character, and of detaining and bringing them under regular adjudication, in proper cases. You are particularly to avoid even the appearance of using force or seduction, with a view to deprive such vessels of their crews and of their passengers, other than persons in the military service of their country.

3. Towards every vessel, and their crews, you are to proceed in exercising the rights of war with all the justice and humanity which characterizes the nation of which you are a member.

4. The master, and one or more of the principal persons belonging to a captured vessel, are to be sent, soon after the capture, to the Judge or Judges of the proper Courts of the United States, to be examined on oath touching the interest or property of the captured vessel and her lading; and, at the same time, are to be delivered to the Judge or Judges, all passes, charter-party, bills of lading, invoices, letters, and other documents and writings, found on board; the said papers to be provided by the affidavit of the commander of the captured vessel, or some of the persons present at the capture, to be produced as they are received, without fraud, addition, subduction, or embezzlement.

By the command of the President of the United States,

JAMES MONROE, Secretary of State.

HYDROGRAPHY, PILOTAGE, &c.

ENGLAND.

THE Trinity-house of Deptford-strond has given notice, that the High Light-house erected on Hurst Beach, to serve as a leading mark with the old Low Light-house, being completed, a light was to be exhibited therein for the first time on the night of Thursday the 27th August, and continued constantly in the night season, for the benefit of navigation. The High Light-house bears from the Low Light-house N.E. by E. $\frac{1}{2}$ E. (by compass) distant 755 feet, and a strong oil light will be exhibited in it, 25 feet higher than the light in the Low Light-house, which latter will be a light of equal brilliancy, and 30 feet above the level of the sea. In sailing through the Needles channel, keep the two Light-houses in one, or (at night) the High Light directly in a line above the Low Light, which will lead ships over the bridge, in a safe channel with five fathoms at low water, and very near in a line with the S.E. side of the Shingles, which is steep to, and must be considered as the boundary line; therefore, the High Light must never be brought to the left, or north-westward of the Low Light; but as soon as the light on the Needles Point bears S.E. you may open the High Light a little to the south-eastward of the Low Light, so as to give a birth to the Shingles as you proceed on to Hurst Beach. The two lights will appear only to the westward; but a light will be shewn from the old Low Light-house, for the navigation above Hurst Point. A chart with sailing directions will shortly be printed, and distributed to the masters and pilots of vessels at the several ports.

NORTH-BRITAIN.

NOTICE TO MARINERS.—The trustees for carrying into effect an Act of Parliament, for rendering the navigation in the Frith and river of Clyde more safe and commodious, have erected a light-house on the point of Toward, a low rocky situation, near the entrance to Rothesay Bay, on the west side of the Frith; and give this public notice, that the same will be lighted on the 1st of November next. Its bearing, coming in channel from the Cumray light-house, is (by compass) N.N.E. $\frac{1}{4}$ E. distance $9\frac{3}{4}$ miles; and from the Clough light-house W.S.W. $\frac{1}{2}$ S. distance $6\frac{3}{4}$ miles. To distinguish the Toward light from the others in the Frith, it is constructed to revolve horizontally, presenting a bright and dim light, alternately, in every direction, except on the north-east side, where so much of it is totally darkened as to prevent its being seen from the rocks called the Captains' Bridges, off Inellan, and the Gantocks, off Denoon; so that vessels navigating along the shore to the northward of this light, by being careful to keep it in sight, will avoid any risk from these rocks.—(*Glasgow*, 7 *September*, 1812.)

FRANCE.

Two English ships of war (Marlborough * and Laurel †), having been totally lost, and one other (Conquistador ‡) much damaged and endangered, owing to the uncertainty attending pilotage among the shoals which lie off that portion of the coast of France which bounds the department of Morbihan; it has been deemed useful to give farther extension to the two former hydrographical articles§ descriptive of a cruising station so much navigated by English ships, by the following extract from a recent publication of much merit:—*

" From Concarueau to Port Louis the coast runs E.S.E. 8 leagues. Port Louis is an excellent harbour, with a citadel and a town on the eastern side, and a large village on the west. But without the port towards the east, are a multitude of rocks under water, which render its entrance rather difficult.† The mark to enter it is to bring the edge of the citadel in a line with St. Catherine, which is a little convent within the river or bay, on the same side as the city, upon a point projecting into the sea, and directly to the east of St. Michael's island. When you are got within the citadel, you cast anchor in 5 or 6 fathoms water, or else run aground under the town, to the north of it, if it be high-tide; for at low water you cannot come under the town, the place being dry at every tide. It is high water here ¼ past 4 o'clock on the days of new and full moon.

" L'Orient is situated about ¼ of a league above Port Louis, at the bottom of the bay [or aestuary] which is formed by the confluence of the Pontscorf and Blavet rivers. It is the place from whence the whole Asiatic trade of the French is [was] carried on.

" * Whether you weigh from the isle of Grouais, or are coming from the offing to pass to the westward of the Truyes [sows] and the Errants, which they call the Great Channel, you are to steer so as to keep the tower of Larmor N.E. northerly, till one of the mills standing eastward of Port Louis be hidden by the southernmost part of the town walls, and the other be well open: by this means you will sail in the mid-channel between the Shisies of Larmor and the Sows. Keeping those marks on as soon as you are so far advanced as to perceive the high land of Pennemane in one with the westernmost corner of the citadel of Port Louis, you will steer in that direction till the west point of St. Michael is brought on with a white mark which lies to the westward of the store-houses at L'Orient: this will carry you safe between the Mare, on which stands a beacon, and

---

* Naval Chronicle, V. 80.   † N.C. XXVII. 228.   ‡ N.C. XXVII. 303.
§ N.C. XXVII. 475. XXVIII. 72.

* *Le Petit Neptune Français*, or " French Coasting Pilot:" revised and augmented by J. F. Dessiou, R.N. *quarto.* London; 1805. (Faden.)

† N.C. XXVII. 453, 509:

* Instructions for the entrance of Port Louis and L'Orient, by Mr. D'Apres de Mannevillette, author of the *Neptune Oriental.*

the foot of the citadel. From this situation you may choose which of the two channels is most convenient, either to the westward of St. Michael, or between that and St. Catherine. In the first case you are to proceed in this track till Queroman mansion-house be brought in a line with the miller's white house that stands by Queroman windmill near the shore, leaving on your starboard side a rock, on which there are only 12 feet at low water, spring-tides, and on your larboard side another rock, called the Hog, which is known by a beacon. Thus you will pass between the Turk's bank and the Quernevel * bank till you have the white mark of the store-house (already mentioned) in one with the single house that stands on the beach: you steer in this manner till athwart St. Michael, and then proceed for the road of Pennemane, leaving on the starboard hand the rock named Pangarne, or Quintrec. In the second case, if you are to pass between St. Michael's island and St. Catherine, when you find yourself in the situation mentioned above, you perceive the corner wall of St. Catherine's garden in one with a white house that stands in the middle of Nezenel town; steering in the direction of this mark, you come athwart the southernmost end of St. Catherine, and then you range along the whole of the place in such a manner as to leave $\frac{2}{3}$ of the Channel towards St. Michael, and $\frac{1}{3}$ towards St. Catherine; this track is to be followed till you discover a little wood in the neighbourhood of Port Louis, called Querbel; through the hole of a stone bridge or causey, which communicates from St. Catherine to the main; in steering thus, Pangarne rock beacon is left on the starboard side; and when you have passed it a ship's length, you steer for the road of Pennemane. It is to be observed, that with a ship drawing above 21 feet water, you cannot make for this road but at high water (spring-tides), in this case you are to anchor at Port Louis. When you pass to the eastward of the Errants (by the middle channel), you must, from as great a distance as you can, bring the town of L'Orient in one with the westernmost bastion of the citadel of Port Louis, and steering thus, leave on the larboard hand the rocks of Bastrene, on which there is a buoy. Sailing on, the Three stones are left on the larboard, and when you have proceeded so far as to bring a fountain on the beach of Gavre in a line with a single tree on the same part of the peninsula to the N. eastward of the village, then you are to steer keeping Larmor windmill on with the two houses which are nearest to the extreme point of Larmor. By this track you come into the great channel at the point from whence you perceive the high land of Pennemane in one with the westernmost corner of the citadel, and then follow the instructions already given. The third entrance, named Gavre channel, is only fit for small vessels; its mark is to keep Larmor windwill in one with the two houses which are nearest to the extreme point; in order to get into the great channel at the place mentioned in the preceding sentence.

" It is high water between Port Louis and L'Orient at $\frac{1}{2}$ past 4 o'clock on the days of new and full moon; and the perpendicular rise of the water is 15 feet in spring-tides.

---

* Mr. D'Apres calls this bank Querso in his plan.

"Directly fronting Port Louis $4\frac{1}{4}$ miles S.W. by S. of the town, lies the isle of Grouais, near $1\frac{1}{4}$ league in length, E.S.E. and W.N.W. with several trees and houses on it. Between this isle and the land, but nearer to the latter, is a bank with only 12 or 13 feet on it at low water; the anchorage is between this bank and the isle in 10, 12, to 15 fathoms, on a bottom of sand and little pebbles resembling coral. Grouais is very clear all round, except on the S.E. where you meet with a bank of rocks, stretching $\frac{1}{2}$ a league in the sea, called *Bout des chats* [cats end.]

"From Port Louis to Beguelonnet, or Beguelan Point, the coast runs S.E. by S. about 5 leagues, being all low land with downs between : about half-way is a big rock above water. From Beguelonnet to Quiberon, or Conguel Point is E. by S. 2 miles. From these points a ledge of rocks stretches nearly to the isle of Houat; through which ledge is a passage called the Teigneuse.

"About 2 leagues S.E. of Point Quiberon lies the N.W. end of Houat, called Point Benneguet : this isle is about a league in length E.S.E. and W.N.W. It is surrounded on the S.E. and N.W. with a multitude of rocks above and under water. N.W. by N. nearly 4 miles from Point Benneguet, and S.E. by S. about 2 miles from Point Conguel lies a high rock called the Teigneuse, or Teignouse, to the southward of which is the pass before mentioned ; it is but little frequented on account of the sunken rocks, which require marks to avoid. The Benneguet pass, near the point of the island is preferable : in these passes the flood sets eastward at the rate of 3 knots. Teigneuse rock is also the mark for passing between Houat and Hédic, distant 1 league S.E. but this channel is very narrow and dangerous, and few ships venture through it except those who are well acquainted. The nearest point of Hedic is encompassed with rocks above and under water, which spread a good quarter of a league in breadth, and almost barring the passage between the two isles render it difficult. Hédic is a round island near $\frac{1}{2}$ a league diameter: it lies within a multitude of rocks above and under water, near which it is not safe to steer : there is, however, good anchorage abreast of them, in 9, or 10 fathoms, on a bottom of sand and mud, a cluster of great rocks called Cardinaux [cardinals] bearing S.S.E. from 3 to 5 miles. These rocks lie $\frac{1}{2}$ a league E. of Hedic ; the largest above water, and some of them extending two good cables-length. There is no passage between Hédic and the Cardinals because of the rocks. When bound for the rivers of Auray, Vannes, Vilaine, or for the Croizic, you pass E. of the Cardinals at the distance of $\frac{3}{4}$ of a league.

"The tides are very strong all along these rocks, and the moon N.E. by E. and S. W. by W. makes high-water.

"Five large leagues S.S.E. of the E. south-eastern end of Grouais is the western point of Belle-isle, called point of Poulains, from a number of rocks lying W. of that of point called Poulains [colts], some above, others under water; but that which stands widest of the rest is a great and high rock above water. On the S. side of Belle-isle is a multitude of other rocks, above and under water, which lie very near the shore. The island is 3 leagues in length, high and steep all round. On the N. side about half-way the island, is situated the town and harbour of Palais, which is the most frequented; you find also another harbour, a little above this, called Sauzon, but seldom visited, though it is better than the former. There are a number of roads for ships at this island, the most frequented of which are those on the northern side under the castle, and a league E. of it. Another good road lies on the E. side of the island, under point Locmaria: the anchorage is 8, 10, or 15 fathoms water, according to the distance from the shore. A little E. of the castle, and ½ a league from shore, lies a rock under water, named Basse Palais, on which are 4½ fathoms at low water; and ¼ a league from shore N.W. off Colts' point, are several rocks on a level with the water, which are very dangerous.

" From the E. end of the Cardinals to the river of Auray, or of Vannes (for the two rivers have but one mouth, called the Morbihan), the course is N. by W. ¼ W. 4½ leagues. On the W. side of the mouth lies a great bank of rocks, with several isles, which extend about ½ a league S. You leave these isles on the larboard side, as you make your entrance, passing between them and Point du Petit-mont, near mid-channel, steering a little nearer the eastern shore. You find in this passage from 7 to 8 fathoms water. When within the said isles and the E. point, you see the mouths of the two rivers. There are a multitude of isles and rocks therein, and the tides are extremely strong and quick, which occasions almost continually a great current of water pouring in or out through the narrow passage, for which reason they are never to be entered without pilots. You may cast anchor any where as well without as within. In entering you must be cautious of a bank on the eastern shore, about 2 miles S. by E. from Point Petit-mont; this bank joins to the land, and extends above ½ a league to sea, westward from the high steeple of St. Gildas. Between the Cardinals and this point, within the compass of the isles Ilonat and Hédic, there is every where good anchorage, in 8, 10, or 12 fathoms, according to the distance from land. The tide flows S.W. by W. and N.E. by E. or it is high water 45 minutes after 3 o'clock on the days of the new and full moon.

" From Point Dousey to the river Vilaine the coast runs about 4¼ leagues E. and from the Cardinals to the river's entrance the course is N.E. by E. 5½ leagues. You must steer wide of Dumet isle, lying between them, and running into a number of sandy points which stretch out to sea ¾ of a league, and require a good berth. The common channel is westward of this isle, and the western side of the river is always taken on account of its cleanness. Then steer a cable's length off the land, or farther if you think fit, till you have the river open; after which you enter through the middle of the channel; for there are rocks on the eastern side of the entrance; when you are within these rocks you may anchor, or else run aground. At low water, ordinary tides, there are from 9 to 10 feet in the mouth of the river. Though directions are here given for those rivers, it is not advisable to enter them without pilots; which are almost constantly attending in their shallops off the Cardinals, for that purpose.

" From the Vilaine to the Croisic the coast runs about 3¾ leagues southward: the land is all low, and at a small distance you see the town of Guerande, with a high pointed steeple; and within the town of Croisic comes in view another high steeple, of stone, called the Tower of Bas; by which marks this coast is easily known. When you pass between the main land and Dumet, you must keep nearer the land than to the isle, because of several banks which run out from the isle towards the coast. From the Cardinals to Croisic the course is about E. ½ S. 4¼ leagues; then you pass between Dumet and a ledge of rocks called the Four * [oven] which lies 1 league W. from Point Croisic; it is dry every tide, and very dangerous. When you have a mind to steer with safety in that passage, you must not bring the high steeple of Bas S.E. of Point Croisic, nor yet unite them in the same line, for you would infallibly run on the Four; but you must keep the steeple N.E. of the point, by which means you will pass the island at a small ½ league. The Four is almost 1½ league in length to the S. and its southern point is 6 leagues from the point of Belle-isle, and 3 leagues S.E. ½ E. from the point of the Cardinals. The entrance of Croisic is extremely difficult, both on account of the rocks which block up that whole haven, and of the great currents inward and outward; it is no sooner high water than the ebb forces back, and one as well as the other carries you directly across the rocks; for which reason, as well as because it drys every tide, this harbour is rarely visited but by small craft. There is a spot within the entrance called the Linigot, where two ships may ride in 10 or 12 fathoms. The exports of this place are white salt, pilchards, and brandy, which come from Nantes. In the course from Belle-isle to Nantes you pass between the point of Croisic and the Four bank, taking care not to approach the point too near, because of some dangerous rocks.

" The moon N.E. by E. and S.W. by W. makes high-water."

S.

AFRICA.

Notice is hereby given, for the information of the masters and pilots of his Majesty's ships, and for the benefit of navigation in general, that the beacon upon the Trident or Whittle Rock, in False Bay, at the Cape of Good Hope, disappeared in the tempestuous weather which preceded the 10th of June last.—(*London Gazette*, 8 *September*.)

The danger most in the way of ships working to or from Semon's bay, is the rock on which the Trident and Asia struck in 1795, and other ships since. It lies 4½ miles E. from the north point of Little Smith's Winkle Bay, and about 8 miles N.N.E.-ward (true) from Cape Point. By compass Cape Point is said to bear from S.W. ¼ W. Cape False S.E. ½ E. Seal island N.E. ¼ N. Muysenberg N. ½ W. and Great Smith's Winkle W.

---

* On the Four shoal the English ship of war Resolution was wrecked in the sea-fight of November, 1759. And the Conquistador was nearly wrecked 3d March, 1812. See Naval Chronicle, XXVII. 303.

PLYMOUTH SOUND with the Projected BREAK-WATER.

Reduced from the Chart ordered by the HOUSE OF COMMONS to be printed 1812.

Published September 30, 1812, by J. Gold, Naval Chronicle Office, 103, Shoe Lane, London.

but these bearings are possibly not very exact. Lieutenant Whittle examined this danger, and found it to be a rocky bank, about ¾ mile broad, on which there is a rock with only 12 feet over it at low water. There are others to the N.W. about one cable's length from it, with 4 and 5 fathoms on them. On the 12-feet rock the angle of Cape Hanglip and Cape Point, taken with a quadrant, was 87°, and the summits of two hills over Fish-hook bay just touching each other. To avoid this dangerous patch, generally called Whittle's rocks, a ship should go to the W. ward of it, keeping within 2 or 3 miles of the land in passing between little and great Smith's-Winkle bays, taking care in passing abreast of it that the angle of Cape False and Cape Point is not increased to 85°. Close to this patch the soundings are 20 and 22 fathoms. The ship Francis struck on a spot stated to be about a mile to the N.-ward of these rocks; but it is probable the bearings were not correctly taken, and that in fact it was one of the northernmost of Whittle's patch on which she struck.—(*Horsburgh*.)

S.

PLATE CCCLXXII.

THE chart of Plymouth Sound, with a delineation of the Plan of the Dyke or Breakwater, forming therein, for shelter to ships at that anchorage, which was laid before the House of Commons, is here presented to the readers of the NAVAL CHRONICLE, upon a reduced scale. The fidelity with which the reduction has been made, by Mr. Rowe (Map and Chart Engraver, of Bedford Street, London) will be found highly creditable to his talents.

The official papers, relative to the Plymouth Breakwater, commence at page 422 of the preceding volume of the NAVAL CHRONICLE; are continued at page 478; and are farther continued at pages 118 and 213 of the present Volume. Of these documents, Mr. Jackson's letters, at pages 122 and 124 of this Volume, particularly refer to the annexed plate. The letter of our Correspondent, W. Y. E. at page 115, containing the distances of the different points, shoals, &c. adjacent to Plymouth Sound, presents an additional illustration.*

In the progress of our review of CAPTAIN MANDERSON's *Twelve Letters*, some comparative statements will be submitted, of the relative advantages of Plymouth, Falmouth, and Scilly, as adapted for the reception, security, &c. of the Royal Navy.

The *Plymouth Chronicle*, of September 15, contained the following

---

* For a View of Plymouth, the Citadel, St. Nicholas Island, Mount Edgcumbe, Staddon Heights, and the Sound, *vide* N. C. VI. 33; for a View of Plymouth Dock, XXVII. 416; and for an historical account of Plymouth, Plymouth Dock, &c. VI. 33, and VII. 125, 130, 236.

notice, respecting some suggestions which have been made, by a Captain Moyle, of the Engineers:—

" The principal improvements in the construction of the Breakwater at this place, suggested by Captain Moyle, and submitted to the Lords of the Admiralty, consist in extending one of the extremities of the present plan to the land, and making a cut across the isthmus to the sea, for the admission of a strong current of backwater, as also the entrance of ships. By the adoption of these suggestions, it is supposed, that the harbour will be rendered more safe and commodious, the ingress and egress of ships of war, in all states of the wind and tide, will be greatly facilitated, the inconvenience to be apprehended from the accumulation of mud and soil will be obviated, and the whole pier will not only be rendered more secure and compact, but completed at one half the estimated expense of the adopted plan."

NAVAL PREMIUMS

Offered in the Year 1812, *by the* SOCIETY, *instituted A.D.* 1754, *for the Encouragement of Arts, Manufactures, and Commerce.*

Claims for the same to be addressed to Dr. C. Taylor, Secretary, in the Adelphi, London.

3. RAISING OAKS. To the person who shall have raised, since the year 1808, the greatest number of oaks, not fewer than five thousand, either from young plants or acorns, in order to secure a succession of oak timber in this kingdom; the gold medal.

4. For the next greatest number, not fewer than three thousand; the silver medal.

38. PRESERVING POTATOES. To the person who shall discover to the Society the best and cheapest method of preserving potatoes, two or more years, perfectly sound, without vegetating, and in every other respect fit for the use of the table; the gold medal, or thirty guineas.

39. For the next greatest quantity, not less than fifty bushels; the silver medal.

42. GAINING LAND FROM THE SEA. To the person who shall produce to the Society an account, verified by actual experiment, of his having gained the greatest quantity of land from the sea, not less than fifty acres, on the coast of Great Britain or Ireland; the gold medal.

60. CULTURE OF HEMP. The Society wishing to encourage the growth of hemp for the use of the navy in every part of the United Empire, offer to the person who shall sow with hemp, in drills at least eighteen inches asunder, the greatest quantity of land in any part of the United Empire, not less than fifty acres statute measure, in the year 1812, and shall at the proper season cause to be plucked the summer hemp (or male hemp bearing no seed), and continue the winter hemp (or female hemp bearing seed), on the ground, until the seed is ripe; the gold medal.

NAVAL PREMIUMS. 235

61. To the person who shall sow with hemp, in drills at least eighteen inches asunder, the next greatest quantity of land in any part of the United Empire, not less than twenty-five acres, statute measure, in the year 1812, and shall at the proper season cause the same to be plucked as above-mentioned; the silver medal.

63. PRESERVING SEEDS OF VEGETABLES. For the best method of preserving the seeds of plants in a state fit for vegetation, a longer time than has hitherto been practised, such method being superior to any known to the public, and verified by sufficient trial; the gold medal, or thirty guineas.

64. PREVENTING THE DRY-ROT IN TIMBER. To the person who shall discover to the Society the cause of the dry-rot in timber, and disclose a certain method of prevention superior to any hitherto known; the gold medal, or thirty guineas.

65. PRESERVING SALTED PROVISIONS FROM BECOMING RANCID OR RUSTY. To the person who shall discover to the Society the best, cheapest, and most efficacious method of preserving salted provisions from becoming rancid or rusty; the gold medal, or thirty guineas.

66. REFINING WHALE OR SEAL OIL. For disclosing to the Society an effectual method of purifying whale or seal oil from the glutinous matter that incrusts the wicks of lamps, and extinguishes the light though fully supplied with oil; the gold medal, or fifty guineas.

71. SUBSTITUTE FOR TAR. To the person who shall invent and discover to the Society the best substitute for Stockholm tar, equal in all its properties to the best of that kind; and prepared from materials the produce of the United Kingdom and its Colonies; the gold medal, or one hundred guineas.

72. TURPENTINE FROM THE SCOTCH FIR, OR PINUS SYLVESTRIS. For the greatest quantity of turpentine, not less than two hundred weight, prepared in Great Britain, from that species of fir called the Scotch fir, or Pinus Sylvestris, Linn.; the gold medal.

73. For the next greatest quantity prepared, not less than one hundred weight, on similar conditions; the silver medal.

N.B. The Society being in possession of the method practised for extracting turpentine from the trees whilst growing, and of samples so procured, information will be given upon the subject, on application for that purpose, at the Society's house.

88. PRESERVING IRON FROM RUST. To the person who shall invent and discover to the Society a cheap composition, superior to any now in use, which shall effectually preserve wrought iron from rust; the gold medal, or fifty guineas.

114. MARINE PAINTING. For the best original painting in oil of a marine subject, the size not less than thirty-six by twenty-eight inches, by persons of either sex, under twenty-five years of age; the lesser gold medal.

115. For the next in merit, the lesser silver medal, on similar conditions.

156. TRANSIT INSTRUMENT. To the person who shall invent and produce to the Society a cheap and portable transit instrument, which may easily be converted into a zenith-sector, capable of being accurately and expeditiously adjusted, for the purpose of finding the latitudes and longitudes of places, and superior to any portable transit-instrument now in use; the gold medal, or forty guineas.

157. TAKING WHALES BY THE GUN-HARPOON. To the person who, in the year 1812, or 1813, shall strike the greatest number of whales, not fewer than three, with the gun-harpoon; ten guineas.

165. EXTINGUISHING FIRES. To the person who shall produce to the Society the best and most effectual method of procuring an immediate supply of water in case of fire, or for the means best calculated to prevent or extinguish accidental fires in buildings, superior to any now in use; the gold medal, or thirty guineas.

168. IMPROVED VENTILATION. To the person who shall invent and produce to the Society a mode of permanently ventilating the apartments in hospitals, workhouses, and other crowded places, superior to any now known or used; the gold medal, or fifty guineas.

171. RAISING THE BODIES OF PERSONS WHO HAVE SUNK UNDER WATER. To the person who shall invent and produce to the Society, a cheap and portable drag, or other machine, superior to those now in use, for the purpose of taking up, in the best and most expeditious manner, and with the least injury, the bodies of persons who have sunk under water; the gold medal, or thirty guineas.

173. TAKING PORPOISES. To the people in any boat or vessel, who, in the year 1812, shall take the greatest number of porpoises on the coast of Great Britain or Ireland, by gun-harpoon, or any other method, not fewer than thirty, for the purpose of extracting oil from them; the gold medal, or thirty pounds.

174. OIL FROM PORPOISES. To the person who shall manufacture the greatest quantity of oil from porpoises taken on the coast of Great Britain or Ireland, in the year 1811, not less than twenty tons; the gold medal, or thirty pounds.

175. CURING HERRINGS. To the person or persons who shall, before January, 1813, cure the greatest quantity of white herrings, not less than thirty barrels, equal in all respects to the best Dutch herrings, the same being caught in the British or Irish Seas, and cured in a British or Irish vessel or port; the gold medal, or fifty guineas.

176. For the next greatest quantity, not less than fifteen barrels; the silver medal, or twenty guineas.

177. NUTMEGS. For the greatest quantity of merchantable nutmegs, not less than ten pounds weight, being the growth of his Majesty's dominions in the West Indies, or any of the British settlements on the coast of Africa, or the several islands adjacent thereto, and equal to those imported from the islands of the East Indies; the gold medal, or fifty guineas.

178. KALI FOR BARILLA. To the person who shall have cultivated, in the Bahama Islands, or any other of his Majesty's dominions in the West Indies, or any of the British settlements on the coast of Africa, or the several islands adjacent thereto, in the year 1811, the greatest quantity of land, not less than two acres, with Spanish kali, fit for the purpose of making barilla ; the gold medal, or thirty guineas.

179. For the next greatest quantity, not less than one acre; the silver medal, or fifteen guineas.

180. DESTROYING THE INSECT COMMONLY CALLED THE BORER. To the person who shall discover to the Society an effectual method of destroying the insect commonly called the borer, which has of late years been so destructive to the sugar canes in the West India Islands, the British settlements on the coast of Africa, and the several islands adjacent thereto ; the gold medal, or fifty guineas.

181. CULTIVATION OF HEMP IN UPPER CANADA. To the person who shall [have sown ?] sow with hemp the greatest quantity of land in the province of Upper Canada, not less than six arpents (each four-fifths of a statute acre), in the year 1811, and shall at the proper season cause to be plucked the summer hemp, or male hemp bearing no seed, and continue the winter hemp, or female hemp bearing seed, on the ground, until the seed is ripe ; the gold medal, or one hundred dollars.

182. To the person who shall [have sown ?] sow with hemp the next greatest quantity of land in the same province of Upper Canada, not less than five arpents, in the year 1811, in the manner above-mentioned ; the silver medal, or eighty dollars.

183. For the next greatest quantity of land, in the same province, and in a similar manner, not less than four arpents ; sixty dollars.

184. For the next greatest quantity of land, in the same province, and in a similar manner, not less than three arpents ; forty dollars.

185. For the next greatest quantity of land, in the same province, and in a similar manner, not less than one arpent; twenty dollars.

186 to 190. IN LOWER CANADA. Premiums exactly similar in all respects to those held out for the province of Upper Canada, are also offered to the province of Lower Canada.

191 to 195. IN NOVA SCOTIA AND NEW BRUNSWIC. Similar premiums in all respects are also offered to the provinces of Nova Scotia, and New Brunswic.

196. IMPORTATION OF HEMP FROM CANADA, NOVA SCOTIA, AND NEW BRUNSWIC. To the master of that vessel which shall bring to this country the greatest quantity of marketable hemp, not less than one hundred tons, in the year 1812, the produce of Upper Canada, or of one of the above-mentioned provinces ; the gold medal.

197. To the master of that vessel which shall bring the next quantity, not less than fifty tons ; the silver medal.

198. SUBSTITUTE FOR HEMP. To the person who, in the year 1812, shall discover and produce to the Society, a substitute for hemp, equally

cheap, durable, and applicable to all the purposes for which hemp is now used; the gold medal, or fifty guineas.

N.B. *The premiums for Nos. 181, to 198, are all extended one year further.*

199. SILK. 'For the greatest quantity of silk proper for manufactures, not less than one hundred pounds weight, produced by any person in Malta, or islands near adjacent thereto, in the possession of Great Britain, in the year 1813, from silk-worms bred there; the gold medal, or fifty guineas.

200. For the next greatest quantity, not less than fifty pounds, on similar conditions; the silver medal, or twenty guineas.

N.B. The same premiums will be given for silk produced in the years 1814 and 1815.

201. BHAUGULPORE COTTON. To the person who shall import into the port of London, in the year 1812, the greatest quantity, not less than one ton, of the Bhaugulpore cotton, from which cloths are made in imitation of nankeen, without dyeing; the gold medal.

202. ANNATTO. To the person who, in the year 1812, shall import into the port of London, from any part of the British settlements in the East Indies, the greatest quantity of annatto not less than five hundred weight; the gold medal.

203. TRUE COCHINEAL. To the person who, in the year 1812, shall import into the port of London, from any part of the British settlements in the East Indies, the greatest quantity of true cochineal, not less than three hundred weight; the gold medal.

N.B. *The premiums from No. 201 to 203 inclusive, are all extended two years further.*

Naval Premiums and Rewards bestowed, in 1812, by the Society of Arts, Manufactures, and Commerce, Adelphi.

To Mr. Henry Parke, Dean Street, Soho, for an original painting of shipping, a view at the Nore. The silver medal.

To Master Frederick Yeates Hurlestone, King-street, Covent Garden, for a drawing of the head of Neptune, a copy. The silver pallet.

To Messrs. Robert and Giles Caymes, of Yeovil, in Somersetshire, for manufacture of sail cloth, proper for the use of the royal navy, and superior to the best Dutch, class 146. The gold medal.

To Mr. Arthur Hodge, Bride-lane, Fleet-street, for a method of preserving butter from becoming rancid in warm weather, or hot climates. Ten guineas.

To Mr. William Bowler, Holborn Hill, for a mechanical method of destroying rats, and other vermin. Ten guineas.

To Mr. William Sampson, No. 20, Great Wild Street, for an ingenious churn, by which butter may be easily and quickly made. The silver medal, and ten guineas.

Naval Poetry.

PORTUGUESE HYMN TO THE VIRGIN MARY,
"THE STAR OF THE SEA."
By the late Dr. Leyden.

STAR of the wide and pathless sea!
  Who lov'st on mariners to shine,
Those votive garments wet, to thee
  We hang, within thy holy shrine;
  When o'er us flash'd the surging brine,
Amid the warring waters tost,
  We call'd no other name but thine,
And hop'd when other hope was lost.
                Ave Maris Stella!

Star of the vast and howling main!
  When dark and lone is all the sky,
And mountain waves, o er ocean's plain,
  Erect their stormy heads on high:
  When virgins for their true loves sigh,
They raise their weeping eyes to thee;
  The Star of ocean heeds their cry,
And saves the found'ring bark at sea.
                Ave Maris Stella!

Star of the dark and stormy sea!
  When wrecking tempests round us rave,
Thy gentle virgin form we see
  Bright rising o'er the hoary wave.
  The howling storms that seem to crave
Their victims, sink in music sweet;
  The surging seas recede to pave
The path beneath thy glistening feet.
                Ave Maris Stella!

Star of the desart waters wild!
  Who pitying hears the seaman's cry,
The God of Mercy, as a child,
  On that chaste bosom loves to lie;
  While soft the chorus of the sky
Their hymns of tender mercy sing,
  And angel voices name on high,
The mother of the heavenly King.
                Ave Maris Stella!

Star of the deep! at that blest name
  The waves sleep silent round the keel,
The tempests wild their fury tame
  That made the deep's foundations reel;
The soft celestial accents steal
So soothing through the realms of woe,
  The newly damned a respite feel
From torture in the depths below.
                   Ave Maris Stella!

Star of the mild and placid seas!
  Whom rainbow rays of mercy crown,
Whose name thy faithful Portuguese,
  O'er all that to the depths go down,
With hymns of grateful transport own:
When gathering clouds obscure their light,
  And Heaven assumes an awful frown,
The star of ocean glitters bright.
                   Ave Maris Stella!

Star of the deep! when angel lyres
  To hymn thy holy name essay,
In vain a mortal harp aspires
  To mingle in the mighty lay!
Mother of God! one living ray
Of hope our grateful bosoms fires,
  When storms and tempests pass away,
To join the bright immortal quires.
                   Ave Maris Stella!

EPITAPH ON ADMIRAL COTTON.

IN this family vault a philosopher lies,
  Who puzzled of Paris the students so wise,
Till at last having tried all the universe round,
That *cotton* could never be *worsted* they found.
                                            S.

Marine Law.

COURT MARTIAL.

JAN. 6.—A Court Martial was held on board H.M.S. Prince of Wales, at Sheerness, for the trial of Lieutenant Richard William Simmonds, commander of the Manly gun-brig, for the loss of that vessel, which was captured on the 2d of September 1811, by three Danish ships of war, each carrying eighteen long eighteen-pounders.

MARINE LAW. 241

The Court was composed of the following members, all post captains:—

Captain LEE, President.

Captains DOUGLAS,   Captains HANCOCK,
——— BINGHAM,   ——— AUSTEN,
——— PROWSE,   ——— PIPON,
——— HATTEY,   ——— HAWTAYNE,
——— Lord G. STEWART,   ——— BURTON.

The Court being duly constituted, the charges were read by the proper officer, and the fact of the capture of the Manly being established in evidence, Lieutenant Simmonds entered upon his defence, in support of which the following, among other documents, were produced and read, viz.

A letter, of which the subjoined is a copy, from Lieutenant Simmonds, to Sir H. E. Stanhope, Bart. commander-in-chief, &c. &c. &c. Sheerness, dated Christiansand, 4th Sept. 1811:—

" SIR—I am extremely sorry I am now under the disagreeable and painful necessity of representing to you, for the information of the Right Hon. the Lords Commissioners of the Admiralty, the particulars of the capture of his Majesty's gun-brig Manly, under my command, with the Chanticleer in sight, by three Danish sloops of war, on the morning of the 2d instant.

" We exchanged numbers with the Chanticleer at 5. 30. P.M. on Sunday the 1st, Drommels bearing north-west by west, distance about twelve leagues, when she made our signal to pass within hail, which I accordingly complied with, and after waiting on Captain Spear, having no surgeon on board the Manly, and both vessels being bound to one port, I thought it prudent, through his advice, to remain in company with the Chanticleer that night, for the purpose of her surgeon visiting my sick people the next morning, Captain Spear informing me at the same time he meant to sail along the coast during the night, and the superior sailing of the Chanticleer occasioned me to carry a press of sail, against a heavy head sea, to keep her company. At one A. M. on Monday, she was a long way a-head; and at two observed three strange sail close to her, but could not now discern which was the Chanticleer. I then made the private night signal, which was answered in that direction, and the four vessels being right a-head, I continued my course, endeavouring to come up with them, as I was certain the Chanticleer must be one. About 3. 30. I observed a firing amongst them, which gave me suspicion that the three strangers must be enemy's vessels, and conceiving from their superior force the Chanticleer must be in a very perilous situation, I was determined, whatever might be the consequence, not to forsake her, but to share the same fate, and continued under all sail, using every exertion in my power to close with them for her assistance; and being confident, from the appearance of the strangers, that their force was more than double ours, both in guns and men, I only thought of selling the Manly, as dear as possible, in her support. I could not, however, distinguish which was the Chanticleer, till after I had received the fire of two of the enemy's vessels, who, I now

Nav. Chron. Vol. XXVIII.

perceived, to be three Danish brigs of war, and which I at that moment did not think proper to return, my only wish being to close the Chanticleer as near as possible, which I also then perceived to be abaft my larboard beam, making sail from the enemy. The largest of their brigs now tacked to close the Manly. I then hauled to the wind, and tacked with our head to the eastward, to join the Chanticleer, if possible; but she still kept her course, steering from the enemy, and seemed to decline, on her part, to renew the action. I had, however, by this time, for her support, placed the Manly in a situation when it was impossible to avoid it, and the largest of the enemy's brigs, which afterwards proved to be the Loland, mounting eighteen long eighteen-pounders, with a complement of one hundred and twenty-five men, commanded by Captain Holm, a post captain, in the Danish navy, coming upon our starboard beam, received her whole broadside, which did us considerable damage. We instantly returned it, when an action commenced, and continued within musket-shot for the space of two hours and twenty-five minutes, when the other two brigs, who had now left off the chase of the Chanticleer, returned to support the Loland, and were within musket-shot, the one endeavouring to take his station on our larboard-bow, the other to supply the place of the Loland, on our beam, who now tacked, and took her station on our starboard-quarter, keeping up a constant fire; nor was it in the smallest degree possible for us to prevent these manœuvres on the part of the enemy, owing to their superior sailing, and we being completely disabled, our head sails being all shot away about the beginning of the action, and afterwards our standing and running rigging, with all the other sails entirely cut to pieces; masts and bowsprit badly wounded in several places, and four guns dismounted, and rendered completely unfit for service; and as the fire of all three brigs would have been opened upon us at a very small distance, within the space of five minutes, they still continuing to close, and our small force consisting then of only 37 men and five boys, the master, midshipman, and three men being absent in detained vessels, the brig in a crippled state, and quite unmanageable, I conceived it would only have been vain presumption on my part, and a cruel sacrifice of the lives of my brave little crew, to have pretended further resistance, against three sloops of war, who now appeared to be heavy vessels, and afterwards proved to mount each 18 long 18-pounders, with a captain and three lieutenants, exclusive of their complement of men, one of them having 125; the other two, 120 each; especially when there was not the smallest hopes of any assistance, or possibility of escape. I was, therefore, reluctantly compelled to submit to their superior force; and although our loss in men was very trifling, having only one killed, and three wounded, yet, from the length of time we were exposed to their fire, and the shattered state of the brig at the close of the action, I have to thank the Almighty no more of them fell. The Loland has also suffered considerably; but of their damages and loss of men, they avoided letting us gain the least information; she has, however, to get a thorough repair, and is this day getting out her fore-mast.

" I should conceive myself extremely remiss in my duty, did I not recommend, in the strongest terms, the steady, cool, and gallant conduct of my small ship's company, during the whole of the action; never did I witness men in better spirits, and the master being absent, as before stated, Mr. Richard Cowan, clerk, having been experienced to the sea for a number of years, and also been a considerable time in his Majesty's service, I therefore ordered him to supply the master's place on the quarter-deck, and his steady conduct and unremitted exertions on this occasion, in the face of so superior an enemy, merit my warmest approbation; nor can I think of closing my letter without recommending him to their Lordships' notice, in the highest sense of the word, as a young man truly worthy and deserving of their countenance, or any favour which they may be pleased to confer upon him at any future period. Mr. Toby, midshipman; also Mr. Kettleby, and Keeble, pilots, for their steady conduct and behaviour likewise, merit great praise.

" The under-mentioned is a list of the killed and wounded, on board the Manly, and likewise of the force of the enemy.

" I have the honour to be, Sir, with the greatest respect, your most obedient, humble servant,

" R. W. SIMMONDS, late Lieut. and Commander of his Majesty's gun-brig Manly."

" *To Sir H. E. Stanhope, Bart.*
Commander-in-chief, &c. Sheerness."

" *A List of the Killed and Wounded, on board the Manly.*

" Wm. M'Queen, seaman, killed.
" John Roke, seaman, wounded.
" Wm. Garton, serjeant of royal marines, wounded, dangerously.
" Thomas Read, private marine, wounded, dangerously.

" *A List of the Force of the Enemy's Vessels.*

" Loland, Captain Holm, 18 long 18-pounders, three lieutenants, and 12 men.
" Alsen, Captain Lutkin, 18 long 18-pounders, three lieutenants, and 120 men.
" Sampsoe, Captain Grothschilling, 18 long 18-pounders, three lieutenants, and 120 men.
" Total of enemy's guns 54, men 377.
" Total of brig Manly's guns 12, men 37, and 5 boys."

Translation of the Enemy's Official Account of the Action.

" *Copenhagen, September* 16, 1811

" The commander-in-chief of the batteries on the Norway coast, Rear-admiral Lutkin, has received a report from Captain Holm, relative to the capture of the enemy's brig Manly.

" I take the liberty to inform you, that while cruising off Arendale, with the brigs Loland, Sampsoe, and Alsen, which you were pleased to put under my command on 1st September, 1811, September the 2d, at two o'clock A.M. having proceeded about eight miles E.S.E. from the isle of Paud, steering W. under easy sail, we observed two sail on the lee quarter, which I supposed, from the signals which they exchanged, to be enemy's vessels. I made the signal to clear for action, hauled our wind, and stood in for the land. At three P.M. the Sampsoe fired a broadside, which was returned by the enemy, and the engagement commenced on both sides. The Loland and Alsen commenced their fire also. A short time after, the brig who had engaged the Sampsoe, tacked and stood away S.E. The Sampsoe stood after her ; the Loland and Alsen kept their wind to near the enemy on their weather-bow. At three A.M. we kept the same course. At dawn of day, we observed both vessels to be enemy's brigs. The vessel which was chased by the Loland steered easterly ; and we also, at four A.M. came alongside of her ; about gun-shot distance we commenced the action. The enemy's vessels had already commenced their fire. At 5. 40. we tacked, with an intention to get under her stern to rake her. At 5. 55. he struck his flag.

" The first lieutenant, Craft, was sent with a party of men to take possession of the vessel ; the second lieutenant, Grove, to bring the officers on board : he returned immediately, and brought with him the commander, Lieutenant Simmonds, who reported her to be the Manly gun-brig, with ten 18-pounder carronades, two long 6-pounders, and 58 men on board. A heavy sea caused both our and the enemy's shot to be fired without effect. The Alsen was, at three A.M. within gun-shot of the brig, which was chased by the Sampsoe ; she kept close to her.

" The first lieutenant, Lutkin, was obliged to return ; a heavy sea being out, he kept to the N.W. endeavouring to assist the Loland, which was then engaged with the enemy's brig. The first lieutenant, Grotschilling, finding that the Sampsoe could not take the brig he was in chase of, he returned, and stood towards us, to assist me to take the Manly. When the Sampsoe and Alsen drew near, I made the signal to assist in manning the prize.

" The Loland has one man killed, but none wounded ; her rigging and sails received very little damage. The Sampsoe and Alsen had neither killed nor wounded ; their vessels were not damaged, and their sails and rigging but trifling. The first lieutenants, Grotschilling and Lutken, have shewn themselves very good officers in manœuvring their ships, and did every thing in their power to capture the other vessel. The second lieutenants, Grove and Fleisher, both behaved themselves gallantly, and the whole of the crew belonging to the Loland shewed much bravery.

" The commanders of the Sampsoe and Alsen give both their officers and crew the highest characters.

" It must be confessed, that it reflects much honour on the commander of the Manly to have made such a resistance. The Manly is much crippled, and there is nothing on board the Manly but what has suffered more or less.

" H. P. HOLM."

MARINE LAW.

Lieutenant Simmonds's Address.

" Mr. PRESIDENT, and Gentlemen of this Honourable Court.—In expressing my humble hope that this Hon. Court will not consider me intruding, by submitting to their perusal, in addition to my public despatch to Vice-admiral Sir Henry Edwin Stanhope, *The Danish Gazette* account, with a translated copy, of the action between his Majesty's late gun-brig Manly, and the Danish sloops of war, on the 2d of September last, in order that if a doubt *can* exist of my having made every exertion in my power, and acted to the best of my judgment, under existing circumstances, to maintain the honour of my King and Country, the enemy's narrative may, at least, be received as admissible evidence; as it is reasonable to conclude, upon grounds of national pride, he would not admit that the action, *by his own account*, continued from 4. 45. to 5. 55. with such a superiority of force. It is unnecessary for me to comment upon the circumstances that brought the Manly into action, further than by saying, when at 3. 15. A.M. I observed the Chanticleer bear down to the three strange sail; and about 15 minutes after saw a firing amongst them, which led me to think the strange sail were enemy's vessels, and if they were so, the Chanticleer must be in a perilous situation, from their superiority of force, I felt most imperiously called upon, by every idea of duty as an officer, and regard to my own character, and the confidence I placed in the bravery of my small crew, to make all possible sail to render her support.

(Signed)   " R. W. SIMMONDS, Commander of his Majesty's late gun-brig Manly."

Judgment.

" The Court having most diligently investigated the whole of the circumstances connected with the capture of the said brig; and having very maturely and deliberately considered the same; are of opinion, that no blame whatever is imputable to the said Lieutenant R. W Simmonds, for the loss of the said brig; and DO MOST HONOURABLY ACQUIT HIM, AND HE IS MOST HONOURABLY ACQUITTED ACCORDINGLY."

The President's Address.

Captain R. Lee, Esq. of his Majesty's ship Monarch, second in command of his Majesty's ships and vessels of war in the river Medway, and at the buoy of the Nore, and President of the Court, at the close of the proceedings, addressed Lieutenant Simmonds, on returning his sword, to the following effect :—

" Lieutenant Simmonds, after your very handsome conduct in defence of his Majesty's late brig Manly, I have great pleasure and gratification in returning you your sword, from a conviction that, whenever you have occasion again to draw it, it will be for your own honour and that of your country.

(Signed)   " R. LEE,
" Captain of his Majesty's ship Monarch."

" *Chatham, Jan. 6th,* 1812."

NAVAL HISTORY OF THE PRESENT YEAR, 1812.

(August—September.)

RETROSPECTIVE AND MISCELLANEOUS.

THE Gleaner has arrived from America, having left New York on the 15th of August, and Halifax on the 26th. She did not, we are now informed, carry out the despatches announcing our revocation of the Orders in Council, and, consequently, has not brought over any determination of the American Government on that particular point. The *National Intelligencer*, however, which is regarded as the organ of the government, breathes a very hostile and determined spirit. " The Orders in Council of the British Government," observes the Editor, " are now no longer a question with the United States. The question of peace now requires only a proper and a vigorous use of the ample means which the government is possessed of, to render it speedy, decisive, and glorious. Peace, when it comes, must bring with it more than the confession of British outrage by the retraction of its avowed tyranny. It is not a mere cessation to do wrong that can now produce a peace—wrongs done must be redressed; and a guarantee must be given in the face of the world, for the restoration of our enslaved citizens, and the respect due to our flag, which, like the soil we inherit, must in future secure all that sails under it. The rights of neutrals must be recognized; and the British, like the first tyrants of the Swiss, must no longer expect a free people to bow down, and worship the symbols of British usurpation."

If we have now to refer to the proofs of the correctness of those opinions which we stated in a preceding part of this Volume,[*] upon the subject of the dispute with America, we beg our readers to be assured, that we do it not in the way of triumph, but from the sincere wish to be instrumental, as far as our humble but honest endeavours can be useful, towards averting that last of national evils, a new war, a war against the descendents of Englishmen, a war against the seat of political and religious freedom We endeavoured to induce our readers to distrust the statements in our public prints as to the power of the English party in the American States. We asserted, that the venal press in England was engaged in propagating a series of deceptions with regard to the sentiments of the people in America. And we gave it as our opinion, that the repeal of our Orders in Council would not be sufficient to restore us to a state of peace with America. In consequence of the infatuation we deplored having prevailed over sound advice, we are now actually in a state of war with our kindred across the Atlantic: while those corrupters and blinders of the people, who have hastened, if not actually produced this war, do yet attempt to make their readers believe, that we are not at war with the republic of America.

---

[*] N. C. XXVIII. 157.

The American Congress declared war; they passed an act,* making war against this United Kingdom; their government issued letters of marque and reprisals; but still our hirelings said there would be no real war. Alas! the folly and falsehood of these opinions.

Those who will not believe the "Instructions for the privateer armed vessels of the United States," signed, " James Monroe, Secretary of State,' and " a proclamation by William Hull, Brigadier-general, and Commander-in-chief of the North-western Army of the United States," would not believe, though one were to rise from the dead. This last address, it is possible, may prove the forerunner of the fall of Canada; which once gone, will never in all probability return to the English crown any more than Hanover. The fact of war being now ascertained beyond all doubt, the next thing for us to think of is the means by which we are to obtain peace with this new and formidable enemy: one requisite towards it, which we hope may be duly considered in the proper quarter. is no longer to affect to treat the matter so lightly as we have been tempted to do.

Both Houses of Congress adjourned on the 6th of July. They meet again on the 2d of November. During the next session they will consist of the same members. The election of new members for the House of Representatives comes on in November next ; and the election of President in December.

The Marquis of Wellington's victory at Salamanca, announced at page 159, has produced very important results. His Lordship entered Madrid on the 12th of August, Joseph Buonaparte precipitately retreating towards Valencia. Having left a considerable force in Madrid, Lord Wellington was at Valladolid on the 8th of September, and the French had retreated in the direction of Burgos.—The siege of Cadiz, which had lasted upwards of two years and a half, was abandoned on the night of the 24th of August ; Marshal Suchet leaving behind him a considerable quantity of stores, ammunition, &c. The allied troops, under the command of General Cruz and Colonel Skerrett, subsequently took the town of Seville by assault, sustaining scarcely any loss. Suchet continued his retreat.—Sir Home Popham continues his exertions on the north coast of Spain.

Letters from Rio Janeiro, dated July 7, announce the intelligence of peace having been restored between the government of Buenos Ayres, and the Portuguese on the opposite shore of La Plata; and that the latter were, in consequence, withdrawing within the limits of their own settlements.

As the Russians continued to retreat, Buonaparte, according to the latest advices from the seat of war in the North, expected to approach near to Moscow about the 6th or 7th of September. The Russians had established lines in front of Moscow, and were also forming an entrenched camp at Mojaisk—An armament, composed of 30,000 Swedes, and 40,000 Russians, was expected to sail from Gottenburgh, about the 20th of September, for the purpose of acting upon the rear of the French army.

---

* N. C. XXVIII., 137.

Parliament was to be dissolved, by Proclamation, on Tuesday, the 29th of September.

The Admiralty has fixed the salaries of the pursers of the smallest class of sloops of war (lately called gun-brigs) at 150*l.* per annum, and put every description of stores on board into their charge. It is said to be Lord Melville's intention to extend this judicious plan throughout the navy, increasing the salaries of these officers according to the rates of the vessels; and also to make a more suitable provision for them when disabled from service. At present, a purser must have been in active service 15 years, before he can receive the superannuation stipend of 40*l.* per annum.

An Expedition, under the command of Captain Owen, of the Cornelia (brother of Commodore Owen), sailed from Batavia on the 16th of February last, to take possession of Palembang, in the island of Banker.

A third Battlion of Royal Marines is to be immediately formed for actual service, the command of which, it is said, will be given to Major Timins. About 300 are arrived from Anholt, who are to constitute a part of the force. That Island is now garrisoned by one of the Garrison Battalions.

His Majesty's schooner Cherub, Lieutenant Nisbett, was upset on the 23d of August, whilst cruising on the American coast, and every soul on board perished.

The Attack gun-brig, Lieutenant R. W. Simmonds, has been lost, after a most gallant action with the Danish gun-boats, in a calm, off Anholt. Lieutenant S. experienced a similar fate last season, in the Baltic, when he commanded the Manly.*

Admiral Thornbrough, who commands on the Cork station, has suggested to the Admiralty, and obtained its sanction, to allow fishermen to provide boys, instead of men, for the naval service.

The following was the amount of the naval force of Britain, according to the returns, up to the 1st of September:—At sea, 101 ships of the line, 10 from 50 to 44 guns, 117 frigates, 105 sloops and yachts, 8 bombs and fire-ships, 127 brigs, 35 cutters, 52 schooners, gun-vessels, luggers, &c.; total, 555.—In port and fitting, 19 of the line, 6 from 50 to 44 guns, 28 frigates, 37 sloops, &c. 22 brigs, 7 cutters, 12 schooners, &c.; total, 131.—Guard-ships, 5 of the line, 1 of 50 guns, 4 frigates, 5 sloops; total 15.—Hospital ships, prison ships, &c. 33 of the line, 3 of 50 guns, 2 frigates, total 38.—In ordinary, and repairing for service, 71 of the line, 12 from 50 to 44 guns, 72 frigates, 32 sloops, &c. 6 bombs, &c. 15 brigs, 1 cutter, 5 schooners, &c.; total, 214.—Building, 31 of the line, 4 of 44 guns, 19 frigates, 6 sloops, 8 brigs; total, 68.—Grand total, 1021.

Captain Talbot, of the Victorious, 74, has been presented by the Board of Admiralty with a gold medal, to be worn with his full uniform, suspended by a ribband from the fourth button-hole, on the left side of the lappel, for his gallant conduct in capturing the Rivoli, of 80 guns, in the

---

* N.C. XXVIII. 241.

Adriatic Gulph.—We thought it belonged only to the Crown to bestow honors on its *Officers* and *servants*.

The Volage, Captain Mackay, with Sir Evan Nepean on board, for Bombay, arrived at the Cape of Good Hope on the 24th June, with three cartel-ships from England, on their return to the East Indies. Admiral Stopford was at the Cape, with the Lion, Nisus, and Galatea. The President left the Cape on the 17th of June, for the Isle of France.

A letter from on board H.M.S. Royal Oak, dated the 6th Sept. off Flushing, contains the following particulars concerning the enemy's fleet in the Scheldt :—" The French fleet here consists of twenty-one sail of the line, nine frigates, and twenty-seven brigs. We have seventeen sail of the line, five frigates, and four brigs. It is not expected that the enemy's fleet will attempt putting to sea this year, as there were lately 2000 of their best sailors marched off to join their army on the frontiers of Russia."

A regulation has lately taken place at the Admiralty, relative to the nomination of assistant-surgeons to dock-yards. They are to be appointed from the list of naval surgeons.

Letters have been received from the Island of Ceylon (by way of the Cape of Good Hope), dated Columbo, in the end of March and the beginning of April. The Africaine, Hon. Captain Rodney, had arrived in Columbo Roads on the 10th of March, having on board Lieutenant-general Brownrigg, the new Governor. She had made a remarkably rapid passage from Madeira, where she arrived from England on the 10th of December, having sailed in the end of November; for several days she made 200 miles a-day by the log, and never saw a single sail during the whole of her voyage, nor had sight of land after she passed St. Nicholas, one of the Cape de Verd Islands, the 20th of December. The Africaine was waiting the arrival of the Owen Glendower, at Columbo, to take orders from Sir Samuel Hood; but if he should not arrive in a certain limited time, Captain Rodney intended to proceed to Madras. All was quiet in India at the date of these letters, according to the information current in Ceylon.

The Queen Charlotte has been lately inspected by Sir William Rule. An extraordinary number of hands is to be employed on her, and she will be ready for sea in three months.

When the Gleaner sailed, much apprehension was felt for the safety of Commodore Rodgers and the American squadron.

The Spartan, Captain E. Brenton, has taken nine American privateers in the Bay of Fundy; and the Pyramus, Captain Dashwood, has taken eight sail of Americans in the Baltic.

Among the prizes carried into Halifax, are two from London, and three from Liverpool, (one of them with a license on board) valued at 200,000*l*.

Nav. Chron. Vol. XXVIII.   K K

Letters on Service,

Copied verbatim from the LONDON GAZETTE.

ADMIRALTY-OFFICE, AUGUST 22, 1812.

Copy of a letter from Vice-admiral Sir James Saumarez, Bart. and K. B. to John Wilson Croker, Esq. dated on board the Victory, in Hawke Road, 12th August, 1812.

SIR,

YOU will please to lay before my Lords Commissioners of the Admiralty, the enclosed letters, which I have received from Rear-admiral Martin, dated the 4th and 5th instant, stating the arrival of the Russian flotilla of gun-boats at Riga, also detailing his proceedings, and stating intelligence of the operations of the armies, and an account of a severe action between Count Witgenstein's corps and Marshal Oudinot, in which the latter was defeated, with the loss of three thousand prisoners and some cannon.

I have the honour to be, &c.
JAS. SAUMAREZ.

Riga, 4th August, 1812.

The Russian gun-boats, so long expected, and at one time so anxiously desired, arrived here on the 31st ultimo, and now form a most important acquisition to the defence of the place.

The way Captain Stewart has conducted himself in the command of the Russian and English gun-boats, is highly praise-worthy, and his unremitting activity, so creditable to the country, has been willingly imitated by the officers and men of the Aboukir and Ranger, who are placed under his orders; they have unquestionably kept the enemy from crossing the river, at the falls above the town, where a body of infantry and horse still remained intrenched; the only time they ever advanced towards the boats they were dispersed in a very few minutes, after losing five men and two horses killed.

General Cravart, who commands the troops of the enemy in this neighbourhood, during the absence of Marshal Macdonald, sent on the 27th ultimo, to summons General Essen to surrender, assigning as a reason for doing so that his battering train would arrive in the course of a fortnight.

There has been a sharp affair in the neighbourhood of Witepsk, where it seems a strong division of the enemy crossed the Duna, and attacked part of the corps of Prince Bagration; but they were repulsed, and pursued across the river to the distance of several miles. The enemy sustained a considerable loss in killed and prisoners, most of them Wirtemberg troops; the Russian loss is not mentioned, except that a General Okuloft was killed.

T. B. MARTIN.
Sir James Saumarez, Bart. &c.

SIR, *Riga, 5th August, 1812.*

I have infinite satisfaction in acquainting you, that a messenger is arrived from General Count Witgenstein, stating, that a severe action was fought between his corps and that under Marshal Oudinot, on the 30th and 31st ult. in the neighbourhood of Polosgh, or Poloch.

It appears that Oudinot had crossed the Duna, and was marching with a view, it is supposed, of coming round upon Riga, and cutting off the communication with Saint Petersburgh, when Count Witgenstein commenced a most spirited attack, and obliged him to re-cross the river, with the loss of three thousand prisoners and some cannon,

The fighting had been very sharp, and the Count was pursuing the enemy when the couriers came away.

The loss of the killed and wounded is not mentioned on either side, except that General Kulnieu of the Russian hussars is killed, and Count Witgenstein slightly wounded.

An official report of this action will probably be published in the course of this evening, and I shall forward it to you to-morrow by a vessel going to Hano.

We have no accounts from the main army since that of the 29th ultimo, which mentioned Prince Bagration having driven the enemy across the river. I have the honour to be, &c.

T. B. MARTIN, Rear-admiral.

Sir James Saumarez, Bart. &c.

P.S. I have this instant received the enclosed from General Essen, confirming what I have stated respecting this affair. T. B. M.

SIR, *Riga, 24th July (5th Aug.) 1812.*

I hasten to communicate to your excellency the intelligence I have just received from General Count Witgenstein. He informs me, that on the 18th and 19th instant, (30th and 31st July), he gained a complete victory over Marshal Oudinot. The battle took place between Schebesch and Polotzk. Three thousand prisoners, two cannons, and a quantity of baggage and ammunition, are unequivocal proofs of his victory. The Count writes, that he is in pursuit of the enemy, and that his advanced-posts are hourly sending in fresh prisoners.

Being desirous of transmitting as soon as possible this agreeable intelligence to General Suchtelen, I venture to request your excellency will forward the inclosed to him by the earliest conveyance. In case you should not at this moment have any vessel disposable, Colonel Ballabin will move Admiral Schesihenkaff to supply one.

I have the honour to be, with high consideration,
Your Excellency's most obedient, humble servant,
ESSEN, Governor of Riga.

To Rear-admiral Martin.

AUGUST 25.

Copy of a letter from Admiral Young to John Wilson Croker, Esq. dated on board H. M. S. the Impregnable, off West Capel, the 20th instant.

SIR,

I enclose, for their Lordships' information, a copy of a letter from Lord George Stuart, captain of H. M. S. Horatio, giving an account of the capture, by the boats of that ship, of two Danish armed vessels, and an American ship, their prize, on the coast of Norway, in which their Lordships will perceive a degree of persevering bravery, in the highest degree honourable to all who were engaged ; but the more their gallant spirit excites admiration, the more it is to be lamented that so many of such brave officers and seamen should be lost to their country.

I have the honour to be, &c.

W. YOUNG.

H. M. S. Horatio, Tromptsen Sound, Coast of Norway,
SIR, *3d August, 1812.*

I have the honour to make known to you, when in execution of your orders, running down the coast of Norway on the 1st instant, in latitude

70° 40′ N., a small sail was seen from the mast-head, close in with the land, which we discovered to be an armed cutter before she disappeared among the rocks. Being anxious to destroy the enemy's cruizers, who have so considerably intercepted our trade in this quarter, I dispatched the barge and three cutters, under the command of my first lieutenant A. M. Hawkins, who gained information on shore that the cutter had gone to a village on an arm of the sea, thirty-five miles in land, where he immediately proceeded, and, at 8 A. M. on the 2d, she was discovered at anchor, together with a schooner and a large ship, which, on the appearance of the boats, presented their broadsides with springs on their cables.

As a strong tide set the boats towards them, Lieutenant Hawkins determined to attack, notwithstanding their advantageous position; at nine the fire commenced on the boats (one of which was dispatched under the directions of Mr. James Crisp, master's-mate, to disperse some small-armed men collected on shore—this he effected, and returned to the attack before the enemy struck), and after a most sanguinary combat, they were carried in that true and gallant style which far surpasses any comment of mine on its merits, or of the characters of the brave fellows employed. They proved to be His Danish Majesty's schooner No. 114, of six six-pounders and thirty men, and cutter No. 97, of four six-pounders and twenty-two men, commanded by Lieutenant Buderhof, a first lieutenant in the Danish navy and commodore of a division of small vessels employed on this coast, in person on board the schooner; and an American ship of about four hundred tons, their prize.

I lament to say that the loss on both sides is severe, and nearly similar. Though I had before had occasion to represent the meritorious conduct of Lieutenant Hawkins, I cannot in this instance sufficiently express my sentiments of his gallantry, as well as that of Lieutenant Masters, second of the Horatio. Lieutenant Hawkins who received a severe wound in the right hand when the boats were advancing, and another in the left arm in the act of boarding, represents the spirited and able support he received from Lieutenant Masters, who was also severely wounded in the right arm, and I must also bear testimony to the merits of this officer. The service has lost a valuable officer in First Lieutenant Syder (royal marines), killed in the act of boarding; and that of a most amiable young man, Mr. James Larans, assistant-surgeon, who soon after died of his wounds. I must also represent the high terms Lieutenant Hawkins speaks of Mr. James Crisp, master's-mate, Mr. William Hughes, boatswain, and Mr. Thomas Fowler, midshipman; the two latter are also severely wounded.

The services of Lieutenants Hawkins and Masters, with the petty officers, and the several instances of spirited behaviour of the seamen and marines, well deserve the encomiums already passed. The unwearied, skilful, and humane attention of Mr. Thomas Bishop, surgeon, to the wounded demand my warmest acknowledgments. Our loss is to be attributed to the desperate resistance made by the Danish Commodore, (who is severely wounded, as well as the commander of the cutter) and the excellent position his vessels were placed in.

The prizes I have directed to North Yarmouth. Herewith I beg to enclose the list of killed and wounded.

I have the honour to be, &c.

G. STUART.

To *Wm. Young, Esq. Admiral of the White, Commander in Chief, &c.*

A List of Killed and Wounded in the Boats of H. M. S. Horatio, employed on the 2d of August, 1812.

Killed.—Oliver Shimmings, quarter-master; George Markham, ditto;

Thomas Arthur, quarter-master's-mate ; Thomas M'Munn, captain of afterguard ; Jeremiah Patience, captain of mast ; James Morris, able seaman ; John Hall, ditto; First Lieutenant George Syder, royal marines; and Richard Carrick, corporal of ditto.

Wounded.—Abraham Mills Hawkins, first lieutenant, severely; Thomas P. Masters, second lieutenant, ditto ; Mr. Hughes, boatswain, ditto ; Mr. Fowler, midshipman, ditto ; Mr. Larans, assistant surgeon. (since dead); James Nightingale, quarter-master, dangerously, (since dead) ; William Hopkins, captain of forecastle, severely; Joseph Day, quarter-gunner, ditto ; Thomas Pearson, able seaman, ditto; John Liade, ditto, ditto ; John Dennis, ditto, ditto ; James Cummins, ditto, ditto ; James Earsley, quarter-gunner, slightly ; James Bridle, ordinary seaman, ditto ; Serjeant Harvey, royal marines, ditto ; and James Stokes, private marine, severely.

Total number of the enemy killed—10.
Total wounded, including officers—13.

G. STUART, Captain.

AUGUST 29.

Copy of a letter from Captain Broke, of H. M. S. Shannon, addressed to Vice-admiral Sawyer, and transmitted to John Wilson Croker, Esq.

H. M. S. Shannon, off New York,
SIR, *July* 16, 1812.

I have the pleasure to inform you, that the Shannon has this day captured, after a smart chace, the United States' brig Nautilus, of sixteen guns and one hundred and six men, commanded by Captain Crane, twenty-four hours out from New York on a cruize, and had taken nothing.
I have the honour to be, &c.

P. B. V. BROKE.

SEPTEMBER 1.

Vice-admiral Sir James Saumarez, Bart. K. B. has transmitted to John Wilson Croker, Esq. a letter from Rear-admiral Martin. of which the following is an extract:

Riga, August 10, 1812.

In my letter to you of the 5th instant, I mentioned, that the division of gun-boats under Captain Stuart, associated with another division under a Russian captain, had proceeded up the Boldero river, to co-operate with a body of troops from this place and the garrison of Dunamunde ; the object of the expedition being, in the first place, to take the enemy by surprise, and, failing in that, to force them back from Schlock, and, if possible, to penetrate to Mittau.

The service chiefly assigned to the British was, to keep in advance, and, if practicable, to destroy the bridges which were convenient for the retreat of the enemy ; and the only bridge (that of Kalnezeen) was speedily and effectually rendered unserviceable.

General Louis, who commanded the troops, gives the highest praise to Captain Stuart, and the British boats employed upon that service.

Copy of a letter from Vice-admiral Sir James Saumarez, Baronet, K. B. to John Wilson Croker, Esq. dated on board the Victory, in Hawke Road, August 20, 1812.

SIR,

I enclose, for the information of the Lords Commissioners of the Admiralty, the copy of a letter I have this morning received from Rear-admiral

Martin, dated the 11th instant, enclosing one (a copy of which is also transmitted herewith) from General Essen, Governor of Riga, communicating intelligence of the continued success of the Russian arms, and the junction of Prince Bagration with the main army at Smolensko, which you will please to lay before their lordships.   I am, &c.

JAS. SAUMAREZ.

SIR,   *Riga, July* 30, 1812.

I lose not a moment in communicating to your Excellency a most agreeable piece of intelligence, which I have just received.

The commander in chief of the third army (General Tormasson), has obtained a victory over the enemy near Cobrin. Four stand of colours, eight pieces of artillery, with one general, in the service of Saxony, seventy officers, and three thousand troops, have fallen into the hands of the conquerors.   I have the honour to be, &c.

ESSEN, Governor of Riga.

Vice-admiral Sir James Saumarez, Bart.
and K. B. &c.

P. S. In addition to the foregoing intelligence, I have to acquaint your Excellency, that the united forces of General Barclay and Prince Bagration are in the neighbourhood of Smolensko. General Platoff commands the combined advanced guard.

Riga, August 11, 1812.

I have the honour to enclose, for your information, a letter which I have this instant received from General Essen, communicating the agreeable intelligence of the continued success of the Russian arms, and the junction of Prince Bagration's corps with the main army at Smolensko.

This information is from the commander in chief, General Barclay de Tolli, who dates his letter the 4th instant, at Smolensko.

In addition to what is mentioned in the general's letter, I learn that General Tormassoff suddenly left the position which he had occupied for some time at Gitomirz or Zitomirz, in order to attack a corps of Saxons, stationed near Kubryn, twenty-four miles from Bryex Litowski, and about one hundred and thirty miles east of Warsaw, where he defeated the enemy, who retired towards Minsk.

Vice-admiral Sir James Saumarez,
Bart, K. B.

Vice-admiral Sir James Saumarez, Bart. K. B. has transmitted to John Wilson Croker, Esq. a letter from Lieutenant J. C. Crawfurd, commanding H. M. gun-brig Wrangler, of which the inclosed is a copy.

H. M. Gun-brig Wrangler, off Seyer Island,
SIR,   *August,* 1812.

In pursuance of your orders of the 14th instant, I proceeded off Randers with your boats, and the cutter of the Locust, but not finding the French lugger there, I proceeded further to the westward off Mariager Fiord, to reconnoitre that port; a small Danish cruiser was perceived coming out, gave chase to her, when she bore up, and ran into Alborg : at night Lieut. Petley, myself, and Mr. Curtis (second master of the locust), thought that she might be carried by the boats, which was agreed upon. Lieutenant Petley then proceeded in shore, with the barge and cutter, in company with the Locust's boats, under charge of Mr. Curtis, her second master.

About two o'clock in the morning they got alongside of her, and carried her from under a very heavy fire from the battery and musketry from Hall's Fort, in the entrance of that river, without the loss of a single man. She is one of those cruisers that have been of great annoyance to our convoys off the Scaw; she mounts two brass six-pounders, one long two-pounder, and small arms, and commanded by Lieutenant Tetens, of the Danish navy, and commodore of a division of gun boats off Flanstrand, with a complement of twenty-two men, who made their escape into the battery of Halle. They found her moored close under the muzzle of the guns of the battery, and could not prevent the lieutenant and men from making their escape, except one man, whom we have a prisoner. I stood in shore, as far as I could with safety, to cover the boats.

I have the honour to be, &c.

J. C. CRAWFORD, Lieut Com.

SEPTEMBER 5.

Copy of a Letter from Vice-admiral Sir James Saumarez, Bart. and K. B. to John Wilson Croker, Esq. dated on board H.M.S. Victory, in Hawke Road, the 27th August, 1812.

SIR,

I herewith enclose a letter I have received from Rear-admiral Martin, dated the 17th instant, on board the Aboukir, off Riga, conveying information of the movements of the Russian forces to that period; by which their lordships will observe, that no event of importance had taken place since the letter I transmitted from the Rear-admiral, dated the 11th instant.

I have the honour to be, &c.

JAS. SAUMAREZ.

SIR, *Aboukir, off Riga Bay, Aug. 17, 1812.*

I have to acquaint you, that couriers arrived last night from Count Wittgenstein and General Barclay De Tolli, by whom we learn that no important affair has yet occurred.

Count Wittgenstein's letter is dated the 13th instant, at a small village called Doschoch, about forty miles this side of Polotzk, to which last place he had pursued Oudinot, and leaving a strong advanced post in front of it, in order to deceive him, the count immediately took a direction with his army towards Draya, to meet Macdonald, of whose departure from this neighbourhood, he had received early intelligence.

Hearing, however, that Marshal Oudinot had obtained a reinforcement of eleven thousand men, he halted, and presently moved forward again in the direction of Polotzk, and falling in with a small French division, he attacked them, and took six hundred prisoners, besides baggage. It was conjectured, that Oudinot had re-crossed the river, and it was ascertained, that his loss, in the late action, had been much more severe than was at first reported.

General Barclay De Tolli's letter, is dated the 10th of August, at Smolensko; it speaks only of an attack made by Count Pahlen's cavalry on the enemy's rear guard, which he drove before him, taking two or three hundred prisoners, and General Sebastiani's carriage with all his papers.

Frequent skirmishes take place, and they are represented as invariably favourable to the Russians, and every thing in the army is going on in a satisfactory way. Several small detachments from this garrison, have been scouring the country, and have destroyed a magazine and taken some prisoners.

I have the honour to be, &c.

T. M. MARTIN, Rear admiral.

Vice-admiral Sir James Saumarez,
  Bart. and K. B. &c.

Extract of a Letter from Commodore Sir Home Popham, to Admiral the Right Honourable Lord Keith, K. B. dated on board H.M.S. Venerable, Bilboa Inlet, 16th August, 1812, and transmitted, by the last mentioned Officer, to John Wilson Croker, Esq.

Yesterday morning, at day dawn, General Renovales attacked the enemy, and his dispositions were so judicious, that he drove him out of the town, from whence he retreated on the high road to Zornosa, and his whole force fell back towards Darango. The Spaniards lost ten men killed, and twenty-three wounded; the enemy certainly lost more, and had six prisoners taken.

Major Williams marched with a strong picquet to examine the country; but as the enemy continued to retreat, he returned to the town of Bilboa in the course of the night.

I directed Captaid Malcolm to take a proportion of gunpowder, with a party of men, to blow up the Moro, as we had completely destroyed every work at Portugalete and its neighbourhood; but as General Renovales preferred doing it himself, I supplied him with powder for that purpose.

SEPTEMBER 12.

Extracts of letters from the Captains of H. M. S. named in the margin*, addressed to Vice-admiral Sawyer, Commander in Chief of H. M. S. and Vessels at Halifax, and transmitted to John Wilson Croker, Esq.

H. M. S. Acasta, at Sea, July 24, 1812.

I beg to acquaint you, that H. M. S. Acasta, under my command, fell in with, and captured this day, in lat. 44° 15′ N. and lon. 62° 30′ W. after a short chase, the American privateer brig Curlew, pierced for twenty guns, but having only sixteen on board, with a complement of one hundred and seventy-two men.

H. M. Sloop Colibri, Cape Sable, bearing West 12 Leagues, July 26, 1812.

I beg leave to acquaint you, that on Sunday at eight A. M. we described two ships to the northward, and a schooner to the S. E., the former apparently steering a course for Halifax; hauled up in chase of the schooner; at noon exchanged numbers with H. M. schooner Bream; wore in chase of the ships to the northward, which we found had hauled up for us, the headmost evidently a man of war with an American ensign, and pendant flying; she soon tacked and made sail from us, with a bark her prize; we continued closing with her, and at a quarter before three o'clock we came alongside, and the action became general, and at three they called out for quarter; brought to, and took possession of the American ship privateer Catherine, from Boston, out eight days, and had taken nothing but the said bark: she is a beautiful and well equipped ship, pierced for sixteen guns, mounting fourteen long six-pounders, and a complement of eighty-eight men, commanded by Francis A. Burnham; she had one man killed, and one wounded; her men ran below, which accounts for their suffering so small a loss.

H. M. Sloop Emulous, at Sea, July 31, 1812.

H. M. sloop under my command, fell in with, yesterday evening, the American privateer brig Gossamer, of fourteen carriage guns, with one hundred men, and after a short chase came up with and captured her: she left Boston on the 24th instant, had made one capture, the ship Mary Anne, of Greenock, from Jamaica bound to Quebec.

---

* Acasta, Colibri, Emulous.

NAVAL HISTORY OF THE PRESENT YEAR, 1812.   257

SEPTEMBER 15.

Extract of a letter from Captain J. G. Bremer, of H. M. Sloop Bermuda, dated off Boulogne the 11th instant, to Vice-admiral Foley, and transmitted, by the last mentioned Officer, to John Wislon Croker, Esq.

I have the honour to inform you, that this morning at daylight, I saw a lugger in the north west, having French colours flying, chased by the Dwarf cutter and Pioneer schooner, the latter vessel far astern.

At ten o'clock the lugger made an ineffectual attempt to cross the Bermuda's bow, and did not surrender till he had received several broadsides of grape, from this vessel.

The utmost gallantry was displayed by every officer and man employed in the boats of the Dwarf and Pioneer and the animated zeal and laborious exertions of Lieutenant Gordon and those who remained on board the cutter, exceed all praise.

The prize is the privateer Le Bon Genie of Boulogne, having on board sixteen guns (four only mounted) and sixty men; she sailed from Boulogne last night, and had not made any captures.

The enemy made a desperate resistance, and his loss has been severe, there being three killed and sixteen wounded, most of them severely.

SEPTEMBER 22.

List of American Privateers taken and destroyed by H.M. Ships and Vessels on the Halifax Station, between 1st July and 25th August, 1812, transmitted by Vice-admiral Sawyer, to J. W. Croker, Esq. in a Letter dated 25th August 1812.

Active schooner, of 2 guns and 20 men, captured by the Spartan, Captain Brenton, 16th July, 1812, off Cape Sable.

Fair Trader schooner, of 1 gun and 20 men, captured by the Indian, Captain Jane, and Plumper, Lieutenant Bray, 16th July, 1812, Bay of Fundy.

Argus schooner, of 1 gun and 23 men, captured by the Plumper, Lieutenant Bray, 17th July, 1812, Bay of Fundy.

Friendship schooner, of 1 gun and 8 men, captured by the Plumper, Lieutenant Bray, 18th July, 1812, Bay of Fundy.

Actress sloop of 4 guns and 53 men, captured by the Spartan, Captain Brenton, 18th July, 1812, off Cape St. Mary.

Intention schooner, of 1 gun, 3 swivels, 29 men, captured by the Spartan, Captain Brenton, 19th July, 1812, off Anapolis.

Gleaner sloop, of 6 guns and 40 men, captured by the Colibri, Captain Thompson, 23d July, 1812, off Cape Sable.

Curlew brig, of 16 guns, 172 men, and 270 tons, captured by the Acasta, Captain Kerr, 24th July, 1812, lat. 44. 15 N. long. 62. 30 W. pierced for 20 guns, off Cape Sable.

Catharine ship, of 14 guns and 88 men, captured by the Colibri, Captain Thompson, 26th July, 1812, off Cape Sable.

Gossamer brig, of 14 guns and 100 men, captured by the Emulous, Captain Mulcaster, 30th July, 1812, off Cape Sable.

Morning Star schooner, of 1 gun, 4 swivels, 50 men, and 70 tons, captured by the Maidstone, Captain Burdet, and Spartan, Captain Brenton, 1st August, 1812, Bay of Fundy; burnt by the boats in a creek called Baily's Mistake.

Polly schooner, of 1 gun, 4 swivels, 40 men, and 60 tons, captured by the Maidstone, Captain Burdet, and Spartan, Captain Brenton, 1st August, 1812, Bay of Fundy; burnt by the boats in a creek called Baily's Mistake.

Commodore Barry, a revenue cutter, of 6 guns, pierced for 10 guns, captured by the Maidstone, Captain Burdet, and Spartan, Captain Brenton, 3d August, 1812, Bay of Fundy; attacked in Little River, and brought out by the boats; the chief part of the crew escaped.

Madison schooner, of 2 guns, captured by the Maidstone, Captain Burdet, and Spartan, Captain Brenton, 3d August 1812, Bay of Fundy; attacked in Little River, and brought out by the boats; the chief part of the crew escaped.

Olive schooner, of 2 guns, captured by the Maidstone, Captain Burdet, and Spartan, Captain Brenton, 3d August 1812, Bay of Fundy; attacked in Little River, and brought out by the boats; the chief part of the crew escaped.

Spence schooner, of 2 guns, captured by the Maidstone, Captain Burdet, and Spartan, Captain Brenton, 3d August, 1812, Bay of Fundy; attacked in Little River, and brought out by the boats; the chief part of the crew escaped.

Polly schooner, of 4 guns and 35 men, captured by the Colibri and Statira, 11th August, 1812, entrance of Bay of Fundy.

Buckskin schooner, of 1 gun, 3 swivels, and 32 men, captured by the Colibri and Statira, 11th August, 1812, off Cape Sable.

Dolphin schooner, of 1 gun, 1 swivel, and 28 men, captured by the Earl Moira, tender to Guerrier, 12th August, 1812, off Shelburne.

Regulator schooner, of 1 gun and 40 men, captured by the Colibri; Captain Thompson, 12th August, 1812, off Cape Sable.

Dolphin schooner, of 2 guns and 48 men, captured by the Colibri and Maidstone, 13th August, 1812, off Cape Sable.

Lewis schooner, of 6 guns and 30 men, captured by the Hope, tender to the Africa, 14th August, 1812, off Halifax.

Pythagoras schooner, of 3 guns and 35 men, captured by the Bream, Lieutenant Timpson, 9th August, 1812, off Shelburne, after an action of 20 minutes; the enemy had 2 men wounded.

Bunker's Hill schooner, of 7 guns and 72 men, captured by the Belvidera, 21st August, 1812, Sambro Light House, N. W. 242 miles.

H. SAWYER, Vice-admiral.

SEPTEMBER 26.

Extract of a Letter from Captain Harper, of H. M. Sloop Saracen, to Admiral Sir Richard Bickerton, Bart. dated Spithead, 23d instant, and transmitted by the last mentioned officer to J. W. Croker. Esq.

Whilst proceeding in pursuance of your orders of the 21st instant, last evening at sunset, thick hazy weather, Beachy Head bearing N. by W. distant seven or eight miles, I observed in the S. S. E. two large luggers, in chase of, and very near, three deep-laden English vessels.

I instantly made all sail for their protection, and, after a short time, but anxious chase, succeeded in capturing Le Courier, French lugger privateer, of 14 guns, and 50 men, commanded by M. Juan, and belonging to Calais. The French captain, and two of the crew, were desperately wounded before they surrendered.

The other lugger, named L'Honorine, of equal force, having got at a great distance whilst securing the one I boarded, and dark night coming on, I am sorry it was not in my power to capture; but I completely drove her off the coast, and I have every reason to believe that the three vessels they were in chase of escaped.

LETTERS ON SERVICE,

Not published in the Gazette.

(COPY.)

His Majesty's cutter Entreprenante, Gibraltar Bay,
SIR, *30th April* 1811.

I beg leave to inform you, that, on the 25th instant, in compliance with your orders, I stood in to Malaga Bay with a flag of truce. At 1. 30. P.M. observed a boat coming out with a flag of truce: not willing to lose time, I met her in my boat, and delivered the letter addressed to General Sebastini, to the Governor of Malaga. He informed me the purport of the letter could not be complied with, without consulting his government; but he wished me to anchor until the next day. This, I told him, I could not do, but must proceed immediately. He then gave me a letter, with a flying seal, for Governor Campbell at Gibraltar, and we parted. Prior to this, I observed two French privateers and a merchant-brig coming into the bay; and before I could get on board, and make sail, one of them anchored close to the Mole-head. These vessels, as I shall state hereafter, were two out of the four French privateers which I engaged off Castle Ferro, on the 12th day of December last.

I have the honour to be, sir,
Your most devoted and obedient humble servant,
PETER WILLIAMS, Lieut. and Commander.

To Commodore C. V. Penrose, Senior Officer, &c. &c. &c.
Gibraltar Bay, H.M.S. San Juan.

His Majesty's cutter Entreprenante, Gibraltar Bay,
SIR, *30th April* 1811.

I have the pleasure to inform you, that, on the 25th instant, at 2. 30. P.M., having all sail set, the wind west, working out of Malaga Bay, I observed a French privateer and her prize coming in. At 3 P.M. the Mole-head bearing N.N.E. two miles, I brought the privateer to action, and in fifteen minutes completely beat her, and drove her on shore. Not having more than quarter less three fathom water, was obliged to tack; fired several shot at her prize, brought her to, boarded her, and took her. She proved to be the Spanish brig St. Joseph, from Cadiz and Gibraltar, bound to Tarragona. The privateer mounted 6 guns and 50 men. The enemy must have suffered very much, our shot having hulled her in many places. It appeared that the enemy's intention, by directing her fire so high, was, to dismast the cutter. It is with great pleasure I inform you, that, during this short action, I had not a man hurt. No praises that I can bestow are adequate to the merits of the officers and crew under my command, for their unremitted exertions in the action, in working the cutter, and taking in tow the prize, in the presence of some hundreds of spectators on the Mole-head of Malaga.

I have the honour to be, Sir,
Your most devoted and obedient humble servant,
PETER WILLIAMS, Lieut. and Commander.

To Commodore C. V. Penrose, Esq. Senior Officer,
&c. &c. &c. H.M.S. San Juan, Gibraltar.

Promotions and Appointments.

Admirals and Captains appointed.

Rear-admiral Charles Tyler, to be commander-in-chief at the Cape of Good Hope, *vice* Stopford; he goes out in the Semiramis.

Rear-admiral Scott to hoist his flag in the Chatham, off the Scheldt.

Captains.—W. R. Montagu, to the Niobe; Deans Dundas, to the Pyramus; the Hon. William Gordon, to the Magicienne; J. A. Gordon, to the Seahorse; James Gordon Brewer, to the Bermuda; C. Dashwood, to the Cressy; J. Temple, to the Armide; J. Dunn, to the Dublin; T. Barclay, to the Success troop ship; A. Lowe, to the Jalouse; G. H. L. Dundas (of the Vengeur), to be pay-captain at Sheerness; David Milne, to the Venerable; K. J. White, to the Thistle; G. C. Sartorious, to the Snap sloop; R. L. Coulson, to the Stork; C. Robb, to the Apelles; B. W. Page, to the Puissant; T. Everard, to the Wasp; John Bayly, to the Alonzo; H. E. R. Baker, to the Dannemark; R. Coote, to the Boxer; Thomas Maling, to the Mulgrave; J. Taylor, to the Espiegle; Sir Thomas Berry, to the Barfleur; C. H. Watson, to the Arachne; James Brisbane, to the Pembroke; J. Wilson, to the Arab; C. H. Reid, to the Fervent; Sir T. Cochrane, to the Surprize; S. Blyth, to the Bozer; E. Tucker, to the Surveillante; R. Mansel, to the Chatham; J. Bissett, to the Royal Sovereign; R. Mainwaring, to the Gorgon H.S.; —— Davis (acting), to the Barbadoes.

Lieutenants, &c. appointed.

William Holmes, to the Saracen; E. Medley, to the Diomede; C. Oakes, to the St. Domingo; G. C. Urmstone, W. Roberts, J. Cairns, to the Marlborough; —— Mercer, to the signal station at Dundee; J. Rowan, to the Dublin; W. Finlaison, to the Nimrod; G. Pedlar, F. C. Annesley, W. H. Ingram, and H. Dawson, to the Grampus; J. Rubridge, to the Rover; H. Entwistle and C. H. Serle, to the Warspite; William Stone (1), to the Royal William; D. Edwards, to the Adamant; R. Coles, to the Melpomene; T. Marshall and R. B. Branch, to the Acorn; R. Watts, to the Fox troop ship; C. Pearson, to the Phœbe; T. P. Baker, to the Barham; J. Smith, to the Pembroke; R. Helpman, to the Fairy; W. Rawlinson and J. Hackett, to the Wasp; John Broderick, to the Iphigenia; T. Trimmer, to the Mulgrave; H. E. F. Pogsone, to the Bramble; H. Tucker, to the Centaur; E. White, to the Horatio; A. Belsey, to the Bold; W. Almer, to the Fervent; G. Fairlip and J. S. Fletcher, to the Cherokee ; J. Wells, to the Freija; J. Scott, to the Marlborough ; J. Campbell, to the Boxer; J. Bury, to the Valiant; J. Davis, to the Fox; P. Maingy, to the Success; J. Thompson, to the Castilian; J. Robinson, to the Semiramis; R. Sainthill, to the Muros; W. B. Ryland, to be flagofficer to Admiral Cockburne; C. R. Norman, to the Queen; N. Glen, to the Alfred; W. Fitzmaurice, J. Pakenham, and J. Coleman, to the Magicienne; H. D. Chads, J. Harrington, and A. Buchanan, to the Java; G. H. Hutchins, to the Standard; F. Beckett, to the Bellona; E. W. Astley, to the Monmouth: W. R. Dawkins, to the Duncan; F. Wemys, to the Swiftsure; G. Hall, to the Adamant; A. G. Clugstone, to the Cordelia; T. Patten, to the Forrester; J. Garland, W. Haswell, J. Townshend, and C. Moorsom, to the Superb; H. Ready, to the Moselle; J. Ferrant, to the Bozer; William Brown, to the

Melpomene; A. Donadieu, R. Mainwaring, C. H. Watson, J. Noyce, A. Westrop, and W. Bryan, to the rank of commander; G. Hutchins and J. Harvey, to the rank of lieutenant.

Pursers.—B. Worth, to the Laurestinus; George Whitbread, to the Dartmouth; William Bowden, to the Fervent; James Gillies, to the Swan; W. Paine, to the Sulphur; J. Collier, to the Saracen; and J. G. Amyott, to the Dover,

Mr. Thomas Glover, to be secretary to Admiral Cockburne.

R. L. Mosse, Esq. eldest son of Captain Mosse, who fell at the destruction of the Danish Fleet under Lord Nelson at Copenhagen, to be clerk of the survey of Portsmouth dock-yard.

A. Keddell, naval store-keeper at Milford, to be clerk of the rope-yard of Portsmouth dock-yard.

Masters.—Isaac Simon, to the Laurestinus; George Turner, to the Barfleur; S. Vale, to the Saracen; J. Bevans, to the Forester; T. Lean, to the Foxhound; T. M. Temple, to the Chatham; A. Louthean, to the Seahorse; James Macullum, to the Arab; J. Hamilton, to the Mulgrave; R. Dobson, to the Apelles; J. Willins, to the Drake; J. Smith, to the Espiegœ; J. Pack, to the Magicienne; S. Stead, to the Superb; John Brown, to the Rosario; R. Hawkey, to the Cherub; J. T. Crout, to the Alfred; J. Osman, to the Puissant; W. Rowe, to be superintending master at Portmouth; James Barrow, to the Melpomene; P. Inskip, to the Bramble; C. Leach, to the Wasp; D. Bevans, to the Surprise; A. M'Kenzie, to the Colossus.

A List of Midshipmen who have passed for Lieutenants in September:

Sheerness.—J. A. Mouatt, H. C. M. Phillips, T. Hare, C. A. Ross, A. Docking, J. T. Hubert, E. J. Crutchley, E. Jennings.

Portsmouth.—J. Delamotte, William Saul, William Salmond, Thomas Moubray.

Plymouth.—Charles Chapman, R. Conner, John Monday, D. Briggs, J. C. Seymour, W. Green, W. Farquharson, James Burton.

Surgeons, &c. appointed.

William Davies, to the Apelles; John Waller, to the Success; George Wardlaw, to the Diomede; James Anderson, to the Fairy; Charles Mayberry, to the Saracen; Thomas Williams, to the Magicienne; Andrew Mannin, to the Nimrod; T. C. Jones, to the Java; William Warden, to the Marlborough; Alexander Montgomery, to the Sabine; Barry O'Meara, to the Rivoli; Andrew Leslie, to the Chatham; George Brander, to the Maria; William Boyd, to the Muros; William Warner, to the Boyne; James Holbrook, to the Surprize; William M'Farland, to the Zenobia; Stephen Sherlock, to the Sheldrake; Scott Brown, to the Superb; J. M. Brydone, to the Mulgrave; James Twaddell, to the Arab; John Stewart, to the Wasp; Robert Evans, to the Belle Poule; Andrew Darling, to the Pembroke; S. J. Swayne, to the Seahorse; P. Reilly, to the Phipps; D. M'Coll, to the Barfleur.

Assistant-Surgeons, &c. appointed.

George Sharp, to the Stag; Joseph M'Gowan, to the Grampus; Henry Brock, to the Valiant; Andrew Barrie, to the Abundance S.S.; Peter Cunningham, to the Marlborough; James Cruickshank and Samuel Alexander, to the Chatham; Andrew Morrison, to the

Triton H.S.; Caleb Emmerson, to the San Juan; Thomas Elder, to the Childers; John Patton, to the Snap; James Clark, to the Horatio; Alexander Dunbar, to the Hearty G.B.; Peter Macdougall, to the Marlborough; John Liddell, to be hospital mate at Yarmouth; Patrick Hill, to be ditto at Stapleton; Robert Cummin, to the Marlborough; Robert Dickson, to the Dannemark; W. S. Winkworth, to be dispenser at Barbadoes; Hon. George Burrowes, to the Manly; Alexander Stewart, to the Mulgrave; James Bootes and John Gillies, to the Barfleur; James M'Ree, to be hospital mate at Portchester; John Riddell, to the Abercrombie; Francis Sankey, to the Pembroke; David Wilkin, to be an hospital mate at Deal; C. Quernel, to the Superb; William Kelly, to be hospital mate at Stapleton; John M'Leay, to be ditto at Haslar; William Anderson, to the Boxer; P. O'Reilly, to the Superb.

BIRTHS.

The lady of Lieutenant Bradley, R.N. of a daughter.

At his house on the Blackheath Road, the lady of William Bayley, Esq. R. N. of a son.

At Chatham, at the house of her father, Commissioner Sir Robert Barlow, Mrs. Byng, the lady of Captain George Byng, of the Warrior, of a son and daughter.

At Bath, the lady of Sir John Gore, of a son.

At Portsea, Mrs. Oglesby, wife of Mr. Oglesby, of H.M.S. Plantagenet, of a son.

Mrs. Lawson Long, wife of Mr. L. Long, purser of H.M.S. Elizabeth, of a daughter.

Aug. 1, at Frederick's-place, Walworth, Mrs. J. T. Lee, of a daughter.

Aug. 16, the lady of Captain J. Stevens, of the Maitland East Indiaman, of a daughter.

Aug. 22, at Fareham, the lady of Captain Mainwaring, R.N. of a son.

Sept. 17, in Great Mary-le-Bone-street, the lady of Captain Rolles, R.N. of a son.

Sept. 20, the wife of Mr. John Panchen, of H.M.'s frigate Phœbe, of a son.

MARRIAGES.

Lately, at Chalton church, J. Inches, Esq. R.N. to Mabella Ann Ovey, youngest daughter of Mr. S. P. Pritchard, commanding H.M.'s store-ship Dromedary.

Lieutenant R. R. Marley, R.N. to Miss Eliza Ann Marshall, of Park-lane, Southsea.

T. Waring, Esq. of the Grove, to Miss Hanmer, only daughter of Job Hanmer, Esq. Captain R.N. of Holbrook-hall, both in Suffolk.

Lieutenant J. Rickman, of the Royal Hospital at Greenwich, aged 78, to Miss Pullibank, daughter of the late Lieutenant Pullibank, R.N. aged 23 years.

J. Baillie, Esq. late secretary to the Hón. Admiral Berkeley, to Lady Burton, widow of Sir J. Burton, of Soho-square.

Lieutenant Turner, R.N. to Miss Walker, daughter of the late Rev. Charles Walker, rector of Cosgrove, Notts.

Aug. 27, at Marlborough, Captain J. A. Gordon (late of H.M.S. Active), to Miss Ward, youngest daughter of John Ward, Esq. of Marlborough.

Aug. 31, Captain Richard Spencer, R.N. to Ann, eldest daughter of Mrs. Lidden, of the Manor, Charmouth, Dorset.

Sept. 26, at Hoddesdon, Herts, Lieutenant and Adjutant Octavius Scott, of the Portsmouth division R.M. to Miss Edwards, of Tottenham, Middlesex.

OBITUARY.

Lately, at Barbados, Mr. Maxwell, navy agent.

At Leith, Mrs. Davies, wife of Mr. W. A. Davies, late secretary to Vice-admiral Otway.

Rear-admiral Laird, father-in-law of Captain Frederick Warren, of H.M.S. Argo.

At Greenwich, Mrs. Walter, relict of the late Captain Walter, R.N.

Miss Stanhope, eldest daughter of Admiral Sir Henry Stanhope, Bart.

Ralph Paine, Esq. formerly storekeeper of his Majesty's Dock-yard at Deptford. He has bequeathed a sum of money to endow an' hospital, to be erected on the New Road, Chatham, for the benefit of the widows of shipwrights. The spot of ground for this purpose he purchased some years ago.

At Meriden, on his road to London, the Hon. Captain I. A. Bennet, R.N. youngest son of the Earl of Tankerville. He lost a leg on the 1st of June, in which action he was a midshipman of the Montague.

At Salisbury, ——— Willoughby, posthumous son of the late Captain Hon. Willoughby Bertie (lost in the Satellite, in December 1810), nephew of the Earl of Abingdon.

Mr. Hansford, master-plumber in Portsmouth Dock-yard. He succeeded to that situation on the death of the former master-plumber, who was lost in the Royal George at Spithead.

Mr. Marshall, many years assistant-surgeon in Portsmouth dock-yard.

Mrs. Martin, mother of John Martin, Esq. of the Navy Pay-office, Portsmouth dock-yard.

At Trelawney, in the Island of Jamaica, in his 33d year, after a short but severe illness, Dr. Charles Truscott, third son of the late Admiral Truscott, of Exeter.

At Greenwich, Mrs. Peach, widow of the Rev. S. Peach, and only daughter of the Rev. Dr. J. Bradley, formerly Royal Astronomer at Greenwich.

Mr. Smith, clerk of the survey of H.M.'s dock-yard, Portsmouth.

At Haslar Hospital, Mr. Thomas Middlemist, purser of H.M.S. Dover.

Miss Betsey Beddek, eldest daughter of Richard Beddek, Esq. of the Royal Naval Hospital, Plymouth.

Early in June, Mrs. Pittman Goode, mother of the lady of Vice-admiral Crown, in the service of the Emperor of Russia, and grandmother to W. J. Cleveland, of the East India Company's service.

June 14, at Jamaica, Captain Edward Rushworth, of H.M.S. Barbados.—This truly estimable young officer, who has been thus prematurely cut off, had not attained his twenty-fifth year. He was the eldest son of Edward Rushworth, Esq. by the Hon. Catherine Rushworth, daughter of the late Lord Holmes, of the Isle of Wight, and grandson of Captain Rushworth, of the Royal Navy, who died in 1780. In the honourable service which he embraced, at a very early period of life, his career was distinguished by an ardent zeal for the glory of his country, in the pursuit of which, he happily, in frequent instances, had opportunities of signalizing himself, both by his personal valour, and the display of that excellent judgment which seems peculiar to a British naval officer; particularly by the capture of the Fort of Batabano, in the Isle of Cuba, in October 1806, and the consequent destruction of the enemies' privateers and ships there:—as mentioned in the Gazette, November 1806.*—For his gallant conduct, the then Board of Admiralty recommended him to Admiral Dacres to be posted. There have been, perhaps, but few young men whose death has been more sincerely lamented than that of Captain Edward Rushworth. His loss has excited the deep regret, of not only his numerous relations, but of a most extended circle of professional and private friends.—His remains were deposited in Jamaica, near those of his maternal great uncle, Admiral Holmes, who died at Jamaica in 1760, when commander-in-chief on that station.—The ceremony was attended by Admiral Stirling, the General and Field Officers, Naval Captains, and other principal Officers of the Navy and Army, as a last tribute of respect to the memory of this young and much-lamented hero.

June 25, at Venice, the French Admiral Villaret Joyeuse, Governor of that city. He commanded for some time the Toulon fleet, and was the officer, we believe, who, in some boasting despatches, accused Nelson of running away from him; which caused the British hero to observe, that he supposed his reputation for courage was too well established to be injured by the lying Frenchman; but if ever he caught Mons. Joyeuse, " he would make him eat his words."

July 4, at Brockhurst Cottage, near Gosport, John Dredge, Esq. forty years in the navy, and purser of H.M.S. Le Pegase.

July 27, at his father's house, Smith-square, Westminster, Captain Waterhouse, R.N.

July 31, at Greenock, aged 98, Lewis Gellie, Esq. R.N. He was a native of Aberdeen, and one of the oldest lieutenants in the navy. He served with Admiral Boscawen, with whom he was a great favourite.

Aug. 1, at Worthing, aged 70 years, Ambrose Serle, Esq. one of the commissioners of the Transport Board.

Aug. 11, at Old Woodstock House, Oxfordshire, Joseph Dewsnap, sen. Esq. father of Lieutenant Joseph Dewsnap, R.N. of the Royal Hospital at Greenwich.

Aug. 19, of a fever, Lieutenant Hare, of the Fervent G.B.

Aug. 26, at Deptford, in child-birth of her tenth child, the lady of Captain H. Garrett, R.N.

Sept. 21, at Walworth, James Dewar, Esq. many years a purser in the Hon. E.I.C.'s service.

Sept. 24, at Portsmouth, Lieutenant Thomas Westoby Kent, R.N. aged 30. His death was occasioned by a handspike falling on his head.

* *Vide* LETTERS ON SERVICE, N. C. XVI. 507.

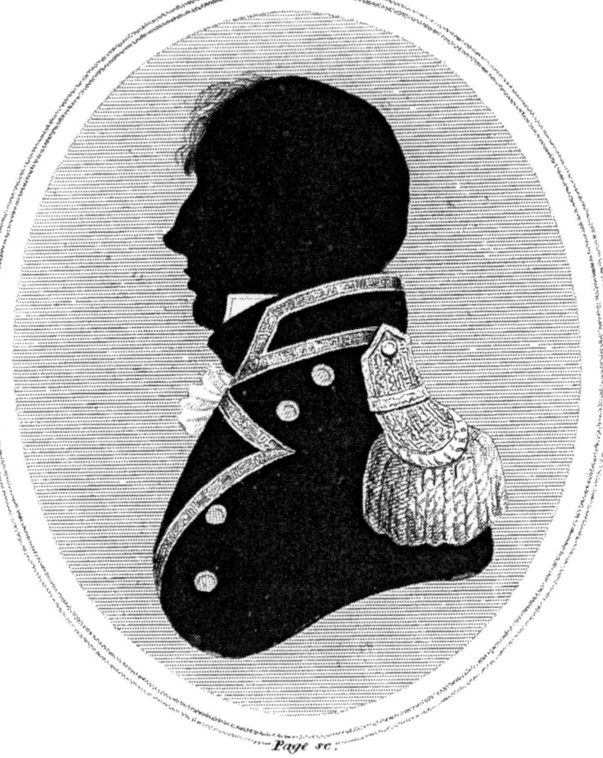

CAPT^N HENRY WHITBY. R.N

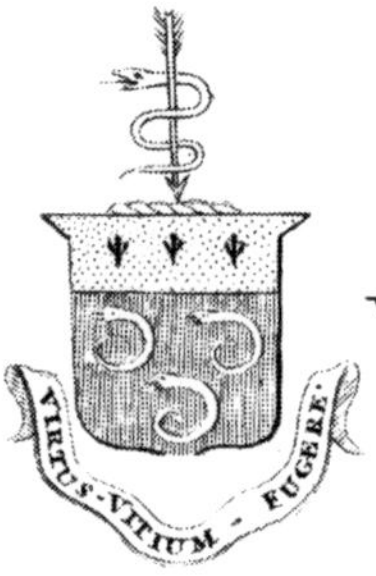

Published October 31st 1812 by Joyce Gold 103 Shoe Lane, Fleet St London.

BIOGRAPHICAL MEMOIR

OF THE LATE

HENRY WHITBY, Esq,

CAPTAIN IN THE ROYAL NAVY.

> " It is not the tear at this moment shed,
> When the cold turf has just been laid o'er him,
> That can tell how belov'd was the soul that's fled,
> Or how deep in our hearts we deplore him."——MOORE.

CAPTAIN HENRY WHITBY, whose career, though short, was such as to give promise of attainment to the highest honours of his profession, was the youngest son of the Reverend Thomas Whitby, by Mabella, youngest daughter of the late John Turton, Esq. of Angrave. He was born on the 21st of July, 1781, at Creswell Hall, his father's seat in the county of Stafford.—His family and connections on both sides were ancient, and had long been established in that part of England. Amongst other relatives, particularly of his own profession, may be mentioned the gallant and noble Earl St. Vincent.*

The period of childhood has generally so many circumstances in common, so few which are worthy of notice as extraordinary, that no surprise will be excited by saying, that young Whitby loved play better than books. Being a healthy and robust boy, he was, in very early youth, designed for the navy. His education was consequently adapted to his future situation in life; and, having acquired the rudiments of latin, &c. at Brewood and Copy Hall schools, in his native county, he was sent to others, where navigation and the preparatory branches of nautical science were taught. Towards the close of the year 1794, or early in 1795, it was judged proper to send him to sea; and one of his brothers (Captain John Whitby†) having about that time returned

---

* For a portrait and memoir of his Lordship, vide N.C. IV. 1.

† Of this officer, who died at Newlands, near Lymington, about the 7th of April, 1806, having recently resigned the command of H.M.S. Gibraltar,

from the East Indies, though a very young man, as flag captain to the Honourable Rear-admiral Cornwallis,* he was received as a midshipman on board the Excellent. While a youngster in the admiral's ship, he so conducted himself as to gain the approbation and favour of that truly brave and gallant officer. It is often in circumstances the most trivial that character is first displayed—At the time of the celebrated retreat of the 17th June, 1795, under the conduct of Admiral Cornwallis, whose flag was then on board the Royal Sovereign,† young Whitby was confined to

from ill health, we take leave to transcribe the following brief, but honourable notice, from our XVth Volume, page 352:—" He was a very excellent officer, and an intimate companion of the brave Admiral Cornwallis, at whose seat he died. Captain Whitby was the eldest son of the Rev. Thomas Whitby, of Cresswell-Hall, near Stafford. He was admitted into the royal navy, at the age of 12 years; from which period, a short interval only excepted, he was continually engaged for twenty years in the active duties of his profession, till about the 20th of March last, when indisposition, from unwearied and unremitted attention, compelled him to solicit, from the Lords of the Admiralty, a short leave of absence from the Gibraltar, of 80 guns; to which ship, from the Ville de Paris, he had been recently appointed. This indisposition, which at first excited no serious apprehension, assumed, after the lapse of some days, a more formidable aspect; and so rapid and overwhelming was its progress, that notwithstanding every effort of medical skill, it soon subdued a very useful and valuable life. So true it is, that in the midst of life we are in death.—In the Minerva frigate, then bearing the flag of the Hon. Admiral Cornwallis, his patron and friend, Captain W. was made post, in 1793 (April 20). Of his professional skill, zeal for the naval service, and constant attention to even the most minute parts of his duty, there is very ample testimony from those, who, from situation, are the most competent judges. His loyalty to his Sovereign, and his attachment to his country and its dearest interests, were ardent and sincere. The powers of the mind, which he was cultivating with assiduous care, were such, that few subjects to which he applied his attention steadily, could elude their grasp. To speculate upon the product of such powers, thus cultivating, is now, alas! as useless as it is vain: equally useless too it is, to lament the loss of one naval character, however considerable, when every British naval officer, and every seaman, is a Hero."

* For a portrait, biographical memoir, &c. of Admiral Cornwallis, vide N. C. VII. 1.; XVII. 202; and XXVII. 360.

† In the VIIth Volume of the NAVAL CHRONICLE, page 141, is a plate, representing the retreat of the British squadron, which consisted of the Royal Sovereign, Mars, Triumph, Brunswick, and Bellerophon, and Pallas and Phaëton frigates. *Vide*, also, N.C. VII. 20; and XXVII. 356.

his hammock with the measles. No sooner, however, did he learn that the French were upon the squadron, with a very superior force, and that some sharp fighting was expected, than he jumped up, and, dressing himself, declared, that, whatever might be the consequence, he would stand by his gun, and share the dangers and the credit of the day. If he did not carry his resolution into effect, it was solely owing to the restraint of positive orders to the contrary. This was an earnest of his future conduct. It was the dawn of that decided bravery, which, upon all occasions, courted danger, and which was, long after, displayed in meridian splendor in that proud and glorious action of frigates off the Island of Lissa, in the Adriatic.

At the end of about two years from his first entering the service, Mr. Whitby was removed into a frigate, as a situation where he might have the advantages of more active employment, and a bolder field for his enterprising spirit. He accordingly served successively in the Alcmene, under Captain Sir Richard Strachan, in the Thalia, in the Triton, &c. till, in the year 1799 (June 4), he was promoted to the rank of lieutenant. Shortly afterwards,[*] he was appointed to the Prince George, line-of-battle ship, then commanded by the late Sir Charles Cotton.[†] This period of his naval life was principally passed in the Channel and Mediterranean. On the latter station, he was in the way of acquiring a great variety of nautical experience and skill; and, besides other engagements, he was as much concerned in the ever-memorable one of the 1st of August, off Aboukir,[‡] under the command of Lord Nelson, as any person in a frigate could well be.—He was a witness how Britons could, and ought to, fight;'* how bravery, well directed, may prove victorious. His ship towed the gallant Nelson out of the scene of action, when the battle ceased, when the triumph was complete.

In the course of the year 1800, Lieutenant Whitby returned to England, in a very indifferent state of health. The air, how-

---

[*] April, 1800.

[†] A portrait and biographical memoir of Sir Charles Cotton's services are given in our XXVIIth Volume, page 353.

[‡] For the official, and other accounts of, and for various particulars relating to, the Battle of the Nile, vide N.C. I. 42, 43, 149, 235, 237, 369; II. 181, 189; XXV. 413.

ever, of his native land, and a quiet life, having, in a few months, re-established his constitution, he was, in April, 1801, appointed to the Leviathan, then bearing the flag of Rear-admiral Duckworth.*—It was in this situation that he was first placed under the immediate command of that distinguished officer, and that he formed an acquaintance, which ripened into intimacy and friendship. Admiral Duckworth, then commanding on the Jamaica station, took the earliest opportunity of raising him to the rank of commander, and made him acting post captain of the Proselyte frigate. That ship, unfortunately, struck, during the night, on a reef of sunken rocks; and, being but in a crazy state, she went to pieces almost instantly. With difficulty the crew were saved: every thing else perished in the waves.—By this unexpected calamity, Mr. Whitby's promotion was retarded; the loss of the Proselyte becoming known to the Admiralty, previously to their confirmation of his rank as post captain, or even as commander. He was, consequently, put back again into the Leviathan, as lieutenant. Such mortifying circumstances are by no means of unusual occurrence in the navy. An accident may defeat the efforts of the greatest zeal; the elements may counteract designs which have been laid with the most mature judgment. While Mr. Whitby, however, suffered mortification and anxiety, he gained caution and experience. Uninterrupted success, in young minds especially, too often engenders temerity: by occasional disasters and reverses of fortune, the greatest commanders, as the greatest monarchs, have been produced.

By the friendship of Admiral Duckworth, Lieutenant Whitby was at length promoted to the rank of commander, and appointed to the Pelican.†—In this vessel, unaided, he carried on the blockade of Aux Cayes with such unremitting diligence and activity, as to reduce the inhabitants to a state of famine, and to terms of almost unconditional surrender.‡

---

* Sir J. T. Duckworth's memoir and portrait are in our XVIIIth Volume, page 1, et seq.

† His commission was confirmed on the 28th of April, 1802; but, we believe, he had been acting commander of the Pelican, from the month of February preceding.

‡ Vide LETTERS ON SERVICE, N. C. XI. 62.—For the whole of the proceedings respecting St. Domingo, vide N. C. X. 333, 334, 335, and 449; XI. 61, 160, 212, to 250; XVIII. 17.

On the 6th of February, 1804, he was promoted to the rank of post captain, and commanded successively the Santa Margaretta, and Desiree frigates, and the Centaur, line-of-battle ship. He commanded the last-mentioned ship, when, during the summer of 1805, Lord Nelson pursued the French fleet from the Mediterranean to the West Indies;* and the Centaur, St. George, and two others, of the line, were ordered to join his Lordship with all possible despatch. Endeavouring to form this junction, they were taken in one of the tremendous hurricanes which commence so suddenly, and increase to such dreadful violence, in those seas. Of the squadron, the Centaur was the most exposed to its destructive rage. Her masts were all carried off like mere twiggs: she was thrown on her beam ends, with a most alarming leak, at an immense distance from any land; and her boats were all stove, and washed overboard. In this awful situation, she lay for many hours, without the least remains of hope, or the slightest expectation of reaching a port in safety. Her companions in danger were spectators of her extreme distress, but were unable to render her the least assistance. By the mercy of Providence, however, the winds were stayed, the fury of the waves abated—The Centaur righted, and being taken in tow by the Eagle, one of the squadron which suffered but slightly, she arrived at Halifax safe, though in a dreadfully shattered condition. Upon this trying occasion, the crew afforded a striking proof of their high state of discipline. In similar dangers, sailors are too apt to resort to liquor, in order to drown in drunkenness their apprehensions of approaching death, or to gratify with impunity a strong propensity to intoxication. In the Centaur, one man only was then guilty of this act of egregious folly; and he was, by the captain's orders, punished on the spot. When prayers and thanksgiving were offered up to the Almighty, for their signal deliverance from the waves, the crew almost to a man were dissolved in tears.

This hurricane, so terrible at the time, led to subsequent events of singular interest to Captain Whitby. It was the cause of his going to Halifax, where Captain Inglefield, whose miraculous escape from the wreck of the old Centaur, in 1782, is so

---

* N. C. XIV. 408.

well known in our naval annals, then resided as commissioner of the navy; and it occasioned a renewal of his acquaintance with that gentleman and his family. An attachment soon took place between Captain Whitby and Catherine Dorothea, the commissioner's youngest daughter, which was confirmed by their union towards the close of the year 1805, or early in 1806.

The Centaur, having been refitted, was ordered to England; but Captain Whitby's stay at Halifax having become desirable to him, he made an exchange into the Leander, of 50 guns, the flagship of the late Sir Andrew Mitchell,* at that time chief on, the Halifax station.

No occurrence worthy of mention took place, till, in April, 1806, some time subsequently to the death of his admiral, he was sent off Sandy Hook, as senior officer of a squadron consisting of the Leander, Cambrian, and Driver sloop of war. He was too well acquainted with the friendship and regard borne to this country by our American brethren; and more particularly with the deceits and frauds practised by the masters of merchantmen, if not to injure us, at least to benefit themselves at our expense, by every possible means—not to examine all vessels which passed his squadron, with a most scrutinizing eye. Having detained some valuable vessels, for having on board contraband goods, he became obnoxious to our trans-atlantic allies. To defend the rights of his country was a most heinous offence, when opposed to their nefarious practices. A man on board one of their coasters having been killed, or reported to have been killed, his death was at once laid to a shot from the Leander; as, about that time, the squadron were firing, to bring-to some homeward-bound American merchantmen, which, fearing the result of a search, obstinately persisted in their course.—A dead body was conveyed ashore, and exposed at New York to public view; an uproar of the most violent kind was excited against the English; the British flag was burnt before the British Consul's house; and some officers of the squadron, who had previously landed for the purchase of provisions, with great difficulty escaped with their lives. Two days elapsed before these circumstances were made known to

---

* Sir Andrew Mitchell's portrait and memoir will be found in our XVIth Volume, page 90.

the senior officer. A strict inquiry was immediately set on foot, as to the probability of a man having been killed by a shot from the Leander; but it appeared almost impossible: at any rate highly improbable; for no vessel, answering the description of the coaster, had been fired at, or had even been seen, by any one on board his Majesty's ships, whilst the firing continued. The elections, however, were then going on at New York, and the party in the French interest were happy to catch at any thing that could serve their purposes against this country.* They demanded Captain Whitby from our government, to try him by their own laws, or to hang him at any rate without justice. Nothing less than his life could satisfy their fury: and, can it be believed, that one of the cabinet of this country, the friend of liberty, and the rights of the British people, then high in office, and the peculiar protector of the heroes of the navy, proposed, or gave it as his opinion, that the demand of the Americans should be acceded to? Can it be possible? It has so been stated, but surely without a foundation in truth! It seems incredible, that an Englishman should be so lost to all sense of justice, so dead to every feeling of honour and humanity, as to entertain, for a single moment, the idea of surrendering to an infuriated people, an officer who was acting in obedience to the orders of his superiors, and zealously protecting the rights of his country. But if the assertion be true, may the recollection make the man blush, who could harbour the thought, particularly when he learns, that the statement of a man having been killed by a shot has since been proved to be a forgery, for the worst of purposes, a falsity of the blackest dye.—Be this, however, as it may, it was finally resolved that Captain Whitby should be tried by a court martial, for the wilful murder of this man, John Pierce, for a violation of the rights of a neutral state, in amity with Great Britain. Accordingly, after some months of very vexatious delay, on the 16th of April, 1807, a court assembled for the purpose, on board H. M. S. Gladiator, at Portsmouth, of which Admiral Montague was president. The trial

---

* A Proclamation of Mr. Jefferson, the President of the United States, prohibiting all intercourse with the Leander, Cambrian, and Driver; and a Memorial of the Mayor, &c. of New York, upon this subject, were inserted in our XVIth Volume, pages 119, and 121.

lasted only two days. Five Americans had been sent over to this country, who deposed to some circumstances which appeared impossible, and to others which were most satisfactorily disproved, by officers of the highest credit, who were present at the transaction. A sentence of acquittal was pronounced by the court; and the president returned Captain Whitby his sword, with the expression of his full assurance, that " it had never been stained in his hands." *

To soothe the Americans, however, he was refused employment. This was the more galling to his high spirit, as he felt, that to put him again into commission was the only mode of fully justifying his conduct to his friends and to his country, from the imputation alleged against him, and of making him some amends for the extreme anxiety and uneasiness, which zeal for the service of his country had occasioned him.—It was at this period, indeed, that his health first became seriously affected. The greater part of his youth having been passed in hot climates, the changes of our variable weather were very sensibly felt by his constitution; and his concern, at being, under such circumstances, thrown out of employment in a profession to which he was devotedly attached, tended much to increase a bilious and rheumatic disorder, which constantly annoyed him.—During this involuntary absence from the service, he passed a domestic life, chiefly in Devonshire, having, with the hard earned profits of his avocation, purchased a small villa in the vicinity of Exeter.

Affairs were in this state, when, in November, 1808, Captain Whitby obtained, from a most authentic source, confidential information, that the man, John Pierce, for whose wilful murder he had been tried, and though acquitted had been kept unemployed, had certainly, not been killed by a shot from the Leander, or from any one of the squadron then acting under his orders. He learned at the same time, that this important fact was fully known to the American ministry, as well as that the most infamous perjury had been committed by those, who endeavoured to swear away

---

* The court martial, holden upon Captain Whitby, was originally published, at length, in the NAVAL CHRONICLE; and, we believe, it has never been before the public in any other form. It is an interesting and highly important document.—*Vide* N.C. XVIII. 72 to 82; and 160 to 175.

his life. This intelligence, so interesting to him, and which he always believed to be the case, though without positive proof in his possession, he, without loss of time, communicated to the first lord of the Admiralty, and, through the secretary of state, to the American minister resident in London. By him, the truth of it was so far admitted, as he allowed, that, on the part of his government, no objection any longer existed, to the *ci-devant* captain of the Leander being again brought into active service against the enemies of his country.*

In February, 1809, he, therefore, received a commission for the Cerberus frigate, of 32 guns, and was ordered to join the fleet in the Baltic, under Sir James Saumarez.† There he was chiefly occupied with the convoy of merchantmen; but, as the autumn advanced, his constitution suffered severely, from a return, with increased violence, of his rheumatic disorder, with the addition of an alarming affection of the bladder. He was scarcely expected to survive from one day to another. Returning home, however, as is usual towards winter, from those northern seas, he was considerably restored, by care and medical skill. But a calamity was preparing for him, which, to his latest hour, he never ceased to lament. He found his wife in an advanced state of consumption, a disease so prevalent in this country, so lingering, so delusive, so generally fatal. She continued some months under the

---

* The subjoined anecdote, relating to Captain Whitby, as we observed on its original insertion in the NAVAL CHRONICLE (XVI. 48) ought to have entitled him to very different treatment, from the American nation and government, to that which he experienced.—When he " commanded La Desiree frigate, at St. Domingo, Dessalines, the black chief, either from information, or suspicion, that an American master of a vessel had smuggled off some French whites, to prevent their falling into his hands, ordered the said master to be hanged in his presence. Captain Whitby, shocked at so horrid a proceeding, with that genuine humanity, and determined resolution, so peculiar to a Briton, sent a boat, manned, and armed, to the rescue of the ill-fated American. Fortunately, the knot slipped, and he was suspended by the chin. A musket was fired to clear the way, the ball of which passed near Dessalines: the boat's crew landed, took down the victim, who soon recovered, and restored him to his ship. Dessalines, instead of resenting this, suffered Captain Whitby to be at all times on shore unmolested, and paid him marked attention."

† A portrait and memoir of Sir James Saumarez appears in N. C. VI. 85.

influence of that dreadful malady, at one time apparently better, then almost overwhelmed with renewed paroxysms, till, on January 17, 1810,* she breathed her last, to the unspeakable anguish of her affectionate, afflicted husband. She left no children to bewail her loss.

To assuage the grief with which he was oppressed, and with hope of recovering from the injurious effects of colder climates, he solicited to be sent to the Mediterranean. The application was received with attention and kindness, and, about the end of March, or early in April, 1810, he sailed in the Cerberus, with a convoy for Cadiz, and proceeded thence to join the Mediterranean squadron, at that time commanded by Admiral Sir Charles Cotton.† On his arrival on that station, he was detached to the Adriatic, where the Cerberus formed part of a squadron of frigates, under the conduct of Captain Hoste, of the Amphion, which were very actively employed in annoying the enemy's trade, and scouring their coast. Several severe actions of boats took place, in which the valour of British sailors was eminently conspicuous, and universally successful. At length, to clear the Gulf of this squadron, and to take possession of the Island of Lissa, the French collected a naval force, so superior, that they considered themselves fully competent to engage, and vanquish our little band. Accordingly, on the 13th of March, 1811, by day-light, they were discovered bearing down in two lines upon our squadron, which instantly formed a close line within gun-shot of the abovementioned island. The enemy, under the command of Commodore Dubordieu, consisted of six frigates, of which four were of the largest class, one brig, two schooners, and two gun-boats, mounting together 272 guns, and having on board, besides their complement of sailors, five hundred soldiers: the British squadron was composed of the Amphion, of 32 guns, Commodore Hoste; the Cerberus, 32, Captain Whitby; the Active, 38, Captain Gordon; and the Volage, of 22, Captain Hornby. A more severe engagement was never fought; a more decisive victory, especially against so great a superiority of force, was never gained. The French commodore was killed early in the day; and his ship, attempting to break the British line, went on shore, and

---

* N.C. XXIII. 88. † N.C. XXVII. 387.

was shortly afterwards set on fire and destroyed by her crew. Two others were captured, a fourth struck, but not being immediately taken possession of (from the want of men), she re-hoisted her colours, bore away, and escaped with the remainder.* Such a triumph was not to be purchased without considerable loss. Where all must have fought like lions, to distinguish any one must appear invidious. Thus much may, however, be said of the Cerberus and her commander, that she went into action 50 men short of her complement, which was but 254, and, when it ceased, she had 80 of the remainder killed, wounded, or at least rendered unfit for immediate duty. How can the demeanor of Captain Whitby on this proud day be better described, than in the following words, transcribed from a letter written after his decease, by a naval man, an eye witness of his conduct?—

" On that glorious day, no man's talents were ever better displayed, or courage more tried—that day, I can with truth and confidence say, was the happiest he ever saw; and, trace our naval history from end to end, it will not be found to contain one individual soul, who ever braved danger with more determined firmness than Captain Whitby. He was an ornament to his profession, an honour to all who knew him; and, had it pleased the Almighty to have restored him once again, it would not have been long before he would have stood one of the very first, and most conspicuous characters that grace our annals."

This gallant squadron had, in a few days, sufficiently repaired the damages which it had sustained, to sail for Malta; where it was received, by all ranks, with the admiration, amounting to enthusiasm, which it so well deserved. †

The Cerberus having been refitted, was ordered—not, indeed, as might reasonably and fairly have been expected, to her former station in the Gulf of Venice, the scene of her triumph, but —to cruize off the island of Corfu, where but little chance existed of active service, or that farther glory might be obtained. Cap-

---

* The official details of this truly great and glorious action, will be found recorded in our XXVth Volume, from page 429 to page 436; and at page 423 of the same Volume, is the *French* account of the action, written by an *Italian* Colonel (Geislenga) as it appeared in the *Moniteur*.

† At page 146 of our XXVIIth Volume, are some *Lines, on the appearance of the Amphion and Squadron, off Malta Harbour*, by E——E R——N, Esq. *a Purser in the Royal Navy*.

tain Whitby was indignant at the Cerberus being thus converted into a guardship, when, from his knowledge of the seas, and the services which he had there performed, he considered himself entitled to the situation, which had become vacant by the return of his friend, Captain Hoste,* to England. He represented his wounded feelings to the commander-in-chief, who could not but admit the justice of his complaint. Just at that time, however, an Admiralty appointment, to the Belle Poule, obliged him to return to his native land; where he arrived, a passenger in the Cambrian, in October, 1811. Here, as may be supposed, he was received with open arms by his family and friends, with every demonstration of admiration and affection. The colours of the Corone, which was first boarded by the Cerberus, on her surrender, were presented by him to the mayor and corporation of the borough of Stafford, and with great pomp and solemnity were hung up in St. Mary's church, in that town. There may they long remain, a prouder, brighter memorial of the valiant and sincerely lamented donor, than the richest specimens of monumental marble!

On his arrival in England, Captain Whitby was informed that the Belle Poule had not been vacated by her commander; and thus he found himself again thrown out of commission; at a time, too, when he least expected it. But having so highly distinguished himself, it was not to be supposed that he could long remain unemployed. At the Admiralty he met with the kindest reception and attentions, and was promised, by Mr. Yorke, the Briton, a beautiful new frigate, then shortly to be launched. In the mean time, at a full meeting of the Lords Commissioners, he was presented by the first lord, with a gold medal and ribband, as an honorary distinction for the active part which he had so ably sustained in the action off Lissa.†

---

* Some particulars relating to Captain Hoste will be found in our XXVIth Volume, page 133.

† It seems not improper, in this place, to refer the reader to an account of the commemoration of the victory of Lissa, under the Broad Oak, of Winwick, in Lancashire, the birth place of Captain Hornby, of the Volage, on the 26th of August, 1811: it will be found in our XXVIIth Volume, page 204.

This reward his friends were led to consider as only an earnest of what he would entitle himself to receive, more particularly as he cherished the laudable ambition of attaining, by zealous and able services for his country, to the highest honours of his profession. But, alas! what is ambition, even the most praiseworthy.—How, in an hour, as a flower of the field before the scythe, is man cut off, and then is seen, is heard no more! With pain and sorrow we approach the period which saw the termination of a life so promising, so short, so deeply to be regretted. Captain Whitby, though naturally of a strong constitution, had for some years laboured under a disease of the bladder, the effect of hot climates and sudden changes. In the Baltic, as well as in the Mediterranean, he had in consequence of it been more than once at the point of death. By the skill and unwearied attention of his surgeon, Mr. David James, his life had been saved and prolonged. But the evil was by no means removed. He was constantly liable to sudden attacks, from which the greatest danger might be apprehended. In the month of February, 1812, unfortunately neglectful of his health, he went on a visit into Devonshire, whence he was sent for to attend the sick bed of a dying sister.* During this painful scene, his affectionate heart was in a constant state of anxiety and grief. If every one around her, friends and acquaintance, domestics and the poor, universally lamented such departed excellence, what must be the affliction of a brother, who had for months been witness of her gradual decline, with alternate hopes of her recovery, and apprehensions, too fully realized, of the fatal crisis! His thoughts and feelings were too powerfully affected, by his ever dear sister's illness and subsequent decease, to admit of proper attention to his own disorder. To divert his mind, however, by the duties of his profession, from sorrow which had then become of no avail, he attended the launch of his ship, at Chatham, in the month of April, and commissioned her a few days after. He enjoyed the sight, and felt an honourable pride in the command of such a frigate, given him as an additional reward for meritorious conduct; and which he was induced to hope would lead him to fur-

---

* Lucy, wife of Edward Berkely Portman, Esq. of Brynnstone, near Blandford, M. P. for the County of Dorset.

ther honours in the service of his native land, and the defeat of England's enemies. He no longer had leisure to recollect that his health was precarious, and required the greatest care. To forward his ship was his principal object; and, occupied by his efforts for that purpose, he was seized with a cold, which attacked his bladder, and produced an inflammation so violent and rapid, that all the skill of his medical attendants could not for a moment arrest its resistless progress.—On Sunday, the 3d of May, was the first day on which any symptoms of danger or alarm had appeared; on the 5th, a mortification had evidently commenced; and, on the following day, about four o'clock in the afternoon, he breathed his last!

Thus died, lamented by all who knew him, on the 6th day of May, 1812, Captain Henry Whitby, in the 31st year of his age. So short was his illness, that intelligence of his dangerous state was unable to reach the greater part of his family, till the mournful crisis had passed. " The last two days of his life," says a letter now before us, " he was attended by the only one of his brothers within reach, who can never forget the agonizing moments which separated from him the companion of his earliest youth, the truly affectionate friend of his riper age;—nor can he ever cease to bear in mind the kind attentions which, in that afflicting situation, he received from Sir Robert Barlow, the commissioner at Chatham, from Captain Spranger, Captain Brenton, and indeed all the naval officers, who were then at that port. He must ever regard them as the strongest proof of the very high esteem in which the deceased was held by his brother officers."

On Monday, the 11th day of May, the remains of Captain Whitby were deposited in St. Margaret's church-yard, Rochester, with all the solemnity of naval and military honours. The body having been removed by day-light to H. M. S. Briton, precisely at twelve o'clock, minute guns firing, it was conveyed, at a slow rate, amidst a long procession of boats, to the stairs of the Victualling Office; where, having been landed, it was carried to the grave by sailors, attended by all the officers of the navy and of the garrison, and by an immense concourse of people.

The following is the order of the procession, after the landing of the body:—

First Division of Boats Crews, two and two.
Firing Party of Royal Marines.
Military.
Midshipmen, two and two.
Subaltern Officers, two and two.
Captains of the Army, and Lieutenants of the Navy,
(Army to the right) two and two.
Undertaker.
Mute.   Mute.
Midshipmen of the Briton, two and two.
Surgeon of the Briton.
Dr. Hope.   Dr. Douglas.
First Lieutenant of the Briton.
Rev. James Jones.   Rev. John Griffiths.

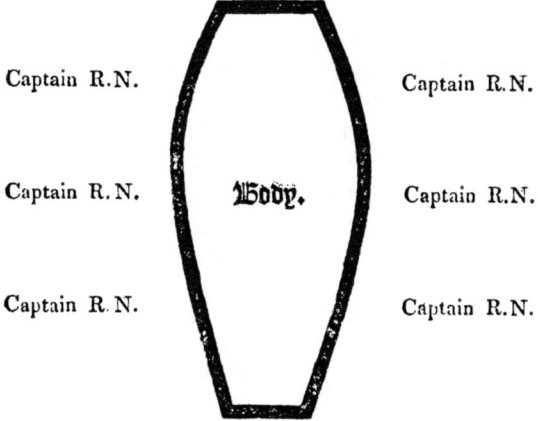

Captain R.N.   Captain R.N.

Captain R.N.   Body.   Captain R.N.

Captain R.N.   Captain R.N.

Mr. Rollier, Midshipman.   Mr. Sherwood, Midshipman.
CHIEF MOURNERS.
Captain George Whitby,   Rev. Edward Whitby,   Captain Northey,
Admiral.   General
Commissioner.
Field Officers and Captains of the Navy, two and two.
Friends of the deceased.
Officers of the Dock-yard, two and two.
Barges Crews, 2d Division.
Marines of the Squadron.

Such was the respect shown by the inhabitants of Rochester to the memory of a brave man, that all the shops by which the procession was to pass, were spontaneously closed by them.

To render justice to the departed subject of this memoir, requires the pen of one who knew him well—who knew him intimately. Fortunately, we are thus enabled to close, with the following animated sketch :—

" Few men, perhaps, ever possessed, in a higher degree, the qualities necessary to form a Hero, and a Christian, than did Captain Henry Whitby. He was zealous, active, enterprising: brave, and collected in the greatest dangers: warm and sincere in his attachments, and of a truly generous disposition. He was a strict disciplinarian: punished from necessity, but rewarded from the joy and fulness of his heart. Too magnanimous to tyrannize where he had power; but too proud to stoop to any man. He might, perhaps, be thought rather hasty in his resentments; but that propensity was infinitely counterbalanced by the steadiness of his friendship. To serve a person who had gained his affection, or merited his regard, he would strain every nerve. But an enemy was soon forgiven. Very few had, to so great a degree, the power of attaching even casual acquaintance. The playful ingenuousness of his manners, the vivacity of his spirits, the information with which his conversation abounded, his natural good nature, and universal wish to oblige, gained him at once the admiration and love of all who knew him. He was constant in his attendance on the duties of religion; and that not from ostentation, but conviction: he had the fear of the Almighty Disposer of Events at all times before his eyes; and neglected not from motives of personal interest his duty to his neighbour. But he had, no doubt, his failings—Perfection is not the lot of man—May they be buried in his grave; may they be blotted by the God of Mercy from the book for ever !"

NAVAL ANECDOTES, COMMERCIAL HINTS, RECOLLECTIONS, &c.

NANTES IN GURGITE VASTO.

DEFENCE OF THE MAY, OF LIVERPOOL.

THE following is a copy of a letter from Captain Affleck, of the ship May, to his owners in Liverpool:—

" DEAR SIRS, " *St. Lucia, 8th August,* 1812.

" I am happy to inform you of the arrival of the ship May here on the 5th. Nothing material occurred on the voyage until the 3d instant, at two P.M. when a vessel was seen from the mast-head, bearing W.N.W. standing to the S.E. the wind at the time E.N.E. a light breeze, our course west, being at the time in the latitude of this island, and about 160 miles to windward. At four P.M. had neared this strange sail so as to see his hull distinctly, and perceived him to be a large schooner, and apparently a vessel of war. Ordered all hands to quarters, and had every thing clear for action. At five he tacked to the northward, and at half-past he tacked again, and came into our wake, when he immediately bore up after us under all sail, with English colours hoisted, and not wishing to let him come too near, fired the stern guns at him, which were immediately returned by his broadside of four guns, and was answered by the May in the same manner. At seven P.M. he hoisted a light, and hailed—" Where is that ship from ?"—I answered from Falmouth, and demanded to know what schooner that was; he replied—" A British man of war," and ordered me on board with my papers immediately.—I told him if he attempted to come a yard nearer he should receive my broadside, but, at that distance, I would send my boat on board, which I did, with my chief mate and two men : his boat immediately returned with six men and an officer, all armed, none of whom were allowed to come on board, except the latter; one who attempted had a pistol put to his breast, and he immediately sat down in the boat. The officer on coming on board told me he was a British privateer, belonging to Bermuda, and insisted on my going on board in his boat with my papers. I told him I was a British letter of marque, and would not quit my vessel, unless to go on board one belonging to his Majesty, and ordered him out of the ship, at the same time desiring him to send my mate and people on board." His boat soon after returned, with the following note :—" Captain Taylor presents his regards to the master of the ship, and insists on his coming on board with his papers, otherwise he may abide by the consequences." My answer was as before, and sent his boat off. He then hailed, declared he would sink me, should I refuse to comply with his request. My answer was, " Fire away !" which was put into execution as soon as his boat reached him, by his broadsides, and showers of musketry, and was as quickly returned by the May. I had now no longer a doubt of his being an American privateer, and on the dawn of day my suspicions were confirmed by his colours. From this time, half-past 7 P.M. till 9 A.M. a fire, with little intermission, was kept up by both vessels; and it appeared during this long action, to be his intention to board the May, which was always frustrated by rounds of grape; until at last he was obliged to haul off in the greatest confusion, with his sails, rigging, and hull dreadfully cut up; and indeed we are in the same situation, having six of our lower shrouds shot away, fore-stay, main-top-mast back-stay, three shots between wind and water, the main-top-mast wounded, and the sails and running rigging cut to pieces, one man killed, and two wounded. It affords me the greatest pleasure to say, that nothing could exceed the coolness and bravery of the few people I had the honour to command.

" I am, Gentlemen, your most obedient servant,
" WILLIAM AFFLECK."

" P.S. The above is a confused account of the action with the American privateer, as I had only a few minutes/notice of this opportunity to write to you by way of Martinico. I have, however, only to add, that had the *May* been armed *with any other guns than those on Colonel Congreve's plan, she must inevitably have been captured*, from the small crew I had on board—one man having been killed, and one wounded, by the first discharge from the privateer, after the return of his boat. The privateer mounted eight guns, and full of men.

" *Killed*—Joseph Rummona, seaman.

" *Wounded*—J. B. Hannah, second mate ; Wm. Walker, apprentice; both slightly, and they are doing well.

" *Prisoners on board the Privateer*—Samuel Hagelhurst, chief mate ; John Erick, and James Antonio, seamen."

FRENCH PRISONERS.

As a proof of the good treatment of the prisoners of war in this country the following comparative statement of those sick and in health will be the best answer to the calumnies of the *Moniteur* :—

Thursday, August 20.

	In Health.	Sick.
On board prison ships in Hamoaze	6,100	61
In Dartmoor *dépôt*	7,500	74

This small proportion of sick is less than the common average of persons not confined as prisoners of war. At Dartmoor *dépôt*, 500 prisoners, such as labourers, carpenters, smiths, &c. are allowed to work from sun-rise to sun-set; they are paid 4d. and 6d. per day, according to their abilities; and have each their daily rations of provisions, *viz.* a pound and a half of bread, half a pound of boiled beef, half a pound of cabbage, and a proportion of soup and small beer. They wear a tin plate in their caps, with the name of the trade they are employed in, and return every evening to the *dépôt* to be mustered.

Early in the month of September, the prisoners at Dartmoor exhibited alarming symptoms of riot. The alleged reason was, their being deprived of their pound and an half of soft bread, and having a pound and an half of biscuit in lieu thereof; the reason of which was, that the bakehouse and all the ovens had been destroyed by fire in the preceding week, and the contractors had not rebuilt them. In consequence of this turbulent behaviour, a detachment of the Cheshire Militia, and of the South-Gloucester Regiment, was drawn up on the walls surrounding the prison; but, although they had loaded their pieces with ball, the prisoners appeared undaunted, and insulted them in the grossest terms. A sentinel on duty had his bayonet wrenched off his piece, yet nobly reserved his fire; an officer, however, followed the Frenchman, struck him over the shoulder with his sword, and brought off the bayonet. The Frenchmen even bared their breasts to the troops, and seemed regardless of danger. The number of prisoners is about 7,500 ; and so menacing was their conduct, that an express was sent off to Plymouth-dock, at eleven o'clock on a Sunday night, soliciting immediate assistance. Three pieces of artillery were in consequence sent off early on Monday morning; and on their arrival at the principal gate, the bars of which, of immense size, had been previously broken by stones hurled against them by the insurgents, they were placed in such directions as completely to command the whole of the prison. This had the desired effect, and order was restored. It is to be noticed, that the allowance of bread at which these men so indignantly spurned, is precisely the same as that which is served out to our own sailors and marines.

METALLIC LIFE-BOAT.

A METALLIC Life-boat, on pneumatic and hydrostatic principles, that will neither sink nor overset, yet serve all the ordinary purposes of ships' boats, either for rowing or sailing, was tried, lately, at London-bridge, on the ebb-tide, during the time of the greatest fall, with her crew on board and filled with water: when she passed through with the greatest safety, and discharged a considerable portion of the water, purposely put into her. This life-boat is described as made of malleable iron, lead, and tin; of twenty feet long, and six feet wide, drawing only ten inches water, with 25 persons, and possessing valves, that without pumping or personal aid, discharge all the water from them. These valves, which act occasionally as pneumatic or air valves, are hydrostatically ballasted with confined water, taken in or put out at pleasure, and are remarkably buoyant and lively in agitated water.

TARRING AND FEATHERING.

THE *Tyne Mercury* presents the following statement relating to the man who, as described at a preceding page,* was tarred and feathered, by the crew of the American frigate Essex, to which he belonged, for avowing himself an Englishman, and refusing to fight against his country:—

" By a New York Paper of the 27th of June, it appears, that a seaman, named Erring, a native of this town, was tarred and feathered by the crew of the Essex frigate, Captain Porter, for refusing to fight against his country. This base conduct excited much indignation at New York, and a statement was published from the man's own deposition, to clear the city from any participation in the affair. The deposition states, that " John Erring was born in Newcastle-upon Tyne, England, that he has resided within the United States since 1800, and has never been naturalized; that on the 14th of October, 1811, he entered on board the Essex, and joined her at Norfolk; that Captain Porter, on the 26th of June, caused all hands to be piped on deck, to take the oath of allegiance to the United States, and gave them to understand, that any man who did not choose to do so should be discharged; that when deponent heard his name called, he told the captain, that being a British subject, he must refuse taking the oath; on which the captain spoke to the petty officers, and told

* Page 199.

them they must pass sentence on him; that they then put him in the petty launch which lay alongside the frigate, and there poured a bucket of tar over him, and then laid on a quantity of feathers, having first stripped him naked from the waist; that they then rowed him ashore stern foremost, and landed him. That he wandered about from street to street, in this condition, not knowing where to go, until Mr. Ford took him into his shop, to save him from the crowd then beginning to gather; that he stayed there until the police magistrate took him away, and put him in the city prison for protection, where he was cleansed and cloathed. None of the citizens molested or insulted him. He says he had a protection, which he bought of a man in Salem, of the same name and description with himself, for 4s. 6d. which he got renewed at the Custom-house, Norfolk.—He says he gave as an additional reason to the captain, why he did not choose to fight against his own country, that if he should be taken prisoner he would certainly be hung."—This story shall be closed by asking the reader a simple question: suppose the captain of an English frigate should suffer his men to tar and feather an American sailor in the port of London, because he would not join in a cruise to fight against his own country, what would you think and say of such an action?"

CAPTURE OF THE ROYAL-BOUNTY.

The subjoined s an extract of a letter, dated St. John's Harbour, 13 August, 1812:—

" On Monday evening last, arrived here Captain Henry Gamble, with part of his crew and passengers, belonging to the ship Royal Bounty, of Leith. This vessel, on her voyage from Hull to Prince Edward's Island, in ballast, was attacked, on the 1st instant, four or five leagues to the southward of St. Peter's, by the Yankee brigantine privateer, of 18 guns, and 120 men. Captain Gamble, being unapprized of the war, was in some degree unprepared for the attack of the American, who chased her under English colours, but, on coming near, hoisted the American flag, and commenced the engagement.

" The Royal Bounty had ten guns, eighteen men, and four passengers, one a female. Captain Gamble sustained the unequal conflict for an hour and a quarter, when, having the boy that was at the helm killed, himself wounded, together with his second mate, boatswain, and cook, the colours were struck. Several shots were fired afterwards, one of which wounded the chief mate. The Americans then took possession, and ordered all the people on board the privateer, where the wounded received surgical assistance, but the others were treated very harshly, having their clothes, some of which they wore, taken from them.

" Two Americans were badly wounded, and it is supposed some were killed, but this was not acknowledged. The American master was quite enraged at the resistance he had met with from Captain Gamble.

" The privateer shortly after boarded the Thetis, of Poole, Captain Pack, from Sidney, with coals, which was set fire to, as well as the Royal Bounty. The crew of the former escaped. At eleven at night Captain

Gamble, with his crew, were set adrift in the boat. They reached the land of Placentia Bay the next morning. After receiving the most hospitable treatment at Lamallin, they were conveyed from thence to Burin, where they also experienced every attention from Mr. Butler and Mr. Harrison, who provided them with a conveyance to St. John's.

" The privateer, we are led to believe, has done a great deal of mischief on the south-west coast, but we hope Captain Cookesley, of the Hazard, who must have been near that part of the coast, will put a stop to his career."

CAPTURE AND RECAPTURE OF THE SYLPH.

SIR HARFORD JONES, the British Ambassador to the Court of Persia, sailed from Portsmouth on the 27th of October, 1807 ; reached Bombay on the 26th of the following April ; arrived at Bushir on the 13th of October, and at Tehran, the present capital of Persia, on the 14th of February, 1809. Two days after the Ambassador had left Bombay, the Sylph, which had on board the Persian Secretary, and some of the presents destined for the Persian monarch, parted company, and nothing was heard of her, until the end of October, when the Nautilus, another vessel belonging to the East India Company, arrived at Bushir. From her, intelligence was obtained of the presence of a number of Joasmee pirates in the Persian gulph, who had attacked the Nautilus, and sustained her fire for five-and-twenty minutes, before they retreated. It turned out, that the Sylph, less fortunate than the Nautilus, had actually been captured by the pirates. The following account of her capture, and recapture, is taken from Mr. MORIER's (Secretary to the Embassy) *Journey through Persia*, &c.

" At the time when the pirates were standing the same course with herself, the Sylph discovered the Nereide bearing down upon her. When the Nereide came close, she hove-to ; but as the commander of the Sylph did not send a boat on board of her, she filled her sails and stood on. When the Nereide had already passed at some distance, the two dows stood towards the Sylph. The Persian Secretary advised the officer of the ship not to permit the dows to approach ; but he would not listen to the suggestion, as he declared they would not touch him. The dows, however, did approach so close, that the Sylph had only time to fire one gun, and to discharge her musketry at them, before they were alongside, and poured aboard her in great and overwhelming numbers. The Persian Secretary, from the concealment to which he had fled, was still able to ascertain, that, as the first act of possession, the Arabs threw water on the ship, to purify it ; they then proceeded to the deliberate murder of the men who were on deck, or discoverable ; that they brought them one by one to the gang-way, and, in the spirit of barbarous fanaticism, cut their throats as sacrifices ; crying out, before the slaughter of each victim, ' Ackbar,' and, when the deed was done, ' *Allah il Allah.*' In the space of an hour they had thus put to death twenty-two persons ; and were proceeding with lights to look for more, when they were astonished by a shot through the' Sylph from the Nereide. On perceiving the disaster of the Sylph, Captain Corbett had immediately hauled up; and though far to the windward, his shot still reached. The Arabs immediately took to their dows, and, elated by the *havock of their success*, (by the success of their havock, we apprehend, it should have been written) made for the Nereide. As soon as Captain Corbett perceived they were bearing down upon him, he ceased firing altogether. The Persian Secretary told us that he saw the dows approach so close to the frigate, that the Arabs were enabled to commence the attack in their usual manner, by throwing stones. Still the Nereide did not fire; till at length, when both dows were fairly alongside, she opened two tremendous broadsides. The Secretary said, he saw one dow disappear totally, and immediately, and the other almost as instantaneously; they went down with the crews crying: 'Allah, Allah, Allah.' Nine men only escaped, who had previously made off in a boat. The Sylph was taken to Muscat, where the Persian Secretary was put on board the Minerva."

CORRESPONDENCE.

MR. EDITOR,

I OBSERVE that you have called the attention of your readers to the subject of the Breakwater in Plymouth Sound ; and considering the magnitude of that work in point of expense, and the essential manner in which it may affect the navy, the public will undoubtedly feel greatly indebted to you for the very marked attention that you have paid to the interests of that branch of the service upon this, as upon so many other occasions.

As the open and fair discussion of works of this nature may be productive of very beneficial, and can scarcely be productive of any evil results, I trust you will afford a place in your publication to the following observations upon the work in question.

Within these few years, a very laudable practice, originally the offspring of individual interest, has been gradually forcing itself into the various departments of the public service. When the execution of a plan has been determined upon, in order to throw upon it whatever lights it may be susceptible of receiving, a general invitation, backed by reward, is held out to all persons to send in plans for the meditated work; and the reward itself is then bestowed on that one among the candidates whose plan is most approved of. No bargain, whether for individuals or for the public, can possibly be more advantageous than this. Genius is stimulated ; merit is rewarded. If the public gains nothing, it loses nothing ; and the advantage, if any, is certain, and may be, and commonly is, a thousand times more than the price paid for it. As a very late instance of the adoption of this mode, it may be sufficient to mention the advertisements that have so recently appeared in the newspapers, offering rewards for plans for penitentiary houses.

Now, if this course be adopted, as it certainly has been, in the instance of works which are neither curious in their nature, fearful as to their result, nor remediless if unattended with success, how much more imperiously is it demanded in the instance of a work which requires for its execution the most eminent scientific knowledge, which may be productive of the most serious mischief, and if not attended with success, be followed by the most disastrous consequences. That this latter is the true character of the work in question, is abundantly shewn by the speech delivered on the subject by Sir Home Popham in his place in the House of Commons.

There publicly warned, and warned also from a variety of private quarters that might be mentioned, what ought to have been the course pursued in order to satisfy the public that the work itself was necessary, and that the mode adopted for carrying it into effect was in every point of view the most advantageous and economical? Ought not all spontaneous information to have been received with avidity, and still more ought not the most effectual measures to have been taken by the usual mode of advertisement, or otherwise, to procure all such as would not otherwise have presented itself? Or, if upon this occasion any reason existed why this mode should not be adopted, and if it was determined in preference to receive only one plan, why should not that plan be submitted to the observation and for the opinion of those who were capable of forming a judgment upon it?

Such, however, with respect to the work in question, has been the mode actually pursued. Confining myself, for the present at least, to so much of the work as belongs immediately to the province of the *Engineer*, and leaving for future observation the other and very distinct part of the work, namely, its probable effect compared with the price paid for it—the Admiralty, avowedly altogether incapable of forming an opinion as to the merits and demerits of whatever plan might be presented to them, apply to an engineer, Mr Rennie (who, undoubtedly, as far as eminence can be truly estimated by extent of employment, is of the very highest eminence in this line of business), and direct him to form a plan for the work in question, which plan having been presented to them, they, utterly ignorant of the subject, decide that it shall be adopted, without any conference or communication whatever with the persons who are paid by the public, on account of their supposed capacity for forming an opinion upon such subjects, I mean various of the members of the Navy Board, and the officers belonging to the Engineer department, or without referring that plan, as they might have done, to other engineers, for their opinion of it!

But admitting that Mr. Rennie is the person of all others upon whose opinion, on this occasion, the public may rely with the most perfect security, still his talents, in this instance, do not appear to have been drawn forth in the manner likely to prove most beneficial to the country, or least unexceptionable to himself. He is forced into the situation (certainly a very unnatural and most painful one), of party and judge in his own cause. Who presents the plan? Mr. Rennie! Who judges of it? Mr. Rennie!! Such is undeniably the fact. The Admiralty, by whose orders the plan is adopted, know nothing of the subject, and they seek no assistance. To reap the full fruit of Mr. Rennie's abilities, and in the most unexceptionable manner, how much preferable would it have been then to have collected the plans of others, to have invited them to sit in judgment over those plans, and to offer written reasons for the preference he might give to one over another: and if, in his own opinion, any plan that he could suggest, would be preferable to those that were presented by others, then to have presented that plan? Whatever advantage there is to be derived from Mr. Rennie's skill would thus have certainly been attained, and without any such objection as that of placing him in the awkward situation above alluded to.

Both the modes that I have just mentioned, of securing for any new project the best consideration, which in the present instance have been so unaccountably departed from, are not only not foreign to the practice of the Admiralty, but they have been followed, and that too in a multitude of instances. To mention only two, and those very recent ones. One of the members of the late, and also of the present Admiralty Board, had become so much enamoured with the model of one of the Danish ships captured in the famous expedition to Copenhagen, as to be very anxious that the plan upon which she had been built should be adopted in our navy; a number of ships were accordingly about to be ordered to be constructed after her model; but a conference on the subject happened to be necessary with the professional members of the Navy Board, and the result was, the utter rejection of the plan, to the very great benefit, as I am credibly informed, of the service. The other instance is still more recent: a plan was proposed by the builder of one of the dock-yards. Mr. Seppings, for placing the cieling of ships diagonally, instead of horizontally; two conferences, consisting each time of very numerous assemblages of persons, and of almost as numerous pursuits and occupations, were held upon the subject, and the result was, the partial adoption of that plan.

But the conduct of the late Admiralty appears to be still more irreconcilable with reason than that of merely not casting about for lights upon this subject; they not only do not invite observation, but, as was observed by Mr. Herbert (of Kerry), in the course of the debate in the House of Commons on this subject, they studiously reject information that is thrust at them, and that too for the very extraordinary reason, that it comes from a public officer, the civil architect and engineer, entrusted, it is admitted, with the execution of other similar and highly important works, but within whose particular department the cognizance of this work, it was said, by the then first lord of the Admiralty, in the course of the debate above alluded to, did not fall. For the purpose of the argument, it may be admitted that the work in question does not belong to the duty of that officer, even that he is expressly precluded by his official instructions from interfering in it, yet is it possible that it should be said that, when proposals are made by him relating to the subject under consideration, that any such extravagant punctilio as that of the work not belonging to his department, should stand in the way of their receiving that consideration to which they were entitled, if not on account of their merit, at least on account of their having come from a person that the public are bound to consider either as unfit for his situation, or, from his continuing to hold that situation, as competent to form an opinion upon the work in question? In one of the two papers presented by that officer, and which were, on the motion of the then first lord of the Admiralty, at the instigation of Mr. Whitbread, printed for the use of the House of Commons, I observe a proposal is made for employing a *floating* Breakwater, and it is mentioned that that plan has been practised, and with very complete success. When is not mentioned; but the place alluded to I believe to be Revel; at least what I am certain of is, that a floating Breakwater is there used, and is found to answer the purpose very perfectly. Now, when it is understood that this floating Breakwater may be formed at a comparatively trifling expense, that if it fails no evil whatever results from it, not even the loss of the timber, for that may afterwards be applied to other uses, does it not strike every man that inquiries ought to have been made from every person, and multitudes there must necessarily be, who could give any information respecting the Revel Breakwater? Or ought not Mr. Rennie, at least, to have been required to make a written report upon that plan, in order that the public might be satisfied either that that plan was impracticable, or, at least, that the one proposed actually to be carried into execution, was so far preferable as to warrant the incurring the great additional expense by which it is to be accomplished?

Luckily, however, the time for all these inquiries, and any others that may suggest themselves, is not yet gone by. The public have still a chance of being relieved, if consistent with the accomplishment of the object in view, from a portion of the vast load of expense, not less, certainly, and probably much more, than 1,500,000*l*. with which they are threatened; or at least, of being satisfied by fair and open discussion (the advantage of which, in his pamphlet on the proposed new Naval Arsenal, was most strenuously inculcated by the late Lord Melville) that the plan proposed is, in every point of view, the most eligible, and the mode of executing it the most economical and most expeditious, and least likely to be attended with any collateral inconveniences. If this were done, they would no doubt submit cheerfully to the additional burthen, that thus comes to be imposed upon them; but, till then, whatever is demanded on this account cannot be expected to be yielded, but with dissatisfaction.

I am, &c. &c.   D.

MR. EDITOR,

LOOKING over some old letters the other day, I found the following account of a gallant action, sustained by the merchant brig Charles, Captain Cromarty, against the French privateer schooner le Vengeance, ff the south side of Jamaica, in the year 1807; which, as it reflects great credit on the master and others who assisted in maintaining a contest for many hours against a superior force, I think you will be of opinion with me, that it deserves a place in your NAVAL CHRONICLE. If so, it is much at your service. C. C.

" I will now relate to you the reason why my last letter was dated from the prison of Trinadad de Cuba, and as I did not mention to your brother in what manner I became a captive, you shall here have the whole account, and as I know you will be gratified, I will not make any apology for being so particular in my detail. Therefore, to commence—I sailed on the 20th May from Port Royal, in a small brig called the Charles, commanded by Mr. Flat Cromarty, a Scotchman, who was good enough to give me a passage. We weighed early in the morning, and by 9 o'clock we had passed the sandy keys that form the south channel into this harbour; the land wind continued to favour us all the forenoon, and about 2 P.M. we got the *Doctor*, or regular sea breeze, which enabled us to double Portland Point. During the night the wind was light and variable, so we did not make much progress; but at daylight found ourselves a little to the westward of Pedro Bluff, becalmed, having lost the air that aided us the preceding hours. At 9 o'clock a suspicious sail was seen to the southward; on observing her through a glass, we were all of opinion that she was one of our cruisers, but a short time after convinced us she was an enemy's vessel, as we plainly descried the tri-coloured flag, and her sweeps, which they were using with every apparent exertion. At twenty minutes after eleven A.M. she was nearly within gun-shot, when she fired her long Tom,* at the same moment hoisting French and Spanish colours. We had at this time all sail set, with our head in shore, but from the lightness of the wind, the brig had not steerage way, which was a very great disadvantage to us, as the privateer, by using her sweeps, might take any position she pleased, while we lay a mere log. Captain Cromarty had previously mentioned his determination to fight the brig as long as he had powder and shot; every one else appeared, indeed, willing to give his aid; but from the great disparity of men, and the apparent worthlessness of the brig's crew, I scarcely entertained a doubt within my own mind, but that she would be captured. However, I was happy to find the men behave so much better than from their appearance I had any occasion to expect, and that the Frenchmen did not take her without a great deal of hard fighting. The Charles's crew consisted of four American black men, four new negroes, and two small English boys; besides which were the master, mate, a young midshipman of the navy, passenger, and myself; in toto—fourteen.—With this motley band we resolved to resist monsieur, who having got within half-pistol shot on our larboard quarter, laid in his sweeps, and commenced action warmly, which was maintained mutually without intermission until half-past two P.M. when our opponent ceased firing, and pulled round with his sweeps, apparently with an intention to be off. At

---

* A term generally used by sailors to distinguish the gun that is placed in the bow of any ship for bringing vessels to.

this movement of his we gave three cheers, and peppered him warmly with canister; but, after a pause, we plainly perceived it to be only a manœuvre, and that his intention was, to board us; having hauled off merely to prepare his small-arm, and cutlass-men. At this interval our helm was put a-lee, with an endeavour to stay the brig, that we might continue to annoy our enemy as much as possible to our advantage, and save the chance of being raked, as he was right a-stern; but our running, and most part of the standing, rigging, was cut, and the wind so light that she would not come sufficiently round to allow the starboard broadside to bear, which the Frenchmen observing, took advantage of, and raked us fore and aft to our hearts content; returning the complement we had but just paid them; after which, they stood for our starboard quarter, with the bloody* flag flying, huzzaing, and firing their long gun, swivels, musketoons, and musketry; we were not intimidated by the ensign of death, but continued to play our guns with great effect, until every cartridge, shot, and wad was expended; and then, having recourse to our muskets (only four in number) they received every grain of powder, and every ball we had to give them; and we should have been proud to have received them at the point of the sword, had there been any for our further defence, but unfortunately there was not one on board. At twenty minutes past four P.M. and after a struggle of five hours, the hottest I ever experienced, necessity alone compelled the British ensign to be hauled down; but I trust you and all our countrymen will do us the justice to believe, that on this occasion the flag was defended as it should be, and that it was not from neglect or want of resistance that it was struck. To my great surprise, after the colour was down, they continued to amuse themselves by firing their large gun and small arms at us, for twenty or thirty minutes; and the dastardly wretches would not board us until every soul went off deck, and even then, they were so alarmed that the muzzles of their blunderbusses and points of their swords were presented to our view, first down hatchways. They obliged us to pull ourselves on board the privateer, during which they fired several shot at the boat, but happily without injuring any of us. Such inhuman and wanton barbarity needs no comment, when we reflect that the performers were men habituated to scenes of rapine, and acts of violence and brutality, therefore callous to all sense of feeling, and possessing neither honour nor humanity. The privateer proved to be the Vengeance,† called by the Spaniards Juliana, mounting four long six-pounders, one long brass eighteen-pounder on a sweep in midships, with swivels, musketoons, and sixty muskets, with a complement of ninety-five men, who were all actually on board, and commanded by an Italian, upwards of eighty years old. They had several men killed and wounded, the number they would not inform us of. It is somewhat singular, that not a man on board the Charles was injured by shot, although

---

* A plain red jack, indicative of no quarter being given, and used by pirates, and French privateers.

† This privateer was afterwards taken by two of H. M. schooners, Gracieuse and Gipsy, off Cape Antonio, after an action of two hours.

there were upwards of twenty round through the hull, quantities of grape, and innumerable musket and musketoon balls in the masts and bulwarks. The Charles was originally a Baltimore schooner, of 90 tons, condemned at Kingston as a prize to one of H. M. ships, and purchased by Sir Simon Clark, Bart. for the purpose of carrying his sugars from the north side to Kingston. She mounted at the time of capture six six-pounder carronades.

Charles, brig—90 tons, 6 six-pounder carronades, 14 men and boys.

Vengeance, schooner—112 tons, 4 long sixes, 1 brass eighteen-pounder, 6 swivels, &c. 95 men.

MR. EDITOR, *September 23, 1812.*

I YESTERDAY went to Deptford, to witness the launch of a new man of war, of 74 guns, called the Devonshire. As it is understood to be the intention of the Admiralty occasionally to nominate for the future his Majesty's ships after the counties and principal towns in England, permit me to suggest, through you, the necessity of avoiding an error into which the builders and painters (perhaps without authority) have fallen on this occasion. I conceive that one object in thus calling ships after towns and counties may be, to induce young seamen to volunteer into that ship which derives its name from the place where such persons reside, or were born. This object, however, is completely done away, when we see on the shield at the head of the ship, as in the instance in question, not the distinguishing ensigns of the *county*, but, forsooth, the heraldic bearings of the *Duke* of Devonshire. However high and exalted the birth of that nobleman may be, assuredly the name has no particular claim on, the gratitude of the naval part of the community; and I am not aware of any interest that can be served, or that any beneficial consequence can result, from thus giving a celebrity of this nature to an individual unconnected with the navy, when there are so many demands on the nation's gratitude in favour of our early, as well as our later navigators.

Perhaps it may be fortunate, that Jack's education seldom enables him to understand latin; otherwise the punning motto * of the Cavendish family, which is conspicuously painted on the shield, might impress him with a principle, which, if generally adhered to by our seamen, would soon reduce our navy to the condition of the Toulon *adventurous* squadron, *whose only safety consists in its avoidance of danger.*

I am, Sir, your's obediently,

W.

MR. EDITOR, *Winchester, 22d September,* 1812.

IN reading the second edition of an account of Marocco, &c. by James Grey Jackson, I perceive that the author professes to be in possession of an infallible remedy for the ophthalmic disease, which so generally attacks

---

* "*Cavendo tutus!*"—Secure by caution.

our seamen in the Mediterranean, called *Nyctalopia*.* " It comes on at dusk, with a defect of vision, the patient being deprived of his sight, so that he cannot see distinctly, even with the assistance of candles." This irksome disease, Mr. Jackson assures us, is cured in 12 hours, by one application of the remedy, which he voluntarily offers to impart to the physician on the Mediterranean station.

It is, therefore, to be hoped, that his Majesty's ministers will avail themselves of the opportunity thus offered, of discovering a remedy of so much national importance, whereby the services of so many hundred sailors will be immediately restored to the public service.

I am, Sir, &c. &c.
NAUTICUS.

MR. EDITOR,   *October 2d*, 1812.

IT is with no small degree of satisfaction, I have observed, that the present First Lord of the Admiralty, who appears disposed to promote the interest and comfort of the officers and seamen of the navy, has already increased the establishment of several of the gun-brigs, and given the command of them to commanders in the navy, with lieutenants under them. Having on a former occasion hazarded an opinion, through the medium of your work, that such a plan was likely to be advantageous, I feel much gratified at seeing it adopted.

Your Correspondent, OCEANUS,† improving on my suggestion for the employment of officers afloat, has most satisfactorily pointed out the propriety of appointing four instead of three lieutenants, to frigates, and I think his remarks so judicious and well timed, that I have not a doubt but that they will come under the eye, and receive the attention of Lord Melville. He has, however, adverted only to a certain description of ships, *viz*. frigates. I am of opinion, that the number of lieutenants might be increased, through ships of every class, and would propose that three decked ships, without flags, should have at least eight lieutenants; 74's, seven; 46's, six; 44's to 32's, four; 32's to 28's, three; sloops, two. By such an arrangement, I conceive, the duty would be more easily, and more comfortably carried on, and a great number of useful officers would be retained in full pay, who would otherwise remain inactive on shore: I believe it is a fact not generally known, that the first lieutenant and the junior of each ship, have not only great responsibility, but a continued series of duties, whether at sea or in harbour, which not being common to the others, becomes very arduous, and often, very irksome to them. By being occasionally divided with the others, it might deprive the first lieutenant of some part of his consequence, which might not be a popular measure; but, adding another officer, and making the duties of the junior lieutenant common to the *two* juniors in rank, would, I apprehend, be an improvement. OCEANUS has very ably shewn

---

* See Jackson's account of Marocco, second edition, page 189.

† See page 107.

the advantages, and necessity of relieving the masters of the navy from the duty of lieutenants, and therefore I will not recur to that part of the subject.

Before I conclude, however, I would beg leave to add my tribute of applause to the conduct of the present First Lord of the Admiralty, for his impartial conduct, in promoting officers of long standing, and those who signalize themselves. It is of great consequence to ensure to naval officers *the certainty* of promotion, if they do their duty; and from the plan now pursued, of promoting so many commanders serving afloat, and first lieutenants of line-of-battle ships, annually, this object may be said to be in a great measure effected. Another part of his conduct I have remarked with high admiration : *viz.* the appointment of post captains, of successful enterprise and bravery, *to new ships*. I need only particularize Captains Hoste, Gordon, Hornby, and the late Captain Whitby; all of whom have had new frigates. Such discrimination must ensure approbation and popularity, from the whole British navy, as it does from the feeble pen of

A FRIEND TO NAVAL MERIT.

P.S. I am convinced that many naval officers might contribute much to the good of the service, by giving useful hints, through your CHRONICLE, founded on experience.

MR. EDITOR, *Port Mahon, Minorca, August* 12, 1812.

THE late brilliant addition to the dress of naval lieutenants, and the neglected state of a class of officers of which I am a member, induce me to request that you will insert the following ideas on the situation of masters in the royal navy.

The respect, and encouragement, to this class of officers, have been gradually declining since the days of Howe and Jervis, and other worthies of the old school, whose names will ever remain sacred to the lovers of their country.—The present masters in the navy may be divided into three classes—first, men who, like the illustrious Cook, have, by their own assiduity and perseverance, acquired a competent share of nautical knowledge, to enable them to discharge their duty with comfort to themselves, and honour to their country. Second, men of reduced families, who, previously to their going to sea, have received a liberal education, and after passing the gradations of mate and master, in the merchant service, have been reduced to comparative poverty, by captures, failures of owners, and other losses incident to the mercantile life. The third and last class are; men, who have served (some double, and others treble) the appointed time, to qualify them for lieutenants in the royal navy; and who, from the exhausted state of the enemy's navy and commerce, added to the want of noble or parliamentary interest, despaired of their services being repaid with a commission; and finding themselves on the summit, or perhaps descending the hill of life, are informed by approaching age, that it is high time to look for some situation that may entitle them to a few shillings half-pay; when nature shall assume her authority over the worn out public servant. Those men, after spending the flower of their youth in the navy, are unacquainted with any other profession; consequently, the only alternative to introduce them to the long sought for wardroom mess and rank is to become a master.

Now, Sir, I appeal to the feeling of your readers, whether such men are not worthy of some little attention from the country; but particularly from the present First Lord of the Admiralty, whose noble father's memory will never be erased from the breasts of British seamen. Should my letter meet the eye of the Noble Lord, before a pause of duty shall enable his Lordship to look into the situation, and security of masters; I trust that it will not be considered presumptive in me to propose an addition to their pay, as well as the privilege of wearing a badge of distinction, similar to that worn by lieutenants; as the equivalent duty of those officers renders it indispensably necessary, as well as political. Such encouragement, I am certain, would be attended with the greatest advantage; namely, men of the first information and experience would be obtained, to navigate our ships; men who, in consequence of the little encouragement to masters, whose summit of promotion is a first rate (dock-yards and store-ships wholly out of the question) lie by, as mates in Kings', or merchants' ships, hoping that some fortunate day may bring a commission for the former, or the command of a ship for the latter.

The numerous applications for masters can be affirmed at the Navy Office, as well as the numbers of young men acting in the capacity of masters whose intentions are, to make a convenience of the service, until the expiration of the established time to qualify them for lieutenants; by these means preventing the encouragement which necessity might urge; as well as holding the situations out of the reach of *passed* masters, numbers of whom, being prevented from going to England to pass for a higher rate, are compelled to remain in small vessels, while those interlopers retain the situation on board some of the finest line-of-battle ships and frigates on this station.

Poor encouragement, indeed, for men who have no other prospect, or income, than that accruing from their situation as masters!

In the hope that these remarks may experience the necessary attention,

I am, Sir, &c.

C. Y. A Master.

PRESERVATION OF SHIPWRECKED MARINERS.

LIEUTENANT BELL.

THE pressure of more temporary matter, prevented the fulfilment of our promise, given at page 311 of the preceding Volume. We now, however, submit the following particulars of Lieutenant Bell's plan, for the preservation of lives, in cases of shipwreck, as they appear in the XXVth Volume of the *Transactions of the Society of Arts*, page 136 :—

" The several trials made before a Committee of the Society at Woolwich, on the 29th of August, 1791, of throwing a line on shore on this principle, were as follow :

" From a boat moored about 250 yards from shore, the shell was thrown 150 yards on shore, with the rope attached to it ; the shell was of cast iron, filled with lead, it weighed 75 pounds, its diameter 8 inches ; the rope in the trial was a deep sea line, of which 160 yards weighed 18lbs. the angle of the mortar from whence the shell was fired, was 45 degrees. By means of the line, Mr. Bell and another man worked themselves on shore upon his raft of casks ; there were many kinks in the rope, which were with ease cleared by Mr. Bell, in which he was assisted by his snatch-blocks.

" The second trial was repeated in a similar manner, and with equal success, the shell falling within a few yards of the former place, the gale of wind was brisk, and the water rough. The direction of the shell was nearly from north to south, and the wind blew nearly north-west.

" In the third trial, the mortar was elevated to 70 degrees ; the rope attached to the shell, was an inch and a half tarred rope, of which every 50 yards weighed 14 pounds and a half ; the shell, of the kind above-mentioned, fell 160 yards from the mortar, and buried itself about two-thirds in the ground ; the line or rope run out was about 200 yards, and it required the force of three men to draw the shell out of the ground at that distance.

" The grommet, in all these trials, was of white three-inch rope ; and in all the above trials by means of the line, two men worked themselves on shore upon the raft ; each charge of powder was 15 ounces.

" A fourth experiment was made by firing, from the same mortar, a grapnel in a wooden case ; it did not retain its hold in the ground so well as the shell ; but amongst the crevices of the rocks, or where the vessel is near shore, will be useful.

" A grapnel of this kind may be fired from a common cannon with an endless rope, running in a pulley or small block fixed thereto, by which a raft may be successively drawn to and from the vessel, either by the persons in the vessel, or those on shore.

" *Observations made by Lieutenant Bell, upon throwing a line on shore in case of a Ship being stranded.*

" 1st. From the proposed construction of the piece of ordnance, intended to throw the shot and line on shore, I suppose it will be between five and six hundred weight.

" The chamber is to contain one pound of powder, and the bore to admit a leaden ball of sixty pounds or upwards ; the length of range, or distance, will depend upon the size of the line made use of ; I suppose it will carry a deep sea-line between three and four hundred yards distance.

" 2d. All ships that have iron ballast, may use this piece as a part of it, and then there would be only the trifling difference of casting so much of the ballast into the form of the piece; the leaden balls may likewise be used as ballast.

" 3d. I am of opinion there are various ways, on board of a ship, that the mortar may be placed in a proper position for firing, without a carriage expressly made for it; it may be placed upon a coil of rope, or its trunnions rested upon coins, or any thing else, whereby the muzzle can be raised so high that the groove upon the trunnion appears vertical, as the piece in that position would be elevated nearly 45 degrees.

" 4th. As I imagine all ships carry deep sea-lines, on that account I made use of it in the experiments at Woolwich, but if it should be thought too short for the distance, any other light line may be added to the length of it.

" 5th. Supposing a ship's owner to purchase such a piece of ordnance with the leaden balls, and a block carriage; I do not think the whole would amount to more than ten or eleven pounds expense.

" 6th. Where a ship is driving or unmanageable near the shore, it would be proper to have the piece loaded, the line reeled upon handspikes or poles, and laid upon the deck ready for firing at any time it might be judged necessary. The hand-spikes or poles, the line is reeled upon, preserve it in an horizontal form; and they are not to be drawn out until the instant of firing: in this manner the line will deliver itself freely.

" The five water-casks should also be prepared in readiness by lashing them together, and a seaman's chest fixed upon the top of them, having part of its ends or sides cut out in order to let out such water as may be thrown into it by the surf. I dare undertake to land with such a float upon a lee shore any where upon the coast, when it might be deemed unsafe for a boat to make good its landing.

" 7th. *There is every reason to conclude, that this contrivance would be very useful at all ports of difficult access, both at home and abroad; where ships are liable to strike ground before they enter the harbour, as Shields Bar, and other similar situations, when a line might be thrown over the ship, which might probably be the means of saving both lives and property; and moreover, if a ship was driven on shore near such a place, the apparatus might easily be removed to afford assistance;* and the whole performance is so exceedingly simple, that any person once seeing it done, would not want any farther instructions."

We have remarked (Vol. XXVII. p. 310) that the main points of difference between Lieutenant Bell's and Captain Manby's plans are :—that, " according to the former, the ball is projected from the ship, to the shore; by the latter, from the shore to the ship; and that, instead of a *common* shot, used by Lieutenant Bell, Captain Manby has adopted a *barbed* shot." In the passage, however, of Lieutenant Bell's observations, which we have distinguished by the italic character. it appears that Lieutenant Bell actually suggested the mode, in certain cases, of projecting the ball *from the shore to the ship*. Nor does the invention of the *barbed* shot seem entirely to have originated with Captain Manby; for, in the engraving, illustrative of Lieutenant Bell's method of throwing a rope on shore, from a stranded vessel, given in the XXVth Volume of the *Transactions of the Society of Arts*, are two figures; one, of *an iron pin*, to be fired from a common cannon, when people happen to be on the beach, to give immediate assistance; the other, of *a grapnel*, also to be fired from a common cannon.

That Captain Manby has improved upon the ideas of Lieutenant Bell, is not denied; but, that his claims to originality of invention are extremely slight, is sufficiently evident by the extracts which we have made from the *Transactions of the Society of Arts*. By referring to the First Volume of the NAVAL CHRONICLE, page 417, it will also be seen, that, as far back as the 19th of March, 1799, the Committee of the Royal Humane Society allotted a prize to a Mr. L. Gramshaw, for his project of conveying a line *by a bow* to the shore; earnestly recommending to him, to consider of the most powerful and practicable projectile force for effecting that desirable purpose.

With respect to Lieutenant Bell, we shall only add, that we should have felt less anxiety respecting the justice which ought to be done to his invention, if death had not prevented him from urging the originality of his claims himself.

CAPTAIN MANBY.

The subjoined account of Captain Manby's late experiments, is copied from the *Times* newspaper, of Monday, May 4, 1812.

" On Saturday considerable numbers were attracted to Hyde Park by Captain Manby's experiments for saving the lives of shipwrecked persons. A little after 12 the Duke of York arrived, and the experiments commenced. The apparatus was placed on the south side of the Serpentine river, on the level bank near the new watercourse; a few of the Guards were stationed round it, to keep off the multitude; and the circle was filled with some of our principal chemists and people of distinction. The ropes attached to the balls were coiled in different forms on the grass. The first experiment was, we presume, merely to shew the range of the mortar, which threw a shell across the river, and to a considerable distance on the rising ground to the north. A shot was then thrown with the rope attached to it, which fell with great precision at the water's edge on the opposite side. The shell was next thrown in the direction of a tree, which was to represent the masts and rigging of a ship in distress. The shell fell entirely over the tree, and left the rope hanging, as was intended, among the branches. The neatness and obvious utility of this experiment excited great admiration. A young person, equipped in the life preserver, then walked into the water, remained perfectly at his ease at a considerable distance from the side, blew a post-horn, moved his arms in all directions with complete facility, and concluded by swimming across in the direction of the buoy which was fixed as the centre of operation. These experiments were exhibited to the whole extent of Captain Manby's inventions. The light-ball, which on occasion of shipwrecks at night is used to point out the vessel to the people on shore, was thrown up to a considerable height, burst at its highest elevation, and poured down a shower of stars, which, in the darkness of a tempestuous night, must have thrown powerful illumination upon its object. The process of discharging ordnance without the application of fire, is one of Captain Manby's inventions, and one which will probably be of signal importance to the service; but the conception of the plan for preserving human life, and that perhaps the most interesting and valuable species of human life, deserves a higher praise than our's. As no country has a finer and more useful race of men exposed to the perils of the sea; there is perhaps no shore on which, from the peculiar nature of its difficulties, the invention can be applied with more entire success. The idea of forming a communication with the vessel when no boat could venture to sea, was of itself honourable to the person who conceived it; but the subsequent arrangements,—the contrivances at once delicate and durable, and the simplicity which now makes the whole apparatus at once within the compass of almost any purse, and the management of almost any hand, finish and complete the merit of the discovery. There is not a shore of Europe on which it may not be established; and we must hope, that no exertion of wise and active humanity will be wanting to its establishment on every perilous district of our own." *

STATE PAPERS.

DISSOLUTION OF PARLIAMENT.

By his Royal Highness the Prince of Wales, Regent of the United Kingdom of Great Britain and Ireland, in the name and on the behalf of his Majesty.

A PROCLAMATION,

For Dissolving this present Parliament, and Declaring the calling of another.

GEORGE, P. R.

WHEREAS we, acting in the name and on the behalf of his Majesty, think fit, by and with the advice of his Majesty's Privy Council, to dissolve this present Parliament, which stands prorogued to Friday, the 2d day of October next; we do therefore, acting as aforesaid, publish this Proclamation, and do hereby dissolve the said Parliament accordingly; and the Lords Spiritual and Temporal, and the Knights, Citizens, and Burgesses, and the Commissioners for Shires and Burghs, of the House of Commons, are discharged from their meeting and attendance on the said

---

* For the particulars of Captain Manby's plan, the reader is referred to the XXIIId Volume of the NAVAL CHRONICLE, page 188.

Friday, the second day of October next: and we being desirous and resolved, as soon as may be, to meet his Majesty's people, and to have their advice in Parliament, do hereby make known to all his Majesty's loving subjects our will and pleasure to call a new Parliament; and do hereby further declare, in the name and on the behalf of his Majesty, that with the advice of his Majesty's Privy Council, We have this day given order, that the Chancellor of that part of the United Kingdom called Great Britain, and the Chancellor of Ireland, do respectively forthwith issue out writs, in due form and according to law, for calling a new Parliament: And we do hereby also, in the name and on the behalf of his Majesty, by this Proclamation under the Great Seal of the United Kingdom, require writs forthwith to be issued accordingly by the said Chancellors respectively, for causing the Lords Spiritual and Temporal and Commons who are to serve in the said Parliament, to be duly returned to, and give their attendance in, the said Parliament; which writs are to be returnable on Tuesday the twenty-fourth day of November next.

Given at the Court at Carlton-house, the twenty-ninth day of September, one thousand eight hundred and twelve, and in the fifty-second year of his Majesty's reign.

GOD SAVE THE KING.

TREATY OF PEACE

Between his Majesty the King of Sweden, and his Majesty the King of the United Kingdom of Great Britain and Ireland.

In the name of the Most Holy and Indivisible Trinity.

His Majesty the King of Sweden, and his Majesty the King of the United Kingdom of Great Britain and Ireland, being equally animated with the desire of re-establishing the ancient relations of friendship and good intercourse between the two Crowns, and their respective States, have appointed to that effect, namely, his Majesty the King of Sweden, the Sieur Laurent, Baron D'Engerstrom, &c. and the Sieur Gustavus, Baron De Wetterstedt, &c.; and the Prince Regent, in the name and on the behalf of his Majesty the King of the United Kingdom of Great Britain and Ireland, Edward Thornton, Esq. which Plenipotentiaries, after exchanging their full powers, drawn up in full and due form, have agreed upon the following articles:—

Art. I. There shall be between their Majesties the King of Sweden and the King of the United Kingdom of Great Britain and Ireland, their heirs and successors, and between their subjects, kingdoms, and states respectively, a firm, true, and inviolable Peace, and a sincere and perfect union and friendship; so that from this moment, every subject of misunderstanding that may have subsisted between them shall be regarded as entirely ceased and destroyed.

II. The relations of friendship and commerce between the two countries shall be re-established on the footing whereon they stood on the first day of January, 1791; and all Treaties and Conventions subsisting between the two States at that epoch shall be regarded as renewed and confirmed, and are, accordingly, by the present Treaty, renewed and confirmed.

III. If, in resentment of the present pacification, and the re-establishment of the good intercourse between the two countries, any power whatsoever make war upon Sweden, his Majesty the King of the United Kingdom of Great Britain and Ireland engages to take measures, in concert with his Majesty the King of Sweden, for the security and independence of his states.

IV. The present treaty shall be ratified by the two contracting parties, and the ratifications exchanged within six weeks, or sooner, if possible.

In faith whereof, we, the undersigned, in virtue of our full powers, have signed the present treaty, and thereto affixed our seals.

Done at Orebro, on the 18th of July, 1812.

   (Signed) Baron D'ENGERSTROM,
         Baron DE WETTERSTEDT,
         EDWARD THORNTON.

[Here follow the ratifications, signed by the Prince Regent on the 4th of August, and by his Swedish Majesty on the 17th of August.]

UPPER CANADA.—Proclamation.

THE unprovoked declaration of war by the United States of America, against the United Kingdom of Great Britain and Ireland, and its dependencies, has been followed by the actual invasion of this province in a remote frontier of the western districts, by a detachment of the United States. The officer commanding that detachment has thought proper to invite his Majesty's subjects, not merely to a quiet and unresisting submission, but insults them with a call to seek voluntarily the protection of his government.

Without condescending to repeat the illiberal epithets, bestowed in this appeal of the American commander to the people of Upper Canada, on the administration of his Majesty, every inhabitant of the province is desired to seek the confutation of such indecent slander in the review of his own particular circumstances. Where is the Canadian subject, who can truly affirm to himself that he has been injured by the government in his person, his property, or his liberty? Where is to be found, in any part of the world, a growth so rapid in prosperity and wealth as this colony exhibits? Settled not thirty years by a band of veterans, exiled from their former possessions on account of their loyalty, not a descendant of these brave people is to be found, who, under the fostering liberality of their Sovereign, has not acquired a property and means of enjoyment, superior to what were possessed by their ancestors. This unequalled prosperity would not have been attained by the utmost liberality of the government, or the persevering industry of the people, had not the maritime power of the mother country secured to its colonies a safe access to every market where the produce of their labour was in request. The unavoidable and immediate consequence of a separation from Great Britain, must be the loss of this inestimable advantage,—and what is offered to you in exchange? To become a territory of the United States, and share with them that exclusion from the ocean which the policy of their government enforces; you are not even flattered with a participation of their boasted independence; and it is but too obvious, that once exchanged from the powerful protection of the United Kingdom, you must be re-annexed to the dominion of France, from which the provinces of Canada were wrested by the arms of Great Britain at a vast expense of blood and treasure, from no other motive than to relieve her ungrateful children from the oppression of a cruel neighbour; this restitution of Canada to the empire of France, was the stipulated reward for the aid afforded to the revolted colonies, now the United States; the debt is still due, and there can be no doubt but the pledge has been renewed as a consideration for commercial advantages, or rather for an expected relaxation in the tyranny of France over the commercial world. Are you prepared, inhabitants of Canada, to become willing subjects, or rather slaves, to the despot who rules the nations of Europe with a rod of iron? If not, arise in a body, exert your energies, co-operate cordially with the King's regular forces, to repel the invader, and do not give cause to your children, when groaning under the oppression of a foreign master, to reproach you with having too easily parted with the richest inheritance of this earth—a participation in the name, character, and freedom of Britain. The same spirit of justice which will make every reasonable allowance for the unsuccessful efforts of zeal and loyalty, will not fail to punish the defalcation of principle. Every Canadian freeholder is by deliberate choice bound, by the most solemn oaths, to defend the Monarchy as well as his own property; to shrink from that engagement is a treason not to be forgiven. Let no man suppose, that if in this unexpected struggle, his Majesty's arms should be compelled to yield to an overwhelming force, that the province will be eventually abandoned; the endeared relation of its first settlers, the intrinsic value of its commerce, and the pretensions of its powerful rival to re-possess the Canadas, are pledges that no peace will be established between the United States and Great Britain and Ireland, of which the restoration of these provinces does not make the most prominent condition.

Be not dismayed at the unjustifiable threat of the commander of the enemy's forces to refuse quarter, should an Indian appear in the ranks. The brave bands of natives which inhabit this colony, were, like his Majesty's subjects, punished for their zeal and fidelity, by the loss of their possessions in the late colonies, and rewarded by his Majesty with lands of superior value in this province.

The faith of the British Government has never yet been violated; they feel that the sod they inherit, is to them and their posterity protected from the base arts so frequently devised to over-reach their simplicity. By what new principle are they to be prohibited from defending their property? If their warfare, from being different to that of the white people, is more terrific to the enemy, let him retrace his steps—they seek him not, and cannot expect to find women and childr n in an invading army; but they are men, and have equal rights with all other men to defend themselves and their property when invaded,—more especially when they find in the enemy's camp a ferocious and mortal foe, using the same warfare which the American commander affects to reprobate.

This inconsistent and unjustifiable threat of refusing quarter, for such a cause as being found in arms with a brother sufferer, in defence of invaded rights, must be exercised with the certain assurance of retaliation, not only in the limited operations of war on this part of the King's dominions, but on every quarter of the globe, for the national character of Britain is not less distinguished for humanity than retributive justice, which will consider the execution of this threat as deliberate murder, for which every subject of the offending power shall make expiation.

ISAAC BROCK, Major-General and President.
Head Quarters, Fort George, July 22, 1812.

By order of his Honour the President,

J. B. GLEGG, Captain.

God save the King.

At the Court at Carlton House, the 29th of September, 1812.

PRESENT,

His Royal Highness the Prince Regent in Council.

WHEREAS by an Act passed in the fifty-second year of his Majesty, intituled, " An Act to repeal so much of an Act of the forty-third of his present Majesty, as permits the importation of goods and commodities from Turkey, Egypt, or the Levant Seas, in foreign ships ; " it is enacted, that the said Act of the forty-third of his present Majesty shall, from and after the first day of November one thousand eight hundred and twelve, be repealed, and such goods and commodities as were thereby allowed to be imported, shall not, after the first day of November aforesaid, be imported into any part of the United Kingdom in any other than British-built ships or vessels, owned, navigated, and registered according to law ; provided nevertheless, that it shall be lawful for his Majesty, by his order in council, to permit during the present hostilities, and until six months after the ratification of a definitive treaty of peace, any goods or commodities heretofore usually imported from Turkey or Egypt, or from any place within the dominions of the Grand Seignor, within the Levant Seas, to be imported in any ship or vessel whatever, navigated with foreign seamen.

And whereas it is found that certain neutral ships or vessels, which had proceeded under the provisions of the before-mentioned Acts, for the purpose of importing goods and commodities, as permitted by the said Acts, into the ports of the United Kingdom, will not be able to arrive in the said ports, previous to the first day of November next :

His Royal Highness the Prince Regent, in the name and on the behalf of his Majesty, is pleased, by and with the advice of his Majesty's Privy Council, to order, and it is hereby ordered, that the goods and commodities aforesaid, permitted to be imported by the aforesaid Acts, shall be permitted and are hereby permitted to be imported in neutral vessels, into any port or ports of the United Kingdom, until the first day of January next; subject to all duties of Customs and Excise, and to all rules and regulations and conditions, and to all penalties and forfeitures, as prescribed by the aforesaid Act passed in the fifty-second year of his present Majesty.

And the Right Honourable the Lords Commissioners of his Majesty's Treasury, his Majesty's principal Secretaries of State, the Lords Commissioners of the Admiralty, and the Judge of the High Court of Admiralty, and the Judges of the Courts of Vice-Admiralty, are to take the necessary measures herein as to them shall respectively appertain.

JAMES BULLER.

At the Court at Carlton House, the 13th of October, 1812,

PRESENT,

His Royal Highness the Prince Regent in Council.

WHEREAS, in consequence of information having been received of a declaration of war by the government of the United States of America against his Majesty, and of the issue of letters of marque and reprisal by the said government against his Majesty and his subjects, an order in council, bearing date the thirty-first of July last, was issued, directing that American ships and goods should be brought in and detained till further orders; and whereas his Royal Highness the Prince Regent, acting in the name and on the behalf of his Majesty, forbore at that time to direct letters of marque and reprisal to be issued against the ships, goods, and citizens of the said United States of America, under the expectation that the said government would, upon the notification of the order in council of the twenty-third of June last, forthwith recall and annul the said declaration of war against his Majesty, and also annul the said letters of marque and reprisal:

And whereas the said government of the United States of America, upon due notification to them of the said order in council of the twenty-third of June last, did not think fit to recall the said declaration of war and letters of marque and reprisal, but have proceeded to condemn and persisted in condemning the ships and property of his Majesty's subjects as prize of war, and have refused to ratify a suspension of arms agreed upon between Lieutenant-general Sir George Prevost, his Majesty's Governor-general of Canada, and General Dearborn, commanding the American forces in the northern provinces of the United States, and have directed hostilities to be recommenced in that quarter:

His Royal Highness the Prince Regent, acting in the name and on the behalf of his Majesty, and with the advice of his Majesty's privy council, is hereby pleased to order, and it is hereby ordered, that general reprisals be granted against the ships, goods, and citizens of the United States of America, and others inhabiting within the territories thereof (save and except any vessels to which his Majesty's license has been granted, or which have been directed to be released from the embargo, and have not terminated the original voyage on which they were detained and released), so that as well his Majesty's fleets and ships, as also all other ships and vessels that shall be commissioned by letters of marque or general reprisals, or otherwise by his Majesty's Commissioners for executing the office of Lord High Admiral of Great Britain, shall and may lawfully seize all ships, vessels, and goods belonging to the government of the United States of America, or the citizens thereof, or others inhabiting within the territories thereof, and bring the same to judgment in any of the Courts of Admiralty within his Majesty's dominions; and to that end his Majesty's advocate-general, with the advocate of the Admiralty, are forthwith to prepare the draught of a commission, and present the same to his Royal Highness the Prince Regent at this Board, authorizing the commissioners for executing the office of Lord High Admiral, or any person or persons by them empowered and appointed, to issue forth and grant letters of marque and reprisals to any of his Majesty's subjects, or others whom the said commissioners shall deem fitly qualified in that behalf, for the apprehending, seizing, and taking the ships, vessels, and goods belonging to the government of the United States of America, or the citizens thereof, or others inhabiting within the countries, territories, or dominions thereof (except as aforesaid), and that such powers and clauses be inserted in the said commission as have been usual, and are according to former precedents; and his Majesty's advocate-general, with the advocate of the Admiralty, are also forthwith to prepare the draught of a commission, and present the same to his Royal Highness the Prince Regent at this Board, authorizing the said commissioners for executing the office of Lord High Admiral, to will and require the High Court of Admiralty of Great Britain, and the lieutenant and judge of the said court, his surrogate or surrogates, as also the several Courts of Admiralty within his Majesty's dominions, to take cognizance of, and judicially proceed upon all and all manner of captures, seizures, prizes, and reprisals of all ships and goods that are or shall be taken, and to hear and determine the same, and, according to the course of Admiralty and the laws of nations, to adjudge and condemn all such ships, vessels, and goods as shall belong to the government of the United States of America, or the citizens thereof, or to others inhabiting within the countries, territories, and dominions thereof (except as aforesaid); and that such powers and clauses be inserted in the said commission as have been usual, and are according to former precedents; and they are likewise to prepare and lay before his Royal Highness the Prince Regent, at this Board, a draught of such instructions as may be proper to be sent to the Courts of Admiralty in his Majesty's foreign governments and plantations, for their guidance herein, as also another draught of instructions for such ships as shall be commissionated for the purpose above-mentioned.

His Royal highness the Prince Regent is nevertheless pleased hereby to declare, in the name and on the behalf of his Majesty, that nothing in this order contained shall be understood to recall or affect the declaration which his Majesty's naval commander on the American station has been authorized to make to the government of the United States of America—namely, that his Royal Highness, animated by a sincere desire to arrest the calamities of war, has authorized the said commander to sign a convention, recalling and annulling, from a day to be named, all hostile orders issued by the respective governments, with a view of restoring without delay the relations of amity and commerce between his Majesty and the United States of America.

From the Court at Carlton-House, the thirteenth of October, one thousand eight hundred and twelve.

CASTLEREAGH. LIVERPOOL.
N VANSITTART, BATHURST.
CHARLES LONG. MELVILLE.
SIDMOUTH.

PROCLAMATION.

By his Excellency Lieutenant-general Sir John Coape Sherbrooke, Knight of the Most Hon. Order of the Bath, Lieut.-governor and Commander-in-chief, in and over his Majesty's Province of Nova Scotia, and its Dependencies, Vice-admiral of the same, &c. &c. &c.

WHEREAS the United States of America have declared war against his Majesty, I have in the present state of public affairs deemed it expedient, by and with the advice and consent of his Majesty's Council, to suspend, for the time being, the sailing of merchant ships and coasting vessels from any of the ports or harbours of the Province, until proper convoys are arranged for their protection and defence. All persons, therefore, concerned, are hereby ordered and directed, on no account to put to sea from any port or harbour of this Province, with any registered ship or vessel, until from and after the twenty-first day of October next, unless a special license for such sailing with convoy, or other special permission, shall have been first obtained from me, or by my order : and I hereby order and command the collectors, and all other officers of the Customs, and naval officers, to abstain from granting clearances outwards to any ship or vessel of the above description, unless a license, as aforesaid, to sail with convoy, shall have been first obtained for that purpose : and all officers, civil and military, under my command, are hereby ordered to use all lawful means in their power, to cause all persons to pay obedience to this Proclamation.

Given under my hand and seal at arms, at Halifax, this 16th day of September, 1812, in the 52d year of his Majesty's reign.

J. C. SHERBROOKE.

By his Excellency's Command,

H. H. COGSWELL

God save the King.

AMERICAN CIRCULAR.

SIR, *Treasury Department, August* 26.

THE Non-Importation Act being still in force, must in every respect be carried into effect. It is your duty to seize and libel British merchandise in whatever manner, and by whomsoever it may be brought or sent into the United States, with the exception only of property captured from the enemy, the importation of which is permitted by the 14th section of the Act concerning letters of marque, prizes, and prize goods.

In the cases which, from peculiar circumstances, may be entitled to relief, this can be granted only by a special Act of Congress, or upon application for a remission of the forfeiture in the manner prescribed by law.

I have the honour to be, &c.

ALBERT GALLATIN,

The Collector of the Customs.

ADDITIONAL INSTRUCTIONS TO THE PUBLIC AND PRIVATE ARMED VESSELS OF THE UNITED STATES.

THE public and private armed vessels of the United States are not to interrupt any vessels belonging to citizens of the United States, coming from British ports to the United States, laden with British merchandise, in consequence of the alleged Repeal of the British Orders in Council; but are, on the contrary, to give aid and assistance to the same, in order that such vessels and their cargoes may be dealt with on their arrival as may be decided by the competent Authorities.

AMERICAN OFFICIAL ACCOUNT OF THE CAPTURE OF H. M. S. GUERRIERE.

United States Frigate Constitution, off Boston,

SIR, *August* 30.

I HAVE the honour to inform you, that on the 19th inst. at 2 P.M. being in lat. 41° 42′ and long. 55° 48 with the Constitution under my command, a sail was discovered from the mast head, bearing E. by S. or E. S. E. but at such a distance we could not tell what she was. All sail was instantly made in chase, and soon found we came up with her. At three P. M. could plainly see that she was a ship on the starboard tack under an easy sail, close on a wind; at half-past three P.M. made her out to be a frigate; continued the chase until we were within about three miles, when I ordered the light sails to be taken in, the courses hauled up, and the ship cleared for action. At this time the chase had backed his main-top-sail, waiting for us to come down. As soon as the Constitution was ready for action, I bore down with an intention to bring him to close action immediately; but on our coming within gun-shot she gave us a broadside, and filled away and wore, giving us a broadside on the other tack, but without effect; her shot falling short. She continued wearing and manœuvring for about three quarters of an hour, to get a raking position, but finding she could not, she bore up, and run under her top-sails and jib, with the wind on the quarter. I immediately made sail to bring the ship up with her, and five minutes before six P.M. being alongside within half-pistol shot, we commenced a heavy fire from all our guns, double shotted with round and grape, and so well directed were they, and so warmly kept up, that in 15 minutes his mizen-mast went by the board, and his main-yard in the slings, and the hull, rigging, and sails, very much torn to pieces. The fire was kept up with equal warmth for 15 minutes longer, when his mainmast and foremast went, taking with them every spar, excepting the bowsprit; on seeing this, we ceased firing, so that in 30 minutes after, we got fairly alongside the enemy: she surrendered, and had not a spar standing, and her hull below and above water so shattered, that a few more broadsides must have carried her down.

After informing you that so fine a ship as the Guerriere, commanded by an able and experienced officer, had been totally dismasted, and otherwise cut to pieces, so as to make her not worth towing into port, in the short space of 30 minutes, you can have no doubt of the gallantry and good conduct of the officers and ship's company I have the honour to command; it only remains, therefore, for me to assure you, that they all fought with great bravery; and it gives me great pleasure to say, that from the smallest boy in the ship to the oldest seaman, not a look of fear was seen. They all went into action giving three cheers, and requesting to be laid close alongside the enemy.

Enclosed I have the honour to send you a list of killed and wounded on board the Constitution, and a report of the damages she has sustained; also a list of killed and wounded on board the enemy, with his quarter bill, &c.

To the Hon. Paul Hamilton, Esq. ISAAC HULL.

PLATE CCCLXXIV.

THIS Plate presents a view of Fort St. Angelo, situated on the Cotonea side of the island of Malta.—A view of Malta, accompanied by an historical description, will be found in our VIIIth Volume, page 121; a view of Fort Ricasoli, and the entrance to the harbour of Valetta, the capital of the Island, in our XXIst Volume, page 213; and a plan of the fortress of Valetta, with many curious historical particulars, in our XXVth Volume, page 480.

Fort St. Angelo, on the Cotonera side, in the Island of Malta.

PHILOSOPHICAL PAPERS.

The Shrouds, Backstays, and Running Rigging of the Tides and Currents, overhauled by HAWSER HANK, *an ancient Mariner, in some Remarks on a Paper which appeared in the Philosophical Magazine for November and December,* 1800; *to which are subjoined Illustrative Extracts from* ST. PIERRE's *Etudes de la Nature.*

HAWSER HANK's SECOND LETTER.*

MR. EDITOR,

THE next passage in Mr. Wood's *Examination of* ST. PIERRE's *Hypothesis*, to which I request your attention, is the following:—

" When compared to wide-mouthed rivers, opening into the direction of the stream of the tide (why appeal to rivers ?), and that high water is some hours after the moon's appulse to the meridian, as it is observed upon all the western coasts of Europe and Africa."—Why so confidently speak of the tides of Africa? Certainly Mr. Wood never was in that quarter of the globe. The greater part of Africa has no tides. From Ireland, to the Cape of Good Hope, the tides gradually decrease. Along the shores of Europe, and on the northern coasts of Africa, they become still less, until they are altogether lost about the 24th degree of northern latitude: about the same latitude to the southward of the equator they are again perceptible, but even at the Cape of Good Hope they are very weak. " In all which," adds Mr. Wood, " a south-west moon makes high water, and the same is said to be the case on the western coast of America : so that tides happen to different places at all distances of the moon from the meridian, and consequently at all hours of the day."

This is very extraordinary : it would appear that gravitation requires time to perform its journies, like heat and light, and that according to the distance, so will be the elapsed time. But to proceed—" To allow the tides their full motion, the space in which they are produced ought to extend from east to west 90 degrees at least—such being the distance between the places most raised and depressed by the moon's influence." According to this doctrine, the tides cannot have their full motion in any part of our hemisphere, because the shores of America are not so distant. " Hence it appears, that such tides can only be produced in large oceans."—I shall here notice a large ocean, which extends from Cape Horn. Examine the movements of that ocean, as recorded in the journals of navigators in those seas : they are not in favour of this conjecture. Will Mr. Woods assert, that the seas in this part of the world, are, in their revolutions, in harmony with the lunar system ? or will he say, the ice is an obstacle to it ? If the ice of the South Sea impede the progress of its waters, of course there must be a flux and reflux at the extremity of

---

* For the First Letter, *vide* page 126 of the preceding Volume.

those immense masses of frozen waters; unless we suppose the icy cupola of the south pole to be a loose floating body, moved from place to place by the waters;—an idea that has never been advanced. However, this flux and reflux of the sea, at the extremities of these ices, was never noticed by Captain Cook, nor by any other navigator in those southern latitudes: but, as Mr. Woods has before remarked, "*that the shoaliness of the sea, and the intercurrent continents, are the reasons why the tides rise but to so very inconsiderable heights.*"—None of these reasons occur in this ocean to prevent its waters from obeying the lunar laws, except its unknown depth, which is little or no reason, although Mr. Wood's insists that it is. Surely, the unknown depth of any ocean, can never prevent the waters on its surface from following the attractive influence of the sun and moon. For example:—we frequently see strong currents on the surface of the waters of the ocean, which do not exist twenty or thirty fathoms deep.— " Those of the Pacific," says Mr. Woods, " exceed those of the Atlantic Ocean."—In what part of the Pacific Ocean are those strong tides, that Mr. Woods speaks of, to be found?—I have always found the tides in the northern latitudes of the Atlantic stronger than the tides in any other part of the world. But systematic men, who are determined to oppose every thing that is not in unison with their favourite plans, are never at a loss to account for any thing:—" Hence also," adds he, " it is obvious why the tides in the Torrid Zone, between Africa and America, where the ocean is narrower" (I wish I had not so many occasions to notice contradiction in Mr. Woods' paper), " are exceeded by those of the temperate zones on either side"—This is very true; they are exceeded in the temperate zones; inasmuch, as there are no tides in the torrid zone, and strong tides in the other zones.—" And hence," continues he, " we may comprehend why the tides are so small in islands at a great distance from the shores; since the waters cannot rise on one shore without descending on the other."—If the sun and moon raise the waters at one place, certainly they must be proportionably depressed at another: consequently, if the waters are raised at any island by the sun and moon, they must be depressed at some other place—suppose ninety degrees distant; consequently there will be high water at 180 degrees, or at its opposite point, which is according to Mr. Woods' own opinion. Now what is to hinder the water from rising on such an island? Will not the waters accumulate, and rise or swell on the waters, in conformity to the laws of attraction? If Mr. Woods will not admit this, he denies what he has all along been endeavouring to prove, the lunar system's existence, which must raise the tides very much on all islands that intercept and oppose the waters of its attraction, particularly in the open ocean:—Such islands, therefore, as are placed in the open ocean, ought to have, according to Mr. Woods' own assertion, ten or twelve feet perpendicular flow; so that at the intermediate island it must continue at a mean height between its elevations on those shores. Certainly this must be the case with regard to all islands that are situated between two continents; but such islands as are placed clear of all continents, in high southern latitudes, for example, must, from their situation, resist the pressure of the waters of the ocean, which, according to the lunar system, are continually running after the moon; and consequently, we may, no... the lunar theory, expect to find very strong tides on the shores of such islands; but our experience hitherto has not proved this. The shoaliness of the sea being brought forward as a reason why tides do not rise in such islands, in the manner we might otherwise expect in conformity to the lunar laws, is by no means a sufficient reason. The question cannot rest on so slender an argument: for we frequently see strong currents running at a prodigious rate in many parts, carrying the waves of the ocean in various directions, contrary to every known system; and those currents are, comparatively, of no depth, some of them not existing 15 fathoms under the surface. Currents are frequently occasioned by the wind, particularly in low latitudes, though many are altogether unaccountable, particularly in calms of long duration.

The tide produced on the western coast of Europe, says Mr. Woods, corresponds to this theory. It certainly does correspond to this theory, in many parts of the western coasts of Europe, though not in every place: for example, the western coast of France, on which some of our ships of war have been lost, and many others got on shore, owing to the uncertainty of its tides; especially in hazy weather, and in the night-time. Mr. Woods, who boasts so much of his systematic knowledge, will perhaps be astonished when told, that seamen prefer their eyesight to system; and have an old and good proverb amongst them, which I hope they will never forget—*That a good look-out is the best reckoning*. But darkness, sometimes, as in the cases I have alluded to, prevents this look-out.—" Thus it is high water," continues Mr. W. " on the western coasts of Ireland, about the third hour after the moon has crossed the meridian, from thence it flows into the adjacent channels as it finds the easiest passage. One current, for example, turns up the south of England, and another by the north of Scotland, taking considerable time to move all this way, and occasioning high water sooner at the places at which it first arrives, and begins to fall at those places, while the current is proceeding to others farther distant in its course; on its return, it is unable to raise a tide, because the water runs faster off than it returns, till, by the propagation of a new tide from the ocean, the current is stopped, and begins to rise again."

" The tide propagated by the moon in the German Ocean, when she is three hours past the meridian, takes 12 hours to come from thence to London Bridge; so that when it is high water there, a new tide has already attained its height in the ocean, and in some intermediate place, it must be low water at the same time. When the tide runs over shoals, and flows upon flat shores, the water is elevated to a greater height than in open and deep oceans, that have steep banks, because the force of its motion is not broken upon level shores, till the water has attained a greater height."— That the waters of the sea delight to rise and swell upon low and level shores more than on its own natural bed, I deny.—That the tides rush over such parts with great violence, in many instances, is notorious; but to say that they accumulate more there, and swell and rise above the level of other parts of the sea, is an absurdity; for, as the sea advances upon the land so must its force necessarily decrease, till, having attained its own level in other places, it ceases to rise altogether. But to proceed: "If a place communicates with two oceans, or by two different openings with the same ocean, one of which affords an easier passage than the other, two tides may arrive at this place in different times, which interfering together, may produce a great variety of phenomena. At several places it is high water three hours before the moon comes to the meridian."—This is really curious, and by the bye, if this had not been *well known*, it would have been *denied* by partizans; "but that tide," adds Mr. Woods, "which the moon *drives* as it were before her, is only the tide opposite to that produced by her, when 9 hours past the opposite meridian. It would be tedious to enumerate all the practical solutions easily deducible."—Recollect, however, that Mr. Woods' deductions are not proofs. It is only to the school of experience that we are to appeal for proofs. If deduction were to be admitted as proof, Mr. W. might cease to be the echo of the lunar party; for the Frenchman, as he is pleased to call St. Pierre, is too powerful for him.

"Deducible from these doctrines," continues he, "is why lakes and seas, such as the Caspian and Mediterranean, the Euxine and the Baltic, have little or no sensible tides; since having no communication, or being connected by very narrow inlets with the great ocean, they cannot receive or discharge water enough to alter their surface sensibly."—Supposing this to be the case, why are not the waters which are already in those vast seas, themselves *bodily* affected by the sun's and moon s gravitation? Some of these seas lie remarkably well for obeying such laws.

"In general," continues he, "when the time of high water at any place is mentioned, it is to be understood on the days of new and full moon; the times of high water in any place fall at nearly the same hours, after a period of about 15 days, or between one spring tide and another." Here ends Mr. Woods' echo, in support of the lunar system; which, in my humble opinion, has not acquired either strength or intelligence from his studied labours; long as he may have been in copying and collecting the fragments exhibited in his paper.

"This theory," says Mr. Woods, "however, is not without objections, which has encouraged a Frenchman of some eminence, to frame a new and singular hypothesis: ascribing all the phenomenon of the tides to the periodical effusions of the polar ices. I shall first mention the most material facts, and considerations, which appear to militate against the common theory, as stated by St. Pierre, and I shall then endeavour to explain the theory he has substituted."

I wish Mr. Woods had endeavoured to explain this new theory; he promised so to do, but he has not kept that promise. I shall not follow him in his quotation of St. Pierre; but will, in my next, consider this new hypothesis, which has so alarmed all our academicians.

[To be continued.]

HYDROGRAPHY, PILOTAGE, &c.

ENGLAND.

DIRECTIONS FOR NAVIGATING BY THE NEW FLOATING LIGHT OFF BEMBRIDGE.*

A FLOATING LIGHT is now moored on Bembridge Ledge at the east end of the Isle of Wight, S.E. 90 fathoms from the true situation of the Nab Buoy, in 5 fathoms at low spring ebbs, with the following angles and compass bearings; *viz.*

Nettlestone Point and St. Helen's Sea Mark	20	27
St. Helen's Sea Mark and Ashdown Beacon	10	44
Ashdown Beacon, and sharp Western Edge of Culver Cliff	29	3
Sharp Western Edge of Culver Cliff and Dun-nose Point	8	42
Nettlestone Point	N. W. Northerly.	
St. Helen's Sea Mark	N. W. b. W. ¼ W.	
Ashdown Beacon	W. b. N. ½ N.	
Culver Cliff sharp Western Edge	W. b. S.	
Dun-nose	W. S. W.	
Betty's Ledge	W. b. S. ⅞ S.	
N. W. Buoy Princessa	S. W. ¼ W.	
S. E. Buoy Princessa	S. S. W. ⅞ S.	
Warner	N. b. W.	
Nettlestone and East Cowes Points in One	N. W.	

The first rise of the land to the right of the high land over Dunnose Point, is on the sharp angle and highest part of the Middle of Culver Cliff. Ships coming from the westward, round the S.E. buoy of the Princessa will be a good berth to the eastward of that shoal when the light bears N. b. E. If the passage between Betty's Ledge and the N.W. buoy of the Princessa must unavoidably be taken in a dark night, ships must bring the light to bear N. E. b. E. ½ E. and must persevere in keeping it upon that bearing, as the tide between Betty's Ledge and the Princessa (on which in many parts there are not more than 19 or 20 feet), runs with a velocity that makes this channel dangerous to ships drawing much water. The light may be passed close on either side; the anchorage in St. Helen's road is in the direction of the Warner Buoy, where the ground is excellent, about one mile from the light. The light was exhibited for the first time, on the night of the 29th September, and will be continued constantly from sun-set to sun-rise, for the benefit of navigation. Masters and pilots are to observe, that two distinct lights are shown from this vessel, in two lanthorns, suspended from two separate masts, at 43 feet distance asunder,

---

* NAVAL CHRONICLE, XXVIII, 129.

and hung at different heights, the one lanthorn at 25 feet, the other at 18 feet height above the vessel's deck; by which this floating light will be readily distinguishable from the Owers floating light, and other lights in that vicinity.—(*Trinity-house.*)

Bembridge point is in latitude 50° 40′ 59″ N. and longitude 1° 3′ 26″ W. from Greenwich. Variation of the compass about 24° W.—(S.)

DIRECTIONS FOR NAVIGATING THE NEEDLES' CHANNEL BY THE IMPROVED LIGHTS AT HURST POINT.[*]

The New or High Light-house is erected upon Hurst Beach, bearing N.E. b. E. ¼ E. (by compass) distant 755 feet from the old or Low Light-house.—Viewed from the bridge, the Low Light appears about 25 feet lower than the Hight Light, and the two lights appear in one.—This must be considered as the boundary line to avoid the S.E. side of the Shingles :— And must not be passed to the westward, or the High Light brought to the left of the Low Light, as the Shingles are steep-to. A Beacon is also erected upon Hurst Beach, from which the High Light bears E.N.E to shew the boundary of the S.E. side of the Chalk Rocks: And this line must not be passed to the west, or the High Light brought to the left of the Beacon, while the Needle Light bears at any point from S.E. b. E. to E.S.E. In coming from the west, when chiefly there is occasion to use the Needles' Passage, observe, that as soon as, in proceeding through the Channel with the Beacon and High Light in one, High-Down, or Nodes, Signal Post, opens to the northward of the high land of Needles' Point, you are then arrived just without the S.W. part of the Chalk Rocks, and the opposite rocks that form the bridge : And it is recommended, that you *then* steer eastward to bring the two lights in one with all expedition, lest you get on the S.E. projection of the Shingles. As the light at Hurst bears N.E. from the Needles' Point, therefore, in coming from the south, you must bring the lights in one, bearing N.E. b. E. ¼ E. steer in for them, as a leading mark, and when the Needles' Light bears S.E. b. E. you are then within the bridge, and may open the High Light a little to the eastward of the Low Light, and steer up the Channel in that direction to Hurst Beach. When, in case of northerly winds, you wish to borrow upon the Chalk Rocks, being to the westward of them, and having the Needles' Point in sight, steer north-eastward until you have Nodes, or High Down, signal, in sight, within the high land of the Needles, bearing about E.S.E. ¼ E — And when Nodes Signal is over the division between the Chalk and Clay Cliffs, which is very distinguishable, which bearing leads to the south extremity of the Chalk Rocks, keep it thus, until the High Light is over the Beacon at Hurst, and then steer east from the intersection of these two bearings, and proceed as before. In working in through the Needles' Passage, which, however, should not be attempted with vessels of great burthen, nor with any (except small vessels) unless there be urgent necessity for it ; it is to be observed : that ships may stretch as far west-

---

[*] N.C. XXVIII. 227.

ward as to bring the Beacon and High Light-house in one, until the Needles' Light bears E.S.E.—but higher up the Channel beyond that bearing, must not stretch farther westward, than to bring the two lights in one, nor farther to the S.E. than to bring the Needles' Light S.S.W. ½ W. Hurst Light-house is in latitude 50° 42' 23,4" N. and longitude 1° 32' 50" W. from Greenwich. With due attention to the preceding directions, there can be no difficulty in sailing outwards by this channel ; only, it is to be observed, that you ought not to bring the lights in one, either in working, or with a fair wind, until you are well below the buoy of the Warden Ledge, or the Needles bears S.S.W. otherwise you will fall into 3¼ fathoms on the east end of the Shingles : for the ebb tide runs strong to the north westward through the North Channel, and upon the east point of the Shingles, which is particularly to be guarded against, being steep-to here, as well as all along the S. E. side ; hence a good berth should be given to that part. The bearings given in these directions are magnetic ; 'and the variation of the compass around the Isle of Wight is about 24° W.

WALES.

The Corporation of Trinity-House, London, has directed proper landmarks or beacons to be erected, to denote the situation of a dangerous sunken rock, called the " Coal," situate near the Skerries Light-house, off the N.E. point of the entrance into Holyhead Harbour ; upon which rock a considerable number of vessels have stricken and been damaged, and others, it is feared, have been totally lost, and their crews perished.

ASIA.—CHINA SEAS.

In a recent hydrographic publication,* the following mention is made of a danger, which has been already recorded in this CHRONICLE,† conformably to the authority of a newspaper printed in Hindostan :—

" I have been favored with a chart of the eastern side of the Bashee islands, by Captain A. Murray, of the E. I. C.'s ship Earl Howe, who sailed close along that side in December, 1805. Captain M. places the northernmost island in 21° 8' N. but this latitude is deduced back from the run *per* log to the southernmost island, close to which the latitude was observed, giving for the most southern part 20° 17' N. I take M. de la Peyrouse's latitude for the northern Bashee, *i. e.* 21° 9¼' N. inasmuch as an error the other way would be the most liable to lead into danger ; and this higher latitude is corroborated by Captain Horsburgh's chart of the Bashees lately published, wherein the most northern Bashee reaches to 21° 10' N.—The most important part of Captain Horsburgh's chart, and to show which was its principal design, is a dangerous reef, situated nearly in mid-channel

---

* Memoir explanatory of a chart of the coast of China, and the sea eastward from the river of Canton to the southern islands of Japan : by James Burney, Esq. of the royal navy." London ; 1811. p. 20.

† N. C. XXIV. 220.

between the North-Bashee and Botel-Tobago-Xema, not before marked in any chart, and of which this is the first public notice given.* Captain H. mentions in his chart, that in January, 1800, the Swedish ship Oster-Gothland, commanded by Captain Gadd, made a reef in latitude 21° 45′ N. by observation, and when in one with the east end of Botel-Tobago-Xema it bore N. ¼ W. In July, 1809, the ship Cumbrian, commanded by Captain Tate, saw a reef, with several of the rocks above water on its western part, lying in the same direction from Botel-Tobago-Xema, but in latitude (deduced from good observations on the preceding and next succeeding noon) 21° 35′ N. Concerning the situation of the reef or reefs I am the more particular, because M. de la Peyrouse was a whole day becalmed in mid-channel between Botel-Tobago-Xema, and the North Bashee, without seeing any reef, although his track, in chart No. 43 of his published voyage, is drawn making a perfect zig-zag over and about the very spots pointed out by Captains Gadd and Tate. This led me to suspect that the south end of Formosa† had been mistaken for Botel-Tobago-Xema, and that the Vele-rete rocks had consequently been supposed a new discovered reef. I communicated my conjectures to Captain H. who was so obliging as to send me very satisfactory extracts from the journals of the above-mentioned ships, whereby it appears that Captain Gadd, steering a westerly course, soon after leaving the reef, made the south end of Formosa, bearing N.W. b. W. and that Captain Tate saw the Northern Bashees at the same time the reef was in sight. Captain H. is of opinion, that the reef seen by the Cumbrian is the same which was seen by the Oster-Gothland. Admitting this to be the case, which is extremely probable, a difference of ten miles in the latitude by observation cannot satisfactorily be accounted for otherwise than by supposing error on each side, and the truth between. I have thought it best to mark both in the chart: but the Directors of the East India Company will see the necessity of causing a channel, now so much frequented by their ships, to be carefully examined and surveyed."

Mr. Horsburgh having been quoted so circumstantially by Captain Burney, in the foregoing extract from his memoir, it may not be amiss to use this opportunity for confronting the two authorities, by giving the former's own words, in his latest work,‡ when describing the places named by the latter.

---

* Captain Burney's memoir, quoted above, is dated January, 1811; and the Cumbrian shoal was noticed in the NAVAL CHRONICLE published on 1st April, 1810.

† This is another instance of the unwarrantable liberty taken by navigators in affixing fanciful names to places. The real name of the island called by the Portuguese "Formosa," is *Pekan*. It is also called in the vernacular idiom *Ty-oan*, or *Tay-wan*.—(S.)

‡ "Directions for sailing to and from the East Indies, China, New-Holland, Cape of Good-hope, and the interjacent ports, &c. by James Horsburgh, F.R.S." In two parts. London, 1809, and 1811. p. 305.

HYDROGRAPHY. 317

"Botel-Tobago-Xima, in latitude 21° 59′ N. and longitude 121° 48′ E. (by chronometers and good observations,* bears from the North Bashee island N.N.W. distant 55 miles, by the transit bearing taken when both were in sight, the latter then bearing S.S.E. and the former N.N.W. It is a high island, 3 or 4 miles in extent, appearing in the form of a saddle, or with a gap in it when viewed from S.S.W. and may be seen 16 or 17 leagues from the mast-head. The high part of the island is crowned with trees, and it is well inhabited, having several large villages on the southern part.

"Little Botel-Tobago-Xima, in latitude 21° 56¼′ N. is a small island of considerable height, with some bushes on it, about 2 or 2½ miles distant to the S. Eastward of the southern part of the great island: a reef projects from its south end about a cable's-length or more, which is steep-to; there being no soundings near these islands.

"Cumbrian's reef, situated about 7 or 8 leagues to the southward of Botel-Tobago-Xima, is very dangerous,† for it lies in the fair channel betwixt that island and the North Bashees. Until Captain Gadd, in the Swedish ship Oster-Gothland, saw it 12th January, 1800, it was not known to exist. There is a chain of high breakers on it, extending nearly E. and W. about a league or more, and several rocks show their heads above water among the breakers: when in one with the east end of Botel-Tobago-Xima, the reef bore N. ¼ W. the body of Little Botel then N. ¾ E. and Captain Gadd made it in latitude 21° 45′ N. This reef was seen in 1808 by Captain Purefoy, of the ship Charlotte, and by Captain Tate, in the Cumbrian, 26th July, 1809. This ship was working out between the islands, with a light easterly wind, and by observations carefully taken at noon on two succeeding days, when not far from the reef, it was found to be in latitude 21° 35′ N. and the longitude is 121° 50′ E. or 2′ eastward of Botel-Tobago-Xima. I have called it the Cumbrian's reef, because Captain Tate assures me that his latitude may be depended on, which places the reef 10 miles more southward than the position assigned to it by the former navigator: for certainly there cannot be two reefs to the S. of Botel-Tobago-Xima,‡ and it is very remarkable that this reef has been so seldom seen, considering its situation.

"Vele-Rete rocks, or reef, in 21° 42′ N. and 121° 3½′ E. is distant about 14 or 15 leagues westward of the Cumbrian's reef; and bears about S. ½ W. from the low S.E. point of Formosa, distant 4½ leagues. This is a mass of rock, some of them above water, and others even with the sur-

---

* De la Peyrouse made its S.E. point in 21° 57′ N. and 121° 52′ E.

† "It was not placed in any charts until I published one recently on a large scale, comprehending all the islands and dangers between Luconia [Luzon] and Formosa; exhibiting their relative situations and their various channels." (*Horsburgh.*)

‡ The hydrographer cannot help pointing out to navigators Captain Burney's caution in preference to Mr. Horsburgh's incredulity; which, it must be remarked, with all due deference to the latter's scientific character, is not the side whereon error may be committed with impunity —(S.)

face, which may be seen 9 or 10 miles; the channel betwixt this danger and the south end of Formosa is about 4 leagues wide, and very safe. Ships passing southward in thick weather should keep towards the North Bashee isles, making allowance for a northerly current, which is generally experienced in light winds, and during the S.W. monsoon. From latitude 21° 15' N. to 21° 20' N. is a good track to preserve when passing between the Bashees and Cumbrian in thick weather. Several ships during light winds have been drifted by the current between Formosa and Botel-Tobago-Xima: the Glatton and Canton were drifted close to a small island in latitude 22° 39' N. which is surrounded by breakers projecting out N.Eastward a considerable way : this island is 14 leagues northward of Botel-Tobago-Xima, and 8 or 9 leagues distant from the east coast of Formosa.

" Formosa is about 70 leagues in length, extending nearly N.N.E. and S.S.W. the land up the country is generally high, but low in some places to sea-ward, with soundings near the shore, particularly on the west side. The southern part has on it a high double-peaked mountain, discernible at 20 leagues distance in clear weather; from whence the land slopes down terminating in a low projecting point, called the South cape, or S.E. point of Formosa. This point is situated in latitude 21° 54' N. and longitude 121° 5' E. (by mean of many observations of ☉ ☽ ✳ and chronometers) and bearing about W. ½ S. from the W. end of Botel-Tobago-Xima, distant 13 leagues. To the N.Eastward of the point there is a village and a harbour for small vessels; and there is said to be soundings near it on the W. side. About 13 leagues N.Westward of the South cape the Lamay island is situated about 3 or 3½ leagues distant from the coast, with soundings between them. About 13 or 14 leagues farther northward lies the harbour of Ty-oan (formerly the Dutch settlement of Fort Zealand) with a table hill inland E.S.Eastward. This harbour and the other inlets along the west coast, are mostly fronted by shoals ; and from the entrance of the river Pon-kan, in latitude 23° 25' N. sand-banks project 3 or 4 leagues into the offing. Ty-oan harbour will not admit vessels that draw above 7 or 8 feet water; and the other inlets are also shoal. Europeans have no intercourse with this island at present."

MAGNETISM.*

On this subject, so interesting to navigation, the NAVAL CHRONICLE has been favoured with an authentic copy of a paper lately addressed to the Admiralty by Captain Flinders, R.N. Prior, however, to making use of which it is thought expedient to make the reader acquainted with certain remarks explanatory of the same subject, that are contained in the introduction to a work of much repute, which the obliging attention of its author, Mr. Horsburgh, has enabled the hydrographer to make habitual reference to; but not more frequent than deserved. These remarks will be found the more appropriate, because, besides being in themselves instructive

---

* NAVAL CHRONICLE II. 50, 51, 421, 424, 505. XX. 21. XXVII. 194.

to the general reader, they make personal allusion to the circum-navigator above-named, and contain a definition of the variation of the compass, which differs from the signification applied to that phrase in common discourse.

" Variation of the compass, when mentioned in this work,[*] is intended only for the navigator to make the proper allowance in steering from one place to another, and not as a guide for estimating the longitude, which was practised about 25 or 30 years ago by mariners, before the use of chronometers and lunar observations became general. In naming the variation, whether east or west, the language in common use has been adopted, in order to prevent mistakes, although it is ambiguous and incorrect, as will be perceived from what follows. When the north end of the magnetic needle, or N. point of the compass, makes an angle with the true meridian or north pole of the world, this angle is called the " variation of the compass." If the magnetic north points to the eastward of the true north, the variation of the compass is said to be westerly; and it is called easterly variation when the magnetic north points to the westward of the true north pole of the world. So, according to the denomination in vulgar use, if understood literally, it names the variation of the true north from the magnetic north, and not the angle of aberration of the magnetic meridian from the true meridian, which is intended. The epitomes commonly used among mariners name the variation as described above; but Euler, and some other mathematicians, in their works, adhere to the language of truth, by calling the variation of the compass easterly, when the magnetic north makes an angle to the eastward of the true meridian, and *vice versa*.[†] That unsettled manner of naming the nature of the variation, creates mistakes among hydrographers in the construction of charts applicable to navigation : in some charts of the British Channel, where the variation of the compass (according to the common terms used) is westerly, the magnetic north is delineated to the eastward of the true meridian, and in others to the westward of the same. This is liable to embarrass young mariners; but it may be observed, that the magnetic north point is generally placed to the westward of the true north, in the

---

[*] " Directions for sailing to and from the East Indies," &c. 1809, 1811.

[†] This is the sense in which the term " variation" is employed, almost without exception, throughout this department of the NAVAL CHRONICLE. And, on account of the ambiguous indefinite terms applied in common parlance to certain other phenomena, which have an important influence over navigation, it may be serviceable to apprize the reader that the method of applying those terms herein adhered to is as follows :—The direction of the wind is named from the point of the compass whence it blows. The direction of the waves, swell, or sea, is named from the point of the compass whence they proceed. The direction of a current is named from the true point to which it is running, except otherwise specified. The course steered by a ship is expressed by compass. The bearings of land taken by a ship are magnetic, if not otherwise stated. The direction of any coast, or bearing of any head-land, or danger from any other land, is the true bearing by the world, subject to similar exception. (S.)

more modern charts constructed for places where the variation is westerly In places where the variation changed quickly, when sailing nearly on a parallel, navigators were formerly eager to embrace its aid in approximating their longitude : but compasses being subject to many errors from various causes, the longitude ascertained by means of the variation, could never be trusted to with any reasonable degree of confidence. The variation of the needle is in a state of continued change in most places of the globe, and there is also a diurnal and annual variation of the variation : besides, the same compasses will alter when taken from one ship into another, and if shifted to different situations in the same ship. In some places of the globe, although a compass be fixed stationary in a ship, the needle seems to be subject to an aberration of several degrees, proportionate to the angle that the ship's head makes with the magnetic pole. This, Captain Flinders found to be the case during his survey of the coasts of New-Holland, which is recorded in the " Philosophical Transactions of the Royal Society," 1805. With the compass placed a-mid-ships in the Investigator, the bearings of points of land on the south coast of New-Holland, taken immediately before and after tacking, differed sometimes 8° or 9° when the ship's head was changed from E. to W. but there was little or no difference when that change was N. or S. This difference in the direction of the magnetic needle from its mean state was easterly when the ship's head was W. and *vice versa*. When the ship's head was N. or S. the needle continued in its mean state, and shewed a variation from the true meridian, nearly equal to the medium between what is shewn when the ship's head was E. and when W. and the aberration of the needle was nearly proportionate to the number of points which the ship's head was from the N. or S. Captain F. is of opinion, that this aberration of the needle was occasioned by a focal point of magnetism, situated nearly in the centre of the ship; that it will decrease to nothing as the magnetic equator is approached; and that on the N. side of the magnetic equator it will be the reverse of that recited above; the N. end of the needle should then be attracted, and the S. end repelled. So that in this case the aberration of the needle from its mean state should be easterly when the ship's head is E. and westerly when it is W. This aberration of the needle arising from a change of the ship's head, will no doubt vary in different ships at the same place, according to their size, and the quantity of iron they contain : but in places near the equator, where there is little variation, this aberration cannot be perceived, and it is probably not general, even in high latitudes, in places where the variation is considerable. With the view to ascertain whether this phenomenon prevailed generally, the author requested Captain P. Heywood, of H.M.S. Polyphemus, moored at Spithead, to take bearings of conspicuous objects on the land, when the ship's head was eastward, and immediately after when it was changed by the tide to the westward; but he could not perceive any aberration of the needle; the bearings of the objects being always nearly the same after allowing for a small change in the situation of the compass, occasioned by the alteration of the ship's place in riding to the flood, or ebb, tide."

MAGNETISM OF SHIPS.

SIR,   *Admiralty Office, 21st September,* 1812.

Captain Matthew Flinders, of the royal navy, having lately brought under the consideration of my-Lords Commissioners of the Admiralty, a series of remarks made by himself with regard to the variation of the Magnetic Needle, under certain circumstances of situation in a ship; a course of experiments was instituted, with the view of ascertaining the particular causes of error to which he had adverted, or of obtaining some general results from an inquiry so intimately connected as this appeared to be with the improvement of navigation.

I transmit to you herewith a copy of the statement which has been prepared by Captain Flinders upon this subject, and I am commanded by their Lordships to call your particular attention thereto, and to signify their desire, that as opportunities shall offer, experiments may be made on board the ship you command: you noting the results thereof in a table of columns, in the manner which he has pointed out, and adding such remarks as may be suggested to yourself, by the particular circumstances under which the experiments shall be made, and transmitting the same to me, for their Lordships' information.   I am, Sir, &c.

(Signed)   JOHN BARROW.

To the respective Captains, Commanders, and Commanding Officers of H. M. Ships and Vessels.

[ENCLOSURE.]

During the course of my voyage in H. M. sloop Investigator, for completing the discovery of New Holland and New South Wales, I remarked that the variation and the bearings of land taken with an azimuth compass upon the binnacle, were very different when the ship's head was in different directions; and, at length, I found that the following circumstances obtained throughout the whole of the observations.

1. When the head was east, the variation differed from the truth; and always on the same side, while the ship remained in the same hemisphere.

2. When the head was west, the differences were equally great; but a contrary way.

3. The head being north or south, made no difference in the variation; and it was then a medium between what was found at east and at west.

4. At the intermediate points, between the magnetic meridian and east or west, the difference from the true variation bore a proportion to the angle made by the ship's head with the meridian. If the head were on the western side, the difference was of the same nature as that when the head was west; if on the east side, as at east.

5. The proportion at the intermediate points obeyed the following law:
As *Radius*,
Is to the difference at east or west (for eight points:)
So is the *sine* of the angle between the ship's head and magnetic meridian to the difference for that angle.

Or if the number of points, which the head was to the right or left of the meridian were taken as a course; and the difference for eight points, reduced to minutes, taken as a distance; then the difference for the number of points was found in the departure column of the traverse table.

6. These differences were of a directly contrary nature in the south, to what they were in the northern hemisphere. In the English Channel, the compass gave *too much* west variation when the head was west; but, in the southern hemisphere, it always gave too little; and the great west variations were found when the head was east.

7. The differences did not change suddenly on crossing the equator; but, all the way from England, they diminished gradually; and, to all appearance, as the dip of the needle diminished. When the south end of the needle began to dip, the differences commenced the other way; and increased gradually as we advanced southward; until, having arrived in Bass' Strait, where the south dip is nearly as great as the north is in England, the differences became almost as great as when we first sailed; but, as I said before, of an opposite nature.

The experiments lately made in England prove, that similar differences, obeying the same laws, take place in most, or all ships of war; and perhaps they do in merchant ships also, for I have found them in vessels of 80 and 25 tons. Differences were also found in other parts, often greater than at the binnacles; but these being of less importance, the differences only which we observed at, or above the binnacles, on changing the ships heads from *east to west*, are here inserted.

	°		
Sheerness, Starling brig, difference of variation	7	29	greater
Helder frigate	13	3	do.
Raisonable, 64, armed *en flûte*	0	42	do.
Portsmouth, Loire frigate	2	7	do.
Devastation bomb	4	2	do.
Plymouth, Orestes brig			Uncertain.
Channel, Investigator armed-ship	8	4	do.

In Captain Cook's ships, the Endeavour and the Resolution, and also in the Discovery, commanded by Captain Vancouver, the differences appear to have been nearly the same as in the Investigator; and also of a contrary nature in the two hemispheres.

The cause of all these changes in a compass on shipboard, and the modes by which they may be obviated, I have endeavoured to explain in the account of the experiments drawn up by order of the Admiralty; and, to obtain further proofs, it is desirable that the differences should be observed in as many ships, and as accurately as possible, in the following manner:

The azimuth compass to be used, should be a good one; the card traversing freely: and if possible, the needle should be retouched with magnetic bars, before the observations are made. A low stand or stool must be prepared; so that when the compass is placed upon it, it may be of the same height with that by which the ship is steered. The binnacle being then taken away, substitute the stand and azimuth compass; or if the sun cannot be there seen all round, fix the stand as near to the situation as it can be seen; but *clear of any iron*, and *exactly amid-ships*. Let azimuths be taken, using both sides of the vane; and this as often as convenient, and with the ship's head in various directions; but more particularly at, and near, east and west; noting the direction of the head to the nearest quarter of a point.

These observations should always be made with the same instrument, and in the same place; and be entered in a table of ten columns, under the following heads:

Time, containing the year, day, and hour.
Latitude, of the place of observation.
Longitude, of ditto.
Dip, of the needle, if an instrument is on board.
*Alt. ☉*cent.*, corrected for dip, refraction, and semidiameter.
Azim. Obsd., being the mean of three or four sights, with each side of the vane.
By whom, mentioning the observer's name against each observation.
Ship's head, the mean of what it was at the beginning and end.
Variation.
Circumstances, specifying if under sail or at anchor: also, whether the ship was steady, or had motion.

At the head of the table should be mentioned the number of guns mounted, and whether the place was at the binnacle; or if not, how far before or abaft it. Observations may be made in other parts of the ship; but these should be kept in a separate table.

A good number of such experiments, carefully made in a variety of ships, and particularly when lying steadily at anchor, would shew whether the differences at the binnacle are usually so great as to cause much error; and, consequently, how far the discovery of them is of importance to ordinary navigation. With marine surveyors, and all officers who wish to fix the position of places or of their ships, by compass bearings, the subject must necessarily be one of much interest.

Mattⁿ. Flinders

London, 26th August, 1812.   Captain R.N.

The Hydrographer of the N.C. deems it proper to state, principally upon the authority of Mr. Horsburgh, that the variation of the compass is not so great as stated in the " British Channel Pilot," and in other books.

---

* The *hour angle* may be substituted, where there is a time-keeper, and when the altitude cannot be observed. If Walker's meridional compass be used, the 5th and 6th observations are unnecessary.

That book says, that the variation in the entrance of the channel was 28° 7′ W. in 1799, that it is continually increasing at the rate of about a degree in every 5½ years, and that it will be necessary to add 11 minutes for every year subsequent to 1799, to obtain the variation at any time pretty exact.—This statement is incorrect; for, according to the observations taken at the apartment of the Royal Society of London, and published in the " Philosophical Transactions," the variation of the magnetic needle in September 1811, was 24° 14′ 2″ W. and is nearly stationary.* According to the same respectable authority, the annual increase, from 1795 to 1802, was 1′ 20″; and from 1802 to 1810, less than 1′. The rule given by the " British Channel Pilot" would make the variation at present 30° 19′ W. in the British Channel: whereas the variation being at London, as above stated, there is great reason to think that it does not exceed 25½°, or 26° at most, in the entrance of the channel. Now, it is generally accounted to be upwards of 28° W. or ¼ point (and in some accounts nearly ½ point) greater than the truth. This occasions ships to approach nearer to the French coast than was intended, when, in steering up channel, they allow 2½ points of variation, or more, as directed by some of the books, and certain charts in general use. In Arrowsmith's new chart of the channel the variation is marked 2¼ points W. which, no doubt, is near the truth. Lieutenant Murdoch Mac Kenzie, marine surveyor to the Admiralty, made the variation 23° W. at Tor-bay, in 1781, and 23° W. at St. Helen's, in 1783. Lieutenant John Murray, in a survey of the coast near Beachy head, made the variation there 23° W. in 1806. Mr. Grœme Spence, who surveyed great part of the English coasts under the direction of the Admiralty, in 1795, made the variation 22° 50′ in the Downs; and he made it 24° 45′ at the Scilly islands in 1792. From 1792 to 1811, a period of 19 years, the total increase of the variation in London has been 27½′ W. this added to the variation observed by Mr. Spence in 1792, at Scilly, will make the variation there 25° 12½′ in 1811, which, probably, approximates the fact; for the annual increase of variation cannot differ much at Scilly from that observed at London, particularly as the quantity is so small on account of the magnetic pole being nearly stationary, and which may be expected soon to acquire a motion eastward. Mr. Horsburgh gives 25¼ W, for the variation near Ushant in 1811. Ships entering the British channel may allow about 26½ of west variation until they approach the Scilly isles; then 25½° in running up to the isle of Wight; and 24° from thence to Denge-ness.

S.

---

* The dip of the needle at the same time and place was 70° 32′ 30″.

NAVAL LITERATURE.

Twelve Letters, addressed to the Right Honourable Spencer Perceval. Wherein a View is taken of the present Magnitude of the British Navy, the Royal Establishments for its Equipment and Reception, compared with those at different periods of its Strength, and with the Demands the Country now has for its Services, and which must continue with her Power: also of the Policy of the Measures about to be adopted for the supplying of the evident Defects in the present Anchorages and Royal Dock Yards. From JAMES MANDERSON, *Esq. Captain in the Royal Navy; Author of " A Letter addressed to the Prime Minister, and First Lord of the Admiralty, on the Extension of the Naval Establishments of the Country;" and of " An Examination into the true Cause of the Stream running through the Gulf of Florida."* 8vo. pp. 150.

(Continued from page 147.)

THE spirit of inquiry, respecting the national advantages which are likely to result from the Plymouth Breakwater, seems to be so completely awake, that it is impossible for Captain Manderson's letters not to attract a very general and extensive notice. It is, indeed, our opinion, that the attention of the public will be more forcibly drawn to them now, than it could possibly be on their first appearance. The readers of the NAVAL CHRONICLE, in particular, from their being in full possession of the official documents upon the subject, will look to them with great interest; and, on that account, we feel it our duty to present a comprehensive and detailed view of Captain Manderson's work. This, in the first instance, we prefer to do, chiefly by the mode of analysis and extract; and, subsequently, under the head of NAVAL AND HYDRAULIC ARCHITECTURE, we shall submit the substance of varous other communications, referring to the general and comparative benefits, that might accrue from naval establishments at Plymouth, Falmouth, &c.

In a preceding part of this Volume,* we noticed the contents of Captain Manderson's five first letters. In his sixth, he proceeds to examine, what probable benefit the country is likely to derive from the execution of a breakwater, or breakwaters, at Plymouth, more than if the proposed expense were to be incurred in the improvement of Falmouth harbour. " Let it be granted," says he " that the undertaking about Plymouth Sound is finished, and that it holds the number of ships proposed; here is all that can be done with it. How is this to supply the urgent want of a western establishment for all naval purposes?" Captain M. next adverts to the known fact, " that Plymouth cannot receive a third part of the ships and vessels of war employed out of the Channel, and that Portsmouth is not sufficient for those it is expected to receive; but that many are sent to the Thames and Medway, and when refitted, are often detained as long by

---

* *Vide* page 143 to 147.

westerly winds before they can get back into the Atlantic, as they might have performed a voyage from the most western harbour in the Channel to the Mediterranean, the West Indies, or even to the Cape of Good Hope."

.... " Because," says he, " there is a naval establishment in Hamoaze, that therefore there ought not to be another near it, let the wants of the country be ever so great and urgent, is a proposition so pregnant with mischief to the essential interests of the British Empire, that perhaps no one will be so hardy as directly to avow the opinion; although indirectly he support it, by raising unfounded calumnies, and making needless objections, against the only harbour the country possesses near it, not much inferior in capacity, but easier by far of entrance, and more favourably situated for communicating with the ocean westward."......... " What difference would it make to Plymouth, whether the ships and vessels [which] it could not contain were sent to Falmouth, Portsmouth, or farther westward? If the harbour to the westward of it were established, it would soon learn, from experience, that its fears had been groundless; that the alarms raised by interested motives had darkened the eyes of its reason; and in time it would stretch out its hand in good neighbourhood."

Captain M. mentions the sum of 500,000*l*. as the probable expense of removing a square mile of the banks in Falmouth harbour; a space which would contain 56 sail of the line at moorings, 110 fathoms from centre to centre of the moorings, and the same distance from the banks; but, as so great a distance from mooring to mooring, and from the banks, would not be necessary, the space would contain 16 more, making a total of 72.

Alluding to Falmouth outer road—a space extending more than a nautical mile from the mouth of the harbour to the Zone reef, he says—

" It would be no chimera to undertake the making of this space a desirable anchorage. It is the most favourable situation on the English coast for taking advantage of all winds to make a passage into the ocean; and without measuring it by line, as Plymouth Sound, it would contain near double the number of ships at their anchors.

" According to the data for estimating the expense in the Sound, to make a breakwater of two thousand yards on the Zone reef, would cost about a million and a half; and to make it as desirable, perhaps, as Spithead, by making a small breakwater at the Outer Manacle rock, called the Penvin, or Vaze, and another to the north-east of the principal breakwater, might not cost more than two millions sterling. When viewing the space, the idea might be thought chimerical; but the great sea that is rolled into Plymouth Sound by south-west gales, is in a great measure broken off here by the land in that direction; and the breakwater on and about the Outer Manacle rock would prevent its effects from being felt in the space mentioned.

" The undertaking might not prove more gigantic or expensive than that in Plymouth Sound; no such lamentable consequences could be apprehended from it as at that place; and there is one thing certain, that it would prove many times more beneficial to the interests of the nation; whether in giving protection to fleets and squadrons, or convoys, destined to the southward and westward. He who attempts to prove the contrary, must begin with denying all the natural consequences arising from the difference of latitude and longitude, the situation of Ushant and the Land's End, and the most important effect of north-west winds when acting upon them."

It has been seen, that, according to Captain M.'s statement, it would require 1,500,000*l*. to render Plymouth Sound capable of accommodating 30 (the official documents, and plan of the breakwater,* say 36) sail of the line; while, for 500,000*l*. Falmouth might be made to receive at least 56 sail; giving the sum of 1,000,000*l*. sterling, and room for 20, or 26 ships, in favour of Falmouth. Having thus settled the point of *expense*, he proceeds, in his seventh letter, to discuss the question, whether the country would eventually derive more *benefit* from such improvements as have been described, at Plymouth or Falmouth. "There are but two arguments," he considers, "that can be produced in favour of Plymouth Sound, which can be supposed to carry any weight; these are, its vicinity to a dock-yard, and ships being enabled to sail from it in south-east winds."—After taking a view of the British navy at different periods, and the establishments provided for making it effective, Captain M. adverts to the report of the Commissioners of Naval Revision, "which asserts, that room would be wanting to lay up *five hundred and thirty-five* ships and vessels of war in peace, *ninety-seven* of which would be of the line; *eighty-eight* frigates, and *three hundred and fifty* sloops of war, gun-brigs, and other small vessels: that is, supposing the peace establishment to consist of twenty sail of the line, fifty frigates, and one hundred sloops and other vessels.

"A retrospective view of peace establishments," continues Captain M. "of the British navy, will be far from giving a correct idea of what may be necessary in the present state of Europe and of the world. That the state of nations will never assume their former appearance, may be safely affirmed; and, therefore, the peace establishment of this country will have more objects to embrace than formerly, and some of greater magnitude. Allowing, then, that it may be found necessary to have an hundred ships and vessels of war more in commission than the number estimated, still, most probably, room would be wanting for the hundred mentioned."

Captain M. states, that, in a former publication, addressed to Mr. Perceval, and to the First Lord of the Admiralty, he has proved, that the deep water in Falmouth harbour will contain at the least 46 sail of the line at moorings, besides other vessels, and leaving the anchorage of Carrack roads clear; and that a wet dock could be made of St. Just creek, which would contain 40 or 50 sail of the line in a state of ordinary, of equipment, or many of them nearly ready for sea, besides offering eligible situations for docks.

"Allowing, then," says he, "that to prepare the harbour and St. Just creek to contain an *hundred sail of the line*, sixty of them ready for sea,

---

* *Vide* N. C. XXVIII. pp. 122, 124, 233.

and that when so prepared, it would contain the same number in a state, of ordinary, besides a proportion of smaller ships and vessels; and that this could be effected for the same expense it will take to secure, as is supposed, *thirty sail of the line* in Plymouth Sound; or even allowing it should cost ONE MILLION MORE to attain this great national object, in a secure western harbour on the meridian of Ushant, situated in the critical pass of the English Channel, and into which the largest ships can sail during all southerly winds at any time of tide, or find a safe anchorage without its entrance, when the wind blows so far within the land that they cannot sail in direct; from which measure would the country reap the greatest advantages?—There may be those who will assert, from the breakwaters in Plymouth Sound. But how many, amongst those whose minds are not blinded by prejudice, or fettered by interest, will believe them? Should any be disposed to find fault with the using of the word *prejudice*, let such say what other term is more applicable to a dislike not founded on reasonable objections.

" It then appears, that if the money to be expended in Plymouth Sound, in executing a measure covered with doubts of an alarming nature, were laid out in preparing Falmout hharbour for the reception of the navy, a great portion of it would not only find a safe port in war, almost touching the Atlantic Ocean, and of easy entrance during all southerly gales, but also a safe retreat during peace; two important acquisitions long desired, and which would set the mind of the nation and of her government at rest on a great and weighty point, if obtained.

" Can any works that shall be executed in Plymouth Sound, let their magnitude be ever so great, offer any such advantages? Its vicinity to a dock-yard is light in the balance against the *national benefits* in the opposite scale, as depots for all kinds of stores could be formed in Falmouth harbour, as well as in Hamoaze, and many of them more conveniently."

In his eighth letter, Captain Manderson inquires into the advantages which Plymouth Sound may be said to offer, in point of sailing from it, over the western harbour. The whole of this letter, which is very long, is exceedingly important, not only to nautical men, but to the government, and to the nation at large. Captain M.'s reasonings on the subject of the winds, are founded on experience, and on recorded facts.

" I have now before me," says he, " a log of their fluctuations in Falmouth harbour, from the 1st of August, 1800, to the 30th of April, 1802; and as it was not taken for any such purpose as that to which it is now applied, there can be no partiality in the account; if any inaccuracy in particular fluctuations, it must be as favourable to one quarter as to another.

" By this log it appears, that from the 1st of August, 1800, to 31st of December, including a period of five months, the winds were sixty-eight days in the south-west quarter, forty-two days in the north-west quarter, and twelve days in the south-east quarter; but not above two days of what may be called south-east winds, and about fourteen days fair for vessels from any port in the Channel.

" From the 1st of January, to the 31st of December, 1801, it appears they were in the south-west quarter one hundred and fifty-two days, in the north-west quarter one hundred and one days, thirty days in the south-east quarter; but not above seven days of south-east winds, and about sixty days fair from all ports.

" From the 1st of January, 1802, to the 30th of April following, in the south-west quarter forty-seven days, in the north-west quarter forty-two days, in the south east quarter seven days, and fair from all ports thirty days; not above two days of what could be properly called south-east winds.

" Those days not reckoned in the account to make up the number included in the period of time, the winds were so variable as not to belong properly to any quarter.

" It then appears, that for a period of time including one year and nine months, or six hundred and thirty-eight days, the winds blew from the western quarters above four hundred and fifty-two days; and in all that time there were not above eight days of proper south-east winds.

" No ships would venture from the Sound with a thick rainy wind, just veered from south-west to south-east, or to south-south-east, and fluctuating southerly, as they would be inevitably pressed on the coast; and if the wind were east-south-east, ships could sail out of Falmouth harbour direct.

" But ships might sail, as they often do, from Falmouth with an unsettled north-west wind ; for they have nothing to fear by the wind veering westerly or southerly, as they can easily run back into port.

" The periods of time in which the winds are stated, may fairly be taken as a criterion for any other period of time. It is true they are not every year alike, some years being more easterly than others ; but the period taken will be found as favourable in that respect as any other in the western parts of the Channel."

Captain Manderson's next object is, to prove, from facts, what effect the general state of the winds on the south coast of our island has upon the movements of our marine.

" I can have no objection," he observes, " to look back for any length of time, as every year would furnish proofs more or less perspicuous; but in order to avoid prolixity as much as possible, I shall only cite a few cases for three years back.

" May 10th, 1808, passed Plymouth, Rear-admiral Bertie, in H.M.S. Leopard, of fifty guns, with an outward-bound East India convoy ; also, H.M.S. President, of thirty-six guns, and Lightning, of eighteen guns, with an outward bound fleet for the Brazils. The same day the wind veered to south-west ; the Leopard and Indiamen kept the sea, but the Lightning put into Falmouth with part of the convoy, and the President keeping out, was forced eastward. On the 15th, sailed from Falmouth the following ships of war, with convoys, which had been forced into that port by contrary winds. Cambrian, with convoy for the Mediterranean ; Amelia and Avenger, with convoy for America; Belette, convoy for the West Indies;

and Lightning, with convoy for the Brazils; but the President did not pass Falmouth until the 17th, with the Serapis store-ship, and twenty-eight sail under convoy.

"On the 25th of September, 1809, H M.S. La Rhin, of thirty-eight guns, sailed from Plymouth, with seven victuallers for the squadron off Rochfort, and was forced into Falmouth by contrary winds on the 27th, whence she could not sail until the 2d of October. The day after she left Plymouth, nine vessels sailed from Falmouth, and made their passage westward. 7th January, 1810, put into 'Falmouth, with contrary winds, the Nonpareil, of sixteen guns, from Plymouth, with six transports under convoy, bound to Gibraltar, with provisions, &c.; on the 5th, had sailed from Falmouth, the Sandwich lugger, of fourteen guns, with nine sail to the westward.

"31st March, 1810, put into Falmouth by contrary winds, H.M. brig Orestes, with the Alligator and Lapwing transports, for Cork, and Devastation bomb for Cadiz; all from Plymouth. On the 29th, had sailed from Falmouth, two packets, one for Lisbon, the other to the Windward Islands, and a brig called the John, to run it to Madeira; all of which made their passage into the ocean, while those from Plymouth could not sail again until the 8th of April.

"12th July, 1810, the Fervent, with a fleet of transports, with provisions, &c. from Plymouth to Cadiz, was forced by contrary winds into Falmouth; on the 11th, had sailed from the latter port, five packets with foreign mails; one for Lisbon, and others westward,. none of which returned; while the Fervent could not put to sea again until the 18th.

"On the 14th of May, 1811, H.M.S. Favourite, and Intelligent gun-brig, with a fleet of transports from Plymouth, having on board the 11th light dragoons, and part of the 11th regiment of foot, bound to Portugal, put into Falmouth with contrary winds. On the 12th, eight vessels had sailed from this harbour to the westward, for Cork, Dublin, &c.

"On the 8th of June, 1811, H.M.S. Leopard, of fifty guns, having on board a detachment of the guards for Cadiz, was forced into Falmouth by contrary winds, and detained until the 12th. On the 7th, sailed from Falmouth, H. M. brig Seaflower, with despatches for Lisbon, one vessel for Cork, one for Dublin, and another for Wales.

"On the 9th of August, 1811, sailed from Falmouth, H.M.S. Mercury and Spitfire, with the Jasper schooner, and a fleet of transports, for Lisbon; on the 2d, had put into Plymouth, with contrary winds, H.M.S. Shannon and Cormorant, Serapis S.S. Diligence S.S. with about forty sail of transports, with troops on board, for Lisbon and Sicily; but did not get to the westward of Falmouth before the 12th.

"If the annals of vessels sailing from, or being as far to the westward as Plymouth, and others sailing at the same time from Falmouth, were to be minutely examined, they could produce a volume of evidence; much of it of greater importance than any of the cases I have noticed. But if the sailing of two vessels at the same time from Plymouth and Falmouth, let them be ever so insignificant in themselves, is often found to cause several days of delay in getting to the westward, the same will hold good in convoys, as is proved from the cases noticed, and also with respect to fleets and squadrons of ships of war."

After some inferences drawn from these facts, Captain M. mentions the following important cases :—

" In 1808, an expedition was formed in Falmouth harbour, and sailed on the 9th of October, under Sir David Baird, on board of one hundred and fifty transports, carrying between twelve and thirteen thousand men, convoyed by H. M. S. Loire, Amelia, and Champion. On the 11th, it made the high land of Corunna; on the 12th, was on the coast of Spain; and, on the 13th, entered the harbour of Corunna. On the same day it sailed, two transports left Plymouth to join it, one of which, having on board part of the 31st regiment of foot, got into Falmouth with the wind at south-west on the 11th, the day the expedition made the high land of Corunna; and the other, called the Charlotte, having on board part of the 26th regiment of foot, got into Falmouth harbour the very day the expedition entered that of Corunna."

" When reinforcements and stores were, as has been reported, urgently required by Lord Wellington's army, they were prepared at Portsmouth with all possible despatch, and sailed with the first favourable wind. On the 1st of February, 1811, the convoy was met by a south-west gale, when nearly off the Lizard, when it run back to Plymouth and Torbay. The Milford East Indiaman was in company, commanded by Captain Lermont, who had in the month of October preceding put into Falmouth harbour with an easterly wind, being homeward-bound from Bombay; he, therefore, now thought it best to take refuge there again (as did some other vessels), declaring, as I have been informed, that he would rather run back to Spithead than trust his ship either in Plymouth Sound or Torbay. So much do men differ in opinion respecting the safety of different anchorages; but experience is to be trusted before opinion. On the 16th of February, a strong gale came on from north-north-west, when H.M.S. Amethyst was unhappily wrecked in Plymouth Sound, with the loss of many valuable lives; similar disasters no breakwater can ever prevent, as the wind blew from the interior, and as it can in no manner soften the rocky ledges, reefs, projections, and ribs, nearly encompassing this anchorage. On this very day, when there was so much just cause for sorrow covering the land, sailed in safety, from the (misnamed dangerous by some men) harbour of Falmouth, the Milford East Indiaman, Duke of Kent packet for the Windward Islands; H. M. S. Fylla, and several merchant vessels; next day the wind was south. On the 21st, the Franchise and transports were again off the Lizard, where they had nearly been three weeks before, and by the wind coming to blow from the south-west, the John and James transport was unfortunately run down in the dark, and between two and three hundred men of the 11th regiment drowned; the Wellington transport, laden with stores, was also run down at the same time, and sunk, the captain and six men drowned. The fleet now put into Falmouth harbour, whence it sailed on the 9th of March, three weeks after the Milford and other vessels.

"A squadron of his Majesty's ships having troops on board, for the more speedily transporting reinforcements to Lord Wellington's army, which sailed from Spithead with the fleet of transports, and was in company when met by a contrary wind, after being near the Lizard, and had taken refuge in Torbay, from which anchorage it proceeded on its destination on the 16th of February (the same day as the vessels mentioned sailed from Falmouth harbour), and is said to have arrived in the Tagus on the 4th of March. Here I would particularly request your attention, for the sake of your country only, and for no other reason, what might be the consequence of sailing from the western harbour, and any other anchorage eastward, at the same time. Although the distance between Torbay and Falmouth harbour be only *twenty five* leagues, and a squadron of his Majesty's ships on an urgent service, may be supposed to make as good way as any of the vessels that sailed from that harbour the same day it left Torbay; yet the Duke of Kent packet, on the 4th of March, was in lat. 29° 42′ north, and long. 25° 17′ west; being then *five hundred and six* leagues south-west by south, one quarter west, from the Lizard, and *three hundred and twenty-one* leagues south-west by west from Lisbon; therefore, she had run above two hundred and forty leagues farther from the anchorage she left, in sixteen days, than the squadron of men of war had from Torbay, as the distance of the latter from Lisbon is about two hundred and sixty leagues ;-but the Duke of Kent was *five hundred and ten* leagues from the western harbour.

"Is not this fact particularly striking? All the art of sophistry cannot strip it of the unspeakable importance it assumes in a national point of view.

"You will no doubt be exceedingly anxious to inquire, from what cause this great difference of situation could proceed? and be ready to imagine that the packet must be an extraordinary fast sailer. But the cause is not included in such a conjecture; the other vessels that sailed on the same day from the same anchorage, no doubt, were nearly in an equal degree advanced on their voyage. It can be easily ascertained where the Milford East Indiaman was on that day, when she shall have returned to England.

"The great difference of situation proceeded from the cause that has been brought into view; the western harbour being on the meridian of Ushant, and the vessels sailing from it getting clear into the ocean before the wind changed to the south-west, and before the squadron could clear the Channel.

"Here, Sir, is a secret of incalculable value to the British Empire, which appears to have been concealed from the eyes of the nation and, her government, and is at this moment endeavoured to be covered with the shade of everlasting oblivion. But there is the squadron entering the Tagus; and there is the packet three hundred and twenty leagues southwest by west from it; and there is the fleet of transports, with troops and stores on board, now in Falmouth harbour, which sailed from Spithead the latter end of January, bound in haste to Lisbon, but cannot *now* leave their present anchorage until the 9th of March, on which day the Duke of Kent is in latitude 23° 12′ north, and longitude 38° 18′ west, or seven hundred and forty-two leagues south-west of the Lizard, and five hundred and eighty-five leagues south-west and by west, half-west, from Lisbon.

" Now, allowing the fleet of transports to have only run two-thirds of the distance that the packet had done on the 9th of March (if they had sailed from Falmouth on the 16th of February), they would have run four hundred and ninety-four leagues from the Lizard, twice the distance from Falmouth to Lisbon; and if bound up the Mediterranean, equal to the distance a fleet of transports might have carried an army from the western harbour as high as Carthagena. Your own knowledge and penetration can clearly discern the consequences of a fact pregnant with important information to the British nation. It requires no professional disquisition to make it more clear; the statesman can better comprehend its magnitude, while professional representations might labour to darken counsel, without communicating the least useful information."

" When Lord Bentinck was charged with an important mission to the Sicilian court, that no delay might be occasioned in getting out of the Channel, as was supposed, when the wind should come fair, the Menelaus frigate was ordered to receive him at Plymouth, where he was detained some time by contrary winds, as were also nine packets at Falmouth. On the 27th of October (1811), the wind came northerly, when the frigate and packets sailed from their different anchorages; two of the latter put back disabled, but seven effected their passage into the ocean. On the 29th, the Menelaus was forced into Falmouth harbour, whence she could not sail until the 7th of November. The Dauntless, with two transports under her convoy, sailed from Plymouth much about the same time as the frigate, and was also obliged to seek refuge in the western harbour on the same day. When the Menelaus sailed from Falmouth on the 7th of November, the Marlborough, one of the packets which left it on the 27th of October, was on that day in latitude 44° 22′ north, and longitude 11° 28′ west; being then one hundred and forty-three leagues south-west by south, half-west, from Falmouth, and one hundred and nineteen leagues south-west, one quarter west, from Ushant.

" The Walsingham, another of the packets that sailed the same day as the Marlborough, on the 7th of November, was in latitude 45° 44′ north, longitude 12° 28′ west; being then one hundred and thirty-three leagues south-west, half west, from Falmouth, and one hundred and fifteen leagues south-west and by west, half west, from Ushant. Another of the packets, called the Speedy, which sailed the same day as the Menelaus from Plymouth, on the 7th of November, at noon, was in lat. 42° 58′ north, long. 9° 26′ west; being then about one hundred and fifty-five leagues south-south-west from Falmouth, and one hundred and twenty-six leagues south-south-west, half west, from Ushant. The other four packets, whose situations I have not ascertained, were no doubt equally distant from the port they left.

" Here, Sir, there is another trial, of a different kind from those before noticed; one as desirable as could be wished; a stout, good-sailing, well manned, and well-handled frigate, despatched on an urgent service, from an anchorage where, it was supposed, she would be in the best situation for clearing the English Channel, is foiled by packets less able to bear up against storms and tempests, and sailing from a harbour which you may have been led to think unfavourably of. All hinged, and will continue to hinge, generally speaking, on northerly winds of short duration, which give to vessels sailing from Falmouth harbour an advantage so clearly decided over those sailing from an anchorage near a degree of longitude farther to the eastward.

" The advantages that may be promised from Plymouth Sound in southeast winds have not once appeared during the last four years; and hence it may be fairly inferred, that they will very seldom appear; and when they do, may not be wanted: while at the same time it is apparent, that northwest winds, which give the western harbour such an important superiority of situation, are frequent almost every month in the year, more especially in blowing weather during winter, spring, and autumn. Which, then, is the safest to form a conclusion from, in a case, the decision of which must be so momentous to the vital interests of the country; from undeniable matter of fact, or the illusory phantom of *prospective speculation* ?

" Another advantage, of no small consideration, which vessels have when sailing from Falmouth harbour over those leaving any other anchorage in the Channel, during north-west winds, is, that they can cover themselves with the land until they shoot from the Lizard in a south-west direction towards the ocean; and this southern promontory of England may be called the advanced post of her most western harbour, to protect it from the advancing billows of the stormy deep."

(To be continued.)

Naval Poetry.

LINES

ADDRESSED TO THE LIEUTENANTS OF THE NAVY, UPON THE CHANGE OF UNIFORM, ADOPTED AUGUST 12TH, 1812.

YE gallant subjects of Old Davy—
    The jolly " Luffs" of Britain's Navy,
Come listen to my lay:
With hope light up your rugged faces,
Like eager cruiser when she chases,
    And chides her tardy way.

As such bold cruiser when she spies
A sail may haply prove a prize,
    And all her canvas crouds,
Dashes the foam aside her bows,
Dispel the gloom about your brows,
    And drive away its clouds.

Attend awhile unto my muse,
For she doth bring you welcome news,
   As you shall quickly own,—
" Restrictions" all have ceased to be ;
And now the Prince, from fetters free,
   Assumes to act alone.

Your claims so often urg'd in vain,
To that bright prize you've bled to gain,
   The Regent Prince admits ;
That you may be allowed to wear
The Epaulet,—badge proud and fair!
   He graciously permits.

When first the quarter-deck you trod,
Resolv'd no more on land to plod
   But boldly tempt the main,
Was not the epaulet the prize
To which you still, with sanguine eyes,
   Looked forward to obtain ?—

Behold then now your wishes gain'd,
Your hopes fulfilled, the prize obtain'd,
   Bestow'd too from the throne .
No more complain of luckless stars,
Or friends unkind, or bootless wars,—
   The epaulet's your own.

No more shall captain, vain and stern,
Nor flippant army subaltern,
   Alone the " bullion" wear ;
No more marine subordinate
On deck display the epaulet,
   The while your shoulder's bare.

No more shall merchant skippers dare
Your button, late usurped, to wear,
   Now more respected grown ;
That button, late an anchor plain,
The regal crown surmounts again,
   To prove you " The King's own."

When landing on some foreign shore,
By Turk inhabited, or Moor,
   Or where rude Indians dwell,—
With deep " salam," and honours meet,
Your rank proclaim'd they now shall greet,
   Nor slight the " white lappel."

No longer at the splendid ball,
Or party, or assembly, shall

  The haughty fair-one scorn you;
For now, as well as soldier fine
Or of militia or the line,
  Shall golden " swab " adorn you,

Now with slash'd-sleeve, and epaulet,
And trim cock'd-hat, with neat rosette,
  You yield the palm to no men:
With regulation sword and knot,
So bold and smart,—you will, I wot,
  Be the delight of women.

No longer will the fair conceal
The preference they ever feel
  For Britain's brave defenders;—
Since these the epaulet display,
They'll soon " cut out," and keep away,
  All other gay pretenders.

For still the fair, like fish, are caught
By bait with shining tinsel fraught.
  (As glitters many a beau!)
Yet not by glare of dress alone
Are Albion's daughters always won,—
  But worth as well as show.

Thus in Golconda's precious mines
The diamond, yet unpolished, shines
  With beams of doubtful light;
But when the lapidary's art
Has wrought away each ruder part
  The gem is lustrous bright.

Right gladly would I tune my lay
To sing of some " increase of pay "
  As well as ornament;
But such the times,—so poor the nation,
'Tis even not in contemplation,
  Which we must all lament.

Now let us sing—" Long live the King! "
Let wardrooms all, and gunrooms, ring
  With this inspiring strain.
Success attend the epaulet!
And may you soon another get,
  Nor let me wish in vain.
          M. M.

NELSON.
A DIRGE.

Saw ye the streets when Nelson died,
   When his funereal train drew near,
The troops arrang'd on every side,
   The people gazing in the rear?

I saw the streets when Nelson died:
   When his funereal car drew near,
Not one brave heart but deeply sigh'd,
   Not one fair cheek without a tear!

A Nation's grief bedew'd his grave;
   Devotion mourn'd him as her own;
For, in the battle, truly brave,
   He fear'd th' Omnipotent alone!

O! how it sooth'd the Hero's shade,
   Though weeping still at Trafalgar,
When in the grave his dust was laid
   With all the pride and pomp of war!

Intomb d in yonder hallow'd fane,
   With requiems due his ashes rest;
Archangels, with a solemn strain,
   Inshrin'd his spirit with the blest!

Nelson! to men and angels dear,
   Thy name shall never, never die!
Britain embalms it with a tear,
   And fame records it with a sigh!

                        JOHN MAYNE.

SONNET,
WRITTEN AT THE EDDYSTONE LIGHT-HOUSE, JULY 7TH, 1812.

" Qui cursu magnum jam præter vectus Ocrinum
   Navita, Dumnoniæ littora curva legis,—
En, tibi, fluctifragi angusto de vertici saxi
   Tollit se in medio vasta columna mari."——Phillimore.

Structure sublime! that o'er the distant wave
   My anxious eye so oft essayed to trace,
Watching, with levelled glass, the bright surge lave
   Thy towering side, and sweep thy rugged base—
At length thy gulph-encircled rock I tread,
   Around whose marge a thousand currents dart,—
While thou, uplifting high thy awful head,
   Seem'st the last boundary of human art!

  Here, as the frail bark braves the western sky,
   And to the fearful night's revolving reign
  Hoarse desolation pours her hollow sigh,
   The flaming silver cheers the lonely main,
  Sways the bold helm, and o'er the yawning grave
   Rises, like Bethlem's star—to guide and save.
Plymouth.   WILLIAM BALL.

LINES

Intended for a Stone to be placed over two Seamen, late belonging to the Swallow,* interred in the Naval Burying Ground at Port Mahon.

  Courses up and topsails handed,
   Life's main-stay-sail carry'd away;
  Weather sheet and bowlines stranded,
   Here death piped thy last belay.

  Of two, the gen'rous and the bold,
   Two tars the Swallow learn'd to prize,
  Whose valour set in splendour mild,
   And left its lustre to the skies.

  What though they boast no titled fame,
   Nor ask the honours titles leave;
  Yet valour and an humble name,
   Might sure an humble portion crave.

  E'en this cold stone by shipmates rais'd,
   To wake no virtues o'er the grave,
  Leaves that to pow'r Almighty prais'd—
   Almighty just—in mercy save—
H. M. S. Swallow, Mediterranean,   X.
 2 *April,* 1812.

SONG.

BY THE LATE CAPTAIN THE HON. CHARLES HERBERT, R. N.

FROM CAMOENS.

  Dear Mother, then say not
   Why will you not stay;
  Love whispers I may not,
   And drives me away:
  'Tis his pleasure decides me
   No will of my own,
  As a sov'reign he guides me,
   I bow to his throne.

---

  * For a brilliant achievement against the enemy performed by this ship, see N. C. XXVIII. 194.

  Who, 'spight of all wailing,
   Commands me to roam,
  With my sailor boy sailing
   Far, far from my home.
  You know Love's a master
   Not kings can controul:
  His fetters bind faster,
   That fix on the soul.

  Then strive not, dear Mother,
   My steps to delay,
  Love points to another,
   And beckons away.
  When my heart thus directs me,
   Why loiter behind?
  Lo! my sailor expects me,
   And fair is the wind.

  Oh! say, ye wide oceans,
   Did ever ye bear
  On your billows' rude motions
   A form half so fair?
  But of hearts, the blind gaoler
   Sets all on a par,
  'Gainst his laws there's no failing,
   So love-borne, I'll roam
  With my sailor boy, sailing
   Far, far from my home.

LINES

WRITTEN IN THE CAVE OF FINGAL.

Dark Staffa, in thy grotto wild,
 How my rapt soul is taught to feel;
O well becomes it Nature's child
 Low in her stateliest shrine to kneel!

Thou art no fiend's nor giant's home—
 Thy piles of dark and solemn grain
Bespeak thy dread and sacred dome
 Great temple of the western main!

For the harp of the air is heard in thee,
Sounding its holiest lullaby.
Far in thy vaults the mermaid sings,
And the sea-bird's note responsive rings;
Yes, the hymn of the winds, and the ocean's roar,
Are heard in thee for evermore!

Tho' other wonders meet mine eye,
From my chill'd heart shall never fly,
Thy arches cavern'd, green and torn,
On Nature's rifted columns borne;
Thy furnac'd pillars, tall and sure,
Propping the wild entaldature
That round each cope and architrave
In awful murmurs weep and rave;
The whirl of Nature's grand turmoil,
Where billows burst and torrents boil
Thro' portals stern and pavements riven,
Uprear'd by Architect of Heaven—
Thro' darken'd domes, and dens of wonder,
And caverns of eternal thunder! J. H.

Marine Law.

COURTS MARTIAL.

APRIL 16.—A court martial assembled this day, and continued, by adjournment, to the 17th, for the purpose of inquiring into the circumstance of H. M. S. Conquistador having struck on a shoal, at the east end of Quiberon Bay, called "Le Four," on the evening of the 3d of March last, and to try her commander, Lord William Stuart, and the other officers of the Conquistador, for not having taken care in the steering and conducting of his Majesty's said ship; and for having, through wilfulness, negligence, and other default, run the said ship on the said shoal or sand; and for having hazarded the said ship, contrary to the 26th article of war.*

PRESIDENT,
Right Honourable Lord KEITH.

MEMBERS,
Sir ROBERT CALDER, Bart.   Admiral DURHAM,
Captain Malcolm, (Captain of the Fleet,)
Captains LINZEE, BAKER, DUNDAS, LLOYD, Sir GEORGE COLLIER,
LAKE, PLAMPIN, BOUVERIE, and BARTON.

The defence made by his Lordship, was to the following effect:—" Conscious of having fulfilled my duty, and confident that no obloquy can attach to my character, it is with mortified feelings that I find myself, with the officers of the ship I command, to day arraigned on a charge of such magnitude as has been just alleged against us; and I cannot but deem it, from my own observation, as well as from the information of others, a

---

* Vide N.C. XXVII. 303, 477; and XXVIII. 228, 232.

novel proceeding for an accident of this nature, to be made the subject of inquiry in the first instance. For more than twenty years my life,has been devoted to the service of my country, with the most ardent desire to contribute to its welfare, and the most zealous attachment to my profession. I must confess, as these reflections press on my mind, that my pride is hurt, and my feelings are wounded, in being reduced to the mortifying situation of becoming an egotist. It is, however, a great source of consolation, that the charges against me are to undergo the decision of officers of such high rank and distinguished merit as are now assembled, and to you, I trust, it will be in my power satisfactorily to prove, that the accident to the Conquistador did not result from wilfulness, negligence, or any other fault; as her course was shaped according to the safe chart furnished by the Admiralty, and every precaution was taken, in the management of the ship, that prudence could dictate, or zeal for the King's service could prescribe; particularly as I had urgent reasons for reaching my destination. It will be also proved to you, that after the occurrence of the accident, every possible exertion was made (exertions, which, I believe, have never been exceeded), not only during the night when the Conquistador unfortunately struck on the shoal, but from that period until her arrival in this harbour, to preserve her to the service. It is with heartfelt pleasure I bear testimony to the prompt and decisive measures of my officers and crew; to their cheerful resignation and general good conduct, as without their efforts, not only the ship would have been lost, but what is dearer than life, our honour also might have been the forfeit, for the censorious world might then have trifled with our characters, without dreading refutation."

His Lordship then stated, that on the 27th of February, Captain Bisset, the senior officer in Basque Road, directed him to proceed to Quiberon-bay, for a particular purpose, which furnished a powerful inducement to an officer anxious to acquire honour, and eager to perform his duty. His Lordship also stated, that at this time he had only 54 tons of water on board, a circumstance which created an additional inducement to him to be prompt in the obedience of orders, in order that his water might be completed, and his ship rendered more efficient; and that, on the 1st of March, he, solely, worked the Conquistador through the Pertius d'Antioch, against an adverse wind, with squally weather, the pilot being then under an arrest; that though the wind blew strong on the shore the whole of the ensuing night, he persevered in going to sea; that on the weather becoming fair about half-past one P.M. on the following day, at which time l'Isle Dieu was reported to be in sight, he employed himself,with the master, in taking the bearings of the land, with scarcely a minute's intermission, till half-past two, when the west end bore east by south, and was distant, according to their computation, nine miles, after which, from rain and thick weather, the land was no longer visible; that the course of the ship was then shaped according to the Admiralty chart, north by east, and this track was even marked out with a pencil; that at the same time he directed the master, on no pretext, to quit the deck, but carefully to watch the steerage of the ship, till she was brought to an anchor; that he repeatedly afterwards marked out on the chart the supposed position of the ship, gave particular orders for the frequent heaving of the log, and, at half-past six, marked, in anticipation, the spot he supposed she would reach at seven, at which hour he ordered the studding-sails to be taken in, when his intention was to govern himself by the soundings, and as there was the appearance of bad weather from the westward, to have anchored, so as to have ensured, at the same time, a drift for the night, and his getting into Quiberon-bay early the following morning. After referring the Court to the ship's log-book, the Admiralty chart, with the Conquistador's track and positions on the 3d of March, and the several testimonies of her officers, his Lordship concluded as follows:—" I refer you to these, under a full conviction that the more scrutinously my conduct is investigated, the more firmly will my justification be established."

" This defence was corroborated by Lieutenant Giddy, Mr. Selly, the master, Lieutenant Lambert, James Lear, quarter-master, James Hewitt, quarter-master, James West, seaman, Surgeon Henderson, and Captain Somerville, who declared, that during the whole of his attendance on the Conquistador, it was impossible any officer could shew more zeal and perseverance than his Lordship. After due deliberation, the Court came to the following

SENTENCE.

" The Court is of opinion, that the service upon which the Conquistador was employed, was important, and that her captain appears to have been urged thereby to use every exertion to execute his orders.

" That the captain and master had a mean opinion of the French pilot's capacity, and having no confidence in him, did not consult him.

" That, although the master appears not to have been sufficiently acquainted with the setting and velocity of the tides, great anxiety and much care were manifested both by the captain and him in attending to the steering, and conducting of the ship in her course, as well as in placing proper persons to look out, and that the master concurred with the captain in thinking that the course was not only proper and safe to be steered, but that the distance might be run with security; that after the ship grounded, the captain shewed great firmness and presence of mind, evinced great professional skill, used uncommon exertions for the recovery of the ship, and in common with all his officers and crew, chearfully underwent the greatest fatigue and privation up to the period of her arrival at Falmouth; that there is not the most distant ground for believing that the said captain, the Right Hon. Lord Wm. Stuart, and the other officers of the Conquistador, did not take care in the steering and conducting the said ship, or that the said ship was through wilfulness, negligence, or other default, run on the said shore or sands, stated to be " La Four," or that she was hazarded contrary to the 26th article of war: and the Court doth in consequence adjudge the said captain, the Right Hon. Lord Wm. Stuart, and the other officers of the Conquistador, to be severally fully acquitted, and the said captain Lord Wm. Stuart and the other officers of the Conquistador, are hereby so severally and fully acquitted accordingly,"

NAVAL HISTORY OF THE PRESENT YEAR, 1812.

(September—October.)

RETROSPECTIVE AND MISCELLANEOUS.

EVER since the 18th of June have the United States of America been at war against England. But it is only since the 13th of October that we have been placed in a corresponding attitude towards that commonwealth, by an order in council; wherein general reprisals are granted against the ships, &c. of the United States, except any vessels sailing under license or special release from embargo: and recognition is explicitly made of a pacific declaration which the English commander-in-chief on the American station has been previously authorized to issue to that government. The former document alluded to is given at length in another part of this volume.

The Prince Regent's declaration of war shews in its concluding paragraph an anxious and laudable readiness to seize the first honourable means of reconciliation. Let a similar spirit animate a majority of the American people, and an opening will soon be afforded to accommodate all differences between us, and to save the American people from that worst of dangers,—French connection. Meanwhile, the first campaign of these lamentable hostilities has been marked by events on land and at sea each respectively diametrically opposite to the public expectation: at least certainly so to the speculations we had formed—One of the continental armies destined for the invasion of Canada, hardly passed the frontiers 'ere it found itself under the necessity of laying down its arms before the small English force that could be hastily assembled for the defence of that province, as much inferior upon paper as it proved itself superior in the field. And for which it has been rewarded in the person of its commanding officer, Major General Isaac Brock, who has been promptly and deservedly named an *extra* knight of the most honourable military order of the Bath.—" The cheap defence of nations!" The unlooked for reverse of the medal is the capture of one of our stoutest frigates, the *Guerriere*, by a single opponent of the same class of ship, commanded by a nephew, bearing the same name, of the invading general against whom the fortune of war proved so adverse in the back-settlements. Disasters of this kind are so rare in our naval annals, that it is not to be wondered at if such a result of a single-ship action, fought under such peculiar circumstances, should have aroused a more than common feeling. The character of the service is so far compromised by it, that we feel ourselves called upon to contribute our humble endeavours to make this event better understood than it seems hitherto to have been. The reader will perhaps attend to the following statement of one jealous of his country's honour.

An English frigate, rated 38 guns, should undoubtedly (barring extraordinary accidents) cope successfully with a 44-gun ship of any nation: but if that 44, by advantage of wind and superior sailing, should be able to chuse her position, and vary her distance as may suit her convenience, it becomes problematical whether an English 38 could conquer her adversary under such circumstances; which seem to have been those attending this action. If, in addition to these advantages, the enemy should have a much more numerous crew, and so superior a weight of metal as the American possessed; then we have little doubt, that ur ess ine critical accident should befal the enemy, such as a shot in the rudder, or the loss of a mast, neither valour nor seamanship can obtain a victory. In this case, it is to be remembered, the accident last mentioned fell to the lot of the English frigate in a triple proportion. It will be found, by multiplying the number of guns on board the respective ships, by the weight of their shot, that at every broadside the Constitution discharged 777 *lbs.* of metal, and that the *Guerriere* discharged but 526 *lbs.* The proportion is as 3 to 2: consequently, if the *Guerriere* had mounted 48 guns of one caliber, the Constitution was armed with the equivalent of 72 similar guns. With this overwhelming superiority of artillery, manned by a crew nearly double to that of the *Guerriere*, affording the means of employing a numerous musketry, with the power of chusing a position, which enabled her to apply her fire in the most destructive direction, it may well be asked whether there was a rational possibility of our countrymen effecting any thing, even if their masts had not gone so early. Had the Constitution been the English frigate, we are confident (without meaning to cast invidious national reflections, particularly in a case where the victors have displayed both bravery, and its usual concomitant, humanity), that in half an hour the *Guerriere* would have been ours, or at the bottom.

Such of our countrymen as are ill-informed of Yankee prowess should remember, that Captain Bingham defended a contemptible brig (*Littlebelt*) against the sister ship of the Constitution (President). At the same time considering that these immense frigates are equal in weight of metal and complement of men to our two-decked fifties, being actually laid down on the keels of seventy fours; the public must make up its mind to hear before long of some farther misfortunes, similar to that of the *Guerriere*, without feeling that any tarnish has been left upon the national Trident. Above all, let not any premature uncharitable censure be cast upon an officer, who, like Captain Dacres, has valiantly defended his flag, who, in yielding to irresistible strength, has presented no durable trophy to the enemy, and who has yet to justify his conduct before the proper tribunal.*

Buonaparte, after much sanguinary fighting, entered Moscow, the ancient capital of Russia, on the 14th of September. It did not enter into the plan of the Russians, that Moscow should be taken; but, when they found that that event was inevitable, they adopted the most prompt and decisive means, for its destruction, by fire. Every thing having been removed, that time would permit, the city was set fire to in many places at the same moment; and, according to the French statements, about 1600

---

* Since this was prepared for the press, accounts have been received of the trial, and honourable acquittal of Captain Dacres. The loss of the Guerriere's masts is attributed more to their " *defective state*," than to the fire of the enemy.

churches, 1000 palaces, and 30,000 sick and wounded Russians, in the hospitals, perished in the flames! The disappointment of the French ruler is, consequently, great; and his head quarters, should he remain at Moscow during the winter, will be far from commodious.

This dreadful calamity, instead of depressing the spirits, or striking a panic into the mind of, the Russian Emperor, seems to have inspired him with more determined resolution, to hold out to the last, and to reject every proposal for accommodation.—Buonaparte remained at Moscow on the 30th of September; at which time, the Russians were understood to hold very strong positions in its neighbourhood.

The Swedish expedition, respecting which so much has been said, has not yet commenced its operations.

Letters on Service,
Copied verbatim from the LONDON GAZETTE.

ADMIRALTY-OFFICE, SEPTEMBER 29, 1812.

VICE-ADMIRAL SIR EDWARD PELLEW has transmitted to John Wilson Croker, Esq. a letter from Captain Dench, of his Majesty's sloop Nautilus, giving an account of his having, on the 21st of July, captured, off Carbonara, the Brave, French privateer, of five guns, and one hundred and twelve men, and re-captured an English merchant vessel, the only prize she had taken.

And also a letter from Captain Hamilton, of H. M. S. Termagant, stating the capture of l'Intrepide, a French privateer, of three guns and forty men, on the 22d of July, off Malaga, by the boats of the Termagant, under the directions of Lieutenant Moorman.

OCTOBER 6.

Vice-admiral Sir Edward Pellew has transmittted to John Wilson Croker, Esq. a letter from Captain Chamberlayne, of H. M. S. Unité, giving an account of the capture of three vessels, of from eighty to one hundred tons, on the 16th of June, in the small port of Badisea, near Otranto, by the boats of the Unité, Orlando, and Cerberus, under the directions of Lieutenant M‘Dougall.

A letter from Captain Hollis, of the Achille, stating, that on the 17th of July, the boats of that ship and the Cerberus captured or destroyed, off Venice, twelve sail of the enemy's trabaccoloes;

And also a letter from Captain Rowley, of the Eagle, reporting the capture, by storm, on the 20th July, and subsequent destruction of the battery of Cape Ceste, in the Adriatic, by a detachment from the 35th regiment, and a party of marines, under Captain Rutherford, of the 35th, embarked in the boats of the Eagle, under Lieutenant Cannon; and the capture by the latter of an enemy's gun-boat on the 22d.

Vice-admiral Sir Edward Pellew has transmitted to John Wilson Croker, Esq. two letters from Captain Sir Peter Parker, of H.M.S. Menelaus, one giving an account of the boats of that ship having, on the 2d of September, under the direction of Lieutenant Mainwaring, brought out from the river Mignone near Civita Vecchia, the St. Esprit, French letter of marque, pierced for twelve guns, but only two mounted:

The other stating, that on the 4th, two of the boats, under Mr. James Saunderson, master's-mate, brought out from the entrance of the Orbitello Lake, La Fidelle, a government transport, loading with ship timber:

And also a letter from Captain Shaw, of H. M. sloop Philomel, giving an account of his having, on the 24th of August, ran on shore a French Polacre privateer, near Valencia, where she was burnt by the crew, on abandoning her.

Vice-admiral Sir Edward Pellew has transmitted to John Wilson Croker. Esq. returns received from Captain Bathurst, of the Fame, and Captain Hamilton, of the Termagant, of seven towers or batteries destroyed on the coast of Valencia, between the 14th and 29th of August, mounting together twenty-one pieces of ordnance.

And a report from Captain Hamilton, of his having, on the 16th, captured two French privateers, one of four and the other of three guns.

Rear-admiral Laugharne has transmitted to John Wilson Croker, Esq. a letter from Captain Sir Peter Parker, of H.M.S. the Menelaus, addressed to Captain Sir Robert Laurie, of the Ajax, giving an account of an attack made by him on a small convoy of the enemy, in the port of St. Stefano, in the bay of Orbitello, on the 10th of August last. A four-gun battery which commanded the right of the harbour was gallantly stormed and taken possession of by the marines, and two vessels in the port were carried by the boats, one of them, a brig of two hundred tons, laden with timbers and beams for a line-of-battle ship, was brought out; the other, a bombard, laden with naval stores, got aground and was scuttled.—Captain Sir Peter Parker highly commends the conduct of all the officers and men employed upon this occasion. The loss sustained by them was one midshipman (Mr. George Thomas Munro), and one seamen killed, and five men wounded.

OCTOBER 10.

Copy of a Letter from Vice-admiral Sawyer to John Wilson Croker, Esq. dated on board H. M. S. Africa, at Halifax, the 15th September 1812.

SIR,

It is with extreme concern I have to request you will be pleased to lay before the Lords Commissioners of the Admiralty the enclosed copy of a letter from Captain Dacres, of H. M. late ship Guerriere, giving an account of his having sustained a close action, of near two hours, on the 19th ult. with the American frigate Constitution, of very superior force, both in guns and men (of the latter almost double), when the Guerriere being totally dismasted, she rolled so deep as to render all further efforts at the guns unavailing, and it became a duty to spare the lives of the remaining part of her valuable crew, by hauling down her colours. The masts fell over the side from which she was about to be engaged, in a very favourable position for raking by the enemy. A few hours after she was in possession of the enemy, it was found impossible to keep her above water; she was, therefore, set fire to and abandoned, which I hope will satisfy their Lordships she was defended to the last.

Captain Dacres has fully detailed the particulars of the action, as well as the very gallant conduct of, and the support he received from, the whole of his officers and ship's company, and I am happy to hear he is, with the rest of the wounded, doing well; they have been treated with the greatest humanity and kindness, and an exchange having been agreed on, I am in daily expectation of their arrival here.

A list of the killed and wounded is herewith sent, which, I regret to say, is very large. I have the honour to be, &c.

H. SAWYER, Vice-admiral.

SIR, *Boston, September* 7, 1812.

I am sorry to inform you of the capture of H. M. late ship Guerriere, by the American frigate Constitution, after a severe action, on the 19th of August, in lat. 40 deg. 20 min. N. and lon. 55 deg. W. At two P. M. being by the wind on the starboard tack, we saw a sail on our weather-beam, bearing down on us. At three made her out to be a man of war, beat to quarters, and prepared for action. At four, she closing fast, wore to prevent her raking us. At ten minutes past four, hoisted our colours, and fired several shot at her; at twenty minutes past four, she hoisted her colours, and returned our fire, wore several times to avoid being raked, exchanging broadsides. At five she closed on our starboard-beam, both keeping up a heavy fire and steering free, his intention being evidently to cross our bow. At twenty minutes past five, our mizen-mast went over the starboard quarter, and brought the ship up in the wind; the enemy then placed himself on our larboard-bow, raking us, a few only of our bow-guns bearing, and his grape and riflemen sweeping our deck. At forty minutes past five, the ship not answering her helm, he attempted to lay us on board; at this time, Mr. Grant, who commanded the forecastle, was carried below, badly wounded. I immediately ordered the marines and boarders from the main deck; the master was at this time shot through the knee, and I received a severe wound in the back. Lieutenant Kent was leading on the boarders, when the ship coming to, we brought some of our bow-guns to bear on her, and had got clear of our opponent, when at twenty minutes past six, our fore and main-masts went over the side, leaving the ship a perfect unmanageable wreck. The frigate shooting ahead, I was in hopes to clear the wreck, and get the ship under command to renew the action, but just as we had cleared the wreck, our spritsail-yard went, and the enemy having rove new braces, &c. wore round within pistol-shot, to rake us, the ship laying in the trough of the sea, and rolling her main-deck guns under water, and all attempts to get her before the wind being fruitless: when calling my few remaining officers together, they were all of opinion that any further resistance would only be a needless waste of lives, I ordered, though reluctantly, the colours to be struck.

The loss of the ship is to be ascribed to the early fall of the mizen-mast, which enabled our opponent to choose his position. I am sorry to say we suffered severely in killed and wounded, and mostly whilst she lay on our bow, from her grape and musketry, in all, fifteen killed, and sixty-three wounded, many of them severely; none of the wounded officers quitted the deck till the firing ceased.

The frigate proved to be the United States ship Constitution, of thirty twenty-four pounders on her main deck, and twenty-four thirty-two pounders and two eighteen-pounders on her upper deck, and four hundred and seventy-six men; her loss in comparison with ours is trifling, about twenty, the first lieutenant of marines and eight killed, and first lieutenant and master of the ship, and eleven men wounded, her lower masts badly wounded, and stern much shattered, and very much cut up about the rigging.

The Guerriere was so cut up, that all attempts to get her in would have been useless. As soon as the wounded were got out of her, they set her on fire, and I feel it my duty to state that the conduct of Captain Hull and his officers to our men has been that of a brave enemy, the greatest care being taken to prevent our men losing the smallest trifle, and the greatest attention being paid to the wounded, who, through the attention and skill of Mr. Irvine, surgeon, I hope will do well.

I hope, though success has not crowned our efforts, you will not think it presumptuous in me to say, the greatest credit is due to the officers and ship's company for their exertions, particularly when exposed to the heavy raking fire of the enemy; I feel particularly obliged for the exertions of Lieutenant Kent, who, though wounded early by a splinter, continued to assist me; in the second lieutenant, the service has suffered a severe loss; Mr. Scott, the master, though wounded, was particularly attentive, and used every exertion in clearing the wreck, as did the warrant officers. Lieutenant Nicholl, of the royal marines, and his party, supported the honourable character of their corps, and they suffered severely. I must recommend Mr. Snow, master's mate, who commanded the foremost main-deck guns, in the absence of Lieutenant Pullman, and the whole after the fall of Lieutenant Ready, to your protection, he having received a severe contusion from a splinter. I must point out Mr. Garby, acting purser, to your notice, who volunteered his services on deck, and commanded the after quarter-deck guns, and was particularly active, as well as Mr. Bannister, midshipman.

I hope, in considering the circumstances, you will think the ship entrusted to my charge was properly defended; the unfortunate loss of our masts, the absence of the third lieutenant, second lieutenant of marines, three midshipmen, and twenty-four men, considerably weakened our crew, and we only mustered at quarters two hundred and forty-four men, and nineteen boys, on coming into action; the enemy had such an advantage from his marines and riflemen, when close, and his superior sailing enabled him to choose his distance.

I enclose herewith a list of killed and wounded on board the Guerriere; and have the honour to be, &c. JAS. R. DACRES.*

A List of Officers, Seamen, and Marines, killed and wounded on board H. M. S. Guerriere, in the action of the 19th August 1812.

Killed.—Henry Ready, second lieutenant; William White, captain of forecastle; George Griffiths, quarter-gunner; Henry Brown, ordinary seaman; William Brown (2), able seaman; Alexander Cowie, ditto; Richard Cheeseman, landman; John Peterson, able seaman; Joseph Tuck, ordinary seaman; Robert Rogers, able seaman; John Smith (2), gunner's-mate; William Baker, ordinary seaman; J. A. Fox, serjeant royal marines; Thomas Pratt, private marine; William Woodcock, ditto.

Wounded.—James Rd. Dacres, Esq. captain severely; Bartholomew Kent, first lieutenant, slightly; Robert Scott. master, severely; Samuel Grant, master's-mate, ditto; William J. Snow, ditto, contusion; James Enslie, midshipman, slightly; Robert Baillie, boatswain's-mate, dangerously; Hugh M'Kinley, ordinary seaman, dangerously; William Stone, captain mast, slightly; Patrick Murphy, quarter-gunner, dangerously; Henry Dent, ordinary seaman, slightly; John Little, able seaman, dangerously; Peter Peterson, ditto, slightly; William Millington, ordinary seaman, dangerously; John O'Hare, ditto, ditto; William Cooper, able seaman, slightly; Laurence Norman, ditto, dangerously; William Jones, landman, slightly; Kenneth M'Donald, able seaman, severely; James Cromwell, quarter-master, severely; Robert Taylor, able seaman, dangerously; Samuel Miller, captain of afterguard, ditto; James Miller, ordinary seaman, ditto; George Read, able seaman, severely; Ralph Williams, ordinary seaman, slightly: Jos. Copland, ditto, dangerously; Henry Virdue, ditto, se-

---

* The Guerriere was originally a French frigate, and captured by the Blanche frigate, Captain Sir T. Lavie, off the Ferroe Islands, after a severe engagement of three quarters of an hour, July 19, 1806. She belonged to a squadron of frigates which had effected their *exit* from a French port, and annoyed our ships employed in the Greenland fishery. The number of guns mounted at that time was fifty, with a complement of 317 men, and commanded by M. Hubert, a Member of the Legion of Honour. In that affair, the enemy lost twenty men killed, and thirty wounded. The number of guns mounted since her accession to our navy, consisted of twenty-eight 18-pounders; sixteen 32-pounders (carronades) and two long 9-pounders—total, 46 guns, with 300 men; though she had not so many on board when she struck was to the Constitution. Captain Dacres is about twenty-eight years of age, and has been upwards of six years a Post-captain. He was recovering from the wound he had received, at the time when the despatches were sent off. Captain Dacres is son to the late Admiral J. R. Dacres, (see Naval Chronicle xxvi, 279) and nephew to Captain R. Dacres, the present governor of the Royal Naval Asylum at Greenwich; of whom a biographical memoir is given in this Chronicle, vol. xxvi. 353.

NAVAL HISTORY OF THE PRESENT YEAR, 1812. 349

verely; Philip Dwyer, landman, slightly; Alexander Ferguson, ordinary seaman, ditto; William Somers, ditto, ditto: John Hebbs, ditto, severely; James Campbell, ditto, ditto; Peter Stemsted, ditto, slightly; Geo. Emmerson, sailmaker, severely; Geo. Meather, able seaman, slightly; Mathew Reardon, ordinary seaman, severely; William Hall, able seaman, slightly; David M'Michan, carpenter's crew, ditto; John Southgate, ordinary seaman, ditto; Thomas Chandlers, landman, severely; John Smith (3), able seaman, ditto; Henry Holt, ordinary seamen, slightly; James Crooks, able seaman, ditto; Antony Griffin, landman, ditto; Thomas Hardy, ordinary seaman, ditto; James Morris, able seaman, ditto; John Sholes, boatswain's-mate, ditto; Thomas Harrington, armourer, slightly; John Roach, ordinary seaman, ditto; Stephen Kelly, boy, ditto; John Robson, marine, severely; Thomas Crowther, ditto, ditto; Roger Spry, ditto. ditto; John Tabe, ditto, dangerously; Melchisedech Archer, ditto, ditto; William Jones, ditto, slightly; John Gos, ditto, dangerously; Thomas Chambers, ditto, severely; Samuel Long, ditto, slightly; J. Fountain, ditto, severely; William Coope, ditto, dangerously; Edward Daken, ditto, ditto; William Ryan, ditto, slightly.
15 killed; 63 wounded.—Total 78

JAMES R. DACRES.
JOHN IRVINE, Surgeon.

A letter has been received at this office from Rear-admiral Cockburn, dated on board the Marlborough, off Scilly, the 4th instant, giving an account of the capture, by that ship, of the Leonore French privateer, of ten guns and eighty men, which had been chased down by the Doterel and Raven sloops.

Promotions and Appointments.

WHITEHALL, SEPTEMBER 29, 1812.

His Royal Highness the Prince Regent has been pleased, in the name and on the behalf of His Majesty, to constitute and appoint the Right Honourable Robert Viscount Melville; William Domett, Esq. Vice-Admiral of the White Squadron of His Majesty's Fleet; Sir Joseph Sidney Yorke, Knight, Rear-Admiral of the White Squadron of His Majesty's Fleet; the Right Honourable William Dundas; George Johnstone Hope, Esq. Rear-Admiral of the White Squadron of His Majesty's Fleet; Sir George Warrender, Bart; and John Osborn, Esq. to be His Majesty's Commissioners for executing the Office of High Admiral of the United Kingdom of Great Britain and Ireland, and the dominions, islands, and territories thereunto belonging.

The Prince-regent has been pleased to appoint R. Allen, Esq. to be H. M. Consul-general in the kingdom of Gallicia, in the principality of the Asturias, and in the territory of Saint-Andero. (*Foreign-Office*; 23 *September.*)

Also Daniel Bayley, Esq. to be Consul-general in Russia. (*F. O. 9. October.*)

The Hon. E. Stewart, one of the Commissioners of the Victualling Board, is appointed to succeed General Phipps, as Paymaster of Royal Marines.

Admirals and Captains appointed.

Captain William Bradley, (omitted in the last general promotion of the 12th of August) to be Rear-admiral of the blue. This Officer was P. C. of 23d June, 1794.

Captains.—C. M. Fabian, to the Diomede; George Robbin, to the Snake; Richard Wales, to the Osprey; Alexander Frazer, to the Redpole; Thomas Groube, to the Calypso; the Hon.—Napier, to the Goshawk; James Dickinson (2), to the Hasty; Murray Maxwell, to the

Dædalus; J. Eveleigh, of the Jasper, tó the Squirrel, for Rank as Post Captain; and to command the Lion; Cornelius Quinton, to the Argo; fitting for the flag of Admiral Stirling; R. Henderson (pro tempore), to the Dublin; William Hall, to the Rolla; Hon. Charles Paget, to the Superb.

Lieutenants, &c. appointed.

J. B. Naylor, to the Melpomene; George Richards, to the Wasp; J. Wigston, to the Magnificent; W. H. Napier, to the Iphigenia; H. Baker, and C. Retorman, to the Queen; E. Kelly, to the York; J. M' Candlish, to the Alfred; W. M'Leod, to the Snap; M. Donellan, to the Childers; J. Randolph, to the Impetueux; J. Imrie, to the Boxer; J Eaton, to the Beaver; J. Nixon Alfred Dale, to the Pembroke; E. Tuberville, J. L. Lascelles, D. Price, G. Pearce, to the Mulgrave; C. Hawkins, to the Cordelia; D. M'Donald, to the Alphea schooner; J. W. Purches, to the Parthian; R. Hooper, to the Insolent; J. C. Woolnough, to the Arab; H. F. Y. Pogson, to command the Bramble schooner; C. Friend, to the Eclipse; R. Woodriff, to the Atalante; J. Judas, to the Vautour; W. J. C. Clerk, to the Puissant; Charles Dendron, to the Dublin; Patrick, D. H. Hay, to the Ramillies; Thomas Lipson, to the Barfleur; Richard Nason, to the Alfred; Edward Mourilyan, to the Hibernia; David Edwards, to the Adamant; Thomas Revans, James Rogers (1), William Matthews, to the Dublin; Robert Patton, to the Doterell; Thomas Pearce, to the Primrose; Charle M'Arthur, to the Mutine; Robert Roberts, to the Barham; Thomas Marshall, to the Acorn; Henry Davis (3), to the Royal Sovereign; Charles Wolridge, Charles Fraser, to the Stag; A. Watson, to the Fawn; J. B. Smith, to the Aboukir; Frederick Noel, to the Prince of Wales; J. H. Plumridge, to the Tremendous; Charles Hammond, to the Nimrod; W. Walford, to the Forrester; Thomas Ireland, to the Thistle; Percy Grace, to the St. Domingo; A. Davies, to the Lyra; G. R. Douglas, to the Surveillante; J. W. Sheriff, to the Racoon John Mein, to the Talbot; Thomas Bury, to the Valiant; John Davies, to the Fox; W. Truss, to the Sea-lark; Alfred Robinson, to the Semiramis; Edward Kelly, to the York; Colin Campbell, to the Boxer; John Hackett, to the Success; W. R. Cooley, to the Paulina; Charles Dickinson, to the Fairy; William Holmes, to the Saracen; W. H. Rowlinson, to the Wasp; James Clayton, to the Apelles; Edward Colman, to the Magicienne; Charles Pearson (1), to the Phœbe; William Fitzmaurice, to the Magicienne; William Baker (1), and J. Bird, to the Queen; Robert Shed, W. E. Fiott, John Studdert, Edward Purcell, to the Chatham; J. Miles, to the Success; John Hill, to the Landrail; Thomas Day, to the Atalante; John P. Baker, to the Barham; Edward Whyte, to the Horatio; Francis Roberts, to the Espiegle; Frederick White, to the Chanticleer; Edward Satterthwaite, to the Warspite; Michael Dickson, to the Warrior; John Steenbergen, to the Colossus; William Knight (3), to the York; J. Miles, to the Surprize; William Woodley, to the Boyne; Thomas Crane, James Garland, R. D. Davis, W. H. Haswell, to the Superb; H. C. Mercer, to the San Josef; James Fegan, to the signal station at St. Martin, in Jersey; Henry Leeke, to the Lion; R. Hetherington, to the Arab; E. P. Forster, to the Tigre; J. Arnold, to the Barfleur; G. Ring (1), to command the Vengeance P.S.; F. Stevenson, to the Sampson P.S.; John Warton, to the Firme; W. C. Harris, to the Kron Princessen; J. Thompson, to the Crown; Thomas Voll, to the Vigilant; A. B. Evans, to the Vengeance; E. B. Davison, to the Oiseau; W. Coet, to the Guildford P.S.; R. Coates, to the Arve Princen; A. Chapman, to the Prothée;

James Harley, to the Suffolk; A. Wilson and A. Mainwaring, to the rank of commander; Mr. Hay, —— Farr, G. B. Hutchins, midshipmen, to the rank of lieutenant.

Pursers.—E. Aldridge, to be purser of the Andromache; C. R. Palmer, to the Pegasus; M. Corney, to the Delight: J. H. Rand, to the Partridge; R. Cotton, to the Dædalus; D. Bradley, to the Bittern; W. H. Hamilton, to the Champion; C. Davies, to the Bold; C. Newman, to the Bermuda; W. Dyer, to the Pheasant; —— Gifford, to the Success; J. Nesbitt, to the Manly; John T. Palmer, to the Nemesis; Thomas Pickstone, to the Pelorus; William Godfree, to the St. Alban's; James Pottinger, to the Java; H. Hoxton, to the Bourbonnaise; J. Williams, to the Heureux; J. Bendock, to the Julia.

Secretary.—J. Dawe, Esq. to Admiral Tyler.

Masters.—J. Seymour, to the Ramillies; T. Playfair, to the Rapid; W. Butcher, to the Stag; Henry Walker, to the Ranger; T. Price, to the Princess Augusta; G. Webster, to the Dædalus; H. Smartley, to the Pembroke; James M'Allum, to the Arab; W. White, to the Bermuda; A. Smyth, to the Ceres; J. Darg, to the Standard; S. M'Beath, to the Magicienne; W. Reardon, to the Indian; J. Weddle, to the Hope; S. Vale, to the Atalante; J. Park, to the Argo; James Craig, to the Egmont; A. Watson, to the Griffin; L. Nicholas, to the Jalouse; W. Moore, to the Andromeda; G. Carrington, to the Revolutionaire.

A List of Midshipmen who have passed for Lieutenants in October.

Sheerness.—G. Vevers, J. Selbie, C. Croker.
Portsmouth.—B. Mainwaring, S. Shave, J. Johnson, E. Ward, W. Morley, W. R. Davis, C. H. Marshall.
Plymouth.—C. Merriman, A. Brown, J. Lawrence, J. Denman, G. J. Speed, L. Grant, J. Taplin, T. Trile, W. Stanbury, R. A. Jackson.

Surgeons, &c. appointed.

Peter Ramsay, to the Cherub; James M'Connell, to the Wizard; Thomas Marchant, to the Zenobia; William Law, to the Calliope; David Williams, to the Pigmy cutter; John Ogilvie, to the Atalante; George Clayton, to the Vulture; Henry Plowman, to the Ramillies; William Hector, to the Indian; James Duthie, to the Crocodile; Patrick Blaikie, to the Sheerwater; James M'Donnell, to the Dædalus; John Laughna, to the Alonzo; Pearce Power, to the Nemesis; W. H. Trotman, to the Portia; James Torrie, to the Bermuda.

Assistant-Surgeons, &c. appointed.

Charles Mortimer, to the Watchful; T. H. Edman, to be an hospital mate at Deal; Henry Barnes, to the Sylvia cutter; Roger Soden, to the Borer; Patrick M'Donough, to the Surprize; W. H. Hume, to the Tigre; Joseph Gay, to the Triton H.S.; M. Capponi, to be a supernumerary-assistant-surgeon to the East Indies; W. T. O. Kane, to the Bulwark; William Hyde, to the Monmouth; John Hicks, to the Dapper G.B.; Thomas Mein, to the Magicienne; George Smith, to the Princess; W. A. Dalziel, to be a supernumerary to Jamaica hospital; Alexander Stewart, to the Seahorse; Alexander Milne, to the Triton H.S.

BIRTHS.

At Kew, the lady of William Robert Gamble, Esq. of a daughter.
Sept. 21, at the Pier House, Ramsgate, the lady of Lieutenant Woolward, R.N. Harbour Master of Ramsgate, of a son and heir.

Sept. 22, at Penzance, Cornwall, the lady of Rear-admiral S. H. Linzee, of a son.

Oct. 20, at Burrough House, Devonshire, the lady of Captain Stanfell, of H.M.S. Druid, of a daughter.

Same day, at Ham Lodge, the lady of Captain Halliday, of H.M.S. Malta, of a daughter.

MARRIAGES.

Lately, James Lewis, Esq. to Miss Mary Little, third daughter of James Little, Esq. of Portsmouth Dock-yard.

At St. Martin's in the Fields, Lieutenant Williams, of the R.M. to Miss Arnold, of Portsea, sister to Lieut. Arnold, R.N.

At Walthamstow, Lieutenant Martin Cole, R.N. to Louisa, youngest daughter of the late P. Laprimandaye, Esq. of Austin-friars.

Sept. 26, at Stirling, William Walker, Esq. Surgeon of the Royal Dock-Yard at Portsmouth, to Miss E. M. Jenison, daughter of the Reverend Austin Jenison.

OBITUARY.

Lately, on the expedition against Palambang, Captain Eaglestone, of H. M. S. Procris.

At Saltash, Lieut. Rea, of the Braave prison-ship. He has left a wife and numerous family.

In Upper Berkeley-street, Mrs. Sheriff, widow of the late Gen. Sheriff, and mother of Capt. Sheriff, R.N.

William Brabazon Wye, Esq. commander of one of his Majesty's Packets.

Aug. 15, on board H.M.S. Fame, of excessive fatigue, endured at Alicant, Captain Sweet, R.M.

Aug. 29, off Toulon, after four days' illness, Captain W. Kent, of H.M.S. Union. His death was communicated by the following extract of a letter from an officer belonging to that ship, dated off Toulon, the 5th of September.

" I am much concerned to inform you of the recent sudden death of our late worthy captain, who departed this transitory scene on the 29th u/t. after a very few days' illness, from an obstinate bowel complaint. He was much beloved by all on board, and his loss we deeply lament. I need not enter into a detail of Captain Kent's malady ; it is satisfactory, however, to reflect, that every aid the medical art could afford, was had recourse to, and a consultation of the medical officers was held, but it pleased Providence to remove him. He was committed to the deep on Sunday last, in the Bay of Roses, with the usual honours. His nephew, Lieutenant, W. G. C. Kent, was anxious to have him buried at Minorca, or in Spain, but he could not accomplish it, and a signal was made from the flag-ship for the ceremony to take place. The first Lieutenant, Mr. James, has the temporary command. We shall never have a man superior to Captain Kent. I feel for his loss as for the nearest relation."

Captain Kent was in the 52d year of his age. He lost his youngest brother, Lieutenant Henry Kent, in 1801, at Aboukir Bay, when commanding his Majesty's armed transport the Dover, and his only surviving brother is Mr. Kent of the R.N. Hospital, Plymouth.

Sept. 8, at Malta, Mr. James Bray, Master-shipright, R.N. and principal in charge of the naval arsenal at that island ; a situation he obtained by the patronage of Sir Sidney Smith, in reward for his meritorious behaviour, at the Siege of St. John of Acre, when carpenter of H.M.S. *Tigre*. (See Gazette letters in Naval Chronicle II, 620.)

CAPT^N. SALUSBURY PRYCE HUMPHREYS. R.N.

London Published Novr. 30th 1812, by Joyce Gold, Naval Chronicle Office, 103, Shoe Lane.

BIOGRAPHICAL MEMOIR

OF

SALUSBURY PRYCE HUMPHREYS, Esq.

CAPTAIN IN THE ROYAL NAVY.

" It is the first duty of an Officer, to support the honour of his Country."

CAPTAIN HUMPHREYS was the officer who commanded H.M.S. Leopard, of 50 guns, at the time of her encounter with the U. S. frigate Chesapeake, in the month of June, 1807. The existing political differences with America—differences which, in some measure, have arisen from that encounter—therefore, render his services a subject of considerable interest to the British public; particularly when it is recollected, that, in executing the orders of his commander-in-chief, to search the Chesapeake for deserters, his conduct was the theme of very general approbation.*

---

* The action between the Leopard and Chesapeake is first noticed in the historical department of the NAVAL CHRONICLE, for the year 1807, at page 64 of the XVIIIth Volume; at page 116 of the same Volume, is an extract of a letter from a gentleman on board H.M.S. Leopard, dated Chesapeake Bay, June 24, 1807, relating the particulars of the encounter; at page 117, will be found Admiral Berkeley's orders to the respective captains, &c. under his command, to search for deserters; at page 118, are inserted the resolutions passed at a general meeting of the citizens of New York, on the 2d of July, in consequence of the action; at page 119, is the Proclamation of the American President, of that date, on the subject; from page 122, to page 128, appears a correspondence between Captain Douglas, of H.M.S. Bellona, and the Mayor of Norfolk, in America; at page 128, is a statement of the American navy, to which is subjoined an estimate of the number of persons composing the crews of the navy of the United States; Cobbett's strictures on the difference with America also commence at page 128; at page 150 are some farther remarks upon the subject; at page 279, is given Mr. Janson's account of the American navy; at page 280, is a report of the annual expenses of the American navy, for the year 1805, also from Mr. Janson's work; at page 290, is a letter, bearing the signature of NAVALIS, on the rights of the British flag; at page 333, are some strictures, elucidating and justifying the conduct of Admiral Berkeley; at page 335 (misprinted 353), commences a very full report—comprising many important official documents of the proceedings of a court martial,

With the time of this gentleman's birth we are unacquainted; but we are informed that he entered the navy in the year 1790, under the auspices of the present Vice-admiral Vashon, with whom he immediately sailed, on board the Ardent, of 64 guns, to the West Indies. From the Ardent, he soon afterwards removed into the Trusty, the flag-ship of the late Sir John Laforey, Bart. then commander-in-chief on that station.*

Passing through an unbroken series of active services, in the several gradations of midshipman, lieutenant, and commander, Captain Humphreys obtained post rank on the 8th of May, 1804; after which, he remained two years unemployed.—In the course of that period he married the eldest daughter and heiress of the late John Tirel Morin, Esq. of Weedon Lodge, Bucks.

In the month of May, 1806, Captain Humphreys was appointed to the Leander, on the Halifax station; but, in a short time, he was removed into the Leopard, of 50 guns, a more efficient ship, which had been sent out from England, to bear the flag of Vice-admiral the honorable G. Berkeley, commander-in-chief on the American station.†

From the circumstance of the admiral living principally on shore, the Leopard was employed as a private ship, in common with the other cruisers; and thus it was, that it fell to the lot of Captain Humphreys to execute the unpleasant duty of searching the U. S. frigate Chesapeake for deserters.

From the official orders of Admiral Berkeley, dated June 1, 1807,‡ it appears that, while the British squadron were at anchor in the Chesapeake, many of their men, subjects of his Britannic

---

holden on board H.M.S. Belleisle, at Halifax, for the trial of Jenkin Ratford, for mutiny, desertion, and contempt, of which he was found guilty, and executed; at page 479, is a letter signed L. T. O. referring to that of NAVALIS, at page 290, on the rights of the British flag; and, in our XIXth Volume, page 36, is another letter from L. T. O. on the same subject.—The whole of the papers and documents here referred to, arose out of, and bore upon, the engagement between the Leopard and Chesapeake; and, consequently, will be found materially to elucidate that affair.

* A memoir of the public services of Admiral Laforey will be found in our XXVth Volume, page 177.

† For a portrait and memoir of Admiral Berkeley, *vide* N. C. XII. 89.

‡ N.C. XVIII. 117.

Majesty, "deserted and entered on board the U. S. frigate, called the Chesapeake, and openly paraded the streets of Norfolk, in sight of their officers, under the American flag, protected by the magistrates of the town, and the recruiting officer belonging to the above-mentioned American frigate, which magistrates and naval officer refused giving them up, although demanded by his Britannic Majesty's consul, as well as the captains of the ships from which the said men had deserted. The captains and commanders of his Majesty s ships and vessels under my command (says Admiral Berkeley, in the official document to which we have alluded) are therefore hereby required and directed, in case of meeting with the American frigate, the Chesapeake, at sea, and without the limits of the United States, to shew to the captain of her this order, and to require to search his ship for the deserters from the before-mentioned ships (Belleisle, Bellona, Triumph, Chichester, Halifax, and Zenobia), and to proceed and search for the same; and if a similar demand should be made by the American, he is to be permitted to search for any deserters from their service, according to the customs and usage of civilized nations, on terms of peace and amity with each other."

Captain Humphreys proceeded in strict conformity to these orders. On the morning of June 22, in obedience to a signal from Captain Douglas, of H.M.S. Bellona, the senior officer of the squadron, he weighed and reconnoitred; and, having arrived off Cape Henry, to the distance of about four or five leagues, he bore up towards the Chesapeake frigate, which had been descried by the Bellona. On arriving within hail, he despatched an officer with Admiral Berkeley's order, and also with a polite note from himself, to the captain of the Chesapeake, expressing a hope, that every circumstance might be adjusted in such a manner, that the harmony subsisting between the two countries might remain undisturbed.*—After an absence of three quarters of an hour, the boat returned, with an answer from Commodore Barron, of the Chesapeake, stating, that he knew of no such men as were described; that the officers, on the recruiting service for the Chesapeake, had been particularly instructed, not to enter any deserters from his Britannic Majesty's ships; and that he had

---

* N.C. XVIII. 339.

been instructed, never to permit the crew of any ship that he might command, to be mustered by any but her own officers.*

On the receipt of Commodore Barron's letter, Captain Humphreys, from motives of humanity, and a desire to prevent bloodshed, endeavoured to make the search, without recurring to more serious measures, by repeatedly hailing, and remonstrating, but without effect. He then directed a shot to be fired across her bow; after which he again hailed, without obtaining a satisfactory answer. He consequently felt himself under the necessity of enforcing his orders, by firing into the Chesapeake: a few shot were returned, none of which struck the Leopard. At the expiration of ten minutes from the first shot being fired, the pendant and ensign of the Chesapeake were lowered, when Captain Humphreys gave the necessary directions for her being searched. Jenkin Ratford, a deserter from the Halifax (afterwards tried, found guilty, and executed), and three deserters from the Melampus, were found on board the Chesapeake. Several other English subjects composed part of her crew; but, as they did not claim the protection of the British flag, and did not fall within the limits of Admiral Berkeley's orders, Captain Humphreys allowed them to remain.—After the search had been made, Commodore Barron wrote a note to Captain Humphreys, stating, that he considered the Chesapeake as his prize, and that he was ready to deliver her to any officer who should be authorized to receive her.† Captain Humphreys observed, in answer, that, having, to the utmost of his power, fulfilled his instructions, he had nothing more to desire; repeating, that he was ready to give every assistance in his power, to the Chesapeake; and deploring that any lives should have been lost in the execution of a service, which might have been adjusted more amicably.†—The subjoined *letters on service*, relating to this affair, did not appear in the Gazette, nor have they before been published.

"*H.M.S. Bellona, off Willoughby's Point, Virginia,*
" SIR,   24*th June*, 1807.

" I have the honour to transmit you, for the information of the Right Hon. the Lords Commissioners of the Admiralty, a copy of my despatch (of yesterday's date) to the Hon. Vice-admiral Berkeley, as also a copy of his order, dated the 1st instant,§ which I hope will fully explain to their

---

* N.C. XVIII. 339.   † *Ibid*, 340   § *Ibid*. 117.

Lordships, the reason why Captain Humphreys felt himself under the necessity of adopting the measures he did, for carrying the commander-in-chief's order into execution. I have the honour to be, Sir,

"Your most obedient humble servant,

J. E. Douglas

" To *William Marsden, Esq. &c. Admiralty,*
London."

" H.M.S. Bellona, off Willoughby's Point, Virginia,
" SIR, 23d June, 1807.

" I have the honour to enclose you a copy of a letter I received this evening,* from Captain Humphreys, of H.M.S. Leopard, representing to me, that in carrying your orders of the 1st instant into execution, he was under the necessity of firing into the U. S. frigate Chesapeake; and am sorry to say, that I have been informed several men were killed and wounded on board her. The Chesapeake is returned to Hampton Roads, and as she passed us this morning, I observed that her hull, masts, and sails had suffered material injury. As Captain Humphreys has so fully explained every circumstance, it becomes unnecessary for me to say more on this subject—only that I beg leave to state, I am perfectly convinced Captain Humphreys could not have fulfilled your instructions, without having recourse to the measures which he adopted.

" I have the honour to be, Sir,
" With the greatest respect,
" Your most obedient humble servant,
(Signed) " J. E. DOUGLAS."

" To the Hon. Vice-admiral Berkeley, &c. Halifax."

The reader now being in full possession of the English documents relative to the action, we shall next insert the American official statements, copied from the papers which were presented to the House of Commons. They are as follow :—

" *Commodore J. Barron to the Secretary of the Navy, on board the U. S. Frigate Chesapeake.*

" SIR, " Chesapeake Bay, June 23d, 1807.

" Yesterday at six A.M. the wind became favourable, and knowing your anxiety that the ship should sail with all possible despatch, we weighed from our station in Hampton Roads and stood to sea. In Lynnhaven bay

---

* N. C. XVIII. 339.

we passed two British ships of war, one of them the Bellona, the other the Melampus, their colours flying, and their appearance friendly. Some time afterwards we observed one of the two line-of-battle ships that lay off Cape Henry, to get under weigh, and stand to sea. At this time the wind became light, and it was not until near four in the afternoon, that the ship under weigh came within hail, Cape Henry then bearing N.W. by W. distant three leagues. The communication which appeared to be her commander's object for speaking the Chesapeake, he said he would send on board—on which I ordered the ship to be hove-to for his convenience. On the arrival of the officer, he presented the enclosed paper (No. 1.)* from the captain of the Leopard, and a copy of an order from Admiral Berkeley,† which another officer afterwards took back, to which I gave the enclosed answer (No. 2)‡, and was waiting for his reply. About this time I observed some appearances of a hostile nature, and said to Captain Gordon, that it was possible they were serious, and requested him to have his men sent to their quarters, with as little noise as possible, not using those ceremonies which we should have done with an avowed enemy, as I fully supposed their arrangements were rather menace than any thing serious. Captain Gordon immediately gave the orders to the officers and men to go to quarters, and have all things in readiness; but before a match could be lighted, or the quarter-bill of any division examined, or the lumber on the gun-deck, such as sails, cables, &c. &c. be cleared, the commander of the Leopard hailed : I could not hear what he said, and was talking to him, as I supposed, when she commenced a heavy fire, which did great execution. It is distressing to me to acknowledge, that I found, from the advantage they had gained over our unprepared and unsuspicious state, I was not warranted in a longer opposition ; nor should I have exposed this ship and crew to so galling a fire, had it not been with a hope of getting the gundeck clear, so as to have made a more formidable defence. Consequently our resistance was but feeble. In about twenty minutes I ordered the colours to be struck, and sent Lieutenant Smith on board the Leopard, to inform her commander, that I considered the Chesapeake her prize ; to this message I received no answer. The Leopard's boat soon after came on board, and the officer who came in her demanded the muster-book ; I replied the ship and books were theirs, and if he expected to see the men, he must find them. They called on the purser, who delivered his book, when the men were examined, and the three men demanded at Washington, and one man more, were taken away. On the departure from the ship, I wrote the commander of the Leopard the enclosed, (No. 3)§ to which I received the answer (No. 4).|| On finding that the men were his

---

* N.C. XVIII. 339.   † *Ib.* 117.   ‡ *Ib.* 339.

§ Considering the Chesapeake as prize to the Leopard, and offering to surrender her.—N. C. XVIII. 340.

|| Declining to have any thing farther to do with the Chesapeake, unless to afford her assistance, the orders of the British admiral having been executed.—N. C. XVIII. 340.

only object, and that he refused to consider the ship his prize, and the officers and crew his prisoners, I called a council of the officers, and requested their opinion relative to the conduct it was now our duty to pursue. The result was, that the ship should return to Hampton Roads, and there wait your further orders.

" Enclosed you have a list of the unfortunate killed and wounded, as also a statement of the damage sustained in the hull, spars, and rigging of the ship.

" I have sent this letter to you by Captain Gordon, in order that you may have an opportunity of getting such further information as you may wish; " I am, Sir, &c.
(Signed) " JAMES BARRON."

" *List of Dead and Wounded, on board the U. S. Frigate Chesapeake, Commodore James Barron.*

" June 23d, 1807.

" *Killed.*—John Lawrence, James Arnold, John Sheckley.

" *Badly Wounded.*—John Haden, Cotton Brown, John Parker, Geo. Percival, Peter Simmons, Rt. M'Donald, Fras. Courhoven, James Eppes.

" *Slightly Wounded.*—Commodore James Barron; midshipman James Broom; Peter Ellison, Wm. Hendricks, Thomas Short, Wm. Moody, David Creighton, John Martyr, Emanuel Fernandes, John Wilson.
(Signed) ' J. G. T. HUNT,
" Surgeon of the U. S. frigate Chesapeake."

" *Survey on the Hull of the Chesapeake.*

" SIR,

" Agreeably to your requisition of this date to us directed, we have taken a strict and careful survey on the hull of the U. S. frigate Chesapeake, and find it as follows :—Twenty-two round shot in the hull ; viz. twenty-one on the starboard, and one on the larboard side.

" Given under our hands on board the late U. S. frigate Chesapeake, June 23d, 1807.
(Signed) " BENJAMIN SMITH, 1st Lieut.
" SIDNEY SMITH, 5th Lieut.
" SAMUEL BROOKE, Master."
" *Captain Charles Gordon.*"

" *Survey on the Masts and Standing Rigging of the Chesapeake.*

" SIR,

" Agreeably to your requisition of this date to us directed, we have taken a strict and careful survey of the masts and standing rigging of the late U. S. frigate Chesapeake, and find them in the following state:

" The fore and main-masts are incapable of being made sea-worthy ; the mizen-mast badly wounded, but not incapable of being repaired on shore ; three starboard and two larboard main-shrouds, two starboard fore-shrouds, two starboard mizen-shrouds, main-top-mast-stay, capbobstay, and starboard main-lift cut away; likewise the middle stay-sail-stay.

" Given under our hands on board the late U. S. frigate Chesapeake, June 23d, 1807.

(Signed) " BENJAMIN SMITH, 1st Lieut.
" SIDNEY SMITH, 5th Lieut.
" SAMUEL BROOKE, Master.

" *To Captain Charles Gordon.*"

" *Survey on Sails, spare Spars, and Boats of the Chesapeake.*

" SIR,

" Agreeably to your requisition of this date to us directed, we have taken a strict and careful survey on the sails, spare spars, and boats of the late U. S. frigate Chesapeake, and find them in the following state:

" In the fore-sail, 4 round-shot holes, 12 grape-shot holes, and the starboard leech cut away; in the main-sail 3 round-shot holes, full of grape ditto, and the foot-rope cut away; main-top-sail 1 round-shot hole; fore-top-mast stay-sail much injured by grape-shot; in the spare fore-top-mast 2 twelve-pound shot holes, which have rendered it entirely unfit for service; main sky-sail-mast cut in two; the 1st cutter slightly injured; the 2d cutter much injured by a shot which went through her, cut both of her masts and 3 of her oars in two.

" Given under our hands on board the late U. S. frigate Chesapeake, June 23d, 1807.

(Signed) " BENJAMIN SMITH, 1st Lieut.
" SIDNEY SMITH, 5th Lieut.
" SAMUEL BROOKE, Master."

" *To Captain Charles Gorden.*"

" *True Copy, taken from the U. S. Frigate Chesapeake's Log-Book.*

" JAMES BARRON, Esq. Commander;
" CHARLES GORDON, Esq. Captain; and
" SAMUEL BROOK, Sailing Master.

" Monday, June 22d, commences with light breezes from the S. and W. and clear weather. At 7 A.M. hoisted out the jolly boat, and hoisted in the 2d cutter; run the jolly-boat up a-stern. At a quarter past seven, weighed anchor, made sail with a pleasant breeze from W.S.W. and stood out for sea. At 9, passed two of H. B. M.'s ships at anchor; stowed the larboard anchor, and secured the boats. At meridian, the Light-house on Cape St. Henry, bore S.W. by S. people employed in clearing ship for sea. This day ended at meridian, and contained 17 hours.

" Tuesday, 23d, commences with light breezes from the S. and W. and clear weather. A ship in sight, apparently standing for us. At 1 P.M. the wind hauled to the N. and E.; in studding-sails, and hauled upon a wind. At half-past 3, the ship came up with us; backed the main-top-sail, and spoke her—was boarded by her: she proved to be the British ship Leopard of 50 guns. They came on board to demand some men who had deserted from the British navy. The commodore refusing to give them up, the boat returned. They ranged alongside of us, and commenced a heavy fire. We being unprepared, and the ship much lumbered, it was impossible to clear her for action in proper time, though every possible exertion was made. Not suspecting an enemy so near, did not begin to clear the decks until the enemy had commenced firing. In about thirty minutes, after receiving much damage in our hull, rigging, and spars, and having three men killed, viz. John Arnold, Peter Shakeley, and John Lawrence, and sixteen wounded, viz. Commodore Barron ; R. Broom, midshipman; John Hadden, Cotton Brown, Peter Ellison, John Parker. George Percival, Peter Somers, William Hendricks, Robert M'Donald, Francis Courhoven, Thomas Short, James Eppes, John Wilson, William Warren, and John Bates ;* and having one gun ready, fired, hauled down our colours. The Leopard ceased firing, and sent her boat on board. Mustered the ship's company. At sun-set they left the ship, taking with them four men ; viz. John Strachan, Daniel Martin, William Ware, and John Wilson. At the same time, Lieutenant Allen went on board the Leopard, and returned at eight o'clock. The Leopard left us, and stood.

"We then made sail, and stood in shore, having 3½ feet water in our hold. Crew employed in pumping and working ship in for Hampton Roads ; got the anchors clear for coming to. At six A.M. took the third reef in the main-top-sail, and set top-gallant-sails. Held a survey on the masts and rigging. At eight A.M. Cape Henry bore S.W. distant four or five miles, employed working the ship in for Hampton Roads. At half-past meridian came to with the starboard anchor in seven fathom water in Hampton Roads."

The serious and violent conduct which ensued, on the part of the inhabitants of Norfolk ; the correspondence between Captain Douglas and the mayor of that town ; † the resolutions of the citizens of New York ; ‡ the Proclamation of Mr. Jefferson,§ &c. are given at length, in an earlier Volume of the NAVAL CHRONICLE. We feel it unnecessary, therefore, in the present instance, to take any farther notice of that particular point, than by inserting the following official letter, from Mr Hamilton, the British Consul at Norfolk, to Captain Douglas :—

" *British Consul's Office, Norfolk, Virginia,*
" SIR, 25th June, 1807.
" I have this moment the honour of your letter of the 23d instant, with the copy of that written to you by Captain Humphreys, explaining the circumstances under which he found himself obliged, in the execution of his orders from the commander-in-chief, to fire into the United States ship of

---

* The names here given will not be found exactly to correspond with those in the return of killed and wounded, in a preceding page ; but, in both instances, they are correctly copied from the Parliamentary papers.—ED.

† N. C. XVIII. 122. ‡ Ib. 118. § Ib. 119.

war the Chesapeake. However sincerely I deplore with you, that a mutual accommodation for the search for deserters being refused by Commodore Barron, under his construction of the orders of his government, rendered it necessary, on the part of the captain of H.M.S. Leopard, in pursuance of his orders, to resort to force, yet I am happy to find, that the firmness and moderation which he employed, previous to the last appeal, were such, as might have been expected from Captain Humphreys, no less as a British officer, than in his individual capacity.

" As after what has taken place, the decision of the question must rest alone with the two governments (as you have very properly observed), I much lament, that the agitation of the popular mind here, should have hurried the people, at a town meeting which was assembled yesterday, into the adoption of some highly improper, and unauthorized resolutions (as anticipating the determination of the government), prohibiting any supplies being furnished to his Majesty's ships, until the pleasure of the Executive should be known, and forbidding, in the mean time, all intercourse from hence with them, as you will more fully remark by the newspaper which I enclose, containing the resolutions; and whereby you will perceive the state of the general sentiment here.—Being desirous to ascertain how far my communication with you was intended to be affected by the suspension of the intercourse, I addressed a letter to the chairman of the committee appointed by the town meeting, of which, and of his reply, you have copies herewith; by the latter you will observe, that the committee permits me to communicate with you by boats from hence (which, under a confidence that no supplies will be attempted to be sent therein), are to pass without examination, as by land from the bay side; but refuses to suffer the schooners in his Majesty's service to pass and repass with my correspondence as heretofore: in the present position of affairs, therefore, I would earnestly recommend your not ordering either of the schooners to Norfolk, or sending any of your officers here, as in the heat and ferment at this time prevailing, I have no doubt that the vessels would be seized, and dismantled, and the officers insulted and ill used, in the extreme, by the populace.

" Your apprehensions that the water casks filling for H. M. ships had been detained were just.—The schooner, with her quantity of casks filled, had sailed from Hampton on the 23d instant, but was obliged by a squall to come to, under Point Comfort, where she was boarded in the night by a party of armed men, who staved all the casks, and carried back the schooner to Hampton; setting the midshipman who was in her ashore at Mr. Thompson's.—A similar outrage took place on board the sloop that was at the wharf at Hampton, a party of men having destroyed the water casks sent by her to be filled also.

" I have already made known to his Majesty's envoy extraordinary (in private communications) the recent occurrences, as far as any sources of information have been open to me. By this night's mail I shall transmit to him officially copies of your letter of the 23d instant, and of Captain Humphreys to you of the 22d, together with such other intelligence as may be necessary.—I believe Mr. Erskine to be at present at Philadelphia, and thither I shall direct to him.

"Captain Gordon, of the Chesapeake, set off I understand on the 23d for Washington.—I will thank you to inquire of Captain Humphreys, and to inform me particularly, how many broadsides or guns were discharged from H.M.S. Leopard, into the U. S. ship Chesapeake, during the ten minutes which elapsed from the commencement of the firing, until the striking of the colours of the American frigate.—My object in this inquiry is to confute some reports on this subject, which I am sure are unfounded, and that have a great tendency to excite and to influence the spirit of animosity, which for the sake of a favourable termination to the present question it is desirable to prevent.

"I have the honour to remain, with perfect truth and regard,

"Sir,

"Your most obedient humble servant,

"*Captain Douglas.*" (Signed)   " JOHN HAMILTON."

Jenkin Ratford, a deserter from the Halifax, who was taken out of the Chesapeake, by Captain Humphreys, was tried by a court martial, holden on board H.M.S. Belleisle, in Halifax harbour, on Wednesday, the 26th of August, 1807; and, the charge against him having been clearly established, he was executed, at the fore-yard arm of the Halifax, on the Monday following.*— The three deserters from the Melampus, who were taken out of the Chesapeake, were also convicted, and sentenced to receive 500 lashes each, but were afterwards pardoned. †

The commander-in-chief's approbation of the conduct of Captain Humphreys, will be seen by the copy of a letter which we here take the liberty of inserting.

" DEAR SIR,   " *Halifax, July 4th*, 1807.

" I received Captain Douglas's account; with your official letter, containing the transaction which took place on the 22d ult. with the American frigate; and as far as I am enabled to judge by it, you have conducted yourself most properly. It is a matter, however, that willl create much discussion, and I trust you have taken minutes of every thing which passed between the time of your boat coming on board, and the time when you were compelled to act with decision. I have despatched a cutter to England with every circumstance which has hitherto reached me, and Mrs. H. is apprized of your perfect safety, and of your having fulfilled my directions. I hope you mind the public accounts which have been published of this affair as little as I do, and must make allowances for the heated state of the populace, in a country where law, and every tie, both civil and religious, is treated so lightly. It is the business of the French party to inflame the minds of the multitude, and possibly it may be the

---

* N.C. XVIII. 342.   † *Ibid.*

inclination of their rulers to fan that flame? The Norfolk newspaper appears to me, to have other views in its abuse of you and the English nation which in due time will be developed. I have left the arrangement of the ships in the Chesapeake to the direction of Captain Douglas, as its operations must be governed so much by local events, that it is impossible for me to give decisive opinions, until I receive his Majesty's ministers' official documents, by which I must be governed in my future conduct.

" I remain, with great truth,
" Yours very sincerely,

(signature)

Into the detail of the voluminous correspondence which ensued, between the respective governments of Great Britain and America, it is here impossible for us to enter. The most conciliatory conduct, however, was, from the first, adopted on the part of his Majesty's ministers; Mr. Secretary Canning explicitly disclaiming the " right to search ships in the national service of any state for deserters;" thereby virtually declaring, that the issuing of orders for that purpose, by Admiral Berkeley, was an illegal and unauthorized act. Still farther to conciliate the American government, the offending admiral was recalled.

The refusal, however, of the United States, to revoke Mr. Jefferson's Proclamation of the 2d of July, 1807 (by which the British navy was interdicted from entering the ports of America)* and the attempt to blend other subjects with the matter immediately in question, rendered it impossible to bring the negociation to an amicable close, in London. At the close of the year 1807, Mr. Rose was, in consequence, despatched, on a special mission to the American government. His exertions were not more successful. By his instructions, he was expressly precluded from entering upon any negociation for the adjustment of the difference arising from the encounter of the Leopard and Chesapeake, as long as the Proclamation alluded to, should remain in force. The American minister on the other hand, contended, that before the Pro-

---

* N. C. XVIII. 119.

clamation should become a subject of discussion, satisfaction should be made for the acknowledged aggression by which it had been preceded—the attack of the Chesapeake by the Leopard—and also for numerous irregularities, alleged to have taken place prior to that event. This opposition of sentiment, and the unwarrantable claims of the American government, prevented even the possibility of a successful negociation; and, after about six weeks had been employed in fruitless efforts, Mr. Rose found himself under the necessity of declaring, that his mission was at an end. His last letter to Mr. Madison, dated Washington, March 17, 1808, presents the following clear and candid summary of the discussions which had taken place.

" Certain deserters from H. M.'s navy, many of them his natural-born subjects, having entered into the service of the United States, were repeatedly and fruitlessly demanded by the British officers, of the recruiting officers of the United States, but were retained in their new service. As it was a matter of notoriety, that several of these deserters were on board the frigate of the United States the Chesapeake, they were demanded of that frigate on the high seas by H.M.S. Leopard, and all knowledge of their presence on board being denied, she was attacked, and four of them, one avowedly a native Englishman, were taken out of her. Without being deterred by the consideration of how far circumstances hostile in their nature had provoked, though they undoubtedly by no means justified, this act of the British officer; his Majesty's government directed, that a positive disavowal of the right of search asserted in this case, and of the act of the British officer as being unauthorized, and a promise of reparation, should be conveyed to the American minister in London, before he had made any representation by order of the United States. This disavowal, made on the 2d of August last, was transmitted by him to his government before the 6th of that month. But before Mr. Monroe had received his orders to demand reparation, his Majesty learnt, with what surprise it is needless to dwell upon, that the President of the United States had interdicted by Proclamation, bearing date the 2d of July, 1807, the entry of all their ports to the whole of his navy. This surprise was certainly increased, when, in the letter delivered by that minister to require redress for the wrong, although it went into details unconnected with it, not only no concern was expressed on the part of the United States, at having felt themselves compelled to enact measures of so much injury and indignity towards a friendly power, but no mention was made of the causes of such measures being resorted to, or even of the fact of their having been adopted. In addition to the embarrassment arising from these circumstances, and the insufficiency of the explanations subsequently given to Mr. Canning, the introduction of a subject foreign to that of the complaint became the main impediment to the success of the discussions which took place in London. When I had the honour to open the negociation with you, Sir, as I had learnt that the President's Proclamation was still in force, it became my duty, conformably to my instructions, to require its recall as a preliminary to further discussion; had it not been in force, I was not ordered to have taken it into consideration in the adjustment of reparation, and it was considered as hardly possible, that it should not have been recalled immediately upon the knowledge of his Majesty's disavowal of the attack upon the Chesapeake, as an unauthorized act. But his Majesty could not suffer the negociation to be carried on in his behalf under an interdict, which even, if justifiable in the first moment of irritation, cannot be continued after the declaration of his Majesty's sentiments upon the transaction, except in a spirit of hostility.

" It might have been fairly contended, that, in the first instance, the exercise of such an act of power before reparation was refused or unduly protracted, was incompatible with the purposes and essence of pacific negociation, and with a demand of redress through that channel; but such have been his Majesty's conciliatory views, that this argument has not been insisted on, although it might now be the more forcibly urged, as it appears that the government of the United States was from the first sensible, that even had the hostility been meditated by the British government, it would not have commenced it in such a manner. But the exception taken, is to the enforcement continued up to the present time, of measures highly unfriendly in their tendency, persisted in, not only after the disavowal in question, the promise of the proffer of suitable reparation, and the renewed assurances of his Majesty's amicable disposition, but after security has been given in a public instrument, bearing date the 16th of October, 1807, that the claim to the seizure of deserters from the national ships of other powers, cannot again be brought forward by his Majesty's naval officers; it is unnecessary to dwell upon the injury and indignity to which his Majesty's service is exposed, both as touching the freedom and security of correspondents of his agents and accredited ministers in the United States, or as resulting from a measure which, in time of war, excludes the whole of his navy from all their ports, which ports are completely open to the fleets of his enemies; it will be sufficient to observe, that even where exemptions from it are granted, they are made subject to such conditions, that of the three last British ships of war which have entered these ports upon public business, two of them, H.M.S. Statira, having on board a minister sent out for the adjustment of the present differences, and a schooner bearing despatches, in consequence of their inability to procure pilots, were obliged to enter these waters without such assistance, and were exposed to considerable danger. Great Britain, by the forms established, could repair the wrong committed, even to the satisfaction of the United States, no otherwise than by the channel of negociation; yet she avowed distinctly that a wrong was committed, and that she was ready to make reparation for it; it cannot, therefore, be contended, that the unavoidable delay of actual reparation, subjected her to the imputation of persisting in an aggression which was disclaimed from the first; if this is true, however much she will regret any impediment in the adjustment of a difference in which the feelings of a nation are so materially interested; can she, consistently with a due care of her own honour and interests, allow it to be concluded on her part, under an adherence to a conduct which has a decided character of enmity in the proceedings held towards her by the other party.

" I know not in what view the perseverance in the President's Proclamation up to this moment can be considered, but in that of a measure of retaliation, or of self-assumed reparation; or a measure intended to compel reparation; unless if it be that, which, if I rightly understand, you define it to be, a measure of precaution.

" If, when a wrong is committed, retaliation is instantly resorted to by the injured party, the door to pacific adjustment is closed, and the means of conciliation are precluded. The right to demand reparation is incompatible with the assumption of it. When parties are in a state of mutual hostility, they are so far on a footing, and as such they may treat; but a party disclaiming every unfriendly intention, and giving unequivocal proofs of an amicable disposition, cannot be expected to treat with another whose conduct towards it has the direct effects of actual hostility: If then the enforcement of the President's Proclamation, up to the present moment, is a measure of self-assumed reparation, it is directly repugnant to the spirit and fact of amicable negociation : if it is a measure to compel reparation it is equally so ; and by the perseverance in it, Great Britain is dispensed with the duty of proffering redress. But, if it is a measure of precaution, in order to secure reparation, or in order to compel it, it falls under the objections I have just stated. If it is a precaution adopted as a guard against acts of violence apprehended on the part of his Majesty's naval officers, it surely cannot be considered as being as effectual a security as that arising from the renewed assurances of his Majesty's friendly disposition, which imply a due observance of the rights of nations with which Great Britain is in amity, by all persons holding authority under his Majesty's government; from the disavowal of the pretension of the search of national ships ; and from the further assurance of that disavowal given in his Majesty's Proclamation of the 16th of October last; neither under these concurrent circumstances can the plea of necessity be maintained; and if such a proceeding has not the plea of necessity, it assumes the character of aggression. If these concurrent securities against such an apprehension have any value, the necessity no longer exists: if they are of no value, negociation cannot be attempted, as the basis upon which it rests, the mutual confidence of the two parties, would be wholly wanting."

We must confess, that we have ever felt, and that we still feel ourselves totally incapable of comprehending upon what principle—upon what law of nature, or of nations—his Majesty's ministers could plead their justification for abandoning the right of search—for conceding what ought never to be conceded by any independent power in existence—for stamping with obloquy the conduct of an officer, whose proceedings had been in the strictest conformity to maritime law. Thus, however, it was ; and, in a Proclamation, of the 16th of October, 1807, for recalling and prohibiting seamen from serving foreign princes and states, were inserted special instructions for his Majesty's captains, masters, &c. with respect to their claiming such natural born subjects of Great Britain, as might be serving on board foreign ships of war, in a state of amity with us. Instead of taking them by force—an acknowledged right, amongst maritime nations—in case of refusal, they were directed to adopt the circuitous mode of transmitting a statement of the refusal, &c. to the British minister residing at the seat of government of the state so refusing, or to the Admiralty at home. " Without dwelling upon the *particularity* of the case of the Leopard and Chesapeake, or on its total want of *precedent*, we must insist, that the conduct of Admiral Berkeley was in the strictest conformity not only to the maritime laws of England, but to the laws of every maritime power in the world. Admiral Berkeley did not claim the *right of search*, as an *exclusive* right ; but in his official orders, expressly observed, that ' if a similar demand should be made by the American, *he is to be permitted to search* for any deserters from their service, *according to the custom and usage of civilized nations on terms of peace and amity with each other.*' This, as we have just observed, was in the strictest conformity to maritime law. Amongst various claims of power, jurisdiction, and of the authority of the lord high admiral, we find the following statement of demand and admission :—' The lord high admiral, by virtue of the authority he derives from the crown, MAY and DOTH require the commanders of our ships of war, to demand seafaring men, who are natural born subjects, from foreign ships, and *upon refusal* (which is a palpable injury to the prince whose subjects they are) *to take them by force.* This is an *undoubted* right of ALL maritime princes whatsoever, and hath been an ancient custom.'—The justice and *legality* of Admiral Berkeley's conduct are, therefore, clearly established ; and any cession of the ' *undoubted*' right here described, is a deterioration of the rights and respectability of the country "*—

---

* N.C. XVIII, 333, 354.

These are the remarks which occurred to us, when the subject first pressed itself on our attention; and, down to the present moment, we have perceived no cause to doubt their accuracy.

By what has been stated, it must be sufficiently evident, that, from the commencement to the close of the affair between the Leopard and Chesapeake, the behaviour of Captain Humphreys was not only unimpeachable, but, in a very high degree, praiseworthy. Notwithstanding this, however, strange as every thinking person must consider it, he has never been favoured with an opportunity of again asserting the superiority of the British flag. Since his return from America, his time has been chiefly spent at Weedon Lodge, near Aylesbury (an estate to which he succeeded on the death of his father-in-law) in the capacity of a private country gentleman.

HERALDRY.

Captain Salusbury Pryce Humphreys, the subject of the preceding memoir, is the third son of the late Rev. E. Humphreys, Rector of Montgomery, in North Wales, and also of Clungurford, near Ludlow, in Shropshire. His eldest brother, who, early in life, changed his name to that of Trevor, is now one of the six residentiary prebendaries of the cathedral of Chester. He married the eldest daughter of the late Chancellor Briggs, of that diocese.

The mother of Captain Humphreys was the eldest daughter, and coheiress, of the late Rev. Salusbury Pryce, D.D. Her only sister, Anne, married the late Lewis Edwards, Esq by whom she has issue several children, the eldest of which married the Hon. Thomas Parker, son to the late, and brother to the present Earl of Macclesfield, by whom she has several children.

Captain Humphreys married, first, in 1805, the daughter of John Tirel Morin, Esq. by whom he has issue one son, Salusbury, upon whom the estate of Weedon Lodge is entailed. He married, secondly, in 1809, Maria, daughter of William Davenport, Esq. of Bramall Hall, Cheshire, by whom he has issue one son, William Davenport, born on the 15th of September, 1811.

NAVAL ANECDOTES, COMMERCIAL HINTS, RECOLLECTIONS, &c.

CAPTURE OF THE GUERRIERE.

IN addition to the American and British official accounts of the capture of H.M.S. Guerriere, by the U.S.S. Constitution, given at pages 307 and 346 we here insert the following statement, for the purpose of comparison, by an officer of the Constitution:—

"Lat. 41° 42' N. long. 55° 33 W. Thursday, August 20, fresh breeze from N.W. and cloudy; at two P.M. discovered a vessel to the southward, made all sail in chase; at three, perceived the chase to be a ship on the starboard tack, close hauled to the wind; hauled S.S.W.; at half-past three, made out the chase to be a frigate; at four, coming up with the chase very fast; at quarter before five, the chase laid her main-top-sail to the mast; took in our top-gallant sails, stay-sails, and flying gib; took a second reef in the top-sails, hauled the courses up, sent the royal yards down, and got all clear for action; beat to quarters, on which the crew gave three cheers; at five, the chase hoisted three English ensigns; at five minutes past five, the enemy commenced firing; at twenty minutes past five, set our colours, one at each mast head, and one at the mizen peak, and began firing on the enemy, and continued to fire occasionally, he wearing very often, and we manœuvering to close with him, and avoid being raked; at six, set the main-top-gallant-sail, the enemy having bore up; at five minutes past six brought the enemy to close action, standing before the wind; at fifteen minutes past six, the enemy's mizen-mast fell over on the starboard side; at twenty minutes past six, finding we were drawing ahead of the enemy, luffed short round his bows to rake him; at twenty-five minutes past six, the enemy fell on board of us, his bowsprit foul of our mizen rigging. We prepared to board, but immediately after, his fore and main-mast went by the board, and it was deemed unnecessary. Our cabin had taken fire from his guns, but soon extinguished without material injury; at thirty minutes past six shot ahead of the enemy, when the firing ceased on both sides; he making the signal of submission, by firing a gun to leeward; set fore-sail and main-sail, and hauled to the eastward to repair damage; all our braces, and much of our standing and running rigging, and some of our spars, being shot away. At seven wore ship, and stood under the lee of the prize; sent our boat on board, which returned at eight, with Captain Dacres, late of his Britannic Majesty's ship Guerriere, mounting 49 carriage guns, and manned with 302 men; got our boats out, and kept them employed in removing the prisoners and baggage from the prize to our own ship. Sent a surgeon's mate to assist in attending the wounded; wearing ship occasionally to keep in the best position to receive the boats. At twenty minutes before two A.M. discovered a sail off the larboard beam, standing to the south; saw all clear for another action; at three the sail stood off again; at daylight, was hailed by the lieutenant on board the prize, who informed he had four feet water in the hold, and that she was in a sinking condition: all hands employed in removing the prisoners, and repairing our own damage, through the remainder of the day. Friday the 21st commenced with light breezes from the northward, and pleasant; our boats and crew employed as before. At three P.M. made the signal of recall for our boats; having received all the prisoners, they immediately left her on fire, and a quarter past three she blew up. Our loss in the action was 7 killed, and 7 wounded; among the former, Lieutenant Bush of marines, and among the latter, Lieutenant Morris, severely,* and Mr. Aylwyn, the master, slightly. On the part of the enemy, 15 men killed, and 64 wounded. Among the latter, Captain Dacres, Lieutenant Kent, 1st; Mr. Scott, master, and master's-mate.

" During her short cruise, the pride of Boston, the Constitution, besides the above gallant achievement, has destroyed two English brigs, one with lumber, the other in ballast, and re-captured the Adeline, of Bath, from London, with dry goods, which had been taken by the British sloop Avenger, Captain Johnson, of 16 guns; and which Captain H. manned, and ordered for America."

ANTISEPTIC.

To prevent the spreading of an infectious fever, take an ounce of saltpetre, to which add as much hot water as will dissolve it; then draw shreds of writing paper through it, and when dry, burn them in the sick room frequently, and occasionally in other parts of the ship.

CURRENTS.

GALWAY, Oct. 19.—A sealed bottle, containing the following, was cast on shore on the island of Innismain, in this bay, on the 3d October, and found by a man of the name of Joyce; it is supposed to have been written in a storm, and when no hope remained for the preservation of the vessel:—

" Lat. 46° 50′ long. 27° W.—On board the ship Orbit, Monday, Nov. 16, 1811, fifteen days from New York, Captain W. Henry Boot, master.—Passengers—William Roberts, jun. William Little, John Lister, W. H. Hart, Wm. C. Cox, Thomas Wright, Dr. William Fraser, John Horsburgh, M. Purveys.—In the above latitude and longitude this bottle was thrown overboard, and should it be picked up, the person or persons will oblige the above by inserting in some of the public journals when and where "—(*Connaught Journal.*)

GOOD SAMARITANS.

AT a Meeting of the Congregate body of Jews, at their Vestry Room, White's-row, Portsea, the 29th of January, 1812:—

" * Now recovering."

Resolved, 1. That the distress of the widows, orphans, and suffering relatives of the crews of his Majesty's ships St. George, Hero, and Defence, lately lost, be of a serious consideration.

2. Resolved therefore, that a sum of thirty pounds be voted towards their relief.

3. That the said sum be paid into the hands of the Worshipful the Mayor of the Borough of Portsmouth, by

L. LAZARUS, President.
G. LEVI, Elder.

NAVAL DEFIANCE.

(From the Philadelphia Democratic Press.)

" A passenger of the brig Lion, from Havannah to New York, captured by the frigate Southampton, Sir James Yeo, is requested to present his compliments to Captain Porter, commander of the American frigate Essex, would be glad to have a *tete-à-tete* any where between the Capes Delaware and Havanna, where he would have the pleasure to break his own sword over his damn'd head, and put him down forward in irons."

In the same Paper the following answer appeared :—

" Captain Porter, of the U. S. frigate Essex, presents his compliments to Sir J. Yeo, commanding his B. M.'s frigate Southampton, and accepts with pleasure his polite invitation. If agreeable to Sir James, Captain Porter would prefer meeting near the Delaware, where Captain P. pledges his honour to Sir James, that no American vessel shall interrupt their *tete-a-tete*.

" The Essex may be known by a flag bearing the motto, " Free Trade and Sailors' Rights," and when this is struck to the Southampton, Captain Porter will deserve the treatment promised by Sir James.

" September 18, 1812."

ALAS! "POOR POLL."

THE latter end of the month of August last (says the *Belfast Newsletter*), at an early hour in the morning, a bird was observed on a tree at a gentleman's house at Byrt ; a clown who lived about the house, as servant, mistook it for a hawk, and shot it, when it proved to be a beautiful green parrot, and had round its neck a gold ring, on which was engraved, " Captain Pakenham, of his Majesty's ship Saldanha." A person in an adjoining field was listening to the bird when it was shot, and thought it was attempting to speak either the Spanish or French language. What seems extraordinary is, that the bird had not been seen in any part of the country before that morning, though the vessel from which it must have escaped, was lost on the 4th of December last, off Lough Swilly. The place where it was killed was about twenty miles from the wreck. Poor Poll and a dog were the only survivors from that ill-fated ship and her gallant crew.*

---

* *Vide* N. C. XXVII. 42.

THE ROYAL GEORGE.

A Mr. Hicks has lately been sounding round the wreck of the Royal George.—It is now thirty years since that ship sunk at her anchors, at Spithead. We understand Mr. H. has laid a plan before the Admiralty Board for removing her from her present situation, which is to be put into execution next spring. The principal part of his plan is said to be, to fix twenty-eight hooks and purchases in the port-holes, on each side, the falls (or ends) of which are to be brought on board two line-of-battle ships, and half of them fastened on the foremost, and half on the aftermost capstan. At low water these purchases are to be hove taught, and, as the tide rises, it is expected the wreck will move from its present position; when the ships to which it will be attached, will drift into shoal water, until the wreck again touches the ground: the tackles will be again hove taught, and thus, by the revolving of the tide, it will be conveyed close to the shore. It is calculated, that by the strength of the hooks, purchases, and the buoyancy of the ships, a weight of 56,000 tons may be lifted; which is more than four times the weight of the wreck. It has been ascertained, that there is very little sand and mud round it. The present position of the wreck is such an injury to the anchorage at Spithead, that the Admiralty, it is said, have determined to afford every assistance to the plan for removing it, by ships, spars, tackling, &c. The estimate of the projector's expenses exceed 13,000*l*. to repay which he is to have the hull of the ship, and whatever may remain in her, including guns, ballast, &c.

"SHIPS, COLONIES, AND, COMMERCE."

An Account of the Amount of Duties paid on Sugar in Great Britain, in the Years ending 5th Jan. 1810, 1811, *and* 1812, *respectively; distinguishing each Quarter.*

GROSS RECEIPT OF DUTIES.

Years.	1809.			1810.			1811.		
	£.	s.	d.	£.	s.	d.	£.	s.	d.
Lady-Day Quarter	624,522	12	8	944,066	7	0	1,013,275	12	9
Mids. Quarter ..	893,516	17	9	928,183	3	4	969,777	4	11
Mich. Quarter ..	1,852,594	0	4	1,920,622	14	11	1,556,622	17	2
Xmas. Quarter ..	1,413,537	7	6	1,051,800	19	9	1,046,343	0	7
Total....	4,784,170	18	3	4,844,673	5	0	4,586,018	15	5

WM. IRVING,
Inspector General of Exports and Imports.
Custom House, London, 4th Feb. 1812.

Statement of the quantity of grain, &c. imported into Great Britain in the last year, extracted from the official returns to Parliament :—

Corn and Grain .... 265,613 qrs.
Meal and Flour 32,581
Rice .... 124,802 cwt.

Of which the total value, at the average market-prices, amounts to 1,092,804*l*,

UNCOMMON CASUALTY BY A STORM AT SEA.

The brigantine George, of New York, John M'Kirdy, master, from Arundel in Norway, bound for the Isle of Man, with deals and fir timber, was lately stranded near the island of Stroma, in the Pentland Firth. She lay on the reef of rocks called the Skerry, on the S.W. point of the island, for some days, but after taking out part of the cargo, was got off, and brought to the harbour of Thurso, where the remainder of the cargo has since been landed. The vessel's hull is considerably damaged, but believed to be capable of being repaired. Happily, no lives were lost, but the master got himself *severely scalded*, by being thrown by a jirk of the main boom upon the boiling coppers, soon after the vessel had struck upon the Skerry.

GREENWICH HOSPITAL.

In the Pediment on the eastern side of King William's square, is an Emblematical Representation of the Death of Lord Nelson, in *Alto-Relievo*.

In the centre is placed Britannia resting upon a rock washed by the ocean, and receiving the dead body of Nelson, delivered to her at the command of Neptune, by one of the attendant Tritons : Victory with her right hand supports the body of the Hero, and with her left resigns to Britannia the Trident of the god, in token of the dominion of the sea. Behind Neptune, who is seated in his shell drawn by Sea-horses, is seen a British Sailor, announcing " Trafalgar," as the scene of the Hero's death.

On the left hand of Britannia is represented a Naval Genius, recording the Victories of the Nile and Copenhagen, before whom is a British Lion, holding in his paws a marine Tablet, inscribed " Nelson's 122 Battles."

Adjoining these are the sister kingdoms, England, Scotland, and Ireland, with their appropriate emblems, the Rose, Thistle, and Shamrock, reclining affectionately on each other, and overcome by feelings of the deepest sorrow.

At one extremity of the Pediment are represented various naval implements of war, the effects of which are shown in the other extremity, in the total destruction of the enemy's fleet at Trafalgar.—A.D. MDCCCXII.

PYROTECHNY.

A gentleman of Portsea, has submitted to government a shell, that at the immense distance of three miles, will explode 20 balls of combustible matter of three inches diameter, and upwards of 1000 musket and pistol balls; these will be scattered on the horizon within a circle whose diameter is 1400 yards.—The weight of the shell will be upwards of $2\frac{1}{2}$ cwt.

INTREPIDITY.

At the beginning of last winter, a brig was one morning observed in distress between Portreath and Hayle.— About ten o'clock, she went on shore a little to the east of Havle Bar, and shortly after, the captain, who belonged to Looe, and whose name was Davis, together with the mate and two boys, were washed overboard and drowned. Two men, all that remained of the crew, were observed by the persons assembled on the beach to get into the rigging, one on the foremast, and the other on the main mast. In this dreadful situation they continued for some time, every wave completely covering them;—the main mast soon went by the board, carrying with it the unfortunate seaman who had taken refuge on it.—Just at this time, a native of St. Ives, who is a very expert swimmer, stripped on the beach, and, to the astonishment of all present, resolutely plunged into the waves, rolling mountains high, carrying with him the end of a rope, which he purposed to fasten round the men on board, and thus enable the persons on shore to extricate them from their perilous situation. This intrepid and humane individual had nearly reached the vessel, when the end of the rope slipped from him, and he was seen for some time, endeavouring to gain the wreck of the mainmast, to which the almost drowned mariner still clung. At length, he reached it, and as each wave washed over them, he was seen cheering the poor fellow by clapping him on the shoulder. On seeing the danger to which all three were now exposed, a young man of the name of Burt, in opposition to the entreaties of his father, who trembled for the safety of his son, braved the fury of the storm, plunged into the billows, and providentially succeeded in conveying the rope to the first adventurer, who immediately fastened it round the almost exhausted sufferer on the main mast, and having also fastened to him a rope from the ship, he was drawn on shore by the people on the beach. The other seaman on the foremast was got on shore in the same manner, and lastly their intrepid deliverers.

CORRESPONDENCE.

MR. EDITOR, *November* 5, 1812.

IN consequence of your Correspondent, A FRIEND TO NAVAL MERIT, having intimated, that much good might be effected by the circulation of useful hints, through the NAVAL CHRONICLE, I take leave to offer a statement, resulting from the experience of an officer, to prove the impossibility of naval lieutenants making their half-pay cover their expenses, though the utmost economy be observed. The manner in which many of those deserving officers, who have not friends or relatives to assist them, are obliged to live, is, I am convinced, not generally known; and I believe it to be a fact, that the greater part of the people of England imagine them to be well provided for. As they rank with captains of the army, they are very naturally thought to be as well paid. But what will be said when this opinion is confuted, and it is made known, that even a militia captain, who has not permanent rank, who has scarcely any duty to perform, who is seldom, if ever, exposed to the inclemency of the weather, and who lives in a state of comparative luxury, enjoying all the comforts of this life, receives from his country a daily pay of ten shillings, whilst the poor unfortunate navy lieutenant, who undergoes the greatest fatigues and privations, is rewarded with only six shillings? Is it because he patiently waits, that his wants are not attended to? Surely it cannot be from the supposition that he is contented, because great bustle and noise are not made to gain an increase of pay. The Lords of the Admiralty must be well acquainted with the pay of every class of officers, and therefore cannot be ignorant of the smallness of that of lieutenants. By the late regulation, a captain's clerk, who is made purser into a gun-brig, receives, when entered in that capacity, though perhaps he may not have been more than two years in the service, forty pounds annually more than a lieutenant, who may have served his country forty years! An assistant surgeon receives seven pounds every year more than the lieutenant who commands him. I beg leave to ask any consistent person, whether this be encouragement for young men to exert themselves in order to support the respectability of the profession to which they are attached? Is it doing justice to that merit which all the world acknowledge them to possess? I will take upon myself to answer, No! On the contrary, it is wounding to their pride; it chills that ardent spirit, which animates their bosoms, and gives energy to their actions; and it is disheartening, and cruel, as they stand a solitary instance of neglect!

To prove, therefore, the insufficiency of the half-pay of lieutenants, it will here be only necessary to present a statement of one year's expense in London, as noted by one of the unfortunate, though not least deserving, of that class of officers, who was in town waiting for employment, and who studied and practised the most rigid economy, in order that he might, if possible, not exceed the sum allowed him for his past services. The nett annual half-pay of an officer, on the four shilling list, amounts to 72*l.* 16*s.* from which the income tax, with two and a half per cent. to his agent, and other deductions, leaves a clear pay of 64*l.*; a sum not equal to that which is paid by most men of fortune to their butlers!

The expense incurred for lodging, at the cheapest rate, amounts to 23*l.* 8*s. per annum;* for breakfast, dinner, coals, and candles, 43*l.* 4*s.*; which, together, make the sum of 66*l.* 12*s.*; two pounds above the clear half-pay! How, then, is that officer, who has not any more money than that which he receives for his past services (and there are many, very many, who have not), to defray the further expenses attendant on life— such as tailor's, shoemaker's, and hatter's bills; the washing of his linen, the blacking of his boots and shoes, and many other expenses that must necessarily be incurred?

I will ask any gentleman, who now may be enjoying all the benefits and comforts arising from affluence, if his income, by some unforeseen misfortune, should be reduced to so small a sum as that which is received by a naval lieutenant, what would be the state of his feelings? Forced to take up his abode in some obscure and wretched part of the town—to be obliged to seek the cheapest chop-house in the city, there to sit down amidst the lowest characters—to eat sparingly, and to drink stale porter, or perhaps table beer—to sneak out of this worse than dog-kennel, for fear of being seen by some of his acquaintances, and to wander up and down the streets, in hope that the passing objects may dissipate his cares, until night, which, though welcome, brings only a temporary relief, as the morrow ushers in a repetition of his sufferings: what, I ask again, must be the state of his feelings? Is it to be supposed that there are men callous enough to endure such privations, without their pride, and every generous quality of the mind being wounded and depressed? Certainly not! Then let the world know, that such as I have described is the unfortunate situation of naval lieutenants: it is thus that they are left unprovided for, unattended to, and neglected; and, although many have unfeelingly observed, that their minds become hardened from their mode of life, I am convinced of the contrary; and, notwithstanding they may have been the greater part of their lives at sea, their feelings are not the less acute.—Have they not been refined by education? Have they not been bred in the school of honour, and are they not, therefore, feelingly alive to every circumstance that may tend to tarnish the character which they are proud of holding— that of gentlemen? But how ill, indeed, has their country provided them with the means of supporting that character!

It is the anxious hope and expectation of every lieutenant in his Majesty's navy, that the late expensive addition to his uniform, will prove the precursor of an increase of full and half-pay; and, from the acknowledged goodness of Lord Melville's heart, I trust that they will not be disappointed.

OCEANUS.

MR. EDITOR, *Oct. 26th, 1812.*

IN looking over a Navy List the other day, it appeared to me that many of the names of our ships, and favourite names, too, of our seamen, are at present engrossed by receiving and prison ships. I think this might be easily remedied, by taking away the names altogether from that description of vessels, and merely numbering them at the respective ports where they are lying. By this means, we might restore such names as the Brunswick, Canada, Captain, Crown, Europe, Glory, Ganges, Grafton, and a great many others, to effective ships. The number of new ships, annually added to our naval strength, would thus, in the course of a very few years, enable us to explode the French names, which I see no necessity for retaining (unless for captured ships), and the favourite names of our navy would continue to ride triumphant on the main.

HEART OF OAK.

MR. EDITOR, *St. Peter's, 5th Oct. 1812.*

THE following anecdote of Captain William Marcus Courtenay, nephew to the gallant officer of that name, who was killed in the year 1793, while commanding the Boston frigate, should not, I think, pass unrecorded. It displays at once, great coolness in battle, uncommon presence of mind, and real nautical wit Your giving it a place in the NAVAL CHRONICLE, will greatly oblige an eye-witness of the transaction.

In the action of the 1st of June, 1794, Captain Courtenay was serving as master's mate on board the Thunderer, then commanded by the present Admiral Albemarle Bertie, one of the ill-fated captains, excluded from the honorary reward of a medal, because, forsooth, no men were killed or wounded on board his ship, although the Thunderer was in the heart of the action, and nobly did her duty. In the midst of the battle, while the Thunderer was warmly engaged, a spent shot, 24-pounder, lodged in the fore-yard. A sailor, finding the shot loose, slipped off his neck-handkerchief, placed the shot in it, and brought it to Mr. Courtenay, who was then quite busy fighting some of the main-deck guns. The shot was surveyed for a moment by the surrounding tars, and the question of "*Who has any chalk?*" was answered by one of the carpenter's crew presenting a piece to the master's mate. The words *Post Paid* were then made legible on the shot; and it was placed in a gun, and immediately returned to the enemy. It is impossible to describe the enthusiasm, the joy, and momentary exultation (to the total exclusion of every other sentiment), that pervaded the whole ship's crew, at this simple but sudden and singular act, the knowledge of which was conveyed from gun to gun with talismanic powers: those only who have witnessed the heart-thrilling effects of three cheers in battle, as conveyed from ship to ship in testimony of each other's prowess or good fortune, can appreciate the value of this kind of stimulus That officer, however, has his tenfold value, who commands with effect, and pleases while he commands. Such is the character universally ascribed to the subject of this anecdote, whose best friends have no other wish than to see him once fairly afloat, where his exertions will soon *Post pay* his appointment, and, his friends have little doubt, speedily make him, a *Post* Captain also.

A CONSTANT READER.

MR. EDITOR, Dover, 2 November, 1812.

ON the 26th of October there issued from the court at Carlton-house, a proclamation of the Prince-regent,* declaring the punishment of death, and all other pains and penalties of high treason and piracy, against all British mariners, &c. who shall enter, or serve, or be found on board any ship or vessel belonging to the United States of America. There is no doubt of this being the law of the land, and applicable to existing circumstances. But on ruminating what I had just been reading, connected with recent trials for similar offences detected at the Isle of France, certain doubts and queries arose in my mind, which I should wish to have settled through the medium of your impartial publication.

It is taken for granted, that if a British subject, and his property, were in the hands of the enemy, our laws would hold him guilty, if to preserve it

---

* See State Papers in a succeeding sheet.

he consented to serve against his native country; to which I do not make objection:—but I ask in what manner a subject so situated ought to be treated on his return home, supposing he had contrived to escape, after sacrificing all he possessed sooner than contract any such dishonourable or illegal engagement? and whether, if he applied to government for aid, the first question would not be, are you not an emigrant? We know the consequence of the answer to that question: still we expect loyalty and attachment, in short, every thing on one side, and nothing on the other.

FABER.

MR. EDITOR, *Plymouth, 30 September, 1812.*

IN reading a newspaper of the 9th instant, I found in it an extract of a letter, dated "Plymouth, September 4, 1812," on the subject of the Plymouth Breakwater. The author of that production has taken great pains to mislead the public, for there is scarcely a word of truth in his statement. He says, that " a wharf of nearly 300 feet, at Oreston quarries, has sunk 20 feet, the curb-stones forming an angle of nearly forty-five degrees inwards; that the backing has also sunk so much as to destroy the rail-road, and, of course, all approach to the wharf from the quarry." He further says, " the middle of the wharf is burst, and that all further progress is become hopeless, while there is little or no wharf left, from whence to ship the stones." I shall first proceed to answer this writer on the subject of the wharf, and will reply to his other mis-statements afterwards.

In making the statement in the way the author has done, respecting the wharfs, the reader will naturally have supposed that the whole of the wharfs, of 300 feet in length, must have been complete for shipping stone, as he says, that the curb-stones have an angle of forty-five degrees inwards, and that the rail-road has been destroyed. Now the fact is, that excepting a very few feet at each end of the wharf, no curb-stones have ever been on the wall, as it has not been built up within six feet of the curb-stone; neither has the wall burst, nor has any rail-way ever been laid to it; and instead of having little or no wharf to ship from, there is at this time 530 feet of wharf completed. The wharf in question certainly has settled about five feet, but it is not given up, as the author states; the men were only taken from it and put on other work, until the wharf had come to a final settlement, which has now taken place.

The author next says, that " this failure must render half the bargemen and workmen useless; that there are twenty hired barges and ten public ones, and that some hundreds of men are employed in blasting, &c. but that all these are unavailing, while there is little or no wharf left from whence to take off the stone."

In reply to this statement, I must observe, that there never have been more than five private vessels at Oreston in the employ of the contractor, on the concerns of the Breakwater; and one of the public vessels he speaks of is at this time building at Portsmouth; another of the number arrived from Woolwich on the 11th instant, being seven days subsequent to the date of this author's letter.—These vessels arrived at Plymouth mere shells, and certain accommodations of course were necessary to be made in them for the officers, men, provisions, and stores, which it was thought advisable to defer until their arrival at Plymouth, in order that they might be completed under the directions of the Superintendant of the Works of the Breakwater; and on completing them it has been found necessary to raise the sills of the stern-ports 14 inches, the expense of which is upon a par, with all the other assertions contained in the letter in question; and further, instead of men being out of employ, more are taken on every day.

I conclude these remarks by stating, that the number of applicants for situations in the Breakwater department have been immense, and a variety of plans of Breakwater have been proposed, differing from each other, as much as all of them have differed from the plan now executing; those whose plans have not been noticed, and others who have failed in obtaining a situation in the concern, must feel considerable disappointment and chagrin; and I make no doubt that the author of the letter would be found in one of those lists; and many others from the same source may, in all probability, obtrude themselves on the public with similar productions.

As a considerable space has been deservedly allotted in the N. C.* to this undertaking, I trust to your well known candor for correcting any error that may creep abroad upon the subject, and shall therefore thank you to give the preceding a place in your publication.

J. WHIDBEY.

MR. EDITOR,   *Plymouth, Nov.* 6, 1812.

NOT in my time (and, I believe, I am the oldest sailor in this town), did I ever witness such a hurricane of wind as was experienced on the 18th and 19th *ultimo*; except a most tremendous gale that happened in the former French war; when H. M. S. Brilliant cut her cables in the Sound, and ran in alongside the Victualling-office; and, at the same time, that ever-to-be-remembered, by me, melancholy event occurred, when the Little Barbican, by a mountainous sea, was made a breach in, and swept away in the vortex; two young gentlemen, Messrs. Collier, being then drowned, whom curiosity had led there to see the effects of the gale; what I mean to infer from this, is, that the very disastrous event, of the mooring breaking in Catwater, and so much injury done to the ships attached to these moorings, will rouse the corporation, merchants, and ship-owners, to persevere in a former determination, of applying to Parliament for a repeal of this obnoxious Act of FETTERING the harbour with mooring-chains; for it NOW must be obvious, that there is little dependence on such moorings, when so many vessels make fast to one ring; for had those ships been

---

* See N. C. XXVII. 487. XXVIII. 118, 128, 213, 233. at which last-mentioned page will be found a chart of Plymouth Sound, with the projected Breakwater.

moored with their own anchors, in that snug situation, no wind could have hurt them, as I experienced in a ship of war that I was master's-mate of, in the above dreadful gale, lying in a tier of shipping in the very identical place. Therefore, let no compromise induce you to relax the smallest tittle of what I conceive to be an unalienable right of this borough, for all ships to anchor where they please in Catwater, without paying for moorings, which would be an eternal tax on trade and commerce, a great injury to the town, and obstruction to the free navigation of the harbour; for where the moorings are laid, and intended to be laid down, no wind can hurt ships when moored with their proper anchors and cables with a good scope; and I quere, if Mr. Blackburn's yard had not been built, if the moorings had ever been thought of. However, I must do the owner of the yard justice to say, that he is a valuable member of society, and in his actions and expressions, of a very conciliatory nature; but I still presume to say, that an Act of the Legislature must be in force, until repealed; and I should think it not in his power to soften it, and it might so happen, that another possessor might not be of so friendly a disposition : in that case, as the law now stands, when so many advantages are held forth to ships lying at those moorings, what is to become of the ship-builders of this town in time of peace?—as foreigners then flock here to get repaired. Now, were I to give my advice, as an old seaman, instead of those moorings, I would wish Lord Boringdon and this town to go hand in hand, and procure an Act of Parliament for the better improving the harbour of Catwater from the great sea running into Deadman's Bay (which, in the course of time, would save a number of lives and ships); to build or sink a breakwater from the west end of Mount Batten, in the direction of the buoy of the Cobler, to a distance of about 250 fathoms, or such distance as would be found most eligible to break off the S. W. winds; which would be of the utmost utility, and make Catwater one of the finest harbours; where frigates and sloops of war could ride in the greatest safety; materials being so handy for completing it, and the money, from the public spirit of this town for improvements, would soon be raised.

AN OLD SAILOR.

MR. EDITOR, Oct. 13, 1812.

THE loss of H. M. frigate Guerriere is no doubt much to be regretted; but she is not in possession of the enemy, she is not a trophy of victory—not a tarnish is to be found upon the trident of the seas—it was nobly wielded by Captain Dacres and his bold companions in arms, and if they did not conquer, they nobly fell. Why, then, should a certain newspaper trace such a sentiment as the following :—" We do not say Captain Dacres deserves to be punished; but this we dare assert, that there are captains in the British navy, who would rather have gone to the bottom, than have struck their colours." Is the editor of the paper alluded to ignorant of the force of the Constitution? does he know that she is as heavy as an English sixty-four? has any person informed him that the upper deck of the Constitution is flush fore and aft, and that she thereby mounts a double tier of guns, like a line-of-battle ship? Does he not feel, does his conscience not tell him, that when a ship has been fought to the last extremity, until resistance is impotent, and perseverance vain, that the captain is responsible for the lives of his crew; and that had Captain Dacres obstinately persisted longer, the blood of every forfeited life would have been upon him, and their valuable services would have been taken from their country, to deck the funeral of the commander?—Had the *Guerriere* gone down from such obstinacy as the Editor alluded to requires, Captain Dacres would have been an executioner. The man who gives no quarter to the wounded, is not worse, than the man, who, to add to his posthumous fame, sacrifices the lives of his vanquished followers. The British admiral's letter is quite satisfactory. But I would advise the said editor to speculate in a privateer; or, if he has a strong imagination, let him fancy himself commanding a frigate in battle—a much larger ship bears down upon him, he fights nobly—but the die of fortune turns against him. He is overpowered by the strength of his antagonist; he is wounded and in agony; yet he fights bravely on; he struggles to the last; resistance becomes incapable of exertion, and hope expires; why then should he not save the remaining lives of his defeated companions; why should he not do as the late captain of the late Guerriere has done, surrender his wreck to the flames of irresistible strength? I am not acquainted with Captain Dacres, or his officers, but in justice to the British navy and its courageous men, I request this letter may be inserted in the NAVAL CHRONICLE. R.

" He that can read and meditate, need not think the evening long, or life irksome; it is, at all times, a fit employment, and a particular solace to him who is bowed down with years. Without this, an old man is but the lame shadow of that which once he was,"

" Study is the guide of youth, to manhood a companion, and to old age a cordial and antidote." OWEN FELTHAM.

Study, well directed, and carried into practice, is the true Christian's best security.

MR. EDITOR,

THAT the writer of the accompanying letter has no claim to erudition, is as evident a truth, as that he possesses a soul that would not disgrace a mitre, or a flag at the main. This honest rough spun piece of intrinsic worth, like the diamond from the mine, wanted but the aid of art to shine forth with the most brilliant lustre. Let the patrons and opposers of the education of the poor, who are capable of reflection, think well of this, and they will quickly be of one mind; or, should there be any contest between them, it would be in the rational and truly Christian-like endeavour to outstrip each other, in their truly laudable efforts to afford the most effective assistance to the plans now carrying into rapid execution, through the means of the " NATIONAL SOCIETY FOR THE EDUCATION OF THE POOR."—This opens a wide field for delightful speculation; but I must not trespass upon your valuable pages. It now, therefore, only remains for me to give you the assurance, that the letter in question is genuine, it being a faithful copy of the original, at that time in the possession of the much-to-be-lamented Captain John Stewart,* late commander of the Seahorse, than whom, a more gallant officer, better seaman, or better man, never honoured one of his Majesty's quarter-decks.—This is a glorious truth, that all Captain S.'s late officers, a noble train of youngsters, and followers of every description, will readily vouch for—though not with a dry eye—for he was at once their father, guide, and friend.

NAUTICUS.

LETTER FROM A SEAMAN ON BOARD THE VICTORY, TO HIS SISTER, AFTER THE BATTLE OF TRAFALGAR.

Victory, Spithead, Dec. 5, 1805.

DEAR SISTER—Comes with my kind love to you hoping that you are in good health, so thank God I am; for I am very certain that it is by his mercy that me and my country is, and you and your religion is kept up; for it has pleased the Almighty God for to give us a complete victory of the combined fleets of France and Spain; for there was a signal for them being out of Cadiz the 19th October, but we did not see them till the 21st in the morning, and about 12 o'clock we gave three cheers, and then the engagement began very hot on both sides, but about 5 o'clock the victory was ours, and twenty sail of the line struck to us. They had 34 sail of the line, and we had 27 of the line, but the worst was of it, the flower of our country Lord Nelson got wounded at twelve minutes past one o'clock, and closed his eyes in the midst of victory.—Dear sister it pleased the Lord to spare my life and my brother Thomas his, for he was with the same gentleman. It was very sharp for us I assure you, for you had not a moment time till it was over, and the twenty-third of the same instant we lit of a most shocking gale of wind, and we expected to go to the bottom, but thanks be to God, he had mercy on us; for every ship of ours got safe into harbour, and all the French but four got knocked to pieces on the rocks. So that is the most I can tell you of it; for the English is in a right cause you may depend on it, or else the Lord would not have had the mercy on us as he has had, for we made five ships strike to the ship has I am in. We had 125 killed and wounded, and 1,500 in the English fleet killed and wounded—and the enemy 12,000: so I shall leave you to judge how your country fights for the religion you enjoy, the laws you possess; and on the other hand how Buonaparte has trampt them causes down in the places he has had concern with, for nothing but torment is going forward. So never think it is disgrace to having brothers in service; but I have had pretty well on it, and when you write to our mother, give my love to my sister Betty and my poor mother, and send me word about her, and you shall have your loving brother's thanks. So must conclude with hoping this will bring you peace and love and unity. Then you and me and our dear mo-

---

* For a biographical memoir and portrait of this officer, see N.C. XXVIII. p. 1.

ther will meet together, to enjoy the fruits of the island as I have been fighting for. My dear I shall just give you a small description of Lord Nelson;* he is a man about five feet seven, very slender, of an affable temper, but a rare man for his country—and has been in 123 actions and skrimmages, and got wounded with a small ball, but it was mortal. It was his last words, that it was his lot for me to go, but I am going to Heaven, but never haul down your colours to France, for your men will stick to you. These words was to Captain Hardy, and so we did, for we came off victorious, and they have behaved well to us, for they wanted to take Lord Nelson from us, but we told captain as we brought him out we would bring him home; so it was so, and he was put into a cask of spirits. So I must conclude.

Your loving brother,
JAMES BAYLEY.

COMMODORE RODGERS'S CRUISE.

MR. EDITOR,

THE American *National Intelligencer* has furnished the following *Extract from the Journal of Commodore Rodgers.*

"*June* 23*d*.—Pleasant breezes from N.W. to W.S.W. at three A.M. spoke an American brig from Madeira, bound to New York, the master of which informed me, that four days before, in lat. 36° long. 67′, he passed a fleet of British merchantmen, under convoy of a frigate and a brig, steering to eastward: I now perceived, that this was the convoy of which I had received intelligence, prior to leaving New York, and shaped our course east in pursuit of them. At six A.M. Nantucket Shoal, bearing N.E. distant 35 miles, saw a large sail in N.E. standing to S.W. which was soon discovered to be a frigate. The signal was made for a general chase, when the several vessels of the squadron took in their studding sails, and made all sail by the wind, on the starboard tack, in pursuit. At a quarter before seven, the chase tacked, made all sail, and stood from us, by the wind on the same tack. At half past eight, he made signals, when, perceiving we were coming up with him, he edged away a point or thereabouts, and set his top-gallant studding sails. At 11, cleared ship for action, in the expectation that we would soon be up with the chase; the breeze about this time, however, began to incline more to the westward, and became lighter, which I soon discovered was comparatively an advantage to our opponent. At a quarter past one P.M. the chase hoisted English colours. At two, the wind veered to the W.S.W. and became lighter. At 20 minutes past four, having got within gun-shot of the enemy, when, perceiving that he was training his chase guns, and in the act, as I supposed, of firing, that the breeze was decreasing, and we now sailed so nearly alike, that to afford him an opportunity of doing the first injury to our spars and rigging, would be to enable him to effect

---

* A portrait and memoir of Lord Nelson are given in our XVIth Volume.

his escape, I gave orders to commence a fire with the bow-chase guns, at his spars and rigging, in the hope of crippling one or the other, so far as to enable us to get alongside. The fire from our bow-chase guns he instantly returned, with those of his stern, which was now kept up by both ships without intermission, until 30 minutes past four P.M. when one of the President's chase guns burst, and killed and wounded sixteen persons, among the latter myself. This was not, however, the most serious injury, as, by the bursting of the gun, and the explosion of the passing box, from which it was served with powder, both the main and forecastle decks, near the gun, were so much shattered, as to prevent the use of the chase gun, on that side, for some time. Our main-deck guns being single shotted, I now gave orders, to put our helm to starboard, and fire the starboard broadside, in the expectation of disabling some of her spars, but did not succeed, although I could discover that his rigging had sustained considerable damage, and that he had received some injury in the stern.

" I now endeavoured, by altering course half a point to port, and wetting our sails, to gain a more effectual position on his starboard quarter, but soon found myself losing ground. After this, a similar attempt was made at his larboard quarter, but without any better success, as the wind, at this time, being very light, and both sailing so nearly alike, that, by making an angle of only half a point from the course he steered, enabled him to augment his distance. No hope was now left of bringing him to close action, except that derived from being to windward, and the expectation the breeze might favour us first. I accordingly gave orders to steer directly after him, and to keep our bow-chase guns playing on his spars and rigging, until our broadside would more effectually reach him. At five, finding from the advantage his stern guns gave him, that he had done considerable injury to our sails and rigging, and being within point blank shot, I gave orders, to put the helm to starboard, and fire our main deck guns; this broadside did some farther damage to his rigging, and I could perceive that his foretop-sail-yard was wounded, but the sea was so very smooth, and the wind so light, that the injury done was not such as materially to affect his sailing. After this broadside, our course was instantly renewed in his wake, under a galling fire from his stern-chase guns, directed at our spars and rigging, and continued until half past six; at which time, being within reach of his grape, and finding our sails, rigging, and several spars, particularly the main-yard, which had little to support it except the lifts and braces, much disabled, I again gave orders to luff across his stern, and gave him a couple of broadsides.

" The enemy, at this time, finding himself so hardly pressed, and seeing, while in the act of firing, our head-sails to the left, and supposing the ship had in a measure, lost the effect of her helm, he gave a broad yaw, with the intention of bringing his broadside to bear ; finding the President, however, answered her helm too quick for this purpose, he immediately reassumed his course, and precipitately fired his four after main-deck guns on the starboard side, although they did not bear upon us at the time, by 25 or 30 degrees, and he now commenced lightening his ship, by throwing overboard all his boats, waste anchors, &c. and by this means, was enabled, by a quarter before seven, to get so far ahead, as to prevent our bow-chase guns doing execution, and I now perceived, with more mortification than words can express, that there was little or no chance left of getting within gun-shot of the enemy again. Under every disadvantage of disabled spars, sails, and rigging, I, however, continued the chase with all the sail we could set until half-past eleven, P.M. when perceiving he had gained upwards of three miles, and not the slightest prospect left of coming up with him, I gave up the pursuit, and made the signal to the other ships as they came up to do the same.

" During the first of the chase, while the breeze was fresh and sailing by the wind, I thought the whole of the squadron gained upon the enemy. It was soon discoverable, however, the advantage he acquired by sailing large, and this I conceived, he must have derived in so great a degree by starting his water, as I could perceive upwards of an hour before we came within gun-shot, water running out of his scuppers.

" While in chase, it was difficult to determine whether our own situation, or that of the other vessels of the squadron, was the most unpleasant. The superior sailing of the President was not such, off the wind, as to enable us to get upon the broadside of the enemy. The situation of the others was not less irksome, as not even the headmost, which was the Congress, was able at any time, to get within less than two gun-shots distant, and even at that but for a very little time." T.

MR. EDITOR, *Aberdeen, 10th November, 1812.*

THE recent occurrence (almost unprecedented in the naval annals of Britain), of the destruction of one of our largest frigates,* by an American ship, rated of equal force, although certainly superior in weight of metal, and number of men, has produced no slight sensation in the mind of every man, interested in the honour of his country, and that of the British navy. The loss, of itself, is little or nothing; but, considering its circumstances, it is of the greatest importance; for has it not occasioned a loss of reputation to our navy, an increase of character to that of the Americans? I suppose, few will hesitate to answer in the affirmative. The captain of the frigate has been honourably acquitted, and no doubt very properly so, for he fought like a brave man, but was unfortunate. His misfortune, however, has produced a stain on our naval arms, which nothing, but the capture or destruction of the American navy, can efface; and towards which, the efforts of our naval force (and a very small part will suffice for the purpose) ought to be *now* seriously directed; for. hitherto, the war with America, on our part, has been one of defence and forbearance, whilst the Americans have been, and still are, straining every nerve, to distress and annoy us, without seeming to have any wish to meet that spirit of conciliation which is shewn towards them by this country. Had we, at a more early period of the season, sent an effective naval force to their

---

* The Guerriere.

coast (for Admiral Sawyer's squadron had sufficient employment in protecting convoys, which it did with success), with orders at once to crush their pigmy fleet, we should not now have to regret the capture of a frigate and sloop of war, nor their having acquired such an addition of nautical skill and science, for their courage was undoubted.

I hope the attention of our naval department will be now seriously directed to this quarter, for although the American navy is small, it has acquired respect, and consideration, from its enemies, by its daring and successful enterprise. Has not their squadron cruised nearly within sight of our shores, and within soundings? Its destruction is, therefore, (if war continue) an object of peculiar importance, and will every day become more so, until effected, as they are now elated with success, and hold our frigates very cheap. Hitherto, we have sent only *two* ships of the line, under Sir John Warren (an officer possessing the full confidence of the country) to the coast of America; several of our largest frigates have also been sent, and more are said to be fitting for that station. I confess I should be happy to see six or seven sail of the line sent thither at once: if this were done, their frigates must remain in port, or come out to meet certain destruction, or capture. Our Baltic fleet are now on the eve of returning, and we can easily detach a part, without inconvenience; for, if the French are meditating to run out a squadron to America, we ought to have a fleet there able to cope with them.

It may be said, the capture of the Guerriere was occasioned by misfortune, and that our other frigates will be more successful. I hope sincerely, I have little doubt they will; else where will be the far-famed spirit and glory of the British flag, which has rode triumphant on the main so long? But the victory will be dearly bought: we cannot expect an easy conquest: the American frigates are much larger, loftier, carry more guns and men, (many, I lament to say, British sailors amongst them), and the Americans themselves, are second to none, but British tars. Under these circumstances, it is in vain to look for the conquest of the American navy by our frigates, without a sacrifice of lives, which I think ought to be avoided, by employing a few ships of the line. No doubt the *elèves* of our immortal Nelson, burn to wipe off the stain, by getting alongside of them, in a well-manned British frigate. When they do, British valour and skill will conquer; but it will be no bloodless conquest, for the Americans have manifestly great advantages, and are manned with *able* seamen. Let us not, however, trifle with them longer, or allow their temerity, in pretending to dispute the command of the ocean with us, to remain longer unpunished.

I am happy to see an addition of a lieutenant and twenty men ordered for the frigates preparing for service on the coast of America. All our frigates there ought to have an increase of establishment: with well manned ships, the followers of the immortal Nelson, if they meet the enemy, on equal terms, will soon humble his arrogant spirit. Fortun will not forsake those " who remember Nelson." I am, &c.

ALBION.

A SERIES OF NAVAL BULLETINS,

INSCRIBED TO BUONAPARTE.

BY LIEUTENANT D. O'BRIEN, R.N.

On escaping from the insults and cruelties, which that naval officer had experienced in France, during his five year's captivity: giving an account of the extraordinary perseverance and fortitude of Lieutenant O'Brien until he at length effected his escape; and detailing, with peculiar interest, the real and wretched situation of many brave Englishmen, who still linger out their miserable existence in the land of tyranny and oppression.

LIEUTENANT O'BRIEN had previously served on board the Hussar frigate, as master's mate; in which capacity he was on board her, when that ship was lost on the Island of Saints, near Brest, Feb. 8, 1804. He drew up this interesting manuscript on board H.M.S. the Warrior, on being appointed lieutenant to her; and transmitted the whole, when finished, to Mr. Whidbey, master attendant at Woolwich, now absent on the important duty of constructing the Breakwater at Plymouth. This gentleman placed it in the hands of an early friend to our CHRONICLE, with permission to lay the whole account before our readers. Mr. Whidbey's opinion of this Narrative may also be subjoined—" I think it is as curious a production as was ever read; it is admirably adapted for the materials of an after-piece, for the stage, and will shew the friends of Buonaparte in England, how their countrymen have been really treated by him. You may depend that the whole account is strictly true."

On receiving this valuable communication, we requested others of our friends to peruse it; all of whom were highly gratified, and urged us to insert it in the CHRONICLE, as the surest means of giving it immediate and extensive publicity. One of these friends, whose literary taste and abilities give peculiar weight to his opinion, thus expressed himself—" I thank you very much for the perusal of the manuscript of Mr. O'Brien, it conveys so naturally the author's real feelings. The story is as interesting as that of Robinson Crusoe, which perhaps from early prejudice, or as I think more probably from its own merit, is the most captivating history that was ever written. I feel convinced, that if Mr. O'Brien's account were published, it would be very generally read."

The following is Lieutenant O'Brien's own address to his readers:—

" I beg to observe, that it was never originally my intention to make the subsequent narrative of my shipwreck, sufferings in captivity, and rescue, public—however, the persuasion of friends prevailed; and I now offer it with the utmost humility and respect, devoid of embellishment and exaggeration, confined simply to facts:—and I trust the penetrating eye will abstain from criticism and censure; considering that I possess not the pen of a ready writer, having quitted both my parents and my studies at a very early period of life, impelled with an ardent desire to begin my career of duty on that element, where I have still the honour of serving my king and my country.

" Should this long Narrative afford the least entertainment to those who peruse it, or prove of the smallest benefit to my fellow creatures in captivity, I shall feel an ample recompence.

" I have the honour to subscribe myself,
" With the greatest respect,

BULLETIN THE FIRST.

To Buonaparte, the Corsican, Emperor and King.

As your Imperial Majesty has long delighted in the composition of endless bulletins, as they are styled, in which truth and candour are never suffered to appear; it may perhaps amuse you, during some of those pauses which occasionally occur in your systematic destruction and humiliation of your fellow creatures, to be enabled to hear a little truth, and to trace the manner in which an humble individual, like myself, bade defiance to your persecution, and has at length returned to his duty as a naval officer, notwithstanding all the dungeons, and fetters, and insults, which distinguish your reign of despotism and tyranny.

' It was on Monday, Sir, the 6th of January, 1804, that our ship, the Hussar, Captain Wilkinson, made sail from Ares Bay, in Spain, with despatches from Sir Edward Pellew, for England, with a fresh breeze from the S.W. Tuesday, 7th, wind and weather nearly the same. At noon (to the best of my recollection), observed, in lat. 46° 50′ Ushant, bearing N. 37° E. distance 113 or 14 miles. Wednesday, 8th, wind and weather the same, steering (as near as I can recollect) N.E. b. E. running nine knots an hour. Every heart elated with joy, expecting in a very few hours to be safe moored in the land of liberty; some employed writing to their friends and relatives: but, alas! Sir, how frail are the hopes of man! how different had our lot been decreed; that happy arrival has, with many, never yet taken place. The miseries and vicissitudes we were doomed to suffer, will amply appear in the subsequent pages. ----------------

At about 10. 45. steering the same course as above mentioned, and running about 7 knots an hour, in dark hazy weather, we struck on the southernmost part of the Saints; beat over an immense reef of rocks; carried away our tiller in several pieces; unshipped the rudder, and from the violence of beating over, damaged the ship's bottom considerably, so that she made a great deal of water. At length we got into deep water, and let go our bower anchors to prevent being dashed to pieces on immense rocks a-head, on which we were fore-reaching.*—Sent top-gallant-yards and masts upon deck, and used every possible means to ease and lighten the ship; the major part of the crew were at the pumps. The remainder, with the officers, were employed as was most expedient—staving the water casks in the hold, shoaring the ship up, as the ebb tide was now making, and she was inclining to starboard. The carpenter reported the ship to be bilged, and we could distinctly hear the rocks grinding and working through her, as the tide fell. At daylight Mr. Weymouth (master) was sent to sound for a passage amongst the rocks, imagining we might be able to buoy the ship through; but he returned without success; though had he succeeded, from the state the ship was in, there could be very little hope of getting her out. A division of the seamen and marines, with their respective officers, were then ordered to go and take possession of the island; that in the last extremity there might be an asylum secured for the crew and officers: the rest of the crew remained at the pumps, but with very little success, as she kept gaining upon them. The island was taken without any opposition, the only people on it being a few distressed fishermen, and their families. About 11 A.M. began to land the crew, no hopes remaining of being able to save our ship. However, the remainder of the people kept still working at the pumps, waiting the return of the boats. At noon the flood making strong, and fore-reaching withal, Captain Wilkinson gave directions to let go the sheet anchor, which was immediately done. Strong gales from the S.W.

Thursday, Feb. 9th, 1804, at about 1 P.M. every body was safe landed, with two or three pigs and some biscuit, which were the only subsistence we had secured. Captain W. and Mr. Weymouth came in the last boat. At about 1. 30. Lieutenant Pridham, Messrs. Carey, Simpson, and Thomas, three warrant officers, with myself, were ordered by the captain to return to the ship; to cut her masts away, and destroy every thing we possibly could get at. On our arrival on board, the water was nearly square with the comings of the lower deck. At about 3. 30. quitted her, having executed with the greatest accuracy the duty we were ordered upon. The wind still increasing, which left us but little hopes of her hanging together for the night. We joined the officers and crew in a little church, and this was the only place on the island where we could conveniently take up our residence. A regular watch being set, sentinels placed, patroles, &c. regulated; the rest of the crew endeavoured to repose themselves, being greatly fatigued. The weather was excessively inclement during the night. At daylight, discovering the ship still apparently whole, Captain W.

---

* Drawing a-head.

despatched Mr. Pridham, and Mr. Mahony, master's-mate, with a party of men, to destroy her by fire. The other officers and people were employed equipping 13 fishing boats, which belonged to the inhabitants, for the purpose of transporting the ship's company, either to our fleet off Brest, or to England, as circumstances might admit. Mr. Pridham and party returned, and the report of the ship's guns announced the execution of the duty they had been sent upon. Friday, the 10th, at about 1. 30. P.M. boats were in readiness; it then blowing hard from the S.W. We all embarked in them. I had the honour to command one, with 25 men; Captain W. with the master, leading in the barge, which was the only ship's boat in company. We made sail out of the little creeks in which the boats had been moored; the sea running excessively high; and at about 2. the barge hauled up to the N.W. We all of course followed. At 2. 30. or 3 o'clock, we bore up again; several of the boats were in distress, being excessively badly found, having neither sails, rigging, nor ground tackling, that could be at all trusted to. Lieutenants Pridham, Lutwidge, and Barker, were to keep a-head, as no other boats had compasses. At about 5. in a very severe squall, with rain, we lost sight of the barge; every body was of opinion that she had overset; and at 5.30. blowing excessively hard, with a heavy shower of rain, we lost sight of all the boats. At about 6. observed St. Mathew's Light on the weather bow. The wind now chopped round to the N.W. in a very heavy squall, which carried away our main-mast in the step* and fore-eye,† and very near swamped us, having almost filled the boat with water. Chipped the heel of the main-mast, and rove the main-eye and halliards forward; which enabled us to set the fore-sail, and keep scudding, running towards Rock Fort, with the expectation of falling in with some of the other boats; but was disappointed. At 11. determined to anchor in the bottom of Bertheaume bay, though very little or no hopes of riding long, our only ground tackling being a small grappling, and a few fathom of 1¼ inch. We fortunately succeeded in bringing up, though most miserably situated. The weather tide running strong against a violent gale from the N.W. occasioned such a sea, as to bury us frequently in its abyss. A.M. at 2. the sea breaking in a most astonishing manner over us, and finding we were driving,‡ and almost touching abaft, expecting every second to be dashed on the rocks a-stern of us; we hauled in briskly on the grappling rope, hoisted the fore-sail, and wore round : paying out the grappling rope just hauled in, until we brought it right over the quarter, which enabled us to get our grappling on board with ease, while we stood over to the Camaret bay side,∥ in the hope of falling in with some little haven to shelter us, or with one of the other boats; but were disappointed in each expectation.

---

* Step, that part of the mast that fixes in the boat.

† Fore-eye, the rope which the fore-sail is hauled up by.

‡ Scudding, running before the wind.

§ When the anchor does not hold.

∥ This was the bay in which the Chevrette lay, when she was cut out: a most desperate and determined affair.

At about 4. 30. finding we advanced towards Brest harbour considerably, we resolved to try the grapnel once more; although we were not in the smallest degree sheltered from the inclemency of the weather, and were placed immediately under a fort, which we distinguished by their lights, that enabled us to see the centinels on their posts walking to and fro. We made, if possible, worse weather here, than at our former anchorage, with the exception that the grapling held. At 7. 30. the wind and weather, if possible, became more inclement than on the preceding night—not a boat of ours in sight; every minute expecting to be hailed by the fort; not a soul among us that could speak a word of French; almost perished and starved from the fatigue and sufferings of the night; the few provisions we had being totally destroyed by the salt water. Seeing no alternative, but the pain and mortification of delivering myself and crew prisoners of war, came at length to that resolution. Accordingly ordered all the small arms to be hove overboard, and at 8. cut the grapling rope, and ran into Brest harbour under the fore-sail. Imagining my crew and myself might be better treated and received on board the commander-in-chief's ship, than a private one, I went alongside the Alexander, which ship bore his flag; where I was received with the utmost civility and attention, provided with a shift of dry clothes, got me instantly a warm draught, and gave each of my men a glass of liquor, and ordered them breakfast, and every thing that was necessary to recruit them. They informed me, that the whole of the boats, except mine and another, from the violence of the weather, arrived in the night; that they had been under the greatest apprehensions for our safety, as it was not supposed possible, from the size of the boats, and the manner they were found,* that they could stand the severity of the night. Lieutenant Barker, Mr. Nepean, midshipman, and Mr. Carey, boatswain, who had been on board one of the other ships, came on board to congratulate me on our safe arrival; and feared very much that Mr. Gordon, midshipman, who commanded the boat missing, was no more.

Saturday, the 11th, (1804) at 2 P.M. we were all sent on shore to the hospital at Brest, which was the place designed for us; each of us being more or less indisposed. I must here observe, to the *credit* of the French seamen, that a small leather trunk, in which I had saved a shift of linen, &c. was taken out of one of my men's hands, for the purpose of saving him trouble, and handed into one of the lower-deck ports: the fellow, who remained on the ship's gangway, supposed it a piece of *kindness*, and imagined it was safely deposited in the boat that was to conduct us on shore; nor was it discovered until the trunk could not be found on our landing; when I immediately exposed the circumstance to the officers who conducted us, who instantly sent on board to have a search, and appeared excessively hurt, at such a piece of villany being committed by one of their crew: assured me the perpetrator should be severely punished, and I should have my things safely returned; this I despaired of very much, though the former I thought might take place. In the mean time, those officers con-

---

* Provided or supplied.

ducted us to the hospital, insisted upon my wearing my sword all the way, which the captain had refused to receive on board; observing, that I had been unfortunately wrecked, and not taken in fight, consequently had no right to lose my sword; and he further remarked, that in his opinion, we ought to be returned to our native country, and should not be considered as prisoners; but added, that the gaoler on shore would deprive me of it; which was afterwards the case. On our arrival at the hospital, or rather prison (as we were closely watched and guarded), the gaoler took away my sword, and appeared very much enraged at my not allowing him to take my belt: this, I observed to him, *could do no mischief*. I now had the inexpressible happiness of shaking hands with all the officers, except Mr. Thomas (carpenter), who was unfortunately drowned in attempting to land in Bertheaume bay, and Mr. Gordon, midshipman, who, I was very much pleased to hear, was safe at Conquet,* where he effected a landing. We expected him and boat's crew round to Brest the following day. On the 14th, we had the pleasure of seeing him and crew safe arrived: they spoke very handsomely of the treatment they received at Conquet, and on the march. I now received part of the things that were in the trunk, and the thief I was informed had run the gauntlet.

We were very well used during our stay here; and were attended by *Religieuses*, or old nuns, which is a general custom in all the French hospitals: they were the most attentive nurses I ever beheld, constantly on the alert, visiting their patients, administering relief wherever it might be wanting, and solacing the comfortless. On the 18th of February we received information that we should commence our march towards our *dépôt* on the following morning; accordingly, on the 19th, we were ordered to prepare, and to be ready at a moment's notice. At about 8, we were all drawn up in the hospital yard: Mr. Mahony and myself placed ourselves, as we were wont, next to the lieutenants (being the senior midshipmen), but to our great surprise, on calling the names over, we were moved, and placed next to the people, together with Mr. Carey, boatswain, and Mr. Simpson, gunner. They at the same time offered us a brown loaf of bread each, for our day's subsistence, which we declined. We demanded an explanation of this conduct; they informed us, we were of a class (master's-mates) different from any in their navy; that we were ranked as adjutants, *sous officiers*,† and they could not alter it, &c. Lieut. Pridham now interfered; who, it appeared, from the preceding night, had been acquainted that we were thus ranked, but not being versed in military regulations, supposed that adjutant was between midshipman and lieutenant, which he (of course) thought our proper place. After remonstrating a long time on the impropriety of our being placed in the ranks, among the people, the officer agreed to go to the minister of marine, to have the business, as he termed it, arranged: he shortly returned—the minister of marine was out, but his head clerk, or secretary, assured us that the

---
* A sea-port town in Passage du Four, about 12 miles west of Brest.

† Considered as serjeants, corporals, &c.

mistake should be rectified, the moment he returned, and that a courier would be despatched after us to the next stage, with another *feuille de route*. Thus far reconciled, we commenced our march, as they informed us, for Verdun, in Lorrain.

At about 7 in the evening (February 19th, 1804), we arrived at our first stage, a village named Landerneau,* about 20 miles N.E. of Brest: I expected every moment the arrival of the courier, so little, Sir, was I then acquainted with French promises, and with the French character. Here we were allowed to mix with the officers, though as a great favour: our allowance was 11 sols per day, and the youngest mid. had fifty. In the morning, at day-light, 20th, commenced our march, rather more dejected than the day before; in the evening we arrived at a small village (Landivisiau +), a distance of 5 or 6 leagues from Landerneau. Here we halted for the night, and the people were placed in stables, barns, &c. At daylight on the 21st commenced our march towards Morlaix. At about 2 in the afternoon, at 4 or 5 miles distance from the town, we were met by a captain of gend'armerie and two gens d'armes,‡ who, we understood afterwards, came out to escort us into town. They had not long joined us, when I happened to discover one of the ship's boys lift his hand to strike one of the young midshipmen. I immediately ran up and chastised the youngster with a switch I fortunately had in my hand; but mark my amazement! when I beheld this blustering captain of gend'armerie foaming at the mouth, and riding up towards me at full speed, with his sword drawn: he appeared in a very great rage, swore vehemently, and wielded his sword repeatedly over my head. As I did not understand a syllable that he spoke, but was certain it must be abusive language, from the passion he put himself into, I (parrot like) repeated his own expressions as well as I could; which irritated him to such a degree, that had not the officer of infantry who was escorting us, and our own officers, interfered, I do not know to what length he might have carried the business. The officer of infantry expostulated with him on the impropriety of drawing his sword upon a naked prisoner, who could not even understand a word that he said; he declared and persisted, that I spoke as good French as he did; that *we* were all prisoners alike; that we were now in a country where *every man enjoyed liberty*, and *he* would take care, that while with him, we should not tyrannize over one another. I observed, there were some of the crew who understood him, and who explained his conversation to the others, which appeared to please them extremely. We had not marched more than a mile, when a circumstance took place, which gave us all a specimen of the *liberty* just boasted of: A poor man, at least 70 years of age, happened to be conducting a cart along the road; and as

---

* A small poor village.

† A village much smaller than Landerneau.

‡ The gend'armerie of France consist of tried experienced soldiers; they have the internal regulation of the country, and are the best and most strict police in the universe.

he was approaching us, this *lover of liberty* called to him to turn his horses and cart aside, until we had passed; but the poor unfortunate old man not hearing, and continuing his way, this brute rode up to him, and beat and mauled the poor old creature so unmercifully, that the seamen literally hissed him, and asked repeatedly if *that was the liberty he so much vaunted about, but a few minutes before ?*

At about five, we arrived at Morlaix :* the people were placed as usual; the officers were allowed to go to a tavern. On inquiry, I found this captain of gend'armerie had been a weaver before the revolution, and got advanced by his perfidy to the rank he then held. I was informed that he visited our people in the night, to induce them to turn traitors, and enter into the French service; but found himself much disappointed, as every proposal he made was rejected with disdain.   had the pleasure of waiting on three countrymen in the evening, who expected to be permitted (hourly) to return to their native country —A Colonel Macnamara, a Mr. Scot, and a Mr. Fiol. They had been detained by your Majesty before war was declared, and were so fortunate as to obtain passports. I availed myself of this opportunity of acquainting my friends with my misfortunes.

The 22d of February, about 8, we again commenced our route; and after a long march, arrived at a small village (Bell'isle en terre) where we remained for the night, disagreeably situated, the village being excessively poor, and small, the people imposing and extorting double price for every thing. However, this I have found since to be general all over France. On the 23d, at the usual hour (about 8), we recommenced our route towards Guingamp,‡ where we arrived tolerably early. It is a spacious town, and appeared well peopled. We rested here during 24 hours, and were pretty well used. On the 25th, at daylight, we recommenced our march towards St. Brieuc, the last town on the sea coast that we had to touch at, and arrived about 4 o'clock. We were very closely guarded, which certainly was necessary, as it was the intention of a great number *to slip their fetters* at this town : however, it proved impossible. We had another guard ordered here, which we all regretted, as the officer who conducted us from Brest to this place, was a perfect gentleman, and preserved the utmost moderation towards the prisoners, who were not, by the bye, at all times very well behaved.

Feb. 26th, at day-light, we recommenced our route with our new guard. About 10, in passing close to the sea, we were halted ; the guard

---

* Morlaix, a sea-port town in the department of Finisterre, with a castle, and tide harbour : the cartels and flags of truce between England and France generally come to this port.

‡ Guingamp is in the department du Cotere du Nord ; the country, though late in the season, appeared very fertile, the peasants excessively poor and distressed.

§ St. Brieuc is in the department of Finisterre, about a mile and a half from the sea.

loaded their pieces, examined their locks, &c. They appeared rather alarmed, though they were nearly as many as the prisoners in number: About 5 we arrived at Lamballe, an ancient little town, the chief of the late Duchy of Penthievre; and which gave the title of Princess to the unfortunate lady who was massacred at Paris, for her inviolable attachment to the late Queen of France. Rennes is about 12 or 13 British leagues S.E. of this town:

On the 27th, at 8, began our march towards Rennes. We rested at Broons, and Mountauban, and arrived at the city of Rennes* the 29th. The *officers* were allowed to go to a tavern, and *we,* who were ranked *as adjutants,* were conducted with the ship's company to the common gaol, where we were continued, notwithstanding a number of representations to the general commanding here, until the 2d of March, having had what they styled, a day's *sejour.* I should much rather we had continued *en route*, as we were placed in this gaol among criminals and malefactors of every denomination, where we found ourselves covered with vermin, in spight of every effort used to avoid it. We had now another guard ordered—joined our officers, and were very much pleased to be once more in the pure air. Marched on towards Vitré,† where we arrived about 8 o'clock at night; having gone over nearly 10 leagues this day. We had great difficulty to get admitted into any of the inns; still more to procure any refreshments. Upon remonstrating with the landlord at the miserable supper he provided us, and the very high price he charged—he called us *English dogs, told us that we ought to have been glad to have got any thing, and the officer was to blame for not placing us in a stable, or in some other place better appropriated for such brutes than an inn—if he had his will, he would very shortly treat us as such dogs merited, &c.*

The river Vilaine runs through Vitré, and there appears to be an abundance of fish in this town. On the 3d of March, at daylight, we quitted our *hospitable* host, a true and worthy subject of your Majesty, and were marched on towards Laval,‡ a tolerably large town on the Mayenne, renowned for its linen manufactories. We arrived about 5 in the evening, and were kept some time in the market-place, as a *spectacle* for the inhabitants, before we were shown to our respective places for the night. Some of the people who could speak English, came to inform us, that our gracious Sovereign had been dead several days, and that the result would be a general peace. We spurned at their intelligence, and assured them we did not give it the smallest credit. From Laval, we passed through

---

* This is an ancient well-known city, in the department of Isle and Vilaine, of which it is the capital; the inhabitants are computed at 36,000; it is seated on the Vilaine, which divides it into two parts. The streets are strait and broad; but they were very narrow before the fire in 1720, which is said to have consumed 850 houses.

† Vitré is in the department of Isle and Vilaine.

‡ The inhabitants of Laval are computed at 25,000 : the neighbouring quarries produce green marble, or black, veined with white.

Prez en paille* to Alençon,† where we arrived on the evening of the 5th. We rested here 24 hours. The lieutenants, midshipmen, &c. on the 7th in the morning, were marched the Paris route; the *adjutants* and half the ship's company towards Rouen, on the northern route to Charlemont, in the department of the Ardennes. I confess this separation grieved me extremely—parting with my messmates and friends, in a foreign country, together with the imposition, and injustice, of being treated in an inferior degree to my brother officers, could not fail of producing that effect of depression so natural to the human mind........From Alençon we passed through Sees, Bernay, and several small villages to Rouen,‡ where we arrived at about 2 in the afternoon of the 12th. We were all put into the common gaol ; and I must not pass over a circumstance that had happened in the morning prior to our arrival : trivial as it was, it will give the reader an idea of French *liberality*. At about 9 in the morning, we had halted in a village on the banks of the Seine, to get some refreshment; the only thing we could procure was bread and eggs, which were served up with large *pewter spoons*. I observed to the French officer, that a small spoon would be much more convenient; upon which he asked the old lady of the house if she had any; she replied in the affirmative; opened a large coffer, and took out six silver tea spoons, which she placed on the table. We finished our repast, called for the bill, and found this parsimonious old wretch had charged us, though poor prisoners, a penny each for the use of the tea-spoons. The officer, quite amazed, asked her, what she could mean by such a demand ? She replied, with *sang froid*, " *You see those Englishmen are so particular, they cannot eat like other people. My spoons have not been out of my chest for a number of years ; and I am determined they shall pay for the trouble they put me to.*" We of course paid her, and wished her a good morning. I observed a number of brigs, and small craft, lying up at Rouen, in a dismantled and neglected state, and could not help expressing my astonishment to one of the Frenchmen, who were confined with us, that those vessels should not have been equipped and sent to sea, or have been employed in some commercial venture. " And where would be the service of attempting it ? " replied the Frenchman, " when the English would have the vessels before they had completed one such voyage."

The prospect down the banks of the Seine was very striking and beautiful. However, the view was shortly of a different nature, and our prospect was changed to the very agreeable one which the inside of the common gaol presented, with the keeper, and his dear companion. They accosted

---

* A small town.

† Alençon is a large town on the river Sarte, in the department de L'Oire, in Normandy. Paris is about 90 miles British, N.E. of Alençon.

‡ Rouen is a large city, the capital of the department of the Lower Seine, situated on that river : its linens, particularly what are called the Siamoise, are much esteemed ; the city, and its 6 suburbs included, are said to contain between 74 and 75,000 inhabitants. There are also manufactories of cloth, oil of vitriol, &c. here.

us in no very pathetic terms, and assured us, that unless we instantly paid for *two* nights' lodgings, we should be placed in the cells along with prisoners, whose society was not over pleasant. We well knew that what those *kind* people said was a law. However, we took the liberty of asking, why they demanded payment for *two* nights; they replied, "you are going to have a *day's rest*, and the officer that escorted you assured us of the fact."

This officer, whose name (to the best of my recollection) was Galway, lived with us in all the small towns we passed through, professed a great deal of friendship for us, while we were paying his expenses, and repeatedly declared, that *he* would prevent our being confined in the gaol of Rouen: that he *himself* would be responsible for us, and we should remain at an inn: but, alas! so shallow was this officer's memory, that he forgot to pay us one day's allowance (the last day), and did not recollect to leave with the officer who succeeded him, the certificates that he had received from our officers, specifying that we were also officers, noticing the mistake at Brest, &c. which would have been of material service; nor do I suppose he *recollected*, that there was a gaol in this city; for we never saw him after we had been placed under lock and key. We of course came into terms with our host and his rib, and paid them two shillings each for the *two nights'* lodging; which pleased them so much, that they conducted us with a great deal of *politesse* to an apartment, in which were two prisoners and three beds; two were pointed out for us; our room mates we discovered were debtors: the landlady very charitably observed that she was certain we were very *faint*, and wanted some refreshment. She would send us a bottle of *good wine*, and some bread for the present, and would procure us, *pauvres enfans*, a comfortable dinner, in about an hour's time; and then she and her husband, after a thousand curtesies and bows, withdrew, not forgetting to turn the key in the door, and to take it with them. We all agreed that this was a considerate, charitable, good woman: but more did we extol her, when we saw the bottle of wine and bread appear—the man who brought it was a smart active turnkey: he informed us, Mistress was very busy cooking dinner for the English captains; that he had the pleasure of waiting very frequently on British officers in that prison—they were very extravagant, liked to live very well, &c. But this conversation did not by any means suit his present guests; so we made signs to the fellow to be off: he quitted us, taking the same precaution that his master had done. Our finances were ebbing fast, and we began to think the dinner that was preparing for us, would help them out amazingly. I have already observed, that we had $5\frac{1}{2}d$ *per diem* allowed us; but we were very frequently cheated even out of that miserable pittance; and had we not each procured a little cash at Morlaix, on our private bills, we should certainly have perished for want. The table was now prepared with a table cloth, a rare article in a common gaol, and in a short time dinner appeared, with two bottles of wine! It consisted of a little fresh fish, and a small joint of boiled mutton: the dishes were cleared in a short time, without the smallest hope of a second course. We were now anxious to know what the generous good dame could or would demand for this *sumptuous* repast; and inquired of our active waiter, who went to his mistress to know : she very kindly replied, not to make ourselves uneasy, it would be time enough the next day. We accordingly waited until the next day; but were determined to have nothing more until we knew the prices. Our fellow prisoners were particularly polite and attentive to us; and gave us a hint, that we were greatly deceived in our opinion of the landlady; which we easily perceived the next morning, when we insisted upon knowing what we had to pay for what *she* called *dinner* and *wine*. She very coolly informed us, fifteen shillings; we imagined it might have been about seven. However, it was in vain to attempt to explain; we paid the bill, and were obliged to be more circumspect. At about 11 o'clock some naval officers came to inspect our people, and gave some of them pieces of money, with an intention to seduce them : this I saw, as it was publicly done in the gaol yard, and I happened to be looking out of the window at the time. I desired them to be particular in what they were about. One man, a Dane, replied, " we will take what money they choose to give us, and that shall be all they will gain by coming here."

On the morning of the 14th of March, about 8 o'clock, a guard of Cuirassiers rode into the yard. The gaoler was very expeditious in giving us notice that they came to conduct us,—so the bills were paid, and every thing settled to this fellow and his good dame's satisfaction. We were then marched down into the yard, and joined by the people: the gaoler observed to the officer and cuirassiers that we were *des bons garçons:* he appeared to be a very affable good kind of fellow, and informed us, that Mr. Galway, his predecessor, left him no certificates, but he assured us, that with him, that should make no difference. All matters being arranged, we commenced our march towards Amiens,* where we arrived on the 16th. Our officer was as good as his word. In the small villages between Rouen and Amiens, he always took us to an inn, and dined with us himself; but in the latter city he could not prevent our being put into gaol. He, however, came frequently to see us, and remained with us some time. Understanding there was an Englishman (a Mr. S. Pratt) who kept an eating-house in this town, we sent to inform him there were some countrymen of his, who wished to speak with him: but it appeared, *he was busy.* However, he sent Mrs. Pratt, who *shed tears* at seeing the distressed condition of her poor countrymen. If she had it in her power, she would give all the seamen shoes and stockings, and a good dinner, that she would : but at all events she would go and get us a dinner instantly—poor dear creatures ! we must be famished !—With a great many more tender expressions, that I cannot at this moment recollect. She took a *cordial leave* of each of us, and said, she would come again late in the evening, lest she might be noticed. But the dinner should be sent as soon as possible—*to her poor*

---

* Amiens is a very ancient town, in the department de La Somme, in Picardie: three branches of the river Somme enter this city: it has manufactories in linen and woollen cloth (established by Colbert), which employ not less than 30,000 people.

dear countrymen. A small leg of roasted mutton arrived, in about an hour, without any kind of vegetables, with a little salt in a piece of paper, two knives and forks, and two bottles of very inferior wine. We expected to have had an opportunity of explaining to the lady in person the excellency of her dinner in the evening; but she never came near her *dear dear countrymen.* She only sent her man with the bill, which exceeded the gaoler's wife's at Rouen.

On the 17th of March, we commenced our route at about 8 in the morning, and at 5 we arrived at Albert,* where we halted for the night. The next morning our officer astonished us with a most elegant breakfast, of every thing the little town could afford; and he appeared under many obligations to us. We made it a point never to allow him to pay when he brought us to an inn, and this was (I believe) by way of return. Throughout Brittany and Normandy, we found an abundance of cyder; their fuel was principally wood: but as we advanced to the eastward, we found beer substituted for cyder, and turf and coals for wood.

[To be continued.]

PLATE CCCLXXVI.

THE annexed view of the Moorish Mosque, on Pan-well river, in India, is from a drawing by Mr. Wm. Westall.—At this mosque, the Mohammedan sailors offer up their prayers to the Prophet for a prosperous voyage. It is about twelve miles from the sea. The river is not navigable any farther inland.

HYDROGRAPHY, PILOTAGE, &c.

MAGNETISM.

THE magnetic researches which formed part of the last hydrographic section of the NAVAL CHRONICLE,† have elicited the following remarks from an officer, who thereby shews himself no less distinguishable for his critical acuteness, than for his professional knowledge.

" Sir ! In the Naval Chronicle for the last month (page 319), under the head HYDROGRAPHY, is an extract from Horsburgh's " Directions for sailing to and from the East Indies ;" a work, in which the well-earned reputation of the author makes error proportionably pernicious, should error be there found. That

---

* A small town; here we saw turf and coals used for the first time since our departure from Brest.

† See page 318 of this Volume.

Mosk in Panwell river Dekkan, India.

part of the extract upon which I propose to make some observations, is as follows:—

" ' If the *magnetic* North, points to the eastward of the true North, the variation of the compass is said to be westerly ; and it is called easterly variation of the compass, when the magnetic North points to the westward of the true North pole of the world. So according to the denomination in *common use,* if understood *literally,* it names the variation of the true North, *from the magnetic North,* and not the angle of aberration of the magnetic meridian *from the true* meridian or pole of the world, which is intended.'

" I have not the Directions by me, but conclude that the extract is correctly made; and, after premising, that a difference of opinion is not inconsistent with that respect which I do certainly entertain for Mr. Horsburgh, as a zealous searcher and promulgator of what he believes to be true and useful, I have to observe, that the above passage appears to me to contain an error; not in any particular part, but throughout ; and, consequently, I believe, that the denominations of the variation in vulgar use are correct: that is, when the magnetic north points to the eastward of the true north, the variation of the compass is said to be, not westerly, as above, but eastward ; and that this is right.

" In allowing the variation upon magnetic courses or bearings, it is admitted that no error exists in the common practice ; and the question, therefore, turns wholly upon the correctness of the denomination. A north course by compass, where there is two points west variation, is N.N.W. true, or by the world. The magnetic north, does it then point to the eastward of the true north, as Mr. Horsburgh says, or does it point westward, as I presume to think ?

" Take two compass cards, and place them one upon the other. Consider the lower card to shew the true points, and the upper one the magnetic, or compass points. Then, since the magnetic north, with two points west variation, is identical with the true N.N.W. place the N. of the upper, or magnetic card, over the N.N.W. of the under, or true card. It will then, as I think, be evident, that the magnetic north points to the westward of the true pole of the world ; and that the denomination in vulgar use, understood literally, is right. If it can be shewn to be otherwise, I shall be happy to see the proofs, and to correct my opinion.

" In another part of the extract from Mr. Horsburgh's work (N. C. page 320), it is mentioned, that Captain P. Heywood, of H.M.S. Polyphemus, made an experiment, at Spithead, to ascertain the change in the variation which might arise from the direction of the ship's head being altered from the eastward to the westward ; ' but he could not perceive any aberration of the needle.' Whoever knows Captain Heywood, will not doubt of his accuracy ; but the compass not being placed upon, or at, the binnacle, it does not solve the question of differences, even for the steering compasses of the Polyphemus. Captain Heywood was present, in May, 1812, when the experiments instituted by order of the Admiralty, were made on board the Devastation bomb, at Spithead ; and I believe it would not now surprise him, more than it would me, if, in his first observations, the variation, instead of being greater when the head was westward, as was the case in the Investigator, he had found it several degrees less ; since the compass was placed in the fore part of the ship, near, or upon, the knight-heads.

" I am, Sir, &c."

Matt^n Flinders

The Hydrographer of the Naval Chronicle."

If praise be due to the writer of the preceding criticism upon the ground of his judgment, it is not less so for liberality and delicacy: as every reader must feel disposed to acknowledge, when informed, that in the genuine spirit of philosophy,. Captain Flinders instructed the editor not to make public use of his letter, until it had been communicated to the author of the work therein commented upon, and opportunity been afforded him of expressing any wishes that its perusal might suggest. This praise-worthy line of conduct has been pursued: and the Hydrographer is enabled to explain that the passage extracted from Horsburgh's 'Sailing Directions,' is founded upon a mistake, the author was led into by trusting to a book consulted some while previous to the time of writing the introduction, in which part of the work it stands as an incidental paragraph; the process of publication, correcting the press, and that most useful one of making an index, going on at the same time: so that the mistake was not perceived till too late to correct; and it being more of speculative than practical importance, it was not noticed among the *errata*. This explanation, which yields not in modesty and candor to the fairness of the criticism, has satisfied the commentator, and leaves the hydrographer only to add, in justice to the NAVAL CHRONICLE, that the phraseology of the 'Directions' in treating that part of the subject of variation, struck him as of such dubious signification, that its discordance with common discourse is specifically alluded to in the introductory paragraph of the article, and the passage itself had been marked for notice in case of entering upon a review of the work, which the pressure of temporary matter has hitherto been the cause of adjourning. It is now rendered the less necessary, by this specific and public discussion of perhaps the only questionable point in a *quarto* volume of more than nine hundred pages; and consequently ought not to diminish the reliance to be placed on the book generally, as the best authority, touching oriental navigation, now extant in the English language.

The extent allotted to this subject in the former section, already refered to, was the occasion of omitting some farther useful observations on the variation of the compass in the British seas, which are contained in the instructions for the pilotage of the North Sea, written nine years ago, to accompany Admiral Knight's surveys of that navigation.

'The variation of the magnetic needle has been found, by numerous observations, to differ in different parts of the North-Sea. The greatest variation prevails in the north-western part of the sea, that is to say, near the islands of Zetland; where it is now [1803] near 29° W. It decreases to the southward; and the mean variation observed by Mr. Downie, in the year 1792, when surveying the Scotish coast, appeared to be 25.° At that time it was, in the mouth of the Thames, rather less than 24°: it is at present in the Swin (or Kings-channel) 24° 30' W. In the year 1799, the mean variation allowed by the French surveyors of the river Scheld was 21° 30'. At that time the variation at London was 24° 15'. Hence, in that year there was in these places a difference of 2° 45', about a quarter of a point on the opposite sides of the sea, nearly in the same parallel of latitude. From the Scheld to the Naze (of Norway) the quantity of variation is nearly the same: and it may be considered generally, as a quarter point less on the eastern than on the western side of the North-sea. The variation, as observed at London in the year 1576, was 11° 15′, or exactly one point E. It has ever since been approaching to the westward, and was in the year 1800, about 24° 17′ W. Its progressive motion in 224 years was therefore 35° 32′, equal to 57′ 6″ in 6 years, or about 1° in 6¼ years. But, as it appears that the progression on the eastern part of the North-sea, is rather slower than on the British coasts, if the mean allowance of 1° be made for every 6½ years, the probable variation of all parts of the North-sea may be obtained for a number of years to come, without deviating so much from the truth as will be of any consequence to the mariner. Hence, according to the average of the last 200 years, the variation now, at the Thames' mouth, 24° 30′, will in the year 1815, be about 26° 30′; and in the year 1828, it will be 28° 30′ &c. But, according to the foregoing observations, it will always be nearly a quarter of a point less on the opposite coasts."

ENGLAND.
THAMES RIVER.

Notice is given to all Masters, Pilots, and others, that the Corporation of the City of London having given directions, in conformity to the representations that have been made to it, of the great convenience that would be derived to the trade of the Port of London, from having mooring chains, with proper bridles and buoys, laid down in Galleon's Reach, in the river Thames, the said moorings have been completed, since August, 1812, and are ready for use. The situations of the three chains are marked by three large floating buoys, and the in-shore mooring anchor is about twenty fathoms from each buoy, and the outside anchor about ten fathoms from each of the said buoys. All pilots and others not using the moorings will be cautious in letting go their anchors within the before-mentioned distances: and those who choose to bring up at the buoys will be charged the following rates, to be paid previous to quitting the moorings, to the person who will be stationed there to receive the same.

Rates.

Vessels of 100 tons, and under, 10s. 6d. for the first day, and 5s. for every day after.
——— 100 to 200 tons, 1l. 1s. 0d. ditto .... and 10s. 6d. ditto.
——— 200 to 300 tons, 1l. 1s. 0d. ditto ...... and 1l. 1s. 0d. ditto.
——— 300 to 500 tons, 1l. 1s. 0d. ditto ...... and 2l. 2s. 0d. ditto.
——— 500 to 800 tons, 2l. 2s. 0d. ditto ...... and 3l. 3s. 0d. ditto.
Colliers, stopping a tide ..... 1l. 1s. 0d.

GENERAL DESCRIPTION OF THE BUOYS IN THE VICINITY OF ORFORD-NESS.

Trinity-House, London, 25th May, 1812.
New Buoy on Aldborough Knapes; * chequered black and white, with

---
* *Vide* N. C. XXVII. 323.

staff and vane. Laid down in April, 1812. This buoy lies upon the eastern edge of the shoal, in 5 fathoms at common spring-ebbs, and about 1½ cable length to the eastward of that part, where the sea breaks the highest in easterly gales. The sand is here about 350 fathoms broad, *viz.* from 5 fathoms on the eastern edge to 5 fathoms on the western; it lies in the direction of N.E. and S.W. nearly, and is $2\frac{1}{4}$ miles in extent, from 5 fathoms on the N.E. end to 5 fathoms on the S.W. It is steep-to on each side; and, at the distance of about one cable's length, in the direction of E.S.E. from the buoy, there are 10 fathoms; and, at the distance of about 2 cables, 14. From the buoy Aldborough-church bears N.W. a little westerly; Orford High Light W. by S.; Orford-church and Castle in one, W. $\frac{1}{4}$ N.; and Iken-church, which has a tower-steeple, nearly N.W. by W., at one-third of the apparent distance from Aldborough-town to Slaughden-houses. The N.W. end of the Knapes bears from the buoy N.E. by N., and its S.W. end W.S.W. From the latter (or S.W. end) in $3\frac{3}{4}$ fathoms, with the High-light W. $\frac{1}{2}$ S., Iken-church is on the southernmost lime-kiln, and a large bluff tree appears at a boat's length open to the right of a large white house at the north end of Aldborough-town, bearing N.W. by N. At the N.W. end, in 5 fathoms, Old Rengham church appears between two woods bearing N.W. by W.

Buoy on the N.E. end of the Shipwash.—A red buoy, laid down in 4 fathoms, with Baudsey-church bearing W. by N. $\frac{1}{2}$ N., distant about 8 miles, and the High-light N. $\frac{1}{2}$ W. $4\frac{3}{4}$ miles. The object of this buoy more particularly is, to enable ships of great draught of water to proceed with safety through the channel between Baudsey-sand and the Shipwash, instead of proceeding through Hosley Bay. In sailing along the Shipwash, care must be taken to give an allowance in the course for the set of the tide, the flood setting about W.S.W., and the ebb E.N.E., which thwart this sand about two points.

Buoy on the S.W. end of the Shipwash.—This buoy, which is white, was laid down in 1802. From the buoy the Sunk-light bears S.W. $\frac{1}{4}$ W. $8\frac{1}{2}$ miles; the buoy on the Gunfleet, W. by S. $7\frac{1}{4}$ miles; the buoy on the Ruff (in its present position), N.W. by W. $3\frac{2}{10}$ miles; the buoy on the Baudsey Sand, north, $4\frac{3}{4}$ miles. The Shipwash is a dangerous bank, as ships coming in from sea have not sufficient warning, by the lead, in approaching it, being steep-to on both sides.

Buoy on the N.E. end of the Whiting.—A white buoy, No. 11, which is laid down within the distance of a mile from the beach. From this buoy Orford-church bears N. by W., and the High-light N.E. $\frac{1}{4}$ N.

Buoy on the elbow of the Whiting.—A white buoy, in 3 fathoms at low water, laid down in 1810, with the following marks: Orford-ness Light-houses in one, bearing N.E. by E. and Orford-castle N. by E., with a white mill a little open to the westward of it.

Buoy on the S.W. end of the Whiting.—A white buoy, in about $3\frac{1}{4}$ fathoms at low water, laid down in 1810. Marks: A white mill in the country a little open to the westward of a white house, and entering on a grove of trees, bearing N. $\frac{1}{4}$ W.; a Mortella-tower to the westward of

Baudsey Point, shutting in with the point; and the Low-light a little open to the southward of the High-light.

Eastern buoy of the middle ground in Hosley Bay.—A black buoy, laid down in 1810, in $3\frac{1}{4}$ fathoms, with the High-light on Orford-ness E. by N.; Orford-castle N.N.E. $\frac{1}{2}$ E.; and the white buoy on the elbow of the Whiting nearly S.S.E.

Western Buoy of the Middle Ground, in Hosley Bay.—A black buoy, laid down in $4\frac{1}{2}$ fathoms, in 1810. Marks: A white mill on with a single house, a little east of a grove of trees, bearing N.W. by N.; the easternmost Mortella-tower at the entrance of Orford Haven, N.W. by W.; and the High-light, E. by N. easterly.

Buoy on the S.W. end of Baudsey Sand.*—A chequered black and white buoy, laid down in 1802; from which the High-light of Orford-ness bears N.E. $\frac{1}{4}$ N. $7\frac{1}{4}$ miles; Baudsey sea-mark, N.W. by N. 4 miles; the buoy of the Ruff, S.W. $\frac{1}{2}$ S. $4\frac{1}{10}$ miles; the Sunk light, S.S.W. $\frac{3}{4}$ W. $12\frac{1}{4}$ miles.

Buoy of the Cutler.—A black buoy was placed on the southern extremity of the Cutler in 1810. This buoy lies in $4\frac{1}{2}$ fathoms, with the following marks: Baudsey-church on with a white house seen over Baudsey-cliff, bearing N. $\frac{1}{2}$ E., and the Low-light a little open to the southward of the High-light.

Buoy of the Ruff or Rough, red, No. 10, was shifted to its present situation in May, 1811, and now lies seven-tenths of a mile to the southeastward of its former situation, in $3\frac{1}{2}$ fathoms at low water, with the following marks and bearings:—buoy of the S.E. Spit of the West Rocks, S.W. $\frac{1}{2}$ W. $2\frac{8}{10}$ miles; Sunk-light, S.S.W. $\frac{3}{4}$ W. 8 miles; buoy on the S.W. end of the Shipwash, S.E. by E. $3\frac{2}{10}$ miles; buoy on the south part of Baudsey Sand, N.E. $\frac{1}{2}$ N. $4\frac{1}{10}$ miles; and Baudsey sea-mark, N. $\frac{1}{4}$ E. $5\frac{9}{10}$ miles.

Buoy on the Eastern Spit of the West Rocks.—Laid down in May, 1811. A black and white buoy, having the words 'West Rocks' marked thereon. It lies in $3\frac{1}{4}$ fathoms at low water, with the following marks, &c.—The Gunfleet Buoy, S.W. $\frac{1}{2}$ W. distant $2\frac{7}{10}$ miles; the Sunk Light, S. by W. $\frac{1}{2}$ W. $5\frac{1}{2}$ miles; the buoy of the Ruff, N.E. $\frac{1}{2}$ E. $2\frac{8}{10}$ miles; the buoy on the S.W. end of the Shipwash, east, $4\frac{3}{4}$ miles; the sea-mark on Baudsey-cliff, N. by E. $\frac{1}{4}$ E. $8\frac{2}{10}$ miles; the Naze-tower, W.N.W. $\frac{1}{4}$ W. $6\frac{1}{10}$ miles.

Buoy on the Cork Ledge.—A white buoy, laid down in May, 1811, with 'Cork Ledge' marked thereon. It lies to the northward, and near the shoalest part, of this knoll, (on which is about 9 feet), in 2 fathoms at low water, with the following marks and bearings:—1. The tower of Harwich-church, about N.W. $\frac{1}{4}$ W. distant $4\frac{2}{10}$ miles, and seen midway in the opening between the high buildings in Landguard Fort, and the Mortella-tower to the right of the fort. 2. Baudsey-church, N.E. by N. distant $4\frac{8}{10}$ miles, and a little to the northward of the signal-staff on the highest part of Baudsey-cliff.

⁎ All the given bearings are compass-bearings, the depths those at low water, and the miles geographic, of 60 to a degree.

---

* NAVAL CHRONICLE, XXII. 476. XXIV. 404.

A comparison of the preceding instructions for sailing in the vicinity of Orford-ness (published by the most eminent authority in England for coasting pilotage), with the following descriptive remarks relating to the same navigation, (abridged from the " Improved directions for the pilotage of the North-sea," &c. published in 1803) may probably be found useful.

The passages from the Swin channel to Orford-ness are formed by several shoals and dangers; before we proceed to the enumeration of which, it is necessary to premise, that in the year 1802, a light vessel was placed at the eastern end of the Sunk. This vessel shews a single light in the night, and a flag at the mast-head during the day. In foggy weather a bell is rung every half-hour, and it strikes six times every ten minutes to distinguish this from other vessels. From hence the beacon on the Gunfleet bears W.N.W. $5\frac{1}{4}$ miles; the Naze tower N.N.W. $\frac{1}{4}$ W. $9\frac{1}{2}$ miles: the buoy on the E. end of the Gunfleet N. by W. 4 miles; the red buoy of the Ruff N.N.E. $8\frac{1}{4}$ miles; the white and black chequered buoy on Baudsey sand N.N.E. $\frac{1}{2}$ E. $12\frac{1}{4}$ miles; Orford-ness N.E. $\frac{1}{4}$ N. 20 miles; the buoy on the Ship-wash N.E. $\frac{1}{4}$ E. $8\frac{1}{2}$ miles; and the Long-sand head E S.E. $4\frac{3}{4}$ miles. In working between the Sunk and the Gunfleet, stand no nearer the former sand than the light bearing E. as the buoy of the Heaps bears from the light about W. $\frac{1}{2}$ S.

The four following shoals lie on the western side of the Sledway or Shipway channel: *viz.* the West-rocks, a rocky shoal dry at low water, more than 3 miles long, and $2\frac{1}{4}$ broad; the channel named Goldener's-gat between this shoal and the Gunfleet, is about $1\frac{1}{2}$ mile wide, and has from 8 to 6 fathoms at low water. The Cork sand lies off the N. side of the West-rocks; and its eastern end bears about N.W. $\frac{1}{2}$ W. from that shoal. It thence extends W. by S. about $2\frac{1}{4}$ miles, and is $1\frac{1}{4}$ mile broad, partly dry at low-water. The Cork ledge is a small shoal of $2\frac{1}{2}$ fathoms, which lies near the N.E. end of the Cork sand. The Rough, or Ruff, is a small hard shoal, of 3 fathoms to the eastward of the West-rocks, and lies about $5\frac{1}{2}$ miles N.E. $\frac{1}{2}$ E. from the Gunfleet buoy: the red buoy on it is to be left on the larboard side: its marks are, Baudsey church N. b. E. $\frac{1}{4}$ E. and Ramsholt church on with 2 trees that stand to the westward of Felixstow cliff. Between the Gunfleet and Ruff are 9, 8, 7, 6, to 5 fathoms at low-water.

On the eastern side of the same channel are 5 other dangers, as follow:—
Baudsey sand is about 3 miles in length, and $\frac{3}{4}$ in breadth near the S.W. end: its direction is nearly E.N.E. and W.S.W. The soundings are very irregular upon this shoal: less than 10 feet at low-water, spring-tides, has not been found any where upon it; but, from the unevenness of the ground, there may be knowls with less water: upon the S. part a white and black chequered buoy is placed, from which the high light of Orford-ness bears N.E. $\frac{1}{4}$ N. $7\frac{1}{2}$ miles; Baudsey beacon N.W. by N. 4 miles; the buoy of the Ruff S.W. $\frac{1}{4}$ W. $3\frac{3}{4}$ miles; the Sunk light S.S.W. $\frac{3}{4}$ W. $12\frac{1}{4}$ miles; the N.E. end of this sand bears from Orford high light S.W. b. S. 5 miles. The Shipwash is a narrow ridge of sand extending about N.E. and S.W. $7\frac{1}{2}$ miles: some parts of it are said to dry in low ebbs, and it is steep-to on both sides. This is a dangerous bank, as ships coming in from

sea have not sufficient warning by the lead in approaching it. A white buoy is placed at the S.W. end, from whence the Sunk light bears S.W. ¼ W. 8½ miles; the buoy on the Gun-fleet W. by S. 7¾ miles; the Ruff N.W. ¼ W. 4 miles; the buoy on Baudsey sand N. 4¾ miles. The N.E. end bears from the high light of Orford 3½ E. 4¾ miles. In sailing along this sand care must be taken to give an allowance in the course for the set of the tide, the floods setting about W.S.W. and the ebb E.N.E. about 2 points athwart the sand. The Kettle-bottom is a small shoal, lying ¾ of a mile to the N.N.W. of Baudsey sand, about which there are very uneven soundings; the least water found was 2½ fathoms, although some part may have less. The Whiting is a narrow bank, with a white buoy on the N.E. end, not a mile distant from the beach; Orford church bearing N. b. W. it extends S.W. b. W. ¼ W. 3 miles: the 2 light-houses on Orford-ness in one leads close upon the inner side; therefore, in working through Hosley bay, the lower or easternmost light must be kept in sight to the northward of the high light. The Cutler is a rocky shoal, with uneven soundings, the outer edge of which is about 2 miles without Baudsey cliff: the lights of Orford in one leads upon the outer part; therefore, in passing it, the lower light should be kept open to the eastward of the high light.

From the Swin to Hosley bay the direct course is nearly N.E. b. N. but allowance must be made for wind and tide; the flood sets S.W. the ebb N.E. From the buoy on the Ruff to Hosley bay the course is nearly N.E. b. N. more or less to the E. or W. according to the tide: the ebb here sets E.N.E. and the flood W.S.W. Between the Ruff and Hosley bay are 5, 10, 8, 7, and 6 fathoms at low water. In turning to windward stand no nearer to the W. end of the Shipwash than till Baudsey church comes on with the N.E. end of the long wood to the eastward of the cliff, bearing N. b. W. ¼ W. nor to the West-rocks than till Alderton church comes on with Baudsey church, appearing then on the rising part of the cliff. Stand no nearer to the West-rocks than 5 fathoms, nor to the Shipwash than 8 fathoms. Having passed the Ruff, stand no nearer to Baudsey sand than till the tree to the northward of Orford church comes near to the W. side of that church; nor to the Cork sand, or, ledge, than till Harwich church-steeple comes on with a brew-house which stands a little to the northward of Landguard fort; in the night stand no nearer than 5 fathoms. About ¼ a mile S.E. from this end of the Cork sand are 8 fathoms in what is called the Cork hole.

The best anchorage in Hosley Bay is with the church and parsonage on with each other, in 5 or 4½ fathoms at low water. In this bay, the tide flows on the full and change days of the moon, at eleven o'clock. A black buoy was laid down at Hosley Bay, in 1801, on the wreck of a Danish brig, which lies sunken at 6½ fathoms, at low water, with the following marks: the northernmost of two trees, called the Hunters, upon Felixstow cliff, just on with Baudsey cliff, bearing W. S. W. southerly; Orford castle, N. N. E ¼ E. and Orford high cliff, N. E. 6. E. ¼ E. Observe, in running up Hosley Bay, to keep the low light a sail's breadth open to the northward of the high one. Above Orford-ness, is a flat, which runs off the shore about two cables length; the bottom is hard, and there are 6 fathoms close to it; you will have 8 fathoms at one cast, and before the lead can be hoven again may be ashore.

From Hosley Bay, bound to sea, after passing the buoy, steer S. E. by E. when, after crossing the spit of the Whiting, you will have 10 fathoms, which is a flat that runs off from the Ness into the stream of the Ship wash. If bound northward, after passing the Ness beware of Aldborough knapes. Orford lights in one, bearing S. W. by W. will lead you clear between that danger and the shore to the westward.

Ships bound from Hosley Bay to the Downs, with an easterly wind, should turn down to Orford-ness with the ebb, and proceed to the eastward of the Ship wash. From Hosley Bay to Orford-ness, the course is E. N. E. and E. by N. but stand no nearer to the Whiting than 8 fathoms. In this channel, a middle ground about half a mile broad, begins to the eastward of the entrance of Orford haven, and extends thence N. E. 2 miles; the passage between this and the Whiting, in the narrowest part, is a mile wide, and has from 6 to 8 fathoms at low-water.

Upon Orford beach, about 400 yards from the sea side, is a good spring of fresh water; the mark to find it is, to bring the mill upon the chancel of the church, which will lead directly to it.

S.

STATE PAPERS.

At the Court at Carlton House, the 29th of September, 1812,

PRESENT,

His Royal Highness the PRINCE REGENT in Council.

WHEREAS his Royal Highness the Prince Regent was pleased, by his Order in Council, in the name and on the behalf of his Majesty, bearing date the twenty-eighth of February, one thousand eight hundred and eleven, to direct that certain questions, in addition to the preliminary questions directed by his Majesty's general Order in Council of the 5th of April, one thousand eight hundred and five, touching the performance of quarantine, should be put to the commander, master, or other person having the charge of any ships or vessels coming from or having touched at any port or place on the continent of America, or the islands adjacent thereto, or coming from, or having touched at, any of the ports in the West Indies; and whereas it is deemed expedient that the following question should be placed at the head of the several questions so directed to be put by the Order in Council of the twenty eighth of February, one thousand eight hundred and eleven, *viz.*

" In the course of your voyage have any persons on board suffered from sickness of any kind; what was the nature of such sickness; and when did it prevail? How many persons were affected by it? And have any of them died in the course of the voyage?"

H. R. H. the Prince Regent is thereupon pleased to order, in the name and on the behalf of his Majesty, and by and with the advice of his Majesty's Privy Council, that the question above set forth be placed at the head of the several questions directed to be put by the afore-mentioned Order in Council of the twenty-eighth of February, one thousand eight hundred and eleven, to the commanders, masters, or other persons having charge of ships or vessels coming from, or having touched at any port or place on the Continent of America, or the islands adjacent thereto, or coming from, or having touched at, any of the ports in the West Indies; and H. R. H. is further pleased to order, in the name and on the behalf of his Majesty, and by and with the advice aforesaid, that such commanders, masters, or other persons having charge of such ships or vessels, shall, upon such question being put by the superintendant of quarantine, or his assistant, or principal officer or other officer of the Customs, authorized by the Commissioners of his Majesty's Customs, or any four or more of them, to act in that behalf give a true answer to the same in writing, or otherwise, and upon oath, or not upon oath, according as he shall be required by such superintendant or his assistant, or principal officer or other officer of the Customs, authorized as aforesaid, under such pains and penalties as are inflicted by an Act passed in the forty-fifth year of his Majesty's reign, intituled, " An Act for making further provision for the effectual performance of quarantine;" and the Right Hon. the Lords Commissioners of his Majesty's Treasury, the Commissioners for executing the office of Lord High Admiral of Great Britain, the Lord Warden of the Cinque Ports, the Master General, and the rest of the principal officers of the Ordnance, his Majesty's Secretary at War, and the Governors and Commanders-in-chief for the time being of the isles of Guernsey, Jersey, Alderney, Sark, and Man, are to give the necessary directions herein as to them may respectively appertain.

JAMES BULLER.

By H. R. H. the PRINCE OF WALES, REGENT of the United Kingdom of Great Britain and Ireland, in the name and on behalf of his Majesty.

A PROCLAMATION,

For granting the Distribution of Prizes during the present Hostilities.

GEORGE, P. R.

WHEREAS by our Order in Council, dated the thirteenth day of October instant, we have ordered that general reprisals be granted against the ships, goods, and citizens of the United States of America (save and except any vessels to which his Majesty's license has been granted, or which have been directed to be released from the embargo, and have not terminated the original voyage in which they were detained and released), so that as well the fleets and ships of his Majesty, as also all other ships and vessels that shall be commissioned by letters of marque or general reprisals, or otherwise by the commissioners for executing the office of lord high admiral of Great Britain, shall and may lawfully seize all ships, vessels, and goods belonging to the government of the United States of America, or to any persons being citizens of the United States of America, or inhabiting within any of the territories thereof, and bring the same to judgment in any of the Courts of Admiralty within his Majesty's dominions duly authorized and required to take cognizance thereof; we being desirous to give due encouragement to his Majesty's faithful subjects who shall lawfully seize the same, and having declared in council, by our order of the thirteenth of October instant, our intentions concerning the distributions of all manner of captures, seizures, prizes, and reprisals of all ships and goods during the present hostilities, do now make known to all his Majesty's loving subjects, and all others whom it may concern, by this our Proclamation, by and with the advice and consent of his Majesty's privy council, that our will and pleasure is, in the name and on behalf of his Majesty, that the net produce of all prizes taken (save as hereinbefore excepted), the right whereof is inherent in his Majesty and his Crown, be given to the takers (save also the produce of such prizes as are or shall be taken by ships or vessels belonging to or hired by, or in the service of, the commissioners of Customs or Excise, the disposition of which we reserve to our farther pleasure, and also save and except as hereinafter mentioned); but subject to the payment of all such or like customs and duties, as the same are now or would have been liable to, if the same were or might have been imported as merchandise; and that the same may be so given in the proportion and manner hereinafter set forth, that is to say,

That all prizes taken by ships and vessels having commissions of letters of marque and reprisals (save and except such prizes as are or shall be taken by the ships or vessels belonging to or hired by, or in the service of, the commissioners aforesaid) may be sold and disposed of by the merchants, owners, fitters, and others to whom such letters of marque and reprisals are granted, for their own use and benefit, after final adjudication, and not before.

And we do hereby further order and direct, that the net produce of all prizes which are or shall be taken by any of his Majesty's ships or vessels of war (save and except when they shall be acting on any conjunct expedition with his Majesty's land forces, in which case we reserve to ourselves the division and distribution of all prizes and booty taken, and also save and except as hereinafter mentioned), shall be for the entire benefit and encouragement of the flag-officers, captains, commanders, and other commissioned officers in his Majesty's pay, and of the seamen, marines, and soldiers on board his Majesty's said ships and vessels at the time of the capture; and that such prizes may be lawfully sold and disposed of by them and their agents, after the same shall have been finally adjudged lawful prize to his Majesty, and not otherwise.

The distribution shall be made as follows; the whole of the net produce being first divided into eight equal parts:—

The captain or captains of any of His Majesty's said ships or vessels of war, or officer commanding such ship or vessel, who shall be actually on board at the taking of any prize, shall have two eighth parts; but in case any such prize shall be taken by any of His Majesty's said ships or vessels of war, under the command of a flag or flags, the flag officer or officers being actually on board, or directing and assisting in the capture, shall have one third of the said two eighth parts; the said one third of such two eighth parts, to be paid to such flag or flag officers, in such proportions, and subject to such regulations, as are herein-after-mentioned.

The sea-lieutenants, captain of marines, and land forces, and master on board, shall have one eighth part, to be equally divided amongst them; but every physician appointed or hereafter to be appointed to a fleet or squadron of His Majesty's ships of war shall, in the distribution of prizes which may hereafter be taken by the ships in which he shall serve, or in which such ship's company shall be entitled to share, be classed with the before-mentioned officers with respect to one eighth part, and be allowed to share equally with them; provided such physician be actually on board at the time of taking such prizes.

The lieutenants and quarter-master of marines, and lieutenants, ensigns, and quarter-masters of land forces, secretaries of admirals, or of commodores with captains under them, second masters of line of battle ships, surgeons, chaplains, pursers, gunners, boatswains, carpenters, masters'-mates, and pilots on board, shall have one eighth part, to be equally divided amongst them.

The other four eighth parts of the prize to be divided into shares, and distributed to the persons composing the remaining part of the crew, in the following proportions; viz. to the first class of petty officers, namely, the midshipmen, surgeon's-assistants, secretaries'-clerks, captain's-clerks, schoolmasters, masters at arms, captain's-coxswains, gunner's-mates, yeomen of the powder room, boatswain's-mates, yeomen of the sheets, carpenter's-mates, quarter-masters, quarter-master's-mates, ship's-corporals, captains of the forecastle, master sail-makers, master-caulkers, master rope-makers, armourers, serjeants of marines and of land forces, four and a half shares each.

To the second class of petty officers; viz. midshipmen, ordinary captains of the foretop, captains of the maintop, captains of the after-guard, captains of the mast, sail-maker's-mates, caulker's-mates, armourer's-mates, ship's-cook, corporals of marines and of land forces, three shares each.

The quarter-gunners, carpenter's-crew, sail-maker's-crew, coxswain's-mates, yeomen of the boatswain's store-room, gunsmiths, coopers, trumpeters, able seamen, ordinary seamen, drummers, private marines, and other soldiers, if doing duty on board in lieu of marines, one and a half share each.

The landsmen, admiral's domestics, and all other ratings not above enumerated, together with all passengers and other persons borne as supernumeraries, and doing duty and assisting on board, one share each, excepting officers acting by order, who are to receive the share of that rank in which they shall be acting.

And young gentlemen, volunteers by order, and the boys of every description, half a share each.

And we do hereby further order, that in the case of cutters, schooners, brigs, and other armed vessels, commanded by lieutenants, the distribution shall be as follows:

First.—That the share of such lieutenants shall be two-eighth parts of the prize, unless such lieutenants shall be under the command of a flag-officer or officers, in which case the flag-officer or officers shall have one-third of the said two-eighths to be divided among such flag-officer or officers, in the same manner as herein directed in the case of captains serving under flag officers.

Secondly—We direct, that the share of the sub-lieutenant, master, and pilot, shall be one eighth; the said eighth, if there be all three such persons on board, to be divided into four parts, two parts to be taken by the sub-lieutenant, one part by the master, and one part by the pilot; if there be only two such persons on board, then the eighth to be divided into three parts, of which two thirds shall go to the person second in command, and one third to the other person; if there be only a sub lieutenant or a master, and no pilot, then the sub-lieutenant or master to take the whole eighth; if there be only a pilot, then such pilot to have one half of the eighth, and the other half to go to Greenwich-hospital.

Thirdly—That the share of the surgeon or surgeon's assistant, where there is no surgeon, midshipmen, clerk, and steward, shall be one eighth.

Fourthly—That the remaining four eighths shall be divided into shares, and distributed to the other part of the crew in the following proportions; viz. the gunner's, boatswain's, and carpenter's mates, yeomen of the sheets, sail maker, quarter master, and quarter master's mates, and serjeant of marines, to receive four and a half shares each.

The corporals of marines three shares each.

The able seamen, ordinary seamen, and marines, one share and a half each.

The landmen, together with passengers and other persons borne as supernumeraries, doing duty, and assisting on board, to receive one share each.

Boys of all descriptions half a share each.

But it is Our intention, nevertheless, that the above distribution shall only extend to such captures as shall be made by any cutter, schooner, brig or armed vessel, without any of His Majesty's ships or vessels of war being present, or within sight of, and adding to the encouragement of the captors, and terror of the enemy; but in case a y such ships or vessels of war shall be present or in sight, that then the officers, pilots, petty officers, and men on board such cutters, schooners, brigs, or armed vessels, shall share in the same proportion as is allowed to persons of the like rank and denomination on board of His Majesty's ships and vessels of war, the sub-lieutenant and master to be considered as warrant officers, and such cutters, schooners, brigs, or armed vessels, shall not in respect to such captures, convey any interest or share to the fla officer or officers under whose orders such cutters; schooners, brigs, and armed vessels may happen to be.

And whereas it is judged expedient, during the present hostilities, to hire into His Majesty's service armed vessels, to be employed as cruisers against the enemy, which vessels are the property of, and their masters and crews are paid by, the owners of whom they are hired, although several of them are commanded by commissioned officers in His Majesty's pay; it is Our further will and pleasure, that the net produce of all prizes taken by such hired armed vessels, except as herein after-mentioned, shall be for the benefit of such commissioned officers in His Majesty's pay, and of the masters and crews on board the said hired armed vessels at the time of the capture; and that such prizes may be lawfully sold and disposed of by them and their agents, after the same shall have been to His Majesty finally adjudged lawful prize, and not otherwise; the distribution whereof shall be as follows:

The whole of the net produce being divided into eight equal parts, the officer commanding any hired armed vessel afore-said, who shall be actually on board at the taking of any prize, shall have two eighths; but in case such hired armed vessel shall be under the command of a flag or flags, the flag officer or officers being actually on board, or directing or assisting in the capture, shall have one third of the said two eighth parts; the said one third of the two eighth parts to be paid to such flag or flag officers in such proportions, and subject to such regulations, as are herein after-mentioned. In case there be acting on board such hired armed vessel, besides the officer commanding the same, one or more commissioned sea lieutenants in His Majesty's pay, such lieutenant or lieutenants shall take one eighth. One eighth shall belong to the master and mate, of which the master shall take two thirds, and the mate one third; but in case there shall be acting on board such hired armed vessel one or more midshipmen, in that case the master shall take one half of the eighth, and the other shall be divided equally between the mate and midshipmen. The remaining four eighth parts shall belong to, and, being divided into shares, be distributed among the other petty officers, men, and boys, in the same proportion as herein before directed with respect to the division of prize money in His Majesty's ships of war. And in case of prizes taken by any hired armed vessel not commanded by any of His Majesty's commissioned officers, one eighth shall belong to the flag-officers, to be divided as aforesaid, in case such hired armed vessel shall be under the command of a flag; one eighth shall belong to the master and mate, of which the master shall take two thirds, and the mate one third; four eighths shall belong to, and be divided among the petty officers and crew, in manner aforesaid. The surplus, the distribution of which is not herein directed, shall remain at our disposal; and, if not disposed of within a year after final adjudication, the same shall belong and be paid to Greenwich-hospital.

And in the case of prizes taken jointly by any of His Majesty's ships of war, or any hired armed vessel, His Majesty's commissioned officer or officers on board such hired armed vessel shall share with the commissioned officer or officers of the same rank on board His Majesty's ship or ships of war being joint captors; the master of such hired armed vessel shall share with the warrant officers; the mate of such hired armed vessel with the first class of petty officers; and the seamen, landmen, and boys, of such hired armed vessel, with persons of the same description on board his Majesty's said ship or ships of war; save and except that, in case such hired armed vessel shall be commanded by one of his Majesty's commissioned officers having the rank of master and commander, and there shall be none of his Majesty's lieutenants on board, or in case such hired armed vessel shall be commanded by the master, in both those cases, the master of such hired armed vessel shall share with the lieutenants of his Majesty's ships of war, and the mate with the warrant officers: and in case any difficulty shall arise in respect to the said distribution, not herein sufficiently provided for, the same shall be referred to the Lords Commissioners of the Admiralty, whose direction thereupon shall be final, and have the same force and effect as if herein inserted.

Provided, that if any officer, being on board any of his Majesty's ships of war at the time of taking any prize, shall have more commissions or offices than one, such officer shall be entitled only to the share or shares of the prizes, which, according to the above-mentioned distribution, shall belong to his superior commission or office.

Provided also, that, in all prizes taken by any of his Majesty's squadrons, ships, or vessels, while acting in conjunction with any squadron, ship, or vessel, of any other power that may be in alliance with his Majesty, a share of such prizes shall be set apart, and be at Our further disposal, equal to that share which the flag and other officers and crews of such squadron, ships, or vessels, would have been entitled to if they had belonged to his Majesty.

And we do hereby strictly enjoin all commanders of his Majesty's ships and vessels of war, taking any prize, to transmit as soon as may be, or cause to be transmitted to the Commissioners of the Navy, a true list of the names of all the officers, seamen, marines, soldiers, and others, who were actually on board his Majesty's ships and vessels of war under their command at the time of the capture; which list shall contain the quality of the service of each person on board, together with the description of the men, taken from the description books of the capturing ship or ships, and their several ratings, and be subscribed by the captains or commanding officer and three or more of the chief officers on board.

And we do hereby require and direct the Commissioners of the Navy, or any three or more of them, to examine or cause to be examined, such lists by the muster books of such ships and vessels of war, and lists annexed thereto, to see that such lists do agree with such muster books and annexed lists, as to the names, qualities or ratings of the officers, seamen, marines, soldiers, and others belonging to such ships and vessels of war; and upon request forthwith to grant a certificate of the truth of any list transmitted to them, to the agents nominated and appointed by the captors to take care and dispose of such prize; and also upon application to them, the said commissioners, to give or cause to be given to the said agents, all such lists from the muster books of any such ships of war, and annexed lists, as the said agents shall find requisite for their direction in paying the produce of such prizes; and otherwise to be aiding and assisting to the said agents, in all such matters as shall be necessary.

We do hereby further will and direct, that the following regulations shall be observed concerning the one third part of the two eighths hereinbefore-mentioned, to be granted to the flag or flag officers, who shall actually be on board at the taking of any prize, or shall be directing or assisting therein:

First—That a captain of a ship shall be deemed to be under the command of a flag, when he shall actually have received some order directly from, or be acting in execution of some order issued by a flag officer; and in the event of his being directed to join a flag-officer on any station, he shall be deemed to be under the command of such flag officer from the time that he arrives within the limits of the station, and shall be considered to continue under the command of the flag-officer of such station, until such captain shall have received some order directly from, or be acting in execution of some order issued by some other flag-officer, or the Lords Commissioners of the Admiralty.

Secondly.—That a flag-officer commander-in-chief, when there is but one flag-officer upon service, shall have to his own use the one-third part of the said two-eighths of the prizes taken by ships and vessels under his command.

Thirdly.—That a flag-officer sent to command on any station, shall have a right to share as commander-in-chief for all prizes taken by ships or vessels employed there, from the time he arrives within the limits of such station; but if a junior flag-officer be sent to relieve a senior, he shall not be entitled to share as commander-in-chief in any prize taken by the squadron, until the command shall be resigned to him, but shall share only as a junior flag-officer until he assumes the command.

Fourthly.—That a commander-in-chief, or other flag-officer, appointed or belonging to any station, and passing through or into any other station, shall not be entitled to share in any prize taken out of the limits of the station to which he is appointed or belongs, by any ship or vessel under the command of a flag-officer of any other station, or under Admiralty orders.

Fifthly.—That when an inferior flag-officer is sent to reinforce a superior flag-officer on any station, the superior flag-officer shall have no right to any share of prizes taken by the inferior flag-officer, before the inferior flag-officer shall arrive within the limits of the station, or shall actually receive some order directly from him, or be acting in execution of some order issued by him; and such inferior flag-officer shall be entitled to his proportion of all captures made by the squadron which he is sent to reinforce, from the time he shall arrive within the limits of the command of such superior flag-officer.

Sixthly.—That a chief flag-officer quitting a station, either to return home, or to assume another command, or otherwise, except upon some particular urgent service, with the intention of returning to the station as soon as such service is performed, shall have no share of prizes taken by the ships or vessels left behind, after he shall have surrendered the command to another flag-officer appointed by the Admiralty to be commander-in-chief of such station, or after he shall have passed the limits of the station, in the event of his leaving the command without being superseded.

Seventhly.—That an inferior flag-officer quitting a station, except when detached by orders from his commander-in-chief out of the limits thereof, upon a special service, with orders to return to such station as soon as such service is performed, shall have no share in prizes taken by the ships and vessels remaining on the station after he shall have passed the limits thereof; and in like manner the flag-officers remaining on the station shall have no share of the prizes taken by such inferior flag-officer, or by the ships and vessels under his immediate command, after he shall have quitted the limits of the station, except when detached as aforesaid.

Eighthly.—That when vessels under the command of a flag which belong to separate stations, shall happen to be joint captors, the captain of each ship shall pay one-third of the share to which he is entitled to the flag-officers of the station to which he belongs; but the captains of vessels under Admiralty orders, being joint captors with other vessels under a flag, shall retain the whole of their share.

Ninthly.—That if a flag-officer is sent to command in the out-ports of this kingdom, he shall have no share of the prizes taken by ships or vessels which have sailed, or shall sail from that port, by order from the Admiralty.

Tenthly.—That when more flag-officers than one serve together, the one-third part of the two-eighth parts of the prizes taken by any ships or vessels of the fleet or squadron, shall be divided in the following proportions: viz. If there be but two flag-officers, the chief shall have two-third parts of the said third of two-eighths, and the other shall have the remaining third-part; but if the number of flag-officers be more than two, the chief shall have only one half, and the other half shall be equally divided among the junior flag-officers.

Eleventhly.—That commodores with captains under them shall be esteemed as flag-officers with respect to the one-third of the two-eighth parts of prizes taken, whether commanding-in-chief or serving under command.

Twelfthly.—That the first captain to the admiral and commander-in-chief of his Majesty's fleet, and also the first captain to a flag-officer, appointed, or hereafter to be appointed, to command a fleet or squadron of ten ships of the line of-battle, or upwards, shall be deemed and taken to be a flag-officer, and shall be entitled to a part or share of prizes as the junior flag-officer of such fleet or squadron.

> Given at the Court at Carlton-house, this twenty-sixth day of October, one thousand eight hundred and twelve, in the fifty-third year of his Majesty's reign.
>
> God save the King.

By H. R. H. the PRINCE OF WALES, REGENT of the United Kingdom of Great Britain and Ireland, in the name and on the behalf of his Majesty.

A PROCLAMATION.

GEORGE, P.R.

WHEREAS we are informed that great numbers of mariners and seafaring men, his Majesty's natural-born subjects, are in the service of divers foreign princes and states, to the prejudice of his Majesty's kingdom; and whereas attempts may be made to seduce some of his Majesty's subjects, contrary to their allegiance and duty to his Majesty, to enter on board ships or vessels of war, or other ships or vessels belonging to the U. S. of America, with intent to commit hostilities against his Majesty or his subjects, or otherwise to adhere or give aid or comfort to his Majesty's enemies upon the sea;. now we, in order that none of his Majesty's subjects may ignorantly incur the guilt and penalties of such breaches of their allegiance and duty, have thought it necessary, in the name and on the behalf of his Majesty, and by and with the advice of his Majesty's privy council, to publish this Proclamation, hereby notifying and declaring, that all persons, being his Majesty's subjects, who shall enter or serve, or be found on board any ships or vessels of war, or other ships or vessels belonging to the U. S. of America, with intent to commit hostilities against his Majesty or his subjects, or who shall otherwise adhere or give aid or comfort to his Majesty's enemies upon the sea, will thereby become liable to suffer the pains of death, and all other pains and penalties of high treason and piracy; and we do hereby declare, in the name and on the behalf of his Majesty, our intention and firm resolution to proceed against all such offenders according to law.

> Given at the Court at Carlton-house, the twenty-sixth day of October, one thousand eight hundred and twelve, and in the fifty-third year of his Majesty's reign.

God save the King.

At the Court at Carlton-House, the 26th day of October, 1812,

PRESENT,

His Royal Highness the PRINCE REGENT in Council.

WHEREAS the time limited by the order of H. R. H. the Prince Regent, in Council, bearing date the eighth day of November last, for the payment of the bounties for the encouragement of seamen and landmen to enter into his Majesty's royal navy, and the rewards for discovering seamen who may conceal themselves, so that such seamen should be taken for his Majesty's service, and also the rewards to persons who should procure the voluntary service of able and ordinary seamen and landmen fit for his Majesty's naval service, and should convey such seamen and landmen on board any of his Majesty's ships and vessels, or to any of his Majesty's sea-officers employed in raising men, will expire on the thirty-first day of December next, which bounties and rewards are as follows; that is to say, To every able seaman, not above the age of fifty, nor under the age of twenty years, who should enter himself to serve in his Majesty's royal navy, a bounty of five pounds; and to every ordinary seaman so entering himself, and not above the age of fifty, nor under the age of twenty years, a bounty of two pounds ten shillings; to every able-bodied landman, not above the age of thirty-five, nor under the age of eighteen years, so entering himself, a bounty of thirty shillings; to every person or persons who shall discover any able or ordinary seaman or seamen who may have concealed him or themselves, so that such seaman or seamen shall be taken for his Majesty's service by any of his Majesty's officers employed to raise men, a reward of three pounds for every such able seaman, and fifty shillings for every such ordinary seaman fit to serve on board his Majesty's ships; to any person or persons who shall procure the voluntary service of able or ordinary seamen or landmen fit for his Majesty's service, and shall convey them on board any of his Majesty's ships or vessels, or to any of his Majesty's sea officers employed in raising men, a reward of three guineas for every such able seaman, and two guineas for every such ordinary seaman, and one guinea for every such landman, together with an allowance at the rate of one penny per mile for each able seaman, ordinary seaman, and landman, for every mile such man may respectively travel to the nearest of his Majesty's ships of war, or nearest place of residence of any of his Majesty's sea officers employed in raising men, provided such man shall be found fit for his Majesty's service, and there shall not be reason to suppose that he is an apprentice: And whereas it is expedient, that the said several bounties, rewards, and travelling allowance should be continued to be paid for some time longer; his Royal Highness the Prince Regent, in the name and on the behalf of his Majesty, and by and with the advice of his Majesty's Privy Council, doth therefore order, and it is hereby accordingly ordered, that the payment of the said bounties, rewards, and travelling allowance, be continued to the thirty-first day of December, one thousand eight hundred and thirteen inclusive; and that the same be paid in the manner specified in his Majesty's several proclamations now in force for the encouragement of seamen and landmen to enter into his Majesty's royal navy, and for the discovering seamen who may conceal themselves, and for giving rewards for procuring the voluntary service of seamen and landmen; whereof all persons concerned are to take notice, and govern themselves accordingly.

JAMES BULLER.

TREATY OF PEACE BETWEEN GREAT BRITAIN AND RUSSIA.

In the name of the Most Holy and Indivisible Trinity!

HIS Majesty the Emperor of all the Russias, and his Majesty the King of the United Kingdom of Great Britain and Ireland, being equally animated with the desire of re-establishing the ancient relations of amity and good understanding between the two kingdoms respectively, have nominated to this effect, as their ministers plenipotentiary; namely, his Majesty the Emperor of all the Russias, the Sieur Peter Suchtelen, Chief of the Department of Engineers, General and Member of the Council of State, &c. and the Sieur Paul Baron de Nicolay, Gentleman of the Bedchamber, &c.; and H. R. H. the Prince Regent, in the name of his Majesty, King of the United Kingdom of Great Britain and Ireland, the Sieur Edward Thornton, Esq. Plenipotentiary from his Britannic Majesty to the King of Sweden.

The said Plenipotentiaries, after exchanging their respective full powers, in good and due form, have agreed upon the following articles:—

I. There shall be between his Majesty the Emperor of all the Russias, and his Majesty the King of the United Kingdoms of Great Britain and Ireland, their heirs and successors, and between their kingdoms and subjects respectively, a firm, true, and inviolable peace, and a sincere and perfect union and amity; so that, from this moment, all subjects of disagreement that may have subsisted between them shall cease.

II. The relations of amity and commerce between the two countries shall be re-established on each side, on the footing of the most favoured nations.

III. If, in resentment of the present re-establishment of peace and good understanding between the two countries, any power whatsoever shall make war upon his Imperial Majesty or his Britannic Majesty, the two contracting Sovereigns agree to act in support of each other for the maintenance and security of their respective kingdoms.

IV. The two high contracting parties reserve to themselves to establish a proper understanding and adjustment, as soon as possible, with respect to all matters which may concern their eventual interests, political as well as commercial.

V. The present Treaty shall be ratified by the two contracting parties, and the ratifications shall be exchanged in six weeks, or sooner, if possible:—

And for the due performance of the same, we sign, in virtue of our full powers, and have signed the present Treaty of Peace, and have thereto affixed our seals.

Done at Orebro, the 6th (18) July, 1812.

SUCHTELEN (L.S.)
PAUL BARON DE NICOLAY.
EDWARD THORNTON (L.S.)

After sufficiently examining the Articles of the present Treaty of Peace, we have approved of the same, which we now confirm, and by these presents most solemnly ratify, in all its tenour; promising on our Imperial part, for us and for our successors, to observe and execute, inviolably, every thing that has been mentioned and repeated in the said Treaty of

Peace. In witness whereof we have signed with our own hand this Imperial Ratification, and have thereto affixed the seal of our Empire.

Done at Kamenroi Ostrow, the 1st of August, 1812, and the twelfth year of our reign.

(Signed)   ALEXANDER.

(Countersigned)   Count ROMANZOW.

PROCLAMATION,

ISSUED BY ADMIRAL SIR J. B. WARREN, ON HIS ARRIVAL AT HALIFAX.

WHEREAS many British seamen are now in the U. S. of America, and several of them by various means have been seduced to serve on board the American ships at war with the United Kingdoms of Great Britain and Ireland, and others who have deserted from his Majesty's service have been forced to serve against their native country; I therefore call upon all British seamen and others, in the present state of the war, and before it may be too late to join the British colours, under which many of them have obtained glory and honour, to repair to any of his Majesty's provinces, garrisons, ships or vessels: and upon giving themselves up, and declaring their sense of error, I pledge myself to obtain for them H. R. H. the Prince Regent's free pardon and forgiveness; and to those who are willing to enter into the British navy, every encouragement they could wish. I trust that every British seaman will unite in supporting the noblest cause that ever called for the efforts of man,—the preservation of the liberties, independence, religion, and laws of all the remaining nations of the world, against the tyranny and despotism of France; and to defend the honour of the British flag upon the seas, at a moment when Providence has blessed her army with success in sustaining the cause of injured Spain and Portugal."

Dated 5th of October, 1812.   (Signed)   J. B. WARREN.

Naval Poetry.

SONG.

I.

BY the friends we have lost,—by the smile we can never
   Again in life's loveliness view;
By the ties of attachment death only could sever,
   Those ties the same hand shall renew:
By the tear we have shed o'er the tomb of the cherish'd,
   O'er days ne'er to bless us again—
Let us still give a sigh to the hope that has perish'd,
   But a smile to the hopes which remain.

II.

Oh still, as the circle of social affection
  Of *some* valued heart is bereft,
While we treasure through life their belov'd recollection,
  Let us cling to the *few* that are *left*:
Down our cheek while the tear-drop of anguish is stealing,
  A solace e'en then it may prove,
To view the sad glance of reciprocal feeling,
  When it beams from the eye that we love.

III.

Oh this is the charm which shall-brighten to-morrow,
  With the joys that we cherish to-day;
'Tis the pilot who steadies our vessel of sorrow,
  'Tis the star which enlightens its way:
And if e'er, o'er the sea of adversity driven,
  That bark has *no* pilot to steer;
That *star* beaming bright from the portals of heaven,
  Shall bid us seek fortitude *there*.

MARY.

THE RETORT COURTEOUS.*

THE boaster Rodgers is gone out,
  Who fought the LITTLE BELT, Sir;
And very brave it was, no doubt,
  So small a craft to pelt, sir.
    Yankee doodle, &c.

But if brave BROKE he chance to meet,
  He'll drub him for his trouble;
And every British heart will beat,
  To pay the bully double.
    Yankee doodle, &c.

Ere this, perhaps, the English flag
  Is waving o'er his poop, sir;
And that same swaggering Yankee rag
  Just under it doth droop, sir.
    Yankee doodle, &c.

---

* N.C. XXVI. 488. Impartiality, and the desire of satisfying the curiosity of all descriptions of readers, induced us to give place to the scurrilous American songster. These lines have been, as is shewn by their date, for some time in our hands; but the name of the hapless *Guerriere* seemed to render their appearance somewhat unseasonable. The real causes of that ship's disaster having since been so satisfactorily accounted for, and her captain and crew having been subjected to the ordeal of martial judgment, and been absolved from misconduct, we no longer withhold this effusion of a nautical bard.

If this should prove to be the case,
  It will not make us wonder;
For long ago the Yankee race
  Have felt the British thunder.
Yankee doodle, &c.

And as the war they did provoke,
  We'll pay them with our cannon;
The first to do it will be BROKE,
  In the gallant ship the SHANNON.
Yankee doodle, &c.

The BELVIDERE and GUERRIERE too,
  Their country's praise will merit;
And every seaman in each crew
  Will shew a Briton's spirit.
Yankee doodle, &c.

Then here's a health to GEORGE the Third,
  And all the British nation;
They'll make the Yankees feel the sword,
  In every place and station.
Yankee doodle, &c.

29, *September*, 1812.   NAVTICVS.

Marine Law.

COURTS MARTIAL.

OCTOBER 2.—A court martial was assembled on board His Majesty's Ship Africa, in Halifax harbour, for the trial of Captain James Richard Dacres, the surviving officers and crew, of H. M.'s late ship the Guerriere, for the surrender of that ship to the U. S. frigate Constitution, on the 19th of August.—The Court was composed of—Vice-admiral Sawyer, president; Captains Sir J. P. Beresford, P. V. B. Broke, J. Bastard, and C. Gill.

The details of the trial have not yet come to hand; but the following is, we believe, a correct copy of the address, which was delivered by Captain Dacres to the Court, after the evidence had been gone through.

" Mr. President and Gentlemen of the Court.—By my letter to Admiral Sawyer, and the narrative of the principal officers, I trust that you will be satisfied that every exertion was used in defending the ship, as long as there was the smallest prospect of resistance being of any use. In my letter, where I mention the boarders being called, it was my intention, after having driven back the enemy, to have boarded in return; and in consequence I ordered down the first lieutenant on the main-deck to send every body up from the guns; but finding his deck filled with men, and every preparation made to receive us, it would have been almost impossible to succeed. I ordered the men down to their quarters, and desired Mr. Kent to direct part of his attention to the main-deck, the lieutenant being killed. The main-mast fell without being struck by a single shot, the heart of the mast being decayed, and it was carried away solely by the weight of the foremast; and though every thing was done, we could not succeed in getting the ship under command; and on the enemy wearing round to rake us, without our being able to make any resistance, and after having used every exertion, to the best of my abilities, I found myself obliged to order the colours to be struck; which nothing but the unmanageable state of the ship (she lying a perfect wreck) could ever have induced me to do, conceiving it was my duty not to sacrifice uselessly the lives of the men, without any prospect of success, or of benefit to their country.

" On the larboard side about thirty shot had taken effect; about five sheets of copper down, and the mizen-mast had knocked a large hole under her starboard counter, and she was so completely shattered, that the enemy found it impossible to refit her sufficiently to attempt carrying her into port, and they set fire to her as soon as they got the wounded out. What considerably weakened my quarters was, permitting the Americans belonging to the ship to quit their quarters, on the enemy hoisting the colours of that nation, which, though it deprived me of the men, I thought it was my duty.

" I felt much shocked, when on board the Constitution, to find a large proportion of this ship's company British seamen, and many of whom I recognised as having been foremost in the attempt to board.

" Notwithstanding the unlucky issue of the affair, such confidence have I in the exertions of the officers and men who belonged to the Guerriere, and I am so aware that the success of my opponent was owing to fortune, that it is my earnest wish, and would be the happiest period of my life, to be once more opposed to the Constitution, with them under my command, in a frigate of similar force to the Guerriere.

" I cannot help noticing, that the attachment of the ship's company in general to the service of their King and Country, reflects on them the highest credit; for though every art was used to encourage them to desert, and to inveigle them into the American service, by high bounties and great promises, by the American officers, in direct contradiction to the declaration to me, that they did not wish such a thing; only eight Englishmen have remained behind, two only of which number have volunteered for their service.

" Leaving the characters of my officers and ship's company, as well as my own, to the decision of this Honourable Court, the justice of whose sentence no person can presume to question, I close my narrative, craving indulgence for having taken up so much of their time."

Having attended to the whole of the evidence, and also to the defence of Captain Dacres, the Court agreed,—" That the surrender of La Guerriere was proper, in order to preserve the lives of her valuable remaining crew; and that her being in that lamentable situation was from the accident of her masts going, which was occasioned more by their *defective state, than from the fire of the enemy*, though so greatly superior in guns and men. The Court do, therefore, unanimously and honourably acquit the said Captain Dacres, the officers, and crew, of H. M.'s late ship La Guerriere; and they are hereby honourably acquitted accordingly.—The Court, at the same time, feel themselves called upon to express the high sense they entertain of the conduct of the ship's company in general, when prisoners, but more particularly of those who withstood the attempts made to shake their loyalty, by offering them high bribes to enter into the land and sea services of the enemy, and they will represent their merit to the commander-in-chief."

BLASPHEMY AND DISLOYALTY.

WE think it our duty to register the following incident, the result of which will shew that our naval officers are not inattentive to the character and conduct of those under their command: it may at the same time prove salutary, as a warning to the inconsiderate, into whose hands it may happen to fall:—

On the 27th of October, 1807, a court-martial, of which Rear-admiral Sir Isaac Coffin was president, was held at Portsmouth, for the trial of the surgeon of H.M.S. Jamaica, for disorderly behaviour, by provoking and insulting speeches and gestures, to the officers, &c. in breach of the articles of war. Among the witnesses called for the defendant, was the purser of the ship—but his evidence was objected to, on the ground, that he had been heard to blaspheme our Saviour Jesus Christ; to villify the character of the Virgin Mary, to ridicule the bible, and say it ought to be burnt by the common hangman; with other grossly atheistical expressions, which decorum forbids us to repeat: it will not be wondered at, that the same person should —— the king, call him an old fool, &c.— The court resolved, that after proof adduced of the infidelity and disloyalty of the purser, his evidence could not be received; and that the president be requested to represent his behaviour to the Lords Commissioners of the Admiralty. The president, accordingly, wrote to their Lordships; and the purser was dismissed H. M.'s service.*

---

* A remark here occurs, of great moment. The effects of genuine religion are ever sure to attract affection and esteem, and in spite of the rough habits and careless conduct of British sailors in some respects, we have never seen them wanting in allowing due honour to the church, to its ministers, or advocates— " These men see the works of the Lord, and his wonders in the deep," and have more serious convictions in their minds, than appearances would lead us to suppose. But when religion degenerates towards the sour discipline of the puritans, or the dogmatic severity of fanatics, the true beauty of holiness is no longer to be seen, and suspicions of hypocrisy and cant are entertained, when in fact there perhaps only exists a mistaken zeal working without true knowledge.

NAVAL HISTORY OF THE PRESENT YEAR, 1812.
(October—November.)
RETROSPECTIVE AND MISCELLANEOUS.

THE new Parliament assembled on Tuesday, the 24th of November; but, as the remainder of the week was wholly occupied in swearing in the members, &c. the regular business of the Session could not commence till Monday, the 30th.

Buonaparte has abandoned Moscow, and retreated, with the whole of his army, towards Poland. The state of the war is generally considered as very favourable towards Russia.

The Mediterranean station has received the accession of a new second-in-command by the arrival of Vice-admiral Sir Sidney Smith, who joined the squadron cruising off Toulon early in October, and shifted his flag from the Tremendous to the Hibernia. The prospects on that station, as relating to the enemy, may be best collected from the following amusing report, extracted from the French papers.

Toulon, Oct. 24.—The Emperor's squadron, which has, during the summer, manœuvred daily in presence of the English squadron, has not discontinued its exercising and manœuvring since the weather has become more severe. On the 21st, Admiral Emeriau exercised only eight frigates, in tacking without the harbour. On the 22d, the enemy's light squadron shewing an intention to attack a convoy, near Ciotat, the admiral despatched Vice-admiral Baudin, with four ships, which, in conjunction with the frigates, repulsed the enemy, and secured the entry of the convoy. The next day the admiral, having his flag on board the Austerlitz, put to sea, with nine ships of the line and seven frigates; the weather was fine, and a breeze at north-west; but the squadron had hardly passed Cape Sicie, when it began to blow a hurricane. Towards midnight the wind blew so violently, that it was necessary to close the port-holes, secure the guns, and take in every reef. In this condition the squadron kept the sea till the next day, the storm not abating.

It was a magnificent spectacle to observe the simultaneous entry of these fifteen large ships of war, three of them three deckers, all tacking to regain the harbour, in a narrow space, which obliged them to veer every instant whilst the violence of the wind, and the heavy sea, augmented the danger, of their running aground, or on board of one another. Thanks to the dexterity in evolutions which this squadron has acquired, no serious consequences ensued; for a slight shock received by the Majestueux and Danube, by running foul during the night should *go for nothing*. During this cruise, the young conscripts experienced 36 hours of tempest, such as they had no former example of, but they supported it well. The enemy's (English) squadron was but just seen, at a great distance; their look out ships might be discerned nearer.

As our navy is the dearest object of national solicitude, whatever tends to its preservation and safety merits approbation, not only upon principles of patriotism, but from motives of affection to those who are more immediately to derive benefit from thence. It is with pleasure, therefore, that we announce the promising state of the breakwater in Plymouth harbour, and assign the small portion of honour which it is in our power to confer, on all those whose skill or industry have contributed in their respective stations to the advancement of so useful an undertaking. The Navy Board is taking the most effectual means for the completion of this great national work; and by the zeal and indefatigable exertions of Mr. Whidbey, to whom the superintendance thereof is confided, the proposed pier-head has already been raised ten feet from the bottom. We are happy, also, to be in some degree able to announce the ultimate success of the plan, by the proofs which it has already afforded of its efficacy; for, during the late tremendous gales of wind, it was observed from shore, that the structure, even in its present state, broke the force of the sea; so that the ships of war, which were moored nearest to it, rode out the gales much more easily than those which were farther in shore. A correspondent, however, has suggested the propriety of displaying floating lights, every dark night, along the line of this undertaking.

The Transport Board intend to supersede those lieutenants who command prison-ships that have their appointments more than three years. It is believed, that it will be eventually found expedient to place the ships on the regular establishment of the navy, and to appoint commanders to them.

Extract of a Letter from an Officer, late belonging to H. M. S. the Guerriere, dated

Halifax, October 15.

" It was extremely fortunate that the American returned to us after we were dismasted, as I have no doubt that the Guerriere would have gone down before we got her in here; so many shot struck her between wind and water, that her hull was nearly shattered to pieces. We were carried to Boston, where I remained about ten days, and was then sent here. God knows what the people of England will think of the capture of the Guerriere, but they certainly cannot expect more than to fight her until she was sinking. No one that has not seen the Constitution would believe there could be such a ship for a frigate, the nearest ship in the British navy, as to her dimensions and tonnage, is the Orion, of 74 guns. She was laid down for a 74-gun ship: is 180 feet long on her upper deck, and 45 feet 10 inches breadth of beam. She has no gang-ways, but two complete decks, the same as a line-of-battle ship, and is 1630 tons burden. We have been so completely occupied in looking out for Commodore Rodgers's squadron, that we have taken very few prizes. The Acasta, Captain Kerr, is out on a cruise. He has taken some good prizes. She is the finest frigate on this station.

A small fishing boat from Nova Scotia, on board of which was the owner, a man 74 years of age, having been captured and sent into Boston, the Bostonians raised a subscription, bought the boat, fitted her out for a three months voyage, and gave her to the poor old man; remarking at the same time, that they were not at war with unarmed fishermen.

Ships of War taken to pieces within the last three months.

	Guns.	
Powerful	74	Built in 1783.
Buckingham (formerly Eagle)	64	Built in 1776.
Diamond	38	Built in 1794.
Gloire	38	Taken by Sir S. Hood's squadron off Rochfort.
Ambuscade (lately French Pomone)	38	Taken by the Alceste and Active.
Alarm	32	Built in 1756.

Sold out of the service.

Diligence	16	Purchased merchant ship.

Ordered to be sold.

L'Aimable	32	Taken in 1783.
Lynx	18	Built in 1792.

Paid off in November.

Foudroyant	80	Implacable	80
St. Albans	64	Standard	64
Polyphemus	64	Dictator	64
Frederickstein	32		

Commissioned.

Barossa	36	Captain Sheriff.
Conflict	16	—— H. L. Baker.
Satellite	18	—— Porteus.

Ordered to be built in India.

Wellesley	74

𝕷etters on 𝕾erbice,
Copied verbatim from the LONDON GAZETTE.

ADMIRALTY-OFFICE, OCTOBER 17, 1812.

VICE-ADMIRAL SIR JAMES SAUMAREZ has transmitted to John Wilson Croker, Esq. a letter from Captain Hooper, of his Majesty's sloop the Raleigh, giving an account of his having, on the 22d of September, run on shore under Easternest, a French privateer, of about one hundred tons.

OCTOBER 24.

Extract of a Letter from Captain Huskisson, of H.M.S. the Barbadoes, to John Wilson Croker, Esq. dated at Sea, August 22, 1812.

I beg you will be pleased to inform my Lords Commissioners of the Admiralty, that in lat. 31° N. long. 75° W. H.M.S. under my command, after a chase of seven hours, this day captured the U. S. revenue schooner, James Madison, commanded by George Brooks, pierced for 14 guns, and had 10 mounted, two of which were thrown overboard in the chase, with a complement of 65 men; out from Savannah seven days, and has made no captures. She is coppered and copper-fastened, is two years old, and sails remarkably fast.

OCTOBER 27.

Despatches, of which the following are copies, were received last night at this office, from Vice-admiral Sir J. Saumarez, K.B. addressed to John Wilson Croker, Esq.

SIR, *Victory in Hawke, Oct. 17, 1812.*

Herewith I enclose, for the information of the Lords Commissioners of the Admiralty, a letter from Captain Stewart, transmitted to me by Rear-admiral Morris, detailing the operations of the flotilla at Riga, on the expedition against Mittau.

The conduct of Captain Brenton and the lieutenants under his orders appears to have been highly meritorious upon this occasion, and I trust will be found to merit the approbation of their lordships.

I am, Sir,
Your obedient humble servant,
JAS. SAUMAREZ.

John Wilson Croker, Esq. &c.
Admiralty.

SIR, *Riga, October 3, 1812.*

In my last I had the honour to inform you, that an attack on the Prussians in this vicinity was intended to take place about the 26th ultimo. A considerable body of troops under Count Steinheil, left Riga on that day, and the gun boats under the command of the English officers accompanied a strong division of forty Russian boats, besides ten launches, under the command of Admiral Muller, up the river Aa.

The enemy had withdrawn his troops from Schlock, and his other posts, on the approach of the boats. We therefore did not meet with any opposition until the 29th, when about five miles below Mittau; the enemy had there placed three different booms across the river, about half a mile distant from each other. Within pistol shot of the third boom, which was very strong, and well constructed, were placed three batteries of four guns each. The booms were soon destroyed, and as we arrived up, the enemy abandoned their positions with such precipitation, that four twenty-four pounders were left in the works.

The English boats were always in advance, and Admiral Muller has desired me to say, how much he is pleased with the exertions of Captain Brenton and the lieutenants employed in the boats.

The flotilla took possession of Mittau about noon; the enemy had not time to remove some very considerable magazines of clothing, grain, and some arms and ammunition. He also left about four hundred sick and wounded in the town. In the evening a detachment of the army entered the town.

The Prussians retreated from Olai upon Bourski, where they had about one hundred and twenty pieces of cannon, intended for the siege of this place; they there received reinforcements on the 29th, which Macdonald had sent them from Jacobstadt.

On the 30th, the Russians were compelled to retire from before a force of twenty-five thousand men, who had nearly eighty pieces of cannon. As the troops had retired to the vicinity of Riga, the flotilla left Mittau in the evening of the 30th, and after destroying a bridge, which had been erected to facilitate the crossing of the troops and artillery, arrived at Danamunde last night,

October 4.—The enemy's works, which were of a considerable strength at Olai, were destroyed.

The loss on the part of the Russians is estimated at two thousand in killed wounded, and missing. The enemy must also have suffered severely and many prisoners are arrived.

I have the honour to be, &c.

Rear-admiral Martin, &c. Aboukir. HEW STEWART.

Vice-admiral Sir James Saumarez has transmitted to John Wilson Croker, Esq. a letter from Captain Ross, of H. M. sloop the Briseis, giving an account of his having on the 9th instant, captured off Rennoe a French cutter privateer, called Le Petit Poucet, of four guns and four swivels, and twenty-three men; and on the 11th driven three others on shore in Hammerhus Bay; they sailed from Rostock and Stralsund some days before, and had not made any capture.

OCTOBER, 31.

Captain Stewart, commanding H. M. S. the Dictator, has transmitted to John Wilson Croker, Esq. a letter from Lieutenant Duell, of that ship, giving an account of his having in one of her boats, on the 6th instant, captured after a short resistance, His Danish Majesty's lugger, No 28, commanded by a lieutenant, and manned with twelve men. No loss was sustained on our side; the enemy had two men killed and three wounded.

NOVEMBER 3.

Vice-admiral Sir James Saumarez has transmitted to John Wilson Croker, Esq. two letters from Captain Chetham, of H. M. S. Hamadryad, dated the 1st and 14th of last month; the former giving an account of the capture off Langeland, of a Danish row boat, carrying two brass guns and a swivel, and about thirty men, by one of the above ship's boats, under the command of Lieutenant Pesley;

The latter stating the capture, by the boats of the Hamadryad and Clio, under Lieutenants Pesley and Cutler, off Hermeren, of a French lugger privateer, called Le Pilotin, carrying four twelve pounder carronades, and thirty-one men; three Danish luggers, of two guns each, came out from Rodlye to support her, but retreated on the advance of the boats.

Captain Chetham highly commends the conduct of Lieutenant Pesley, and the others engaged on these occasions, in which one man only was wounded.

Sir James Saumarez has also transmitted a letter from Captain Bowles, of H. M. S. Aquilon, reporting the capture by the Sheldrake sloop, off Meen Island, of L'Aimable D'Hervilly, French privateer, of four swivels and between twenty and thirty men, who escaped on shore.

NOVEMBER 14.

Vice-admiral Sir Edward Pellew has transmitted to John Wilson Croker, Esq. a letter, from Captain Hoste, of H. M. S. the Bachante, giving an account of his having, on the 26th of July, captured off Cape St. Vito,

La Victoiré, a French privateer, of three guns and thirty five men, out twelve days from Naples, and had not made any capture.

NOVEMBER 17.

Copy of a Letter from Vice-admiral Sir Edward Pellew, Bart. Commander-in-Chief of H. M. Ships and Vessels in the Mediterranean, to John Wilson Croker, Esq. dated on board the Caledonia, off Toulon, October 12, 1812.

SIR,

I have the honour to enclose a letter from Captain Codrington, detailing a service lately performed in concert with the Baron D'Eroles, highly creditable to those officers. I have the honour to be, &c.

EDWARD PELLEW.

SIR, *Blake, Salon Bay, Sept. 27, 1812.*

I have the honour to inform you, that according to a plan previously arranged between the Baron D'Eroles and myself, a joint attack was made last night on the Puerto of Tarragona, and the Mole swept of all vessels and boats which had there sought protection. The Blake and Franchise left this anchorage after dark, and the Baron marched from Reus at nine o'clock, P. M. when the Jubilee, in consequence of publishing the New Constitution, made such a movement the less to be expected. The boats of the two ships reached the Francoli at about one o'clock, and shortly afterwards the Baron having properly posted his troops for intercepting any sortie which might be made by the garrison, and for cutting off the retreat of such people as might be in the vessels and lower town, gave the concerted signal for the boats to open their fire. The enemy were taken so completely by surprise, that some time elapsed before they returned a shot: and I understand, General Bartoletti, the governor, actually mounted his horse without boots or stockings. Seeing only the fire of the boats, about two hundred grenadiers came out of the town, but being met by a volley of musketry, from a small party of the Spanish troops in ambush at the Capuchin Convent, and being then charged with the bayonet, those who were able made the best of their way back again. The position of the Olive, occupied by a party of Briballu (Calagirats) was carried in the mean time in a very animated manner; and several false attacks on the walls of the fortress attracted the attention of the enemy, and occasioned a brisk fire of cannon from their whole line. The boats then pulled into the Mole, and having finished the operation allotted to them, notwithstanding an angry discharge of shot and shells from the town, the troops retired to Reus, and the ships anchored with the prizes in Tarragona Bay.

The Franchise was extremely well placed by Captain Birch off the Mole Head, for giving such assistance as might have been wanted; and I have reason to be much pleased with the conduct of Lieutenant Hughes, senior lieutenant of this ship, who commanded, and the whole of the officers and seamen who acted under his orders in the boats, for the exactness with which they executed the duties allotted them, without injury to the operations of the troops, and for the great activity which they shewed in bringing out the prizes.

My anxiety to afford all the aid which any unforeseen occurrence might require, and to be ready to profit by any favourable result which might lead to an attack of more importance, induced me to push the Blake forwards towards the Milagro. But notwithstanding that the light of the moon enabled the enemy to direct their shot with considerable precision, she was struck only by one, which passed through the main top sail.

It would be great presumption in me to offer an opinion on the military conduct of the Baron D'Eroles, who gains the respect and regard of all who act with him, as well as all who act under his orders. But I cannot refuse myself the pleasure of remarking, that such was the secrecy and silence of his march, that when the troops and boats were each contiguous to the other in their appointed stations, each doubted the other's arrival, until the concerted signal was made; and such was the steadiness and good order of the troops, who killed or drove back by the bayonet all the force of the enemy which ventured to oppose them, that not a single mistake occurred. It is also highly gratifying to me to record the confident reliance which each service placed on the conduct of the other. And the Baron has done us the honour to consent to the voluntary and magnanimous request of the officers and crews of the two ships, that the whole of whatever benefit may arise from the sale of the prizes shall be given to his troops, in admiration of the valour and the discipline which they shewed upon the occasion.

The loss of the enemy must have been considerable, although it is impossible to ascertain it, on account of the darkness of the night; and the operation under the walls of their own garrison having terminated before day-light. That of the Spaniards amounted to three killed and eight wounded, mostly by the bayonet; amongst us there was not the smallest casualty whatever.

Underneath is a list of the vessels brought out.

I have the honour to be, &c.

EDW. CODRINGTON.

No. 1, a bombard about 60 tons; 2, a lugger 50 tons: 3, a felucca 30 tons: 4, ditto 30 tons; 5, ditto 20 tons. A launch and five small boats.

Extract of a letter from Captain Usher, of H. M. S. the Hyacinth, addressed to Vice-admiral Sir Edward Pellew, and transmitted by him to John Wilson Croker, Esq.

Hyacinth, Malaga Mole, 6th Sept. 1812.

I had the honour to inform you, by my letter of the 11th ultimo, that I sailed from Gibraltar, immediately on learning that America had declared war, and I have now great pleasure in acquainting you, that the whole of the Americans that were on their way down the Mediterranean have been captured by the Mediterranean cruisers, as nothing has arrived at Gibraltar but wh t has been sent in by us, a list of which I have the honour to enclose.

Owing to calms, I did not get abreast of Malaga till the 1st inst. where I was joined by Captain Sibley, and we immediately pushed in to reconnoitre, and on standing in for that purpose, I met the Governor and heads of the departments of Malaga coming out to me, and they informed me that the enemy had retreated, after having blown up the works of the Castle of Gibralfaro.

I have great pleasure in acquainting you that the enemy's privateers have not captured a single merchantman since the affair of the 29th of April.

Copy of a Letter from Captain Peyton, of H.M.S. the Minstrel, addressed to Vice-Admiral Sir Edward Pellew, and transmitted to John Wilson Croker, Esq.

SIR,   H.M.S. *Minstrel, off Valencia*, 30th Sept. 1812.

In obedience to your orders to cruize between Denia and Valentia, for the purpose of intercepting supplies going to the enemy, I beg leave to inform, that on the evening of the 29th I received information of the enemy having laden six vessels with shells at Valencia for Peniscola; the weather being favourable, I conceived it practicable to bring them out, or destroy them. I dispatched the boats of this ship, under the direction of Lieutenant George Thomas, assisted by Messrs. Linns, Oliver, and Smith, midshipmen, for that purpose, keeping the ship close in shore for their protection. They succeeded in bringing out four of them; a fifth was in our possession, when unfortunately the wind shifted suddenly round to the S.E. with a heavy squall, when she grounded, and am sorry to add, was retaken, with three of our men on board, The bravery evinced by the officers and men employed was very conspicuous. The vessels were moored head and stern to the shore, between two batteries of two 24-pounders and two mortars, with a strong garrison in the Grao; their sails unbent and rudders unshipped. Our loss, with the exception of the prisoners, is only one man wounded, I hope not dangerously. I beg leave to return a list of the wounded and prisoners. I am, &c.

J. S. PEYTON, Captain.

A List of the Wounded and Prisoners.

Alexander M'Kenzie, cooper, severely wounded; Thomas Middleton, able, prisoner; Thomas Butcher, marine, ditto; Samuel Thomas, ditto, ditto.

Vice-admiral Sir Edward Pellew has transmitted to John Wilson Croker, Esq. a letter from Captain Adderley, of H.M. sloop Crocus, giving an account of his having, on the 4th of September last, captured the French Settee privateer, Le Formica, of two guns and twenty-five men, out three months from Genoa, without making any capture; the crew escaped in the boats to the Barbary shore.

Copy of a Letter from Lieutenant Loch, acting in command of H.M. Sloop the Rover, addressed to Admiral Lord Keith, and transmitted by his Lordship to John Wilson Croker, Esq.

MY LORD,
H.M. Sloop Rover, 18 leagues W. by N. of Cordoban Light, 21st October, 1812.

I beg leave to acquaint your Lordship, of H.M. brig under my command having this day detained the American schooner, letter of marque, Experiment, Rider master, after a chase of nine hours, mounting six nine-pounders carronades, and seventeen men, from Charlestown thirty-one days, bound to Bour eaux, laden with cotton and rice, and had not made any capture during the voyage.

I have the honour to be, &c.

F. E. LOCH.

Copy of a Letter from Captain Hope, of H.M.S. the Salsette, to John Wilson Croker, Esq. dated at the Motherbank, the 14th Instant.

SIR,

I beg to acquaint you, for the information of the Lords Commissioners of the Admiralty, that Le Mercure, French lugger privateer of sixteen guns and seventy men, was yesterday captured off the west end of the Isle of Wight, by H.M.S. under my command.

I have the honour to be, &c.

HENRY HOPE, Captain.

LETTERS ON SERVICE,

Not published in the Gazette.

(COPY.)

SIR,　　　　　　　　　　*Wyborg, in Jutland, Aug. 26,* 1812.

I am sorry of being under the disagreeable and painful necessity of transmitting to you, for the information of my Lords Commissioners of the Admiralty, the particulars of the capture of his Majesty's brig, the Attack, late under my command, in an action with the Danish flotilla.

In pursuance of the directions of Captain Chetham, of his Majesty's ship Hamadryad, on Sunday the 16th inst. I proceeded off Randers' Flord for the purpose of recalling the Wrangler and Hamadryad's barge and cutter, and on Tuesday the 18th inst. having performed that service, and taken the barge in tow, and being on my return to join the squadron off Sayer, at eleven o'clock, P.M. Foreness, bearing W.N.W. about six or seven miles, with light airs from the E.N.E. and at intervals calm, we observed two boats, which I supposed to be gun-vessels, in that direction. I cleared for action, and, in about twenty minutes, they commenced a very heavy cannonading upon us. Owing to the darkness of the night, I could not then ascertain their number, but from the heavy fire I received, apparently from ten or twelve gun-vessels; we immediately returned their fire, and continued engaging them, until forty minutes past one o'clock, when they ceased firing, and, as I have since found, were joined by another division of gun-vessels, who I had observed firing at the Wrangler; a light breeze springing up, I immediately endeavoured to avail myself of the opportunity of closing the Wrangler, and got out the sweeps, and ordered the barge ahead to for that purpose; but owing to a strong current from the S.E. and it again falling calm, I found it impracticable. I shortly after lost sight of the Wrangler.

We employed ourselves in knotting and splicing the rigging, the sails, standing and running rigging being entirely cut to pieces, the main boom shot away, the gaff down, the foremast and bowsprit nearly gone, two guns dismounted, and a great number of shot between wind and water.

At ten minutes past two, the whole having formed a crescent upon our larboard beam, bow, and quarter; and by so doing, keeping us between themselves and the shore; then commenced the action with a heavy fire of round, grape, and grenadoes, within pistol shot. I continued engaging them until twenty minutes past three o'clock, when, it being still quite calm, the brig a complete wreck, quite unmanageable, and in a sinking state, I was reluctantly compelled to surrender to their very superior force, conceiving any further resistance, when there was not a possibility of an escape, would be a vain sacrifice of my brave crew.

I have to regret to state the loss of two brave men killed, and twelve wounded, several of them dangerously, a list of whom I subjoin: and I have to thank the Almighty no more of them fell under so severe a fire. As to the loss of the enemy, they studiously avoided my gaining any information of.

When the force opposed to us is considered, 14 gun-vessels, mounting two 24 pounders, and two howitzers, and a complement of from 65 to 70 men each, besides four large row-boats, carrying swivels and howitzers, and I having only 49 men, including the Hamadryad's boat's crew, Mr. Couney, the master, with eight men, having been previously captured, whilst rowing guard off Hielam, and an officer and six men being with a prize in England, I doubt not to prove to the satisfaction of my king and country that I had no alternative left.

And if it is possible a doubt can exist of my not maintaining the honour of the British flag to the utmost, I beg leave to transmit *The Danish Gazette* account of the action; where the enemy, notwithstanding their national pride, with candour admit, that we obstinately engaged them for nearly four hours, when I hailed to inform them we had struck, the colours being twice shot away.

I should be extremely remiss in my duty, did I not recommend to their lordships' notice, in the strongest terms, the spirited conduct and able assistance I received from Mr. Charles Heal, master's mate of the Hamadryad; and from Mr. George Harper, pilot of the Attack, who received a severe contusion early in the action, but kept his station to the last, and the conduct of the whole of the seamen and royal marines of my brave little crew was such as meet my warmest approbation; never did I witness men in better spirits.

I have the honour to be, Sir, your obedient humble servant,

R. W. SIMMONDS,* Lieut. and Commander.

To Sir J. Saumarez, Bart. K.B. Vice-admiral of the Red, and Commander-in-chief of a Squadron of H. M.'s Ships and Vessels employed on a particular service.

Return of Killed and Wounded on board of H. M. Brig Attack, in action with 14 Danish Gun-vessels off Foreness, on the night of the 18th August, 1812:

Killed.—William Davidson, gunner's-mate of the Attack; William Shrowder, seaman of the Hamadryad.

Wounded.—Mr. George Harper, pilot, a severe contusion; Wm. Walker, landsman of the Attack, dangerously wounded; Edward Lightbourne, ordinary, ditto, ditto, ditto; Nathaniel Philbrooke, able, ditto, ditto, ditto; William Gayley, boy, ditto, ditto; Samuel Brown, able, ditto, severely wounded; Joseph Mathers, seaman of the Hamadryad, ditto; James Endoll, ditto, ditto, ditto; James M'Kenzie, marine of the Attack, ditto; George Withert, boy, ditto, ditto; James Mealey, marine, ditto, slightly wounded; Thomas Wilson, able, ditto, ditto; Andrew Ewell, quartermaster of the Hamadryad, wrist broke; John Eversim, seaman, ditto, slightly.

R. W. SIMMONDS, Lieut. and Commander.

---

* Lieutenant Simmonds was, after a diligent investigation, and mature deliberation on all the circumstances connected with the capture of the Attack, most honourably acquitted by a court martial, held on board the Cressy, in Wingo Sound, on the 19th of September. Lieut. S. is the officer who brought out a large transport from under the batteries of Boulogne, and while under the protection of a large French lugger and privateer, on the evening of the 4th July last, for which service he received the approbation of the Admiralty. This exploit was effected by the Attack's gig, with only six men on board, and is recorded in *The London Gazette* of Tuesday, the 7th July. The court-martial held on this officer for the loss, by capture, of H.M.S. Manly, is reported at the 240th page of the present volume.

Promotions and Appointments.

WHITEHALL, NOVEMBER 3, 1812.

His Royal Highness the Prince Regent has been pleased, in the name and on the behalf of his Majesty, to grant the dignity of a Baronet of the United Kingdom of Great Britain and Ireland to the following Gentlemen respectively, and the heirs male of their bodies, lawfully begotten; viz.—

Albemarle Bertie, Esq. Vice-admiral of the Red Squadron of his Majesty's Fleet.

Jahleel Brenton, Esq. Post Captain in the Royal Navy.

Gilbert Blane, of Blanefield, in the county of Ayr, and of Culverlands, in the county of Berks, Doctor of Physic, and one of the Physicians in Ordinary to his Royal Highness the Prince Regent.

WHITEHALL, OCTOBER 31, 1812.

His Royal Highness the Prince Regent has been pleased, in the name and on the behalf of his Majesty, to constitute and appoint Sir Rupert George, Bart. James Bowen, Esq. the Honourable John Douglas, John Harness, Doctor in Physic, the Honourable Courtenay Boyle, and William Boothby, Esq. to be his Majesty's Commissioners for conducting the Transport Service, for the care of sick and wounded seamen, and for the care and custody of prisoners of war.

Admirals and Captains appointed.

Rear-admiral J. Surridge is appointed flag-officer and commander-in-chief at Chatham.

Rear-admiral S. H. Linzee, and Rear-admiral E. J. Foote, to command in the Mediterranean; Captain Bourchier, to be Rear-admiral Foote's flag-captain.

Captains.—Richard Arthur, to the Andromeda; J. C. Woolcombe, to the Revolutionaire; J. Sheriff, to the Barossa; H. J. Baker, to the Conflict; John Porteus, to the Satellite; Robert Roiles, to the Union; Hon. G. H. Dundas, to the Edinburgh; Thomas Usher, to the Euryalus; J. L. Manley, posted, and to act in the Hyacinth; Fleetwood Pellew, to the Iphigenia; W. Stewart, to the Revenge; C. P. B. Bateman, to the Stately; John Keenan, to the Ætna bomb; Charles Reid, to the Fervent; A. Browne, to be agent for prisoners of war at Valleyfield.

Royal Marines.—Captains Hole, to the Invisible; Baillie, to the Malta; and Cummins, to the Royal George.—Lieutenants Henderson, to the Alcmene; and Hall, to the Curaçoa.

J. Hollingworth, Esq. son of Mr. Hollingworth, late of the Admiralty Office, is appointed storekeeper of Plymouth Dock-yard, *vice* Salt, who retires on account of ill health.

Lieutenants, &c. appointed.

B. Aplin to the Armide; Thomas G. Allen, to the Lion; Samuel Allen, to the Fawn; William Alner, to the Fervent; R. J. Alleyn, to the Abercromby; R. Anderson, to the Indian; Paul Bagwell, midshipman, to be a lieutenant; Thomas Blackstone, to the Argo; John Broderick, to the Iphigenia; Henry W. Bishop, and George D. Barclay, to the Barfleur; Charles Bostock, to the Pembroke; Richard Bridges, to the Helicon; Richard Bastard, to the Queen; C. P. Coffin, to the Tuscan; James Clisteron, to the Argo; Lewis Cross, to the Apelles; Thomas Carew, to the Impregnable; Christopher Claxton, to the Ramillies; James Drewitt, to the rank of commander; Norwich Duff, to the Seahorse; Charles Dennison, to the Dublin; Thomas Denston, to the Sparrow; John G. Davis, to the Fervent; Thomas D. Dabine, to the Raven; Thomas Evans (2), to the Barfleur; Cyrus Ellicott, to the Diomede; John Eveleigh, to the Lion; E. P. Forster, to the Tigre; George Franklyn, to the Victorious; R. Gambier, to the rank of commander; Elias Thomas Gill, to the Fox; John Geddes, to the Ramillies; Hon. John Gredon, to the Revolutionaire; J. W. Green, to the Hasty; Robert Holman, to the Salvador del Mundo; C. Hole, to command the Badger, *pro tempore*; Joseph Hitchins, to the Duncan; John C. Hickman, to the Dædalus; Henry Hoskin, to the Bedford; Thomas Janverin, to the Christian VII; G. C. Johnstone, to the Echo; E. Kelly, to the York; W. Knight (3), to the York; W. Lock, to the St. Damaso; Richard Lloyd, to the Fawn; Paul S. Laurence, to the Ramillies; S. P. Lound, to the Sarpedon; Robert Loney, to the Reindeer; H. P. Lew, to the Cordelia; W. Langdon, to the Bermuda; ———— M'Culloch, to be a commander; Duncan Menzies, to El Firme; James M'Arthur, to the Vigilant; J. Molesworth, to the Myrtle; W. Milne, to the Argo; Duncan M'Donald, to the Alphea cutter; William Matthews, to the Andromeda; Martin Miller, to the Christian VII.; John A. Morrell, to the Dublin; H. E. Napier, to the Minerva; G. M. M'Kinley Pedder, to the Niemen; Charles Pollard, to the Argo; George A. Pratt, to the Seahorse; Richard Pococke, to the Revolutionaire; Charles Payne, to the Barfleur; Robert Peter, to the Diomede; C. Robinson, to the Port Mahon; J. B. Rose, to the Centaur; William Rosson, to command the St. Damaso P.S.; William Smith, to the Alert; Sir John Gordon Sinclair, to the Redwing; John Simpson (3), to the Vigilant P.S.: John Smith (7), to the Pembroke; W. Stopford, to the Chanticleer; Samuel Sisson, to the Fylla; John Stiles, to the Dublin; George Smithers, to the Goldfinch; Robert Stuart, to the Abercromby; Clines Steele, to the Barfleur; William Styles, to the Braave; John Sadler, to the Princess: Isaac Strutt, to command the Niger P.S.; J. Simpson (2), to command the Caton P.S.; William Stone, to be second lieutenant of the St. Ysidro; J. Towne, midshipman, to be a lieutenant; Thomas Trimmer, to the Mulgrave; Richard Thorold, to the Pembroke; John Hugh Tripp, to the Ramillies; Charles Tamm, to the Beagle; H. P. Tozer, agent for prisoners of war on parole at Oswestry; C. Thompson, agent for prisoners of war on parole at Odiham; Thomas Voll, to the Vigilant; F. Voller, to the Guildford, P. S.; Andrew Vincent, to the Belle Poule; Henry Walker, to the Beaver; H. S. Wilson, to the Bahama, P.S.; I. R. Woodruff, to the Savage; Thomas Woodyatt, to the Dædalus; Robert Watts, to the Fortunée; William Weiss, to the Pelican; Thomas L. Wilkinson, to the Andromeda; J.

Wilson, agent for prisoners on parole at Bridgnorth; R. Westbrook, agent for prisoners of war on parole at Reading; Stephen Donovan, to the Veteran P. S.; Edward Cawkitts, to the Hector P.S.; James Cairns, agent to prisoners of war on parole at Peebles; William Beckett, to be second lieutenant of the Ganges P.S.; Grant Allen, to the Pegase P. S.; S. Perdrian, to be second lieutenant of the St. Damaso P. S.; A. Parry to be second lieutenant of the Niger P. S.; Edward Lyon, to command the St. Ysidro P.S.; George King, to be second lieutenant of the Ferme P. S. since removed to command the Vengeance P. S.; Edward Hartley, to be second lieutenant of the St. Antonio, P. S.; John Hobbs, to be second lieutenant of the Genereux P. S.; Jeffry Gawen, to be agent to prisoners of war on parole at Chesterfield.

Mr. William Green, to be mate of the revenue cutter Roebuck, Captain Bore; employed in the quarantine service.

Pursers.—W. Davidson, to the Culloden; Nathaniel Haydon, to the Greyhound; John Norcock, to the Ceylon; J. Young, to the Argo.

Masters.—W. F. Baker, to the Barossa; W. White, to the Heron; W. Rickman, to the Venus; C. Warren, to the Cygnet; A. Rickards, to the Barfleur; W. Reardon, to the Argo; R. A. Bryden, to the Indian; G. H. Cole, to the Daphne; T. Playfair, to the Rapid; J. Speveling, to the Northumberland; G. Cole, to the Revolutionaire.

A List of Midshipmen who have passed for Lieutenants in November.

Sheerness.—R. Hutchinson, C. Andros, E. Fayerman, W. Vale, Hon. F. Napier, S. Chick, D. Peake, R. Henderson, J. Johnston, A. F. Yearman, E. Garrett.

Portsmouth.—J. B. Elliott, T. Simmonds, W. Usher, T. Hammond, J. Carter.

Plymouth.—R. Daniel, G. P. Trownsell, E. Postlethwaite, J. D. Haswell, R. Barclay, G. Chalmers.

Surgeons, &c. appointed.

John Dickson, to the Franchise; George M'Clure, to the Heron; John Rose, to the Colossus; Henry Osborne, to the Irresistible; Luke Fynn, to the Fyen; Richard Thompson, to the Bahama; Thomas Galloway, to the Vengeance, P. S.; John Finucane, to the Assistance; John Briggs to the Oiseau; William Stanbridge, to the Hector; William Gregory, to the Nassau; Alexander Torbitt, to the Warrior; John Richardson, (1) to the Glory; Thomas Jackson, to the Sheldrake; G. M. Caldwell, to the Volcano; John Dickson, (1) to the Franchise; Alexander Stewart, to the Cordelia; John Clarke and Pearce Power, to the Wolverine; William Stenhouse, to the Revenge; George Parsons, to the Galatea; William Craig, to the Decoy; John Simpson, to the Rose; Thomas Reynolds, to the Andromeda; O. Pinco, to the Revolutionaire; James Doble, (2) to the Nemesis; William Cullen, to the Opossum; Thomas Davis, to the Eclipse; James Dickson, (1) to the Port Mahon; Richard Coniby, to the Pelican; Thomas Marryatt, to the Barfleur; Thomas Stewart, to the Barossa; Edmund James, to the Bermuda; J. E. Risk, to the Ganges; Robert Nairn, to the Centaur; Thomas Gray to the Port Mahon; Lindsey Sims, to the Diadem; ——

Ross, to the Union; —— Stormouth, to the Curaçoa; —— Harris, to the Hibernia; —— Crew, to the Invincible.

Assistant-Surgeons, &c. appointed.

Charles Inches, to be hospital mate at Yarmouth Hospital; W. Dennison, to the Hasty; William Todd, to the Olympia; Robert Paisley, to the Mulgrave; William Hoggan, to the Medusa; Elias Ryall, to the Barbara; Henry Barnes, to the Protector; Robert Williams, to the Impregnable; John Grieg, to the Resolute;· John Thompson, to the Fervent, G.B.; Patrick Clarke, to the Revolutionaire; S. H. Wolley, to the Barossa; David Bennett, to be hospital mate at Deal; John Wilson, to Yarmouth Hospital; James Nicol, to the Wrangler, G.B.; George Cunningham, to the Batavier, H. S.; John Beatty, to be hospital-mate at Perth; Campbell Francis, to the Hannibal; Godfrey Baldamus, to the Enchantress; John Way, to the Conflict, G.B.; John Smith, to the Desirée; Ebenezer Johnstone, to the Victorious; H. Hollyman, to the Centaur; Thomas Waugh, to the Ramillies; Alexander Laughlin, to the Dædalus; John Milligan, to the Adamant; John Baxter, to the Sussex, H. S.; John Brenmer, to the Mulgrave; Robert Dick, to the Shamrock; John Taylor, to the Sealark.

BIRTHS.

At Marmion Cottage, the lady of Lieut. Arnold, R.N. of a daughter.

Oct. 24. At Midhurst, the lady of Captain T. Gordon Caulfield, of a son.

Nov. 18. At Deal, the lady of Samuel Giles, Esq. purser of H.M.S. Valiant, of a son and daughter.

MARRIAGES.

Lately, at Halifax, Mr. Suther, surgeon, of H.M.S. Æolus, to Miss McGory, only daughter of Mr. McGory, merchant, at Halifax.

At Gottenburgh, Thomas Todd Walton, Esq. his Britannic Majesty's agent for packets, to Catherine Eliza, eldest daughter of Thomas Todd, Esq. of Durham.

Mr. F. Bone, purser of the Helicon sloop of war, to Sarah, eldest daughter of Thomas Graham, Esq. of St. Mary's, Scilly.

Lieutenant J. W. Rouse, R.N. to Miss Peggy Dunstone, niece to Mrs. Wood, of the Post-office, Falmouth.

Major Richdale, of the 70th Regt. to Mrs. Bushby, widow of Captain John Bushby, R.N.

Jan. 8, at the British residency in Bagdaad, Asiatic Turkey, Captain Sir William Wiseman, Bart. R.N. to Catherine, daughter of Sir James Mackintosh, Knt.

Oct. 1, Mr. W. Phipps, of Cork-street, Burlington-gardens, to the Right Hon. the lady Baroness Howe, eldest daughter of the late Admiral Earl Howe, and widow of the Hon. Penn Ashton Curzon.

NAVAL HISTORY OF THE PRESENT YEAR, 1812. 439

Same day, Lieutenant John Geddes, R.N. to Mrs. Mary Ann Cleverton, of Portsea.

Sept. 24. At Reading, Richard Westbrook, Esq. to Sarah Ann, eldest daughter of the late Capt. Alexander Cuming, of the Hon. E. I. C's. S. Castle Eden.

Oct. 13, at St. Mary-le-bone church, Mr. Charles Gardiner, to Cecilia Mary, only daughter of Captain Hugh Baikie, R.N.

Oct. 17, at St. George's Church, Hanover-square, J. Slight, Esq. Storekeeper of H.M.'s Victualling-yard, to Miss Sophia Pawrie, of Woolwich.

Oct. 19, at Uplyme, Gustavus Stupart, Esq. Captain, R.N. to Miss Hyndman.

Nov. 10. At Guernsey, Capt. Butter, of the Wiltshire Militia, to Eliza, only daughter of Capt. Dobree, R.N.

Nov. 14. At Plymouth, Captain Henry Jane, of H.M.S. Indian, to Miss Jane Prynn, of Torpoint, sister to Doctor Prynn of Plymouth.

OBITUARY.

Sept. 11. At the House of Industry, Lincoln, in the 95th year of his age, Mr. Wm. North, mariner. He served as quarter-master in Admiral Byng's fleet, and was an evidence on that unfortunate gentleman's trial.

15. At Bristol, in an apoplectic fit, preceded by repeated strokes of the palsy, Capt. George Miller, R.N. lately of H.M.S. Thetis.

17. Lieut. L. M. Yates, R.N. of H.M.S. Menelaus, son of Mr. T. L. Yates, purser of H.M.S. Hibernia. He was shot through the head, in an attack upon the port of Mejan, in the Bay of Marseilles.—At the same time, one seaman was killed, and five marines were wounded.

26. At Guernsey, after a short illness, aged 20, Mary, eldest daughter of vice-admiral Sir James Saumarez, K.B. Bart. &c.

Oct. 1. At Carrackmaross, in Ireland, the widow of the Rev. E. M. Ennis, and mother of Capt. Ennis, R.M. aged 73.

2. Mr. Wm. Neales, midshipman of H.M.S. Crescent, and son of Mr. W. Wm. Neales, of Plymouth. He was unfortunately killed by a grape shot in attempting to save one of the last Baltic convoy that had been driven ashore on the island of Langland, in the Great Belt. He had handsomely volunteered on this service, and finding it impossible to get the ship off, had succeeded in setting her on fire; but as he was pushing off with his brave comrades, the enemy brought down several field-pieces, by the fire of which he and four others lost their lives.

10. In consequence of a wound received in a duel with Lieut. Wm. Stuart, R.M. on the 8th, Lieut. J. Bagnold (or Bagnell), R.M. This fatal event originated in a dispute respecting a woman of light character. Lieut. B. was in the 30th year of his age. He married a daughter of the Rev. Dr. Ashe, of Chippenham, where she now lives, and by whom he had two children, who died. The parties were the most intimate

friends previously to this dispute; and the unfortunate survivor is inconsolable.* The Coroner's Jury returned a verdict of *Wilful Murder* against Lieut. W. Stuart, and against Lieut. John O'Hanlon, who was second to Lieut. B. for aiding and abetting the same.—No part of the evidence involved, or legally ascertained, the second of Lieut. Stuart. The parties concerned were bound over to appear against Lieuts. Stuart and O'Hanlon at the next county assizes.

14. Isaac Judd, Esq. many years first assistant clerk in the Secretary's department of the Transport Office, for sick and wounded seamen.

Nov. 8. In Edward-street, Cavendish-square, London, Capt. Robert Curry, R.N. aged 80. This officer's first commission as lieutenant was dated 8th November 1756, and he was superannuated with the rank of commander on 21st September 1796.

20. At his house at Hereford, in the 63d year of his age, Charles Papps Price, Esq. Captain R.N.

On the 24th of December last, in the prime of life, by a fall from his horse, near his seat, Swilly Farm, in New South Wales, Captain Austen Forrest, brother of Diggory Forrest, Esq. secretary to the Commander in Chief at this port. Capt. Forrest was an officer of distinguished merit and ability, in the East India Company's naval service, and to his enterprising spirit the world is indebted for the discovery of some islands in the Indian Seas, while traversing them in an open boat after the loss of the Sidney. For this discovery, he received the thanks of the Governor-General. Capt. Forrest settled about three years since in New South Wales, where he purchased the valuable estates belonging to the late Governor Hunter, and married Miss Matcham Pitt, cousin of the immortal Nelson.

In February last, in the East Indies, Lieut. G. Cunningham, R.M. son of the late Sir W. Cunningham.

Lately, off Java, Mr. Johnson, second lieutenant; Mr. Simpson, master; and Mr. Holland, purser, of H.M.S. Bucephalus; also, Lieut. J. Peed, of the Modeste, who was desperately wounded in boarding a pirate off Java. The Hesper has lost 80 men, a lieutenant, and all her midshipmen.

At Plymouth, Lieut. Rea, of the Braave prison-ship.

In Finsbury-square, aged 67, Capt. Thos. Newton, late of the Royal Navy.

Sarah, the wife of Mr. Moss, of the navy office, and second daughter of Mr. Leave, surveyor, of Featherstone-Buildings.

Mrs. Farquharson, widow of the late Dr. Farquharson, M.D. Commissioner to the Sick and Hurt Board.

Aged 17, Miss Jane Bury, second daughter of Adm. Incledon Bury, of Denniton-house, near Barnstaple.

---

* Capt. T. M. Bagnold, R.M. not long since, was presented with an honorary medal, by the Society for the encouragement of Arts, for his invention of a gun and carriage, for the purpose of clearing the enemy's tops of marksmen in close action. (*Vide* N. C. XXV. 386). We know not whether that gentleman were a relative of the deceased.

BIOGRAPHICAL MEMOIR

OF

JAMES HORSBURGH, Esq. F.R.S.

HYDROGRAPHER TO THE EAST INDIA COMPANY.

> ——————————" Many a time,
> Mounting the mast-tower-top, with eager ken
> They gaz'd, and fancied, in the distant sky,
> Their promised shore beneath the evening cloud,
> Or seen, low lying, through the haze of morn."
>
> SOUTHEY.——*Madoc.*

WHEN reflection turns to the difficulties and dangers attendant on early navigation ;—when we contemplate the comparative safety with which the waters of the globe are now traversed—a safety for which we are indebted solely to the efforts of hydrographical science—too high a praise can scarcely be accorded to the labourers in that extensive field. The names of Columbus, De Gama, Magelhaens, Drake, Dampier, Cooke, &c. will ever be pronounced with reverence, by a grateful world. Nor is the meed of applause due only to those who have " ventured, where never keel had cut the deep before." They who can successfully follow great leaders, must themselves possess a proportionate degree of greatness ; and, while the discoverer of a new country is hailed with general acclamation, the man who carefully traces, and accurately marks the situation of a destructive rock or shoal, is entitled to share the public gratitude.

The attention of the NAVAL CHRONICLER to the records of hydrographical science—throughout the preceding five or six volumes in particular—must have attracted the notice of even the most cursory reader. Under a strong sense of their great and general importance, we were induced thus to notice the subject, in the Preface to a recent Volume : *—

---

* N. C. XXV. p. ii.

"We hope our increased industry in the collection of geographic materials, does not escape the attention of our professional and scientific reader. "Hydrography" has become an established head in the three last volumes: but we regret to say, contributions towards it are far from commensurate with our wishes to render it more and more interesting: and we are farther led to deplore this deficiency of assistance from our naval friends, because we are convinced that the want of a known common *focus* of nautical information, has contributed to perpetuate the infancy of science, and the perennial succession of error: thus it has been that inventions have become fugitive, and discoveries are endlessly *re*-discovered. Not that we, by any means, advise every ship-master who can just write his own log-book, to hand his own name down to posterity, affixed to every ten yards of land he happens to get sight of for the first time in his life; to entertain the world with the terrific *phenomena* of every gale of wind; or to harrow our feelings with the *pathos* of short allowance. But the foundation for a sober and lasting system must be laid by the diligence and ingenuity of enthusiastic observers, and by recording these *data* we hope to be instrumental in giving form and stability to a part of science at present in an imperfect state. We therefore again present the NAVAL CHRONICLE to travellers and navigators, as the safest depository for such memoranda, and renew our solicitations to naval officers, for hydrographical contributions, unchecked by any literary diffidence, as to the form or style of their documents: while we hope our correspondents on shore will lend their aid towards collecting, arranging, disposing, and condensing the details connected with the progress of this science, which are dispersed through a multitude of works in various languages,—in literary journals—in the memoirs of academies—and in the transactions of learned societies."

Notwithstanding this, and other successive calls,[*] five of our correspondents, comprehending the subject of the present memoir,

---

[*] The preface to Vol. XXVI. contains the following exhortations:— "The great and serious importance of the hydrographical department, becomes monthly more and more conspicuous. It comprehends not only the geographical sites of places, but many local observations, which are interesting to navigation in general. Under this head are also collected all notices to mariners, appertaining to pilotage, &c.—For his very valuable contributions to this department, we beg leave to return our most grateful thanks to J. S. S. To Captain Flinders, and to Colonel Oliver, commanding-in-chief at the Molucca Isles, we are also much indebted."—Again; in the preface to N. C. Vol. XXVII. the same subject is followed up thus:— "The hydrographical department of the NAVAL CHRONICLE continues to increase in importance and in value; for which the grateful thanks of the Editor are again chiefly due to the indefatigable friendship of J. S. S."

are the only persons who have been stimulated to active and direct contribution.

In the confident hope, however, that these examples will yet be productive of a desired effect, we proceed to sketch a concise memorial of Mr. Horsburgh, to whom the nautical profession, and the public at large, are eminently indebted.

James Horsburgh was born at Ely, in the county of Fife, North Britain, on the 23d of September, 1762. His parents were pious, and respectable, but not opulent. They sent him to school at an early period; and, at the age of sixteen, having acquired the elements of mathematical science, of book-keeping, and the theoretical part of navigation, he was apprenticed to Messrs. James and William Wood, of Ely. During a servitude of three years, he sailed in several vessels, chiefly in the coal-trade, from Newcastle, and the Firth of Forth, to Hamburgh, Holland, and Ostend. In May, 1780, he was captured by a French ship, of 20 guns, close to the island of Walcheren; and, in consequence, was detained a short time in prison, at Dunkirk.

After his liberation, Mr. Horsburgh made a voyage to the West Indies; and, on his return to London, he proceeded to Calcutta. Shortly after his arrival at that port, his friend, Mr. David Briggs, then ship-builder there, obtained him the appointment of third mate, in the ship Nancy, bound to Bombay. This was in August, 1784. He continued to sail about two years from the port of Calcutta; and, in the month of May, 1786, when proceeding from Batavia towards Ceylon, in the capacity of first mate of the Atlas, he had the misfortune to be wrecked upon the Island Diego-Garcia. It deserves to be remarked, that this disaster resulted from the erroneousness of the charts then in use; a circumstance which first induced Mr. Horsburgh to think of preserving and arranging such observations as might in future occur to him, relative to the improvement of navigation. "The Atlas," says Mr. Horsburgh,* "was wrecked on the S.E. side of the island [Diego Garcia] about half an hour before day-light, May 30th, 1786, in which vessel I was at the time. The charts on board were very erroneous in the delineation of the Chagos Islands and

* *Vide* " Directions for sailing to and from the East Indies, China, &c." page 132; note.

Banks; and the commander trusting too much to dead reckoning, was steering with confidence to make Ady or Candy (which do not exist) for a new departure, being in their longitude nearly, by account, and bound to Ceylon; but, unfortunately, a cloud over Diego Garcia prevented the helmsman from discerning it (the officer of the watch being asleep), till we were on the reef close to the shore; the masts, rudder, and every thing above deck, went with the first surge; the second lifted the vessel over the outer rocks, and threw her in toward the beach, it being high water, and the vessel in ballast; otherwise, she must have been dashed in pieces by two or three surfs on the outer part of the reef, and every person on board have perished. We had been set 4° to the westward of account in the passage from Bencoolen of 20 days."

From Diego-Garcia he went to Bombay, where, as second mate, he joined the Gunjavar, bound to China, a large ship belonging to Chillaby, a respectable Mohammedan merchant, of Surat. At China he became first mate; and he continued to sail from Bombay to China, and sometimes to Bengal, as first mate of several large ships, upwards of ten years.

In 1791, he joined the Anna, in which he made two voyages to China, by eastern routes. On those occasions, he availed himself of the opportunities which occurred, of making many observations, in parts that were but little frequented by navigators.— By the assistance of books, he had previously exercised himself in the computations of lunar observations, in the use of chronometers, &c. in which he had not been instructed during the course of his juvenile education. He also *taught himself* drawing, and etching, and spherics, from Robertson's " Elements of Navigation." When in port, he generally occupied himself, after the hours of duty, till long after the midnight hour, in the laudable endeavour to perfect himself in those useful attainments.

The observations which Mr. Horsburgh made, during these two voyages to China, enabled him to construct three charts; one, of the Strait of Macassar; another, of the western sides of the Phillippine Islands; and the third, of the track from Dampier's Strait, through the Pitt's Passage, towards Batavia, accompanied by a memoir of sailing directions.

These labours he presented to Mr. Thomas Bruce (then resident at Canton, and now at Grangemuir, in Fifeshire) a gentleman who had previously been his ship-mate, and with whom he had been in the habits of intimate friendship, from his first arrival in India. Mr. Bruce having shewn the manuscripts to several commanders of the E. I. Company's ships, and to Mr. James Drummond, afterwards chief of the factory, they were transmitted to Mr. Alexander Dalrymple, at that time Hydrographer to the Company, and were published, with the approbation of the Court of Directors, for the use of their regular ships. The author's satisfaction upon this occasion was materially heightened, by his receiving a letter of thanks from the Honourable Court, with a small pecuniary present for the purchase of nautical instruments.

In the year 1796, Mr. Horsburgh arrived in England, as first mate of the Carron, a ship belonging to Messrs. Bruce, Fawcett, and Co. of Bombay. Shortly after his arrival, he saw Mr. Dalrymple, by whom he was introduced to Sir Joseph Banks, to Dr. Maskelyne (the astronomer-royal), and to several other scientific gentlemen. In proof of the estimation in which his talents and general character were holden by them, it is sufficient to say, that, to the present moment, he is distinguished by the patronage of the President of the Royal Society; and that, until their decease, he was equally honoured by the friendship of Dr. Maskelyne, Mr. Cavendish, and others.

The Carron having been hired as a transport, to carry out troops for the expeditions which had been projected against the islands of Trinidad and Porto-Rico, he proceeded with her to the West-Indies, whence he returned to England, after an absence of ten months. He then sailed for Bombay; and on his arrival there, in April, 1798, he obtained the command of the Anna, his old ship, which also belonged to Messrs. Bruce, Fawcett, and Co.

In the Anna, Mr. Horsburgh made several voyages to China, Bengal, and Madras; and two to England—one, from China direct, and one from Bombay.

The astronomical clock, made by L. Berthoud, for the ships which went in search of De la Peyrouse, having been brought to Bombay, and put up for sale, after the return of the ships from their expedition to Batavia, Mr. Horsburgh became the purchaser. This clock, which had an excellent composition pendulum, he generally set up at Bombay, and at Canton, when opportunity offered, to assist him in ascertaining the rates of his chronometers, and in observing a series of the eclipses of Jupiter's satellites, at each of those places, which he transmitted to the astronomer-royal. The Anna, however, seldom remained in port a sufficient time to afford a long series of observations of this nature. Of the celerity with which that vessel performed her voyages, the following instance may be mentioned.—She left the Lizard Point on the 20th of April, 1802 ; anchored at Bombay, on the 31st of July ; discharged 900 tons of European cargo, reloaded with cotton, and sailed on the 25th of August ; arrived in Canton river on the 30th of September ; remained there two months and three days ; sailed, with a heavy cargo, on the 3d of December ; anchored at Bombay, on the 11th of January, 1803 ; and, in eight days, cleared the ship : the whole time, after leaving the Lizard Point, amounting to exactly nine months !

From the commencement of April, 1802, to the middle of February, 1804, Mr. Horsburgh kept a register of the rise and fall of the mercury, in two marine barometers, taken every four hours, day and night, at sea and in port. This experiment, as it may be termed, proved the regular ebb and flow of the mercury, twice every twenty-four hours, in the open sea, from 26 degrees north, to 26 degrees of south, latitude ; and that it was diminished, or, sometimes, entirely obstructed, in rivers, harbours, or narrow straits, by the influence of the land ; a fact which seems not to have been previously known. Mr. Horsburgh presented his register to the Royal Society, and an abstract thereof was recorded in the *Philosophical Transactions* for 1805.

Mr. Horsburgh's next production was a chart of the strait of Allas ; which, with some smaller surveys, he transmitted to his late friend Mr. Dalrymple, by whom they were engraved.

He returned to England in the year 1805 ; and, having prepared his manuscripts, and other materials, he, with all practicable diligence, published the following charts, &c.

A Chart of the China Sea, on two sheets, on a scale of two inches to a degree.

A Chart of Malacca Strait, on two sheets, on a large scale.

A Chart of the entrance of Sincapour Strait.

A Chart of Bombay Harbour, with Views of the Land.

A Book of Memoirs, to accompany the above Charts, explanatory of the Indian Navigation, and Eastern Passages to China.

New editions of the above have been published, corrected to the year 1812. Mr. Horsburgh has also since published the following:—

A Chart, on two sheets, from latitude 38° south to the Equator; comprising the Cape of Good Hope, the East Coast of Africa, the Madagascar Archipelago, &c.

A Chart of the Peninsula of Hindoostan, and the islands of the Chagos, the Maldiva, and Laccadiva Archipelago, and Ceylon.

A small Chart of the Islands and Channels between Luçonia and Formosa.

In addition to the publications here enumerated, Mr. Horsburgh is understood now to have in hand, a Chart of the Peninsula and Islands beyond the Ganges, extending from Point Palmiras to the Islands Hainan and Borneo, and from latitude 23° north, to 13° south.

Mr. Horsburgh had the good fortune to sail for England, from China, in the Cirencester, Captain Thomas Robertson; a gentleman of great benevolence and sincerity. Captain P. Heywood, of the royal navy, was also his fellow passenger; and, from that experienced and intelligent officer, while arranging his works for publication, he derived great assistance. Since that period, too, he has frequently benefited by useful communications from the same friendly source.

After his arrival in England, (in 1805) he presented some papers to Sir Joseph Banks, which are embodied in the *Philosophical Transactions* for 1810, through the medium of a paper on luminous animals, by J. Macartney, Esq. where a description is given of luminous marine animals, discovered by the President of the Royal Society, Mr. Forster, Mr. Horsburgh, and others. Some papers which he gave to Mr. William Nicholson, are recorded in Volumes XIII. XIV. and XV. of the *Philosophical and Chemical Journal*, published under that writer's name.

Captain Robertson, with whom Mr. Horsburgh returned from India, shortly after his arrival in this country, introduced him to Captain Joseph Cotton, Deputy-Master of the Trinity-House, and also a Director of the East India Company. This gentleman, distinguished by his desire for the promotion of science, and every thing connected with the improvement of navigation, has, by his continued support, greatly facilitated the publication of

Mr. Horsburgh's various professional works. Of these, the one which bears the following title, is the principal: *Directions for sailing to and from the East Indies, China, New-Holland, Cape of Good Hope, and the interjacent Ports, compiled chiefly from Original Journals and Observations made during twenty-one years' experience in navigating those Seas."*

To this publication, on which Mr. Horsburgh bestowed nearly five years incessant labour, appears a very modest preface, as follows :—

" This work commenced at the solicitation of some navigators, who frequent the Oriental Seas. However incompetent to the task, my chief aim has been to trace out error, and approximate truth; how far this is accomplished, a judicious public, and the commanders and officers who frequent those seas, will decide.

" In pointing out inaccuracies in other nautical works, I have endeavoured to avoid giving cause of displeasure to any of the publishers; but having once suffered shipwreck, by the inaccuracy of the charts in general use, I considered it my duty to point out to other navigators such errors as were perceived, to prevent them, if possible, from a similar misfortune.

" To those navigators frequenting the Oriental Seas, who may have opportunity to discover errors in this work, and communicate them to the author, he will consider himself much indebted, and receive such communication with gratitude."

" SAVILE-ROW, WALWORTH,
  April 4*th*, 1809."

In his Introduction, Mr. Horsburgh gives instructions from the Channel to Madeira, and the Canaries: these are followed by a table compiled from the journals of 238 ships, defining the equatorial limits of the trade winds during every month in the year, with directions for sailing from the Cape Verd across the equator. Here the author's barometrical observations, with those of Captain Flinders, were of great advantage. Next follow directions for sailing to the coast of Brazil, the river Plata, and the islands of Ascension and St. Helena, with a comparison of the eastern and western passages to the latter; winds and currents in the gulf of Guinea, and the west coast of Africa. To these succeed courses from Brazil, touching the islands Tristan d'Acunha, Gough's, &c. to the Cape of Good Hope, with descriptions of the winds and weather there, and dangers in passing eastward;

thence to Van-Diemen's land, through Bass's strait, with details of the islands, winds, and weather, in that ocean, and to the southeast of New Holland, and ample descriptions of the seas and islands to Sunda strait, Java, and the more eastward islands. The prevailing winds in the Indian seas are next fully described, with directions for sailing from the Cape of Good Hope to the different parts of India, by various routes, according to the season of the year; describing the coasts of Madagascar, Mahée islands, archipelagos, or islands in those seas, the harbours, channels, &c. and of the islands of Roderigo, Mauritius, and Bourbon. Mr. Horsburgh then directs the navigator through the Mozambique channel, along the coasts of Africa, the Red sea, Strait of Babelmandel, coasts of Abyssinia, Arabia, Persian gulf, Socotra, and coast of Asia, to Bombay, Comorin, Ceylon, Coromandel, to Bengal, entrance of the river Hoogly, with the Maldiva and Laccadiva islands. The currents, winds, tides, shoals, &c. in all these places, are minutely and accurately described, and the seaman will find ample directions for sailing from the 50th degree north to the 40th degree south latitude, and between the 60th west and 150th east longitude. All the harbours, islands, &c. in this vast track, especially in the Southern, Atlantic, and Indian oceans, extending to the China sea, are distinctly illustrated, and more than usual care seems to have been employed in obtaining the latitudes and longitudes of all the headlands, principal islands, and dangerous places.—One important object of this work is, by giving the geographical descriptions of every perilous place of note, to enable the navigator to sail, free from the apprehension of danger, without any assistance from charts, should none happen to be at hand.—Those parts of the work which are described from Mr. Horsburgh's own observations are the China sea,* Malacca strait, Malabar coast, Bombay Harbour, and Bay of Bengal.—It must be added, that the author's original remarks on the winds and currents will be found worthy the attention of practical seamen, while the philosopher and

---

* In the XVth Volume of the NAVAL CHRONICLE, page 461, is a list of vessels lost in the China sea; accompanied by remarks relative to the treacherous disposition of the Malays, communicated by Mr. Horsburgh.

meteorologist will regard them as valuable *data*, whence he may be enabled to illustrate some of the yet undefined phenomena of nature.—In addition to a copious index and table of contents, it deserves to be mentioned, that, to facilitate the finding of any particular article that may be required—a point frequently of the utmost utility when at sea, and in critical situations—the work is printed with side notes, and with the names of places in capitals.

We must not close this memoir, without adverting to the circumstance, noticed at large in a preceding page,* of Captain Burney's caution of placing the Cumbrian's shoal in two different parts of his chart. On points of this nature, we believe it to be Mr. Horsburgh's opinion, founded on his own long nautical experience, that more misfortunes result from the *timidity*, than from the *temerity* of navigators; and that, in dispersing many imaginary islands and shoals, delineated in various charts, but which have no real existence, his publications have been chiefly serviceable to navigators.

The greater part of our readers, we apprehend, while they applaud the candour of this sentiment, will not be disposed to subscribe implicitly to its justness.

We have to add, that, in the spring of 1806 (on, or about the 15th of March), Mr. Horsburgh had the honour of being elected a Fellow of the Royal Society.

He had also the good fortune to preserve the patronage of the Court of Directors of the East India Company, who, in October, 1810, appointed him to succeed their deceased hydrographer. He continues in that situation, fulfilling the expectations of his friends and patrons; and, by the industry and ability which he has manifested, in all that relates to the navigation of the eastern hemisphere, and in the works of nautical science, the world at large has an opportunity of forming its judgment of the discrimination which placed him in so useful and important an office.

Besides the two well-known sects of naturalists denominated " Physiognomists " and " Craniologists," there exists a third, the members of which profess to study individual character through the medium of the hand-writing, and who may therefore be appro-

---

* N. C. XXVIII. 316.

priately styled "*Graphologists:*" it has been deemed expedient to gratify the curiosity of this class of our readers, by subjoining the following imitation of Mr. Horsburgh's *autograph*:

NAVAL ANECDOTES, COMMERCIAL HINTS, RECOLLECTIONS, &c.

ACTION BETWEEN H.M.S SOUTHAMPTON, CAPTAIN SIR J. L. YEO, AND THE HAYTIAN FRIGATE L'AMETHYSTE.

OF this action, which took place in the month of February, 1812, no official or detailed account has hitherto appeared in this country. Through the attention of a Correspondent, we are enabled to supply the deficiency, by a series of statements from the *Kingston Royal Gazette.*

That Journal, of the date of February 15, first presents the following account:—

" The Southampton frigate, of 32 guns, Capt. Sir James Lucas Yeo, Knt. came to anchor at Port Royal yesterday, with L'Amethyste, Haytian frigate, which surrendered to her after an engagement of a considerable time. We have been favoured with the following particulars of the action, from a very respectable source:

' On the morning of the 3d inst. the Southampton, while cruising on the south side of the island of Guanaboa, fell in with a large frigate, a ship corvette, and an armed brig. On hailing the frigate, she answered " from Aux Cayes."—Sir James Lucas Yeo then sent on board, desiring her commander to wait on him with his papers; this he declined, but sent his second captain with an order, signed by a General Borgellat, calling himself general-in-chief of the south of Hayti. Sir James knowing of no authority this Monsieur Borgellat had to send armed vessels to sea, replied, that without intending to use the least violence, he felt it his duty to send the frigate and the rest of the squadron to Jamaica, for instructions from his commanding officer, and gave the captain of the frigate five minutes to consider of the message. An officer was accordingly sent on board to wait the time, but before three of the five minutes were expired, the officer was told, that the captain would rather sink than comply with his demand; and requesting that, if he meant to enforce it, he would fire a gun a-head of the frigate. Almost immediately afterwards the Southampton's bow-gun was fired, and nearly at the same instant a mutual broadside was exchanged; the crew of the frigate made several efforts to board, but were frustrated in their attempts by the superiority of the Southampton's manœuvres. From half-past six till near eight the action was severe, during which period the corvette and brig made sail, and escaped under the batteries of Maraguana. The main and mizen-masts of the enemy's frigate were presently shot away, and so were the colours early in the action; her shattered condition induced Sir James to hail, to know if she had surrendered, which was answered in the affirmative. Soon afterwards, the foremast and bowsprit went over the side.

' The above frigate was under Petion's colours, is called L'Amethyste, mounts 44 guns, eight 24 and eighteen 12 (French) pounders, on her main-deck, 14 32-pound carronades on her quarter-deck, and four 12-pounder long guns on her forecastle. She was commanded by a white Frenchman, named Gaspard, who was killed in the action, a notorious commander of privateers, and her complement was 400 seamen, besides 300 troops on board, a renegado set, consisting of Frenchmen, Americans, and all nations. She had 105 killed, and 120 wounded, many of whom have since died. The Southampton had only one man killed, and a midshipman and nine men wounded. The prisoners were landed at Maraguana on the 5th.'

To this statement in the *Kingston Gazette*, succeeds a short account of Gaspard, the captain of L'Amethyste, as follows :—

" The above Mons. Le Gaspard was, we presume, the same person who was in the service of Petion, and formerly commanded a ship which was purchased here, called the Lady Frances, and which he afterwards fitted out as a corvette. In 1809 he had a squadron, consisting of one ship, two brigs, three schooners, and a cutter, under his command; and the avowed principle of this man and his adherents was, that in the event of proving unsuccessful in battle with Christophe's cruisers, rather than be made prisoners, they would set fire to their vessels: an instance of this sort occurred about this period, and which we have heard related by him with evident marks of satisfaction: the mate of Goodall brought a large schooner, belonging to the above squadron, to action, which was contested by her with savage ferocity for a long time—at last the mate (whose name we forget) with a party of his men, succeeded in boarding the schooner, and had subdued her crew, when her commander, whose name was Donacour, went below, set fire to the magazine, and blew the vessel up, and every soul on board perished. Such is the savage mode of warfare carried on by these ignorant people; and perhaps had not Le Gaspard fallen before the conclusion of the action with the Southampton, he might have attempted to commit a similar act of barbarity on board L'Amethyste.

" L'Amethyste, we understand, was taken into Port-au-Prince after the action, when the commandant of the place denied having any knowledge of her. She was formerly in our service, and was purchased in England for Christophe about two years ago."

The next week's *Kingston Gazette* (February 22) furnishes the subjoined details:—

" Since our last, we have obtained the following additional particulars of the engagement of L'Amethyste with the Southampton frigate, by the deposition of two American seamen (blacks), who were on board the former vessel when it took place : ' That she had no commission ; that she sailed under the colours of Petion, but had colours of different nations on board ; that the command of her was given to Gaspard, by the commandant of Maraguana, about three weeks previous to the action ; that there were between 600 and 700 seamen and marines, including officers, on board, all natives of St. Domingo, excepting a few Americans—part of them were put on board at Cape François, and the remainder at Maraguana ; that the frigate lately belonged to Christophe, but her officers (with the exception of the commander) and crew revolted, and carried her into the above port; that she had 44 guns mounted, with a proportionate quantity of small arms and ammunition, and was so armed for the purpose of making prizes, and plundering what vessels they might fall in with; that, on the morning of the 3d inst. the Southampton frigate came down on her, and hailed—what ship? upon which the commander of L'Amethyste replied, that she was a ship from Aux Cayes. He was then requested to repair on board the British frigate with his papers : this he declined doing, as also to accompany the Southampton to Port Royal, declaring that he would sooner fight, as he was sure the British frigate could not take him; upon which a gun was fired a-head of L'Amethyste, which vessel immediately returned three, and continued firing till she struck.'

" After L'Amethyste was taken possession of by the Southampton, all the prisoners, with the exception of eight brought down here, *viz.* one white, a mulatto, and six blacks, were sent on shore in boats at Maraguana, Petit-Goave, and Port-au-Prince, most of whom are stated to be Americans, and said they were compelled by force to embark on board L'Amethyste. Monsieur Gaspard was not killed during the action, but so severely wounded, that it was expected he could not survive, and was among the number landed : although he has the appearance of being white, he is of colour, and is well known in this city, having formerly commanded the ship Lady Frances, which was purchased at this port, and fitted out as a corvette, as stated in our last. He was once in the service of Petion, and is a man of desperate and determined character ; and there is little doubt, if all the officers on board L'Amethyste had not been dreadfully wounded, that she would have been blown up before she surrendered, as part of a train of powder was laid towards her magazine when the Southampton took possession of her.—Monsieur Borgellat was born at Aux Cayes, and gained by some means command of the department of the South, after the death of Rigaud. After the engagement, L'Amethyste was taken into Port-au-Prince, and rigged jury-masts, &c. to bring her to this port. It is said that Petion and Christophe both disclaim her having any authority from them to cruise. After L'Amethyste came into possession of Mons. Borgellat, her name was changed to L'Heureuse Re-Union.

" The corvette and brigs, which were in company with L'Amethyste when the Southampton fell in with her, had recently been captured by her, and she was proceeding to Maraguana. They were part of Christophe's squadron with them, and had been taken by surprise.

" The Haytian schooner Clara, in four days from Aux Cayes, having on board an officer from Mons. Borgellat and Mr. Robert Edgar, the former with despatches to Vice-admiral Stirling, and the latter with a memorial from the British merchants resident at Aux Cayes, arrived at Port Royal on Saturday morning, but no person from her was allowed to have communication with the shore. The Clara sailed the same evening on her return, but unluckily got ashore on the South Shoals on the following morning, and was totally lost. The people who were on board, nine in number, were saved by fishing canoes, and brought to Port Royal.

" The despatches to Admiral Stirling, we understand, contained a circumstantial narrative respecting L'Amethyste, from the period of her revolting against Christophe, to the time of her capture, and required some explanation for the attack on her.

" The memorial states, that without pretending to call in question the propriety of the capture of L'Amethyste, or in any way dictating what should be done, it is presumed that conciliatory measures are necessary to insure respect to British persons and property."

The succeeding number of the *Kingston Gazette* (February 29) notices an account of the action, given in the Port-au-Prince paper, in the following manner :—

" The *Echo*, or *National Gazette* of Port-au-Prince, of the 16th inst, details the rencontre between the Southampton and L'Amethyste exactly as we have already given it to our readers, except that it adds, ' that Sir James Lucas Yeo told the Haytian officer, that he knew of no authority that empowered General Borgellat to send a squadron to sea, and that his precise orders were to respect *only* the flags of Petion and Christophe ; that he was consequently under the necessity of detaining the frigate and other vessels, and that he advised the Haytian commander to avoid unnecessary bloodshed, and follow him quietly to Jamaica, where his Admiral and General Borgellat might decide the validity of the capture ; but should he refuse this friendly offer, he would be compelled to use force, and he gave the Haytian five minutes to determine ; he at the same time sent a British officer alongside the Haytian frigate, to await their commander's resolution, where he had scarcely arrived, when Bigot imperiously desired him to retire, and the captain declared that he would much sooner sink his vessel than deliver it up (the second captain observed that as the English frigate carried only twelve-pounders, she would easily be taken), and that he waited only for a signal from the British captain to commence action.

" After detailing the result of the affair, as has already been stated, the Gazette proceeds as follows :

' We learn that, in consequence of the above affair, General Borgellat has caused all the English in his power to be put in prison, but though we have received this information by three different arrivals, we still hope it may not be true, as it certainly would be as unjust as unexampled, that the persons or properties of innocent individuals should suffer for acts in which they had no part.

' The law of civilized nations allows to the individuals of every nation, even after the declaration of war, time to collect their property and retire to their own country.

' Buonaparte, it is true, violated this law, by imprisoning all the British subjects in France at the declaration of the war. Does General Borgellat wish to make use of the French Emperor's measures? We hope no Haytian will imitate the example of this rapacious usurper, who wishes to corrupt them, that he may more easily execute his old project of destroying Hayti.

' The question of right in this affair rests simply on the following point. Has General Borgellat been recognized by the English government as commander-in-chief of the South of Hayti? If he has not, his squadron could only be regarded by that nation as piratical; consequently the conduct of the commander of his Britannic Majesty's frigate is sanctioned by the law of nations. If, on the contrary, General Borgellat has been recognized by the British government, it is a discussion which ought to be decided between the two governments.

' Did the American government seize the persons and properties of the English in the United States, in the affair of the Chesapeake and the Leopard? No. In the recent affair of the President and Little Belt, were the peaceable Americans resident in England molested? No. When Touissant's squadron, which carried troops for the conquest of the South, was captured by an English frigate, did he arrest all the English subjects? No. This chief, when he found that he had never been recognized by the government of Great Britain, was convinced of the legality of the capture, and renounced all claim to the vessels, which were declared good prizes in the island of Jamaica.'"

⁎ The Editor of the NAVAL CHRONICLE will feel much obliged, if, in addition to the above particulars of the action, &c. any of his Correspondents can favour him with the result of the investigation, which, it is presumed, must have taken place on the subject.

PRESENTATION OF A SWORD TO SIR JAMES SAUMAREZ.

PREVIOUSLY to Vice-admiral Sir James Saumarez leaving Gottenburgh, he received a most superb sword, which was delivered to him by Baron Essen, aid-de-camp to the Crown Prince (Bernadotte), accompanied by a flattering letter from his Royal Highness, expressive of the sense which the Swedish government entertained of the Admiral's merits. The whole of the hilt is elegantly set with brilliants, of exquisite workmanship, and of great value. The following is a copy of the letter with which the present was accompanied :—

" MR. ADMIRAL SAUMAREZ.—You have conciliated the esteem of the King, during the period in which the British fleets have been stationed on the coasts of the kingdom. His Majesty, wishing to give you a proof of his regard, ordered me, on my arrival at Gottenburgh, to present you with a sword, as a testimony of the sentiments by which he is actuated. I sincerely regret, that in fulfilling his Majesty's orders, unexpected avocations have deprived me of the pleasure of a personal interview; but I have sent to your Excellency Baron D'Essen, my aid-de-camp, who will have the honour to place in your hands the sword destined for you by the King, and will communicate every thing that I have directed him to say to your Excellency on my behalf.

" Receive, Mr. Admiral Saumarez, the assurance of my high consideration. " Your affectionate,

" *Stockholm, Oct.* 20, 1812." " CHARLES JEAN."

The following is a copy of the Admiral's reply:—

" *H. B. M. S. Victory, Hawke Road, Oct.* 21.

" Sir.—I had the honour to receive yesterday the letter your Royal Highness has graciously been pleased to address to me, together with the sword which his Majesty the King of Sweden has had the condescending goodness to honour me with, for the services rendered to Sweden, during the time I have had the honour to command his Majesty's forces in the Baltic. Too happy that my services should have been found deserving so distinguished a mark of his Royal favour, I receive the sword as a pledge of the alliance that so happily exists between Sweden and Great Britain, and I hope never to draw it but for the honour and defence of Sweden, united with England. Whilst I sincerely regret circumstances have not permitted me to pay my humble respects to your Royal Highness, I cannot sufficiently express the sense I feel for the gracious manner in which your Royal Highness has been pleased to signify to me the King's most gracious intention, and for the very flattering expressions conveyed to me from your Royal Highness by Baron D'Essen.

" I have the honour to be, with the highest respect,

" Your Royal Highness's devoted most obedient humble servant,

(Signed) " JAMES SAUMAREZ."

ADMIRAL BERKELEY.

Previously to the Hon. Admiral Berkeley quitting the command of his Majesty's squadron at Lisbon, he received addresses from the British Consul-general and merchants of that city; also one from the British merchants of Oporto; of which the following are copies:—

" *Lisbon, July* 2, 1812.

" Sir,—We, his Majesty's consul-general and the British merchants resident in this city, being informed that your Excellency is about to retire from the command of his Majesty's squadron on this station, beg leave to offer our sincere acknowledgments for the unremitting attention your Excellency has invariably shewn to the protection of our commercial interests, during the period of your command, particularly by the prompt attention your Excellency has ever shewn to our applications for convoys.

" We feel we should be deficient in the duty we owe to ourselves, and to the nation to which we have the honour to belong, did we not thus publicly express our sentiments, and assure your Excellency that we shall ever entertain a grateful remembrance of the zeal you have evinced in the promotion of our interests, and that of the British trade in general, in this country.

" Permit us further to add our unfeigned wishes for the health, happiness, and prosperity of your Excellency, and much-esteemed amiable family; and with the highest respect and consideration,
" We beg leave to subscribe ourselves,
(Signed by the Consul-general, John Jeffery, Esq. and Merchants of Lisbon.)
" *Oporto, June* 25, 1812.

" Sir,—I have the honour to transmit a copy of a resolution passed at a general meeting of the British merchants, residing in this place, held at my office on the 25th of June, 1812, on being informed that you were on the eve of departure for England, to which I beg to add my full participation in the sentiments therein expressed, and the high respect with which I subscribe myself,
" JOHN ALVEY, acting Vice-consul."

" *Oporto, June* 25, 1812.

" *Resolved.*—That John Alvey, Esq. acting vice-consul, be requested to convey to Admiral Berkeley the thanks of the undersigned British merchants, residing in this place, for the very marked attention uniformly experienced by them in the protection of their trade and the promotion of their interests, during his command on this station; and although they feel the expression of their sentiments to be a very inadequate proof of their acknowledgment, they trust it will nevertheless be accepted, in testimony of their sincere gratitude and respect."

(The signatures of the merchants follow.)

ADMIRAL LEGGE.

The constitutional magistracy of Cadiz have expressed their gratitude to the late British naval commander-in-chief, at Cadiz, in the following warm and handsome terms :—
" *Cadiz, September* 18, 1812.

" Excellent Sir,—The bravery and enthusiasm with which the illustrious seamen of the naval forces under your Excellency's command have contributed towards the defence of Cadiz, and their hearty union with the Spanish naval force, in all the fatigues and dangers during the siege of this island by the enemy's troops, excite in such a manner the gratitude of the inhabitants, that language is insufficient to express the succours and effectual assistances which your Excellency has afforded in all enterprises, and your heroic constancy in annoying the enemy at all points of the opposite coasts, occasioning to them irreparable losses, which will always occupy the memory of the Cadizians, by whom the illustrious name of your Excellency, and your meritorious Subalterns, will be an object of the most grateful remembrance. The constitutional magistracy of this city wishes to convey, in this paper, with its true efficacy, the esteem and regard of the people of Cadiz for such famous warriors; but which cannot be done to the full extent of their desires: they beg that your Excellency would be pleased to receive the heartfelt expressions of their eternal gratitude.

" Your Excellency, a happy witness of the good conduct of your subaltern officers, of their valour, and indefatigable zeal; knowing the merit of your worthy officers; and affected also with the distinction with which the people of Cadiz beholds them; will have the goodness to signify to them, in the name of the municipal body, who are their representatives, their sincere demonstrations of gratitude. Cadiz, free from the treacherous siege with which the enemy has molested it during thirty months, now enjoys the satisfaction of seeing its independence secure, and a wise constitution restores to the Spaniards their liberty and their rights. These advantages, as well national as allied, are owing to the brave defenders of this island, the English marine, which hath taken so active a part in all operations, not only has deserved the esteem and gratitude of the inhabitants of Cadiz, but also hath rendered itself entitled to the rewards and distinctions of the English nation.

" If your Excellency, by the knowledge of the merit of the captains, officers, and ships' companies of the vessels under your command, especially those of the flotilla, and of the great fatigues they have undergone in the midst of the greatest dangers, would be pleased to intercede in favour of those meritorious officers, the City of Cadiz, which is so much interested for their welfare, will have the satisfaction of seeing rewards distributed as a recompence for such signal services.

" The constitutional magistracy of this city, have the honour to depute to your Excellency a legation, who by word of mouth, will express the sincere gratitude of the people of Cadiz, and the high consideration with which their representatives offer to your Excellency their respects.

" May God preserve your Excellency many years.

" CAYETANO VALDES, President."

" *To his Excellency A. K. Legge.*"

" *H. B. M. S. Revenge, Cadiz Bay, Sept.* 22, 1812.

" Most Excellent Sirs,—I beg, in the name of myself, and the officers and men I have the honour to command, to thank you for the handsome mark of attention you have been pleased to shew us, by sending a deputation from your body on board the Revenge; an honour we shall ever consider with the highest esteem and gratitude to the loyal and patriotic inhabitants of this noble city.

" In all our endeavours to prevent this city from falling into the iron grasp of the most despotic tyranny that ever disgraced mankind, we have been animated by the example of firmness, constancy, and devotion to the great and glorious cause in which we are mutually engaged, so eminently shewn by the brave people of Cadiz during such a length of time, under circumstances the most distressing and irritating, and to that of the Royal Spanish Marine, with whom we have ever had a pride in co-operating

" The services of the British officers and men who have so long served in the flotilla in whose welfare you have been kindly pleased to interest yourselves, are duly appreciated by me, and I have not failed to represent them to the notice of the British government.

" That this noble city may long enjoy prosperity, and that freedom which its inhabitants so richly deserve, is, gentlemen, the sincere wish and prayer of your devoted and very obedient humble servant,

" A. K. LEGGE,
" Rear-ad. Com. H. B. Majesty's ships in Cadiz Bay."
" Their Excellencies the Aejantamiente of Cadiz."

GALLANT ACTION.

About the middle of November last, in the evening, a boy, named Massey, fell overboard from H. M. S. Christian VII. lying in the Downs.—It was nearly dark at the time, blowing very hard, and a strong lee tide; circumstances of themselves sufficient to preclude a hope of his being saved; but the cries of the poor little fellow, whilst struggling in the water, being heard by Mr. Chien, 2d master; and Messrs. Howell and Cornwell, midshipmen, who were on the lower deck at the time, they instantly, at the most imminent risk of their own lives, leaped overboard (boots and all on). Before they reached the boy he disappeared; but Mr. Chien, by diving, brought him up three times, and the others helped to support him, but from the heavy sea running, all were soon exhausted, the boy was drowned, and the others, after being driven by the rapidity of the tide nearly a mile from the ship, were, with the greatest difficulty, picked up, almost in a state of insensibility, but were fortunately recovered.

POLITICAL IMPORTANCE OF THE ISLAND OF MALTA.*

The Maltese depended in former times upon the crown of Sicily, but as a free people, enjoying peculiar laws and privileges. The island was given under certain conditions, one of which was, that the privilege of the Maltese should be preserved, by Charles V. to the knights of St. John. The Order violated, in many respects, the privileges of the Maltese, especially under the grand master, Rohan, who abolished, about thirty years ago, the *consiglio popolare*. The Order afterwards, in 1798, betrayed the Maltese and the fortresses into the hands of the French, and quitted the island. The Maltese rose up, when left to themselves, and carried on a bloody war against the French, during two years, in which they lost themselves 20,000 men, but succeeded in reducing the enemy to the last extremity. At this time a British squadron appearing off the island, the French took the opportunity of surrendering to the English, in order to escape the vengeance which they dreaded from the Maltese. The Maltese acquiesced in the

---

* N. C. VIII. 121; XXI. 213; XXV. 480; XXVIII. 308.

surrender, under an assurance, that they should be incorporated with the British empire, their old privileges respected, and a suitable constitution established. Mr. Cameron was appointed his Majesty's civil commissioner, and published a proclamation to that effect, but the island, in breach of these assurances, was made over by the peace of Amiens to the Order of St. John, whom the Maltese detested, and whom they would not allow to come amongst them, during their war against the French. Sir A. Ball, whom during that war they had constituted their leader, he having offered his services to them as a volunteer, was appointed ambassador to the new grand master; but the peace of Amiens being broken, things returned again to their former state, and Sir A. Ball was appointed commissioner. In this situation he became unpopular amongst his former constituents, having suppressed the assembly of which he had been chosen by them president, and complaints were from time to time preferred against his conduct. They were not, however, regarded, nor has any constitution yet been established. The Maltese have therefore claimed, in steady terms, the performance of the conditions, in which alone they consented to accept the sovereignty of Great Britain. The matter, we understand, is likely to be brought before Parliament. There have appeared, at former periods, various publications on this subject. The above statement is taken principally from materials for a history of Malta, compiled by a Mr. Eton, and from a memoir upon the political state of Malta, published in 1807, by Mr. Dillon, a gentleman of the English bar, the same, we believe, who is the author of various publications on the Coronation Oath, and the Catholic Question.

MODE OF EXTINGUISHING FIRE.

THE application of pot-ash forms a cheap and easy method of extinguishing fire. This was tried at the fire which happened some years ago in Greenock, at the foot of the Highland Close; the roof had fallen, but the flame was very high, extending over the adjoining houses, as the wind directed, and threatening the destruction of the whole street of Broad Close, It was midnight; but the streets were so illuminated that a pin might have been discerned. The impregnated water was no sooner thrown in, than all was darkness and smoke; the fire was completely extinguished. The process is very simple: at one end of the fire engine a large tub was placed, into which all the water was thrown, and from it, by two men, one on each side, with buckets, the engine was supplied. To the tub was attached a barrel of sweated American pot-ash, placed under the charge of one man, who, by handfuls, continued liberally to throw the ashes into the water, where they were soon dissolved.

CAPTAIN KRUSENSTERN.

THE Russian circumnavigator, Krusenstern, in the relation of his voyage round the world (recently published in Russ and German), gives a faithful account of the failure of the principal object of his expedition, which was to establish commercial relations between Japan and Russia. " The Emperor of Japan (he says) caused it to be notified to the commissioners whom I carried, that his subjects traded only with the Dutch and Chinese. As to the Russians, he begged them to return to their own country, and, if they valued their lives, never to come back." The two vessels in which Captain Krusenstern performed his voyage, were called the Neva and the Nadessa (Hope): they were English built, and all the equipments of his sailors were purchased in this country.

BRINE'S SIGNAL LANTHORN.

A NEW-INVENTED signal lanthorn, by Mr. Brine, of Portsea, has recently been exhibited on board the commander-in-chief's ship, at Spithead, and much approved for the simplicity of its construction and great utility, as no weather can affect the light, which is fully adequate to all purposes of night signal.

CORRESPONDENCE.

MR. EDITOR, *Lloyd's C. H. 10 December.*

THE space allotted in your last publication, to intelligence from the United-States of America, and more specifically to the roving cruise of Commodore Rodgers, encourages me to contribute the following literal copies from the newspapers recently arrived from that country. The first in order relates to the proceedings of a single American corsair, which might fairly enough have been quoted in contradiction to the parliamentary flourish of the Admiralty, as to the adequate appropriation of naval force in that quarter. Ten or a dozen frigates stationed during the autumn between the Azores, Bermudas, and Madeira, would have completely paralyzed those predatory operations from which our new trans-atlantic adversaries have derived so much benefit, and, above all, encouragement in the outset. Perhaps those who manage this branch may condescend to learn wisdom from dear-bought experience even at the eleventh hour.

The concluding extract, consists of correspondence between our admiral lately commanding on the Newfoundland station, and certain officers of the American States, and will perhaps be found interesting, as throwing light upon the unusual circumstances attending the capture and subsequent employment of the late English ship of war Alert, and as demonstrating the liberal spirit by which the consequential evils of war are tempered in the naval hostility on both sides. It is instructive to look over your enemy's book at all events.

TRITON.

" Arrived at Newburyport, on 23d September, the privateer brig Decatur, Nichols, from a cruise of 47 days, having captured 11 sail of English vessels, two of which (the Duke of Savoy and Elizabeth) arrived several days since Aug. 23, she took brig Pomona, of 2 guns, from Aberdeen, for the River St. Lawrence, and after disarming her, sent her to Halifax, as a cartel, with prisoners. 26th, took brig Devonshire, from Teignmouth for St. John, loaded with green fish, and sent her to France, to sell her cargo; brig Concord, from do. for do. in ballast, and burnt; brig Hope, from do. for do. sent her to Halifax as a cartel. 30th, took barque Wm. and Charlotte, from Quebec for Portsmouth, (E.) with 500 tons timber, deals, &c. mounting 4 6-pounders, &c. and ordered her for the 1st port. Sept. 1, in about long. 30, fell in with the St. Thomas fleet, and captured the ship Diana, 370 tons, loaded with sugar and rum, bound to Liverpool, mounting ten 9 and 12-pounders, &c.; brig Fame, of 180 tons, for Dublin, loaded with rum and sugar, 2 guns—ordered both for the first port in the U. S. 6th, took ship Commerce (Watts, late master), from Demerara for Glasgow, 390 tons, and 14 9 and 6-pounders; loaded with sugar, rum, cotton, and coffee, and ordered her for the first port. [Had an engagement of about 35 minutes with this ship, in which her captain was killed by a cannon ball, 3 men killed, and 2 badly wounded; the masts, hull, &c. considerably injured, and some of the guns dismounted.—When she was first taken in with, Captain Watts requested the Decatur to send her boat on board, which was complied with, but the lieutenant who went in her was detained, and put into the hold of the vessel, and orders given to fire into the boat, but Captain Nichols was too quick for him.]

The Decatur engaged a brig, belonging to the above fleet, under the guns of the commodore's ship, but thinking the hazard too great to attempt boarding her, let her pass. She has made 120 prisoners, 60 of whom were sent to Halifax, and the remainder are on board; has only 20 of her crew on board, 81 being absent in prizes, and arrived previous to her. She has not lost a man during the cruise; has been to the longitude of about 20°, lat. 46°, thence run down the Western Islands, over the Grand Banks, by Halifax, and home. Has been chased by several men of war, but escaped from them. Her sailing greatly exceeds the expectations of her owners. She came into Newburyport in a very handsome style, with about 50 flags, of various kinds, displayed on board of her."—(*New-York Evening Post: 28 September.)*

"*From the Democratic Press.*

"We have been obligingly furnished with copies of the following letters, which we publish with pleasure, in the belief that the information in them will be, particularly that under date of the 31st of August, of much value to our armed vessels public and private.

"COPY

Of a letter from Admiral Sir J. T. Duckworth, commanding his Britannic Majesty's naval forces at Newfoundland, to D. Porter, Esq. commanding the U. S. frigate Essex.

"SIR,   "St. John's, *Newfoundland, August* 5, 1812.

"Your letter of the 2d inst. was delivered to me yesterday by Mr. M'Knight, midshipman of the United-States' frigate the Essex, under your command.

"I am sensible of the good disposition that you have evinced to alleviate the distresses of war, and would gladly have embraced your proposal for an exchange of the prisoners that we have respectively made; but I am sorry to say, that at the present moment, and under the peculiar circumstances of the case, it is not in my power to do so.

"In the first place, I have not yet received those instructions from my government which I consider necessary for the guidance of my conduct in respect to any such arrangement; and in the next, the officer whom you charged with the British prisoners has only delivered to me a list of their names, without producing any of their persons, acquainting me that they had taken the vessel from him, and put into another port of this island.

"I can only therefore assure you, that I shall report the matter fully to his Majesty's government, transmitting a copy of your letter, and of the list of British prisoners by which it is accompanied.

"I have had the pleasure of forwarding to Halifax the young gentleman you sent to me; an opportunity having already occurred—And I have written to the commander-in-chief on that station, requesting that he will endeavour to provide the means of his conveyance to the United States.

"I have the honour to be, Sir,
"Your most obedient humble servant,

J. T. Duckworth

"To Captain Porter, commandant of the U. S. frigate the Essex."

Extract of a letter from Admiral Sir J. T. Duckworth, to the Hon. Secretary of the Navy of the United-States, dated,

"*St. John's, Newfoundland, August* 31, 1812.

"A vessel captured, as the Alert has been, could not have been vested with the character of a cartel, until she had entered a port of the nation by which she had been captured, and been regularly fitted out from thence. For every prize might otherwise be provided with a flag of truce, and proposals for an exchange of prisoners; and rendered thus effectually secure against the possibility of recapture: while the cruising ship would be enabled to keep at sea with an undiminished crew; the cartels being always navigated by the prisoners of war.

"It is utterly inconsistent with the laws of war to recognize the principle upon which this arrangement has been made.

"Nevertheless I am willing to give a proof at once of my respect for the liberality with which the captain of the Essex has acted, in more than one instance, towards the British subjects who have fallen into his hands; of the sacred obligation that is always felt, to fulfil the engagements of a British officer; and of my confidence in the disposition of His Royal Highness the Prince Regent, to allay the violence of war, by encouraging a reciprocation of that courtesy by which its pressure upon individuals may be so essentially diminished.

"On the 4th of this month, a midshipman of the Essex arrived, and presented to me a letter from his captain, proposing an exchange for 86 British prisoners. The midshipman had, however, been placed alone in the charge of one of the captured vessels, with 86 prisoners, to conduct them to this port. A list of 40 prisoners of the same description, disposed of in the same manner, has been sent to me by the commander of the American private armed schooner the Rossie.

"It is incumbent upon me to protest in the strongest manner against the practice of conducting exchanges upon terms like these; and to signify to you, that it will be utterly impossible for me to incur, in future, the responsibility of assenting to them."—(*N. Y. E. P.* 30 *Sept.*)

MR. EDITOR, *Dover,* 1 *December,* 1812.

PERHAPS some of your nautical readers may be induced to employ part of a leisure evening at sea, in solving the following two mathematical questions, connected with naval architecture and navigation :—

1.—A given cone is placed in water with its *vertex* downwards: what part of the *axis* will be immersed if the specific gravity of the fluid be to that of the cone as 8 to 5?

2.—What time in the forenoon of the 16th of November, 1811, in latitude 53° 24' N. was the area of the shadow of a globe, placed on a horizontal plane in the sun-shine, equal to it's superficial content?

I take this opportunity of reminding those members of the naval profession who are addicted to astronomical pursuits, that the almanacs announce four eclipses during the coming year, 1813; *viz.*

February 1.— ☉ rises eclipsed at 7h. 28m. partly visible at Greenwich.

February 15.— ☾ is eclipsed at 8h. 36m. A.M. but invisible to us, being after that satellite is set below our horizon.

July 27.— ☉ eclipsed at 2h. 43m. P.M. invisible here.

August 12.— ☾ eclipsed at 1h. 41m. A.M. visible.

It is not requisite to dwell upon the utility to science of correctly observing such phenomena in different parts of the world : but it may perhaps not occur of itself to nautical observers to transmit their astronomical notes made on such occasions for the purpose of comparative publication in the N. C. as the common centre of information interesting to navigators, I hope they will attend to this hint from

COPERNICK.

MR. EDITOR,

I SHOULD feel myself particularly obliged to any of your correspondents, who would inform me,—

1. What is supposed to be the amount of the losses sustained by British subjects, by confiscation, in Denmark, in consequence of the expedition to Copenhagen ; and of the seizure of Danish ships and cargoes in the ports of this kingdom, previously to a declaration of war against Denmark?

2. The value of the Danish ships and cargoes, seized by our government, and of the seizures made at Copenhagen, previously to the declaration of war against Denmark; or, in other words, the amount of the so called Danish droits?

3. Whether the British subjects, whose property the Danes confiscated, in consequence of the seizure of Danish property by the British government, have received any indemnification, or any promise of indemnification, out of the fund of the Danish droits?

4. Whether any appropriations, and what, have been made out of the fund of the Danish droits?

5. What is the amount of the sums, which have been given to the Duke

of York, Princess of Wales, &c. out of the fund of droits? And more particularly if these presents were made out of the general fund of droits, or specifically out of the Danish droits?

6. What is the present amount of the general fund of droits?

7. What was the date (I think, some time in 1808) of the motion made by Lord Sidmouth, in the House of Lords, for keeping unappropriated the funds arising from the sale of the Danish ships and cargoes, so seized, with a view to restore them to Denmark? on which occasion, he proposed to retain out of that fund, sufficient to indemnify the British merchants and manufacturers, who had been reduced to ruin by the confiscation of their property in Denmark; and which latter proposal was opposed by Lord Hawkesbury, on the ground that this fund belonging entirely to his Majesty, the subject ought not to be entertained by parliament; and, for the rest, that the sufferings of the British subjects on this occasion, were of a nature, that should induce them to rely with confidence on the generosity of his Majesty.

8. Whether the sufferings of these British subjects have ever come to the knowledge of his Majesty? D. F.

** Connected, in some measure, with this subject, is the following letter, which, since the receipt of the above, has appeared in one of the public prints, addressed to Mr. Brand, M.P.

" SIR,

" By the question which you put the other day to the Chancellor of the Exchequer, relative to his laying before the house an account of the droits of Admiralty, previously to granting the supplies, I conclude it is your intention to found some motion on that statement, for the purpose of making that fund available for the public service—a measure in which you will have the countenance of every enlightened patriot. There is one circumstance, however, involving very important interests, which I trust you will not overlook on that occasion : I mean the losses which a great many British merchants suffered by confiscation in Denmark, and who conceive that no appropriation of the Danish droits can be more just and honourable than in indemnifying them for the losses which were brought on them by the very cause, nay in consequence of the very cause, which produced to his Majesty the same fund of droits. Whatever may be the result of any attempt to bring this enormous sum under the controul of parliament, I call on you most solemnly, on behalf of a great body of my much-injured fellow-subjects, to lift your voice against any further dilapidation of this fund of Danish droits, until the sufferers in question have received out of it every shilling of their losses. The British government, previously to a declaration of war, seize on the Danish property in this kingdom, amounting to a sum, which has been stated, in parliament, at 1,600,000*l*. The Danish government, in consequence of this, confiscate all British property in Denmark, amounting to about 280,000*l*. The two governments have, therefore, made a noble booty, while individuals in both countries have been ruined. This is a crying enormity, which I trust will shortly be laid before the public in all its nakedness. A. F. Z."

MR. EDITOR, Aberdeen, 6th December, 1812.

I have lately taken more than one opportunity, through the channel of your highly useful, and, to naval characters, most interesting work, of stating my sentiments, with respect to the propriety of employing additional lieutenants and commanders in our men of war; and I certainly feel much satisfaction in perceiving, that my sentiments have been in unison with those of the present board of Admiralty, who have made several important and useful alterations, within the last two or three months, by which many meritorious and deserving officers will be put in commission. The success of my former suggestions induces me to submit, with all possible deference, to the respectable board before mentioned, a few remarks on the situation of that class of officers denominated masters, in the royal navy, whose merits and services are generally acknowledged, but who have been far from meeting with the encouragement and protection to which the arduous and highly important nature of the duties of their station appear to give them a just claim. It has occurred to me, from perusing a letter in the NAVAL CHRONICLE, signed "A MASTER IN THE NAVY,"* that, after serving six years, masters ought to rank as lieutenants (passing for that rank the same as midshipmen), and, from that period, although still serving as masters, become eligible for obtaining the rank of commanders, when they may have distinguished themselves, or their services have entitled them to such promotion. At present, every lieutenant, I believe, is superior to the masters of our men of war. I would propose that, after the master passes for lieutenant, he should rank as such according to the date of his examination; that his commission be made out for master and lieutenant; and that the pay and allowances (which are too small both in army and navy), be made exactly alike. Were this plan to be introduced, it might lead, in a few years, to what I should consider as a still greater improvement; viz. the incorporation of masters with lieutenants, and committing the duties of the former, as now established, to the second lieutenant of the ship, or making them common to all, except in time of action, when they should devolve entirely on one,—the second lieutenant. I am certain that we should, if this were the case, have many more thorough-bred seamen, and first rate navigators, than we have; as every officer must then depend on himself, and on his own nautical knowledge, without having the master to consult.

An improvement is also much wanted with respect to *midshipmen*. Many young men, after serving, often, instead of six, ten, or twelve years, find it impossible to obtain commissions as lieutenants, although they have passed for that rank years before. I would propose, that, after passing,

---

* *Vide* page 295.

they should *all* become master's mates, with some additional pay, who do not immediately receive lieutenants commissions; and, after serving two, or at the utmost three, years in that capacity, they should, on certificate of such service to their captains' satisfaction, become *entitled* to their commissions as lieutenants, without any farther delay. I am persuaded that such an arrangement as this is very much wanted; for many young men of merit quit the king's service, in disgust, for that of the merchants, from finding it impossible to obtain promotion.

In the hope that these hints may attract the notice of the Admiralty board, and prove serviceable, I am, &c.

A FRIEND TO NAVAL MERIT.

MR. EDITOR,

I OBSERVE that several new frigates, of 38 and 36 guns, are to be immediately built of fir, to be finished in twelve months. They are no doubt wanted, particularly in consequence of the war with America; and I would therefore suggest, that they be built on a scale enabling them to cope with the American frigates. Perhaps this is intended. At present, our frigates are no match for the Americans. I hope also they will receive British names, and the French nomenclature soon become out of fashion in the navy. We have at present above 20 sail of the line, and 50 frigates in commission, with French or other foreign names; and we seem to have forgotten our own sea-port towns, counties, and even some of our naval heroes: for instance, Effingham, Torrington, Barrington, &c. Any thing rather than French: it is no longer, thanks to our brave seamen, a novelty to see a French man of war captured by a British ship, therefore there is no longer any necessity for retaining the French name, to let it be known that she was taken from the enemy.

BRITANNICUS.

MR. EDITOR,

I TRANSMIT some extracts of letters from an officer in the squadron cruizing off Venice, for the purpose of being inserted in your NAVAL CHRONICLE. J. J.

1812.—August. I am now at the end of business, and commence intelligence;—being off Venice, cannot do better than say a word or two about it. We reconnoitre it now and then, going within four miles of the entrance of Port, called Mala moco, and from the mast head see every thing in the harbour; but the city is low, and of mean appearance. The chu c ι towers being not only like pepper boxes, but those too without any kind of ornament; one only, out of 32, being a stone cupola, a very diminutive imitation of St. Paul's,* without the lanthorn, ball, cross, &c. Small islands, not $\frac{1}{4}$ of a mile in breadth, extend many miles along the coast, and defend

---

* London.

the Lagunes of Venice from ships,* or tempests from without. The French have a rear-admiral's flag flying on board an 80-gun ship, and a 74 and one frigate are besides ready for sea, and several small vessels of war. Two 74's ready for fitting in the arsenal, but they have such shallow water, that they are under the necessity of bringing their 74's over the bar of Mala moco, on kamels, a contrivance used by the Dutch.† The ships being built, are not manned, and *so well officered,* that a mid. who deserted from them some days ago, says, he has served two years, and was never at sea. I am not able to give you any further information about them, but that they are, as well as all the inhabitants of these parts in general, dissatisfied with the French government, which is a military despotism of the most arbitrary description. Every sort of public authority is executed by soldiers—As for instance, the news here is, that the Russians have defeated the French, Murat drowned, Boney prisoner—in short, of the worst ‡ description. The public authorities, therefore, ordered the public not to speak at all of the news, which is accordingly done—for the talking on the subject would only entitle those who do so, to the honour of execution by a military commission. Let John Bull beware. No person dares speak on any subject in Italy, not authorized by the public functionaries, it being constantly attended with the trifling inconvenience of being shot or plundered. The taxes are levied by the military, who charge for their trouble pretty handsomely—non-payment is attended with going into the army. Let Johnny beware again. With the mid. who deserted from the frigate t'other day, came a mate and boat's crew—Italians—sick of French fraternization. I took a small vessel the other day, under French colours, in our boats. The master was half-owner, belonging to Trieste. This man had some time ago supplied Captain Hoste with some provisions; the French discovered this, and kept the poor devil two years in confinement in irons, in the fortress of Trieste, and he only escaped shooting by the interference of the principal men of the town.

Sept. 27.—You will possibly see by the Gazette, that we have taken a valuable convoy of 16 vessels; and the Eagle§ lost her first lieutenant in the affair. But we have since experienced dreadful weather, and only one is yet arrived safe at Lissa. We are consequently in the most anxious state about the men on board them. We have seen one or two bottom up. Nothing I have yet seen equals the changeable and stormy weather in these seas; thunder, lightning, and rain, being the usual accompaniments.

Oct. 15.—I mentioned in my last our having taken a convoy of oil vessels, and the death of the Eagle's 1st lieutenant. I have to add, 8 or 9 have foundered, and we have to regret the loss of about 40 of the ship's company, either drowned or prisoners.

---

* Attacks by shipping. † Also by the Russians. ‡ For the French. § 74.

MR. EDITOR,

UPON inquiry, I find that the frigate, on board of which the late Captain (then Lieutenant) Whitby served, at the time of the battle of Aboukir, did not join Lord Nelson's fleet till after the action.

In troubling you with this correction, allow me also to notice an error of the press in the memoir of Captain Whitby, page 265, where Angrave, mentioned as the place of his birth, should have been printed Augrave.

I am, &c.

* * * * * * * * * * * *.

*** On referring to the Ist Volume of the NAVAL CHRONICLE, page 65, it will be seen, that there was no frigate whatever attached to the squadron which achieved the victory of Aboukir. According to Lord Nelson's official return, the Leander, of 50 guns, and the Mutine, of 14, were the only ships present of a lower rate than line-of-battle. The Leander, notwithstanding her comparatively inferior force, took her station in the line, and anchored athwart hawse of the French admiral.* The Mutine remained outside, to assist the Culloden, which had grounded. The Vanguard, bearing the commander-in-chief's flag, anchored the first ship outside of the enemy's line, and remained there till the close of the action.—ED.

A SERIES OF NAVAL BULLETINS,
BY LIEUTENANT D. O'BRIEN, R. N.

(Continued from page 400.)

BULLETIN THE SECOND.

FROM Albert we marched to Bapaume;† the road was excessively dirty and bad. Our men were so exceedingly weak this day, the weather being very inclement, raining incessantly, that the officer made some of his cuirassiers take three or four of them behind them, on their horses. It was about four in the afternoon when we arrived. The officer took us to a tavern; we were dripping wet. We were shewn into a spacious

---

* N. C. I. 54.

† A small fortified town in the department of Pas de Calais; the inhabitants boast that it has never been taken: the Duke of York was very near it in 1793, they informed us.

apartment, where a large table was laid out, and a number of genteel looking citizens were sitting round a stove, that was fixed in the centre of the room: they did not appear to take the smallest notice of us, nor to make room even for the officer, who was wet to the skin: however, he took the liberty of requesting they would allow him to approach, which they did, with seeming reluctance. We now endeavoured to dry ourselves, and get into the best plight we could; having ordered, at the same time, something for dinner, or rather supper, as it was about 7 o'clock. We were given to understand that it was the election day for a new mayor, in consequence of which the aldermen, &c. had ordered a dinner, which being served up, left us in full possession of the stove; a circumstance that pleased us greatly. Those gentlemen did not, in point of appetite, appear to deviate from their namesakes in a certain great metropolis, although I could not perceive that they had any turtle soup: champagne appeared to be the only wine they relished. Our supper was served us on a small table near the stove: those gents, as they became moistened with the generous juice of the grapé, condescended to become more familiar with the English prisoners and their officer; insisted upon touching glasses, and even on drinking champagne with them: and in the course of the night, those very people, who on our arrival had not vouchsafed to treat us with common civility, became so excessively pressing and free, that they absolutely proved a great annoyance. They even lavished, in their cups, a number of encomiums on the *noble nation* we belonged to—" *What a great pity*," said they, " *it was, that Englishmen and Frenchmen were not unanimous; they would then carry every thing before them, and conquer the whole world.*"

Our officer now informed us, that he was not allowed to conduct us any further—that he had applied to go with us all the way, but without effect. He appeared very much hurt at being denied, and took his leave of us for the night, declaring that he would see us in the morning before we parted. At daylight, on the 19th of March, a serjeant came to apprize us, that he was come with a guard of dragoons to conduct us to Cambray. So we instantly got up, and made every arrangement. , Our old officer appeared, and recommended us strongly to the serjeant; took an affectionate farewell of each, and literally shed tears at quitting us. We regretted his loss very much—he was tender-hearted and compassionate, and reflected honour on the nation that gave him birth, though certainly an exception to the generality of your Majesty's subjects. The people were so much attached to him, that he had not the smallest trouble; they did exactly as he wished.

At about half-past 8, in a most inclement morning, the wind right in our teeth; hailing and raining, without intermission, our poor crew all ranked, and miserably clad, we commenced our march towards Cambray,*

---

* This was formerly a very renowned city: it has a fort and citadel, and was once strongly fortified; but at present the walls are decaying, and in ruins. It is seated on the Scheldt, famous for the manufacturing of cambrics, which took their name from that city.

under an escort of dragoons; where we arrived about four in the afternoon, in a horrible state, all over mud and dirt. We were marched through the town, and placed in the citadel. The captains, as they styled us, were permitted to stop at the Cantine, but our poor seamen were put into a *souteraine*, where we endeavoured to procure them some fresh straw, which they rolled themselves up in, after refreshing themselves with a sort of soup, which we also provided for them. This was what the French call *soupe grasse*, made in the following manner :—They fill a large pot, or *marmite*, with water; when it begins to boil, they throw a handful or two of salt into it, agreeably to the quantity of water, chop up some cabbage, or herbs, which they also put in : and last of all, a ball of hogs-lard, kitchen stuff, dripping, or any other grease they may have. They then allow this soup to boil until the herbs, &c. are well done; then they serve it up in soup-plates or dishes, having previously bread cut in very thin slices in the said plates, &c. ; and charge twopence, and sometimes more, for each plate-ful. I have seen our landlady at Sees, a village near Rouen, after she had cooked us some beef-steaks, put all the gravy into the pan, fill it up with water; and, after she had kept the pan boiling for some minutes, she poured the whole contents into a large pot of water which she had boiling on the fire, previously prepared with salt and herbs, as before observed ; this she served out as soup to our poor seamen, at a most exorbitant price. We remained at Cambray until the 21st. when a severe frost, with snow, set in ; and we had to march, with the wind and snow, and hail at intervals, right in our faces, to Landrecy,* a distance of near six British leagues : our people were put into the gaol, and we were allowed the *honour* of stopping at the *palais national* tavern. They were very fair here in their demands. At daylight, March 22d, we commenced our route to Avesnes, where we arrived at about four ; they put us all indiscriminately into the town gaol. About five, the town major came to speak with us, and obtained us permission to go to a certain inn, which he pointed out, and where we were egregiously imposed on. The 23d we had another guard of dragoons, under the command of a serjeant, to escort us to our *dépôt*. At about three, we arrived at a poor little village called Hirson ; where, having no gaol, they billeted the seamen and us upon the inhabitants. We were quartered in a collar-maker's house. The poor people were extremely civil, and procured us tolerably good beds ; every other necessary they provided us with, we paid for. Next morning, the 24th of March, we took our leave of the collar-maker and family, and in the afternoon, at about four, arrived at a village named Maubert Fontaine ; a place still more poor and miserable than Hirson, where we were also billeted : the people with whom we were placed, were very great impostors, extorting double price for every thing. The next

---

* This town is in the north department, and late province of Hainhault ; the fortifications are very much neglected : it was taken by the allies, after a severe bombardment, in 1794, but retaken in three months afterwards.

morning, however, we parted, and proceeded to Rocroy,* where we arrived early, being a short march; our people were put into gaol; we made interest to be allowed an inn, and remained here 24 hours. Our landlord was a consummate scoundrel, he took every occasion of imposing on, and insulting us. On the morning of our departure, he produced us a sum total, of an enormous amount, without detailing the particular things supplied. We expostulated with him upon the enormity of the sum, and wished to know what such a demand could be occasioned by, as we were particularly economical, our funds being very low. He flatly refused any explanation, insisted upon payment, and used innumerable insulting and provoking epithets. We were obliged to comply, and recommenced our route to a small village called Fumy,† one stage from Givet, or Charlemont, our *dépôt*. We arrived here early, and were billeted; the people extremely civil. Next morning, the 28th of March, at 8 o'clock, commenced our last day's march. At about three (a short march), we arrived at our destination,‡ a distance of near seven hundred

---

* This town is in the department of Ardennes, tolerable well fortified, celebrated for the victory gained by the Prince of Conde (then Duke of Enghein) over the Spaniards, in 1645.

† Situated on the brink of the Meuse: there are famous slate quarries here.

‡ Givet is a fortified town in the department of Ardennes, and bishoprick of Liege, divided into two by the Meuse. That on the south side is called Little Givet: this town is commanded by a very strong fort and citadel (Charlemont) built upon an immense rock; the fortifications were constructed by Vauban, famous for his genius as an engineer. We never were allowed to enter the citadel, consequently were ignorant of the force or number of guns mounted on it. It was attacked by the allies in 1794, from an eminence on the south side of the river, but without effect.

The communication between Great and Little Givet is kept up by means of a ponton bridge; the centre boats are placed so as to be hauled out occasionally, to admit vessels to pass up and down, which frequently happens. There are passage boats that sail regularly between this town and Namur, which is ten or twelve leagues N.E. of it. Little Givet is chiefly inhabited by tanners, who carry on an extensive trade in this part of the country; they are greatly at a loss in the currying part of their business. Those people appeared very much disposed to be friendly with us; but we were kept so very close and strict, that it was impossible to form any acquaintance. Every necessary of life is cheap in this town; their beer is tolerably good. Wine is rather dear, as there are very few vineyards. We discovered a vast difference in the nature of the soil here, and that of the countries of the west, *viz*. Brittany, Normandy, and Picardie; this appearing much more barren and sterile. I have often observed with surprise how singularly neglectful they were of the fortifications of the town, and how particularly attentive with respect to Charlemont, the citadel. Our prisoners, at the commencement, were confined in this place; but when they became numerous, they were moved down to the horse barracks, from a dread, I suppose, of their revolting some day, and taking possession of that town and all. Had they once possession of one, the other would be entirely at their mercy and disposal. During our stay at this *dépôt*, four of the seamen escaped from their prison, two of

miles from Brest. We found the ship's company of H. M. frigates la Minerve, Captain Brenton, and Shannon, Captain Gower, with a number of men belonging to the merchants' service, here. A Mr Bradshaw, one of Captain B.'s clerks, visited us; he had permission to live in town, being acting in the situation of commissary to Captain Brenton; through him we were introduced to Captain Petervin, of the *gendarmerie* who was commandant of the prisoners of war. Our names and descriptions were taken, a Jersey man, named Garree, was interpreter,—the commandant appeared at a loss what to do with us; we were sent on the footing of private sailors to him; he appeared to be unwilling to put us with the people; hesitated and appeared undecided. However, at length, he agreed that we should go to the Stag's Head Tavern, as we appeared very much fatigued after so long a march. We accordingly proceeded, with Mr. Bradshaw, our guide, after returning Mons. le Commandant a thousand thanks for his condescension. This we found a very decent tavern, and the first in the town, which inspired us with an idea that this officer harboured *a good opinion of the adjutants.*—We ordered a tolerably good dinner. Mr. Bradshaw cut his mutton with us, and assured us that the commandant would permit us to lodge in the town. This intelligence exhilarated our drooping spirits prodigiously; we ordered an additional bottle of wine on the strength of it, and passed the evening as chearfully as circumstances would admit.

The next day, we waited with Mr. Bradshaw on the commandant; he received us with that politeness peculiar to his country.—We explained, through the interpreter, the cruelty of being sent to the seaman's *dépôt*, and treated differently from our brother officers: he agreed that our complaints were just, assured us he would immediately write to General Wirrion, at Verdun (who was commander-in-chief over the British prisoners), and state the case to him: at the same time he advised us to write to our commanding officer, and he would have our letter forwarded; desired us to remain quiet at our tavern, and he would do every thing in his power to alleviate our distresses. We returned him a thousand thanks, took our leave, and returned *à la tête de Cerf.*------------------------------------

Upon an overhauling of our finances, we had the mortification to find, that we could not remain many days at a tavern—not having a farthing allowed us for our subsistence; the 5½d. subsided the moment we arrived at the dépôt. Mr. Bradshaw could not render us any pecuniary assistance, without Captain Brenton's permission. Consequently our situation was becoming every moment worse and worse. As lodgings, we were informed,

---

whom belonged to our late frigate. On their being missed the following morning, parties of *gensd'armes* on horseback were despatched by the commandant to search for them in all directions; with strict orders to mutilate, *and in fact not to bring them back alive ;*—" that it might prove an example (using his own expressions) to the rest of the prisoners."—However, fortunately for those poor fellows, they escaped their pursuers, at least for that time.—The commandant was also frequently in the habit of riding into the prison yard, and taking his pistols out of the holsters, examining the priming, &c. This chiefly happened in the evening—the prisoners could not avoid laughing at such foolish conduct.

were excessively cheap in the town, we concluded that we had better apply to the commandant for leave to hire a couple of rooms, with cooking utensils, &c. than to continue any longer as we were. However, we dreaded that he might order us into the barracks with the people, if we commenced so early to demand favours. We therefore agreed to be extremely economical, and to wait a few days longer. Those days being expired, we made the intended application, and with success. He approved of our plan, and gave us written permission to walk about the town. This he took entirely upon his own shoulders, and assured us, that he relied upon our honour, not to go without the limits of the town : if we abused this indulgence, he should be severely punished. We declared our intentions were not to cause him the smallest trouble or uneasiness, which we were particular in attending to. This same day we hired two rooms at a Madame De Garde's, the widow of a ci-devant general. She provided us with two beds, for us four, cooking utensils, and every thing necessary for housekeeping, and at a very moderate price. We acquainted Mons. le Commandant of our success: he congratulated us greatly, but appeared to be sorry that we lodged in this old lady's house, as he observed she was *une jacobine*, and of *the old school*. We liked the old dame the better for this information, but were extremely cautious in mentioning it. Our *ménage* commenced the following morning. We took it by rotation to cook for the day. This, however, was remedied in a short time, as we were allowed our captain's steward, whose name was Allen, an infirm elderly man, to live with us, and cook, &c. for us. Our dishes were not very exquisite—soup and bouilli, with vegetables, were our daily fare, and this we feared could not continue long.

(1804.) No answer to the letters from Verdun ; the month's rent due ; finances extremely low. We solicited Mr. Bradshaw to allow us a pound of meat a day, as he did the private sailors: he could not conform to this request, without the sanction of Captain B. He wrote instantly respecting it, and received a favourable answer by return of post ; which proved of material service to *the poor adjutants*. We repeatedly wrote to be removed to the officers' *dépôt*, at Verdun, but did not receive any answer until the latter end of May. I am of opinion that a number of our letters never came to hand. Lieutenant Pridham, in his answer, gave us every expectation of being shortly removed, assured us that Captain Brenton and he were using every exertion to have us removed, and our rank rectified. On the 4th of June, the anniversary of his Majesty's birth-day, low as our pecuniary circumstances were, we contrived to give the commandant and paymaster of the *dépôt* a dinner. The latter, whose name was Payne, we had received many civilities from: the day passed very agreeably, until about sun-set, the time settled for locking the seamen up in their different apartments ; when they gave three cheers in commemoration of the day that gave their gracious Sovereign birth, and hauled in the colours of all nations, made by themselves, that they had kept all day streaming out of each window, taking care to have the French tri-coloured flag under all ; which was never noticed by either commandant or guards. The cheers of nearly a thousand men made no little noise ; they resounded hideously in our ears as we sat at table, our lodging being contiguous: the commandant was greatly alarmed, imagined that the seamen had revolted, and had actually got out of prison: so great was this officer's hurry, that he made but *one step* from the *top* of the stairs to the *bottom.* We had a little trouble in getting him on his legs again, and were greatly rejoiced in finding that he had received no injury from this *step*—assuring him there was no foundation whatever for his fears. However, he would be convinced in person, therefore went to the prison, and was highly pleased to find every thing perfectly tranquil. Being returned, he observed that the English were *des braves gens,* and he would drink another glass of wine in commemoration of King George's birth-day. The national dish, roast beef, with plum pudding, was not forgotten upon this occasion. Monsieur liked the well-done, or outside part of the former, extremely; but the latter, neither of our guests would touch for a long time. At last, by dint of persuasion, they condescended to taste it, and so sudden was the transition made upon them by this taste, that we had some pains to secure ourselves a part, though it was a pretty sizeable pudding. They exclaimed, as they gulped it down, " *Sacre bleu comme il est bon."*—" *Ma foi oui,"* repeated the other alternately. We felt highly pleased at the sight, and laughed heartily.

At a late hour, or rather, in regard to the morning, an early one, *Messieurs* took their leave, evidently in great spirits, and we retired to rest.

Since our arrival at this *dépôt,* several of the stoutest, and apparently most healthy of our men, died of a fever, supposed to be caught in some of the gaols on the road; our poor servant Allen was seized with it, and expired in a few days..........In the latter part of June, our commandant appeared much altered, and became extremely distant; we were at a loss to know the cause of so sudden a change. Mr. Bradshaw informed us, that he once observed to him, " that the English officers (as he was kind enough to style us) were excessively proud. I never meet them, but I take my hat off, whilst they only lift theirs." Admitting this to have been the case, we had a better opinion of him, than to suppose that so trivial a matter could cause so great an alteration in his behaviour. He one night sent a guard of gend'armes to take us from our lodging to the guard-house, for being in the streets after 9 o'clock; when it is scarcely dark at this season of the year; although we had no regular time prescribed by him to be in doors: there we remained, on a cold pavement, all night, at a loss to know what we had been guilty of. Our guards assured us, it was merely the caprice of the commandant. At noon Mr. Bradshaw visited us, without giving us any hopes of release. The commandant informed him, that we were confined for not answering a centinel on his post, who had hailed us: this we denied, as we had not passed one that night. Mons. Brasseur, the second in command, then came to see us, and expressed great sorrow at seeing us confined without cause; he waited on the commandant, became responsible for our conduct, and had us moved to our lodgings, where we were ordered to continue without stirring out, until further orders.

Our poor landlady received us with the greatest joy imaginable, bathed us with her tears, and had some refreshments ready, although she had sent us a very good breakfast to the guard-house by her own son. In three days we were once more liberated, but were always confined whenever a religious procession, or any amusement, took place, which, at this particular time, was very frequent. Our chief amusement was a game at billiards, and a walk round the ramparts, or rather ruins. We frequently met with military officers at the billiard table, who always behaved with the strictest politeness, and made us an offer of the table the moment we entered the room; which, of course, was declined, until they had finished. I purchased a grammar and dictionary, with an idea of learning French, and also begged of the lady at the library, to choose me an easy French book, that I might begin translating, which she had the kindness to do; but to my surprise, her choice was a collection of obscenity, which obliged me to return it, to have it changed. She then gave me a novel, and laughed heartily at my disapproving of her book, as she termed it. We were constantly, from the commandant's conduct of late, under apprehensions of being close confined with the people; he appeared more inveterate against me, than against any of the others. However, about the 10th, or 12th of July, we received a letter from our commanding officer at Verdun, stating, that General Wirrion had at last sent an order for Mr. Mahony and me, to be conducted to Verdun *dépôt*; but not a word about either the boatswain or gunner.* The commandant received the order by the same post. Mr. Bradshaw received also directions from Captain Brenton, to supply us with cash to enable us to proceed; all this intelligence arriving at the same time, nearly overwhelmed us with joy; but the other poor fellows, who were to remain, were disconsolate, fearing much the commandant's severity when we quitted them.

1804.—The 16th of July, was the day appointed for our departure. Mr. Mahony had a bad foot, in consequence of which a cart was ordered, which carried us both. Every thing was now arranged; and we had previously been permitted to see our ship's company, a pleasure we had been deprived of for some weeks. We took an affectionate farewell of our shipmates and landlady, and began our route under the escort of two gend'armes.

[To be continued.]

---

* Those poor fellows, we had the inexpressible sorrow of seeing pass through Verdun, in less than three months after we quitted them, together with two of our seamen, that I observed had escaped from Givet prison; they were arrested close to the water side, near Dunkirk, and were on their way to Bitche to be punished. Garree, the Jersey man, who acted as interpreter, through some pique, informed the commandant, that the boatswain and gunner had an idea of making their escape: he gave him credit for this information, and despatched these poor fellows to a *dépôt* of punishment, where they remained for two years and a half, which caused the death of the boatswain. This very scoundrel, the informer, a few days after their departure, made his escape, and arrived safe at Jersey.

PLATE CCCLXXVII.

APE'S HILL, or Mont de Singe, is the Mount Abyla, or Abila, of the ancients, and was one of the reputed Pillars of Hercules, as Calpe, now Gibraltar, was the other. The Spaniards recognize it under the name of Sierra Ximea; and, in the old Flemish book of pilotage, entituled, " Le Nouveau et Grand Illuminant Flambeau de la Mer," published in 1689, it is called Schemincquel. It is situated in the empire of Morocco, on the Strait of Gibraltar, about 10 or 12 miles E N.E. from Al-cassar. It is nearly S. from the S.W. cape of Gibraltar bay, on the European shore. A small island lies near the coast, off the W. side of this lofty mountain, near which is 15 fathoms water; and, in a shallow bay, on the E. side, there are from 7 to 12 fathoms. From Alcassar to Ape's Hill, the ebb, which begins to run westward at 4 o'clock, at spring tides, is very narrow along shore. At this part, the tides differ considerably from those in the middle of the strait.

We shall avail ourselves of the present opportunity, to notice one or two other places, in this neighbourhood, on the African shore.—Cape Spartel, the south western promontory of the Strait of Gibraltar, lies in latitude 30° 46' N. and longitude 5° 7' 12" W. from Greenwich.

Ceuta, according to French authority, is in latitude 35° 54' N. and in longitude 7° 36' W. from Paris. From Cape Spartel to Ceuta point, the extreme length of the strait is seven marine leagues.

The best survey of this coast, is that which was made by Captain (now Admiral) John Knight, in the year 1799. According to observations subjoined to that survey, the bays of Ceuta and Tetuan afford anchorage from 18 to 22 fathoms, with good shelter from westerly winds; but, when the easterly, or "levant" winds spring up, it is necessary to get under weigh. In June, 1799, the English fleet, under Admiral Lord Keith, anchored here, and was plentifully supplied with water from the river Mazari, near Tetuan.—The magnetic variation, at the period alluded to, was 2 points westerly.

As a naval and military station, Ceuta is of more importance than Gibraltar, and is, in fact, the key of the strait; inasmuch as the navigation thereof is carried on nearer to the African than to the European shore.

For this place, by a suitable equivalent, it would, in the opinion of many, be highly desirable to effect an exchange with Spain, when saved from French sovereignty.—Gibraltar, perhaps, important as it is, might be offered; for it is a possession of more glory than advantage; and, in our hands, will ever, under a settled order of things, be a bar to cordial connection between the two nations. This consideration appears to deserve the notice of the English ministry. A project was on foot; for possessing ourselves of Ceuta, by a *coup de main*, in 1808 ; but, being too long delayed—as is frequently the case, in this country of deliberation and preparation, where the phrase, " secret expedition," means any thing rather than secret or expeditious—it proved abortive.

Ceuta was conquered from the Moors, by Henry, Duke of Viseu (who died in 1463) son of King John the Ist of Portugal. It continued a possession of that crown, till the revolution of 1640, when it fell to Spain, and was finally ceded to that country, by the treaty of Lisbon, in the year 1688. It withstood a vigorous siege by the Moors, in 1697.

HYDROGRAPHY, PILOTAGE, &c.

ENGLAND.

WIGHT, ISLE.

6th November, 1812.

PURSUANT to the directions of the Lords-Commissioners of the Admiralty, the Red Buoy of the Nab, going into St. Helen's, and the Light-Vessel lately stationed there, are both removed rather more than half a mile to the south-westward (by compass), of the situation where they respectively were placed, according to the former notice from the Trinity-House.* The buoy now lies on the west :—and the Light-Vessel on the east edge of the Nab Rock, about 80 fathoms asunder :—It is therefore to be particularly observed, that ships now must not pass between the Buoy and the Light-Vessel. Notices, containing farther particulars, with instructions, will forthwith be published and distributed for the information of the masters and pilots of H. M.'s ships, and of navigation in general.

ST. GEORGE'S, (or IRISH) CHANNEL.

13th November, 1812.

THE Light-House, on the Smalls, in St. George's Channel, has received so much damage in the late tempestuous gales, as to render it impracticable to exhibit any light therein during the present winter : but every necessary preparation will be made for reinstating the Light-house, and renewing the exhibition of the light, as early as possible in the ensuing summer.

---

* See N. C. XXVIII. pp. 129, 313,

ATLANTIC OCEAN.

AZORES.

The islet of *Sabrina*, near the island of St. Michael, which owed its origin to a sub-marine volcano, has gradually disappeared, since the month of October, 1811, leaving an extensive shoal.* Smoke was discovered still issuing out of the sea in February last, near the spot where this phenomenon appeared.—(*Edinburgh Correspondent*, 24 October, 1812.)

AFRICA.

CAPE OF GOOD-HOPE.

Whereas the coast to the N.-Westward of the Cape of Good-hope has been already described;† and as a chart of this promontory and circumjacent coast forms the concluding embellishment of the present volume,‡ it has been deemed also the most appropriate subject for hydrographic selection. The following descriptive remarks upon this important position are adopted for the most part from the works of the present intelligent hydrographer to the East India Company.

Dassen, or Coney, island is the only remarkable object between Saldanha and Table bays, being 6 leagues southward from the former, and 9 N.N.Westward from Robben isle at the entrance of the latter: it is a low sandy islet, about 4 or 5 miles from the main land, dangerous and rocky on its western side; but there is understood to be anchorage within it. Between this place and Table bay the water has a black stagnated appearance. This part of the coast is of moderate height: but the land contiguous to Table bay is so remarkable that it cannot be mistaken, and appears like an island, when seen from sea at a considerable distance. The highest part, from whence the bay derives its name, is situated at the S. part of it right over Cape-town: it is 3,500 feet high, level on the top, and falls down nearly perpendicular at the E. end, till it joins the Devil's mount, a rugged peaked mountain, nearly as high as the former; and separated from it by a small gap. The W. end of Table mountain is also nearly perpendicular from the top to a considerable distance, and then has an abrupt declivity till it joins the base of another rocky, conical mount, called the Sugar-loaf, or Lion's head; which is about 2100 feet high. On the summit of this latter there is a signal-flag generally displayed when a ship appears; in some places it is so steep that it can only be ascended by steps cut in the soil. This is joined on the N. side by an oblong mount, about 1000 feet high, called, from a fancied resemblance, the Lion's rump. The Lion is on the W. and S.W. sides of the bay, as the Table and Devil are on the S. side. On the E. side commences the low sandy isthmus

---

* N.C. XXVIII. 57.

† For the hydrography of Saldanha, and a chart of that bay, see pp. 129, 148. of this volume.

‡ Plate CCCLXXVIII.

between Cape-town and False bay. The land from Table mountain southward to the extremity called the Cape of Good-hope, is high and uneven. When, during the summer months the Table begins to be covered with a white cloud, it indicates a strong S.E. or E.S.E. wind. In January, February, and March, these winds blow sometimes with great fury over the before-mentioned mountains, and through the gap between them, driving the white clouds like wool in rolling fleeces over the perpendicular sides of the table. Ships therefore ought to moor with good cables, for they are liable to drive and bring both anchors a-head: in fact they have been known to be driven from Table bay by these S. Easters with all their anchors down, and not to regain the anchorage till after five or six days. When the Table is free from clouds the S. Easter will be mild, and then a gentle sea-breeze generally blows in on the W. side of the bay, while there is a fresh S.E. breeze prevailing from the E. side of it half-way across during most of the day. The prevailing winds, at Table bay and near the Cape of Good-hope are from S.E. and S. during summer; the S.E. winds blowing more or less in every month of the year, and generally bringing settled weather: these winds extend more than 200 leagues to the eastward of the cape. N.E. winds are less frequent than any, and never continue long. In May, June, July, August, the W. and S.W. winds blow strong, attended with cloudy weather and fogs; but the most violent winds during these months are the N. Westers; which frequently blow in severe storms for several days together, with a clouded sky, and sometimes accompanied with lightning, hail, or rain. These winds extend as far as latitude 27° S. in the track towards St. Helena, and prevail far to the westward, but much farther eastward of the Cape, blowing generally with most violence near the land. The summer is from October to April; in which season it has been thought safe to sojourn in Table-bay, notwithstanding ships have suffered by N.W. gales in November, particularly in that month of the year 1799, when H.M.S. Sceptre and several others were wrecked. These N.W. gales are occasionally experienced about the Cape in every season of the year; and although ships have been driven on shore by them, more than once in the month of April, the Dutch fixed on the 10th May for all ships to leave this place, as the period when the strong N.W. winds might be daily expected. Such a mountainous sea is forced into the bay by some of those storms, that it is almost impossible for any ship to withstand them. The early navigators to India seem often to have touched at Table-bay for refreshment in the winter months; and in cases of exigency ships still sometimes put in there during that season, notwithstanding the extreme risk of N.W. gales. Although an eddy current may be setting along shore southward from Dassen isle to Table bay, the regular current at the same time often sets round the Cape to the N. Westward, as far as the high land on the W. side of Table-bay: ships therefore should endeavour to make the land to the southward of the entrance if bound into the bay, particularly if the wind inclines to the S.W. From the Cape to Table bay the shore is mostly steep, and may be approached within 1½ or 2 miles distant, in sailing along towards Green point, the northern extremity of the peninsula. About 3 leagues southward from this point, at the N. end of an excavation in the land, Hout bay is situated. It is said this bay can afford shelter from all winds; but it can only be to a small number of ships, as it is rather confined, and has a reef of rocks at the entrance. A ship in passing the points which form this bay, should keep 1½ or 2 miles from the land, to give a berth to some straggling rocks detached from the shore; and she may keep about the same distance from it till she reaches a low verdant point (of the same name) to avoid some rocks at a small distance from the shore between the Sugar-loaf and Green point : most of these are above water, and within half a mile of the shore : the depths of water at about 1 or 2 miles off, from 50 to 60 fathoms.

Robben, or Penguin, island,* is low and flat, distant about 5 miles northward from Green point: this last may be approached near, the soundings being regular towards it; but the island must not be passed nearer than 2 miles, on account of a sunken rock called the Whale, about 1½ mile distant from it's S. extreme, on which the sea breaks when there is much swell; at other times it is not perceivable. A ship may borrow on the point to 10, 9, or 8 fathoms without danger, then steer towards the shipping in the road with regular soundings of 8, 7, or 6 fathoms. In the fair season regular sea-breezes from W. prevail in the mornings, which continue till noon or longer; these are followed by easterly winds from the land, which blow fresh during the afternoon, and frequently till the return of the sea-breeze on the following morning. The S.Easter sometimes comes from the land with great fury : it is, therefore, prudent to take a reef, or even two, in the top-sails, before a ship reaches Green point, if it be near or past noon. By neglecting this precaution when rounding the point with all sail set in a light breeze, ships have been seen suddenly to meet the fiery S.Easter on opening the bay, and be compelled to let every thing fly to save their masts; and one of these ships, whilst the people were aloft securing the sails, ran nearly a-shore on the E. side of the bay, in the act of veering. If abreast of the point a ship should meet such a blast too strong for her to work to windward, she ought to bear away, and anchor under the island : or if well in the bay, she may run for the channel between the island and the main, and anchor in 8 or 9 fathoms, at ¾ of a mile distant from its eastern shore; where she may lie till the morning, when the S.Westerly breezes will enable her to weigh and run for the usual anchorage before Cape-town. The S.Easters have been known to blow so strong, that a ship could not effectuate the preceding manœuvre, but was driven to sea till the violence of the wind abated. The other resource in these cases is to make short tacks to the southward of Green point, under the lee of the high land, until the S.Easter should subside; and this seems preferable to the risk of losing an anchor by endeavouring to bring up in a strong gale. All ships going into Table bay should use the channel

---

* The disappearance of this island by means of volcanic convulsion, is recorded amongst other contemporaneous gleanings, in Vol. XXIII. p. 187 : but seems to rest on dubious authority ; or at most the submersion must have been of partial extent.

between the point and island: but for going outwards, the channel to the E. of the island is most proper; for the S.E. winds blowing out of the bay produce a partial current or outset between the island and the northern shore; whereas the current frequently sets past Green point into the bay to replace the quantity of water thus displaced.

"After working from Dassen island to the entrance of Table bay, in January, 1798," says Mr. Horsburgh, " we observed in the morning that it was calm under the high land in the S. channel; but a steady light breeze was perceived on the water between Penguin island and the N. shore. To preserve the breeze we proceeded to work in by the N. channel. About 2 P.M. the S.Easter came to blow strong, carried away our top-sail-sheets, and we were obliged to close reef the top-sails, when beating through between the island and the main. We found a lee current while the wind was strong, and gained little ground until it moderated, about 8 P.M. In beating through, we did not stand nearer to the island than 8 fathoms; the soundings were from 8 to 12 fathoms, sandy ground, but did not decrease much in nearing the main. From where we tacked on each side the depths were generally from $9\frac{1}{2}$ to 11 and 12 fathoms across the channel. On the main, three rocky points project a small distance from a sandy beach; near these, several sunken rocks were seen shining under water, distant $\frac{1}{4}$ of a mile or more from the shore. Near the outermost of these points we shoaled from 10 to $7\frac{1}{2}$ fathoms at a cast; whilst in stays I perceived some rocks under water about 2 cable-lengths within us, which render it unsafe to make too free with the shore in this part. The reef placed in the charts, projecting about a mile from the E. part of the island, was not discernible." Between Green point and Penguin island the ground is foul: should a ship be driven by the swell towards the Whale in a calm, and be obliged to anchor, the stream-anchor will be the most convenient for this purpose, where the ground is rocky. The proper anchorage in the bay abreast the town is sandy bottom; the W. side of it is clear ground all over. In the summer months a ship may moor in 7, 6, or 5 fathoms, with Green point N.W. $\frac{1}{2}$ N. the body of Table mountain S.W. $\frac{1}{4}$ S. and the flag-staff on Lion's mount W. $\frac{1}{2}$ S. Off shore from $\frac{1}{2}$ to 1 mile, and from the town 1 or $1\frac{1}{4}$ mile. When N.W. winds are expected, do not anchor under 6 or $6\frac{1}{4}$ fathoms; in which depth the swell runs more regular than in shallow water. At these times ships should ride with a whole cable, or more; for they are liable to drive if the anchors be not well seated in the sand; and when a ship drives, it is difficult to bring her up, as the anchors scrape along the surface of the sand, and do not take hold while the heavy seas are striking against her. The best ground is from 5 to $7\frac{1}{2}$ fathoms: when so far out as to have the Lion's head in one with, or open to the northward of the Lion's rump, the ground is rocky quite across the bay. Table bay is an excellent place for obtaining refreshments; the water is good; but wood is scarce. Sheep are to be had in abundance, at moderate prices; also other provision of various kinds; particularly vegetables and fruits, which are good. The water is conducted in pipes to the wooden pier; where boats fill it by hoses, leading from the conduits to their casks. The atmosphere is generally cool in the night, although the sandy soil is often greatly heated by the sun's rays: this occasions hot gusts of wind to blow out of Table bay, in the evenings. In this bay it is difficult to obtain rates for chronometers on ship-board in the fair season ; for correct altitudes of the sun cannot be obtained, owing to the mutability of refraction near the horizon. During seven days stay here, Mr. H. took nearly 100 sets of fore-noon and afternoon altitudes of ☉ to regulate 7 chronometers; but did not get their rates very exact. Objects in the horizon at the entrance of the bay were sometimes reflected double; the picture of a vessel under sail was seen in the atmosphere above her, and other objects variously represented. Therefore it is advisable, if a ship doth remain several days at this place, to land the chronometers, and correct their rates by altitudes taken upon an artificial horizon, or else in a basin of water on ship-board, when there be little wind. The longitude of Cape-town probably is not yet definitively ascertained. Comparative determinations of its geographic site will be given, together with those of other remarkable positions in its vicinity, at the end of this memoir. The tide seldom rises more than 5 feet perpendicular in Table bay; high-water at half-past 2 o'clock full and change of ☾. Ships moor with their anchors about N.W. and S.E. The variation of the compass has been ascertained by the mean of many morning azimuths, taken by two compasses, to be as here-under:—

Table mountain E. 12 leagues, variation 25° 40′ W. February 1798.
———————— 14 ————, ———— 25° 40′ ———————— 1800.

The Cape of Good-hope is the southern point of the peninsula which separates False and Table bays from each other : but the popular notion of its being the southern-most extremity of the African continent is erroneous, inasmuch as Cape Agulhas (whose name is corruptly changed by English mariners into *Lagullas*), bears from it E. 20° S. distant 30 leagues.† From Table bay southward the land is rugged, and of considerable height, ending in hummocks at the Cape-point.

False bay is formed by Cape of Good-hope on W. side, and by Cape False E.ward. This latter is a steep bluff, resembling a wedge, which may be seen at 8 leagues distance, and appears to hang over westward when viewed from S. It was named Hanglip by the Dutch, and is sometimes called Hottentot's point. The entrance of the bay from cape to cape is about 5 leagues, nearly on the same parallel. It extends N.ward into the land about 5½ leagues, being a large open gulf of a square form, comprehending several small bays within it's limits. The dangers to be avoided, yet known to navigators, are found on the western side, that is to say: the Bellows is a large rock even with the water's edge, about 2½ or 3 miles from the Cape point proper, bearing S. b. W. true. In 1803, when the Bellows rock was on with the Cape by compass, it bore N. 35° E. and in one with the western extreme N. 17° W. the Cape then bearing N. variation being 26° W. On this rock the sea generally breaks. About 2 miles or

---

† The meaning of the Portuguese word Agulhas is " needles." In 1598, the magnetic variation at this cape was 30′ W. at Cape of Good-hope 25′ E. and at Cape False, 0.

more N.E. is another sunken rock, called the Anvil, distant about 2 miles from the Cape: there is a passage between these rocks, and between them and the land, with soundings from 20 to 7 fathoms; but these passages are not frequented, the current running strong, and the bottom being rocky. In August, 1778, the Colebrook was lost on an unknown rock, said to be 1½ league N.E.Easterly from the Bellows. By many navigators this is thought to have been the Anvil, the true position seems not exactly known: it is said by Captain Fraser to bear S E. by E. from the Cape; by Colebrook's journal S.E. 4 miles; Mr. Bligh places it E.S.E. 2′ S. and Captain Huddart thinks it about E. from the same point, variation allowed. There is thought to be 14 feet water on the Anvil, but its bearing is so differently stated, that there is ground to suspect the existence of another rock hereabouts. When the Colebrook struck, the Royal-Admiral passed between the rock and the land: the former ship had 30 fathoms water before and after striking. Across the entrance of False bay the depths of water are from 40 to 50 fathoms; but a little westward of mid-channel there is a rocky bank, with soundings on it from 16 to 30 fathoms, having 45 and 46 within it, and 60 without, southward. The middle and eastern parts of the bay are deemed free from dangers; but the ground is foul and improper for anchorage. If a ship coming from the W. with a N.W. wind be bound into the bay, she may pass southward of the Bellows at discretional distance: when abreast of it at 2 or 3 miles, the course ought to be E.S.E. to E. b. S. by compass, till she has run 5 or 6 miles: she may then haul up E.N.E. and N.E. taking care not approach to the Cape point nearer than 5 miles, till it bears W.N.W. by compass: being then to the northward of the Anvil or Colebrook rocks, she may haul in to 2 or 3 miles from the western shore into moderate depths for anchoring. On the western side of False bay, a ridge of rugged mountains is perceivable, extending to the northward as far as Table bay. On the eastern shore is a similar ridge, reaching to the head of the bay. The Table mountain is discernible in clear weather at 60 miles distance southward, and is seen very distinctly from the entrance of False bay. The space between the ridges at the head of the bay is low, the mountains seen over it being at a great distance in-land. About 4 leagues from the Cape, near the N.W. corner of False bay, at the foot of the highest mountain on the coast, is situated Simon's, or Semon's bay. Ships put into this anchorage when Table bay is unsafe, from April to September; but in every month of the year this is considered as a place of safety, although it is open to N.Easterly winds, because these seldom or never blow strong; so that this cove may be considered as a secure retreat for ships in most seasons of the year; but it cannot afford shelter from the S.E. winds to more than 13 or 14 sail. Refreshments and provisions are supplied from the interior and Cape town, distant from hence about 6 leagues: water, of a good quality, is conveniently obtained. At a small distance from the S. point of this bay, there is an islet, or rock, in the form of a barn, called Noah's-ark; About a mile N.N.Eastward from this, a small reef lies near the water's edge, called Roman rocks; between these two dangers is the usual channel for ships. From Roman rocks E N.E. about 2 leagues lies Seal island, surrounded by rocks above and under water, some of which extend 2 and 3 miles southward, and near 4 miles eastward; breakers are always seen when the sea runs high. In 1795, the Warren-Hastings struck on one of the southernmost patches, whilst in stays: False cape S. b. E. ¾ E. by compass, Cape point S.W. ¼ W. a high peak at the bottom of False bay N. b. W. and the shipping in Simon's bay W. b. N. ¾ N. Ships turning to windward in False bay should not approach Seal island nearer than 4 miles on the S. side, or 3 on the S.W. But the danger most in the way of ships working to or from Simon's bay is the rock on which the Trident and Asia struck in 1795, and other ships since. This, however, has been so amply described at a preceding page (232) of this volume,* that we need not at present revert to it, except to state, that subsequent to the last publication of the N. C. the Hydrographer has been favoured with the following additional memorandum relating to the Trident, or Whittle, rocks, which were recently given to an eminent navigator when upon the spot. The marks are (by compass) as follow:—

  Cape point .... S.W. ½ W.
  Noah's-ark, 6 or 6½ miles .... N.W. b. N.
  Cape Hanglip .... S.E. ¾ S.
  Muysenberg, houses .... N. ¼ W.

The situation is 4 miles from the western shore; and it has 12 feet on it at low water.

A ship coming into False bay from the E. with a S.W. or Westerly wind, should steer for the middle of the bay, or for the western side; when the Cape point bears, by compass, W. by N. she is clear to the northward of the Anvil, or other supposed dangers in that vicinity, and she may then borrow within 2 miles of the shore, or even less if requisite. When about 6 miles within the Cape point, and abreast of the rocky hill over little Smith's-winkle bay, she ought not to stand farther from the shore than 3 miles, in passing Whittle's rocks; and should it fall calm, she may chuse a proper depth for anchorage on the western shore. Ships may pass to the eastward of the rocks, and between them and the reef of Seal island: but for strangers the western channel seems preferable, the land affording sufficient guidance. After passing Whittle's rocks, a ship may continue to steer or work about 2 miles from the western shore. On approaching Simon's bay, Noah's-ark will be discerned off the S. point; but the most conspicuous marks are white sandy downs, appearing like snow, in the hollows between the mountains to the N.W. of Noah's-ark. This islet, which is of level out-line, is steep-to, having 9 fathoms close to it; the soundings in the channel between it and Roman rocks are from 10 to 15 fathoms: from hence a ship should steer direct for the white marks above-mentioned, till she reaches the anchorage. A ship working with a N.W. wind, may proceed by the outer channel, which is much wider than the channel between the Roman rocks and Noah's-ark, taking care not to

---

* Also see N.C. II. 260.

borrow very close to the N.W. side of the former, as a rock, with 3 or 4 fathoms on it, is said to lie at a small distance from them in that direction. To work into False bay, to the eastward of Whittle's rocks, a ship should not bring Cape point to the S.W. by S. by compass, till Noah's-ark bears N.W. by W. and when on the starboard tack bring Noah's-ark nothing to the N. of this bearing, by which Whittle's rocks will be avoided; but she must not stand far northward to Seal island, on one of the sunken rocks connected wherewith the Warren Hastings struck, as has already been mentioned. In Simon's bay the depths of water are 8, 9, and 10 fathoms: a good berth for a large ship is Noah's-ark, on with Cape Hanglip S. 35° E. by compass, and the north battery N. 13° W. off shore about 1 mile; or a ship making a long stay may moor farther in, with Cape Hanglip shut in by the S. point of Simon's bay; but it is best to chuse a distance convenient to have room in case of driving; although the bottom is good, and the anchors hold well when seated in it. Ships moor in this road N.W. and S E with the stoutest ground tackle to N.W. from May to September, and *vice-versâ* during the above months: but during those months Table bay is to be preferred. In Simon's bay it is high water at ½ past 3 o'clock, full and change of ☾: the rise and fall seldom exceed 3 feet, and little current is perceptible. From October to April, S.Easterly winds prevail, but do not continue longer than 5 or 6 days at a time, and are constantly succeeded by variable winds. In Simon's bay it frequently happens that these winds, after blowing very strong for a day and part of the night, abate towards morning, and as in Table bay are succeeded by a land-breeze from N. N. W. By taking the advantage to weigh with the first of this breeze, a ship sometimes may get to sea before the return of the S.Easterly wind; if she cannot clear the land before that wind sets in, the most prudent plan is to return to the anchorage. Ships bound eastward should leave the bay when N.W. winds begin to blow; if bound westward, in the winter season, they ought to remain till these winds are on the decline, and get under sail when they shift to westward, as it is probable they will veer from W. to S.S.W. and S. which will be favourable for doubling the Cape. Ships from the E. bound into False or Table bays, when the S.E. winds prevail in the summer months, should take care not to fall to leeward of the Cape, for frequently it will be found difficult to gain the former bay, if a ship makes the land about the Cape, bearing to the eastward during strong S.E. winds. Several ships from India, at different times, bound into Table bay with stores, have been obliged to bear away for St. Helena; having made the high land about the Cape bearing eastward, they apprehended too much time would be lost by endeavouring to reach the bay.

The Cape of Good-hope is frequently the boundary of very different kinds of climate, for ships homeward-bound have in general unsettled cloudy weather, and the winds variable to the eastward of it; but so soon as they get round to the westward of this promontory, the weather generally becomes favourable, with a steady S.Easterly wind; this may be expected more particularly in the summer season.

Geographical sites of places mentioned in the preceding memoir.

Names.	Authorities.	Latitude S.	Longitudes E. from Greenwich. Meridional	Time. h. m. s.
Dassen, isle	Horsburgh	33 24 0		
Cape, town	De La Caille		18 26 0	
——	Mason and Dixon		18 27 0	
——	recent observations		18 32 0	
——	Requisite Tables, 1802.	33 55 42	18 23 7	1 13 32
——	Mean of several chronometers from Table bay to St. Helena*		18 34 0	
——	Horsburgh: mean of 6 meridional altitudes ☉	33 58 0	18 28 30	
——	Conn. des Tems, 1803†	33 55 15	18 24 0	
Cape of Good-hope	——	34 29 0	18 23 15	1 13 33
——	Horsburgh‡	34 27 0	18 31 30	
Simon's bay	——	34 15 0		
Cape False	Requisite Tables	34 16 0	18 44 0	1 14 56
False bay	——	34 10 0	18 33 0	1 14 12
Cape Agulhas	Horsburgh	34 58 30	20 18 0	

S.

STATE PAPERS.

St. James's, November 30, 1812.

THIS day his Royal Highness the Prince Regent proceeded in state from St. James's palace to the House of Lords, where he arrived at a quarter before two o'clock; and having alighted from the state coach, he was received at the portico by the great officers and others, and proceeding to the robing room in the usual manner, his Royal Highness was there robed, his hat on his head, and the procession moved into the house in the following order :—

---

* The measurement was 24° 11', during a run of 13 days; and James-town is allowed for in 5° 36' 30" W.

† The calculation of the longitude from this authority is founded on the allowance of 2° 20' 15" difference between Paris and Greenwich.

‡ In computing the longitude of the Cape, Mr. Horsburgh has adopted the mean quoted above for the town, and added thereto 3' difference from thence.

Officers of the Household.
Pursuivants.
Heralds.
Peers.
Norroy, King of Arms.
The Lord Privy Seal.
The Lord President of the Council.
The Lord Chancellor.

| Serjeant at Arms. | Black Rod.
 The Earl Marshal with his Staff.
 The Coronet of His Royal Highness the Prince of Wales, borne by the Earl of Yarmouth.
 The Cap of Maintenance, borne by the Marquess of Winchester. | Garter.
 The Deputy Lord Great Chamberlain.
 His Majesty's Crown, borne by Earl Powlett, K.T.
 The Sword of State, borne by the Earl of Liverpool. | Serjeants at Arms. |

His Royal Highness the
PRINCE REGENT.

His Royal Highness seated on the Throne, the great officers and others standing on the right and left, the Commons were summoned by black rod, and the speaker, attended by the members, being at the bar, his Royal Highness delivered the following most gracious Speech, in the name and on the behalf of his Majesty, to both Houses of Parliament:—

My Lords, and Gentlemen,

It is with the deepest concern that I am obliged to announce to you, at the opening of this parliament, the continuance of his Majesty's lamented indisposition, and the diminution of the hopes which I have most anxiously entertained of his recovery.

The situation of public affairs has induced me to take the earliest opportunity of meeting you after the late elections. I am persuaded you will cordially participate in the satisfaction which I derive from the improvement of our prospects during the course of the present year.

The valour and intrepidity displayed by his Majesty's forces, and those of his allies, in the Peninsula, on so many occasions during this campaign, and the consummate skill and judgment with which the operations have been conducted by General the Marquess of Wellington, have led to consequences of the utmost importance to the common cause.

By transferring the war into the interior of Spain, and by the glorious and ever-memorable victory obtained at Salamanca, he has compelled the enemy to raise the siege of Cadiz; and the southern provinces of that kingdom have been delivered from the power and arms of France.

Although I cannot but regret that the efforts of the enemy, combined with a view to one great operation, have rendered it necessary to withdraw from the siege of Burgos, and to evacuate Madrid, for the purpose of concentrating the main body of the allied forces; these efforts of the enemy have, nevertheless, been attended with important sacrifices on their part, which must materially contribute to extend the resources, and facilitate the exertions of the Spanish nation.

I am confident I may rely on your determination to continue to afford every aid in support of a contest which has first given to the continent of Europe the example of persevering and successful resistance to the power of France, and on which not only the independence of the nations of the peninsula, but the best interests of his Majesty's dominions, essentially depend.

I have great pleasure in communicating to you, that the relations of peace and friendship have been restored between his Majesty and the Courts of St. Petersburgh and Stockholm.

I have directed copies of the treaties to be laid before you.

In a contest for his own sovereign rights, and for the independence of his dominions, the Emperor of Russia has had to oppose a large proportion of the military power of the French government, assisted by its allies, and by the tributary states dependent upon it.

The resistance which he has opposed to so formidable a combination, cannot fail to excite sentiments of lasting admiration.

By his own magnanimity and perseverance, by the zeal and disinterestedness of all ranks of his subjects, and by the gallantry, firmness, and intrepidity of his forces, the presumptuous expectations of the enemy have been signally disappointed.

The enthusiasm of the Russian nation has increased with the difficulties of the contest, and with the dangers with which they were surrounded. They have submitted to sacrifices of which there are few examples in the history of the world; and I indulge the confident hope, that the determined perseverance of his Imperial Majesty will be crowned with ultimate success; and that this contest, in its result, will have the effect of establishing, upon a foundation never to be shaken, the security and independence of the Russian empire.

The proof of confidence which I have received from his Imperial Majesty in the measure which he has adopted of sending his fleets to the ports of this country, is in the highest degree gratifying to me; and his Imperial Majesty may most fully rely on my fixed determination to afford him the most cordial support in the great contest in which he is engaged.

I have the satisfaction further to acquaint you, that I have concluded a treaty with his Sicilian Majesty, supplementary to the treaties of 1808 and 1809.

As soon as the ratifications shall have been exchanged, I will direct a copy of this treaty to be laid before you.

My object has been to provide for the more extensive application of the military force of the Sicilian government to offensive operations; a measure which, combined with the liberal and enlightened principles which happily prevail in the councils of his Sicilian Majesty, is calculated, I trust, to augment his power and resources, and at the same time to render them essentially serviceable to the common cause.

The declaration of war by the government of the United States of America, was made under circumstances which might have afforded a reasonable expectation that the amicable relations between the two nations would not long be interrupted. It is with sincere regret that I am obliged to acquaint you, that the conduct and pretensions of that government have hitherto prevented the conclusion of any pacific arrangement.

Their measures of hostility have been principally directed against the adjoining British provinces, and every effort has been made to seduce the inhabitants of them from their allegiance to his Majesty.

The proofs, however, which I have received of loyalty and attachment from his Majesty's subjects in North America, are highly satisfactory.

The attempts of the enemy to invade upper Canada have not only proved abortive, but by the judicious arrangements of the governor-general and by the skill and decision with which the military operations have been conducted, the forces of the enemy assembled for that purpose in one quarter, have been compelled to capitulate, and in another have been completely defeated.

My best efforts are not wanting for the restoration of the relations of peace and amity between the two countries; but until this object can be obtained without sacrificing the maritime rights of Great Britain, I shall rely upon your cordial support in a vigorous prosecution of the war.

Gentlemen of the House of Commons,

I have directed the estimates for the services of the ensuing year to be laid before you, and I entertain no doubt of your readiness to furnish such supplies as may enable me to provide for the great interests committed to my charge, and afford the best prospect of bringing the contest in which his Majesty is engaged to a successful termination.

My Lords, and Gentlemen,

The approaching expiration of the charter of the East India Company, renders it necessary that I should call your early attention to the propriety of providing effectually for the future government of the provinces of India.

In considering the variety of interests which are connected with this important subject, I rely on your wisdom for making such an arrangement as may best promote the prosperity of the British possessions in that quarter, and at the same time secure the greatest advantages to the commerce and revenue of his Majesty's dominions,

I have derived great satisfaction from the success of the measures which have been adopted for suppressing the spirit of outrage and insubordination which had appeared in some parts of the country, and from the disposition which has been manifested to take advantage of the indemnity held out to the deluded by the wisdom and benevolence of parliament.

I trust I shall never have occasion to lament the recurrence of atrocities so repugnant to the British character; and that all his Majesty's subjects will be impressed with the conviction that the happiness of individuals, and the welfare of the state, equally depend upon a strict obedience to the laws, and an attachment to our excellent constitution.

In the loyalty of his Majesty's people, and in the wisdom of parliament, I have reason to place the fullest confidence. The same firmness and perseverance which have been manifested on so many and such trying occasions, will not, I am persuaded, be wanting, at a time when the eyes of all Europe, and of the world, are fixed upon you. I can assure you, that in the exercise of the great trust reposed in me, I have no sentiment so near my heart as the desire to promote, by every means in my power, the real prosperity and lasting happiness of his Majesty's subjects.

At the Court at Carlton-House, the 28th of February, 1811,

PRESENT,

His Royal Highness the PRINCE REGENT in Council.

WHEREAS his Majesty was pleased, by his general order in Council of the 5th of April, 1805, touching the performance of quarantine, to direct, that where any ship or vessel shall attempt to enter into any port or place in Great Britain, or the islands of Jersey, Guernsey, Alderney, Sark, or Man, whether such port or place shall have been appointed for the performance of quarantine or not, the superintendant of quarantine or his assistant (if there shall be such superintendant or assistant at such port or place), or, if not, the principal officer of H. M.'s Customs at such port or place, or such officer of the Customs as shall be authorized by the commissioners of the Customs, or any four or more of them to act in that behalf, shall go off to such ship or vessel, and shall, at a convenient distance from such ship or vessel, keeping to windward, demand of the commander, master, or other person having charge of such ship or vessel, answers to certain preliminary questions therein set forth : and whereas it is deemed expedient, that in the case of ships coming from, or having touched at any port or place on the continent of America, or the islands adjacent thereto, or coming from or having touched at any of the ports in the West Indies, the following questions, in addition to the said preliminary questions, should be put to the commander, master, or other person having the charge of such ships ; *viz.*

Q. How long after sailing from your port of lading, or having touched at any port on the continent of America, or the islands adjacent thereto, or any of the ports in the West Indies, was the first appearance of disease observed ?

Q. How had the persons attacked been employed before they came on board ?

Q. Had they been employed in loading or unloading the ship before she left the port ?

Q. Had the place which they inhabited before they sailed the reputation of being healthy ? or was it subject particularly to the remittent fever incident to the country ?

Q. Had the fever been frequent in the place before the ship sailed ?

Q. Did the persons who were ill on board your ship fall sick nearly about the same time, or within a few days of each other; or did the disorder spread successively from one to another, and increase considerably or did it abate gradually, and cease to multiply as the distance from the ports you sailed from or touched at as aforesaid increased ?

Q. What was the greatest number of persons ill at the most sickly period of your voyage?

Q. What were the whole number of persons on board your ship when you sailed ?

Q. What is the whole number of persons now ill on board your ship ?

Q. Can you state what were the symptoms of illness with which your crew was first attacked, and what was the daily succession and change in them till their death ?

Q. Whether any and what medicines have been used, and what methods have been adopted to prevent its spreading among the crew ?

Q. Whether attention has been paid to cleanliness and ventilation on board your ship ?

His Royal Highness the Prince Regent is thereupon pleased to order, in the name and on the behalf of his Majesty, and by and with the advice of his Majesty's privy council, that the questions above set forth, in addition to the preliminary questions directed by his Majesty's general order in council of the 5th of April, 1805, respecting the performance of quarantine, be put to the commanders, masters, or other persons having charge of ships or vessels coming from or having touched at any port or place on the continent of America, or the islands adjacent thereto, or coming from or having touched at any of the ports in the West Indies ; and his Royal Highness is further pleased to order, in the name and on the behalf of his Majesty, and by and with the advice aforesaid, that such commanders, masters, or other persons having charge of such ships or vessels, shall, upon such questions being put by the superintendant of quarantine, or his assistant, or principal officer, or other officer of the Customs, authorized by the commissioners of his Majesty's Customs, or any four or more of them, to act in that behalf, give a true answer to the same in writing, or otherwise, and upon oath, or not upon oath, according as he shall be required by such superintendant, or his assistant or principal officer, or other officer of the Customs authorized as aforesaid, under such pains and penalties as are inflicted by an act passed in the forty-fifth year of his Majesty's reign, intituled, "An Act for making further Provision for the effectual performance of Quarantine." And the right honourable the lords commissioners of his Majesty's Treasury, the commissioners for executing the office of lord high admiral of Great Britain, the lord warden of the Cinque Ports, the master-general, and the rest of the principal officers of the Ordnance, his Majesty's secretary at war, and the governors and commanders-in-chief, for the time being, of the isles of Guernsey, Jersey, Alderney, Sark, and Man, are to give the necessary directions herein as to them may respectively appertain.*

W. FAWKENER.

SLAVE TRADE.

MAURITIUS GOVERNMENT NOTIFICATION.

UNDER existing circumstances, his excellency the governor deems it proper to give publicity to the following correspondence, addressed to him by his excellency Rear-admiral Stopford, accompanied by an extract of an act of parliament recently passed in the imperial parliament, enacting fresh penalties against any farther traffic in slaves.

By order of his excellency the governor,
(Signed) A. BARRY, Chief Sec. to Gov.
Port Louis, Isle Mauritius, 15th May, 1812.

SIR, *H. M. S. Lion, Table Bay, Feb.* 13, 1812.

In order to remove any misapprehension in the minds of the inhabitants of the isle of France, relative to the effect likely to be produced by the decision of the court of Vice-Admiralty on the subject of La Prudente, detained as prize when clandestinely endeavouring to introduce slaves into the isle of France, but which vessel has been restored by the decision of this court; and in order to give full notice, that the slave trade shall not be allowed to be carried on contrary to law, notwithstanding the encouragement given to it by this decision, I have to request that your excellency will be pleased to announce in any public and effectual manner you may think proper, my firm determination to resist any encroachment of the law upon this subject, and to direct all such vessels clandestinely endeavouring to introduce slaves into the isles of France and Bourbon to be detained, and to await the decision of the high court of Admiralty in England.

I have the honour to be, &c.
ROBERT STOPFORD, Rear-admiral.
His Excellency Governor Farquhar, &c.

SIR, *H. M. S. Lion, Table Bay, Feb.* 17, 1812.

Having just received from England an act of parliament, enacting fresh penalties against any further traffic in slaves, and as I conceive the earliest information of such an act to be essentially necessary at the islands under your excellency's government, I send copies of the clauses more particularly relating thereto, and regret that I cannot send you the act itself, being only supplied with one copy of it.

---

* For the State Paper, properly forming the sequel to this, *vide* page 408.

Your excellency will therefore see the utter impossibility of my granting any permission or authority to the commanders of his Majesty's ships under my orders to grant any passport, or in any way suffer the admission of slaves into the islands under your excellency's government, without submitting myself to the penalty of this very strong and positive act of parliament.

I have therefore sent orders to the senior officer at Port Louis, to seize all vessels and slaves that he may meet.

I have the honour to be, &c.

ROBERT STOPFORD, Rear-admiral.

His Excellency Governor Farquhar, &c.

(Here follows the extract of the act of parliament.)

His excellency the governor having received intelligence, through a private channel, that regulations have been made for the trade between England and these colonies, and considering that the information may be relied upon, though not yet officially communicated to this government, hastens to notify, for the satisfaction of the merchants, planters, and other inhabitants of these islands who-n it may concern, that the same commerce will be free to every individual, making application to be allowed to carry it on, and subject only to the same regulations as the commerce of private merchants between other parts of India to and from England; save, however, that the merchandise is to be freighted on ships, supplied either by the India Company, or by individuals who may desire to furnish and send the same as their own private property, under licenses to be obtained for that purpose from or through the special orders of the East India Company; the commerce between these colonies and India remaining as heretofore.

By order of his excellency the governor,

(Signed)   A. BARRY, Chief Sec. to Government.

Port Louis, Isle Mauritius, 15th May, 1812.

AMERICA.

Extracts from a Memorial, addressed to the President of the United States, by more than 1500 of the Inhabitants of the County of Rockingham, in New Hampshire, on the 5th day of August, 1812.

" WE have witnessed, with sincere and deep regret, a system of policy pursued by the general government, from the embargo of 1807, to the present time, tending most obviously, in our view, to the destruction of the commerce of these states.

" The alarm excited in our minds by the favourite and long continued " Restrictive System," is raised still higher by the late declaration of war against Great Britain; an event which, we believe, in the present defenceless circumstances of the country, will be productive of evils of incalculable magnitude.

" The impressment of our seamen, which forms the most plausible and popular of the alleged causes of war, we believe to have been the subject of great misrepresentation. The number of these cases has been extravagantly exaggerated. Every inquiry on the subject strengthens our conviction, that the reputed number bears little relation to the true number. We are among those to whom instances of impressment, if they did actually exist to any considerable extent, must be known; yet we cannot find them out. Some of the members of this meeting have been constantly employed in commercial pursuits, and have had ships on the ocean from the peace of 1783, until the ocean became unnavigable, as to us, by the embargo of 1807; and yet during all that time have never suffered the loss of one native American seaman by impressment. Other members of this meeting have, as masters of vessels, long inhabited as it were, on the seas, and have been visited hundreds of times by British ships of war, and never had an American seamen taken from them by impressment.

" If so many of our seafaring fellow citizens were actually in bondage, they must have been taken from the inhabitants of the Atlantic coast. They would be from among our brethren, sons, relations, and friends.

" It is well worthy of notice, that the greatest apparent feeling on this subject of impressments, and the greatest disposition to wage war on that account, are entertained by the representatives of those states which have no seamen at all of their own; while those sections of the community, in which more than three-fourths of the mariners of the United States have their homes, are, by great majorities, against that war, among the professed objects of which, the release of impressed seamen forms so principal a figure.

" It is well known that England pretends to no right of impressing our seamen. She insists only that she has a right to the service of her own subjects, in time of war, even though found serving on board the merchant ships of other nations. This claim we suppose to be neither unfounded nor novel. It is recognized by the public law of Europe, and of the civilized world. Writers of the highest authority maintain, that the right belongs to all nations. For the same reason, say they, that the father of a family may demand the aid of his children to defend himself and his house, a nation may call home her subjects to her defence and protection in time of war.

" But if this were not so, is our nation to plunge into a ruinous war, in order to settle a question of relative right between the government of a foreign nation and the subjects of that government? Are we to fight the battles of British seamen? Nay more—are we to espouse their cause, in opposition to the cause of our native mariners?

" Fatal, indeed, would it be to the important interests of the navigating states, if the consequence of this war should be, that the American flag shall give the American character to all who sail under it, and thus invite thousands of foreign seamen to enter into our service, and thrust aside our own native citizens.

" England has always professed a willingness to adjust this subject by amicable arrangement. She has repeatedly called on us to do our part towards effecting such adjustment. She has reminded us of the facility, we may say the falsity, with which American protections are obtained; of the frequent instances, in which Irishmen, and even men that cannot speak a word of our language, are found with American protections in their pockets. She has expressly and officially offered to prohibit, by severe laws, all impressment from American vessels, if the American government would enact laws prohibiting American officers from granting protections or certificates of citizenship to British subjects. She has, also, through her minister, offered to restore *every native seaman* that our government could name, as being under impressment. For years preceding the declaration of war, our government has been, in a manner, silent on this subject. When the arrangement was made with Mr. Erskine, the present administration themselves did not consider any existing difficulties on the subject of impressment as insuperable obstacles to peace.

" The blockade, and orders in council,—the other causes of war, bear no better examination than the subject of impressment. The blockade, now so grievous to be endured, we know was regarded, at the time it was laid, as a measure favourable to our interests. We know this, upon the express declaration of Mr. Munroe, then our minister in England. We have his own words, that it would be regarded " in a favourable light," and that it " promised to be highly satisfactory to our commercial interests."

" By what train of reasoning this favour is now turned into an injury, and an injury of such magnitude as to justify war, we are utterly at a loss to comprehend.

" We are equally unsatisfied with the arguments used, to prove that the decrees of France were repealed in November, 1810. Against such supposed repeal of the French decrees, we have the express declaration of the French government itself, as late as March, 1812, alleging that those decrees did then exist. We have also had daily evidence of their operation, in the destruction of our property; and some members of this meeting have convictions of the existence and operation of those decrees, down to the very moment of our declaration of war; which convictions being produced by great and repeated personal losses, in the seizures, detention, confiscation, and burnings, under those very decrees, are not likely to be removed, by any ingenious comments on the terms of an ambiguous, deceptive and fallacious instrument, like the Duke of Cadore's letter.

" The conduct of France, in relation to the repeal of her edicts, exhibits to our view, a scene of the most contemptible fraud and juggling, that ever disgraced the court of any nation.

" The British orders in council, we are informed, are now revoked. We cannot but lament, that the declaration of war was forced and hurried, as if to put us beyond the benefit of favourable events. Every attempt at postponement was ineffectual; and the question was taken, at a moment, when, perhaps, a month's delay would have removed the principal ground of complaint, and averted the awful calamity.

CAPE OF GOOD HOPE.

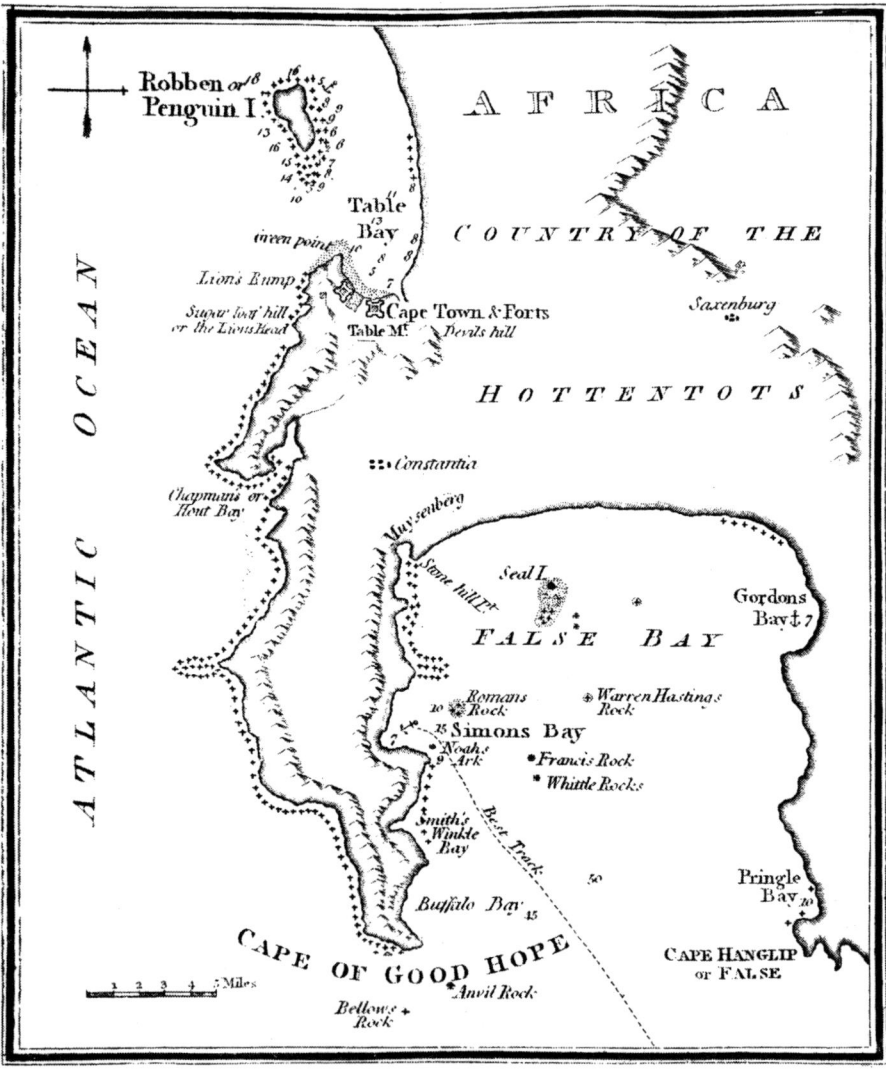

"But although we lament the present war, on all accounts, yet do we deprecate it most of all, as we view in it, as we fear, the harbinger of French alliance.

"On the subject of any French connection, either close or more remote, we have made up our minds. *We will, in no event, assist in uniting the Republic of America, with the military despotism of France.* We will have no connection with her principles or her power. If her armed troops, under whatever name or *character, should come here, we shall regard them as enemies.* No pressure, domestic or foreign, shall ever compel us to connect our interests with those of the house of Corsica; or to yoke ourselves to the triumphal car of the conqueror and the tyrant of Europe."

PLATE CCCLXXVIII.

THE NAVAL CHRONICLE already contains such full and important information, relating to the Cape of Good Hope,* that, in addition to the hydrographical details, commencing at page 479 of the present Volume, we must here be as concise as propriety will admit.

This promontory was reached, by Bartholomew Diaz, in the year 1486, or 1487; but it was first doubled, by Vasco de Gama, in 1494. Diaz called it *Cabo de las Tormentas*, or the Cape of Tempests; on the return of that navigator, it received its present prophetic name from Emanuel, King of Portugal.

The Cape and its vicinity were formerly much infested with lions, tigers, wolves, &c.; but, in proportion as the population of a settlement increases, such animals always retire, and their numbers are now so small, and they keep at so great a distance, that the inhabitants have very little cause for alarm. Wild game, however, is still plentiful; and the number of antelopes and deer is prodigious. There are also elephants, rhinoceroses, elks, &c. Among the rare birds which are found at the Cape, the indicator, or honey bird, deserves notice. This is a small brownish bird, of the cuckow *genus*, which, having observed a nest of honey, immediately flies in search of some human creature, to whom, by its fluttering, whistling, and chirping, it communicates the discovery. It then leads the way directly towards the place, flying from bush to bush, or from one ant-hill to another; and, when close to the nest, it remains still and silent. When the

---

* In Vol. III. page 361, are some particulars relating to the natural products of the Cape; in Vol. V. page 417, is a View of the Cape, accompanied by historical and descriptive details; in Vol. X. page 8, *et seq.* inserted in the memoir of Admiral Lord Keith, are the official accounts of its capture, by that officer, in the year 1795; in Vol. XI. page 14, is an account of the slaves at the Cape; in Vol. XII. page 380, is a second View of the Cape, and a South Whaler; in Vol. XIV. page 194, are *Considerations on the comparative value of the Cape of Good Hope and the Island of St. Helena;* and, in Vol. XV. pp. 248, 250, 261, are the official statements of the capture of the Cape, by Commodore Sir Home Popham, and Major-general Sir David Baird, in 1806.

honey has been removed, the indicator flies to feast on the remains. By similar conduct it is also said to point out, with equal certainty, the dens of lions and other beasts of prey.

Timber, from want of cultivation, is a scarce and expensive article. Corn is now generally grown beyond the isthmus and along the western coast, on the farther side of the great north and south chain of mountains, beyond which, the remote districts furnish a supply of horses, sheep, and horned cattle. Most of the European, and several of the tropical fruits, have been introduced into the colony, and cultivated with success. Peaches and apricots, when in season, are sold at the rate of a shilling per hundred.

In addition to butcher's meat and game, the market of Cape Town * is constantly supplied with various sorts of sea-fish, which are caught in the bay; and there is seldom any deficiency of European vegetables for the table.

In the year 1795, the British government, with the view of effecting the capture of the Cape of Good Hope, sent out a military force, under the orders of General Craig, protected by a squadron commanded by the present Admiral Lord Keith, and the late Admiral (then Commodore) Blanket. This expedition, the strength of which had not been proportioned to the magnitude of the enterprise, was fortunately reinforced, after its arrival; and its object was consequently effected, in the surrender of the whole colony, by capitulation, in the month of September†.—The captors remained in quiet possession of the settlement for upwards of ten months, when a Dutch squadron arrived, with the vain hope of dispossessing them. It fell into the hands of those against whom its efforts were intended to be directed; ‡ and, from that period, until the treaty of Amiens, when the settlement was restored to the Dutch, its possessors enjoyed a tolerable degree of tranquility; the inhabitants also enjoying, under the mild auspices of the British government, that freedom and happiness to which they had before been strangers.

Several warm debates took place in the British parliament, as to the propriety of restoring the Cape of Good Hope to the Dutch; and it was the opinion of many of the best informed men in the country, that it ought on no account, to be given up. Its surrender, indeed, could only be considered as a sacrifice to Buonaparte, with the view of obtaining peace.

The inhabitants of the settlement were decidedly in favour of the English; and very little doubt can be entertained, that, had the attempt been made, it might have been in our hands at the commencement of the present war; but, probably for some state reason, no effort was made to obtain it until the autumn of 1805. An expedition was then sent out, the naval part of which was entrusted to Commodore Sir Home Popham, while the command of the troops, consisting of between four and five

---

* Cape Town, as will be seen by referring to the chart, is situated on the S.E. angle of Table bay. A plan of the castle, or fortress, which was erected by the Dutch, will be given, at a future period, in the NAVAL CHRONICLE.

† N. C. X. 8, *et seq.*

‡ N. C. V. 421.

thousand effective men, were given to Major-general Sir David Baird. This force arrived in Table Bay on the 4th of January, 1806; and, on the 18th of the same month, the Dutch governor (Jansens) having signed a capitulation for a general surrender, Britain was once more possessed of one of the most important settlements in the world.*

As a naval station, the Cape is extremely valuable, on account of the facility with which our cruisers may be despatched thence, either to India or to America; and from the shelter which it affords to shipping, when distressed by the violent storms that frequently occur in those latitudes. Had the French, or their vassals the Dutch, been permitted to hold the Cape, France possessing at the same time the Isle of France and the Mauritius,† and the Rio de la Plata belonging to Spain, over whose movements she, very recently, had an implicit controul, our trade must have been materially injured. The enemy, by keeping cruising squadrons at those places, would have had our homeward-bound shipping so completely within their power, as scarcely to afford them the possibility of escaping. No ships, but those of England, can attempt a voyage to the East Indies, on account of its length, without some such convenient place as the Cape of Good Hope to stop at for refreshment. To English sailors, from their habitual hardiness, and from the peculiar advantages which they enjoy respecting the plentifulness and superior quality of their provisions, such a half-way port might not perhaps be of much consequence; but as our ships have frequently a number of Lascars, or unseasoned troops on board, it becomes highly necessary for their relief.

The cheapness of provisions at this settlement, is another argument much in its favour. "In the year 1797," says Mr. Barrow, "the squadron consumed 1,085,266 pounds of fresh meat, and 1,167,995 pounds of biscuit, or about 3000 pounds of each a day; besides 184,358 pounds of soft bread, 217,813 pounds of flour, and 1,066 bushels of wheat: it consumed, moreover, 1,226,738 pints of wine, and 244,904 pints of spirits; together with a considerable quantity of butter, vinegar, raisins, peas and beans; all the produce of the colony, and all of them articles which were to be procured at a moderate rate. I conclude, from the quantity expended, that in this year, the squadron, supposing it to consist of 3000

---

* N. C. XV. 248, 250, 261.

† It is not very long since Buonaparte announced the comparative impregnability of the isles of France and Bourbon, to reduce which, the occupation of an army of 30,000 men, for six months, was pronounced necessary. It has since appeared, according to their own consistent statements, that the garrisons of all the "*small French colonies*"—Martinique, Guadaloupe, the isle of Re-union (Bourbon), and the isle of France—"*could not have amounted at most to more than 2,000 men!*" If the islands here mentioned are the small colonies, we should be glad to have the larger ones pointed out. Buonaparte suddenly discovered, on the capture of the isle of France, &c. that all these colonies "furnished nothing to the parent state"—that they cost France twenty millions a year—and that their produce was already so cheap in London, that it would not pay the expense of carriage to Europe. To this notable discovery, the old fable of the "Fox and the Grapes" furnishes a very satisfactory answer.

men, was subsisted mostly on Cape produce; and, therefore, it cost the government little more than one-fourth part of what it would have done on most other stations."

The Cape, as a military station, is also highly important. According to Mr. Barrow, in the whole seven years that we before retained possession of this settlement, the military department cost no more than 1,789,181*l.* or 255,597*l.* on an annual average. This was during a time of war, while we maintained there an army of 5000 men, and were at the expense of erecting a number of fortifications. It is estimated that, in peace, the contingencies and extraordinaries of the army would not amount to above 25,000*l.* or 30,000*l.* yearly; and that this sum, as well as all the demands of the civil department, might, by proper management, be defrayed out of the revenues of the colony. The air of the Cape is particularly salutary and beneficial to troops, after their passage from Europe; and to invalids, who may be returning from India. The mildness of the climate renders the Cape a wholesome and commodious station, for forces that may be destined for the East or West Indies; and enables the recruit to undergo the fatigues of drilling with a comparative degree of ease, that would be impracticable in tropical latitudes. Consumptive complaints are prevalent at the Cape; but they are thought to proceed chiefly from the sudden change of temperature, especially from heat to cold. Dropsy is a very general disease in middle-aged subjects; and from apoplexy, schirrosities of the liver, &c. the natural consequences of intemperance, instances of longevity are extremely rare, few exceeding the period of sixty years. The mortality in Cape Town, during an average of eight years, while it was in possession of the English, was about five in two hundred among the white inhabitants, and under three in a hundred among the slaves.

In a commercial point of view, this settlement is of less consequence, though capable of much improvement. It might be made an important *dépôt* for British trade with America; and, if well supplied with British and India goods, the clandestine trade which is carried on under neutral colours would be destroyed, because the traders could not afford to sell at so low a price as the East India Company. As a *dépôt* for the Southern Whale Fishery, so important to the commerce and navigation of Britain, the Cape might be rendered essentially useful.

It is stated, in an early Volume of the NAVAL CHRONICLE,* that, at the beginning of the last century, when Governor Van-Der-Stel planted the vineyards of Constantia, whence, as is well known, the most delicious wines are annually brought to Europe, he caused a basket of earth to be taken up, at the distance of every hundred roods, for a considerable tract of country round the Cape. On that spot, the soil of which was found to be the least brackish, the vineyards were planted. His excellency, the present governor, impressed with the idea, that, in the present—and probably future—state of intercourse between Great Britain and France, the Cape wines might be rendered capable of superseding those of the latter country, has issued instructions † for improving and extending the cultiva-

---

* III. 361. † February 14, 1812.

tion of the vine, for preparing the fruit, &c.; and has also offered gold medals, of considerable value, to such of the inhabitants as may be most successful in their efforts, with respect to the greatest quantity, and finest quality of their wines. Should these endeavours succeed, with wine, it may not unreasonably be expected, that Britain will derive a supply of brandy also, from the Cape; and thus would her independence on France, for those productions, be secured in perpetuity.

Marine Law.

COURTS MARTIAL.

A COURT MARTIAL was some time since holden, in the Downs (Admiral Foley, president), on Lieutenant Richard Stewart Gamage, of H.M.S. Griffon, for stabbing a serjeant of marines belonging to that ship, which caused his death. The minutes of the trial have not appeared; but, from the following defence, which the prisoner delivered, the reader will become sufficiently acquainted with the facts of the case:—

" *Mr. President, and Gentlemen of this Hon. Court,*

" It is with the utmost poignancy of feeling, with the deepest bitterness and regret, that I appear before you in my present awful and unfortunate situation. To the wretch hardened in crimes, and growing grey in the pursuits of villany, the recollection of having actually deprived a fellow-creature of existence, the divine gift of the Creator, must ever crowd his imagination with a load of the most intolerable ideas.

" How then can any power of language express the multiplied pains of my situation, the pangs of remorse which swell in my bosom, with the most heart-rending sensations on the remembrance of the past, through an unpremeditated and deeply-lamented act, which has led to this investigation. Ah, God! could years of banishment and pain atone for the mania of a moment, could tears of blood, or sobs of acutest grief, recall the flighted spirit, the scorpion's sting, which now rankles in my bosom, might be removed, and the fever of a young man be succeeded by peace of mind and the sweetness of content: but, alas! what human power can re-kindle the vital spark, or illuminate the faded eye; the flood of affliction, and the humane tear, are in vain; they rend my soul, but yield no consolation to its wound.

" Thus, though impressed with the deepest contrition, my imagination *recoils* with horror and indignation at the horrid crime of *murder*,—though the unfortunate man did indeed fall by my hand, the violent mutinous tenor of his conduct, heightened by the most aggravated circumstances to me, his commanding-officer, in the act of carrying on the duties of my situation, worked me to a phrenzy of passion, in the tempest of which, he fell a sad victim of his own consummate obstinacy. Of a very different nature from the whirlwind of rage by which he was swept from among men, is the prepense malice of the deliberate and insidious murderer.

" God Almighty knows my heart bleeds at the recital, but it is a duty I owe to myself, and to the world, to draw your attention to my situation as a first-lieutenant, and the consequent provocation ; and I fondly hope this honourable court will accompany me in my feelings as an officer, and as a man. A complaint had been made to me by the carpenter of the ship, of the deceased, who had conducted himself in the most riotous and disorderly manner to the said person : weighing the circumstances, I, with a lenity natural to me, and which I trust I shall prove to have ever been my character, from high evidence, ordered him a slight punishment, too trifling in its nature, and not unbecoming his situation as a soldier, merely to walk the quarter-deck with a musket in his hand, and to which I was induced, by a prepossession in his favour, and a wish to preserve him from condign punishment, which must have been the consequence, if the regular steps had been taken. When, with insufferable contempt, better expressed by the carriage, and demure countenance and eye, than by language, he impertinently refused to submit ; I again and again commanded further compliance, the same provocation was renewed—I flew to my weapon, and here before God and my country, I most solemnly disclaim any intention to endanger the life of the deceased, and declare I meant simply to intimidate, and thereby force obedience to my orders. Acting on this principle, I several times struck the musket, which the deceased held in his hand, and desired him to walk about—this seemingly had the desired effect—he shouldered arms, and my sword was returned to its scabbard. But in the very same moment, my soul still glowing with indignation at his outrageous audacity of air and aspect, he again refused compliance, and dared me to the fatal act. The imposing attitude of the man, the fierce arrangement of his features, his high ingratitude and disdain working on my imagination, already infuriated by irritated exasperation, that like a flash of lightning across my brain, reason forsook its seat, raging madness usurped the sway, and my sword, obeying its hurried mandate, was passed into his body.

" Cruel! cruel! most cruel sword! which at once plunged him into eternity—to appear unprepared before his God—and me into the deepest gloom of misery and remorse. I trust I do not exhaust the indulgence of this honourable court with a repetition of my regrets—what bosom can deny the sigh, or what eye the tear, when charged with the death of a fellow-creature, under any circumstances ? The full heart feels relief on the heaving forth of its sorrows ; and though no pencil can pourtray the anguish which preys upon my mind at this moment, yet I feel some consolation in thinking that this man was formerly the object of my lenity— when, from motives of compassion, and the just sense I entertained of his professional abilities, I had shielded him from punishment, though implicated in the serious charge of mutiny. From this circumstance, I hope it will appear to this honourable court, that there was no premeditated malice against this unhappy victim of my misguided passion—and that a moment's cool reflection would have rather induced me to stretch forth that arm for his preservation instead of his destruction.

"I cannot look back on the unhappy event without suffering the most painful sensations, not only as respects the deed itself, but also as regards a sort of unhappy destiny, and not as a casual occurrence. God forbid that I should for a moment dare to arraign, or even to call in question, the justice of an everlasting Providence: but if ever fate preponderated the action of an individual, or hurried him to a crisis, some unknown power with cruel and desperate sway, tyrannized on that lamented day over the affections of my heart, and dashed its calm placidity with the tumultuous waves of violence and rage.

"I must claim the indulgence of this honourable court for occupying so much of its valuable time, if I have deviated from the subject before them: but when they recollect the very critical situation in which I am placed, I hope they will be ready to pity and forgive the wanderings of the mind. I shall beg leave to call the attention of the court to the testimonies I shall advance to prove the general calmness and indulgence of my temper towards every one in public and private. I have more particularly at this time to lament the death of my much respected friend and commander, Captain Rushbrooke, as also the absence of Admiral Dixon from this country; but yet I trust I shall still be able, from the testimony of Captains Trollope and Braimer, and another officer in the court, and of many of my messmates and brother officers,—and what must tend still more to convince this honourable court of the extent of my clemency as it respects my conduct to those placed under my command, together with my other depositions, the leading men of the Griffon are also ready to bear testimony. I trust the warm and artless effusions of their manly and unsophisticated hearts, will sufficiently convince this honourable court of the repugnance of my nature to the act; and that nothing but the irritating conduct of the deceased could have made me outstep the bounds of reason and justice.

"A seeming obedience returned the blade unpolluted to its sheath, when an unexpected recurrence of the offence, under aggravated circumstances, overwhelmed at once my discretion and my judgment, and drove me on to commit the horrid deed with which I stand arraigned at the bar of this honourable court. When I turn my thoughts towards the melancholy catastrophe, the retrospect is agonizing in the extreme, but I look forward to whatever may be the result of this court martial, with becoming deference and resignation, which can only proceed from a conscience awakened to its guilt, and assisted by the Divine Power. I feel supported by the confidence of ever having acted on humane and honourable principles—I know myself incapable of committing an ill action, and am horrorstruck at the magnitude of this.

"I trust there is not a spectator in this court, who does not believe these emotions to be the genuine inmates of my breast—if there be any amongst them of a contrary opinion, I address them in the language of the Apostle, 'Would to God you were all together such as I am, except these bonds.'

" Mr. President, and Gentlemen of this Hon. Court, in your hands I place my honour and my existence, the hopes and fears of my family, and all that is valuable to the officer, the gentleman, and the man; fully sensible they can be no where so safely confided as to the breasts of those of my own profession, the pride and boast of my country, and the terror of its foes. I have proved before you, as before my God, the case of my unfortunate situation, and whilst you decide on my future destiny, I earnestly entreat you to remember, ' That earthly power doth then shew likest God's, when mercy seasons justice.' "

The court, after due deliberation upon the case, adjudged Lieutenant Gamage to be *Guilty of Murder*; regarding, him, however, as a fit object of royal clemency. The case, we understand, was laid before the law-officers of the crown ; the utmost intercession was made in behalf of the prisoner ; and a letter from the whole of the ship's company of the Griffon was sent, praying a pardon, but without effect. He consequently suffered the sentence of the law, on board of the Griffon, in the Downs, on the morning of Monday, the 23d of November.—On the Saturday preceding, the following *general memorandum* was issued :—

GENERAL MEMORANDUM.

Impregnable, in the Downs, 21*st November,* 1812.

Lieutenant Richard Stewart Gamage, of his Majesty's brig Griffon, having been adjudged, by a court-martial, to suffer death, for having murdered a serjeant of the royal marines of that brig, the lords-commissioners of the Admiralty have directed that he shall be executed on Monday morning next, on board the Griffon.

When the signal for the punishment is made, two boats (kept quite ready) manned and armed, are to proceed from every ship to the Griffon, the officers commanding them being directed to obey such orders as they may receive from her captain. All works are immediately to cease, and the crew of every ship is to be turned up to observe the execution ; and, that the attention of the officers and ships companies may not be diverted from the melancholy scene, nor the salutary reflections to which it may give occasion, be interrupted, no work is to be begun till after the body has been lowered down. Soon after the execution shall have taken place, while the body is still hanging, the 28th article of war, and so much of the latter part of the 19th article as relates to the behaving with contempt to a superior officer, shall be read to the ship's company, and immediately after them, the following admonition, with such additional observations as the captain may think proper, to impress strongly on the minds of the officers and all the crew, the necessity of a strict attention to discipline, and a perfect obedience to the laws.

To be read to the Ship's Company.

The commander-in-chief most earnestly desires to direct the particular attention of the fleet to the melancholy scene they are now called to attend ; a scene which offers a strong, and, much he hopes, an impressive lesson to every person in it; a lesson to all who are to command, and to all who are to obey. Lieutenant Gamage is represented by every person who knew him, and by the unanimous voice of the ship's company of the Griffon, as a humane, compassionate man; a kind, and indulgent officer; yet, for want of that guard which all men should ever keep over their passions, this kind, humane, compassionate man, commits the dreadful crime of murder! Let his example strike deep into the minds of all who witness his unhappy end; and, whatever their general disposition may be, let them learn from him, that, if they are not always watchful to restrain their passion within its proper bounds, one moment of intemperate anger may destroy the hopes of a well spent, honourable life, and bring them to an untimely and disgraceful death; and let those who are to obey, learn from the conduct of the serjeant, the fatal effects which may result from contempt of, and insolent conduct toward, their superiors. By repeated insolence, the serjeant overcame the kind and gentle disposition of Lieutenant Gamage, and, by irritating and inflaming his passion, occasioned his own death. The commander-in-chief hopes this afflicting lesson may not be offered in vain; but that, seriously contemplating the awful example before them, every officer, and every man, will learn from it, never to suffer himself to be driven, by ill-governed passion, to treat with cruelty or violence, those over whom he is to command; nor by disobedience or disrespect, to rouse the passion of those whom it is his duty to respect and to obey.

(Signed) WILLIAM YOUNG.

The respective Captains and Commanders.

The subjoined letter, recording the particulars of this unfortunate young man's last moments, appears to have been written from the best information:—

" *Downs, November* 24, 1812.

" Poor Gamage was executed yesterday on board the Griffon. He had encouraged the thought that mercy would be extended to him, and he seemed very composed until he was informed that no hopes of life remained. The thoughts of suffering such an ignominious death were too much for his feelings, and he became almost incapable of receiving those instructions and consolations which his unfortunate situation required. He was attended almost every day, from the time of his trial until his execution, by the Rev. W. Elliot, chaplain of the Royal Oak,—a gentleman so well informed in the principles of religion himself, and so under the influence of his holy office, as to be fitted for a dying sinner's friend. He found considerable difficulty in depriving him of some false notions of honour, which had much agitated his mind; but at length these forsook him, and he embraced those truths which are the sinner's only hope. When the 9 o'clock gun fired,—the signal for boats to assemble, he said to Mr. Elliot, who had hold of his hand, ' See, I don't tremble, do I?' " At half-past nine, Capt. Trollope, and all his messmates, assembled with him, and joined in prayer. He then said he was perfectly ready. After Captain Trollope had read the warrant, he walked up, without the least assistance, and placed himself firmly on the fatal spot. As he passed along the deck, the sentinels saluted him by carrying arms! When his arms were seized behind him, he very deliberately gave his pocket handkerchief, and desired his hands might be tied also. A great weight was then attached to his feet, and a black handkerchief was put over his face—the gun fired—and he was launched into eternity without a struggle, amidst the sorrowful tears of every man on board the Griffon, and the surrounding spectators. The evening before his execution, he took leave of the ship's company, and wrote a very long and affectionate letter to his sister. Thus was cut off, in the prime of an honourable life, an officer, the characteristic of whose mind was mildness and humanity; but who, in a sudden paroxysm of passion, committed that crime which divine disapprobation has denounced with death—' He that ruleth his spirit, is better than he that taketh a city.'"

The body was taken on shore for interment at two o'clock, and was received at landing by Peter Dower, Esq. governor of the Navy Hospital, who, with a number of naval and military officers, attended this unfortunate young gentleman's remains to the burial ground at the rear of the hospital, where they were deposited. Captain Trollope, and the officers of the Griffon, with several of the crew, were present, and bore ample testimony, by their appearance, to the regret they felt at his untimely fate.

Lieutenant Gamage's seniority of rank was from the 26th of August, 1808.

At a court martial recently holden at Newfoundland, to inquire into the circumstances attending the capture of the Alert sloop of war, by the American frigate Essex, Lieutenant Duncan, senior lieutenant of the Alert, was found guilty of disobedience of orders, and not rendering that assistance to Captain Laugharne that he ought to have done; and he was sentenced to be dismissed from H. M.'s service. Captain Laugharne, his other officers, and crew, were all most *honourably acquitted*. Rear-admiral Carpenter (then captain of the Antelope) sat as president.

PLATE CCCLXXIX.

BEING THE FRONTISPIECE TO THIS VOLUME.

REPRESENTATION of the monument, designed and executed by G. Bacon, which has been erected in St. Paul's Cathedral, to the memory of Captain George Duff, R.N. who fell in the battle of Trafalgar.*

---

* For a portrait and memoir of Captain Duff, *vide* N.C. XV. 265.

NAVAL HISTORY OF THE PRESENT YEAR, 1812.

(November—December.)
RETROSPECTIVE AND MISCELLANEOUS.

THE *London Gazette* of December 26 contained an official notice, that the necessary measures had been taken, by the command of his Royal Highness the Prince Regent, for the blockade of the ports and harbours of the bay of the Chesapeake, and of the river Delaware, in the United States of America, as follows :

"*Foreign Office*, December 26, 1812.

" His Royal Highness the Prince Regent, acting in the name and on the behalf of his Majesty, has been pleased to cause it to be signified, by Lord Viscount Castlereagh, his Majesty's Principal Secretary of State for Foreign Affairs, to the Ministers of Friendly Powers residing at this Court, that the necessary measures have been taken, by the command of his Royal Highness, for the Blockade of the ports and harbours of the bay of the Chesapeake and of the river Delaware, in the United States of America; and that from this time all the measures authorized by the Law of Nations will be adopted and executed, with respect to all vessels which may attempt to violate the said blockade."

It is our painful duty to announce the capture of another British frigate by the Americans. In latitude 29° N. longitude 29° 30' W. the Macedonian, of 38 guns and 300 men, commanded by Captain Carden, was fallen in with, on the 25th of October, by the United States, American frigate, of 55 guns and 478 picked men, commanded by Commodore Decatur; and, after a sanguinary action of two hours and ten minutes, in which she had 36 men killed, 36 severely, and 32 slightly wounded, she was compelled to surrender.

H. M.'s brig Frolic, which was captured by the American sloop of war Wasp, has been retaken, together with the Wasp, by H.M.S. Poictiers.

It is with regret we state the loss of the Belette sloop of war, Captain Sloane. She was appointed to lead the Russian ships through the S. W. passage of Anholt, when she unfortunately got on shore on the rocks, off the Island of Lessoe (in the Cattegat), and all the officers and crew perished, except five men.

By letters received from the masters of vessels bound for this country, but detained at Matwyck for want of convoy, we learn. that the admiral commanding the last division of the Russian fleet, and the minister of marine, had both agreed that the whole of the homeward-bound vessels remaining in Cronstadt should be convoyed home by the former. The captain of H.M.S. Snipe, however, on learning this circumstance, positively forbade any of these vessels to avail themselves of the protection thus generously conceded. They are in conquence wintering at Matwyck and Carlscrona.

Ships Paid off in November.

Guns.

Victory	100	At Portsmouth.
Alfred	74	ditto.
Doris	36	At Plymouth.

Ships commissioned in November.

Heron	18	Captain M'Culloch.
Shamrock	14	—— Green.

Ship taken to pieces in November.
Hound bomb.

Ships launched in November.

Medway	74	Indus		74
Lacedemonian	38	Perseus		22

Ordered to be built in India.

Amphitrite	38	Victor		18

Ships to undock in January, having undergone a thorough repair.

Rivoli	74	Albion		74
Madagascar	38	Amphion		32
Havoc	14	Archer		14

The Benbow ...... 74, and Despatch ...... 18, to be launched in January.

The Melampus, 36 guns, is gone from Hamoaze into Catwater, to be repaired at Blackburn's yard.

The Hebe, 32 guns, at Deptford, is ordered to be sold.

The following ships have sailed to re-enforce Sir J. B. Warren on the American station:

Marlborough	74	Rear-admiral Cockburn.	
Victorious	74	Captain Talbot.	
Ramillies	74	——	Sir T. Hardy.
Cumberland	74	——	Baker.
Seahorse	38	——	Gordon.
Sybil	38	——	Upton.
Surprise	38	——	Sir T. Cochrane.
Syren	32	——	Woolcombe.
Minerva	32	——	Hawkins.
Peacocke	18	——	Peake.
Atalanta	18	——	Hickey.
Indian	18	——	James.

Government have ordered twelve new frigates to be immediately built of fir timber; some to be ready in twelve months, and named as follows:—Hebrus, Pactolus, Eurydanus, Niger, Tagus, Tiber, &c. &c. Of these, five are to be built at Blackwall, one at Deptford, one at Northfleet, one at the Isle of Wight, and two at Limehouse.

Letters on Service,

Copied verbatim from the LONDON GAZETTE.

ADMIRALTY-OFFICE, NOVEMBER 28, 1812.

ADMIRAL SIR JOHN THOMAS DUCKWORTH, Commander in Chief of H.M. ships and vessels at Newfoundland, has transmitted to John Wilson Croker, Esq. a list of thirty-three American vessels detained, and two English vessels (taken by American privateers) re-captured, by the squadron under his command.

Copy of a Letter from Captain Hockings, of H.M. sloop the Dominica, addressed to Rear-Admiral Sir Francis Laforey, and transmitted by the latter to John Wilson Croker, Esq.

H. M. ship Dominica, St. Thomas's,
SIR, Sept. 12, 1812.

I have the satisfaction to acquaint you of the capture of the American schooner Providence, privateer of Providence, by H.M. sloop Dominica, under my command, yesterday, the 11th, in latitude 19 deg. and longitude 63 deg. 15 min. after an anxious chase of ten hours. She is pierced for twelve guns, but has only four, having thrown the rest overboard, and a complement of sixty men; has been out thirty days, but has made no captures.

I have the honour to be, &c.
ROBT. HOCKINGS, Commander.

DECEMBER 5.

Extract of a Letter from Captain Swan, of H.M. sloop the Bellette, addressed to Captain Serrell, of the Helder, and transmitted by Rear-Admiral Hope to John Wilson Croker, Esq.

H.M. sloop Bellette, off Romsoe,
30th October, 1812.

In executing your orders last evening, to protect the rear of convoy, I beg leave to acquaint you that Mr. James Turnbull, acting master of this sloop, in the yawl, boarded and captured in a very gallant manner, after a short but spirited resistance, a Danish row-boat, with a lieutenant and fifteen men, armed with two 2-pounders, small-arms, &c. The Danes had five men badly wounded.

DECEMBER 12.

Rear-admiral Fremantle has transmitted to John Wilson Croker, Esq. a letter from Captain Taylor, of H.M.S. the Apollo, giving an account of his having, on the 20th of September, off Corfu, captured the Ulysse xebec, of 6 guns, and 56 men, commanded by Mons. Oletta, commander of a division of gun-boats belonging to that island:

And also a letter from Captain Andrew, of H. M.'s sloop Weazle, stating, that the boats of that vessel had captured, on the 21st and 22d of August, between Parga and Corfu, a bombard laden with oil, and an armed settee with letters and passengers.

DECEMBER 19.

Admiral Sir Richard Bickerton has transmitted to John Wilson Croker, Esq. a letter from Captain Hichens, of H. M.'s sloop Zephyr, giving an account of his having, on the 10th instant, captured the American letter of marque schooner Antelope, of ten guns, and thirty-two men, bound with a cargo from New York to Bourdeaux.

DECEMBER 22.

Admiral Lord Keith has transmitted to John Wilson Croker, Esq. a Letter from Captain Tobin, of H.M. ship Andromache, senior officer, off the Gironde, stating that the Briton had, on the 15th instant, captured the Sans Souci French privateer, of fourteen guns and one hundred and twenty men, belonging to St. Maloe's.

Promotions and Appointments.

Admirals and Captains appointed.

Rear-admiral Cockburn, to succeed Vice-admiral Sawyer, as commander-in-chief on the Halifax station.

Rear-admiral J. Nicholl Morris is appointed commander-in-chief in the Baltic during the remainder of the season.

Captain S. Malcolm hoists a broad pendant on board the San Josef, Captain Jackson, during the absence of Lord Keith from the Channel fleet.

Sir Edmund Nagle, Knt. to hoist his flag in the Antelope, as commander-in-chief at Newfoundland, *vice* Sir J. T. Duckworth: E. Hawker to be his captain.

Captains.—A. Brine, to the Sterling Castle; P. Carteret, to the Pomone; W. M'Culloch, to the Heron; —— Butcher (acting) to the Barham; Donald M'Leod, to the Princess; Andrew Green, to the Shamrock; Phipps Hornby, to the Stag; Sir John Gore, to the Revenge; James Rattray, to the Contest; James Tillard, to the St. Juan; Robert Riddell, to the Britomart: C. Hobart, to the Muros; John Forbes, to the Insolent; James Prevost, to the Ceres; —— Carroll, to the Volcano; R. Gambier, to the Pelorus; John Bowen, to the Salcette; C. Hope, to the Lacedemonian; —— Robilliard, and J. Griffith, to the rank of post captain; —— Allen, to be agent for prisoners of war at Newfoundland.

Lieutenants, &c. appointed.

W. E. H. Allen, to the Cygnet; James Atkins (1), to the Clarence; R. J. Alleyn, to the Hotspur; —— Athill, to the Malta; A. Burgh, to the Heron; George Bague, to the Cygnet; Dennis Bolton, to the Valiant; Thomas Blackistone, to the Revenge; Thomas Blake, to the Cadmus; H. Bagot, mid. of the Revenge, to be a lieutenant; John Brenton, lieutenant, to the rank of commander; J. Burrowes, H. Bolton, mids, to be lieutenants; —— Broderick, to the Loire; George Bateman, mids. of the Aimable, to be a lieutenant; —— Boxer, to the Hibernia; E. W.

NAVAL HISTORY OF THE PRESENT YEAR, 1812. 511

Cook, to the Orestes; Walter Croker, to the Iphigenia; —— Curry, to the Contest; Edroin Callaway, to the Regulus; A. Clugstone, to the Bedford; Edward Chappel, to the Rosamond; J. Crook, to the Thames; Wm. Cullis, to the Wasp; Charles Crowdy, to the Sterling Castle; Smith Cobb, to be a commander; Charles Dobree, to be a commander; Davis Hamilton, mid. to be a lieutenant; Joseph Dodd, to the Elephant; L. Dennys, to the Horatio; R H. Drake, to the Barham; —— Douglas, to be flag-lieurenant to Lord A. Beauclerc; Thomas Dundas, to the Peacock; James Edgecumbe, to the Shamrock; James Eickie, to the Pembroke; Thomas Edmonds, to the Cornwall; H. A. Elliott, to the Cornwall; F. W. Ellis, mid. to be a lieutenant; J Gramshaw, to the Hibernia; Thomas S. Griffinhoofe, to the Ville de Paris; Samuel Greenaway, to the Revolutionaire; Wm. Gilpin, mid. of the Shannon, to be a lieutenant; George Hawkins, to the Conquistadore; C. B. Harvey, to the Hibernia; Wm. Handly, midshipman of the Atlas, to be a lieutenant; Hon. T. L. Irby, to the Sybille; Thomas Jeff, to the Sparrow; L. Jackson, to the Revenge; J. Knapman, to the Albicore; Walter Kirby, to the Satellite; John Law, midshipman of the Calcutta, to be a lieutenant; William Lemesurier, to the Princess; Charles Lechmere, to the Barossa; R. J. Lewin, to the Minerva; John Lapslie, to the Woodlark; Nagle Lock, midshipman, to be a lieutenant; Jeremiah Mahoney, midshipman of the Hussar, to be a lieutenant; B. Molesworth, to the Sterling Castle; Herbert Mackworth, to the Hibernia; C. Maitland, R. C. M'Crae, midshipmen of the Victory, to be lieutenants; Henry Masterman Marshall, to the Royal William; Joseph Magin, to the Griffon; M. Montague, to the Barossa; W. S. Millett, to the Abercromby; F. P. Cellerton, midshipman, to be lieutenant; Andrew Munroe, midshipman of the Ranger, to be a lieutenant; J. Ormsby, midshipman of the Victory, to be a lieutenant; William Poore, to the Chanticleer; Edward Phillips, to the Rose; J. Packman, of the Magnificent, to be a lieutenant; J. H. Plumridge, to the Hibernia; Robert Patton, to be flag-lieutenant to Rear-admiral Foote; S. Perdrian, to the Waldemaar; John Pitts, to the Banterer; Wm. Richardson (2), to the Revenge; John Roberts (2), to the Bittern; H. R. Richards, to the Alfred; Richard Rawle, to the Doris; R. C. Ross, and J. Rapsley, to the Woodlark; Thomas Scott, to the Conflict; J. H. Servant, to the Sceptre; Charles Sommerville, to the Ætna; Sir J. G. Sinclair, Bart. to the rank of commander, and to command the Redwing; George Simmonds, to the Salcette; Wm. Harris Smith, to the Fox; J. R. Smith, (flag-lieutenant to Rear-admiral Martin), to the rank of commander; Charles Sterling, midshipman, to be a lieutenant; Thomas Sparks, P. Saumarez, midshipmen of the Victory, to the rank of lieutenants; —— Tollman, to the Royal William; Charles F. Turner, to the Rolla; W. G. Thomas, to the Ætna; George Vallock, to the Orestes; H. Wertlake, midshipman of the Dover, to be a lieutenant; Charles West, to the Irresistible; P. Wallis, to the Romulus; E. B. Watson, to the Devastation; Samuel Wriford, to the Pembroke; W. West, to the Ville de Paris; J. R. T. Wright, to the Hibernia; William Walker, to the Beaver; R. A. Wadham, to the signal station at Fort Cumberland.

Pursers.—R. H. Goddard, to the Doris; M. Fogarty, to the Medway; F. Moriarty, to the Shamrock; G. D. Dowell, to the Cornelia; J. Worsfold, to the Woodlark; Edward Bell, to the Bahama; W. Elliott, to the Bucephalus; Benjamin Nicholson, to the Carriere; John Tackle, to the Sussex, hospital ship; —— Stowe, to the Calliope.

Secretaries.—M. De Coetlegon, to Admiral Surridge; W. Harris, to Admiral Foote.

M. Edgecumbe, clerk of the rope-yard, Chatham dock-yard, to be clerk of the survey at Plymouth.

J. Manley, from the victualling-yard, Deptford, to be clerk of survey of Chatham dock-yard.

Masters—Robert Dodd, to the Bermuda; J. Tower, to the Plover; A. Shennan, to the Irresistible; P. Black, to the Despatch; W. B. Wise, to the Revenge; J. Trelwing, to the Tweed; W. Speed, to the Eclipse; J. Keale, to the Iphigenia; W. Moore, to the Daphne; James Boyd, to the Pomone; G. Stuart, to the Royal Oak; T. Weatherall, to the Galatea; J. Perriam, to the Stork; G. H. Cole, to the Andromeda; C. Warren, to the Cygnet; M. Wilkinson, to the Britomart.

A list of midshipmen, who have passed for lieutenants in December:

Sheerness.—J. G. K. Podmore, E. Roberts, T. Ramsey, R. Saumarez.

Portsmouth.—W. H. Peters, R. Edwards, C. Woods, W. F. Jebb, W. D. Evance, G. W. Courtenay, D. Sherlock.

Plymouth.—J. Marshall, P. Harden, J. Robinson, C. Holroyd, W. H. Kemble, R. Hare, R. Fuller, J. Harding, R. Harris, A. Miller.

Surgeons, &c. appointed.

Richard Bacon, to the Sheldrake; Thomas Jackson, to the Parthian; Robert Barnfield, to the Warrior; Wm. Bland, to the Hesper; J. P. Druris, to the Prometheus; John Richardson (2), to the Cruizer, gun-brig; Robert Williams, to the Waldemaar; J. H. Kent, to the Plover; Morgan Finucane, to the Niger, prison ship; William Ralfe, to be dispenser at Malta; Gabriel Johnstone, to the Ceres; Alexander Torbitt, James Hall (2), and N. M. Cox, to attend the sick of the Russian fleet.

Assistant-surgeons, &c. appointed.

Michael Quin, to the Revenge; William Plampin, to the Latona; Wm Clause, to the naval hospital at Jamaica; William Watt, to the Aboukir; Wm. M'Intyre, to the Ramillies; James Morice, to be hospital mate at Haslar; John O'Donnell, to the Pembroke; George Beauchamp, to the Viper cutter; Henry Ellis, to the naval hospital at Jamaica; A. C. Hyndman, to the Sealark; Donald Kennedy, to the Namur; John Breist, to the Resolute; John Greig, to the Gladiator; James Scott, to the Zealous; Thomas Hunter, John Temple, and John Beckett, to attend on the sick of the Russian fleet.

BIRTHS.

In Keppel-street, Brunswick-square, the lady of Captain C. Austen, R.N. of a son.

Nov. 22, at Emsworth, the lady of Captain Hayes, R.N. of a daughter.

25. At Hampton Court Palace, the lady of Captain Walker, R.N. of a son.

27. The lady of Thomas Grant, Esq. clerk of the cheque of his Majesty's dock-yard, Portsmouth, of a daughter.

Same day, at Newtown, Mrs. Lane, wife of Mr. Lane, purser of H. M. S. Narcissus (now in the West Indies), of a daughter.

MARRIAGES.

At St. John's, Newfoundland, Mr. Thomas Downer, assistant-surgeon of H.M.S. Antelope, to Miss Biddy Walsh, of St. John's.

Archibald Christie, Esq. eldest son of Admiral Christie, of Baberton, N.B. to Maria, only daughter of the late George Reeves, Esq. of Langley.

At Plymouth, Lieutenant George Gill, R.M. to Mary, youngest daughter of James Clark, Esq. of Anderton, in the county of Cornwall.

At Plymouth, George Foster, Esq. clerk in the dock-yard, to Miss A. Carswell, second daughter of Mr. Carswell, at Pound.

Nov. 5, at Alverstoke, G. A. Colman, Esq. R.N. to Miss Rosa Maria Bayley, youngest daughter of the late Hon. Captain P. Bayley, R.N.

25. Major Minto, of the royal marine artillery, to Miss Little, of Grove Hill, Camberwell.

28. John Day, Esq. naval storekeeper at North Yarmouth, to Miss Slade, daughter of J. Slade, Esq. merchant, Plymouth.

Dec. 3. Captain F. Beaufort, R.N. to Alicia Madelena, eldest daughter of Leatock Wilson, Esq. of Harley-street, London.

10. John Charles Blake, purser of H.M.S. Pyramus, to Maria, daughter of Mr. Charles Windle, of Leeds.

19. At Bishop's Hall, near Taunton, Henry Lark, Esq. of Upper Bedford-place, to Mary, only daughter of St. Albyn Gravenor, Esq. of Taunton Castle, Somerset.

OBITUARY.

On the coast of Catalonia, in his 22d year, Lieutenant George Sandys, of H.M.S. Bustard. His death was occasioned by falling overboard in a gale of wind, and every effort to save him proved ineffectual.

On his passage from Heligoland, Captain Hunt, of H.M.S. Britomart.

At Smyrna, where he had arrived in attempting to get to England, after a captivity of eight years and three months in a French prison, Captain Strauchan, formerly of the Jane, of Berwick.

At Swaffham, Lieutenant E. Towle, of H. M. S. Beaver.

In London, aged 21 years Mr. J. S. Brooking, of the Navy Office, son of Nicholas Brooking, Esq. collector of the Customs, Dartmouth.

At Gosport, Mr. Lilly, gunner of one of his Majesty's ships in ordinary at Portsmouth.

Oct. 28. At Olmedo, in Spain, in consequence of wounds received by him in an action with the French, Lieutenant Wm. Lockhart, of the 16th light dragoons, son of the late Rear-admiral Lockhart.

Dec. 6. At Gosport, the infant son of Captain Ballard, R.N.

7. At Stonehouse, Mrs. Glynn, wife of Captain Glynn, R.N.

8. At Penzance, Richard M'Killop, Esq. R.N. aged 44 years.

12. In Upper Wimpole-street, Mrs. Milbanke, widow of the late Admiral Mark Milbanke.

17. W. Bennicke, Esq. purser of H.M.S. Britannia.

INDEX

TO

THE TWENTY-EIGHTH VOLUME.

A.

ABERCROMBIE, General, death of, 12.
Actions—between the Belvidera and an American squadron, 104. The Swallow and two French ships, 194. The Guerriere and Constitution, 307, 347, 370, 426. The Attack and a Danish flotilla, 433. The Southampton and L'Amethyste, 451.
Adair, Mr. eulogium by, on the late Capt. Stewart, 37.
America, particulars relating to, 49, 73, 132, 137, 138, 139, 157, 222, 224, 226, 246, 257, 301, 306, 307, 343, 370, 384, 386, 408, 409, 417, 420, 426, 461, 462, 463, 495, 507.
America *versus* France, 49.
Angelo, St. view of the fortress of, 308.
Antiseptic, 371.
Ape's Hill, view and description of, 477.
Arab, loss of the, 4.
Arts, Society of, 234.
Attack, loss of the, 433.

B.

Badere Zaffer, capture of the, 34.
BALCHEN, Sir John, memoir of, 89. Commands the Virgin and the Chester, ib. Engages the Dunkirk squadron, 90. Commands the Orford, 93. Serves in the Baltic, 94. Promoted to a flag, 95. Sent to the Mediterranean to reinforce Admiral Haddock, 96. Made governor of Greenwich Hospital, and knighted, 97. Sails for Portugal in the Victory, and releases Sir Charles Hardy, 99. Loss of, on his return to England, ib. Inscription on the monument of, in Westminster Abbey, 100.
Bampfield, Mr. on preserving the health of mariners, 57.
Baronets, new naval, 435.
Belchier, Capt. effusion of, 109.
Bell, Lieut. (See Mariners.)
Belvidera, action between the, and an American squadron, 104.
Berkely, Admiral, *fac simile* of the handwriting of, 364. Presentation of addresses to, 456.
Bilbao, naval proceedings at, 78.

Biographical interrogatories, 114.
Boulogne, attack on, 17.
Blasphemy, dismissal from the service for, 424.
Brine's signal lanthorn, 461.

C.

Caledonia and Hibernia, comparative dimensions of the, 126.
Ceuta, particulars relating to, 477.
Charles, the, defence of, 289.
Chatham, the, 51.
Charlotte, Queen, destruction of the, 7.
Chesapeak, the, and Leopard, particulars relating to the action, &c. between, 354 to 369.
Chesapeake and Delaware, blockade of the, 507.
Christopher, St. view and description of the island of, 116.
Clark, John, intrepidity of, 193.
Cline, Mr. humanity of, 459.
Coghlan, Capt. J. anecdotes of, 200.
Cole, Capt. Sir C. presentation of an address to, 101.
Constitution, accidents on board of the, 193.
CORRESPONDENCE, 54, 107, 204, 286, 375, 461.
———————, naval conjugal, 51.
Courtenay, Capt. W. M. anecdote of, 377.
COURTS MARTIAL—(See Marine Law.)
Currents and tides, remarks on, 309, 371.
Cyclades, population of the, 30.

D.

Daly, J. heroic death of, 203.
Danish droits, queries respecting, 464.
DARTMOUTH, Admiral Lord, portrait and memoir of, 177. Enters the service, under Sir Edward Spragge, 179. Commands the Pembroke and the Fairfax, ib. Made lieutenant-general of the ordnance, ib. Distinguishes himself in the battle of Solebay, 180. Serves in the York, and the Royal Catharine, 182. Made governor of Portsmouth, 184. Appointed colonel of a regiment of foot. Made master general of the ordnance, sworn a member of the privy council, created a peer, and appointed commander-in-chief of an expedition against Tangier, 185. Made constable

of the Tower, 186. Supersedes Sir Robert Strickland, 187. Confinement and death of, in the Tower, 188. Heraldic particulars of, 189.

Defence, loss of the, 210.

Defiance, naval, 372.

Delaware (see Chesapeake.)

Devonshire, launch of the, 292.

Douglas, Capt. J. E. *fac simile* of the hand-writing of, 357.

Drowning, means to prevent, 48

Duckworth, Sir J. T. official letters of, relating to an exchange of prisoners with America, 462, 463. *Fac simile* of the hand-writing of, 463.

Duff, Capt. Geo. monument erected to the memory of (Frontispice,) 369.

Dundas, Capt. T. pyrotechnical invention of, 198.

E.

East India ship-building, 125.

Eclipses, the, for 1813, 464.

Edwards, Commodore. account of, 90.

Egypt, expedition to, 10.

F.

Fac similia.---J. Stewart, 17. J. E. Douglas, 357. G. Berkely, 364. M. Flinders, 401. D. O'Brien, 389. J. Horsburgh, 451. J. T. Duckworth, 463.

Falmouth, superiority of, to Plymouth, 325.

Fire-arms, improvement in, 48.

Fire, mode of extinguishing, 460.

Flinders. Capt. 318, 321, 400. *Fac simile* of the hand-writing of, 323, 401.

G.

Gamage. Lieut. trial and execution of, for murder, 501.

George, the Royal, intention of raising, 373.

Good Hope, the Cape of, hydrographical details relating to, 478. Chart and description of, 497.

Gordon, Mr. A. testimony in favour of, 112.

Greenwich Hospital, 374.

Guerriere, La, capture of, 307, 347, 370, 381, 386, 426.

H.

Hake, method of catching, 50.

Hawser Hank, letter of, respecting tides and currents, 309.

Hibernia (See Caledonia.)

HORSBURGH, J. Esq. biographical memoir of, 441. Birth, education, early employment, capture, and shipwreck of, 443. Hydrographical pursuits of, 444. Introduced to Sir J. Banks, &c. 445. Purchases Berthoud's astronomical clock ib. Experiments of, on marine barometers, 446. List of the publications of, 446, 447. Writes a paper on luminous marine animals, 447. Preface of, to his *Sailing Directions*, with a summary of the contents of that work, 448. Elected a fellow of the Royal Society, and appointed hydrographer to the East India Company, 450. *Fac simile* of the hand-writing of, 451.

HUMPHREYS, Capt. S. P. portrait and memoir of, 358. Enters the service, attains the rank of post captain, commands the Leander, and, subsequently, the Leopard, 354. Engages the Chesapeake, 354, to 364. Heraldic particulars of, 369.

HYDROGRAPHY.—Sumatra, 70, 129. Atlantic Ocean, 71. France, 72, 228. Isle of Wight, 129, 313, 478. Hurst Beach, 227, 314. Navigation of the Frith and Clyde, 227. Whittle Rock, 232. Semon's Bay, 232. Holyhead Harbour, 315. China Seas, 315. Magnetism, 318, 400. River Thames, 402. Orford-ness, 403. St. George's Channel, 478. Azores---Isle of Sabrina, 479. Cape of Good Hope, 479.

I.

Ichthyology, 102.

Ignition, spontaneous, 202.

Impulse, extraordinary, 106.

India ships, missing, 49.

Interrogatories (See Biographical.)

Intrepidity, instances of, 374, 459.

J.

Java, prize-money, 192.

Joke, a sailor's, 102.

Junck, Jack, journal of, 52.

K.

Krusenstern, Capt. 460.

L.

Languillia, attack on the batteries of, 160, 167.

Legge, Admiral, presentation of addresses to, 457.

Lequitio, naval proceedings at, 74.

Leopard (See Chesapeake.)

Letter to the Editor, from Mulciber, enclosing Captain Tillard's narrative, concerning a submarine volcano, near the Island of St. Michael, 54.

—— to the same, from Mr. R. W. Bampfield, surgeon of H. M. S. Warrior, on the mode adopted by him for preserving the health of mariners on long voyages, 57.

—— to the same, from Ypsilon, enclosing an epitaph on Capt. Shipley, 63.

—— to the same, relating to an extraordinary phenomenon at Nevis, 64.

—— to the same, from Oceanus, suggesting the employment of additional lieutenants on board sloops of war, &c. 107.

INDEX

Letter to the same, enclosing a military effusion by Captain Belchier, 108,
—— from Justicius to the first lord of the Admiralty, respecting the widows and orphans of officers slain in action, 109.
—— to the Editor, enclosing a testimony in favour of Mr. A. Gordon, 112.
—— to the same, enclosing a narrative of John Anderson one of the survivors of the crew of the St. George, 113.
—— to the same, from Plutarch, enclosing biographical interrogatories, 114.
—— to the same, stating the distances of the different points, shoals, &c. of the intended Breakwater, Plymouth Sound, 115.
—— to the same, from Mr. Toupin of Exmouth, recording the appearance of a mermaid, 204.
—— to the same, by Muzzle to Muzzle, suggesting improvements in military tactics, 208.
—— to the same, from Capt. W. H. B. Tremlet, on the affairs of the Peninsula, 208.
—— to the same, enclosing the narrative of Joseph Page, one of the survivors of the Defence, 210.
—— from Tom Starbord, to the first lord of the Admiralty, respecting the pay and half-pay of lieutenants, 212.
—— to the Editor, on the Breakwater in Plymouth Sound, 286
—— to the same, enclosing Capt. Cromarty's account of the defence of the Charles, 289.
—— to the same, on the launch of the Devonshire, 292.
—— to the same, on the cure of the Ophthalmic disease, 292.
—— to the same, from a Friend to Naval Merit, suggesting the employment of an additional number of lieutenants on board line of battle ships, &c, 293.
—— to the same, on the situation of masters in the Royal Navy, 294.
—— to the same, on the impossibility of naval lieutenants living on their half-pay, 375.
—— to the same, respecting favourite names of ships of war, 377.
—— to the same, with an anecdote of Capt. W. M. Courtenay, 377.
—— to the same, on the proclamation declaring the punishment of death on all British mariners found on board vessels belonging to the United States of America, 379.
—— to the same, by Mr. Whidbey, on the Plymouth breakwater, 379.
—— to the same, describing a hurricane, 380.

Letter to the same, on the loss of the Guerriere, 381, 386.
—— to the same, enclosing a letter from a seaman to his sister, relating to the battle of Trafalgar, 382.
—— to the same, enclosing an account of Commodore Rodgers's cruise, 384.
—— to the same, with extracts from American newspapers and letters, from Sir J. T. Duckworth, relating to the exchange of prisoners with America, 461.
—— to the same, proposing mathematical queries, and announcing the eclipses for the year 1813. 464.
—— to the same, requesting information respecting the Danish droits, 464.
—— to the same, proposing new regulations in favour of masters and midshipmen in the royal navy, 466.
—— to the same, suggesting the abolition of the French nomenclature in the British navy, 467.
—— t the same, with extracts of letters from the squadron cruising off Venice, 467.
—— to the same, correcting an error in the memoir of Capt. Whitby, 469.
Licenses, commercial, 48.
Life boat, metallic, 283.
Linzee, Capt. attempted assassination of, 197.
Lieutenants, suggestions for the employment of an additional number of, 107, 293. Pay and half pay of, 212.
Love, Mr. praiseworthy conduct of, 200.

M.

Magnetism, 318.
Malta, political importance of, 459.
Manby, Capt. (See Mariners.)
MARINE LAW, Report, of the French minister of marine, relative to the proceedings of La Renommée, La Neride, and La Clorinde, 151, Court martial on Lieut. R. W. Simmonds, for the loss of the Manly, 240. Court martial on Lord W. Stuart, for running the Conquistador on a shoal, 340. Court martial on Capt. J. R. Dacres, for the loss of the Guerriere, 422. Dismissal of the purser of H. M. S. Jamaica, for blasphemy and disloyalty, 424. Acquittal of Lieut. R. W. Simmons, for the loss of the Attack gun-brig, 433. Trial and execution of Lieut. Gamage, for the murder of a serjeant of marines, 501.
Mariners, shipwrecked, Lieut. Bell's, and Capt. Manby's plans for the preservation of, 295, 298.
Masters, situation of in the navy, 294. Proposed regulation in favour of, 466.
May, the, defence of, 280.

INDEX.

Macedonian, capture of the, 507.
Memorial, American, against the war, 495.
Mermaid, appearance of a, 204, 206.
Midshipmen, proposed regulation in favour of, 466.
Mosque, Moorish, view of a, 400.

N.

Narrative, melancholy and interesting, 196.
NAVAL ANECDOTES, COMMERCIAL HINTS, RECOLLECTIONS, &c. 48, 101, 192, 28, 370, 451.
——ARCHITECTURE, 115, 118, 125, 126, 128, 143, 213, 233.
——HISTORY OF THE YEAR 1812. 73, 157, 246, 343, 425, 507.
——LITERATURE.— Manderson's twelve letters to Mr. Perceval, 143, 325.
——POETRY.—Adelmorn and Angeline, 148. Portuguese hymn to the Virgin Mary, 239. Epitaph on Admiral Cotton, 240. Address to the lieutenants of the navy, on the change of uniform, 334. Nelson, a dirge, 337 Sonnet written at the Eddystone light-house, 337. Lines on two seamen, late of the Swallow, 338. Song, from Camoens, ib. Lines written in the cave of Fingal, 339. Song, 420. The Retort Courteous, 421.
Navy, Turkish, account of the, 43.
Nelson, Lord, 374.
Nevis, extraordinary phenomenon at, 64.
Nomenclature, French, suggestion for abolishing the, in the British navy, 467.

O.

Oak, Royal, 52.
O'Brien, Lieut. D. naval bulletins of, 388, 469. *Fac simile* of the hand-writing of, 389.
Orphans and widows, suggestions for the relief of, 109.
Ophthalmia, cure of, 292.

P.

Parliament, prorogation of, 141. Dissolution of, 299.
————, Regent's Speech on opening the new, 488.
Parrot, Captain Pakenham's, fate of, 372.
Plymouth Breakwater, 115, 118, 128, 143, 213, 233, 286, 379, 426.
Polly, the, discovery of the wreck of, 198.
Premiums, naval, 234.
Prisoners, French, 282.
Prisoners, Irish, 103.
Prizes, proclamation for granting the distribution of, 409.
Puerto Santo, view and description of, 53.
Pyrotechny, 374.

Q.

Quarantine, questions relating to, 405, 491
Queries, mathematical, 464.
————, respecting the Danish droits, 464.

R.

Rodgers, Commodore, account of the cruise of, 384.
Royal Bounty, capture of the, 284.
Riga, naval proceedings at, 428.
Ruse de Guerre, legitimate, 48.
Russia, treaty of peace with, 418.

S.

Sabrina, islet of, disappearance of the, 479.
Sailor's life, both sides of a, 105.
Saldanha Bay, chart and description of, 148.
Scaldings! 374.
Samaritans, good, 371.
Saumarez, Sir J. presentation of a sword to, 455.
Sheldrake's improvement in mechanic power, 200.
Shipley, Captain Conway, epitaph on, 64.
Ships, colonies, and commerce, 102, 373.
Ships of war sold, &c. 427, 508
Signal lanthorn (see Brine's).
Simmonds, Lieut. R. W. 240, 433.
Slave trade, 493.
Solebay, battle of, 180.
Southampton, action between the, and L'Amethyste, 451.
South Wales, New, state of, 193.
Spain, naval proceedings on the coast of, 74, 78, 164, 171.
Spartel, Cape, 477.
STATE PAPERS.— Declarations of the members of her Majesty's Council respecting the state of his Majesty's health, 69. Message of the president of the United States to Congress, 132. Declaration of war between Great Britain and America, 137. Proclamations by General Sir J. C. Sherbrooke, 138, 306. Order for a general embargo on American shipping, 138. Admiralty order for the revocation of licences, 139. Peace between Great Britain, Russia, and Sweden, 139. Opening of the Swedish port, 140. Revocation of the order for reprisals against Russia, 140. Royal speech on the prorogation of parliament, 141. War between America and Algiers, 222. Malta trade, 223. Act to prohibit American vessels from trading with the enemies of the United States, 224. Instructions for American privateers, 226, 307. Dissolution of parliament, 299. Peace

between Great Britain and Sweden, 300. Proclamation by Major-general Brock, in Upper Canada, 301. Importation of goods from the Levant, 303. General reprisals against America, 304. American circular, relative to the seizure of British merchandise, 307. American official account of the capture of the Guerriere, 307. Quarantine questions, 408. Distribution of prizes, 409. British subjects serving foreign states, 417. Treaty of peace between Great Britain and Russia, 418. Proclamation by Sir J. B. Warren, inviting the return of British seamen from the service of America, 420. Regent's speech, on opening the new parliament, 488. Quarantine questions, 491. Correspondence on the slave trade, 493. American memorial against the war, 494.

STEWART, Captain J. portrait and memoir of, 1. Enters the service in the Rose, ib. Serves in the Discovery, 2. Becomes acquainted with Lord Camelford, 4. Made lieutenant in the Arab, ib. Shipwrecked, and made prisoner, on the French coast, ib. Serves in the Revolutionaire, Queen Charlotte, Formidable, Tonnant, Foudroyant, and Barfleur, 5. Conduct of, at the destruction of the Queen Charlotte, 7. Employed on shore, at Leghorn, 9. Commands the Mondovi sloop, ib. Cruises off Lisbon and Oporto, and sails on the Egyptian expedition, 10. Made post in the Africaine frigate, 12. Commands the Europe and the Ceres, 12, 13. Letters of, to J. Loch, Esq. 15, 17. Fac simile of the hand-writing of, 17. Employed in the attack on Boulogne, ib. Resignation of, from illness, 18. Commands the Sea-horse, 19. Conduct of, in the Archipelago, 19 to 32. Arrives at Malta, 33. Captures the Badera Zaffer, Turkish frigate, 34. Receives a medal from the King, 36. Account of the services of, by Mr. Adair, 37. Sends an account of the Turkish navy to Lord Collingwood, 43. Captures the islands of Pinnosa and Gianuti, 45. Anecdote of, ib. Brings home Lord Amherst, 46. Death, and interment of, in Westminster Abbey, ib. Heraldic particulars of, 47.

St. George, the, loss of, 113.
Stuart, Lord W. (see Marine Law.)
Sugar, duties paid on, 373.
Swallow, H. M. S. action between the, and two French ships, 194.
Sylph, capture and re-capture of the, 285.

T.

Tactics, military, improvements in, suggested, 206.
Tarragona, capture of, 430.
Tarring and feathering, 199, 283.
Telegraph, nocturnal, 192.
Thames, projected transformation of the, 199.
Tides, (see Currents.)
Tillard, Captain, narrative of, concerning a sub-marine volcano, near the island of St. Michael, 54.
Toulon, manœuvres of the French fleet at, 425.
Trafalgar, letters relating to the battle of, 383.
Transport Board, list of the new, 435.
Tremlett, Captain, on the affairs of the Peninsula, 208.

V.

Venice, extracts of letters from off, 467.

W.

Warren, Sir J. B. proclamation by, inviting the return of British seamen from the service of America, 420.
Water, improvement in the keeping of, 102.
Watkins, Captain, account of, 191.
Whidbey, Mr. on the Plymouth Breakwater, 379.
WHITBY, Captain Henry, portrait and memoir of, 265. Enters the service in the Excellent, 266. Conduct of, in Admiral Cornwallis's retreat, 267. Made lieutenant, ib. Serves in the Prince George and Leviathan, 267, 268. Wrecked in the Proselyte, 268. Made commander in the Pelican, 268. Made post-captain, 269. Commands the Santa Margaretta, Desirée, and Centaur, ib. Goes to Halifax, ib. Marries Miss Inglefield, 270. Commands the Leander, ib. Trial of, for the alleged murder of an American seaman, 272. Appointed to the Cerberus, 273. Serves in the Baltic, ib. Participates in Captain Hoste's action in the Adriatic, 274. Nominated to the Belle Poule and to the Briton, 276. Death of, 278. Character of, 280. Corrections in the memoirs of, 469.
Widows, (see Orphans.)
Wilde, Captain, account of, 191.

INDEX.

GAZETTE LETTERS.

ADDERSLEY, Capt. 432
Bathurst, Capt. 346
Andrew, Capt. 510.
Bowles, Capt. 428
Bray, Lieut. 257
Bremer, Capt. G. H. 257
Brenton, Capt. 257
Burdet, Capt. 257
Campbell, Capt. 75, 162, 167
Cockburn, Rear-adm. 349
Codrington, Capt. 428
Chamberlayne, Capt. 345
Chetham, Capt. 428
Crawford, Lieut. 254
Cutler, Lieut. 428
Dacres, Capt. 346
Dench, Capt. 345
Dixon, Lieut. W. H. 163
Dabbs, Lieut. 75
Douglas, H. 172
Dawn, Capt. 164
Duckworth, Sir J. T. 509.
Eager, Lieut. 75
Essen, Lieut.-gen. 171, 251, 254
Hamilton, Capt. 345, 346
Harper, Capt. 258

Hichens, Capt. 510.
Hockings, Capt. R. 509.
Hollis, Capt. 345
Hooper, Capt. 427
Hope, Capt. 163, 432
Hopkins, Capt. 74
Hoste, Capt. 428
Huskisson, Capt. 427
Jane, Capt. 257
Keith, Lord, 171
Ker, Capt. 257
Lennock, Capt. 78
Locke, Lieut. 432
Mainwaring, Lieut. 346
Martin, Rear-adm. 169,170, 250, 253, 255
Moresby, Capt. 164
Mulcaster, Capt. 257
Murray, Adm. 164
Napier, Capt. 162, 163
Nicholas, Capt. 162
Osborne, Lieut. J. J. 163
Parker, Sir P. 345
Pellew, Admiral, 160, 163, 164
Pesley, Lieut. 428
Peyton, Capt. 431
Philips, Lieut. C. 163

Popham, Sir H. 74, 79, 164, 171, 216
Rea, Capt. 160
Robilliard, Capt. 82
Rowley, Capt. 160, 162, 345
Ross, Capt. 83, 428
Saumarez, Adm. 176, 250, 253
Sawyer, Vice-adm. 257, 346
Saunderson, Mr. 346
Shaw, Capt. 346
Simmonds, Lieut. 77, 434
Stewart, Capt. J. P. 75, 80, 81, 82, 427
Stuart, Lord, G. 252, 253
Taylor, Capt. 509.
Thomas, Capt. 75
Thompson, Capt. 257
Thornborough, Adm. 164
Timpson, Lieut. 257
Tobin, Capt. 510.
Usher, Capt. 75, 431
Waldegrave, Hon. Capt. 167
Warrand, Lieut. T. 166, 167
Weir, H. Capt. 82, 83
Williams, Lieut. P. 258
Willis, Capt. 171
Young, Adm. 78, 251

PROMOTIONS AND APPOINTMENTS.

ACKLAND, E. 175
Adams, Lieut. 174
Aiton, Mr. W. 86
Aldridge, Mr. 351
Alexander, Mr. 86, 261
Allen, R. Esq. 349
——, Lieut. 510
——, Lieut. S. 436
——, Lieut. T. G. 436
——, Lieut. G. 437
——, Lieut. W. E. H. 510
Alleyn, Lieut. 436
——, Lieut. R. J. 510
Allison, Mr. 86
Alltoft, Mr. 85
Almer, Lieut. W. 260
——, W. 436
Alms, Adm. J. 173

Amyott, Mr. 261
Anderson, Mr. 86, 261, 262
———, Lieut. 436
Andross, C. 437
Angus, Mr. J. 86
Annesley, Lieut. F. C. 260
Appleby, J. T. 85
Aplin, Lieut. 436
Arnold, Lieut. J. 350
Arthur, Capt. R. 435
———, Lieut. J. 436
Ashford, Mr. 175
Astley, Lieut. A. W. 260
Atchison, Capt. A. 174
Athill, Lieut. 510
Atkins, Lieut. J. 510
Ault, Mr. J. J. 85
Autrige, Capt. W. 174

Aylmer, Adm. 173
Ayres, Mr. J. 175
Bacon, R. 512
Bagot, Lieut. H. 510
Bague, Lieut. G. 510
Bagwell, Lieut. P. 436
Baillie, Mr. H. 86
——, Capt. 435
Baker, Mr. 85, 175, 437
——, Capt. E. R. 173
——, Lieut. T. P. 260
——, Capt. H. E. R. 260
——, Lieut. H. 350
——, Lieut. J. P. 350
——, Lieut. W. 350
——, Capt. 435
Baldamus, Mr. 438

INDEX.

Ball, Lieut. 174
Bamber, Mr. H. 65
Barclay, Capt. T. 260
Barclay, R. 437
———, Lieut. 436
Barker, W. 175
———, Capt. J 174
Barnes, Mr. 86, 351, 437
———, P. 175
Barnfield, R. 512
Barrie, Mr. 261
———, Capt. R. 174
Barron, T. D. 86
Barrow, Mr. 261
Barton, Capt. B. 173
Bassan, 174
Bastard, Lieut. 436
Bateman, Capt. C. P. B. 435
Boteman, G. 510
Batton C. 85
Baxter, Mr. 438
Bayley, D. Esq. 349
Bayley, Capt. J. 260
Bayne, Lieut. G. 510
Bayntun, Capt. 173
Beasley, T. 175
Beatty, Mr. 85, 438
Beauchamp, C. P. 512
Beauclerc, Lord, A. 173
Beckett, J. 512
———, Mr. 86
———, Lieut. 174, 437
Bedford, Capt. W. 173
———, Capt. J. 174
Bell, E. 511
Belsey, Lieut. A. 260
Bendock, Mr. J. 351
Bennet, Mr. A. 86
———, Lieut. C. 174
———, Mr. 437
Berry, Capt. Sir T. 260
Bertie, Vice-adm. 435
Bevans, Mr. 261
Bigland, Lieut. 174
Bignall, Lieut. G. 84
Bird, Lieut. J. 350
Bishop, Mr. 175
——— -, Lieut. 436
Bisset, Capt. J. 260
Black, Mr. J. 86
———, Mr. 86
———, P. 512
Blackistone, Lieut. T. 510
Blackstone, Lieut. 436
Blaikie, Mr. P. 351
Blake, Lieut. T. 510
Bland, W. 512
Blane, Dr. G. 435
Blaney, Lieut. 174
Bligh, Adm. 173
Bluett, Capt. B. S. 84
Blythe, Mr. 85
———, Capt. S. 260

Bolton, Lieut. D. 510
———, Lieut. H. 510
Boyer, Adm. 173
Bootes, Mr. 262
Boothby, W. Esq. 435
Borrowes, Lieut. J. 510
Bostock, Lieut. 436
Bourchier, Capt. 435
Bowden, Mr. 261
Bowen, Lieut. C. H. 84
———, Mr. 86
———, R. 86
———, J. Esq. 435
Bowen, Lieut. J. 510
Bowlby, G. H. 85
Boxer, Lieut. 510
Boyd, J. 512
———, Mr. 261
Boyce, W. 175
Boyle, Hon. C. 435
Boyles, Adm. 173
Bradley, Mr. 351
———, Capt. W. 349
Branch, Lieut. 260
Brander, Mr. 261
Brane, Lieut. A. 510
Breist, J. 512
Brenmer, Mr. 438
Brenton, J. Esq. 435
———, Lieut. J. 510
Brewer, Capt. J. G. 260
Bridges, Lieut. 436
Briggs, Mr. 261, 437
Brine, Capt. A. 174
Brisbane, Capt. J. 174, 260
Brocke, Mr. 261
Broderick, Lieut. 436, 510
Broughton, Capt. J. 173
Brawn, W. C. 86
Brown, Adm. 173
———, Lieut. 260
———, Mr. 261
———, A. 351
———, Mr. S. 261
———, Capt. A. 435
Bruff, Mr. 85
Bryan, Mr. J. 85
———, Lieut. 261
Brydon, Mr. 437
Brydone, Mr. 86, 261
Buchannan, Lieut. 174, 260
Buller, Adm. Sir E. 173
Bulteel, Adm. 173
Bunster, G. 86
Burnie, Mr. 86
Burns, Mr. 85
Burdon, Adm. 173
Burgh, Lieut. A. 510
Burnside, Mr. 86
Burrell, Mr. 86
Burrowes, Mr. 262
Burton, Mr. 261
Bury, Adm. 173

Bury, Lieut. J. 260
———, Lieut. T. 350
Butcher, Lieut. 510
-- ———, Mr. 351
Caie, Mr. J. 86
Cairnes, Lieut. J. 260, 463
Calaway, Lieut. E. 511
Caldwell, Mr. G. M. 437
Cameron, Mr. 86
Campbell, Mr. 86
———, Mr. J. 86
———, Lieut. J. 174, 260
———, Lieut. C. 350
Candlish Lieut. J. M. 350
Capponi, Mr 351
Carpenter, Capt. 173
Carew, T. 86
———, Lieut. 436
Carrol, Capt. 510
Carruthers, Mr. 86
Carter, J. 84, 437
Carteret, Capt. P. 510
Canners, Lieut. 174
Cawkitts, Lieut. 436
Cellerton, F. P. 511
Chadds, Lieut. 174, 260
Chalmers, G. 437
Chambers, Capt. S. 174
Chapman, Lieut. A. 350
———, Mr. 261
Chappel, Lieut. E. 511
Charlesson, R. 175
Chick, S. 437
Chrystie, Lieut. J. 85
Clark, Mr. 86, 261
Clarke, Rev. J. S. 172
———, Mr. 437
Clause, W. 512
Clay, Capt. E. S. 174
Clayton, Lieut. J. 350
———, Mr. G. 351
Claxton, C. Lieut. 436
Clerk, Lieut, W. C. 350
Clifford, Capt. A. W. J. 174
Clinch, Capt. T. 174
Clisteron, 436
Clugstone, Lieut. A. 511
Carney, Mr. 351
Coates, Lieut. R. 350
Cobb, Lieut. 174
———, Lieut. S. 511
Cockburn, Adm. 173
———, Capt. G. 173
Cochrane, Capt. T. B. 174
Cochran, Capt. Sir T. 260
Cockburn, Adm. 510
Coe, Mr. W. 85
Coett, Lieut. W. 350
Coffin Lieut. 436
Cole, Mr. 86, 437
———, G. H. 512
Coles, Lieut. R. 260
Collier, Lieut. 175

INDEX.

Collier, Mr. 261
Coleman, Lieut. J. 260
Colman, Lieut. E. 350
Compton, Mr. 86
Comby, Mr. R. 437
Conner, Mr. 261
Cook, Lieut. E. W. 511
Coole, Capt. R. 260
Cooley, Lieut. W. R. 250
Cope, A. T. 85
Coppin, F. 85
Copplestone, Mr. 175
Corson, W. 86
———, Mr. 86
Cotton, Mr. R. 351
Coulson, Capt. R. L. 260
Cowan, Lieut. 174
Courtenay, G. W. 512
Cox, N. M. 512
Craig, Mr. W. 437
Crane, Lieut. T. 350
Crawley, Adm. 173
Crew, Mr. 437
Crisp, Mr. T. 85
Croke, Lieut. 174
Croker, C. 351
———, Lieut. W. 511
Crook, Lieut. J. 511
Cross, Lieut. 436
Crout, Mr. 85, 261
Crowdy, Lieut. C. 511
Cruickshank, Mr. 261
Crutchley, Mr. 261
Cubit, Mr. 85
Cullen, Mr. W. 437
Cullip, Lieut. W. 511
Cumming, Mr. 86
Cummin, Mr. 262
Cummins, Capt. 435
Cunningham, Capt. 174
——————, Mr. 261
——————, Mr. 437
Cupples, Mr. W. 86
Currie, Mr. 175
Curry, Lieut. 511
Curtis, Mr. 86
Dabine, Lieut. 436
Dale, Lieut. J. N. A. 350
Dall, Mr. 35, 175
Dalziel, Mr. W. A. 351
Daniel, R. 437
Dashwood, Capt. C. 260
Darley, A. 85
Darling, Mr. A. 261
Dartler, Mr. W. 86
Davies, Mr. W. 261
———, Lieut. 350
———, Mr. C. 351
Davidson, Mr. 437
Davis, Lieut. 176
———, Capt. 260
———, Capt. R. D. 350

Davis, Lieut. H. 350
———, W. B. 251
———, Lieut. 436
———, Mr. T. 437
Davison, Lieut. E. B. 350
Dawe, J. Esq. 351
Dawkins, Lieut. 260
Dawson, J. Lieut. 84
———, Lieut. H. 260
Day, Lieut T. 350
Deans, Adm. 172
De Coetlegon, M. 511
Delamotte, Mr. 261
Dendron, Lieut. 350
Denman, J. 351
Dennis, E. 85
———, Lieut. L. 511
Dennison, Lieut. 436
Denston, Lieut. 175, 436
Derewzey, Lieut. 175
Dick, Mr. 175, 438
Dickenson, Lieut. T. 84
———, Lieut. C. 350
———, Capt. 349
Dickson, Capt. E. S. 174
———, Mr. 262
———, Lieut. M. 350
———, Mr. J. 437
Dilkes, Adm. 173
Dobie, Mr. J. 437
Dobree, Lieut. C. 511
Dobson, Mr. 261
Docking, Mr. 261
Dodd, Lieut. J. 511
———, R. 512
Domet, Wm. Esq. 349
Donellan, Lieut. M. 350
Donadieu, Lieut. A. 261
Donovan, Lieut. S. 436
Douglas, Lieut. 511
———, Lieut. G. R. 350
———, Hon. J. 435
Dowell, G. D. 511
Down, Capt. E. A. 174
Drake, Lieut. R. H. 511
Drewit, Lieut. 436
Druris, J. P. 512
Duckworth, Sir J. T. 510
Duff, Lieut. 436
Dunbore, Mr. 261
Duncan, Mr. W. 175
Dundas, Capt. G. H. L. 260
———, Capt. D. 260
———, Rt. Hon. W 349
———, Hon. Capt. 435
———, Lieut. T. 511
Dunn, J. 85
———, Mr. 175
———, Capt. J. 260
Duthie, Mr. J. 351
Durham, Adm. 173
Dyer, Mr. W 351

Easto, R. 86
Eaton, Lieut. J. 350
Edgecumbe, Lieut. J. 511
————, M. 512
Edman, Mr. T. H. 351
Edmonds, Mr. W. 175
————, Lieut. T. 511
Edward, Lieut. D. 260
Edwards, Lieut. 175, 350
————, R. 512
Eichey, Lieut. J. 511
Elder, Mr. 261
Ellicot, Lieut. 436
————, Capt. E. 174
Elliott, J. B. 437
————, Lieut. H. A. 511
————, W. 511
Ellis, F. W. 511
———, H. 512
Emmerson, Mr. 261
Entwistle, Lieut. H. 260
Evance, W. D. 512
Evans, Lieut. T. 84
———, Lieut. A. B. 350
———, Mr. R. 86, 261
———, Lieut. 436
Eyre, G. P. 85
———, Lieut. 175
Eveleigh, Capt. J. 350
————, Lieut. 436
Everard, Capt. T. 260
Fabian, Capt. 349
Fairlip, Lieut. G. 260
Fancourt, Adm. 173
Farr, Mr. W. 175
Farquarson, Mr. 261
Faulkner, J. 85
Fayerman, Adm. 173
————, E. 437
Fead, Lieut. 174
Fegan, Lieut. J. 350
Ferrant, Lieut. 260
Ferrier, Adm. 173
Findley, Mr. 86
Finlaison, Lieut. W. 260
Finucane, Mr. J. 437
————, N. 512
Fiott, Lieut. E. 350
Fitzmaurice, Mr. 85
——————, Lieut. W. 260
——————, Lieut. W. 350
Fletcher, Lieut. J. S, 260
Flyn, W. 85
Flynn, Capt. T. 174
Fogarty, M. 511
Foley, Capt. 84
———, Adm. 173
Fonereaux, J. 85
Foote, Capt. E. J. 173
———, E. J. Adm. 435
Forbes, Capt. J. 510
Forster, Lieut. 350, 436

Fortescue, H. 175
Fowler, T. 85
Franklyn, Lieut G. 436
Francis, Mr. 438
Fraser, J. 85, 86
———, Adm. 173
Frazer, Capt. A 349
Freeman, R. 85
Fremantle, Adm. 173
Friend, Lieut. C. 350
Fuller, R. 512
Fynn, Mr. L. 437
Gabrel, Lieut. J. W. 85
Galloway, Rt. Hon. Earl, 173
———, Mr. T. 437
Gambier, Lieut. 436
———, Capt. R. 510
Gardiner, Lieut. T. 84
Gardner, Capt. Hon. F. H. 173
Garland, Lieut. 260, 350
Garson, Mr. 175
Garrett, E. 437
Gay, Mr. 351
Gawen, Lieut. G. 437
Geyt, Capt. G. L. 174
Geddes, Lieut. 436
George, Sir R. 435
Gibbs, R. 85
Gifford, Capt. J. 174
———, Mr. 351
Gill, Capt. G. 174
———, Lieut. 436
Gilchrist, Mr. 86
Gillies, Mr. 261
Gilpin, W. 511
Glascock, Lieut. G. 85
Glasson, Mr. 86
Glen, Mr. J. 175
———, Lieut. N. 260
Glover, Mr. T. 261
Goddard, R. H. 511
Greig, J. 512
Godfree, Mr. 351
Godwin, Mr. 175
Goldsmith, J. 85
Gooch, Mr. J. 175
Gordon, Mr. 86
———, Lieut. 174
———, Capt. J. A. 260
———. Hon. W. 84, 260
Gore, Capt. Sir J. 173
———, Sir J. 510
Grace, Lieut. P. 350
Graham, Capt. J. 84
———, Mr. W. 86
Gramshaw, H. J. 511
Gransden, Mr. 175
Grant, Lieut. 351
———, Mr. 85
Graves, Sir T. 172

Gray, Mr. 86, 437
Gredon, Hon. J. 436
Gregory, Adm. 173
———, Mr. W. 437
Green, Lieut. 84, 436
———, Mr. 261, 437
———, Mr. W. 175
———, Capt. A. 510
Greenly, Sir I. C. 172
Greenway, H. S. 511
Grey, Capt. E. 174
Grieg, Mr. 437
Griffinhoof, H. 511
Griffiths, Mr. J. 86
———, Capt. 173
———, Capt. J. 510
Grindall, Adm 173
Gritton, Mr. 175
Grose, Mr. 175
Groube, Capt. T. 349
Guthrie, Mr. J. 175
Hackett, Lieut. J. 260, 350
Haig, R. Esq. 85
Haines, Mr. 85
Halkett, Capt, 173
Hall, Lieut. 174, 175, 260
———, Capt. W. 350
———, J. 512
Hallowell, Adm. 173
Halstead, Adm. 173
Hamilton, Mr. 261
———, Adm. 173
———, Mr. W. H. 351
———, Lieut. D. 511
Hammond, Lieut. C. 350
———, T. 437
Handly, W. 511
Hanswell, 85
Hanwell, Capt. 173, 174
Harden, P. 512
Harding, J. 512
Hardy, Capt. Sir T. 173
Hare, Mr. 261
———, R. 512
Harfield, Mr. 85
Hargood, Adm. 173
Harley, Lieut. J. 350
Harness, Dr. 435
Harper, Capt. J. 174
Harris, Capt. G. 173
———, Mr. 175, 437
———, Lieut. W. C. 350
———, W. 511
———, R. 512
Harrington, Lieut. 260
Harrison, Mr. 175
Hartley, Lieut. 437
Harvey, Lieut. 261
———, Capt. J. 173
———, Adm. E. 173
———, Lieut. C. B. 511
Haswell, Lieut. 260, 350

Haswell, J. D. 437
Hawke, Mr. 86
Hawker, Capt. E. 510
Hawkey, Mr. 261
Hawkins, Lieut. C. 350
———, Lieut. G. 511
Hay, Lieut. 350
———, Mr. 351
Haydon, Mr. 437
Hayes, Capt. G. 174
Hea, R. 86
Head, Capt. M. 84
Hearding, Capt. G. 174
Heastie, Mr. 86
Hector, Mr. W. 351
Hellard, Capt. W. 174
———, Lieut. 174
Helpman, Lieut. R. 260
Henderson, Mr. 86
———, R. 350, 437
Henry, A. 85
Hepburn, Mr. 85
Heron, Mr. T. 86
Herringham, Lieut. 174
Hetherington, Lieut. R. 350
Hewit, Capt. J. 84
Hewitt, 85
———, Lieut. 174
Hewitson, Mr. 86
Hewson, Lieut. 174
Hickman, Lieut. 436
Hicks, Mr. 351
Hill, Mr. 86. 262
———, Lieut. J. 350
Hire, Capt. G. A. 84
Hitchens, Lieut. J. 436
Hoare, Lieut. H. W. 84
Hobart, Capt. C. 510
Hobbs, Lieut. J. 437
Hodgson, Mr. 175
Hoggan, Mr. 437
Holbrook, Mr. 261
Hole, Capt. 435
———, J. 436
Hollingworth, J. Esq. 435
Holman, Lieut. 436
Holmes, Lieut. W. 260, 350
Holroyd, C. 512
Hooper, Lieut. R. 350
Hope, Capt. W. J. 173
———, G. J. Esq. 349
———. Capt. C. 510
Hornby, Capt. 174
———, Capt. P. 510
Hoskin, Lieut. 436
Hotham, Capt. W. 173
Houghton, Lieut. 174
Hoxton, Mr. 351
Huber, Mr. 261
Hughes, Lieut. 174
Hulber, G. Esq. 175

INDEX.

Hume, Mr. 351
Humphry, W. W. 85
Hunter, T. 512
Huntingdon, Mr. 85
Hutchins, Lieut. 260, 261
———, Mr. 351
Hutchinson, R. 437
Hyde, Mr. 351
Hyndman, A. C. 512
Imrie, Lieut. J. 350
Inches, Mr. 437
Inger, Mr. J. J. 86
Inglis, G. 85
Ingram, Lieut. W. H. 260
Inskip, Mr. 85, 261
Ireland, Lieut. T. 350
Irly, Lieut. T. L. 511
Jacob, E. H. 175
Jackson, J. 86
———, Lieut. 174
———, R. A. 351
———, Mr. T. 437
———, Lieut. L. 511
———, 512
Jager, Lieut. T. 174
James, Mr. D. 175
———, Mr. E. 437
Jamison, Mr. W. 86
Jane, J. 175
Janverin, Lieut. 436
Jebb, W. F. 512
Jeff, Lieut. T. 511
Jenkinson, Lieut. 175
Jennings, Mr. 261
John, Mr. L. 85
Johnson, J. 351
Johnston, Mr. 175, 438
———, Lieut. G. C. 436
Johnstone, W. 85
———, J. 437
———, G. 512
Jones, Mr. J. 85
———, Mr. T. C. 261
———, Adm. 173
———, Mr. T. 86
Joyce, Mr. 86
Judas, Lieut. J. 350
Kane, Mr. 351
Keale, J, 512
Keane, E. 175
Keddell, Mr. A. 261
Keeling, Lieut. 175
Keeman, Capt. 435
Keenah, 85
Keilly, Mr. 86
Kellet, A. H. 85
Kelly, Mr. 262
———, Lieut. E. 350, 436
Kemble, W. H. 512
Kennedy, E. 85
———, D. 512
Kent, Capt. W. 84

Kent, J. H. 512
———, Lieut. 174
Kift, Mr. 86
King, Sir R. 173
———, Capt A. 174
———, Lieut. G. 437
Kirby, Lieut. W. 511
Kirkley, Mr. 85
Kissock, Mr. 86
Knapman, Lieut. J. 511
Knight, Lieut. W. 350, 436
Knowles, Adm. Sir C. 172
Kortwright, Lieut. N. 84
Laforey, Adm. 173
Lamb, Mr. 175
Lambert, Lieut. 171
———, Capt. H. 173
Lane, Mr. 175
Langdon, 436
Lapsley, Lieut. J. 511
Lascelles, Lieut. J. L. 350
Laughlin, Mr. 438
Laughna, Mr. J. 351
Laurence, Lieut. 436
———, J. 351
Law, Mr. W. 351
———, J. 511
Lawson, Mr. S. 175
Leach, Mr. 85, 261
Lean, Mr. 251
Lechmere, Adm. 173
Lechmere, Lieut. C. 511
Lee, Capt. R. 173
Leeke, Lieut. H. 350
Legge, Hon. A. K. 173
Le Mesurier, Lieut. W. 511
Leshie, Capt. S. 174
Lesby, Mr. 175
Leslie, Mr. A. 261
Lew, Lieut. 436
Lewin, Lieut. R. J. 511
Lewis, Mr. 85
Liddall, Mr. 262
Lind, Mr. J. 175
Link, S. 175
Linton, Mr. 86
Linzee, Capt. S. H. 173
———, Adm. 435
Lipson, Lieut, T. 350
Lloyd, Lieut. 436
Lock, Lieut. 436
———, N. 511
Loney, Lieut. 436
Lound, Lieut. 436
Louthean, Mr. 261
Lowe, Capt. A. 261
Luke, Adm. 173
Lyford, H. J. Capt. 174
Lyon, Mr. P. 86
———, Lieut. E. 437
Macdougall, Mr. 261

Macdowal, Mr. 86
Mackworth, Lieut. H. 511
Macullum, Mr. 261
Magin, Lieut. J. 511
Maguire, Mr. 86
Mahoney, J. 511
Maingy, Lieut. P. 260
Mainwaring, Capt. R. 260
———, Lieut. R. 261
———, B. 351
———, Lieut. A. 351
Maitland, C. 511
Malcolm, Capt. S. 510
Maling, Capt. T. 260
Mann, Adm. 172
Manley, Adm. 173
———, Capt. 435
———, J. 512
Mannin, Mr. A. 175, 261
Mansel, Capt. R. 260
Marchant, Mr. T. 351
Marryatt, Mr. T. 437
Marshall, Lieut. T. 260, 350
———, C. H. 351
Martin, Adm. 173
Mathews, Lieut. 350, 436
Maxwell, Capt. M. 349
May, Mr. J. 175
Mayberry, Mr. C. 261
M'Allum, Mr. 351
Marshall, Lieut. H. 511
———, J. 512
M'Arthur, Lieut. 350
M'Call, Mr. D. 261
M'Cleod, Capt. D. 510
M'Clure, 437
M'Conkey, Mr. 175
M'Connell, Mr. J. 351
M'Crea, R. C. 511
M'Crery, Lieut. D. 174
M'Culloch, Capt. W. 510
M'Cullock, 85, 436
M'Donald, Capt. C. 174
———, Lieut. 436
———, D. Lieut. 350
———, Mr. J. 351
M'Donough, Mr. 351
M'Dougall, Adm. J. 173
M'Farland, Mr. 261
M'Gowan, Mr. 175, 261
M'Intyre, W. 512
M'Keen, Mr. J. 86
M'Kenzie, Mr. 85, 261
M'Kinley, Lieut. 436
M'Lean, Mr. 85
M'Leay, Mr. 262
M'Leod, Mr. J. 86
———, Lieut. W. 350
M'Pherson, Mr. A. 86
M'Ree, Mr. 262
M'Roberts, Mr. 86
Medley, Lieut. E. 260

INDEX.

Mick, Lieut. 174
Mein, Lieut. J. 350
——, Mr. 351
Melville, Rt. Hon. Vis. 349
Menzies, Lieut. 436
Mercer, Lieut. 260, 350
Merriman, C. 351
Michod, Mr. J. P. L. 86
Miles, Lieut. J. 350
Miller, Mr. 175
——, Lieut. 436
——, A. 512
Millet, Mr. 175
——, Lieut. W. S. 511
Milligan, Mr. 438
Milne, Capt. D. 173, 261
——, Mr. 351
——, Lieut. 436
Milner, Capt. A. 174
Mitchell, Capt. N. 174
Molesworth, Lieut. 436
——————, Lieut. B. 511
Monatt. J. A. 261
Monday, Mr. 261
Montague, E. 175
—— ——, Lieut. M. 511
Montgomery, Mr. A. 261
Moore, Capt. G. 173
————, Lieut. 174
————, Lieut. J. A. 84, 175
————, W. 512
Moorsom, Adm. 173
——————, Lieut. 260
Morley, W. R. 351
Morrell, Lieut. 436
Morris, Capt. G. H. 174
———, Adm. 173
———, Adm. J. N. 510
Morrice, J. 512
Morrison, Mr. 261
Mortimer, Mr. C. 351
Mosse, R. L. Esq. 261
Mott, Capt. A. 174
Moubray, Capt. G. 174
————, Mr. 261
Mourilyan, Lieut. E. 350
Munroe, A. 511
Murphy, Mr. 85
Nagle, Adm. Sir E. 173, 510
Nairn, Mr. R. 437
Napier, Hon. Capt. 349
————, Lieut 350, 436
————, Hon. E. 437
Nash, W. 175
Nason, Lieut. R. 350
Naughton, Mr. J. 175
Naylor, Lieut. J. B. 350
Neale, Sir H. 173
Nesbitt, Mr. 351
Newman, Mr. C. 351
Nichol, Mr. 86, 437
Nicholson, B. 511

Noel, Lieut. F. 350
Noreack, Mr. 437
Norie, Mr. 175
Norman, Mr. 86
————, Lieut. C. R. 260
Norton, Lieut. 175
Noyce, Lieut. 261
Oake, Lieut. 84
Oakes, Lieut. C. 260
O'Gara, Mr. 86
O'Donnell, Y. 512
Ogilvie, Lieut. D. 84
————, Mr. J. 351
O'Meara, Mr. B. 261
Osborne, Adm. 173
————, J. Esq. 349
————, H. 437
Osman, Mr. 261
O'Reilly, Mr. 262
Ormsby, J. 511
Otway, R. 85
Overy, Mr. J. 85
Owen, Capt. 174
Pack, Mr. 261
Packman, J. 511
Paddon, Lieut. 175
Padmore, J. G. K. 512
Page, Capt. B. W. 260
Paget, Hon Capt. 84, 350
Paine, Mr. 261
Paisley, Mr. 437
Pakenham, Lieut. 174, 260
——————, Hon. T. 172
Palmer, Mr. 351
Parsons, Mr. G. 437
Parry, Lieut. A. 437
Pater, Capt. C. D. 174
Paterson, Mr. 86
————, Capt. C. W. 173
Patrickson, Mr. A. 86
Patten, Lieut. T. 260
————, Mr. 261
————, Lieut. 174, 350
Patton, Lieut. R. 511
Paulet, Capt. Lord H. 173
Payne, C. W. 85
———, Lieut. 436
Peake, Mr. W. 85
———, D. 437
Pearson, Lieut. C. 260, 350
Pearth, Mr. 175
Pechell, Lieut. 174
————, Capt. 174
Pedlar, Lieut. 260
Pellew, Sir. F. 173
————, Capt. F. 435
Perdrian, Lieut. 437
——————, Lieut. S. 511
Perkins, Mr. J. M. 85
Perriam, J. 512
Peter, Lieut. R. 436
Peters, W. H. 512

Petit, Lieut. J. 84
Petre, Mr. 85
Petrie, Mr. W. 86
Phillips, Mr. H. C. M. 261
————, Lieut. E. 511.
Pickmore, Adm. 173
Pickstone, Mr. 351
Pidlaw, Lieut. 174
Pierce, Lieut. G. 350
————, Lieut. T. 350
Pierrepont, Capt. W. 173
Pinco, Mr. O. 437
Pitt, Lieut. J. 511
Plampin, Mr. 86
————, W. 512
Playfair, Mr. 351, 437
Plowman, Mr. H. 351
Plumridge, Lieut. 350
——————, Lieut. J. H. 511
Pocoke, 436
Pogson, Lieut. 174, 350
Pogsone, Lieut. H. E. F. 260
Pollard, Lieut. C. 436
Pollock, Mr. 86
Popham, Sir H. 173
Poore, Lieut. W. 511
Porteus, Capt. 435
Postlewaite, E. 437
Pottinger, Mr. 351
Power, Mr. 86
————, Mr. P. 351, 437
Pratt, Lieut. 436
Prevost, Capt. D. 510
Price, Mr. 86, 351
————, Lieut. D. 350
Pringle, Capt. 174
Purvis, Adm. 173
Purches, Lieut. J. W. 350
Purcell, Lieut. E. 350
Quernel, Mr. 262
Quin, M. 512
Quinton, Capt. C. 350
Rae, Mr. 86
Ralfe, W. 512
Ralle, Lieut. R. 511
Ramsay, D. 85
Ramsey, Mr. P. 351
————, T. 512
Rand, Mr. J. H. 351
Randall, Lieut. 84, 174
Randolph, C. G. 85
Randolf, Lieut. 350
Rapsley, Lieut. J. 511
Rattray, Capt. J. 510
Rawlinson, Lieut. W. 260
Raynham, M. 84
Read, Lieut. 85
Ready, Lieut. H. 260
Reardon, Mr. 437
Reed, Mr. T. 85
Reeve, Lieut. J. 85
Reid, Mr. 86

INDEX.

Reid, Lieut. 175
———, Capt. C. H. 260
———, Capt. C. 435
Reilly, Mr. 261
Retorman, Lieut. C. 350
Renans, Lieut. 350
Reynolds, Mr. T. 437
Rice, D. 85
Richards, Mr. 85
———, Lieut. G. 350
Richards, Lieut. H. R. 511
Richardson, Mr. J. 437
————, J. 512
————, Lieut. W. 511
Riddell, Capt. R. 510
Rickards, Mr. 437
Rickman, Mr. 437
Riddell, Mr. 262
Ring, Lieut. 350
Risk, Mr. J. E. 437
Rivers, Mr. 85
Robarts, Lieut. F. 350
———, E. 512
Robb, Capt. C. 260
Roberts, Lieut. 174, 175
————, Lieut. W. 260
————, Lieut. R. 350
————, Lieut. J. 511
Robertson, Mr. 85, 86
————, Lieut. 174
Robbin, Capt. 349
Robilliard, Capt. 510
Robinson, Mr. 175
————, Adm. 173
————; Lieut. J. 260
————, Lieut. A. 350
————, Lieut. 436
————, J. 512
Roche, Mr. 86
Rogan, Mr. R. H. 86
Rokely, Lieut. 174
Rolfe, W. 86
Rolles, Capt. 435
Roper, Lieut. 174
Rose, Lieut. J. B. 436
———, J. 437
Ross, Mr. J. 85
———, Mr. A. 86, 175
———, Capt. C. 173
———, Mr. 261
———, Lieut. R. C. 511
Rosser, Mr. 86
Rosson, Lieut. 436
Rothery, J. H. 86
Rowan, Lieut. J. 260
Rowe, Mr. 261
Rowlinson, Lieut. W. H. 350
Rubridge, Lieut. J. 260
Ruckhurst, Mr. 85
Russel, Adm. 172
———, Mr. 175

Rust, R. 85
Rutherford, Mr. G. S. 86
Ryall, Mr. 437
Rye, Capt. P. 174
Ryland, Lieut. 260
Sadler, Lieut. J. 436
Sainthill, R. 260
Salmon, Mr. 261
Salt, Esq. 435
Sankey, Mr. 262
Sartorius, Capt. G. C. 260
————, Capt. G. R. 174
Satterthwaite, Lieut. E. 350
Saule, Mr. 261
Saumarez, P. 511
————, R. 512
Schaw, Mr. 86
Schomberg, Capt. A. W. 174
Scott, Mr. 85
———, Mr. E. 85
———, Mr. J. 86
———, Capt. M. H. 173
———, Rear-adm. 260
———, Lieut. J. 260
———, J. 512
———, Lieut. T. 511
Seed, Mr. 175
Selbie, J. 351
Selby, Mr. 85
Serle, Lieut. C. H. 260
Servant, Lieut. J. H. 511
Sewell, Lieut. H. F. 174
Seymour, Mr. 261, 351
Sharp, Mr. 261
Shave, S. 351
Shed, Lieut. R. 350
Sheriff, Lieut. J. W. 350
———, Capt. 435
Sherlock, D. 512
Sherlocke, Mr. 261
Sherratt, Mr. 86
Shippard, Capt. A. 174
Shipton, Lieut. J. 84
Shivers, Adm. 173
Shoveller, Mr. W. 86
Sibly, Capt. E. R. 174
Simmonds, Mr. 437
————, Lieut. G. 511
Simmons, Mr. J. H. 85
Simms, Mr. L. 437
Simon, C. 85
———, Mr. 261
Simpson, Lieut. J. 436
————, Mr. J. 437
Sinclair, Sir J. G. 436
————, Sir J. G. 511
Sissons, Lieut. 174
Sisson, Lieut. S. 436
Smartly, Mr. 351
Smith, Capt. C. T. 84
———, Lieut. J. 85, 260, 436
———, Sir W. S. 84, 173

Smith, Mr. 261, 351, 438
———, Adm. 172
———, Lieut. 175
———, Lieut. J. B. 350
———, Lieut. W. 436
———, Lieut. J. R. 511
———, Lieut. W. H. 511
Smithers, Lieut. 486
Soden, Mr. R. 351
Summerville, Lieut. G. 511
Sparke, Mr. 175
Sparks, T. 511
Speare, R. Esq. 175
Speed, G. J. 351
———, W. 512
Speer, Mr. J. 86
Spence, Mr. 85
———, Lieut. 174
Speveling, Mr. 437
Squire, Lieut. H. 174
———, Capt. 174
Squires, Mr. 85
Stanbridge, Mr. W. 437
Stanbury, W. 351
Stanhope, Sir H. E. 172
————, Lieut. E. H. 174
Stapleton, 85
Stead, S. 261
Steenbergen, Lieut. J. 350
Stenhouse, Mr. W. 437
Stephens, Adm. 173
Stephenson, Mr. 175
Sterling, C. 511
Stevenson, Lieut. F. 350
Stewart, Mr. 261, 262, 351
————, Hon. E. 349
————, Capt. W. 435
————, Mr. A. 437
————, Mr. T. 437
Stiles, Lieut. 436
Stiff, Mr. 175
Stodart, Mr. 86
Stoddart, Lieut. 175
Stokes, P. 175
Stone, Mr. T. 85
———, Lieut. 174
———, Lieut. W. 260, 436
Stopford, Adm. 173
————, Lieut. 436
Stormouth, Mr. 86, 437
Stowe, Mr. 511
Strachan, Sir R. 173
Strode, Mr. 85
Stuart, Mr. 85
———, Lieut. 436
———, G. 512
Studdart, Lieut. 350
Surridge, Capt. T. 173
————, Rear-adm. 435
Swann, R. C. 86
Swayne, Mr. 261
Tackle, Mr. 175

INDEX.

Tackle, G. 511
Tamm, Lieut. 436
Taplin, J. 351
Taylor, Adm. 173
———, Capt. J. 260
———, Mr. 438
Temple, Mr. 86, 261
———, Capt. J. 260
———, J. 512
Thomas, Mr. 86
———, Lieut. W. G. 511
Thompson, Lieut. J. 84, 260, 350
———, Mr. T. 85, 86
———, Adm. 173
———, Capt. J. 174
———, Lieut. C. 436
———, Mr. J. 437
———, Mr. R. 437
Thorold, Lieut. 436
Tilford, Mr. 85
Tillard, Capt. J. 510
Todd, Mr. J. 86, 437
Tollman, Lieut. 511
Torbitt, Mr. A. 437. 512
Torrie, Mr. J. 351
Tower, J. 512
Towne, Lieut. W. 436
Townshend, Lieut. 260
Tozer, Lieut. H. P. 436
Trelwing, J. 512
Trile, T. 351
Trimmer, Lieut. T. 260, 436
Tripp, Lieut. 436
Trollope, Sir H. 172
Trotman, Mr. W. H. 175, 351
Trownsell, G. P. 437
Truss, Lieut. W. 350
Tuberville, Lieut. E. 350
Tucker, Mr. 85
———, Lieut. H. 260
———, Capt. E. 260
Turner, Mr. 85, 261
Twaddle, Mr. 261
Tyler, Rear-adm. 260
Tymon, Mr. 86
Vale, Mr. 261
———, W. 437
Vallack, Lieut. G. 511
Veitch, Capt. J. 174
Vevers, G. 351
Vincent, Lieut. A. 436

Voll, Lieut. T. 350, 436
Voller, Lieut. 436
Uniacke, R. 86
Urmstone, Lieut. C. G. 260
Urniston, Lieut. 174
Usher, Capt. 435
Usher, W. 437
Wadham, Lieut. R. A. 84, 511
Wales, Capt. R. 349
Walford, Lieut. W. 350
Walker, Mr. 351
———, Lieut. H. 436
Walker, Lieut. W. 511
Wallace, Lieut. P. 511
Waller, Mr. J. 261
Walsh, Mr. P. 86
Ward, E. 351
Warden, Mr. W. 261
Wardlane, Mr. 261
Warkman, Mr. J. 175
Warner, Mr. 261
Warrand, Capt. T. 174
———, Lieut. 175
Warren, Adm. Sir J. B. 173
———, Mr. 437
———, C. 512
Warrender, Sir G. 349
Warsfold, Lieut. 511
Warton, Lieut. J. 350
Watson, Mr. 86, 175
———, C. H. 260, 261
———, Lieut. R. 350
———, Lieut. E. B. 511
Watt, W. 512
Watts, Lieut. 174, 260, 436
Waugh, Mr. 438
Way, Mr. 438
Weatherhall, T. 512
Webster, Mr. 86, 351
West, Lieut. C. 511
———, Lieut. W. 511
Wertlake, H. 511
Weir, Capt. H. 174
Weiss, Lieut. 436
Wells, Adm. 173
———, Lieut. J. 260
Wemys, Lieut. 260
West, W. 86
Westbrooke, Lieut. R. 436
Westphall, Lieut. 174
Westrop, Lieut. 261
Whinyates, Capt. 174
Whitbread, Mr. 261

White, Lieut. 174, 260
———, Capt. K. J. 260
———, Mr. W. 437
Whitmore, N. C. 86
Whitshed, Adm. 172
Whyte, Lieut. E. 350
Wigstone, Lieut. J. 350
Wily, Mr. 85
Wilkin, Mr. 262
Wilkinson, J. Esq. 85
———, Lieut. 174, 436
———, N. 512
Willes, G. W. Esq. 84
Williams, Mr. 86 175, 437
———, Mr. E. 86
———, Mr. J. 86, 351
———, Mr. T. 261
———, Mr. D. 351
———, Sir. T. 173
———, Lieut. 175
———, R. 512
Williamson, Mr. 85
Willins, Mr. 175, 261
Wills, Mr. 175
Wilshire, Mr. 85
Wilson, Capt. J. 260
———, Lieut. A. 351
———, Lieut. J. 436
———, Lieut. 436
———, Mr. J. 437
Winkworth, Mr. 262
Wise, Lieut. 174
———, W. B. 512
Wobridge, Lieut. 350
Wolley, Mr. 437
Wood, Mr. 86
———, J. 86
Woodley, Lieut. 175, 350
Woodriffe, Lieut. 350, 436
Woods, C. 512.
Woodyatt, Lieut. 436
Woolcombe, Capt. 435
Woolnorth, Lieut. 350
Worth, Mr. 85, 261
Wray, Lieut. 174
Wrifford, Lieut. S. 511
Wright, P. 175
———, Lieut. J. R. T. 511
Wyndam, Capt. G. 84
Yeams, Mr. 85
Yearman, A. F. 437
Yorke, Sir J. S. 173, 349
Young, Mr. 437

INDEX.

BIRTHS.

ARNOLD, 438
  Austen, 512
Bailey, 87
Ballard, 37
Bayley, 262
Bradley, 262
Burt, 176.
Byng, 262
Caulfield, 438
Douglas, 176
Gamble, 351
Gardner, 176

Grant, 512.
Giles, 438
Gore, 262
Halliday, 352
Hayes, 512.
Lambert, 176
Lee, 262
Lane, 512
Linzee, 352
Long, 262
Mainwaring, 262
Oglesby, 262

Panchen, 262
Parker, 87
Prevost, 87
Rolles, 262
Stanfell, 352
Stevens, 262
Upton, 176
Wainwright, 87
Walker, 512
Williamson, 87
Wise, 176
Woolward, 351

MARRIAGES.

BAILLIE, J. Esq. 176, 262
Beaufort, Capt. F. 513
Blake, Mr. J. C. 513
Bone, Mr. F. 438
Butter, Capt. 439
Christie, A. Esq. 513
Cochrane, Hon. B. 176
Cole, Lieut. M. 352
Colman, G. A. Esq. 513
Coombe, Major, W. M. 176
Davies, Lieut. H. 176
Day, J. Esq. 513
Downer, Mr. T. 513
Euston, Earl of, 87
Foster, G. Esq. 513
Gardiner, Mr. C. 439
Geddes, Lieut. 439
Gill, Lieut. G. 513

Gordon, Capt. J. A. 263
Harding, J. Esq. 87
Inches, J. Esq. 262
Jane, Capt. 439
Jessop, Mr. 87
Laffer, P. Esq. 176
Lark, H. Esq. 513
Lewis, J. Esq. 352
Lipsom, Lieut. 176
Marley, Lieut. 262
Minto, Major, 513
Nesbitt, W. Esq. 176
Phipps, Mr. W. 438
Richdale, Major, 438
Rickman, Lieut. 262
Rouse, Lieut. 438
Scott, Lieut. 263
Shoveller, Mr. 87

Slight, J. Esq. 439
Spencer, Capt. R. 263
Stupart, Capt. 439
Suther, Mr. 438
Turner, Lieut. 263
Waldegrave, Hon. W. 87, 176
Walker, W. Esq. 352
Walpole, Rt. Hon. Lord, 176
Walton, T. T. Esq. 438
Waring, T. Esq. 262
Westbrooke, R. Esq. 439
Williams, C. Esq. 176
———, Lieut. 352
Wining, Lieut. 87
Wiseman, Sir W. 438
Young, Capt. 87

OBITUARY.

ATKINSON, Mr. G. 88
  Bailward, Mr. 88
Bagnold, Lieut. 439
Ballard, ———, 513
Beddeck, Miss, 263
Bennet, Hon. Capt. I. A. 263

Bennicke, W. Esq. 513
Bray, Mr. J. 352
Bridges, Rev. B. J. 88
Brooking, Mr. J. S. 513
Bury, Miss, 440
Byng, J. Esq. 176
Crane, Mr. 88

Cunningham, Lieut. G. 440
Curry, Capt. 440
Davies, Mrs. 263
Dewar, J. Esq. 264
Dewsnap, J. Esq. 264
Dredge, J: Esq. 88, 264
Eaglestone, Capt. 352

INDEX.

Ennis, Mrs. 439
Farquarson, Mrs. 440
Forrest, Capt. A. 440
Garrett, the Lady of Capt. 264
Gellie, L. Esq. 264
Gifferena, G. Esq. 88
Glinn, Mrs. 513
Goode, Mrs. 263
Hamilton, Mr. 87
Hansford, Mr. 263
Hardyman, Lieut.-Col. 176
Hare, Lieut. 264
Harrington, Lieut. 88
Heacock, Lieut. 88
Hunt, Capt. 513
Jardine, Capt. 88
Jocelyne, Hon. J. B, 88
Johnstone, Mr. 440
Joyeuse, Adm. V. 264
Judd, T. Esq. 438
Keats, Rev. R. 88
Kent, Lieut. T. W. 264
———, Capt. W. 352
Laird, Rear.adm. 263
Lilly, Mr. 513
Lockhart, Lieut. W. 513
Marshall, Mr. 263
Martin, Mrs. 263
M'Cleverty, Mrs. 88
M'Killop, R. Esq. 513
Maxwell, Mr. 263
Middlemist, Mr. 263
Milbanke, Mrs. 513
Miller, Capt. 439
Moss, Mrs. 443
Neales, Mr. 439
Newton, Capt. 440
North, Mr. W. 439
Paine, R. Esq. 263
Parker, Lieut. 88
Peach, Mrs. 263
Perkins, Capt. 88
Price,—, 88
———, C. P. Esq. 440
Rea, Lieut. 352, 440
Rushworth, Capt. 264
Sandys, Lieut. G. 513
Saumarez, Miss, 439
Serle, A. Esq. 264
Sheriff, Mrs. 352
Smith, Mrs.
Stanhope, Miss, 263
Stewart, Mrs. 176
Strauchan, Capt. 513
Sweet, Capt. 352
Towle, Lieut. E. 513
Truscott, Dr. C. 263
Walter, Mrs. 263
Waterhouse, Capt. 264
Willoughby,—- 268
Winter, Adm. De. 88
Wye, W. B. 352

Printed by Joyce Gold, 103, Shoe-lane, London.

Lightning Source UK Ltd.
Milton Keynes UK
07 December 2010

164019UK00001B/42/P